THE PHENOMENAL SELF

The Phenomenal Self

BARRY DAINTON

OXFORD

UNIVERSITY PRESS

OXFORD
UNIVERSITY PRESS

Great Clarendon Street, Oxford OX2 6DP

Oxford University Press is a department of the University of Oxford.
It furthers the University's objective of excellence in research, scholarship,
and education by publishing worldwide in

Oxford New York

Auckland Cape Town Dar es Salaam Hong Kong Karachi
Kuala Lumpur Madrid Melbourne Mexico City Nairobi
New Delhi Shanghai Taipei Toronto

With offices in

Argentina Austria Brazil Chile Czech Republic France Greece
Guatemala Hungary Italy Japan Poland Portugal Singapore
South Korea Switzerland Thailand Turkey Ukraine Vietnam

Oxford is a registered trade mark of Oxford University Press
in the UK and in certain other countries

Published in the United States
by Oxford University Press Inc., New York

British Library Cataloguing in Publication Data

Data available

Library of Congress Cataloging in Publication Data
Dainton, Barry, 1958-
The phenomenal self / Barry Dainton.
p. cm.
Includes bibliographical references and index.
ISBN-13: 978-0-19-928884-7
1. Self (Philosophy) 2. Phenomenalism. 3. Phenomenology. 4. Self. I. Title.
BD450.D263 2008
126—dc22
2008002539

Typeset by Laserwords Private Limited, Chennai, India
Printed in Great Britain
on acid-free paper by
Biddles Ltd, King's Lynn, Norfolk

ISBN 978–0–19–928884–7

1 3 5 7 9 10 8 6 4 2

Contents

List of Figures

For Gwynneth

Preface

But what positive meaning has the Soul, when scrutinized,
but the *ground of possibility* of the thought?

William James

When pondering the question 'What kind of thing am I?' most of us find
ourselves pulled in different directions. In many respects we seem to be perfectly
ordinary material things. We can see ourselves in mirrors; we have a certain shape,
size and weight, and our bodies are composed of the same kind of elementary
ingredients as tables and chairs. But in other respects it seems that we are not
ordinary material things—or that we do not think of ourselves as such. We
have minds, and most material things (or so most of us believe) do not. No
less importantly, most of us have little or no difficulty in imagining ourselves
surviving transformations and displacements that no ordinary material object
could possibly survive. I may not believe it likely to happen, but I have no
difficulty in making sense of the possibility that I could be given the form of a
dolphin, or changed into a sentient tree (or even a sentient lump of silicon) and
so discover what it is like to be physically very different from how I actually am.
It is equally easy to imagine myself enjoying an afterlife in a non-physical realm,
or waking up to find that I already exist in a non-physical realm and have been
merely dreaming that I am a human being. How could such fates be conceivable
possibilities *for me* if I am an ordinary material being?

There are different ways of responding to this tension. Some say that we are
in fact perfectly ordinary material things—human animals, or brains, say—and
attempt to explain away any considerations which seem to suggest otherwise. At
the other extreme are those who hold that the self is an entity of an entirely
non-physical kind, an immaterial soul or somesuch. And then there are those who
opt for a middle way, and try to do equal justice to the competing considerations.
One influential strategy for bringing about the reconciliation, pioneered by
Locke, is to try to show that we are entities whose existence and persistence
conditions are unlike those of any ordinary material thing, and which are also
such as to permit most (if not all) of the transformations we can so easily envisage
ourselves surviving. If this could be established, then we could be confident that
we are entities of a distinctive kind, even if we turn out to be composed of the
same elementary ingredients as hunks of wood or lumps of cheese. As for the
terms in which our identity conditions should be formulated, the direction in
which we should move is obvious. What sets us apart from ordinary material

things is the fact that we possess minds and they do not; when we envisage ourselves surviving some radical transformation we generally envisage our *mental life* continuing on. (I can envisage myself surviving in the form of a tree, but only if the tree has the ability to think or feel.) Hence it seems clear that we should seek to define our identity conditions in mentalistic terms. And this is precisely the line that Locke took: 'That with which the *consciousness* of this present thinking thing can join itself, makes the same *Person*, and is one *self* with it, and with nothing else; and so attributes to it *self*, and owns all the Actions of that thing as its own, as far as that consciousness reaches, and no farther; as every one who reflects will perceive' (*Essay*, II, XXVII, §17).

Leaving to one side the difficult issue of what Locke meant by 'consciousness' in passages such as this, the potential advantages of this general approach are clear and significant. If a viable theory along Lockean lines could be developed, the competing ways in which we conceive of ourselves would be largely reconciled. Such a theory also offers the prospect of a quite general account of what a *minded being* is, an account that is not restricted to human kind. This is a definite advantage, for there is no reason to think that persons are confined to human form. Our universe could easily contain many forms of conscious intelligence that are very unlike human beings; if it does, then there are actually existing persons (or selves) of the non-human variety. But even if it does not, many of the non-human creatures familiar from fictional tales are manifestly people, so it is clear that concepts such as 'person' or 'self' are sufficiently general as to have application outwith the human sphere. Those who follow in Locke's footsteps seek to elucidate the persistence conditions associated with these concepts in purely mentalistic terms.

This book is an attempt to develop a neo-Lockean account of the self. But if my approach is entirely orthodox, the destination to which it leads is not.

Starting from the question 'What form of mental continuity is necessary and sufficient to keep me in existence?' the answer given by most contemporary neo-Lockeans is psychological continuity. The latter consists (roughly speaking) of causal relations between psychological states: if a person at some future time has memories, beliefs, intentions, values, and personality traits which are both similar to, and causally dependent on my current memories, beliefs, values, etc., then that person is me. This approach can seem very plausible. Any future person who is strongly psychologically continuous with will very likely believe themselves to be me (assuming they have not been supplied with information to the contrary), and they might easily be able to convince others that they were me. But appearances can be deceptive, and I believe this is a case in point. If we pay due heed to sorts of change we can conceive ourselves as surviving—in just the way Locke urged—then the psychological approach soon starts to look problematic. For just as it is conceivable that we could survive radical changes in our physical constitution, it is equally conceivable that we could survive radical changes in our psychological constitution—changes which rupture psychological continuity. Why suppose the relevant changes are survivable? Because they could conceivably occur without rupturing a further and different form of mental continuity: experiential continuity, the sort of continuity we find in our streams of consciousness, from moment to moment. This sort of continuity is sufficient to keep a person in existence, even in the absence of continuities of the psychological kind. Or so I will argue.

If this is right, the lesson seems clear. Rather than trading in psychological continuity, neo-Lockeans should seek to define our persistence conditions in terms of experiential (or phenomenal) continuity. The latter seems more intimately related to our continued existence than the sort of causal relationships psychological theorists focus upon. Developing a viable account grounded in this sort of continuity—an 'experience-based' account as I will call it—may not be a straightforward business, not least because an explanation of how we survive periods of unconsciousness will be needed (assuming we do in fact survive such periods). But if the various difficulties could be overcome in a satisfactory manner the benefits would be substantial: we would have a theory which allows us to survive a far greater range of those changes we can easily conceive ourselves surviving than the better-known alternatives. And while such a theory would clearly be superior to the alternatives when judged by Lockean standards, it could well be a better theory by any standards.[1]

Given the approach I will be pursuing, I will inevitably be spending a good deal of time talking about experience. But my focus will be narrow. In order to provide the experience-based approach with firm foundations, I will try to establish that the experiences in our ordinary streams of consciousness are bound together by a *phenomenal* unifying relationship that is distinct from the relationships of causal dependency that psychological theorists rely upon.[2] I will also spend some time exploring the various forms of interdependencies which exist among experiences in the same stream of consciousness. This topic has significant implications for the kind of unity things such as ourselves might possess, and this issue is in turn relevant to the sort of *things* we can reasonably take ourselves to be.

One topic about which I have little to say is the relationship between consciousness and the physical. Since I believe attempts to reduce the phenomenal

[1] Or at least when judged by *one* of Locke's standards. Locke was certainly interested in finding an account which accommodated the sorts of changes we could conceive ourselves surviving, but he also lay great store on finding an account which could accommodate our intuitions concerning the just distribution of punishment and reward. Hence the emphasis he placed on experiential memory: it can easily seem wrong to punish a person for a crime they cannot remember having committed (at least if retribution is the goal—deterrence is another matter). Since I am primarily seeking an account which accommodates our survival intuitions, my approach is at most *neo-Lockean*.

[2] This terminology may seem puzzling. Given that experiences belong to the realm of the psychological, aren't continuities in (or amongst) experiences forms of psychological continuity? They certainly can be regarded as such, provided 'psychological' is construed in a broad way, as roughly synonymous with 'mental'. However, experiential continuity of the kind I will be concerned with is distinct from what is called 'psychological continuity' in much of the personal identity literature. Hence my choice of terminology.

to the non-phenomenal are bound to fail, I adopt a stance of full-blooded realism with regard to the phenomenal. I take conscious states to be just as real, just as much parts of concrete reality, as protons and electrons, or stars and planets. But as is all too familiar, adopting a non-reductionist view of consciousness makes it very difficult to comprehend how consciousness fits into the material world as we know it. There are various proposals. Some hold that experiences are non-physical particulars, others that they are states of non-physical substances. Others argue, rightly in my view, that our current conception of the physical is less than fully adequate, and so we cannot as yet rule out the possibility that some (or all) physical things have a phenomenal aspect. A more speculative proposal is that the physical and phenomenal both arise out of some more fundamental mode of reality, one that is neither physical nor phenomenal in itself. A less speculative (but more pessimistic) proposal is that there is no deep problem concerning the relationship between consciousness and matter, it is just that our minds are singularly ill-equipped to understand what this relationship is.[3]

Since I cannot see that we are yet in a position to know which of these proposals is true, or closest to it, I remain largely neutral on this issue. My working hypothesis is that our consciousness is causally dependent on activity in our brains. Or to put it another way, that our brains have the capacity to produce experience. In adopting this position I do not take a view on the issue of whether phenomenal states are material or immaterial in themselves. Nothing I have to say hangs on this question. Although I assume that our consciousness is generated by our brains, I would not want to claim that human (or animal) brains are the *only* things that possess the capacity to generate consciousness; as things stand, we do not know enough about the matter-consciousness relationship to know what sort of (physical) thing can sustain consciousness. Nor do I assume that we have infallible access to all aspects of our experience; it is one thing to know what an experience is like, simply by having it, it is another to know how best to describe it, and mistakes are possible.

While this *moderately naturalistic* position (as I will refer to it) is fairly common these days, it is by no means universally accepted. In the philosophy of mind, at any rate, many contemporary philosophers opt for a less moderate form of naturalism: they take the view that some form of reductionism about experiential states and properties must be true. Given this, it is worth noting right at the outset that adopting a reductionist stance towards the phenomenal by no means rules out adopting an experience-based approach to the issue of personal identity. Reductionists can accept a theory formulated in terms of phenomenal states and relations, and *then* bring their preferred mode of reduction into play. From a reductionist standpoint, an analysis formulated in phenomenal terms can be true,

---

[3] For the latter view see McGinn (1989); for more optimistic and constructive proposals of the sort I have in mind see Chalmers (1996), Lockwood (1989, 1993), McGinn (1993), Strawson (1994), Unger (1999).

it is just not metaphysically fundamental. From a non-reductionist standpoint, of course, the analysis in phenomenal terms *is* fundamental.

Moderate naturalism may be neutral with regard to claims concerning the precise way in which the phenomenal and physical are related, but it is by no means compatible with every position on this issue, for it may well be incompatible with the stronger forms of substance dualism. I do not regard this as a disadvantage, for as things currently stand, I do not think there is any compelling reason to believe the stronger forms of dualism are true. Even if it could be established that experiences are non-physical, the doctrine that experiences are states of immaterial *substances* requires further justification—and for reasons that will emerge, I am not persuaded by some of the arguments that are commonly used to support this doctrine. But even if these arguments (or some variants thereof) were persuasive, there would still remain a very pertinent question, raised by Locke, and later by Kant. Suppose my consciousness does in fact reside in a particular immaterial substance, is it necessarily to be confined to *one* such substance? Can we rule out the possibility of a single subject's mental life being sustained by a succession of immaterial substances? Since it is not obvious that we can, defining the persistence conditions of subjects in terms of mental continuity is an option even substance dualists should take seriously.

I may not devote much time to substance dualism *per se*, but I do spend some time considering whether certain claims commonly associated with the doctrine can be defended within the rather different framework of moderate naturalism. The relevant claims are these: first, that our continued existence is an absolute or all-or-nothing affair, and second, that selves are not only genuine *things*, they are metaphysically *simple* things. These claims are of course connected: it is difficult to see how the existence of a thing which is metaphysically simple (in the sense of lacking constituent parts) can be anything other than an all-or-nothing affair. It is also by no means obvious how either of these claims could be true if we reject the doctrine that experiences are states of a primitive (and probably immaterial) particular, and hold instead that they are entirely the product of neural activity within our brains. Indeed, we shall see that the doctrines of absoluteness and simplicity may well ultimately not be sustainable in an unqualified form within a moderately naturalistic framework. However, we shall also see that something surprisingly close to them might be. In pursuing these investigations I was motivated by a suspicion that the appeal of these doctrines might have two sources rather than just one: various metaphysical inklings or inclinations certainly play a role, but perhaps certain features of our ordinary experience also lend them plausibility. The conclusions I reach suggest there may well be an element of truth in this.

The question of how there can be conscious subjects in a material universe is one of the great mysteries associated with the self. Although I make no attempt to solve this problem here, there are other puzzles I do not ignore. One such is the relationship between selves and their states of consciousness. There is a significant sense in which we know what it is like to *be* a self simply by virtue of being conscious, and starting from this premise some argue that we are acquainted with our selves (or some aspect of them) in our experience. How else would we know as much as we do about the sort of things we are? While this can seem plausible, there are others who maintain that the self cannot possibly be apprehended in introspection because it is what is doing the apprehending. If Hume had grasped this point (a familiar line of argument runs) he would not have expected to find his self among the contents of his consciousness, and so he would not have felt obliged to draw the absurd conclusion that his self did not exist: to suppose the self does not exist because one does not encounter it in one's experience is akin to concluding that one must be blind because one cannot see one's eyes. The conception of the self as an observer or witness, a point-centre of awareness or apprehension, is a familiar one, and it too can seem quite compelling. Clearly, these opposing views—the self as something which features in experience, and the self as non-apprehended apprehender—cannot both be correct. The impasse can be resolved, I suggest, by achieving an adequate conception of the structure and composition of our streams of consciousness, and drawing some basic distinctions.

Although I work on the assumption that our experiences are causally dependent on our brains, I devote little time to the findings of neuroscience, psychology or cognitive science. It is not that these are irrelevant, far from it; a more comprehensive treatment would certainly incorporate them. One reason for this omission is that the relevant empirical results need careful evaluation before their import is clear, and the book is long enough as it is. But secondly, and no less importantly, I think there is some point in trying to ascertain what can be said about the self from the standpoint of ordinary experience, of the kind most of us have most of the time. This is of some interest in its own right—at least for beings such as ourselves—but it may also offer some clues as to what selves *in general* are like. The character of ordinary human experience may well be an imperfect guide to those features that are common to consciousness in all its forms (if there are such), but I can see no reason for supposing that abnormal or atypical forms of human consciousness will be a better guide.

Of course many of those working in the field of cognitive science also have more general aspirations. To take just one relevant example, entities possessing minds can possess very different levels of cognitive sophistication, and consequently have the capacity to be 'self-aware' in very different ways. A cat in hot pursuit of a mouse may well have a (probably non-conceptual) awareness of itself as something distinct from its environment and prey, but this form of self-consciousness is different from that enjoyed by a three-year old child, and different again from that of a typical adult human reflecting on how their life has gone. Arriving at a detailed understanding of the different modes of self-awareness is an important task; many of the relevant distinctions are applicable across species, and progress has been made.[4] However, for reasons which will emerge, I suspect that these sorts of cognitive abilities are non-essential attributes of conscious subjects, at least if these are conceived in the most general and fundamental way. If this is right, then to arrive at an understanding of what the persistence of such subjects essentially requires and involves, we must concentrate on the most basic and universal features of conscious life, features that can plausibly be regarded as common to the experience of all subjects, irrespective of their cognitive sophistication. Some might be sceptical about the prospects of such a narrowly focused approach delivering any interesting or worthwhile results, but I hope that what follows demonstrates that this scepticism is misplaced.

There is a further topic about which I have little say: the nature of persistence, what persistence involves. This has been much-discussed in recent years, and much of the debate has revolved around two competing views about the nature of persisting things. Advocates of the more traditional 'endurance' theory hold that a typical material object is a three-dimensional entity that persists by being wholly present at a succession of different times. In the opposing camp are the subscribers to the 'perdurance' theory, according to which ordinary material objects are four-dimensional entities, things that extend through time as well as space. For a perdurantist, the table I see before me is not the whole table, but just a temporal part of the table. Endurantists, on the other hand, claim that things such as tables do not possess temporal parts; if this is the case, then my table cannot have parts of itself located at other times, and so it is the *whole* table that is sitting there in front of me. Interesting and important though these issues are, I have opted not to engage with them here.[5] Although the standard of the recent debates has been such that many aspects of these complex issues are much better understood than they were, it is still too early to declare a clear winner. Indeed, it may well be that there will not be a clear victor: we may end up with two (or more) general theories of persistence, each of which makes sense on its own terms, each of which can handle the various puzzle cases that arise, albeit in different ways. For this reason I have remained as neutral as possible on this issue too, and have tried to develop an account of the self that can be accepted by endurantists and perdurantists alike.

That said, I do not ignore general ontological issues entirely. A complaint frequently lodged against those who adopt the neo-Lockean approach is that by focusing very narrowly on issues of persistence they give insufficient thought to what selves actually *are*, and as a consequence remain oblivious to the ontologically problematic nature of the sort of account they provide. Although there is some justice in this complaint, I think an ontologically viable account

---

[4] See for example Metzinger (2003) and Bermúdez (1998); both authors present a good deal of relevant empirical data, as well as analyses of different modes of self-consciousness.

[5] Haslanger (2003) provides a good introduction to the various positions, as does Sider (2001), albeit from a partisan perspective.

along neo-Lockean lines can be developed, probably in more than one way, and I give some indications as to how this might be done. Even so, some readers may feel short-changed in this regard. The issue of whether or not it makes sense to think that material entities can coincide has been much debated recently, and I do move rather quickly through some difficult and much-disputed territory. This (perhaps unseemly) haste was motivated by a number of considerations. My decision to remain as neutral as possible on the nature of persistence played a role, as did the fact that I have nothing novel to add to the recent debates (I do have something to say about the extent to which neo-Lockeans need to commit themselves to coinciding entities in the first place, but that is a different matter.) And while a fuller treatment of the ontological options may have been beneficial for those who are unfamiliar with the relevant literature, it would also have led to other topics receiving less attention. If our understanding of the self is to advance, progress needs to be made on two fronts: general metaphysics certainly, but also the philosophy of mind. So whilst not ignoring general ontological issues, I also spend some time trying to integrate my account of the self in a more general view of the mental. As is usually the case when fighting on two fronts, certain sacrifices had to be made.

If ontological issues loom larger in the later parts of the book, the earlier parts are taken up with other matters. I open proceedings in Chapter 1 by arguing that thought experiments have a legitimate but limited role to play in our investigations into our own nature. After a brief outline of the orthodox psychological continuity approach, I develop a series of imaginary scenarios aimed at establishing, first, that the psychological approach lacks the intuitive appeal often claimed for it, and second, that an account grounded in experiential continuity would have considerably greater credibility—provided of course that it could be developed in a satisfactory manner. When the orthodox Lockean methodology is taken as far as it can go, it ends up pointing in different direction than is usually supposed.

Although some of the scenarios I deploy in reaching this conclusion may strike some as being more than usually far-fetched, the envisaged states of affairs are all clearly and easily *imaginable*, and at this preliminary state of proceedings that is all that matters. That said, such scenarios are not to everyone's taste, and when considering how best to present the main lines of argument in the book, I did consider adopting a purely metaphysical approach. Rather than starting off in a traditional Lockean vein, with a consideration of various more or less speculative imaginary cases, I would have directly addressed a question along the lines of: 'Given a particular conception of consciousness, and the kind of unity to be found in consciousness, what metaphysical account of the self can we provide?' Most of the book can certainly be viewed as a response to this question. I opted to take the Lockean route primarily because it is still not uncommon to find the experience-based approach largely or completely ignored in neo-Lockean circles, where the psychological approach continues to dominate. It is worth noting too that some of the terminology that I introduce when outlining these scenarios is also put to use in several subsequent stages of the discussion.

The topic of personal identity features scarcely at all in Chapters 2 and 3, yet these chapters play a central role in the overall argument. In them I try to do two things: achieve a reasonably clear and accurate picture of the synchronic and diachronic unity to be found in a typical stream of consciousness, and establish that these unities are a consequence of phenomenal relationships. These inquiries are largely conducted from a phenomenological perspective, but since it is phenomenal unity and continuity that are at issue, this is inevitable. I start by looking at the unity of consciousness at a given time, and argue that this is best understood as being the product of a primitive inter-experiential relationship, *co-consciousness*. This conclusion is reached after alternative accounts are found wanting. I then move on to diachronic unity, and try to reach an understanding of how our experience can have the dynamic temporal characteristics that it so evidently has. How can we make sense of the flux and flow that we find in experience, and which make the 'stream' metaphor so apt? How is it possible for us to directly apprehend change and persistence? How are the successive phases of our streams of consciousness related? I conclude that to account for the diachronic unity of consciousness we need appeal to nothing more than co-consciousness, albeit in its diachronic form. Both synchronic and diachronic unity are thus accounted for in essentially the same way.[6]

Establishing that the experiences within a stream of consciousness are bound together by a basic experiential relationship is a very useful result. It means that we can account for the unity of consciousness at and over time without appealing to the causal relationships that are constitutive of psychological continuity. Co-streamal experiences may be causally related in any number of ways, but they are also connected by a relationship of a purely phenomenal kind, and this phenomenal relationship is sufficient in itself to generate phenomenal unity and continuity. This result also means that we can account for the unity of consciousness without invoking the self. Instead of saying 'to be unified experiences must belong to the same subject' we can say 'experiences are unified when they are co-conscious'. Finally, but no less importantly, since it is very plausible to suppose that experiences found in unified states and streams of consciousness have a common subject, we have a non-question begging criterion for assigning experiences to subjects: experiences can have a common owner

---

[6] The particular conception of phenomenal unity is defended at greater length in my *Stream of Consciousness* (Dainton, 2000). Although the present work builds on the latter, it is entirely self-contained, the relevant doctrines and arguments being expounded anew where necessary. The general account of our persistence conditions that I will be developing here does not require all the doctrines I defend in *Stream of Consciousness*—indeed, with appropriate modifications, the general account could easily be adapted to a range of views concerning the structure and unity of consciousness. But as will become clear, if what I say about the unity of consciousness (and particularly *diachronic* unity) is along the right lines, my account of our persistence conditions rests on very solid foundations indeed.

without being co-conscious, but there is little doubt that experiences that are in fact co-conscious are also consubjective.

This simple and direct connection between the notion of a subject of experience and co-consciousness turns out to be all that is needed to construct an account of the conditions under which a subject of experience can continue to exist through periods of unconsciousness. What is a subject of experience if not a being that has the *capacity* to have experiences? How are capacities for experience related when they belong to the same subject at any given time? An obvious and compelling answer: they can contribute to streams of unified consciousness. The bulk of Chapter 4 is taken up with explaining and elaborating this basic picture. There are in fact a number of ways in which the basic picture can be elaborated, and after introducing a few of these in a cursory way I explore one approach in more detail. (This makes for a longer exposition, but ultimately—I hope—a more accessible one; there are benefits to viewing things from different angles.) I call the resulting account *the C-theory*. I further distinguish two forms of the C-theory. In its narrow (less ambitious) guise it offers no more than an account of our persistence-conditions; in its broader (more ambitious) guise it provides an account of what we are.

Addressing the self from the standpoint of experience is scarcely a new approach, even if it has been neglected somewhat of late. In Chapter 5 I assess some alternative experience-based conceptions, and argue for the superiority of the C-theory. Among the alternatives examined are the theories of John Foster and Galen Strawson. Interruptions in consciousness pose a problem for all experience-based approaches. Experiences in a single uninterrupted stream of consciousness pose little or no difficulty—such experiences are unified experientially, and they can be ascribed to a single subject on this basis—but experiences in streams separated by an interval during which their subject is unconscious are evidently not unified in this sort of way. So on what experiential basis can such streams be assigned a common owner? Foster has an elegant solution to this problem, involving possible extensions of earlier streams which join with later streams. However this solution can be developed in two quite different ways, and it turns out that both versions are problematic, albeit for different reasons. Strawson sidesteps the problem altogether by holding that we have much shorter life-spans than we normally suppose, spans which are far shorter than typical streams of consciousness (or what are normally thought of as such). Not surprisingly, Strawson also holds that our streams of consciousness are far less unified than has often been supposed. I suggest that he is wrong about this. A very different approach—one that is a good deal closer to my own—is elaborated by Peter Unger in his *Identity, Consciousness and Value* (1990). Unger and I start from similar premises: he too adopts a robust realism with regard to the experiential, and he holds that, so far as our persistence is concerned, it is the preservation of experiential capacities that primarily matters. But Unger also argues that there are powerful material constraints on our persistence. More specifically, he maintains that there are circumstances in which we could cease to exist even if our streams of consciousness continued to flow on without interruption. I suggest Unger's position is afflicted by an internal tension, and argue in favour of an entirely unrestricted and purely experiential account of our persistence conditions.

The chapters which follow are devoted to further refining the C-theory. In Chapter 6 the focus is on the relationship between the phenomenal and non-phenomenal parts of the mind, and the similarities and differences between the C-theory and the more familiar psychological continuity approach. So far as the first of these issues is concerned, there is little one can say that is not controversial, and since the issue is a difficult one I will be looking at it from different angles. But the general conception I will be outlining (in §6.5) at least has the merit of a reasonably familiar one in recent philosophy of mind—at least in non-reductionist circles—even if it has not yet loomed large in the personal identity literature. Drawing on this conception, I suggest that the C-theory can be thought of as a causal theory, albeit of a distinctive kind, and go on to distinguish three distinct types of mental subject. With these clarifications out of the way, I turn to the issue of how much of what matters in life resides in the continuities with which the C-theory is concerned. One way of bringing this issue into clear relief is by contemplating cases in which experiential and psychological continuities diverge—a comparatively unfamiliar form of mental bifurcation, but one that seems at least conceivable.[7] I suggest that in such cases all our deepest identity-related concerns remain locked onto the experiential continuities. It may well be that not everyone will share my intuitions on this score. But at the very least I hope to establish that the continuities targeted by the C-theory have a significant degree of importance, and this alone is sufficient to establish that psychological continuity is not the only mental continuity which matters.

Chapter 7 deals with some pressing questions concerning the way the C-theory applies to ourselves. What does embodiment require and involve? What is the relationship between an embodied human subject and the human animal which sustains such a subject's mental capacities? After developing an account of embodiment which does not require subjects actually to be *in* their bodies, I respond to the objection that neo-Lockean accounts of the self inevitably double the number of subjects there actually are—the 'too many thinkers' or 'too many subjects' problem, as it is sometimes called.

I begin Chapter 8 by considering how little can a subject possess by way of experiential capacities and still exist. How *simple* can a subject be? I then move on to consider whether a subject's experience is necessarily the product of experiential capacities. In addressing these questions I introduce some strange and improbable

---

[7] Is such a bifurcation actually possible? Perhaps, but we will need to know more about these different aspects of the mind—and how they relate to their physical underpinnings—before we will be in a position to draw any firm conclusions.

scenarios, but for anyone intent on exploring the ramifications of the experience-based approach as fully as possible such excursions into wilder metaphysical territories are difficult to avoid. In any event, although these scenarios do point to some surprising conclusions, these may not be as unacceptable as they first appear, or so I argue. I close with a brief examination of another difficult topic: whether a partially unified consciousness is possible. If the answer to this question is 'no' then there is a sense in which selves are necessarily simpler than they would be if the answer were 'yes'.

The theme of simplicity is considered from another angle in Chapter 9. One way for an object to be metaphysically simple is to lack parts, in the manner of a geometrical point. But larger compound objects can be simple too, in one sense at least, provided their parts are such they cannot be separated from the wholes to which they belong. It is widely supposed, for example, that psychological systems are composed of parts that are heavily interdependent. I argue that systems of experiential capacities are also heavily interdependent, and that some of these interdependencies arise from purely phenomenal considerations: they are a consequence of the various forms of interdependency (or holism) that are to be found among the constituents of unified conscious states. The interdependencies are sufficiently deep and pervasive that the relevant systems of capacities (and hence our selves) are composed of parts that are inseparable from their wholes—quite *how* inseparable depends on how finely we choose to individuate the items in question.

I then turn, in Chapter 10, to the question of whether subject-identity is absolute or not. The question here is how sharp the temporal boundaries of a subject's existence are, when viewed from the perspective of the C-theory. Can we fade into or out of existence, or are the boundaries of our lives utterly sharp? I suggest the answer is by no means clear-cut. One difficulty is arriving at a general understanding of the conditions under which potentialities can persist through trying circumstances. A second and even more difficult question is whether or not the kind of potential for experience our brains possess is all-or-nothing, a question in which we have some personal interest. I argue that while we can in fact reasonably take our experiential capacities to be all-or-nothing, so doing is not without its difficulties.

Having explored the C-theory in some detail, I turn in Chapter 11 to possible objections. Some maintain that it is illegitimate to specify the identity conditions of mental subjects in terms of mental states since the latter are ontologically dependent on the former. I suggest this objection is less than compelling. Next I consider whether the C-theory provides us with a believable account of the sort of thing we are. Is the notion that we are essentially nothing more than clusters of mental capacities really one we can live with? Are such things really *things*? I suggest that, in one important sense at least, they are. By way of further support for my approach, I suggest there may be worlds which consist of nothing but capacities, of one kind or another. I also consider the issue of whether or not the C-theory should be classed as 'reductionist'—but since some philosophers regard reductionism as a virtue rather than a vice, this discussion is relegated to an appendix. (I suggest that the C-theory *is* reductionist, in several senses, but not in ways that are in any way problematic.)

Up to this point I have been working on the assumption that, providing a subject's stream of consciousness flows smoothly on, without interruption, there is no doubt whatsoever that its subject continues to exist. This assumption is put under pressure by the possibility of fission. What if one's stream of consciousness were to smoothly branch? What if a single self were to divide into two? Does the thesis that phenomenal continuity is subject-preserving collapse at this point? It might be thought that it must, since it is widely believed that if one subject were to divide into two, the resulting subjects must be distinct from the original subject since they are obviously distinct from one another—they are *two*, not *one*. I argue against this (and other) views of fission in Chapter 12, and provide an interpretation which allows us to regard the products of fission as identical with both one another and the subject who divided into them. I conclude with a brief look at fusion, and suggest that it too is susceptible to the same treatment.

The stance I adopt with regard to fission (and fusion) is undeniably a radical one. However, anyone not convinced by my arguments for the claim that identity on the one hand, and the mental continuities normally sufficient for identity on the other, remain locked together during fission (or fusion) cases should not feel obliged to shun the C-theory for this reason alone. First because there are other interpretations of fission which deliver the same result (although these also have their disadvantages). But secondly, and perhaps more importantly, the bulk of what I have to say can easily be transposed to another key. It has become customary to distinguish between identity and 'what matters'—that is those features of our lives that we most value, or are most concerned about. I present the C-theory in the guise of an account of our identity conditions, but it can function perfectly well as an account of what we most care about. There are different senses of 'what matters', and I do not claim that the continuities at the heart of the C-theory are equally relevant to them all; but I think they are certainly relevant to some of the most significant. It is certainly possible to follow those who (like Parfit) regard the possibility of fission to reveal that identity and what matters can come apart, and then take the C-theory as one's guide to what matters.

A word on terminology. The terms 'person', 'self', and 'subject' are used in different ways by different philosophers; some treat them all as synonymous, others do not. I follow the latter practice. The issue of the conditions under which we ourselves will continue to exist is usually called the problem of 'personal identity'. While this is understandable, it can be confusing. If our concern is with our own personal survival, paradoxical though it might sound, it is not clear that we should be concerned to discover the conditions under which *persons* persist. Personhood is often taken to require the possession of certain characteristics,

characteristics which (on the face of it) are not essential to our own personal survival. Locke defined a person as a 'thinking intelligent being that has reason and reflection and can consider itself as itself, the same thinking thing in different times and places.'⁸ A person in this sense is a being (not necessarily human) equipped with a fairly sophisticated degree of mentality. Is the possession of this degree of intellect necessary for our own survival? Not obviously. We did not possess this degree of sophistication when very young (it is natural to think) and perhaps many of us will lose this degree of sophistication before we die (it is natural to fear). If this is right, we are not essentially persons in the Lockean sense. The same applies to another sense of the term, to which Locke also drew attention. 'Personhood' is sometimes used to denote a status conferred upon an entity when it is the bearer of certain moral or legal rights and obligations. What counts as a person in this sense will of course vary from culture to culture, and from time to time. In some cases, entities that are not human beings, and not sentient, are classed as persons, for example, companies and other institutions. In other cases, some perfectly fit and healthy human beings will be classed as persons, while others will—for whatever reason—be classed as 'non-persons'. In these cases, it seems obvious that the legal or moral status of personhood may be conferred or withdrawn without affecting the continued existence of its bearer. Of course, if you were to become a non-person in the moral or judicial sense, you might be so distraught that you would do away with yourself; but in these circumstances it is your own actions that lead to your death, not your changed status.

If an inquiry into the existence and persistence conditions of persons is intended to be an inquiry into our own identity conditions, then a 'person' is something that we must each of us be essentially; personhood in this sense will not be a property that we can continue to exist without possessing, or continue to possess without continuing to exist. While it is possible to use 'person' in this way, it is somewhat strained, and the risk of confusion or misunderstanding remains. Consequently, as may already have become clear, I have opted to talk only of 'selves' and 'subjects'. I treat these as interchangeable. This policy too may not be to everyone's liking. As some use the term, to be a 'self' it is necessary to possess the capacity to be aware that one is a self. On this view, selves necessarily possess the ability to be self-conscious, whereas mere subjects of experience do not. As already indicated, I do not believe that *we* are essentially self-conscious beings, for reasons which will become clear, and since it would be odd indeed to hold that a self is not essentially a self, I prefer not to confine selves in this way.

Simplifying only a little, my answer to the question 'What are we?' is that we are subjects of experience, beings whose sole essential attribute is the ability to have experiences of one kind or another. Not surprisingly, this answer is entirely unoriginal; Descartes would probably have said much the same. But there is a

---

⁸ *Essay* II, XXII, §9.

difference: my account, unlike that of Descartes, is thoroughly naturalistic, or as naturalistic as it is possible to be while taking experience seriously, in that I assume throughout that our capacity for consciousness is physically grounded, and this difference is significant. Combining an experiential approach to the self with a naturalistic world-view means confronting hard (perhaps insoluble) problems, but it is also liberating. The widespread suspicion regarding consciousness that held sway for much of the last century has meant that many important issues and approaches have not received the attention they should have. So far as the self is concerned, no doubt there are many paths yet to explore, paths quite different from those I pursue here, and as of now we can only guess where these further investigations will lead. Nonetheless, if we are anything like the beings we seem to be, I would be surprised if all the core elements of the present account were to prove entirely redundant or mistaken.

Acknowledgements

This book has had a long gestation—longer by far than I once would have thought possible—and I am grateful to everyone who has supplied me with ideas, criticism and encouragement during this time. Particular thanks to Tim Bayne, John Foster, Richard Gaskin, Logi Gunnarsson, Howard Robinson, Galen Strawson, Nicholas Nathan, and Graham Nerlich. Much of the final draft was completed during periods of leave made possible by the AHRC and the University of Liverpool. I am grateful to both.

In several parts of the book I have drawn on ideas developed in 'Survival and Experience', *Proceedings of the Aristotelian Society* (1996), 'The Self and the Phenomenal', *Ratio* (2004) and 'Consciousness as a Guide to Personal Persistence' (co-author Tim Bayne), *Australasian Journal of Philosophy*, (2005). Much of 'Time and Division', *Ratio* (1992) has found its way into Chapter 12. I am grateful for permission to use this material here.

1
Mind and Self

An appealingly straightforward approach to the question 'What sort of thing am I?' takes zoology as its guide. According to those who adopt this approach we are essentially human beings, and since human beings are animals of a particular kind, our identity conditions are those of a particular kind of animal. For obvious reasons this position is sometimes called *animalism*. Since proponents of animalism can admit the possibility of non-human persons—for example aliens belonging to a different species of animal—to be a *person* or *self* on this view it is not necessary to be human. Some animalists are prepared to admit the possibility of persons who are not animals at all: perhaps one day sentient robots will be constructed, beings who are sufficiently like us mentally that it would be unreasonable to regard them as anything other than persons. Such possibilities are compatible with the claim that those of us who *are* animals of a particular species are essentially such. It follows from this claim that those persons who are human beings are essentially such, and hence that particular *human persons*, as we might call them, are identical with particular animals belonging to the species *homo sapiens*. In virtue of being identical with a particular animal, a human person cannot ever be anything other than a particular animal. This means there is no possibility of our surviving the death (or at least the irreversible annihilation) of our bodies.[1]

Animalism has some significant points in its favour. There is no uncontroversial evidence that beings such as ourselves exist prior to our biological beginnings, or after our biological deaths. The only reliable way we have of tracing the extent of a person's life is by tracing the career of a particular human organism. If animalism were true, we would have a simple and straightforward explanation of why what we normally take to be good evidence for personal persistence is just that. Also, for what it is worth, human beings are unproblematically and unambiguously *entities*, with well-defined kind–membership conditions. For those attracted to materialism as a general metaphysical framework, the fact that human beings

---

[1] Recent defenders of this position (or variants of it) include: Ayers (1991: volume II, part III), Johnston (1987), Olson (1997, 2003), Snowdon (1990, 1991), van Inwagen (1990), Wiggins (2001).

are a scientifically recognized zoological kind is in itself a point in favour of this conception of (human) personhood.

But for all these advantages, animalism begins to look distinctly implausible as soon as we look at imaginary cases. A good many relevant scenarios have been devised, but for present purposes one will suffice.

Research continues on nanotechnology. The aim is to develop nanomachines, machines just like any other, except in size: a nanomachine is a complex molecule, several orders of magnitude smaller than a typical living cell, designed and built to do a specific job of work. Let us jump to a time, perhaps in the not too far distant future, when nanotechnology has been developed much further than at present. Given their size, nanomachines are well suited to numerous medical applications; they can, for example, bore through a cell wall and carry out highly specific modifications to cell nuclei. But they can do much more. Certain nanomachines can disassemble entire cells, and use their component atomic and molecular parts to build a replacement, a wholly new kind of artefact, but one which exactly imitates the biochemical behaviour of the cell it replaces. These artificial cells, let us suppose, are wholly *non-biological* molecular machines. The point of having certain groups of one's cells replaced in this manner is their longevity: the replacements are much more reliable, over a much longer period, than the cell-systems they replace. Given the tendency of our bodies and brains to deteriorate somewhat in our later years, the nervous system is an obvious candidate for nanomechanical replacement. Indeed, this sort of procedure has already been given a name in the philosophical literature: *neuron replacement therapy*, or NRT.[2] For present purposes, however, it will prove useful to focus on a more extensive procedure, one in which each and every cell in the recipient's body is replaced. Call this *cell replacement therapy*, or CRT. The therapy is simple enough to carry out. A single syringe can contain many millions of nanomachines in liquid suspension; once injected, these devices self-replicate many times over, using our ordinary bodily materials (and possibly some specially ingested ingredients) for raw material. They then circulate round the bloodstream until they find their target cells. The nanomachines then get to work. Each cell is replaced by a similarly sized non-biological device, one that is connected up to its neighbouring cells in just the same ways as the original. Given their size, nanomachines work very quickly. Given this speed, and their vast number, the whole process is complete within five or six hours, and at any one time only a few per cent of one's bodily system is incapacitated. Since the procedure is usually completely painless, most recipients choose to remain conscious throughout.

Having decided to undergo the procedure yourself, you make the same choice—in the unlikely event of a problem arising, being awake significantly

---

[2] For example, in one form or another: Searle (1992), Kirk (1994: 88–9), Chalmers (1996: ch. 7), Garrett (1998: 49–50).

increases the chances of early detection. The solution is injected; you sit down and wait for the first signs that the nanomachines are at work: although you are not expecting to feel significant discomfort, you do expect to feel *something*. Remarkably, you feel nothing unusual whatsoever. No itches or tingles, no numbness or paralysis or loss of motor function, no interruptions or distortions in visual or auditory experience; so far as you can tell, your memory and intellectual abilities continue to function normally. It is as though nothing out of the ordinary were happening. Yet, as tests a few hours later reveal, the procedure has been a complete success: all your original cells have been replaced with non-biological machinery. Although you feel the same as usual, and your outward appearance is superficially unchanged, you are no longer an organism, no longer a human being.

The import of this case is evident. If events were to unfold in the way described, it seems clear that you would survive the envisaged procedure. It seems clear that you would survive because it seems obvious that you would continue to exist throughout. After all, you—and it seems clear that it *is* you—continue to think thoughts, to take decisions, to move about, to remember your past, to have perceptual experiences, all without any discernible interruption throughout the period during which the transformation takes place. However, if you do survive the procedure it is difficult to see how you could be a human being. Like all animals, human beings are biological organisms, but the entity created by the procedure is not an organism, it is entirely non-biological in nature. If you could outlast the human animal that you are currently most intimately associated with, you and this animal cannot be one and the same thing.

Can it really be so easy? Can we reasonably hope to learn significant truths about ourselves by doing no more than consulting our intuitive reactions to fictitious scenarios? Is it reasonable or realistic to suppose that our intuitive responses are keyed into metaphysical or scientific truth? How could they be? Understandably, some claim that we cannot rely on our intuitions to any significant extent—see, for example, Wilkes (1988), Johnston (1987), and Gendler (1998). Of those who take this view some maintain that we must look to the natural sciences in order to discover what we are; others insist that we must rely solely on metaphysics. But I think a more moderate line is reasonable. While I agree that it would be a mistake to expect too much from thought-experimentation, I also think it would be a mistake to eschew it completely.

One reason for this is the simple fact the imaginary cases found in the literature on personal identity often do generate extremely powerful intuitive responses. Upon being introduced to certain sorts of scenario, many of us clearly feel that it is entirely obvious that such and such a process would (or would not) be fatal to the subject concerned. The CRT procedure, for instance, if it were to unfold in the way just described, seems clearly survivable. There are many equally unambiguous scenarios. If my head were successfully transplanted onto another (headless) human body, it strikes me as obvious that I would survive the operation, and have a (mostly) new body—and I am not alone, most people take a similar view.

Secondly, and no less importantly, the use of thought experiments in an inquiry into our persistence conditions is underpinned by a clear rationale. A typical human life is woven from several different strands, some organic, some mental. Even if in reality these modes of continuity are not separable, by considering imaginary cases in which they do come apart we may be able to learn something about those elements of our lives we regard as most essential to our survival. If we can effortlessly envisage surviving a procedure which eliminates one specific continuity, we have grounds for supposing that this continuity will not feature in a readily acceptable account of what our persistence requires. If, on the other hand, we find it impossible to imagine ourselves surviving such a rupture, we have grounds for supposing the opposite. If we want a believable account of our persistence conditions, an account in which we can recognize ourselves, then it would surely be foolhardy to ignore evidence such as this. Especially since it is not unreasonable to suppose that we do have some insight into our own existence and persistence conditions. We are, after all, entities of an unusual kind: we are beings with consciousness and self-consciousness, and as such we have a unique perspective on what our existence and persistence involves. This is not to say that we have complete knowledge or understanding of the kind of things we are (e.g. introspection does not reveal to us that we have a brain), but in virtue of this unique inside perspective we have resources to draw on when we ponder the question of what our continued existence requires that we lack in other cases. This inside knowledge, limited as it may be, is inevitably going to inform our intuitive responses. Since our first-hand experience of the general character of what it is like for beings like us to exist and persist is likely to be broadly similar, whatever impact this experience has on our survival-intuitions is also likely to be broadly similar.

That said, it would be unreasonable to expect universal agreement with respect to each and every case. There are several related reasons for this.

Prior theoretical commitments are one potential source of disagreement. Different conceptions of the sort of thing we are obviously have different consequences with regard to the sorts of transformation that we could survive. Of those who are already firmly committed to some such conception, there will be some who are able temporarily to suspend their commitment when contemplating imaginary cases, but there may be others unable or unwilling to do so, with obvious consequences. However, I suspect that only a small minority of interested parties fall into the latter camp. If we come to believe a particular doctrine is false, most of us retain the ability to appreciate why others find it attractive.[3]

---

[3] This suspicion finds confirmation in the recent literature. Despite their animalist sympathies, philosophers such as Olson (1997), van Inwagen (1990), and Wiggins (2001) clearly appreciate the intuitive appeal of the Lockean position.

There is a second cause of intuitive divergence, one whose influence is likely to be more extensive. Before we are introduced to the philosophical literature, most of us will have encountered several different conceptions of the self and its possible fates: we are all familiar with fictional tales featuring princesses being turned into frogs and back again, for example, or people being killed but returning as ghosts, vampires, or demons. By uncritically and repeatedly accepting that such transformations are intelligible (which we often do, if only to allow the story to flow), our pretheoretical sense of the possible courses our lives could take is likely to alter and expand. As a result, our immediate intuitive responses to the kinds of thought experiments employed by philosophers is liable to be both permissive and varied—we haven't all been exposed to the same tales, and for one reason or another we won't all have found the same tales equally convincing.

Of course the intermingling of concept and belief, and the ensuing problem of separating the meaning of a word from the long-sedimented accretions of popular lore concerning what it denotes, is encountered elsewhere in philosophy, but it may well be that the problem is unusually acute in the current context. Few of us, for instance, will have encountered different conceptions of what constitutes *knowledge* prior to being introduced to the philosophical literature; nearly all of us have encountered a variety of conceptions of what persons are, or might be. But in acknowledging this we should also recognize that the resulting differences in our intuitive responses are likely to be quite small. It is true that there is endless variety to be found in folk tales, myths and fictions, but when it comes to implicit conceptions of the self, this variety occurs within quite narrow constraints. There are numberless tales of people living on as animals, demons, spirits, and (in recent years) as computer-sustained software entities. Where are the tales of people living on as ordinary (unaugmented, mindless) puddles, rocks, or rainbows? So far as our own nature is concerned, in attempting to locate the bounds of plausibility by the use of thought experiments, philosophers are to a large extent exploring territory already mapped out in fiction.

There is a further limitation on what we can learn from imaginary cases. Theories of the self are vulnerable on two fronts. We want an account that feels plausible, that accords with our deeper instincts and beliefs about the kind of thing we are. But we also want an account that is acceptable on general philosophical grounds, an account that is internally coherent and which also meshes with our wider philosophical commitments. An approach that is attractive on the intuitive level will not ultimately prove to be acceptable if it should turn out that it cannot be developed in a metaphysically satisfactory way. There is no guarantee whatsoever that the conception of the self and self-identity which best satisfies our intuitions will prove to be acceptable on broader metaphysical grounds.

However, while this is true, if the account which proves most appealing on the intuitive level also turns out to be unacceptable when broader metaphysical considerations are taken into account, we need not feel obliged henceforth to shun the use of thought experiments entirely. It would simply mean that we need to take a step back and try to develop an account which combines as much intuitive plausibility as possible with metaphysical soundness. Here yet a further factor enters the equation. The ineliminable role of wider philosophical considerations inevitably means that a final consensus is likely to elude us. People who bring different philosophical commitments to the table when assessing competing accounts of the self may well reach different verdicts on their overall merits, even if they agree on the degree to which each account is intuitively appealing. Since opinion on many central philosophical issues remains divided, and is likely to remain so, it would be unwise to expect a convergence of views as to the nature of the self any time soon, even if consensus could be reached on what a maximally appealing account might look like.

Where does this leave us? Taken together, these various points suggest that it is reasonable to suppose that thought experiments will have a limited but valuable role to play in our inquiry. Even if there is unlikely to be a complete consensus about each and every case, our intuitive responses to scenarios in which the various strands of our lives are pulled apart may still provide us with at least a rough idea of the sort of approach that is likely to prove most plausible, that accords with the most deeply and universally held features of our understanding of the kind of beings we are. Thought experimentation can thus provide us with some idea of where we should start and the direction in which we should move. If it can deliver no more, this is already something worth having. Thereafter imaginary cases should take more of a back-seat role; the detailed elaboration and refinement of our account is a theoretical task requiring metaphysical imagination and analysis, and those with different metaphysical preferences may well move off in different directions. Even so, when engaged in the task of elaboration, the insights gleaned from imaginary cases remain relevant. We may be looking for an account of the sort of thing we are that is metaphysically coherent, but we also want an account that we can believe.

Needless to say, the proof of the pudding is in the eating. My aim in this opening chapter is to show that our responses to imaginary cases *do* provide a useful point of departure.

1.2. PSYCHOLOGICAL CONTINUITY

In one sense the envisaged CRT procedure puts an end to your life, in another it does not. The process gradually extinguishes all biological life in your body, but it does not affect your mental life in the slightest: for as was stipulated, your memories, personality and intellectual abilities are unchanged, and you remain fully conscious throughout. The fact that we can easily imagine ourselves surviving such a procedure suggests that we regard the preservation of our mind, or mental life, as sufficient for our own continued existence. A variant of our original scenario suggests that the preservation of our mental life is also necessary for our continued existence. Imagine undergoing the *neuron* replacement therapy (or NRT) we encountered earlier, the procedure which converts only your neural cells into non-biological equivalents, leaving the rest of your body intact. Unfortunately, the procedure goes badly wrong, and most of your brain is converted to an inert homogeneous jelly; the only parts which still work are the lower brain regions responsible for autonomic bodily functioning. The upshot is that your mind and mental states are completely and permanently annihilated, but your body continues to live on, albeit in a mindless unconscious way. I think it fair to say that most of us would regard such an outcome as fatal to ourselves, if not our bodies.

Among Western philosophers it was probably Locke who first fully grasped the implications of the notion that mental continuity alone is necessary and sufficient for our continued existence. Locke realized that provided our mental life continues on, we believe we will remain in existence, irrespective of what houses or sustains our mental life.[4] It seems quite conceivable that a single persisting mind—and hence a single self or person—could inhabit a succession of entirely different material bodies, or equally, for those who believe in their existence, a succession of numerically distinct immaterial souls. The latter is no more difficult to imagine than the former. (Just imagine that the soul housing your mental life has been replaced every ten seconds for the past half hour without this being noticeable; once again, it seems obvious that you have survived this series of substitutions because it seems plain that you have remained in existence for the past half hour.) Thus was the Lockean project born: providing an account of our persistence conditions in terms of mental continuity, without essential reference to any entity which happens to house or support our mental life. Only an account along these lines can hope to do justice to our conception of the kind of thing we are. Or so those who follow in Locke's footsteps maintain.

There are, however, different forms of mental continuity, and consequently there are different ways in which a Lockean (or neo-Lockean) account of our identity conditions can be developed. The currently dominant approach—a direct descendant of Locke's own memory-based account—is usually known as the *psychological continuity* theory. There are several variants, but all share some core features. I will deal with the variants in due course, but first the basics, starting with the intuitive underpinning.

Since most of us believe that our brains sustain our minds, it is not surprising that most of us believe that we go wherever our brains go. Suppose that when you fell asleep last night you were drugged then kidnapped, and your brain was successfully transplanted into my body; something similar happened to me, with

---

[4] 'Upon separation of this little Finger, should this consciousness go along with the little Finger, and leave the rest of the Body, 'tis evident that the little Finger would be the *Person*, the *same Person*; and *self* then would have nothing to do with the rest of the Body.' *Essay* XXVII, §17

the difference that my brain was transplanted into your body. When waking up this morning we would both have a nasty surprise. Apart from a bad headache, we would find ourselves in a different body—on looking in the mirror you would see my face staring back at you, and I would see yours. A perturbing scenario, but a perfectly intelligible one. Now imagine a variant. Suppose a device is developed which produces just the same *psychological* effects as a brain-exchange, but without the surgery. There is no removal or exchange of brains or neural tissue. Rather, the device works by scanning and recording the neural structures responsible for psychological states such as memories, intentions and beliefs, along with hopes, fears, personality traits, and so forth, in each of two brains. The device then puts these recordings to work, causing each brain to enter into a psychological configuration that is all but indistinguishable from that previously instantiated in the other. Let us suppose, as previously, that you and I will both be drugged and kidnapped when we fall asleep tonight, but this time, instead of a brain-exchange we are subjected to a psychology-exchange: the device is used to impose your psychology onto my brain, and mine onto yours. If we again suppose that neither of us received advance warning of what was to happen, then it is plausible to think that we would each have a nasty surprise the next morning. I wake up in your body, I look in the mirror and am shocked to see your face—I wonder what on earth has happened; if it were not for the absence of surgical scarring I might even suppose that my brain had been transplanted into someone else's body! You have parallel reactions. We each believe that we have changed bodies. Scenarios of this kind, when formulated in this kind of way, make it very plausible to think that a psychological transfer would produce the same effect as a brain transplant: it is easy to believe that you really have moved into my body, and that I really have moved into your body.

So much for the intuitive rationale for the psychological theory; the scenario just outlined is essentially Locke's famous Prince–Cobbler case in modern dress. But what of the theory itself? Locke proposed a memory-based account.[5] If a Cobbler comes to have the Prince's memories, and the Prince the Cobbler's, then the two have exchanged bodies. In short, people go where their memories go. But from the purely intuitive point of view this is implausible. Most of us can easily conceive of surviving the loss of our memories—we do not regard amnesia as a life- or existence-threatening occurrence—also, most of us believe that we existed as infants, prior to the acquisition of any significant memories. The proposal is also problematic on a more theoretical level: how do we distinguish genuine

---

[5] Or at least, this is how Locke is often construed. What Locke really intended is less than clear, for as Barresi and Martin point out 'the simple memory-interpretation of Locke is at best radically incomplete. For central to Locke's account of the self is the idea that consciousness is reflexive and that it plays a dual role in self-constitution: it is what unifies a person not only *over* time but also *at* a time. Memory-interpretations, whether simple or not, do not explain how consciousness plays this dual role. Even so, it is clear that an important part of what Locke meant by *consciousness* plays this dual role' (Barresi and Martin 2003: 37).

memory-transfers from cases where people become deranged and come to have a set of illusory memories? Locke was silent on such questions; the contemporary psychological continuity theory was developed to answer them.

The story usually runs something like this.[6] Psychological states include not only memories but beliefs, intentions, desires, hopes, fears, likes and dislikes, and the various character traits. Let us focus on a single psychological state, the belief that I currently have that Everest is the highest mountain. If some future person Y also believes that Everest is the highest mountain, and this belief is causally related in an appropriate way to my Everest-belief, this person will be *psychologically connected* with me. If Y has other beliefs that I share, and these beliefs are causally related to mine in the right sort of way, then each of these common beliefs will constitute a psychological connection too. The same applies for my other psychological states. I can remember blowing out the candles on my seventh birthday; if Y has a memory with the same content, and this memory is causally related to my memory in the right kind of way, this is a further psychological connection. For any psychological state S that I have, if Y has a state with the same content, and this state is causally related to S in the right sort of way, then this link between myself and Y constitutes a psychological connection. The fact that I am psychologically connected with Y does not mean we are psychologically indistinguishable. I may have many psychological states that Y lacks, and vice-versa, but the fact that we *are* psychologically connected means that we have *some* psychological states in common. Now consider a case in which an earlier and a later person are not directly psychologically connected at all. Z is a person who lives in Y's future. Although Z and Y are psychologically connected to quite a high degree, there are no psychological connections whatsoever between myself and Z. I share many states with Y, but Y shares none of these states with Z—this is possible since Y has many states that I lack. Although I am not directly psychologically connected with Z, I am connected with Z *indirectly*, via the psychological connections both of us have with Y. This sort of indirect connectedness is called *psychological continuity*. More generally, psychologically continuity is constituted from overlapping chains of direct psychological connections.

So much for the terminology. So far as personal persistence is concerned, the proposal is this: an earlier person P is identical with a later person Q if and only if P is psychologically continuous with Q. Since psychological continuity includes a wide variety of different psychological states, there is no longer any danger of amnesia being fatal. Amnesiacs can no longer remember episodes from their past life, but they do not lose all their psychological states; many factual beliefs remain intact, as do personality traits, some likes and dislikes, and various mental abilities. These are enough to secure psychological connectedness and continuity from the early stages of childhood to the final stages of adulthood.

---

[6] See, for example, Lewis (1976*b*), Shoemaker (1984), Parfit (1984).

I have presented the theory in a schematic form so as to bring out as clearly as possible its defining trait: it is essentially a *causal* theory of survival. Psychological continuity is built from overlapping chains of psychological connections, and the latter are forged from relations of causal dependency holding between earlier and later psychological states. The causal ingredient fulfils two roles. Any account of self-identity has to have the means to distinguish duplicates from the real thing; similarity alone, even exact similarity, does not make for identity. Suppose I were to die tomorrow, by falling under the proverbial omnibus; a week later, by a freak coincidence, vast numbers of elementary particles converge and combine to produce a being who is exactly like me on the psychological level. Is this person me? There is no reason to think so. Is this person psychologically continuous with me? No, because the requisite causal dependencies between our psychological states do not exist. The same causal dependencies serve a second function: circularity prevention. The psychological continuity theorist wants to explain our persistence in terms of the persistence of psychological states. Suppose I currently have the intention to visit Berlin. Under what circumstances will this token belief continue to exist? A natural answer is that *I* will continue to exist, and continue intending to visit Berlin. A similar story can be told about other states. My memory of blowing out candles on my seventh birthday is another token state; for this state to exist at some future time, *I* will have to exist at that time, and still be able to remember the experience in question. If this account is correct, psychological connectedness presupposes sameness of person, and if we cannot state the conditions under which psychological connections hold without appealing to personal identity, an account of personal identity rooted in psychological connectedness would be circular. Hence the appeal to causality. If we can explain the persistence of token psychological states in causal terms, without appealing to sameness of self, we can explain psychological continuity and connectedness in a non-circular way. Whether this is really possible is a substantive issue, all that matters for our purposes is that most psychological continuity theorists believe that it is possible.

I will call this approach the causal-psychological theory, or the *P-theory* for short; I will also refer to psychological continuity as *P-continuity*. Thus far I have provided only the bare outlines of the P-theory, and as is no doubt obvious, the core idea can be developed in a number of different ways.

One question concerns how much connectedness is required for survival. Some P-theorists take the view that for a future person to be me, that person must be quite like me psychologically; they must possess a good many of my memories, beliefs, intentions, and the like. If this is the case, survival requires a good deal of connectedness. But many P-theorists take a different view. They are prepared to allow that a person's psychology can change a great deal over time, perhaps totally. Provided these changes do not happen too suddenly, provided there is a good deal of connectedness over the short term, a future person could be me even if there are no direct psychological connections linking us. I will be linked to this future person by P-continuity, and this is enough to guarantee my survival. There is plenty of room for P-theorists of this persuasion to disagree about the rate of psychological transformation that is consistent with survival, but I will not try to adjudicate on this issue—I simply note that the P-theorist has room for manoeuvre here.

Another significant dimension of variation concerns the kind of causal relation that is needed for psychological connectedness. The latter has to be caused in the right sort of way, and different views as to what the right sort of cause can be have different implications for the relationship between ourselves and our brains. Following Parfit (1984, §78), we can distinguish between the *Narrow* and *Wide* versions of the P-theory. Narrow P-theorists hold that for P-continuity to be person-preserving it must be caused in the usual sort of way, in our case by a single human brain. Wide P-theorists are more liberal, and allow non-standard causes, for example the psychology-exchange device we encountered earlier.

Although both versions of the P-theory may well be coherent, it does not follow they are equally well-motivated. Wide and Narrow theorists both begin from the premise that so far as survival is concerned, it is mental continuity that is of crucial importance. But if mentalistic considerations are paramount, it is not at all obvious why we should accord any particular significance to *brains* as a means of securing the required causal relations. Narrow theorists could insist that their view represents a sensible compromise between the conservative implications of body- or brain-based accounts and the radical implications of the Wide approach. But since they agree with the Wide theorists that the brain is only relevant to survival because of its role in securing P-continuity, it is hard to see why they should insist that sameness of brain is *necessary* for survival. If P-continuity has primary importance, why should we regard a process which gradually turned an organic brain into an inorganic one be fatal if P-continuity is unperturbed by the process?

Since it is the Wide P-theory that looks to have greater intuitive appeal—and intuitive appeal is what we are currently looking for—it is this version I shall concentrate on.

1.3. FIRST DOUBTS

If the P-theory were true, it would have a number of intriguing consequences, not the least of which is the prospect of travel at lightspeed via *informational teleportation*. This putative mode of getting around—variants of which are now familiar from both science fiction and philosophy—works as follows. A person—you, let's suppose—is subjected to a scanning process of an unusually probing kind: it reveals and records every detail concerning the atomic (and sub-atomic) composition and structure of your body and brain. As soon as the scan is completed, your body is instantly (and painlessly) annihilated, and the resultant information transmitted to some distant location by radio waves. The matter and energy produced when your body is annihilated are not transmitted to the distant location, these resources are put to good use locally: they are turned into organic fertilizer. Once received, the information from your scan is used to construct a physical replica of you from a fresh supply of matter and energy. The construction process is very fast; it takes only a few seconds. This replica is very similar to you physiologically and neurologically: the 'new you' is a conscious being, psychologically indistinguishable from the 'old you'. The question, of course, is whether the new you *is* you, or merely a replica of you. Is teleportation a way of getting about, or an expensive way of committing suicide?

The verdict of the Wide version of the P-theory is clear: since the causal relations between the original and reconstituted versions of you are direct enough to guarantee your survival, this form of teleportation should be regarded as a mode of transportation. But most of us, when first encountering this kind of story, do not find the answer obvious at all. The notion that *some* form of teleportation may be survivable is by no means entirely unbelievable. The characters in the various *Star Trek* series have no qualms about using their 'transporter' system, and viewers tacitly assume *that* system, however it works (the details are usually left unclear) must be person-preserving—why else would anyone use it? But when the core mechanics of purely informational teleportation are made explicit, it is very easy to believe that the newly-constructed you is merely a replica of you, rather than you yourself. At the very least, this fact suggests the P-theory does not possess the intuitive plausibility it initially promised, and which we are currently seeking. Moreover, such doubts can easily be strengthened. It suffices to consider a scenario where the upshot so far as P-continuity is concerned is precisely the same as in teleportation, but where the technology is less bedazzling.

For reasons we need not enter into, you are anaesthetized and then deep frozen. When fully hardened, your body is fed head-first through something resembling a bacon-slicer. By the time your feet have passed through this machine your body has been sliced into about fifty thousand very thin slices. Over some years, each of these slices is studied in great detail, using a variety of techniques. The aim is to draw up a complete map of the cellular composition and structure of a typical human body. These techniques are destructive, so by the time the map is complete none of your tissues remains intact. The map contains so much information that to store it in standard book form would require hundreds of volumes and an exorbitant quantity of paper, but it can fit easily onto one of the latest-generation optical discs. These discs become the standard anatomy text for medical students, and soon there are thousands of copies, all over the world. As the years pass, and re-constructive sub-cellular medicine blossoms, it becomes possible to use the map of your body to build an exact physical replica of it. So efficient are these techniques, the replicas produced are conscious beings who exactly resemble you psychologically (so far as anyone can tell). The excitement and controversy this procedure initially provoked have long since blown over, and the procedure is now a standard lab exercise for students the world over: a replica of you is brought into being a couple of times a week, on average. Most of these replicas are near-perfect; they awake believing themselves to be you, and are psychologically indistinguishable from you (or just about—lab exercises sometimes go awry). Happily (or not) few survive long: a couple of hours after regaining consciousness, the reanimated versions of you are painlessly put to sleep, and thereafter used for dissection practice.

You may find this scenario somewhat morbid. You may well find the idea of having your deeply anaesthetized body put through a sophisticated bacon-slicer an unpleasant prospect, but how do you feel about the subsequent reanimations? Do you feel personally concerned with the fates of the thousands of copies that will be made of you? I suspect not, for it seems clear that these are *merely* copies of you. They are replicas not the real thing. However, if the P-theory were true—at least in its Wide guise—this is not how you ought to feel. The template of your body stored on disc is causally connected to you in a very direct way; had your psychology been in any way different than it was, the neural map stored on the discs would be different in a corresponding manner. The causal connections between you and your replicas in this case is as direct as in the case of informational teleportation. If the latter is person-preserving, then the procedure just envisaged should be too. But it clearly is not.

Confronted by scenarios such as these, the P-theorist could respond along these lines: 'So what? Some truths of metaphysics are hard to believe or unpalatable. Out intuitions are not an infallible guide to truth, far from it.' And of course this is a perfectly respectable position to take. But in the present context it is damaging, for we are currently looking for no more than an intuitively compelling basis upon which to construct an account of the kind of thing we are, and it seems that the P-theory is a good deal less intuitively compelling than it initially seemed.

In what direction should we move? It might seem that our responses to the bacon-slicer example are pointing us towards some form of physical continuity account, or the P-theory in its Narrow form. No one thinks that informational teleportation is a way of moving physical objects. If a lump of granite is broken down into its constituent atoms and these are scattered, or turned into energy or fertilizer, it is clear that the lump no longer exists, and there is no temptation to suppose that a replica of the lump constructed from a previous scan is identical with the original. The same applies for a hunk of meat. If teleportation destroys us, rather than preserves us, then perhaps we are akin to hunks of meat or lumps of granite. However, for reasons already noted, no account along these lines will be a plausible candidate for a neo-Lockean account of the self. It is simply too easy to envisage surviving any amount of physical or material disruption or discontinuity. The mind-preserving CRT procedure looks to be eminently survivable, and the same applies to more radical procedures where the replacement of physical constituents occurs at an even faster rate: so long as there is no mental disruption, it is hard to believe such procedures would be fatal.

In any event, such a response would be premature. As a further cluster of thought experiments will make clear, P-theorists are right to think that a mentalistic account of survival is more believable than the alternatives; where they go wrong is in equating the self-preserving form of mental continuity with P-continuity.

1.4. SOME VARIETIES OF VIRTUAL LIFE

Virtual reality is now a familiar concept. The state-of-the art at present is quite primitive, but still capable of producing impressive effects. A moderately sophisticated set-up comprises a suit fitted with sensory pads, and a visor fitted with video-display units, both connected up to a computer. On donning the visor you see a computer-generated landscape stretching out before you, populated with three-dimensional objects. Should you turn your head, the sensory pads pick up the speed and degree of movement, and the computer quickly changes the visual display in a corresponding manner, so as to create the impression that you are exploring a stationary outer environment with your eyes. If you walk towards an object, you see it getting closer and larger—the changes in perspective are entirely realistic. If you see a solid cube on a table-like object in front of you, and reach forwards to pick it up, you see a hand stretching forward, its movements corresponding to the movements you intend and feel; and when you grasp the cube, you see it move in just the way a real object would when picked up. These relatively simple tricks produce a powerful illusion of being in a world there waiting to be explored; but this entirely 'virtual' world does not exist outside the computer's memory and your own experience. There are clearly limitations on this sort of procedure. Even if entirely realistic visual and auditory stimuli could be provided by means of a headset, it seems unlikely that fully realistic tactile illusions could be provided by a computer-controlled mechanical suit. Even if such a suit could reproduce the effect of picking up a heavy object, it is hard to see how it could reproduce the patterns of pressures and textures felt by our skins as we swim through water (say). To produce a fully life-like illusion of being in a world (a world very much like the real world), virtual reality technology will very likely have to abandon complicated suits, and, bypassing the body's sensory organs, work instead directly on the brain, or at least the nerves leading from the spinal cord and sense organs to the brain, and those parts of the brain involved in bodily movements.

I will call this hypothetical future development of virtual reality technology *virtual reality of the second degree*, or VR-2. All we have at present is a fairly primitive level of VR-1, virtual reality of the first degree, which produces its illusions by stimulating the body's sense organs, rather than operating directly upon the brain. We do not know enough about the brain to know what sorts of neurophysiological intervention would be needed to produce a completely realistic illusion of living and moving about in a complex physical world, and even if we knew we would not be able to carry such interventions out; and no doubt the computer resources needed would be considerable. But this is only an imaginary case, so let us suppose these difficulties have been overcome. Someone hooked up to a VR-2 device would be in a position akin to that of the traditional vat-brained subject, or a victim of the Cartesian Evil Demon. Their sensory experience would be indistinguishable, phenomenologically at least, from that of someone inhabiting an external world of the kind they seem to be inhabiting, but the world they seem to be inhabiting is not the real world, it is merely an illusion. VR-2 technology might provide lucrative commercial possibilities. It would, for example, be far cheaper to visit distant lands by immersing oneself in an appropriate VR-2 program than visiting them in person. The effect would be somewhat similar to playing one of today's more sophisticated computer role-playing games, but far more life-like. On entering such a program, you find yourself in an unfamiliar environment, and have to decide what to do; the way your 'trip' unfolds depends partly on the choices you make—the program is equipped to deal with whatever you elect to do, and furnishes you with perceptual experiences appropriate to both your artificial environment and your actions.

Now although the environments our hypothetical VR-2 subjects seem to inhabit are illusory, the subjects themselves certainly exist. (Their experience might be indistinguishable in all phenomenological respects from yours or mine at this very moment, and the notion that *we* do not exist, in the midst of having experiences such as *these*, is difficult to take seriously.) VR-2 subjects also have psychological systems similar to yours or mine—their memories, beliefs, intentions, and personality traits are all intact. Because of this, in assessing the importance of P-continuity, it will prove useful to take a further step, and consider *virtual reality of the third degree*, or VR-3.

In this significantly more sophisticated system, when a subject is connected to the VR-device, not only is a completely realistic virtual environment generated, as previously, but the subject is also furnished with new memories, beliefs, intentions, personality traits, etc.—a whole new psychology, one whose constituent states are not causally dependent upon those they replace. The replacement psychology is not installed instantly, but it is accomplished speedily, in a matter of a few minutes. On being informed that they can expect to experience nothing more than a few moments of mild anxiety and bewilderment, most VR-3 users understandably opt to remain fully conscious throughout the transition. So advanced are the machine–brain interfacing technology in VR-3 devices, this is quite feasible.

By way of an illustration, let us suppose that you have long been an aficionado of VR-2 adventures and you decide to take another trip. Having always been fascinated by the Second World War, you opt to spend a week as a WW2 submarine commander. If you choose the VR-2 option, you retain your current memories and personality traits; if you choose the VR-3 option, your current memories and personality traits are wiped from your brain (and stored in the computer's memory) and your brain is furnished with an entirely different psychology, of the kind a typical WW2 submarine commander might well have had. Since you have already been on several VR-2 vacations, you choose the VR-3 option and its promise of a far more immersive experience. You are connected to the machine, the technician tells you the program is about to begin, and as the echo of his words fades, you find yourself on the windswept deck of a submarine at sea, the freezing salty spray lashing your face as the surprisingly small vessel courses through the heavy sea—there is no trace of your previous environment, or the VR-3 machine. For a few moments you feel surprised by this sudden transition, and the entirely realistic character of the illusion, but then a sailor speaks to you, and you find yourself replying, and any sense of passively witnessing a life-like illusion disappears: you are soon completely absorbed by the task in hand, your previous life utterly forgotten. A week later, while in the midst of dealing with a serious depth-charge attack, you find yourself transported from your command post in the bowels of your shuddering submarine to the quiet of what seems to be a warm bed. After a few moments of bafflement, you remember, everything. Your original memories, beliefs and personality are back in place, you remember the sudden transition to the deck of the submarine as the program began its run, and everything that has happened over the past week—and remembering the damp, the cold, the terror, the adventure of it all, you decide it was worth every penny. You have not only looked through the eyes of a submarine commander—a VR-2 simulation would provide that—you have experienced what it was like to *be* one.

Embarking on a VR-3 adventure involves undergoing what is in effect a fast and drastic brainwashing. When the simulation begins, your original psychology, down to the last detail, is quickly removed and replaced. As was stipulated, the new (and possibly very different) psychology is in no way causally dependent upon your original psychology, and so psychological continuity is ruptured. From the perspective of the P-theory, the consequences of this are dramatic. Narrow P-theorists will perhaps most plausibly view the rupture as lethal, since on this view P-continuity and sameness of body are necessary for survival, and P-continuity has been ruptured. Another option for the Narrow P-theorist is to say that you enjoy an intermittent existence: you cease to exist when the initial psychological transfer takes place, and when your original psychology is returned to your body, you return to existence—in between times a distinct subject occupied your body. Wide P-theorists have the option of holding that you are transferred into computer memory, where you persist in a dormant state until your psychology is returned to your body and reactivated. But since each of these interpretations entails that you do not proceed to experience the WW2 adventure—you are either dead, enjoying a temporary period of non-existence, or stored away in computer memory—none is in the least plausible. Or at least, none of these interpretations seems in the least plausible if we clearly stipulate that the envisaged VR-3 process accomplishes the psychological transfer *without interrupting the flow of your experience*, which is how we are construing this process. In the VR-3 scenario just outlined it was stated that as your psychology was replaced you remained fully conscious throughout, that is you had an uninterrupted succession (or stream) of bodily sensations, perceptual experiences, thoughts, memories, and emotions. The perceptual experiences were (seemingly) of a transition between two very different environments, but there was no interruption of experiential continuity: you were always experiencing *something*, and hence the transition itself was something you directly experienced. That fast and dramatic changes in perceptual content can be experienced is something we all know. Just think of what it is like to watch an action movie, or dive into a swimming pool: in both cases there are fast and extensive changes in the contents of experience, but there is no loss (or total interruption) of consciousness—the sudden and dramatic changes are themselves *experienced*.

More pertinent to the scenario we have been considering, the transitional phases in the VR-3 scenario would be subjectively similar to the experience of waking from a vivid dream. It is easy to imagine the relevant sort of case: one moment you are dreaming you are an officer aboard a WW2 submarine, and fully immersed in that world, with no (available) knowledge of your normal life, then you start to awake. After a few moments of confusion, *experienced* confusion, you are back snug in your bed, the submarine adventure already quickly receding. Since most of us have been woken up in the midst of vivid dreams, most of us have had experiences of this kind (even in the absence of VR-3 machinery), and we all know that transitions of this character can be directly experienced. The transition occurs as part of an uninterrupted stream of consciousness in which each phase seamlessly slides into its successor.[7] The envisaged VR-3 process is rather more extreme, but it is phenomenologically similar, and easily imaginable.

---

[7] We can say that we are *conscious* of such transitions, provided 'conscious' is construed in the right way. A person can 'be conscious' in the sense of *being awake* (*rather than asleep*), but they can also 'be conscious' in the sense of *continuing to have experiences of some kind*. The two senses do not always coincide: a person who is dreaming is conscious in the latter of these senses but not the former. Note also that there is, in principle, no need for the VR-3 induced rupture in psychological continuity to be accompanied by any dramatic changes in the qualitative character of a subject's experience. Suppose you opt for a 'lucky dip' VR-3 trip: your new psychology and virtual environment are randomly selected, from a vast array of permissible permutations of the relevant parameters. By a sheer fluke, the randomly generated psychology you are supplied with is an exact replica of your original psychology, and the virtual environment you are located within is—again by sheer fluke—an exact copy of your actual environment. Improbable but not impossible. And given the way the replacement psychology is created, it is not causally dependent in any way on your original psychology, and so not psychologically continuous with it. But while this new variant makes it particularly easy to envisage oneself surviving ruptures in psychological continuity—if the replacement is instantaneous, it need not impinge in any way on the flow of one's consciousness—it is also useful to appreciate that processes which replace one's psychology *and also* significantly alter the character of one's experience are eminently survivable, provided no rupture in phenomenal continuity occurs. This is why in the main text I have been concentrating on the more dramatic kind of VR-3 trip.

The idea that we would not or could not survive such a process is difficult to take seriously.

I plead guilty to the charge of having presented this scenario in a question-begging way—I assumed without question that *you* were present at each stage of the procedure. But given the fact that you are indisputably present at the outset, and that the stream of consciousness you have at the outset flows on without interruption, isn't assumption eminently justified? The idea that a stream of consciousness starts off as yours, and ends up as somebody else's seems absurd—at the very least it is radically counterintuitive. And don't forget: it is with intuitive plausibility (and implausibility) that we are concerned at present.

VR-3 scenarios illustrate ways in which aspects of our minds or mental life could diverge. They also show that it is easy to envisage ourselves (a) surviving ruptures in psychological continuity, and (b) surviving massive and sudden psychological change—survival without psychological similarity. What VR-3 scenarios do not do is illustrate survival in the absence of any psychological system whatsoever. A more radical procedure than any yet considered does illustrate this, and so further undermines the P-theory.

When you embark on your VR-3 adventure you are provided with new beliefs, memories, and personality traits, and left free to act as you wish: the actions you undertake are the causal product of your artificially implanted psychology, they are not dictated by the VR-3 program; the latter simply detects and responds to the courses of action you undertake, providing you with perceptual experiences appropriate to your freely chosen decisions and actions, as they unfold in your virtual environment. You behave in accord with a newly installed psychology, rather than your original, but there is a real sense in which it is still you who is calling the shots. Since a VR-3 device has to be sophisticated enough to quickly generate life-like experiences in response to a subject's often unpredictable choices and actions, there would be obvious advantages in developing technology capable of generating *virtual reality of the fourth degree*. It is only with this development that survival without anything we might call a psychological system becomes a reality.

On being plugged into a VR-4 machine you find yourself slipping quickly (but consciously) into the scenario and psychology you have selected. The available options in these respects are similar to those offered by VR-3 programs, but with one significant difference: the VR-4 program does not install a new psychology into your brain, it completely bypasses your own psychology, and furnishes you with an uninterrupted flow of experience that is entirely computer-driven. Moreover, this stream of consciousness is no longer the product of activity going on within your brain, it too is entirely machine-generated. Having discovered the fundamental physical principles responsible for the generation of phenomenal consciousness, the designers of VR-4 machinery decided to avoid the risks associated with directly manipulating people's brain activity for long periods.

When you embark on your VR-4 trip, your stream of consciousness is, in effect, *lifted* from your brain and seamlessly joined to a stream of consciousness that is machine-produced. Your brain, meanwhile, lapses into a profound coma-like condition. None of this is noticeable from the inside, as it were. Your experience is seamlessly continuous throughout, just as it is on a VR-3 excursion. So, having embarked on your VR-4 trip, it seems to you, phenomenologically, that you are having adventures in your chosen locale (although you won't remember choosing it), and you do so from within a psychology that may be quite different from your own (although you won't be aware of this at the time); furthermore, you have experiences of (or *as* of) choosing certain courses of action, deliberating over what to do, weighing up the odds before you leap, and reaping the consequences of your decisions. But although the phenomenological character of your experience is just as it would be if your decisions were the upshot of a set of causally efficacious beliefs, desires, and personality traits, in reality your *entire* stream of consciousness is computer generated, so the experiences you have are wholly determined in advance; you experience and 'do' nothing that is not present on the program being run on the VR-4 device.

To make matters more concrete, suppose your VR-3 generated submarine adventure had been recorded, down to every last thought, feeling, volition, and experience. The contents of this recording were not pre-programmed, since the VR-3 machine generated experiences in response to how you acted from moment to moment, and your actions were the unpredictable upshot of your own distinctive neurological characteristics combined with the implanted psychology. However, the availability of VR-4 technology means absolutely anyone can enjoy exactly the same adventure—hook them up to the machine and play them the recording, and they experience everything you experienced; where you agonized over a decision, they agonize over it. There is a difference: whereas you actually took these decisions, they only seem to; but this difference is not something detectable at the phenomenological level. The same applies to understanding and cognition. A subject enjoying a VR-4 trip thinks meaningful thoughts and understands other people's utterances, or at least they seem to: their understanding-experience is just like yours or mine.[8] The experience of a VR-4

---

[8] I use this term in Strawson's sense, to refer to the various forms of consciousness associated with what we might call the 'experience of meaning' in its diverse forms (contentful thoughts, written and spoken words): 'To talk of understanding-experience, then, is not to commit oneself to the implausible view that there is some single qualitative type of experience that anyone who has understanding-experience must have. It is not to commit oneself to the view that particular qualitative experiences invariably go with understanding particular sentences. Nor is it to commit oneself to the view that understanding-experience involves any kind of inner mental theatre. The point is simply this: there is in the normal case something it is like, experientially, to understand a sentence, spoken or read. You have just done so and are continuing to do so. Your doing so is not nothing, experientially. It is part of the current *course of your experience*, part of the content of your conscious life, and it is happening now.' (Strawson 1994: 7)

subject may only be *as if* understanding is taking place, and the same applies to other forms of cognition, but this is all that is required for a phenomenologically realistic trip. From the phenomenological perspective, a VR-4 adventure is just as full and vivid as your current experience, in every respect.

We are assuming—as in previous cases—that you slip into your VR-4 adventure without any interruption in phenomenal continuity (and as before, this is something that we simply stipulate—there is no doubt about it, your stream of consciousness flows on, without interruption). Consequently, it seems clear, intuitively speaking, that *you* slip into the adventure, that the experiences delivered by the program are experiences you have. But when you are immersed in a VR-4 program, your stream of consciousness is completely controlled down to the last detail by the program, and as a consequence, the course of your experience is independent of what is going on around you (i.e. independent of the kinds of events you could ordinarily perceive) and also independent of your beliefs, memories and personality traits. Your stream of consciousness is divorced from both the external environment and the rest of your mind (the psychological system that remains latent in your body). By focusing on an uninterrupted stream of consciousness, life in the absence of anything resembling an ordinary psychological system becomes easily imaginable.

To bring the ramifications of this into clear relief let us vary the scenario a little. While you are enjoying your VR-4 submarine adventure, a rare accident happens: the life-support equipment keeping your body in a healthy condition breaks down, and your brain is irreparably damaged. Your psychology is irreparably destroyed; your memories, beliefs, and personality traits are irretrievably lost. However, since your stream of consciousness is being wholly sustained and produced by a VR-4 device, you are oblivious to all this: you are still at sea, trying to ensure that your craft and crew survive the depth-charges exploding all about. Or so it seems to you—your experience is as full-bloodedly realistic as any *real* submariner's ever was. But things have changed; you can never be returned to your body and brain to take up the life you left behind. Happily, things are not as bad as they might be. The legal situation is clear. Before embarking on your VR-4 holiday, you signed a standard contract. This contract allows VR-4 holidaymakers to determine the course of action that should be taken in the event of their re-embodiment becoming impracticable, for whatever reason. Two options are available. The first is to have one's stream of consciousness discontinued immediately. The second is to continue on with the VR-4 adventure. This involves living out the remainder of one's days within the virtual world that one chose to visit only temporarily. Anyone choosing this options is guaranteed an eventful and rewarding life, and a peaceful death at a respectable age. Not surprisingly, many choose the latter option—since the first amounts to instant death. This is the option *you* chose before embarking on your submarine trip. You have another thirty years or so ahead of you.

1.5. STRANDS UNTANGLED

Life as nothing but a series of experiences, a stream of unified consciousness, flowing on in the absence of any psychology may be imaginable, but it is not necessarily possible. The same applies to a life consisting of a stream of consciousness flowing smoothly over total ruptures in the causal relations between psychological states that are required for P-continuity. There is no reason to think VR-3 or VR-4 devices will ever be constructed, or could ever be constructed. Such devices would certainly require technology far in advance of anything currently available, and given that we know so little about how our brains generate experiences, we are not yet in a position to speculate with any confidence about quite how far neural-interface technology could be taken.

Setting technological considerations aside, the situation is scarcely any more clear from a purely philosophical standpoint. Scenarios in which experiential and psychological continuity come apart are certainly easy to *imagine*, and it is not difficult to see why. First of all, psychological continuity is largely a subterranean phenomenon, at least from an experiential standpoint. Psychological states such as beliefs, memories, intentions, desires can all manifest themselves in consciousness; they do so all the time. But typically only a tiny portion of our psychological system is manifest in our experience at any one moment (think of all the memories you have that are *not* reflected in your current experience). Since the bulk of our psychological systems at any given time are concealed behind the scenes, as it were, it is by no means obviously absurd to suppose that sizeable portions of these systems could be replaced without this impinging on the character of our experience. (In an analogous vein, imagine gazing up at the moon; as you keep it clearly in view, isn't it perfectly possible that technologically advanced aliens are rapidly removing 99 per cent of the moon's mass? Provided they take steps to ensure that the visible surface of the moon remains unchanged, would you be any the wiser?)

There is a second, and perhaps more important reason why it is so easy to imagine experiential and psychological continuities coming apart. As Hume noted, relationships of causal dependency are neither observable nor introspectible. If from a phenomenological perspective causal relations are always and necessarily invisible, it is scarcely surprising that we can easily imagine our experience remaining unaltered in the absence of such relations. But imaginability is one thing, possibility another. Many imaginable states of affairs are not nomologically possible, and at least some states of affairs are imaginable without being logically possible. Consequently, from the fact that scenarios in which streams of consciousness flow on in the absence of psychological and biological continuities are readily imaginable, we cannot conclude—at least without further argument—that such cases are really possible, in any significant sense. In fact, given our current state of knowledge, I do not think we can be confident about what the precise relationship between the phenomenal and non-phenomenal aspects of the mind really is.[9]

But so far as present purposes are concerned, all this is largely irrelevant. The various scenarios just outlined were not intended to establish the real possibility—whether nomological, logical, or conceptual—of the different strands of our life becoming separated from one another. Their purpose is the much less ambitious one of making it easier for us to appreciate which of the easily distinguishable strands of life seems most intimately bound up with our survival, and the answer seems clear. There is not one type of mental continuity, there are two. In addition to the continuities forged by relations of causal dependency between earlier and later mental states, there are also continuities in our conscious experience that we are acquainted with throughout our waking hours, continuities in our perceptual experience, in our bodily experience, in our thoughts, feelings, volitions, and mental imagery. These *phenomenal* or *experiential* continuities are normally accompanied by physical and psychological continuity. But as our thought experiments have revealed, phenomenal continuity all by itself seems sufficient to keep us in existence: from a purely intuitive standpoint it is implausible to suppose that ruptures in physical or causal (and hence psychological) continuity that do not impinge upon the flow of phenomenal consciousness could put an end to our existence. Irrespective of whether such ruptures are in any sense really possible—a controversial matter, philosophically speaking—this result suggests that we should explore the possibility of framing an account of our persistence conditions in terms of experiential continuity, as opposed to continuities of any other kind. Or at least, it suggests that anyone seeking to elaborate an account along Lockean lines should move in this direction. In developing such an account it would, of course, be useful to know the precise relationship between the phenomenal, causal, and material aspects of mind—only then would we know whether it is really possible (logically, metaphysically, or nomologically) for the corresponding continuities to diverge. But the project of trying to specify our persistence conditions in phenomenal terms can be pursued perfectly well in the absence of this knowledge. Lockeans who favour the psychological approach often do so without committing themselves to any particular view of the relationship between the physical and the psychological—why shouldn't Lockeans who find the phenomenal approach appealing do likewise?[10] Even if it should

---

[9] It could easily turn out that the question 'Can the two aspects of mind really come apart?' lacks a straightforward answer. To illustrate, suppose Chalmers' non-reductive functionalism turns out to be correct. Then (I take it) the phenomenal and causal/functional aspects of mind would be nomologically inseparable in this world. But since in this theoretical framework the phenomeno-functional connections which hold in this world are only contingent, there are other possible worlds where the two forms of mentality can and do come apart.

[10] Those who extend reductive causal conceptions of the mental to the phenomenal realm (e.g. analytic functionalists) will insist that it is incoherent to suppose that experiential continuity could

turn out to be *logically* impossible for phenomenal continuity to diverge from causal or organic continuities, it would be wrong to conclude that these different continuities must all be of equal significance. Things of different kinds can be inseparably locked together without being equal in all other respects: there is no such thing as a painting without edges, but this does not mean that the edges of a painting possess the same aesthetic value as what they surround.[11]

Although I am not claiming (here at least) that we can use thought experiments of the kind we have been considering to discover deep metaphysical truths about the nature of the mental, I am claiming that they can provide useful insights into what is most relevant (and irrelevant) to our continued existence. Consequently I am open to this sort of objection:

Devising tales which contrive to give the impression that experiential continuity can be sufficient for our persistence even in the absence of other continuities establishes nothing, for it is also possible to devise tales which would leave the vast bulk of readers with the impression that so far as our continued existence is concerned, experiential continuity is mere flotsam in comparison with psychological or physical continuities. Suppose, for example, that each day at noon, your stream of consciousness is instantaneously transferred into my body (and starts to be sustained by my brain), and my stream of consciousness is instantaneously transferred into your body (and starts to be sustained by your brain). Since these changes never impinge on our psychological systems, we are completely unaware of these movements, and so too is everyone else. It would surely be absurd to hold that, under these circumstances, you and I are exchanging bodies on a regular basis.

No doubt narratives could be developed which make experiential continuity seem largely (perhaps even entirely) inconsequential so far as facts about personal identity are concerned could be developed, but this is only to be expected: skilled story-tellers often do succeed in making the implausible seem plausible—at least within the confines of the tale they are telling. But what matters for present purposes is whether experiential continuity *still* seems unimportant when our attention is drawn to it—when it is given just as much prominence in a description of what is happening as psychological and physical continuities. It is hard to see how it could. Just imagine that the stream of uninterrupted consciousness which features in the scenario under consideration starts off as

obtain in the absence of relationships of causal dependency. It goes without saying that this variety of reductionism is controversial—and as I said in the *Preface*, I am working on the assumption that reductionism about the phenomenal is false. Nonetheless, it is worth (re)emphasizing the point that subscribing to some version of causal reductionism is perfectly compatible with attempting to define our persistence conditions in experiential rather than psychological terms. Functionalists, after all, do not deny that experiential states exist, they just give a causal account of what their existence involves.

[11] If our streams of consciousness turn out to be identical with certain physical continuities, then the latter will of course have the same significance (so far as our persistence is concerned) as the former—but since they are numerically identical, and (now) known to be so, this is only to be expected.

yours, and ask yourself whether you can make sense of its ceasing to be yours, irrespective of what happens at the physical or psychological levels. As we have just seen in connection with the VR-3 and VR-4 scenarios, it is by no means impossible to imagine one's stream of consciousness continuing on through radical changes in accompanying psychological dispositions. Given this, we can easily make sense of the idea that—in the scenario just outlined—you and I *do* change bodies each day, even if no one notices. It is also worth pointing out here that subscribing to the psychological or bodily continuity theories provides no immunity to difficult-to-discern changes in facts pertaining to personal persistence. Suppose at noon today your body was annihilated and instantly replaced by an exact replica, or that you underwent an instantaneous brainwashing, and receive a new psychology that is very similar to your original psychology (even though the former is causally independent of the latter). Such replacements may well go entirely unnoticed, from first- as well as third-person perspectives, but according to the theories in question they are not survivable.[12]

The rationale for favouring the phenomenal can be put in a slightly different and somewhat stronger way. A claim that our persistence consists in the holding of some mental or physical relationship between earlier and later selves will only be readily believable if the presence of this relationship at least makes the identity claim readily intelligible. But it would be better if we could start off from a stronger position. For an account to be maximally plausible, the identity-conferring relationship should be such that if it holds between an earlier self X and a later self Y, it is *impossible for us seriously to doubt* that X and Y are one and the same. We have seen that if X and Y are linked by psychological continuity alone—as in the informational teletransportation scenario—not only is it possible to doubt whether X and Y are numerically identical, the claim that they are identical can be hard to take seriously. The same applies to any form of material continuity in the absence of mental continuity—as we saw in connection with the NRT-procedure which went wrong, it is by no means obvious that a person can survive the total and permanent obliteration of their mind. The situation is

---

[12] The point can be illustrated in a further way. In his well-known and influential article 'The self and the future' (1970), Bernard Williams discusses a pair of imaginary cases in a way which threatens to undermine the Lockean methodology. When a psychological transfer case is presented in one way, it seems intuitively clear that the original persons go with their psychologies into new bodies; when essentially the same case is presented in a different way, it seems intuitively clear that the persons involved remain in their original bodies, and are merely brainwashed. If our intuitions can be so easily manipulated, how can they be trusted? Doesn't the fact that we can seriously doubt that a psychological transfer can succeed in shifting *ourselves* into another body indicate that deep down we are committed to a bodily continuity theory of our persistence? Not in the least, for there is a significant omission in Williams' presentations: no mention whatsoever is made of *phenomenal* continuity. If the scenarios are presented in such a way that it is clear what happens to the subjects' streams of consciousness—that is to say whether they remain in the original body, or move into a new body—all ambiguities are eliminated: it is immediately clear what happens to whom, it is immediately clear that experiential continuity trumps other sorts of continuity. See Dainton and Bayne (2005) for a more thorough discussion of Williams' argument.

very different when X and Y are linked by phenomenal continuity, when X and Y are subjects of a single uninterrupted stream of consciousness—irrespective of what changes or discontinuities occur on the material or psychological levels. When an earlier and a later self are connected in this way, it is very hard, perhaps impossible, to believe that they are anything other than one and the same. Hence, if we are seeking to build on foundations that are as intuitively appealing as possible—that are as *credible* as possible—there is a strong case for looking beyond material and psychological continuities, and focusing first on continuities of the phenomenal variety.

It is one thing to say that experience (or the capacity for it) matters more than anything else when it comes to our continued existence, it is quite another to say that the character of our experience is *all* that matters to us. VR-4 devices are what Nozick called *experience-machines*. Nozick introduced the idea of an experience-machine to make just this point: 'We learn that something matters to us in addition to experience by imagining an experience-machine and then realizing that we would not use it . . . . What is most disturbing about them is their living of our lives for us.'[13] Nozick also mentions the fact that we want to do certain things—make differences to the world and other people—over and above merely having the experience (as) of doing them. This is all true. Given the choice of a very pleasant and interesting life spent entirely hooked up to an experience-machine, and a significantly less pleasant and interesting life lived in the real world, few of us would volunteer for the former. But the crucial point is that we regard the machine-generated life *as a life*, and a life *we* could lead. Being permanently attached to an experience-machine and having a purely virtual (rather than a biological) life is not a fate many of us would choose—but it is very different from non-existence.

Descartes maintained that a being capable of conscious thought could be certain of one thing: its own existence *as* a conscious being. This plausible claim can be broadened: for as long as it *remains* conscious, a conscious being can be confident of its own persistence, its own continued existence as a conscious being. Since I would not want to claim that conscious beings or subjects of experience are necessarily self-conscious, we can re-phrase thus: a conscious being can be confident that it will continue to exist for as long as it remains conscious, for as long as it continues to have experiences. This yields a principle that is as simple as it is clear:

Experiences in the same stream of consciousness belong to the same self or subject.

Or in more succinct form, where 'consubjective' is taken to mean 'belongs to the same self or subject':

The S-thesis: co-streamal experiences are consubjective.

---

[13] See Nozick (1975: 44). Nozick also considers a *transformation machine*, which turns you (physically) into whatever sort of entity you choose to be, and the *results machine*, which turns the world into what you want it to be.

Further investigation will be required before we can be confident that the S-thesis is in fact true, but it certainly has a good deal of plausibility. Try to imagine a scenario in which your stream of consciousness flows on in an ordinary straightforward fashion but *fails to take you with it*. The notion that one could be left behind in this way seems absurd, as absurd as supposing one could cease to exist without ever losing consciousness. Suppose you have been granted the power to experience moving in any way that you desire, at any speed, in any direction. It is easy to imagine oneself finding out it what it would be like to zoom backward or forward across time, or to shoot across to the other side of galaxy in a matter of seconds, or to slide into other dimensions or parallel universes. Can you imagine picking up so much speed that you find out what it is like to leave your stream of consciousness behind? If you think you can imagine what it would be like to do precisely this, are you sure you are not just imagining *extending* your current stream in some unusual way?

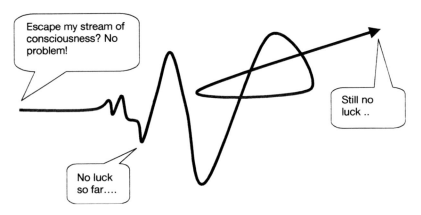

Figure 1.1 Attempting the impossible

While I think Descartes was right to emphasize the close connection between selfhood and experience, I am not inclined to follow him all the way. Phenomenal continuity may provide us with a uniquely compelling guide to our own persistence, but it looks to be at best a sufficient condition for it.[14] Experiences in a single uninterrupted stream of consciousness may be linked by phenomenal continuity—each brief phase is experienced as sliding into the next—but experiences in distinct streams are not. If I lapsed into dreamless sleep last night, the experiences I am having today are not phenomenally continuous with those I had yesterday. Unless we hold (as Descartes notoriously did) that despite

---

[14] Here, as elsewhere in these preliminary remarks, I am ignoring the problems posed by the putative possibility of fission, which I will come to later on.

appearances to the contrary we are in fact continuously conscious throughout our lives, or that our lives are much shorter than most of us believe, then it is hard to see how phenomenal continuity could be a necessary condition for survival. If distinct streams of consciousness (streams separated by gaps in consciousness) can be consubjective, we need an account, preferably an informative account, of how this can be so. I will refer to this as the 'bridge-problem'.

It is certainly true that it is not obvious how the bridge-problem can be solved by appealing to experiential continuities—the problem exists precisely because there are times in our lives when such continuities are absent! Nonetheless, the link between experiential continuity and survival is so strong, that it is reasonable to think that this form of continuity might at least form the *basis* for a credible account of our identity conditions. It certainly seems reasonable to suppose that an account along these lines, provided it can overcome the bridge-problem without straying too far from its phenomenal foundations, will be more believable than an account built on any other basis. For this reason such an account along these lines—a *experience-based* or *phenomenalist* account, as I will sometimes call it—is well worth pursuing. The guiding tenet of this approach is straightforward: in formulating an account of our existence and persistence conditions we should appeal, so far as is possible, to nothing more than phenomenal unity and continuity.

2
Phenomenal Unity

2.1. EXPERIENCE

An experience-based approach to the self may have distinct advantages over the alternatives, but as every builder knows, the stability of a structure depends upon the strength of its foundations. Before embarking on the constructive phase of operations I am going to spend some time on the foundations. This chapter and the next are devoted to the unity we find in our experience, both at and over time. I am not going to attempt to provide a very detailed characterization of these modes of unity. For present purposes this is not needed.[1] My aims are more modest: I will defend, albeit in outline form, a general conception of both synchronic and diachronic phenomenal unity. Since this conception accounts for the unity and continuity of consciousness without appealing to anything external to consciousness, it is well-suited to serving as the basis for a phenomenalist account of the self and its persistence conditions.

So far as synchronic unity is concerned, the topic I will be concerned with in this chapter, although I take it as obvious that such a unity exists, there are very different views as to its nature, and some of these have significant implications for the kind of thing that selves could be. I will be arguing against several such views, and in favour of an alternative, simpler, account. Although the latter has certain implications for the structure of consciousness (not least by accounting for phenomenal unity without appealing to anything external to experience) it does not in itself compel the adoption of any particular conception of what selves are—phenomenological considerations (even broadly construed) can take one a certain distance, but not all the way. Diachronic unity poses difficulties of a different kind. Most would agree that from moment to moment our typical streams of consciousness seem continuous: each brief phase of our experience appears to slide seamlessly into its successor. These transitions appear so smooth that it is phenomenologically unrealistic to talk of discernibly distinct 'phases' at all; for the most part our consciousness unfolds as a continuous flow. Discontinuities in the contents of our experiences do occur—as when we hear a sudden and unexpected loud bang, or put our hand on a hot stove

---

[1] For a fuller account see Dainton (2000), and for further elaborations and clarifications Dainton (2003a, 2003b, 2003c, 2003d).

and feel a sudden and intense pain—but these discontinuities do not (usually) interrupt the overall continuity of our consciousness: sudden interruptions of this kind generally occur against the backdrop of an uninterrupted flow of bodily sensations and perceptual experiences in other sensory modalities. (Being pulled from a day-dream by a sudden loud BANG is not at all like regaining consciousness after deep dreamless sleep.) That our streams of consciousness *seem* continuous is something few would be inclined to deny, but explaining how this is possible is a notoriously difficult task, and some very different theories have been proposed. Some of these theories deny that the successive parts of our streams of consciousness are in fact unified experientially, despite appearances to the contrary. I will argue that accounts of this kind are mistaken. According to the view of diachronic unity I will be defending, the neighbouring (brief) parts of a stream of consciousness *are* unified by direct experiential connections. Once again phenomenal unity—this time in its diachronic form—is accommodated without appealing to anything external to the phenomenal sphere.

Before proceeding a few further preliminaries are in order. I set out some of my starting assumptions in the *Preface*, there are others—of a less general kind—that also need to be put on record.

As may well already be clear, as I use the terms, the realms of the experiential and the phenomenal are co-extensive: I take an *experience* to be any item or state with a phenomenal character, and something has a character of this type if there is something that it is like to have it. 'Consciousness' and 'experience' are similarly related, for by 'consciousness' I always mean *phenomenal* consciousness, and for something to be conscious in this sense there must be something that it is like to have it. A phenomenal *object* is any part of an experience, and the features of such objects are phenomenal *properties* (or *characteristics*). I allow the expression *phenomenal content* to range over phenomenal objects and phenomenal properties.

These preferences with regard to these terms is by no means uncommon these days, but it has implications that are worth noting. Some philosophers prefer to work with a narrow conception of consciousness. Typically starting from the premise—by no means implausible, on the face of it—that conscious states differ from their non-conscious counterparts by virtue of the fact that we are *aware* of the former but not the latter, these philosophers then put a substantive gloss on 'awareness'. Some hold that to be aware of something, in the relevant sense, we have to pay attention to it; others say that we have to think about it. There is no harm at all in registering the differences between these different ways of being conscious, but from a phenomenological standpoint at least, these restrictive policies seem implausible and unmotivated. This is easily appreciated with the help of a few examples. If on a busy street the traffic noise is such that I have to strain to hear what a friend is saying, my auditory experience is clearly not confined to my friend's voice. I continue to hear the traffic noise (alas) even though I am not thinking about it or attending to it. Similarly, if my attention becomes intently focused on a drop of rainwater slowly running down the outside of my window, my visual experience does not narrow down so that I see nothing but the raindrop: I continue to see the window, the walls on either side, and what lies beyond; I continue to hear the traffic noise outside; I continue to have a range of bodily and emotional feelings. I do not notice these peripheral experiences, I pay no attention to them; I am not thinking about them, but they are there nonetheless. Since a complete description of what it is like to be me at the time in question would include these experiences, it seems perverse to hold that they are not parts of my consciousness—if my consciousness *were* restricted to what I am attending to, or thinking about, it would be very different from how it is.[2]

For these reasons, it seems far more natural to construe 'consciousness' in a broad fashion, so as to embrace experiences that we do not pay attention to, as well as experiences to which we do pay attention, in one way or another. So far as individuation is concerned, it is common practice to assume that experiences owe their individuality to their *precise phenomenal character*, their *time of occurrence* and their *subject*. For most practical purposes this is unproblematic, but in the context of an inquiry into the nature of subjects it is less than ideal. If we assume at the outset that experiences are dependent in this way upon subjects, certain metaphysical options are closed off before we have even begun. The subject-dependent status of experience is a significant and controversial hypothesis that has to be argued for, not simply assumed in advance. Consequently, I will work on the less theoretically charged assumption that experiences owe their individuality to their precise phenomenal character, their time of occurrence and their *physical basis*. If E_1 and E_2 are two simultaneously occurring experiences with the same phenomenal character, to be distinct they must be grounded in different physical systems, or different parts or aspects of the same physical system. (In the human

---

[2] There is, of course, more to be said on this topic. For some thoughts on *how* we can know this see Dainton (2000: ch. 2). Note that it is possible to hold (as I do) that our experience is not confined to what we are paying attention to without also committing oneself to what Noë calls the 'snapshot' conception: 'According to a conception of visual experience that has been widely held by perceptual theorists, you open your eyes and—presto!—you enjoy a richly detailed picture-like experience of the world, one that represents the world in sharp focus, uniform detail, and high resolution from the centre to the periphery' (Noë 2002: 2). The snapshot conception does not accord with the phenomenology: the unattended parts of the visual field are *not* in sharp focus (at least in my case). Noë goes on to get the phenomenology right: 'But surely it is a basic fact of our phenomenology that we enjoy a perceptual awareness of at least some unattended feature of the scene . . . I may look at you, attending only to you. But I also have a sense of the presence of the wall behind you, of its colour, of its distance from you.' (Noë 2002: 8) He goes (at least partly) astray when he equates the perceiving of the visual background with the sense we have that a whole cat is present even when we perceive only those parts of it which are not concealed by the fence behind which it is sitting. Unlike the unseen parts of the cat, the visual background *is* seen—it is present in experience, even if not in a very detailed way. For some relevant empirical work (involving subjects being randomly 'beeped' and asked to record what they were experiencing at the time) see Schwitzgebel (2007: 25): 'My participants exited the experiment with a moderate view of some sort, thinking that experience extends beyond the field of attention but does not occur in every major modality 100 per cent of the time.'

case, the relevant system is the brain or nervous system.) This will serve for most purposes, although alternative schemes are required to deal with certain exotic cases.[3] Given my agnostic stance with regard to the matter–consciousness relationship, I take no firm line on the issue of precisely what is involved in experiences having a physical basis. If experiences are themselves physical then the relationship may well be identity. If experiences are non-physical the relationship is presumably causal. But it may be that the relationship is best conceptualized in some other way—a way we have yet to discover.

As for what counts as *an* experience, I take a pragmatic stance. For some purposes it may be appropriate to regard the entirety of what I am experiencing at a given time to be a single experience, for other purposes it may be more useful to regard the contents of my visual field as a single experience, and likewise for the other sensory modalities; for other purposes—for example when I both see and hear a dog barking—it may be useful to regard combination experiences in different modalities that happen to be associated with a common object (or cause) to be single experiences. In short, there are many ways to divide a typical complete state of consciousness into parts, and I will not be assuming there is any privileged way of so doing.

Questions about counting aside, quite what can be regarded as 'an experience' is affected by the view one takes of perception. Whereas direct (or naïve) realists hold that the immediate objects of perceptual awareness are physical objects or their surfaces, representational (or Lockean-style indirect) realists hold that the immediate objects of perception are phenomenal items, generated by our brains in response to incoming stimuli. There is no denying that the indirect realist theory is counterintuitive. The phenomenology of visual experience is such that our eyes seem to be (more or less) transparent windows onto the world; the material objects we see in our environments seem to be right there, present before us *in propria persona*—it is by no means obvious that all we are (directly) apprehending are brain-generated experiential representations rather than the physical things themselves. Nonetheless, since I think direct realism is ultimately very hard to defend, I will be assuming in what follows that some form of the representational theory *is* true, and hence that the objects we are immediately aware of in our perception—for example the yellow wall visible a few feet away from me, the sound of my neighbour's dog barking—are themselves phenomenal items possessing phenomenal properties, and as such parts of my overall state of consciousness.[4] Although this assumption significantly influences what I take

---

[3] For instance, if there are possible worlds consisting of nothing but experiences, and experiences are non-physical, then it will obviously be impossible to individuate otherwise indistinguishable experiences by reference to their physical basis. In such cases, taking experiences to be basic for purposes of individuation seems legitimate—certainly as legitimate as taking material objects to be basic in universes containing nothing but material objects.

[4] I do not think direct realism succumbs to a single knock-down argument; my adherence to the Lockean view is motivated by a number of considerations which—so far as I can see—all

our states of consciousness to include, and some of the ways I will be describing them, many of my main lines of argument do not depend upon it, and direct realists should be able to translate most of the relevant doctrines into their own preferred terms. More specifically, if it is possible to develop a version of direct realism which is compatible with the unity and continuity we find in our typical streams of consciousness, then it should be possible to translate the claims I will be making in this chapter and the next into terms acceptable to the direct realist—assuming, that is, that these claims are themselves adequate to the phenomena.[5]

Although Lockean-style indirect realism is sometimes known as the *representational* theory, it is important to distinguish this position from the 'representationalism' found in contemporary philosophy of mind and cognitive science, the standpoint advocated by Harman (1990), Dretske (1995), and Tye (1995). There is a good deal to be said about this approach, but I am going to concern myself here with just one aspect of it: the claim that we are not in any significant sense aware of any of our experiences. According to latter-day representationalists, in our perceptual experience we are aware of our surroundings in virtue of being aware of representations of them, but we have no awareness of the representations themselves (the latter are thus 'transparent'), but only of the *content* of these representations, that is how they represent the world as being.[6] To appreciate how this is supposed to work out in practice, take

point in the same general direction. If the conceptions of matter to be found in contemporary physics are along roughly the right lines then medium-sized material objects are more akin to volumes of empty space permeated by force-fields than 'solids' as we intuitively conceive them. This point alone does something to undermine the plausibility of direct realism: anyone who takes science seriously already has reason to think that the objects we perceive are radically unlike how we perceive them to be. There is also the familiar point that life-like hallucinations are possible, so we know that our brains can generate real-seeming environments all by themselves. And the fact that the causal processes involved in seeing and hearing are analogous to the processes which result in the production of states such as pain—that is states which are (fairly) obviously phenomenal. We feel a nettle's sting when our skin is irritated by an acid and electrical signals are sent to our brains' pain-centres via our nerves; we see the colours in a rainbow when appropriate patterns of electromagnetic radiation interact with the nerve cells in our retinas, triggering a cascade of neural processes in the various visual systems in our brains, processes which terminate in the production of visual experience. Where's the difference? But no one thinks that pains are out there on the surfaces of nettle leaves, waiting for us to sense them. As for the question of why direct realism seems true, there is surely no real mystery here. Since our sensory systems evolved to inform us of goings-on in the world about us, it would be surprising if it were otherwise: real snakes often have a dangerous bite, representations of snakes do not. It is in our interests to believe the world is as we see it—or as our experience presents it. For more on these themes see Robinson (1994), Foster (2000), and Chalmers (2004).

[5] Some arguments later in the book rely on claims about how different parts of our overall experiential states are interrelated (e.g. §8.6, §9.5). While these are less resistant to translation into terms the direct realist would find acceptable, the general approach to our persistence conditions that I will be advocating does not depend on these arguments.

[6] Here is Tye expounding the doctrine: 'Visual experiences are like sheets of glass. Peer as hard as you like via introspection, focus your attention any way you please, and you will only come across surfaces, volumes, films, and their apparent qualities. Visual experiences are transparent to

the experience of seeing a red balloon floating against a blue sky. For an indirect realist of the Lockean variety the blue expanse and the red sphere (or circle) are themselves experiences, by virtue of being *parts* of their subject's overall state of consciousness at the time in question, and these experiences possess a certain spatial relationship to one another. The representationalist will describe matters in a different way: in being aware of the balloon, we are not aware of an experience (or any part of an experience), we are aware of *the balloon itself* (construed as a material object), since the content of our experience is (roughly speaking) 'a red balloon floating across the sky'. Now of course Lockean indirect realists can agree that the relevant experience (as they would construe things) indeed has this representational content: this experience is naturally regarded as presenting a red balloon floating across the sky. However, they also hold that this content is embodied in (or associated with) a vehicle that is *not* transparent: namely, an expanse of phenomenal blue containing a circle (or sphere) of phenomenal red. The Lockean will readily concede we can (and usually do) take these phenomenal items to be things in the world—representationalists are quite right about this. But the Lockean will further, and I think rightly, insist that we are also able to effect a switch of perspective and view these same items *as* phenomenal items, if we so choose. The 'transparency' of what carries representational content is thus dependent on whether we adopt a stance of naïve phenomenology (we take our experiences at face value) or critical phenomenology (we allow broader philosophical commitments to affect how we view our experience). So far as I can see, *both* ways of talking about experience are perfectly intelligible and equally legitimate. Accordingly, I see no reason to eschew all talk of experience in favour of talk about what experiences present. Representationalists who are alert to the nuances of phenomenology are well aware of the unity and continuity to be found in our experiences (or as they would put it) among the objects and qualities represented in our experiences (see Tye 2003). If representationalism can be developed in a way which is adequate to the phenomena, then it should be possible to re-state the phenomenological claims I will be making over the course of this chapter and the next in terms representationalists are prepared to accept.[7]

---

their subjects. We are not introspectively aware of our visual experiences any more than we are perceptually aware of transparent sheets of glass. If we try to focus on our experiences, we "see" right through them to the world outside. By being aware of the qualities apparently possessed by surfaces, volumes, etc., we become aware that we are undergoing visual experiences. But we are not aware of the experiences themselves' (2003: 24).

[7] I cannot myself see how representationalists can (i) save the phenomena, that is provide an account of what our ordinary experience is like that is phenomenologically adequate, (ii) reject direct realism, and (iii) also hold that the representations which present the world to us are transparent, and so lacking in discernible phenomenal features—just where do the phenomenal features we directly apprehend in our experience come from? Given (ii), it cannot be our physical surroundings, and given (iii) it cannot be the mental representations which supposedly represent the world. But I will not press this point here.

Our sensory and perceptual experiences are significant parts of our consciousness at any one time, but it is important to stress that they are not the only parts. We often tend to overlook the full range of bodily experiences. In addition to bodily sensations, feelings of warmth, pressure and the like, there are also various kinds of proprioceptive experience—the sense we have of how our limbs are disposed, or how our bodies are oriented. There are also mental images, conscious thoughts, and emotional feelings. Also easily overlooked are the range of 'fringe' feelings, for example the intuitive sense that we have seen someone's face before, or that we know the answer to a question, or that things are proceeding as they should, or shouldn't. A temporal cross-section of a typical stream of consciousness will contain experiences of all these varied kinds.

Moreover, and relevantly to present purposes, each and every part of such cross-sections are unified: our experiences at any one time are experienced *as* unified. We all know what it is like to see a cat crossing a road; we all know what it is like to see a cat crossing a road while hearing a plane pass overhead. In the one case there is a visual experience, in the other there is a visual experience *and* an auditory experience, and the latter experiences are experienced as occurring together in a single episode of consciousness—they are, in short, *co-conscious*. Even if we cannot characterize it in an informative way, we all know what it is like for auditory and visual experiences to be co-conscious; we all know what it is like for conscious thoughts and stinging-sensations to be co-conscious; we know what it is like for conscious thoughts, stinging-sensations, and visual experiences of cats crossing roads to be co-conscious. At least as a first approximation, all our experiences are co-conscious with one another at any given time; all exist as parts of unified states of consciousness. This applies to the experiences to which we are paying attention or thinking about, and those to which we are not. Indeed, those experiences we do attend to are themselves co-conscious with those to which we are not attending: the phenomenal foreground and the phenomenal background are unified in our overall consciousness.

The question we need to focus on is this: what phenomenal binding agent is responsible for this unity? What is the phenomenal adhesive, as it were, that binds our consciousness together?

2.2. PHENOMENAL SPACE

There may well be regions of our expanding universe—distant galaxies moving rapidly apart, for instance—that are not in direct causal contact with other regions. We are happy to regard such regions as parts of the same universe because, despite their mutual causal isolation, they are spatially related, and by definition objects that are spatially related exist within the same space. In the physical realm, space is a unifying agent like no other. Might the same apply in the phenomenal realm?

On the face of it, the suggestion is by no means absurd. Much of our experience is certainly spatially extended.[8] This is obvious in the case of vision (think of gazing at a big blue sky) and only slightly less obvious in the case of hearing, but many bodily sensations possess also some spatial extension (think of sliding into a hot bath) as do many mental images. The spatial character of our consciousness does not end here. Many of our experiences possess intrinsic spatial extension but many are also spatially related, both within sense-modes and across them. When I hear a person speaking on my right and a car passing to my left, I have two spatially related auditory experiences; when I have these auditory experiences while watching a bird fly overhead, my auditory and visual experiences are spatially related. Moreover, and equally obviously, the space in which we see and hear things is also the space which our bodies seem to inhabit. Not all our experience has discernible spatial extension or a fully precise spatial location—for example a vague feeling of unease, most conscious thoughts—but merely by virtue of seeming to occur within our bodies (or heads) such experiences are spatially related to all our other experiences.

The space within which our experience unfolds may be phenomenal rather than (or as well as) physical, but it cannot be denied that most of our experiences (or many of their contents) are spatially related, and consequently it is not obviously absurd to hold that the unity of consciousness is a product of its spatial character. Hence we arrive at what we can call the *space-thesis*, according to which experiences (or their contents) cannot be co-conscious *unless* they are phenomeno-spatially related, and they are co-conscious only *because* they are phenomeno-spatially related. For the space-thesis to be true it is not enough for most of a subject's experiences to be spatially related for most of the time, it must be impossible for a subject's experiences to be co-conscious *without* being phenomeno-spatially related. Hence the question we need to address is whether it is possible for experiences (or their contents) to be co-conscious without being phenomeno-spatially related. Although the issue is a difficult one to resolve with certainty, I can see two reasons for thinking this might indeed be possible.

First of all, the spatial characteristics of different kinds of experience can vary enormously, likewise the strength of their spatial relatedness. Imagine looking at a chess board. Not only are the squares of phenomenal colour which feature in your experience spatially extended and precisely demarcated, their mutual spatial relations to one another could not be clearer. The spatial features of non-sensory experiences, such as conscious thoughts and certain moods or emotions, are far less well-defined. Under normal conditions, the latter sort of state seems to be located in our bodily sense-fields, albeit not very precisely, and as a consequence they inherit spatial relations to all other parts of our current experience. This last

---

[8] Or if you prefer 'Many of the contents of our experience are spatially extended'—some reasons for not distinguishing between experiences and experiential contents will emerge in the later parts of this chapter.

fact is suggestive. What spatial characteristics would wholly non-sensory forms of consciousness possess in the total absence of perceptual and bodily experience? The answer could well be: none whatsoever. Imagine that you become reduced to a disembodied (but still functioning) brain. You are no longer capable of having any form of sensory experience, not even in the form of mental images or memories (you suffered some brain damage during the operation); you no longer have any bodily sense-field, not even of the phantom variety. But you can still think non-imagistic thoughts, and still feel certain emotions. Given the absence of perceptual and bodily experience, and assuming that you have no idea where your brain now is—you are not in any kind of contact with the outside world—it seems unlikely that you would have the impression that your experience is occurring at any particular place in physical space. You would very likely *feel* as disembodied as you actually are—or more so, since although you know you must still have a brain, you can no longer perceive it. Now, when in this disembodied condition, would you have any impression that you yourself are extended in space? Would your thoughts and feelings seem to be occurring in a phenomenal space of any kind? It is hard to see why or how they could. In the absence of a phenomenal space, although your thoughts and feelings are just as co-conscious as they ever were, would they seem to be *spatially related* to one another in any way whatsoever? Again, it is difficult to see why or how they could. If experience can be radically non-spatial in this sort of way, and it seems quite plausible to suppose that it can be, then the space-thesis is false.

There is a second route to this conclusion. Although our sensory experiences are fully integrated spatially, it could easily be that this is due to contingent features of our makeup. We are spatially localized beings; our various sense organs are all on the surfaces of our bodies, and our bodies are unified material objects which occupy a comparatively small volume of space. Since we perceive the world from the vantage point of a single spatial location, it is to be expected that our perceptual experiences are spatially unified: our senses have evolved so as to provide us with an accurate guide to our surroundings, and our surroundings are spatially unified. But must all conscious beings be spatially localized in this way? There is no obvious reason to think so. To pick on just one of many conceivable examples, there might well be worlds (possible or actual) where conscious beings live deep underground, and only perceive the surface via several widely-spaced eyes protruding through their planet's surface on long flexible stalks. Since the eyes of such a creature view the world from very different locations, if the resulting visual experiences *were* spatially integrated they would, in effect, be misrepresenting how things are. It would be better by far for the various 'scenes' to be experienced together, co-consciously, but without being spatially superimposed. If such beings could exist or evolve, their sensory consciousness would be unified without being spatially integrated.

This is purely speculative, of course, but the speculation is not entirely idle, for it is not difficult to imagine one's own experience coming close to having a similar form. As research over several decades has confirmed, those accustomed to using 'telepresence' technology often experience mild forms of apparent bi-location. An engineer who is closely monitoring the progress of remotely controlled submarines will at times have a strong sense they are themselves present underwater, negotiating a path along the ocean floor, despite knowing full well that they are safely ashore in a comfortable warm dry control room. Surgeons who carry out operations by video-link often feel that they are in direct physical contact with a patient who in reality is hundreds or thousands of miles away, and they continue to have this feeling while conversing with people who really are a few feet away—despite seemingly being present elsewhere, they also remain aware of their real surroundings, albeit at the margins of their awareness. These effects are to a considerable degree attention-dependent; as attention to the task in hand or scene in view waxes and wanes, participants typically feel their subjective location—the place where they feel themselves to be located—shifting back and forth between real and virtual environments; but on occasion they may also feel as if they are suspended somewhere in between, or in both places at once (Biocca 1997). While in this state, such subjects have a consciousness that is spatially disunified (at least largely), but which is also unified: the experiences associated with each environment are co-conscious.

Given the limitations of the currently available technology, it is not surprising that these effects tend to be transitory and unstable—that people rarely feel themselves *fully* immersed in their virtual environments for long. As the machines get better, this might easily change.

Consider, for example, the gymnasium. These days they are often extremely noisy places to be, and since many gym users prefer their own choice of music, they wear headphones as they exercise, hooked up to personal music systems. In a few years time the VR-3 technology we have already encountered may make a more complete escape from one's surroundings possible. Let us suppose that you frequently avail yourself of this technology. During your regular lunchtime gym session, while continuing to pedal away on your exercise machine, you opt to make use of your VR-3 cranial implant to take an extremely lifelike virtual tour around one of the world's greatest museums. (You are not always so high-minded: you spent your previous exercise session at a rock concert.) The museum is a communal virtual environment, and you are supplied with a manifest virtual presence within it—an 'avatar' in the form of a head which moves about in accord with your wishes. As well as providing you with an audio-visual viewpoint, you can also use this virtual head to converse with other (virtual) visitors. Back in the gym your body continues to be a source of bodily feeling, but nothing more: the virtual reality device temporarily numbs your head and 'suspends' your biological eyes and ears—for the duration of the trip you are only able to see and hear through your *virtual* eyes and ears, and although you can talk, you can only do so by using your virtual mouth.

As you explore the museum, moving back and forth, viewing paintings from different angles, conversing with other viewers—their avatars also take the form of roving heads—you continue to have a background awareness of your body back in the gym, pedalling away. But you have little or no sense that *you yourself* are in the gym (even though you know full well that in one sense that is precisely where you are). Why? Because you have the strong impression that your thinking (and willing, and mental imaging) is taking place precisely where it usually does: a couple of inches behind your eyes and between your ears, and these seem to be unambiguously located in the museum. Phenomenologically speaking you now have *two* different spatial locations, and the spatial relationship between these locations is tenuous. For despite remaining dimly aware of your body, you have no sense of where your body is located in relation to your audio-visual viewpoint: you can feel your legs pumping away on the exercise machine, but you have no idea as to which direction your head would have to move in order to meet up with your body; similarly, you have no idea as to which direction, or how far, your body would have to move in order to reconnect with your head. Consequently there are no spatial relations (of the phenomenal variety) linking your bodily and audio-visual experiences.

Although you spend most of your exercise session in the museum (subjectively speaking), every now and again you direct the focus of your attention onto your bodily experience, just to make sure that everything is as it should be on that front. The consequences are dramatic. As the focus of your attention shifts, as your audio-visual experience of the museum recedes to the periphery as your bodily experience comes to the fore, there is a corresponding shift in your subjective location: you come to have a vivid sense of *being in* your body once again. Such shifts do not involve any sense of moving *through* space, they simply involve a change in where you seem to be. And of course, when 'in' your body you have no sense as to which direction you would have to move in order to reconnect with the audio-visual perspective of your head. On yet other occasions you try to pay equal attention to your bodily and your audio-visual experiences; you find it difficult to divide your attention in this way, and even when you succeed you cannot sustain it for long. But when you do succeed, you seem (fleetingly) to be equally present in both the gym and the museum, even though you have no sense of where these locations are relative to one another.

For present purposes, what is of interest about this type of scenario is not that it seems possible to envisage oneself seemingly existing at two separate and distant locations, it is that it seems conceivable that one's total state of consciousness could be divided into parts that are not spatially connected, phenomenally speaking, despite being fully co-conscious. By 'conceivable' here I mean 'reasonable to think possible', rather than 'clearly imaginable'. I for one cannot clearly imagine what it would be like for my consciousness to be divided into spatially isolated parts. But I can come close to it. When reflecting on scenarios of this type, it seems very plausible to think that experiences *could* be co-conscious despite being spatially unconnected with one another. As for why this seems plausible, it may in large part be due to our intuitive insight into the nature of the co-consciousness relationship itself. We know what it is like for experiences to be co-conscious, and we know experiences can be fully and vividly co-conscious even when their apparent spatial relations are extremely weak or vague—for example sounds do not need to have a precise spatial location to be experienced together, certain bodily sensations likewise—and this suggests that co-consciousness itself is not essentially spatial in nature, even though the experiences it connects usually are spatially related.[9]

In any event, these considerations, combined with the apparent possibility of wholly non-spatial modes of consciousness being co-conscious, strongly suggest that the space-thesis is false. At the very least, so long as we confine ourselves to broadly phenomenological factors, as we are currently doing, we have no good reason for supposing it to be true.

2.3. SELF AND AWARENESS

I want to look at a second account of the synchronic unity of consciousness, an account that has substantive implications for what selves are. Although I will be arguing that this account is even more problematic than the space-thesis, it is nonetheless well worth examining. The reason for this is simply that the account in question can seem very compelling—or at least, it can when we are considering the self from a purely experiential perspective.

As noted in §2.1, some have found it plausible to hold that we are conscious of something only if we are *aware* of it. Anyone subscribing to this view has what may seem to be an account of the unity of consciousness that is both simple and appealing: they can hold that experiences (or their contents) are unified when, and only when, they fall under a single awareness. If this were the case, and if mental states have to fall under an awareness in order to be conscious at all, it is to be expected that our experience is as unified as it is. Unity and consciousness would necessarily be found together because both essentially depend on awareness; a single agency or mechanism would be responsible for the existence *and* the unity of conscious experiences. However, as I also noted, there are different views as to the kind of awareness which supposedly renders contents conscious. In the light of our current concerns, and assumptions, we can rule out several of these. Consider first the doctrine that paying attention to (or thinking about) experiences renders the latter conscious in a distinctive way. Perhaps so, but since it is typically the case that all parts of our experience are

---

[9] For a more detailed treatment of these themes see Dainton (2000: ch. 3, 2003*b*, 2003*c*). This result has implications that I will be exploring further in Chapter 5.

unified—including those parts that are the objects of our thought or attention and those parts that are not—we cannot explicate phenomenal unity in terms of this sort of awareness.[10] The same applies to introspective awareness, at least of the contrastive type, the type which focuses on some parts of our experience at the expense of the remainder. The co-consciousness of the unintrospected regions of our experience cannot be accounted for by awareness in this guise, and the same applies to the co-consciousness of these regions with the parts of our experience which *are* introspected.[11]

Clearly, if a form of awareness is responsible for phenomenal unity, it must extend to all parts of our experience, and account for the manner in which these parts are experienced together. There is a form of awareness which, if it existed, might well satisfy these conditions. There is a tradition according to which all conscious states comprise two distinct elements: one or more phenomenal contents, together with an act of pure apprehension or sensing which the relevant contents fall under. The phenomenal contents are instantiations of phenomenal properties (assuming the representational theory of perception), whereas the 'pure sensing' is construed as a quasi-perceptual form of direct awareness that ranges over inner objects (such as thoughts and mental images) as well as seemingly outer ones (what we see and hear). In effect, the doctrine takes the direct (or naïve) realist view of ordinary visual perceptual experience—an unmediated apprehension of material objects—and generalizes it to all forms of experience. A version of this view dates back at least as far as Locke, who wrote: 'Consciousness is the perception of what passes in a man's own Mind' (*Essay*, II, I, §19). It lives on in the guise of the 'higher-order sense' theories, whose contemporary

[10] This is something of an oversimplification. Proponents of 'higher-order thought' theories—see, for example, Rosenthal (1986)—hold that the thoughts which render experiences conscious are themselves usually *unconscious*. But while this view may successfully explain why parts of our experience we don't seem to be thinking about can be conscious—assuming experiences actually do need to be thought about in order to be conscious—it is by no means obvious that it can explain the overall unity of consciousness. The higher-order thought theorist will claim that a collection of experiences is unified if and only if they are all objects of a single higher-order thought. But as Rosenthal himself concedes (2003: 330) there is probably no single higher-order thought which takes in all our conscious states. And even if there were, it is implausible in the extreme to hold that the phenomenal bonds between our experiences are constituted by a higher-order state that is itself entirely *unconscious* for the most part! This applies equally to those versions of the higher-order theory which appeal to potential higher-order conscious thoughts, as opposed to *actual* but unconscious higher-order thoughts—see, for example, Carruthers (2000). For more on this theme see Dainton (2003c).

[11] This too is something of an oversimplification, for rather than explicating the unity of consciousness in terms of introspection, we could turn to *introspectibility*: we might say that experiences are unified if and only if they are *potential* objects of introspection. This proposal is also problematic, for several reasons, although there are also complications which I will not enter into here—see Gilmore (2003) and Dainton (2003d). These aside, it is more plausible by far to suppose that a collection of experiences are jointly introspectible in virtue of the fact that they are unified, rather than to suppose that a collection of experiences are unified only in virtue of the fact that they could be introspected, but are not.

defenders include Armstrong and Lycan.[12] I will call this doctrine the 'naïve perceptual' (or NP-) model of consciousness, and use *awareness** to refer to the relevant form of apprehension.

Now, whatever one might think of it as a general account of the structure of consciousness, the NP-model does provide a natural and seemingly promising account of the unity of consciousness. A unified state of consciousness is simply a collection of contents presented to a single awareness*, and since awareness* is itself a conscious apprehending, we have an account of why the various parts of a unified state of consciousness are *experienced* together. In short, contents are co-conscious if and only if they fall under a single awareness*. No less significantly, the NP-model also yields a distinctive conception of the self. If the NP-model is true, what could be more natural than to identify selves with enduring point-centres of pure awareness*? By so doing we not only fully satisfy the ownership doctrine—the claim that we are things that *have* experiences—we can also solve Hume's puzzle. Hume was seeking his self among the contents of his consciousness, but failed to find what he was looking for. If selves are what such contents are presented to, Hume's quest was doomed to fail. Not only was he was looking in the wrong place, he was trying to see something that by its very nature cannot be seen. The NP-model thus provides a plausible explanation of the supposed elusiveness of the self.

As well as satisfying these desiderata, the proposal has a good deal of appeal on the intuitive level. Mark Johnston has argued that our responses to the imaginary cases (of the sort employed in the personal identity literature) reveal a commitment to what he calls a 'bare locus' of mental life. Since Johnston takes a bare locus to be a 'constant that-to-which-experience-presents' (1987, 1992*a*: 593), it is hard to see how bare loci can be anything other than centres of pure awareness*. For Johnston the appeal of the bare locus conception lies in the fact that it allows us to survive any amount of physical and psychological disruption: provided that we are aware* of something—anything—we remain in existence, irrespective of what else might befall us. With just a little effort, it is also possible to envisage ourselves continuing to exist as *nothing but* a disembodied point of view. We came close to this in the previous section, when imagining what life might be like as a roving head. Being a disembodied bare locus—a *bare point of view*, as we might call it—would be rather like this, but with one significant difference: the relevant points of view would not be rooted in a *head*. Hence if you were to be reduced to such a condition, although you would be able to perceive your surroundings from a single point of view, if you were to look in a

---

[12] For example, Lycan (1996: ch. 2, 1997: 755–6) and Armstrong (1997: 724). It should be noted that not all higher-order sense theorists construe the objects of awareness in the manner I do; it is perfectly possible to combine the view with a direct realist conception of perceptual experience, according to which we directly apprehend the material objects in our environments.

mirror you would see only the wall opposite, you would not detect any trace of yourself at all.

2.4. A SUPERFLUOUS SELF

The doctrine that selves are enduring loci of awareness* may be appealing in some respects, but it is only a viable option if the NP-model is true—if consciousness does have an awareness-content structure, and awareness* itself actually exists. I cannot see any reason to suppose the NP-model is in fact true. Awareness* is superfluous, both phenomenologically and ontologically. Let us begin with the phenomenology.

Since awareness* itself is supposedly 'pure' in the sense of lacking any intrinsic phenomenal qualities of its own, it makes no positive phenomenological contribution to consciousness: it does not influence the character of what we experience. This is not necessarily a fatal flaw—as already noted, proponents of the NP-model hold that it is a mistake to expect to find awareness* among the contents of consciousness—but it does invite a question: 'Would our experience as a whole be any different if awareness* were absent? How could we tell if it were missing? Or non-existent?' Of course, this question invites the response: 'In the absence of awareness* there simply can't be any conscious experience!' Leaving this claim aside—I will be evaluating it shortly—the imperceptible character of awareness* nonetheless makes for a difficulty for the NP-theorist. Given that awareness* is entirely characterless, whatever it is about our experience which is suggestive of an awareness*–content divide must entirely belong to the *contents* of consciousness. Being featureless, awareness* can contribute nothing to the phenomenological case for its own existence. This at least weakens the case for the NP-model. Why believe consciousness has elements or structures that cannot be discerned *in* consciousness?

This point would be strengthened if we could identify which aspects or features of our experience can make the NP-model seem plausible. The complete story is probably a complex one, but some of the more important sources are not difficult to discern.

First, and most obviously, much of our ordinary experience is perceptual, and as I have already noted, from a phenomenological standpoint the direct realist view of ordinary perception is very plausible. Our eyes and ears do seem to provide us with unmediated access to what we see and hear, and accordingly it seems perfectly natural to say that we are directly aware of what we perceive. If I explore my surroundings by slowly turning my head and looking all around, it can indeed seem that I am directing a beam of apprehending awareness onto the world about me. But such appearances can be accounted for without positing awareness*. When I look at the wall opposite I seem to be seeing something that is external to me and quite independent of me. I am 'directly aware' of the wall but only in the sense that I seem to be *seeing the wall* itself. The immediacy of the experience—the lack of any experienced *inter*mediaries between myself and what I see—is a characteristic feature of how my visual sense functions; when I slowly turn my head, the 'awareness' that I am employing is simply my sense of sight. Similar remarks could be made for hearing and touch. Our seemingly being directly aware of what we perceive can be fully explained by appealing to nothing more than the typical characteristics of our various perceptual experiences and the powers of our various sensory systems. The positing of an additional and all-embracing mode of awareness* is superfluous.

A second source of the NP-model's appeal lies in the phenomenology of attention. We can attend to any region of our experience, and when we do so it often seems like we are 'seeing' what is there for the first time. And in a sense we are: when some feature of what is there comes to our notice for the first time. But ordinary forms of attending have their own qualitative character—unlike the NP-theorists' awareness*—and generally speaking they are directed at only some parts of our experience at any given time, not all of them.

Thirdly, and perhaps most importantly, there are the so-called 'fringe feelings' that accompany our sensory experiences and conscious thoughts. Think of what it is like to see a face and know that you have seen it before, without being able to quite place it. Compare this with what it is like to know that a certain word just isn't right, or is right. Or think of what it is like to carry out a task with the reassuring feeling that everything is proceeding as it should—or with the feeling that it isn't. In each of these cases (and in many others of the same genre) there is a feeling or intuition with a quite specific character, a feeling whose significance is entirely unambiguous, but one that does not possess a qualitative character of a sensory kind—fringe contents typically have no definite spatial location, size, or colour, for instance. Such feelings are easily overlooked, but when our attention is drawn to them it soon becomes apparent that they are commonplace; indeed, they are significant ingredients in our overall consciousness.[13] As for their relevance to the topic in hand, when pondering our natures as conscious beings, most of us have no difficulty in accepting the claim that there is something more to us than the various contents we are currently aware of, likewise the claim that we are active apprehending somethings that are distinct from these contents. Mangan suggests that non-sensory fringe contents often have a function similar to that of the on-screen menus in a word processor: they provide an indication, in consciousness, of the various kinds of cognitive resources that can be called on, if needed—like the menus, they let us know what is available in an economical way: consciousness (like the screen) is left largely free for more pressing matters (current sensory experience, the document being worked on). It is very plausible to suppose that a significant part of our

---

[13] William James' exploration of the fringe is to be found in the 'Principles of Tendency' section of the *Principles*. For more on the topic see Epstein (2000) and especially Mangan (2001).

abiding 'sense of having or being a self' is largely due to the continual presence of non-sensory 'pointers' in our consciousness: these fringe-components together provide us with an intuitive understanding of our undeployed potential, they make us aware that there is more to our minds (to ourselves) than is occurring in current consciousness—this 'sense of there being more' is quite definite, and continually present in ordinary experience, albeit in a non-sensory form.

In a more concrete and directly relevant vein, it can seem as though a centre of receptivity, of *openness*, lies at the hub of our experience. Just think of what it is like to be in a quiet room, listening intently for the slightest noise, or gazing keenly at a night sky in an attempt to see the most distant stars, or waiting for a toothache to strike again. Having recognized the existence and significance of fringe feelings we can account for these facts without recourse to the additional (and introspectively invisible) level of consciousness posited by the NP-theorist. There is indeed an additional 'something' in consciousness; not a point-centre of pure awareness*, but simply fringe feelings of various types, some more ubiquitous than others. Among the most significant in the present context are the feelings associated with conditions such as these: *being in a state of readiness, opening or straining one's senses, being prepared for the unexpected, being determined or resolute, potency: having the sense that one is mentally or physically energized, that one is equipped for the task in hand, that one is about to act.* Wouldn't the presence of these and similar feelings be sufficient to give rise to the sense that we are active apprehending subjects? What else could possibly be needed? Imagine your consciousness being gradually emptied of all content until all that remains is a single solitary fringe feeling: *being ready for whatever comes next.* If we try to imagine ourselves existing in the form of a 'pure locus of awareness', don't we end up imagining something along these lines? If so, 'pure' does not really mean 'devoid of all content', it simply means 'devoid of all *non-fringe* content'.[14]

I do not pretend that this diagnosis is complete; there may be other reasons why the NP-model can seem appealing, but taken together, the three factors just outlined go quite a long way towards explaining how it might seem as though our experience harbours an awareness*–content divide, even if in fact it does not. But I will not dwell on these diagnostic issues further, for there are quite different reasons for being suspicious of the NP-model, and its associated conception of the self.

Let us start with the latter. The notion that there is nothing more to ourselves than our current experiences is intuitively implausible; it is natural to suppose that we are things that *have* or *own* experiences, and hence are in some ontologically significant manner distinct from them. I suggested earlier that the bare locus conception—construed as the doctrine that we are centres of awareness*—conforms to this natural view. And in one sense it clearly does: by hypothesis, awareness* is distinct from the contents it apprehends. Distinct

---

[14] This paragraph is borrowed from Dainton (2004).

perhaps, but could a locus of awareness* exist *independently* of any phenomenal content? Could a *bare* awareness* exist? It is difficult to see how it could. Since awareness* is entirely featureless, there cannot possibly be anything that it is like to be a bare awareness*. From a phenomenological standpoint, the condition of being a bare awareness* would be indistinguishable from non-existence. Why suppose such a thing could exist? If we do suppose such a thing could exist, *what is it* that we are supposing exists? If we conclude that a bare awareness* is an impossibility, we should accept that (conscious) selves can only exist in the presence of phenomenal contents.

Proponents of awareness* might well be prepared to live with this loss of autonomy with regard to the contents of consciousness. But issues of dependency arise in another way. We can ask whether awareness* can exist independently of phenomenal contents, but we can also ask whether phenomenal contents can exist independently of awareness*. Proponents of the NP-model (especially those who also embrace the Lockean view of perceptual experience) may well strongly incline to the view that contents are essentially awareness*-dependent. I suggested above that given the featureless character of awareness*, the NP-theorist is vulnerable to the charge of redundancy: why think the character of our consciousness would be in the least different if awareness* were absent? Why suppose something exists if it makes no difference to anything? But if phenomenal properties can only be realized in the presence of awareness*, the redundancy charge is countered. In the absence of awareness* there simply could not be any experience, of any kind. However, the claim that phenomenal contents are awareness*-dependent is a decidedly non-trivial claim. Why believe it to be true? I cannot see any reason for believing the thesis to be true.

Is the awareness*-dependency thesis a conceptual truth? It seems not. What is self-contradictory or incoherent in supposing that phenomenal contents can exist, and constitute experiences, all by themselves? Someone might say: 'But it's a nonsense to suppose someone could have an experience without being *aware* that they are having it!' There is an uncontroversial sense in which this is true. The claim can be reformulated thus: 'Any experience has a discernible impact upon the overall character of its subject's overall consciousness'. While the latter claim is very plausible, to suppose that 'aware' here refers to a featureless additional ingredient in consciousness is to take a further and contentious step—indeed, it is to beg the question. In defence of the dependency claim it could be objected:

Phenomenal contents *can't* exist all by themselves, they can't be 'self-revealing', they need to be apprehended *by* someone or something in order to *be experienced*.

As with the previous objection, there is a reading of this claim that is very compelling: we could take it to mean that any experience is had by some *subject*. This may well be true, but again it does not follow that the subject of experience is awareness*—other options exist, for example the subject of experience could be a human animal, or a brain, or an immaterial soul—or something different

again and rather less obvious. In short, simply to assume the subject is awareness*
is to beg the question.

If the dependency thesis is not a conceptual truth, perhaps it is supported by
empirical considerations. Perhaps, but it is difficult to see how this could be. The
problem, once again, lies with the complete transparency of awareness*. Given
the depths of current ignorance concerning the relationship between matter
and consciousness, the only available empirical evidence for the dependency
thesis is phenomenological. But how could there possibly be *phenomenological*
evidence that content depends for its existence on the presence of something
which *cannot* be detected *in* experience? If someone were to say 'The character
of my experience gives me reason to believe that phenomenal red can only exist
in the presence of X, which is entirely featureless and undetectable', we would
not take them seriously. The awareness*-dependency thesis, construed as rooted
in phenomenology, is precisely analogous.

If we reject the dependency thesis—which in the absence of any supporting
considerations, I think we should—then the redundancy charge against the
NP-theorist resurfaces with renewed vigour. If phenomenal contents can exist
just as they are in the absence of awareness*, then our streams of consciousness
could be just as they are (phenomenologically) in the absence of awareness*.
Given this, what reason do we have for supposing an entity as strange as
awareness* exists in addition to phenomenal contents? Worse still, if we suppose
awareness* *does* exist, we effectively double the number of conscious subjects.
There are the subjects whose experience is made up of the phenomenal contents
of streams of consciousness, and there are the subjects whose experience consists
in the awareness* of these contents. Ontological absurdity aside, this result has
the worrying consequence that we cannot know which type of subject we are.

2.5. SIMPLICITY AND UNITY

The upshot of the preceding discussions seems clear: we should reject awareness*,
and the NP-model along with it. So doing brings a double reward. It makes for a
significant ontological saving. It also makes it possible to adopt a simpler—and
therefore (all else being equal) preferable—conception of what experience
involves or requires. The NP-theorist holds that phenomenal contents only
become experiences when apprehended by a higher-order awareness. Once we
reject this conception we are free to regard phenomenal contents as intrinsically
conscious items—as experiences in their own right. According to this view,
nothing needs to be added to a phenomenal content to turn it into an experience:
any and all instantiations of phenomenal properties are fully-fledged conscious
experiences. I call this the *Simple Conception* of consciousness.

Those who subscribe to this one-level view of consciousness are sometimes said to be committed to conceiving of phenomenal items as being

'self-intimating'—mental states fall into this category if they are such that their owners cannot fail to know that they are in them—and there is a sense in which this is correct. It certainly follows from the Simple Conception that no phenomenal content can fail to register in its subject's consciousness if by 'register' we mean no more than 'contribute towards the overall character of what it is like to be that subject at that time'. However, contents can register in this minimal way without being *cognitively* registered in any discernible way. It does not follow from the Simple Conception that subjects have exhaustive or infallible propositional knowledge about all parts and aspects of their experience at any one time. Since we lack such knowledge, this is just as well. (And of course our lack of such knowledge is entirely compatible with our being fully *acquainted* with the phenomenal character of our total states of consciousness: we can (and do) know what our experience is like in this sense even though we cannot usually fully *describe* it.) The related claim that phenomenal items are 'self-revealing' has to be treated in a similarly circumspect way. If such items are experiences in their own right, then there is a sense in which they are self-revealing: they do not need to be apprehended by a separate faculty of awareness in order to be conscious. But in another sense the claim is wrong: phenomenal contents do not need to be *revealed to* a self—conceived as some separate apprehending agency—in order to be conscious.[15]

A further consequence of the Simple Conception is worth noting. In a manner of speaking, experience is *self-constituting*. By this I don't mean that a self is nothing but a collection of experiences—whether the bundle-view is correct or not I leave open at this stage. I mean rather that what it *feels* like to be a self is entirely explicable solely in terms of the phenomenal character of the contents of consciousness, no additional level of awareness or apprehension is involved or required. Of course, quite what it feels like to be a conscious self varies enormously. Often we are entirely *un*self-conscious—for example when wholly engaged in some practical task; on other occasions we can be

---

[15] Hence I think Ryle was essentially correct when he said: 'A person's present thinkings, feelings and willings, his perceivings, rememberings and imaginings, are intrinsically "phosphorescent"; their existence and their nature are inevitably betrayed to their owner. The inner life is a stream of consciousness of such a sort that it would be absurd to suggest that the mind whose inner life is that stream might be unaware of what is passing down it' (1949: 13). Or at least it is so long as 'aware' is construed in the right sort of (minimalist) way. (Ryle may have been mistaken in rejecting as much of the 'Official Doctrine' as he did, but he was right in rejecting some of it: our cognitive access to our experience is by no means infallible.) So far as I can see, there is nothing wrong with the 'phosphoresence' metaphor either, but it should be borne in mind that experiences of *all* kinds are intrinsically conscious—and hence that sounds (as heard), conscious thoughts, and bodily sensations are all equally 'illuminated' in their own distinctive ways. The general view of experience I am advocating here may be controversial, but it is by no means unique or unfamiliar: Zahavi (2005: 23, 42) argues that a 'one-level' conception of consciousness is standard amongst classical phenomenologists, and what Zahavi calls the 'one-level' conception is very similar to the Simple Conception. (Zahavi combines the one-level view with the doctrine that all experiences are minimally self-conscious. I have my doubts about the latter: see §8.2.)

intensely self-conscious—for example when engaged in philosophically driven introspective activities. It matters not. Provided we construe 'content' in a suitably broad way—so as to include conscious thoughts, volitions, acts of attention, all manner of bodily and fringe feelings—what it feels like to be a (conscious) self, in any condition or mood, can be captured or created simply by organizing an appropriate collection of phenomenal items into a single unified state. In this manner (if in no other) the experiential self, the self as manifest in experience, is fully *reducible to* its experiences at any one time.

This point brings into focus the question of unity once more. If phenomenal unity is not essentially spatial in nature, if it is not a product of attention or introspection, if it is not a consequence of contents falling under a single locus of higher-order awareness, what can we say about it? In the absence of any viable alternative, the best course is simply to regard it as a primitive feature of experience. A unified state of consciousness simply consists of experiential parts that are all linked to one another by co-consciousness, where the latter is the relationship of 'experienced togetherness' with which we are all so familiar; in this sense (if no other) experience can correctly be regarded as *self-unifying*. According to the Simple Conception (as I will henceforth use the phrase) a compound conscious state consists of nothing more than experiences, and the unity of these experience is the product of relationships of co-consciousness among its constituent parts. In this manner experience unifies itself without recourse to any entity or agency external to experience.

This is not to say that everything external to a given state of consciousness is irrelevant to that state's unity—in our case, phenomenal unity is presumably a product of activities within our brains, and there is a story to be told about how our brains manage to do what they do—but we can comprehend why it is that our states of consciousness *seem* unified by appealing solely to relationships between the parts of these states. The fact that our states of consciousness are self-unifying (in the sense just introduced) is of obvious relevance to my larger project of explicating the persistence conditions of selves in terms of experiential relationships and continuities. It may well be the case that synchronically unified experiences necessarily belong to the same subject, but we can state the conditions under which experiences are so unified without appealing to subjects: experiences are unified if, and only if, they are co-conscious. The fact that the co-consciousness relationship is (on the face of it) quite distinct from the relationship 'belonging to the same subject' is an additional bonus.

A few further words on the nature and character of this unifying relationship. Co-consciousness connects experiences, but it is important to note that it accomplishes this without featuring *in* experience, as a distinct experiential item with its own distinctive phenomenal features. When two experiences are co-conscious they are experienced together, but this togetherness is not the product of a third experience which comes between the two, it is a direct (unmediated, experientially speaking) relationship between the two experiences themselves. Co-consciousness has no phenomenal features of its own—it is not an experience in its own right—rather it is the way in which experiences are related when they are experienced together (and we all know precisely what it is like for experiences to be related in this way).[16]

As a means of bringing the distinctive character of co-consciousness into clear relief, it is useful to focus on the way contents in different sense modalities are experienced together, for example one's current visual and bodily experience. It is important to realize, however, that co-consciousness is not a binary relationship between distinct sense modalities. First of all, it is not confined to sensory experience. My visual experience at the current time is co-conscious with my auditory, bodily, and olfactory experiences, but it is also co-conscious with my conscious thoughts, mental images and various fringe feelings. Second, it operates within experiential modalities as well as between them. The various sounds I am currently hearing are co-conscious with one another; the upper and lower parts of my visual field are co-conscious with one another, and the same obviously applies to the various elements of my bodily experience and my mental images, and so forth. Quite generally, irrespective of how we divide our overall experience at any one time into parts—and as I noted earlier, there may well be no one best way of doing this—each part is co-consciousness with every other part. Of course, this pervasive all-embracing unity is just what one would expect if all parts of our experience were apprehended by some external higher-order awareness of the sort posited by the NP-model. But once the far-reaching character of the co-consciousness relation is appreciated, it is clear that no such external unifying agency is required to render phenomenal unity intelligible.[17]

---

[16] This is why conceiving of phenomenal unity in this sort of way is not vulnerable to the regress objection one of encounters in this context. for example 'the unity . . . of consciousness cannot be accounted for in terms of the subjective contents of consciousness because the same question of unity . . . arises again for any such contents' Hurley (1998: 5); see also Tye (2003: 22). The co-consciousness relationship is *not* just another experience for which the question of unity immediately arises; it is simply that relationship which connects experiences when they are experienced together.

[17] While I believe that explicating phenomenal unity in terms of the co-consciousness relationship is illuminating, I would not want to claim that it is the only useful way of approaching matters. Bayne and Chalmers (2003) develop an account of synchronic unity that makes no mention of co-consciousness whatsoever. Their basic idea is that a collection of conscious states is phenomenally unified only if they are encompassed by, or subsumed in, a single conscious state. A collection of states is subsumed in a single state only if there is something that it is like for a subject to be in all of them at once—only if they have a 'conjoint phenomenology'. The claim that all of a subject's experiences at any one time are phenomenally unified can then be formulated thus: 'For any set of phenomenal states of a subject at a time, the subject has a phenomenal state that subsumes each of the states in that set' (Bayne and Chalmers 2003: section 6). From these premises Bayne and Chalmers go on to develop a variety of interesting formulations, theses and analyses. However, despite the differences—see Bayne (2001) for some contrasts—the co-consciousness and subsumptive approaches agree on one key issue: phenomenal unity is a product of experienced relationships between conscious states, it is not imposed from above or from without. Conscious states have a conjoint phenomenology if and only if they are experienced together—that is if they are mutually co-conscious.

We will be considering further ramifications of this way of thinking about phenomenal unity in due course. I will conclude here by mentioning just one issue that is of some significance. Let us say that a state of consciousness is *strongly unified* if all of its parts are mutually co-conscious, and *weakly unified* if each part is co-conscious with at least one other part, but some parts are not co-conscious with other parts. The simplest example of a weakly unified state is one divided into three regions, E_1, E_2, and E_3, where E_1 is co-conscious with E_2, E_2 is co-conscious with E_3, but E_1 and E_3 are not co-conscious. I have assumed thus far that our own states are strongly unified, and that is certainly how things seem, at least ordinarily. But is this always or necessarily the case? Or is it possible for a state of consciousness to be only weakly unified? The answer to this question depends on whether the co-consciousness relation is transitive or not. This is a difficult issue to resolve with any degree of certainty, but for the moment I will assume that it is. My grounds for so doing are simply that it is all but impossible to conceive how co-consciousness could fail to be transitive. If experiences E_1 and E_2 are unified by co-consciousness they form, in effect, a *single* experiential state, all of whose parts are fully and mutually co-conscious with one another, and as a consequence it is not obvious that an additional experience could be co-conscious with one part of this state without also being co-conscious with the remainder. (I will be looking at this issue in more detail in Chapter 8.)

Whatever its other merits, the assumption of transitivity delivers a satisfyingly neat state of affairs. I will use the expression *total experience* to refer to any collection C of experiences that satisfies the following conditions: (i) the members of C are all mutually co-conscious (i.e. each experience in C is co-conscious with every other experience in C), and (ii) the collection is not a part of any more extensive collection of experiences that are all mutually co-conscious. If co-consciousness is transitive, then since it is also plausible to suppose that it is reflexive and symmetrical, it is an equivalence relation. As such it partitions the totality of experiences into mutually exclusive ensembles, each of which is a total experience. If we further assume that each total experience belongs to a distinct subject, then we have a tidy, and on the face of it plausible, way of assigning experiences to subjects. Whether this simple picture is correct is another matter.

3
Phenomenal Continuity

3.1. A CONSTRAINT

Now that we have a reasonably adequate understanding of what the synchronic unity of consciousness involves, we can turn our attention to its diachronic counterpart. What phenomenal relationships unify our streams of consciousness from moment to moment? According to James consciousness 'does not appear to itself chopped up in bits. Such words as "chain" or "train" do not describe it fitly as it presents itself in the first instance. It is nothing jointed; it flows' (1952: 155). It is easy to see what James means.

Our experience typically exhibits a combination of change and stability, and for the most part the change occurs in a continuous fashion. Think of what it is like to listen to a police siren gradually recede into the distance, or to see a ship slowly drifting across a bay, or to feel the burn of a strong mint on one's tongue, or to run one's finger along a smooth slab of marble. In these cases, and untold others, the continuity in and of our experience is obvious. There are, of course, discontinuities too. We can switch in an instant from thinking about one thing to thinking about a quite different thing; when looking around a room we can let our eyes sweep slowly around, or we can let them jump—seemingly instantaneously—from one place to another and then another and then back again. On other occasions the discontinuities are due to objects themselves: fast-moving small lizards can seemingly vanish from view only to reappear an instant later at a different location. But generally speaking, these localized discontinuities—whether in thought, sensation, or perception—take place against the backdrop of a largely continuous expanse of bodily and emotional feeling. So for example, as my eyes leap hither and thither around the room, my mild sense of boredom remains, and my bodily feelings—of being *upright*, of feeling my hands in my pockets and the floor pushing up against my feet—remain largely constant, and constantly *present* in my experience, even though I am not paying attention to them.

In attempting to get to grips with the diachronic phenomenal unity the continuity of our ordinary streams of consciousness—the lack of discernible gaps—is comparatively unproblematic. The deeper difficulties all stem from the fact that we seem to be directly aware of change and persistence. When I hold my hand before my eyes, slowly clenching and then unclenching my fist, I *see* my fingers move—I experience their motion with as much immediacy as their colour or shape. The same applies to the boat I see drifting across the bay, or to the waxing and waning of the police siren—we directly experience change in all our sensory modalities, just as we do in our conscious thinking and our mental images. The experience of persistence is just as real as that of change, it is just less obvious: think of what it is like to hear the noise of distant traffic droning on and on, or to stare for several minutes at the unchanging whiteness of a ceiling, or to put your hand in a fast running stream and feel the water flowing around your fingers. In cases such as these, there is little or no variation in the content of our experience, but we are nonetheless aware—even if only inattentively—of a continuous replacement or renewal of phenomenal content, whether auditory, visual, or tactile. Otherwise unchanging experiences exhibit *experienced passage* or *phenomenal flow*.

As for why the presence of change and persistence in experience is problematic, it suffices to ask oneself this: 'Are we directly aware of the past or the future?' The common sense answer, of course, is that we are not: we can anticipate the future and remember the past, but we are *directly* aware only of what is present. Quibbles deriving from the finite speed of signal transmission aside, this may seem self-evidently true: we may commonly perceive events which occurred hundreds or thousands of years ago (every time we see distant stars in the night sky), but our *experience* is nonetheless confined to the present. But of course the present, strictly speaking, has no temporal depth, it is no more than a durationless dividing line between past and future. Hence the problem. If our immediate experience really is confined to the present, how can it also contain directly experienced change and persistence, given that the latter both require some interval of time in which to occur? Now it is certainly true that the period of time through which our direct awareness appears to extend—the duration of the so-called 'specious' (or 'phenomenal') present—is comparatively short. Psychological research suggests that it typically only lasts for a second or so, and introspection—in my case at least—tends to confirm this.[1] But brevity does not

---

[1] This is an oversimplification: estimates of the duration of the specious present in the psychology literature range from a fraction of a second to half a minute. But it is plausible to think that the longer estimates are concerned with temporal units that are easily remembered or cognitively significant in some way, rather than the span of immediate awareness. As Lockwood (2005: 370–1) puts it: 'Even the shortest number that James mentions, of 3.6 seconds, is too long, on the face of it, to be a credible figure for the span of the specious present. But as for the largest figure that James cites, a hefty 12 seconds, this is simply preposterous. These figures must surely relate, not to the span of the specious present . . . but to the time interval within which, *with the aid of memory*, a subject can unify the presented material in the form of an overall pattern or structure that the mind can grasp as a whole. This is the concept of a time gestalt; and the ability to form such gestalts is an essential precondition for appreciating music or sustaining the simplest conversation.'

make for unreality. How can a temporally extended experience of *any* duration exist within a durationless instant?

A good deal of ingenuity has been expended on this problem over the years, and some quite elaborate models of the temporal structure of experience. I will not be exploring these here.[2] My aim is the more limited one of making a case for this claim:

The Diachronic Co-consciousness Constraint: (DCC): any phenomenologically plausible account of phenomenal continuity must acknowledge that all the successive brief phases in a typical stream of consciousness are connected by co-consciousness.

Or to put it another way, the unity of phenomenal consciousness over time is due to the same binding agent as the unity of consciousness at a time. If DDC could be established we would have at least the beginnings of an experience-based account of our persistence conditions: we could state the conditions under which experiences belong to a single stream of consciousness—and so the same self or subject—without appealing to anything external to experience.

If DCC strikes you as being obviously true, so much the better. But obvious or not, the majority of the more influential accounts of phenomenal continuity reject it, explicitly or implicitly. The best way of establishing the strength of the case for DDC is to reveal the unacceptable features of those accounts of phenomenal continuity which fail to conform to it.

3.2. MEMORY

It might seem that our direct experience of change and persistence can be explained in a very simple and straightforward way: by appealing to the fact that, generally speaking, we are *continuously* awake and aware throughout our waking hours. But this is wrong. The reason why is often encapsulated in slogans such as 'a succession of experiences does not make for an experience of succession'. It may initially be tempting to suppose that the experience of seeing a dog running across a field consists of nothing but a gap-free succession of momentary (or minimally brief) experiences, each presenting the dog at a slightly different location. However, as a little reflection reveals, such a succession would not in itself constitute an experience of *seeing the dog in motion*. This is obviously the case if we suppose each of these momentary experiences occurs in a stream of consciousness belonging to a different person, but it holds

---

[2] For surveys of relevant work in philosophy and psychology see Miller (1984), Le Poidevin (2000), Gallagher (1998), Dainton (2000, 2003*a*), Pöppel (1985).

equally for the single-person case. The phenomenal content of each momentary experience is a static visual presentation of a dog, an image that is motion-free. A succession of experiences of this kind, irrespective of how tightly packed in time, can never amount to anything more than what it is: a series (perhaps a gap-free continuous series) of static phenomenal images. In actual fact, of course, if we are shown a succession of suitably related still images on a physical screen at a sufficiently fast rate (more than ten per second or so) then we have an experience of motion that is indistinguishable from the real thing—this effect is the basis of cinema and television. But in this sort of case the static onscreen images themselves have no phenomenal reality, all we *see* are dynamic phenomenal images generated by our brains. The point thus remains: a succession of still images that *are perceived as such* do not and cannot amount to a direct experience of motion. And what goes for motion goes for change and persistence generally.

One response to this difficulty is to retain the idea that a stream of consciousness is composed of a continuous succession of momentary (or minimally brief) experiential phases, but to hold that each of these phases is accompanied by (or includes) a memory of some or all of the immediately preceding phases. The presence of these short-term memories accounts for the sense we have that our experience is phenomenally continuous, as well as our (apparently) direct experience of change and persistence. Mellor propounds an account along these lines: 'our experience of the direction of time demands nothing more than an accumulation of memories, of memories of memories, and so on. This . . . is what makes the flow of time seem to take us into the future rather than back into the past' (1998: 123). Suppose, for example, that we hear a sequence of notes *do-re-mi*, and each note is quite short, and is immediately followed by its successor. Mellor explains the resulting experience of succession thus: we first hear *do*; we then hear *re* and while doing so we consciously remember having just heard *do*; we then hear *mi*, and as we do so we consciously remember having heard *re* while remembering having just heard *do*. And so on: the nested short-term memories do not extend back very far—our consciousness would be flooded with them if they did—but they do not need to extend back very far in order to do the job required.

The memory-based theory is economical, and it may seem quite promising. After all, our personal memories provide us with the most obvious experiential link with times other than the present. The memory-based theory is also of particular interest in the current context. We are investigating phenomenal continuity because this form of continuity seems more intimately bound up with our continued existence than any other. In reaching this conclusion we considered and rejected Locke's memory-based approach and its contemporary successor, the P-theory. If it were to turn out that phenomenal continuity is itself a product of short-term memories, a form of the P-theory might well turn out to be vindicated: after all, short-term memories are a form of psychological connection, not too distantly related to the long-term memories that Locke placed at the heart of his account.

But for better or for worse, this way of resuscitating the P-theory is not very promising. Memory will undoubtedly loom large in any remotely plausible story of our longer-term relationship with time—of how it is that we feel ourselves to be living at the driving edge of a life-process spanning a number of years—but it does not play a comparably crucial role in our moment-to-moment short-term experience of change and persistence. Consider first the phenomenology. I know what it is like to hear *do-re*. I know what it is like to hear first *do*, then *re* accompanied by a memory of hearing *do*. But I also know what it is like to hear first *do* then *re* accompanied by a memory of hearing *fa*—or a bird-call, or a firecracker exploding. Yet in each of these cases the auditory phenomenal character of the succession *do-re* is much the same. Quite generally, our immediate experience of change seems largely unaffected by what we are consciously remembering at the time. But clearly, if anything like Mellor's account is along the right lines, it shouldn't be.

There are other difficulties. The claim that my experience of *do* being followed by *re* consists of my hearing first *do*, then *re* accompanied by an acoustic memory-image of *do* may seem entirely plausible. After all, the hearing of one sound often is accompanied by a memory of a preceding sound. But in fact, this sort of example lends the memory-theory a plausibility it does not really deserve. For in reality, the (live) experience of *re* and the memory-image of *do* are experiential contents with some temporal depth, contents that are experienced as extended wholes lasting some (short) period of time. For the memory-theory to be viable—for it to be a *complete* account of phenomenal temporality—it must explain the apparent temporal depth of *individual tones* in terms of nested memories as well. But how plausible is it to suppose that the experience of *do* consists of a succession of strictly momentary or durationless tones, each of which is accompanied by a collection of nested memories, each of which is of further durationless tones? It is far from obvious that the notion of a *durationless* auditory sensation makes any sense in the first place. Even if we suppose such things could exist, it is far from obvious how adding them together could create sensations which possess genuine temporal depth. The memory-theorist could maintain that while experiences themselves are durationless, the memories which accompany them are not. But this position too is dubious in the extreme. If we never experience any change or duration first hand, isn't it incoherent to suppose that change or duration are *remembered*? In reply the memory-theorist might hold that the relevant short-term memories images have phenomenal features additional to those possessed by the original experiences: so although we do not directly experience an extended tones, we have memory-like acoustic images which do possess genuine temporal depth. But as Foster notes (1979, 1991: 246), since it is now being conceded that we *can* directly experience duration and change—albeit in the form of a memory-like mental image—it would be perverse to deny that we have this sort of experience when we seem to, that is when we are actually hearing (or seeing, or feeling) things persist or change.

In short, since it is difficult to see how the memory-theorist can do full justice to the temporal features of experience we must look for an alternative account of phenomenal continuity. In fact we are not yet entirely done with the memory-based approach, for some of the more sophisticated theories we will be looking at shortly can be viewed as variants on the same theme. But as we shall see, these are afflicted by difficulties that are no less serious than those which afflict the theory in its simpler forms.

3.3. CHUNKS, APPREHENSIONS
AND REPRESENTATIONS

A viable explanation of the temporal features of experience needs a better account of the specious present than the memory-based theory provides: a way must be found of fully acknowledging that we *directly* experience change and persistence. One option—defended by Whitehead (1929) and Sprigge (1983, 1993), amongst others—is to hold that a stream of consciousness consists of a series of distinct temporally extended *chunks* or *pulses* of experience. Each individual pulse is a distinct specious present, and will typically include numerous instances of directly experienced change or persistence, even though it is short-lived. Since the temporally separated contents of such pulses are *experienced together* even though they are spread through (a brief interval of) time they are *co-conscious*, albeit diachronically. According to this view, a typical stream of consciousness consists of a succession of pulses, laid out end to end, in the manner of a line of bricks in a wall. To take a simple case, consider hearing a rendition of *do-re-mi-fa-so-la*. If we assume each tone occupies half the duration of a specious present, this short stretch of experience will consist of three pulses, thus:

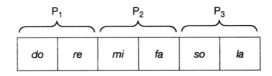

Figure 3.1 Streamal structure: the pulse view

At first view the pulse theory may seem to provide what we are looking for. There are no gaps between any of notes depicted in Figure 3.1, so the theory seems compatible with the continuity of our experience, and the fact that the pulses are temporally extended means that it is able to accommodate directly experienced change and persistence. What else is needed?

A good deal. The trouble with the pulse theory is that while it fully recognizes the existence of some specious presents, it ignores the existence of others. Consider again the experienced succession *do-re-mi-fa-so-la*, and let us again suppose this divides into pulses in the way shown. We do experience *do* flowing into *re*, and *mi* flowing into *fa*, and *so* flowing into *la*. The pulse theorist gets this just right. However, if we hear the notes sung in fairly quick succession we hear *each* note flowing into its successor. So in addition to the transitions just recognized, we also directly experience *re* flowing into *mi* and *fa* flowing into *so*. There are thus two phenomenal presents in this simple example, two experienced transitions that the pulse theorist entirely fails to recognize.

Confronted with this objection, pulse theorists could appeal to memory. They could hold that pulse P_2, for example, consists not just of the experienced transition *mi-fa* but also a short-term memory impression of *do-re*. But as we have already seen, appealing to memory in this way is problematic. Since the transition between *re* and *mi* is not experienced, it cannot be remembered. Moreover, even if we suppose apparent memories of the appropriate kind are in fact present, due perhaps to a confabulatory cognitive mechanism, it remains the case that the pulse theory fails to recognize relationships of co-consciousness that actually exist, that are actually experienced. In this connection it is crucial to distinguish two types of experiential succession. Focusing solely on the transition between the experiences of *re* and *mi*, here is what the pulse theorist is now proposing:

[. . . *re*] [*mi* . . . + memory of *do-re*]

As the square brackets indicate, *re* and *mi* occur in entirely distinct pulses of experience, and the kind of directly experienced transition that connects *do* with *re* and *mi* with *fa* is entirely absent. The contention that our streams of consciousness are composed of successions of discrete elements of this kind is surely very implausible: given the absence of any direct experiential connection between *re* and *mi*, from a purely phenomenal perspective, they might as well exist in different universes. Or to put it another way, if the pulse theory were correct, and experiences just like these *did* exist in two different universes (or in the same universe a million years apart), they would jointly constitute a genuine stream of consciousness. This is surely absurd, but it is what the theory we are considering entails. According to the pulse theorist the only phenomenal relationship that holds between successive and distinct specious presents is qualitative similarity—either amongst experiences themselves, or experiences and subsequent memory impressions—and qualitative similarity is a relationship which can hold between specious presents in different universes.[3]

---

[3] I will be saying more about this sort of case in §3.5.

It is useful to contrast the succession we have just been considering with another, where the focus is again confined to the transition between *re* and *mi*, but we now suppose that these experiences occur within a single pulse, and *mi* is accompanied by a memory-impression of the preceding stream-phase:

[*re-mi* + memory of *do-re*]

Here an experience of *re* flows into (and hence is co-conscious with) an experience of *mi*, and the latter is accompanied by a memory of just having heard *do-re*. Although the presence of the memory impression accompanying *mi* will obviously make a difference to the overall experience of continuity here, it does not constitute it entirely: in addition to the memory there is the directly experienced transition between *re* and *mi*, a transition that is entirely ignored by the pulse theorist.

We have been considering an artificially simple example, but these considerations retain their force in the context of streams of consciousness whose contents are as varied and complex as our own. Quite generally, the pulse theory ignores or misrepresents approximately half of experienced transitions that are to be found in our streams of consciousness. Clearly, this is not nearly good enough.

Desperate straits call for desperate remedies. By way of a reply, pulse theorists could insist that the problematic transitions are illusory, and hence that all the actual phenomenal transitions are in fact accommodated by their theory. We seem to hear *do* flowing into *re*, and we also seem to hear hearing *re* flowing into *mi*, but whereas in the first case the impression is accurate, in the second it is not. More generally, experienced transitions within pulses are as they appear, those between pulses are not.

This suggestion is far-fetched to say the least. The claim that two experiences 'seem the same' can be construed in two ways. It can mean that the experiences are phenomenally identical, in the sense of possessing exactly the same phenomenal properties; alternatively it can mean that the experiences are *judged* or *believed* by their subject to be qualitatively identical. When 'seems the same' is construed in the former way, the proposal is simply incoherent. If the experiences of hearing *do-re* and *re-mi* are phenomenally indistinguishable with regard their experienced continuity—if in each case the first experience really is directly diachronically co-conscious with the second—then they clearly do not differ in the way being proposed. Hence the claim must be that in both cases we mistakenly believe or judge that the transitions are of the same kind when in fact they are not.

Mistakes are always possible, even when it comes to describing the character of one's own experience, at least in the case of fallible beings such as ourselves. But to postulate such a widespread and dramatic delusion as the one being envisaged here seems singularly under-motivated to say the least. We are being asked to accept that our ability to discriminate between real and apparent phenomenal transitions is error-prone in a remarkably systematic fashion: we get it right when we judge that *do* and *re* are co-conscious, we get it wrong when we judge that *re* and *mi* are co-conscious, even when we are doing our utmost to detect any difference in the character of the transition but fail to do so. And similarly for all the successive phases (or pulses) in our streams of consciousness. This hypothesis may not be beyond the bounds of logical possibility, but it is sufficiently implausible as to require considerable supporting evidence before it would merit being taken seriously. What reason have we been given for supposing that we are deluded in this manner? It is easy to believe we occasionally make mistakes when we try to describe subtle nuances in our experience, especially if we do so in a careless or absentminded manner, but it is less easy to believe we could fail to detect seismic variations of the kind we are concerned with here. It is one thing to misdescribe the precise character of a phenomenal content, or to misjudge quite how one content is related to another—it is often not obvious precisely how faint sounds are spatially related—but it is another thing entirely to be wrong about whether two highly conspicuous phenomenal contents are experienced together or not. As I listen to the succession of tones I hear *do* flowing into *re* flowing into *mi* flowing into *fa*—try as I might, I can discern no difference in the character of the transitions; each successive phase of my experience is directly co-conscious with its successor. In analogous fashion, when I look at the white ceiling above me I am aware of a spatially continuous spread of colour: the right-hand region is continuous and co-conscious with the central portion, and the latter is continuous and co-conscious with the left-hand region. The notion that I am mistaken about these elementary phenomeno-spatial properties and relations is difficult to take seriously. The same applies to their temporal counterparts.

Perhaps I am guilty of dwelling too long on the obvious, but there is a reason for so doing. The difficulty which afflicts the pulse theory—the phenomenologically unrealistic disintegration of streams of consciousness into isolated phases—also afflicts other accounts of phenomenal temporality, as we shall see. So let us press on.

An alternative to the pulse theory, elaborated by Broad (1923), relies on a version of the awareness-content model of consciousness. If a spatially extended phenomenal content can be apprehended as a whole by a single act of awareness, why can't a temporally extended content be so too? Perhaps a specious present consists of a temporal spread of content that is apprehended as a whole by a single momentary act of awareness. A significant advantage of this proposal is that it provides a (seemingly) appealing account of how change and per-sistence *can* be directly apprehended: the earlier and later phases of an event are presented *together* to a single locus of awareness. But of course, this expla-nation is only as secure as the awareness-content (or NP-) model itself, and as we saw in §2.4, this model is suspect. In any event, as can be seen from Figure 3.2, drawing on the resources of the awareness-content conception does not automatically result in an improvement on what the pulse theorist had to offer.

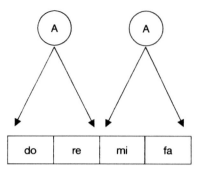

Figure 3.2 The momentary awareness + extended contents model

Act of awareness A_1 apprehends *do-re* in one specious present, and act of awareness A_2 apprehends *mi-fa* in a second specious present. As with the pulse theory, some transitions are recognized and accounted for, others are not. Since *do-re* and *mi-fa* fall into wholly distinct specious presents, *re* cannot be experienced as flowing into *mi*, despite the fact that it *is* experienced as doing precisely that.

Broad saw the difficulty and tried to overcome it. In order to restore full flow, as it were, he suggested that the contents of neighbouring acts overlap, in the manner indicated in Figure 3.3.

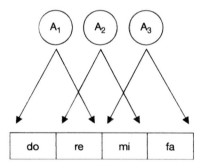

Figure 3.3 Broad's version

Whereas previously the transition between *re* and *mi* was entirely ignored, it is now fully acknowledged and apprehended: by the additional act of awareness A_2. If we suppose, as Broad did, that successive acts are densely packed, we can—it seems—capture every experienced succession, and so do full justice to the phenomenological character of our experience.

In fact, while in one respect Broad's proposal is a genuine advance over the pulse theory—all specious presents are now duly recognized—in other respects it is no advance at all. Is the new model phenomenologically adequate? It is not obvious that it is. Since *re* is experienced by act of awareness A₁ *and also* by the act of awareness A₂, it seems that *re* is experienced twice-over, when in reality it is experienced just once. And of course what goes for *re* goes for every tone in the series, and for every brief phase of any stream of consciousness.[4] There is worse to come. The pulse theory fragments consciousness, but a case can be made for thinking that Broad's model does so too. We are being asked to accept that a stream of consciousness consists of a succession of acts of awareness, each taking in slightly different spreads of content. The fact that numerically the same contents are to be found in successive or neighbouring acts provides for unity (or partial identity) at the level of contents, but there is no trace of unity to be found at the level of *awareness*. A₁ and A₂ may take in a common content—*re*—but *qua* episodes of awareness they are entirely distinct. (Since they are both momentary, there is no possibility of partial overlap.) What reason do we have for thinking that a succession of discrete acts of this sort could constitute phenomenally *continuous* consciousness of the sort we are so familiar with? So far as I can see, none whatsoever. If you had an experience with content *do-re* and I had an experience with content *re-mi*, the result would obviously not be an experience of *do-re-mi*. Broad's proposal seems to generate an analogous consequence. It multiplies specious presents, but it fails to provide a satisfactory account of how successive specious presents are related to one another.[5]

In his later writings on temporal awareness Broad adopted a very different approach, variants of which have also been developed by Husserl, Ward, and more recently, Lockwood.[6] The new account does away with acts of awareness stretching out across time to apprehend temporally extended expanses of content.

---

[4] Tye has recently argued that since the experiencing of *re* by A₁ and the experiencing of *re* by A₂ are (seemingly) of the same tone occurring at the same time the duplication would go unnoticed: 'I hear a click [or tone] twice in that there are two times at which an act of hearing a click occurs . . . . But [there is] no time between them at which I experience that there is no click. Indeed, there is no time between these two times at which anything is experientially represented by hearing. So, I do not hear a click *as* occurring twice' (2003: 94). Perhaps the account can be developed in such a way that the repetitions go unnoticed, but the repetitions are nonetheless occurring, which makes the proposal profligate to say the least: don't forget that (on Broad's version at any rate) there are *many* additional acts between A₁ and A₂, so *re* is experienced many times over (not just twice), and what goes for *re* goes for each short stretch of experience. For a fuller account of Broad see Dainton (2000: ch. 6).

[5] We could posit a higher-order act to unify A₁ and A₂, but so doing further complicates the structure of consciousness. Moreover, the scope of the higher-order act would need to be at least twice that of the specious present we are familiar with, and this leads to a new difficulty: if such higher-order acts of awareness exist, why is the specious present as short as it seems to be? The difficulties do not stop here. To prevent the disconnection problem afflicting the higher-order acts as well as their first-order counterparts, there would need to be acts of awareness of a still higher-order, and the latter would need unifying by acts of a still higher-order—this ascent leads ineluctably to a single act which embraces the entirety of a stream of consciousness. But again, if such acts exist, why is it that we do not experience all parts of our streams of consciousness together, in a *totum simul*—a mode of experience usually ascribed only to God-like beings?

[6] E.g., Broad (1938, volume 2), Lockwood (1989), Husserl (1991), Ward (1918).

It is now supposed that streams of consciousness are composed of successions of durationless phases, each of which is a specious present. Although each specious present occupies only a moment of real time, their contents are such that they appear to us to be temporally extended. A typical specious present comprises a momentary 'real' experience together with a *representation* of what has just been experienced. The representations in neighbouring specious presents vary in a systematic fashion, as depicted in a simplified way in Figure 3.4.

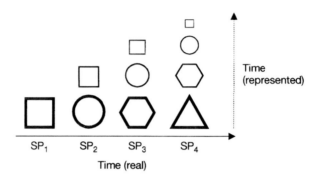

Figure 3.4 The representational conception

Imagine that you are shown a succession of shapes on a screen: a square followed by a circle, then a hexagon, then a triangle. These are indicated by the bold shapes at the bottom of the figure. Although the actual experience of the square occurs in SP_1, the first specious present, it does not entirely vanish from your consciousness. In the specious presents that follow, successively modified representations of the square are to be found; the modifications are such that the square appears less and less present, with the effect that it seems to sink further into the past, before disappearing from consciousness altogether—in the figure, smaller size indicates greater 'pastness'. As can be seen, when the triangle is perceived, in SP_4, it is accompanied by a representation of the three preceding shapes, each appearing under a different temporal mode of presentation.

This 'representationalist' account of temporal awareness is, in effect, a variant of the memory theory we considered earlier. The temporal 'depth' of experience is now being furnished, not by ordinary memories, but by a distinctive *sui generis* mode of mental representation.[7] Quite how these representations achieve what they do is by no means obvious. How can presently occurring contents appear to

---

[7] I call this model 'representationalist' because the recent past features in experience in the form of a representation, rather than being directly presented or apprehended—this position should not be equated with the representationalism of the Harman–Dretske–Tye variety mentioned in §2.1. The representations I am envisaging are usually transparent, but we can become aware of them if we abandon the naïve phenomenological standpoint in favour of its critical (or informed) counterpart;

be located in the past? Although different theorists have attempted to answer this question in different ways, the various proposals on offer are open to objections of one kind or another. However, there is no need to venture into these murky waters here.[8] The sophistication of some of its variants notwithstanding, the representationalist proposal is fundamentally flawed, in a manner that should by now be obvious.

Look again at the specious presents in Figure 3.4—represented in schematic guise by the four columns. It is true that the contents of the earlier specious presents is reflected in those that come later. It is true—if only by hypothesis—that each specious present appears to its subject to possess genuine temporal depth, even though it is in fact momentary. However, is it not also true that each specious present is an *entirely distinct experience* in its own right? Broad's earlier account at least posited an overlap at the level of the contents apprehended by neighbouring acts of awareness, but even that connection is now absent: successive momentary stream-phases have numerically distinct contents. Once again, the difficulty is not with transitions *within* specious presents, but rather with transitions *between* them. Phenomenal continuity is not confined to single specious presents, it also connects and binds successive specious presents. When we hear a melody we hear *each* note flow into its successor; when we see a sequence of illuminated shapes, we see *each* shape being replaced by its successor. None of this would be possible if our streams of consciousness were constructed of discrete experientially isolated fragments in the manner proposed by representationalists. Like those which came before, this latest proposal is disastrously flawed: it fails to save the phenomena.

3.4. OVERLAP AND FLOW

Although a good deal more could be said about each of the preceding theories, this brief survey suffices to bring out the force of two key points. For an account of the temporal structure of consciousness to be phenomenologically acceptable—for it to do full justice to phenomenal continuity—it must first of all render intelligible the fact that we directly experience change and persistence over short intervals: we need an adequate account of the specious present. The simple memory theory we looked at first signally fails in this respect. But secondly,

---

also, I am not assuming that the phenomenal features of these representations can be explicated solely in terms of their intentional content.

[8] Broad appealed to a quality of 'presentedness', which comes in different degrees; the less presentedness a content possesses, the more past it appears. As Husserl noted, it is not obvious how any presently presented sensory quality can perform the task required, and preferred to talk instead of 'retentions', which serve to make us aware of the recent past. Quite how these are supposed to function, however, is also unclear. For further discussion see Gallagher (1998, 2003), Dainton (2003a), Zahavi (2005: ch. 3)

and no less importantly, we need an explanation of how neighbouring specious presents are related to one another, and this explanation must accommodate all the instances of experienced change and persistence that we find in our ordinary streams of consciousness. More specifically, it must find a way of accommodating what I earlier called the *Diachronic Co-consciousness Constraint* (DCC), according to which all the successive brief phases of a typical stream of consciousness are connected by co-consciousness. As we have seen, even if Broad's early and later efforts provide a believable account of individual specious presents (and it is by no means clear that they do), they certainly fail to provide an adequate explanation of the transitions between specious presents. The failing in each case is the same: contents *within* specious presents are allowed to be co-conscious (allowing change and persistence to be directly experienced), but contents in successive specious presents are not and *cannot* be co-conscious. If our streams of consciousness were fragmented in this fashion they could not possibly have the continuously flowing character that they in fact possess.

The bare outline of a better account, one which does conform to DCC, is not difficult to find. When discussing the pulse account we considered the experienced succession *do-re-mi-fa* which divided into two specious presents P_1: [*do-re*] and P_2: [*mi-fa*]. Since in P_1 the transition from *do* to *re* is directly experienced, the experience of *do* and the experience of *re* are co-conscious. Since *do* is experienced as coming after *re* they are not synchronically co-conscious, but they are *diachronically* co-conscious. The two tones are experienced *together*, but in succession rather than simultaneously: the tone *do* is experienced as giving way to, or flowing into, *re*, not as occurring at the same time as *re*. The tones *mi* and *fa* in P_2 are similarly related. Now, as we saw, the pulse account is flawed because it fails to acknowledge the fact that in addition to directly experiencing the transitions *do-re* and *mi-fa*, we also directly experience the transition *re-mi*. There is an obvious remedy for this failing: we need simply introduce into our account an additional pulse of experience, an additional specious present—call it P_X—whose content is *re-mi*. Since we do in fact experience *re* giving way to *mi* this is clearly a step in the right direction, but it may also seem problematic. If the experience of *do-re-mi-fa* consisted of three separate specious presents, P_1: [*do-re*], P_X: [*re-mi*], P_2: [*mi-fa*] then not only would both *re* and *mi* would be experienced twice over—when in fact they are heard only once—but we would once again have a fragmented stream of consciousness. Each experienced transition gets experienced in some specious present, but there are no experiential connections *between* neighbouring specious presents.

These two difficulties can be resolved by a single correction. Rather than supposing that P_X is a numerically distinct experience that exists in addition to P_1 and P_2, we simply hold that the *re* which appears in P_X is the very same token experience as the *re* that occurs in P_1, and in similar fashion that the *mi* in P_X is the very same token experience as the *mi* in P_2. P_X exists, but it is wholly composed of the second part of P_1 and the first part of P_2.

If neighbouring specious presents *overlap by sharing common parts* in this manner, then both our difficulties are resolved. Not only is each streamal phase experienced only once, as it should be, but now there are also direct phenomenal connections between all neighbouring streamal phases: *do* is co-conscious with *re*, *re* is co-conscious with *mi*, *mi* is co-conscious with *fa*, and so forth—as seen in Figure 3.5. Given that we are assuming that the scope of the diachronic co-consciousness relationship (and so the extent of the specious present) does not extend beyond any two tones in our scale, we do not get the phenomenologically unrealistic result that tones separated by greater intervals than this—such as *do* and *mi*, or *fa* and *la*—are experienced together. Successive specious presents coincide, but only partially. For obvious reasons I call this the *overlap model* of phenomenal continuity.[9]

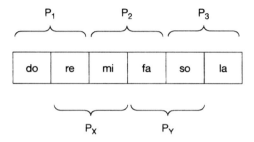

Figure 3.5 The overlap model (in schematic form)

The overlap model is the only account we have encountered thus far that conforms to DCC. Since it is difficult to see how DCC can be satisfied in any other way—that is without positing specious presents which partially overlap by sharing common parts or phases—it is difficult to see how our streams of consciousness could fail to be so structured. This said, the theory does possess a number of intriguing features, some of which are somewhat counterintuitive, at least initially.

In §2.5 I used the term 'total experience' to refer to groups of experiences that are all mutually co-conscious, and that are not parts of any larger group of experiences that are all mutually co-conscious. In that context, where the focus was exclusively on synchronic unity, the experiences in question were momentary or of minimally brief duration. Now that we have expanded our

---

[9] The possibility of this approach was noted by Russell: 'If A, B and C succeed one another rapidly, A and B may be parts of one sensation, and likewise B and C, while A and C are not part of one sensation. . . . In such a case, A and B belong to the same [specious] present, and likewise B and C, but not A and C . . . two presents may overlap without coinciding' (1984: 78). Versions of the doctrine have been propounded on several occasions by Foster (1979, 1982, 1985, 1991); it is also discussed in Lockwood (1989: ch. 15; 2005: ch. 17). For a more detailed examination see Dainton (2000, ch. 7, and 2003*a*).

focus so as to include the temporal dimension, it is clear that total experiences properly so-called are temporally extended. What I have thus far been calling 'specious presents' are nothing more or less than temporally extended total experiences: they consist of temporal spreads of content whose parts are all mutually co-conscious (either synchronically or diachronically) and which are not part of any larger spread of content possessing parts that are all mutually co-conscious. I also suggested in §2.5 that it is difficult to imagine how the synchronic co-consciousness could fail to be transitive. In the diachronic case a very different situation obtains: here failures in transitivity are the norm. Recall our simple example, where *do* is co-conscious with *re, re* is co-conscious with *mi*, but *do* is not co-conscious with *mi*. Quite generally, any two partially overlapping specious presents will contain three experiential parts such that the first is co-conscious with the second, the second is co-conscious with the third, but where the first and third are not co-conscious. Far from being puzzling, however, these breakdowns of transitivity are only to be expected, given what our experience is like. If diachronic co-consciousness were transitive, each part of an extended stream of consciousness would be directly co-conscious with every other part, which is evidently not the case. Moreover, it would be impossible for us to experience contents *passing through* our consciousness in the way we do: think of the way *do* is experienced as giving way to *re* which in turn gives way for *mi*, and so forth. This is only possible because *do* and *mi* are not experienced together, as co-conscious. Needless to say, the intimate link between failures of transitivity and a distinctively temporal feature of consciousness provides some support for the contention that co-consciousness in the synchronic case, amongst simultaneous contents, cannot fail to be transitive.

Two further features of the overlap model should be noted. Thus far we have been working with an artificially simple example. In reality, our streams of consciousness are not usually as simple as *do-re-mi*, their contents are far more complex, varied and irregular. Nor are specious presents distributed in the way depicted in Figure 3.5: separated from their immediate neighbours by equally sized temporal intervals. If they were then some phenomenal successions—such as the one starting half of the way through *do* and continuing on to half of the way through *mi*—would not be experienced. This problem does not arise if we suppose immediately adjacent specious presents are so close together that if they were any closer they would no longer seem to occur in succession. Just how close together would they need to be for this to happen? For human subjects, psychological research into time perception suggests an answer of around 30msec. This is the extent of the so-called *order threshold*: it is only when stimuli are separated by more than this interval that subjects perceive them as occurring in a definite temporal order (Ruhnau 1995). A few of these additional specious presents are indicated in Figure 3.6. If this liberal profusion of distinct specious presents is not obvious in our experience, it is because so many so very nearly overlap one another completely.

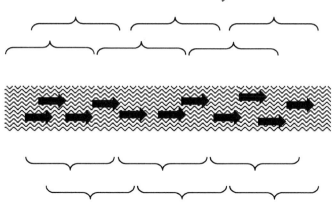

Figure 3.6 A more realistic depiction of the overlap model: incorporating phenomenal flow and more densley packed specious presents

It could be objected that *no* overlaps of this kind are ever discernible in our experience, and in one sense this is true. If a sheet of yellow-coloured glass spatially overlaps a sheet of blue-coloured glass, the region of overlap is easy to see. When held up to the light the region where one sheet is superimposed over the other is markedly different in colour from the areas on either side, which remain yellow and blue. But partially overlapping specious presents are not related in this way. Rather than two numerically distinct experiences which are somehow superimposed (over a brief interval time), in the region of overlap we have only a single experience, an experience that forms a part of two (or more) specious presents. This sort of overlap—by way of sharing of parts, rather than superposition—does not impact on the intrinsic properties of the experiences concerned, and in this respect it is indiscernible. But in another respect the existence of the overlapping structures is readily discernible: when we hear *do-re-mi*, we hear *do* flowing into *re*, and *re* flowing into *mi*, and the *re* which follows *do* is the very same token experience as the *re* which is followed by *mi*. This sort of structure is ubiquitous in our experience; this sort of structure consists of temporally extended experiences which overlap by sharing common parts.

The second point concerns what I earlier called 'phenomenal passage'. Consider again the experienced succession *do-re*. Since the co-consciousness relationship is symmetrical, if *do* is co-conscious with *re* in a single temporally extended total experience, then *re* is equally well co-conscious with *do*. Given this, why is it that we hear *do* flowing into, or being followed by *re*? Our experience seems to flow or unfold in just one direction, but how can this be if co-consciousness itself is symmetrical and hence bi-directional? Short-term memory no doubt plays a role here, as do a variety of fringe-type experiences: anticipatory feelings, the feeling of going forth confidently or hesitantly, inklings that something good or bad is about to happen, and so on. But I suspect that the primary factor responsible for phenomenal passage is simply the distinctively temporal character of phenomenal contents themselves. A directed dynamic flowing quality is built into phenomenal contents as diverse as sounds, pains, visual experiences of motion and rest, bodily and emotional feelings. Just think of what it is like to feel an intense toothache: the throbbing *ongoing* character of the experience is part of the phenomenal fabric of the pain sensation. Much the same applies to the phenomenal contents associated with hearing a piercing whistle, or seeing a bird swoop down to make a kill. Co-consciousness does not in itself explain the inherently directional character of experience, but it does not need to. What it does provide is a unified phenomenal framework within which contents possessing a directional intrinsic character can exist within phenomenally continuous streams of consciousness. This framework is illustrated in Figure 3.6: the dynamic (flowing) character of contents housed within overlapping specious presents is represented by the small arrows.

We can also put the co-consciousness relationship to work in defining in more precise terms what a *stream* of consciousness is, and what is required for experiences to belong to the same stream—or be *co-streamal*, as I shall sometimes put it. We saw earlier that a specious present is a temporally extended total experience. An experience of this kind is a temporally extended distribution of phenomenal contents that are (i) all mutually co-conscious, and (ii) not parts of any larger distribution of mutually co-conscious contents. As we have seen latterly, a stream of consciousness consists of a series of partially overlapping specious presents. Consequently, a *complete* stream of consciousness is simply a maximal chain of overlapping specious presents. We can also say that experiences are co-streamal if and only if they are directly or *indirectly* co-conscious. Experiences are related in the latter way if they are connected by overlapping chains of direct co-consciousness.

3.5. PHENOMENAL CUTS

The overlap model is fully compatible with DCC, the Diachronic Co-consciousness Constraint. Indeed, since to conform to the latter an account of the diachronic unity of consciousness must acknowledge that successive specious presents are connected by co-consciousness, DCC requires the overlap model, or something very much like it. There is, however, a line of argument which might seem to undermine DCC. Here is one way of formulating it:

Suppose that at precisely noon today, just as you are about to cross a busy street, you are vaporized, instantaneously, by a devastatingly powerful laser beam. Although your annihilation brings your stream of consciousness to an immediate halt, it does not affect in the slightest the character of your experience leading up to this event. How could it? Are we to suppose that your pre-noon experience is affected by events that have yet to occur, via some mysterious channel of backwards causation? Assuming not, it seems that your experience leading up to the moment of your annihilation is just as it would have been if the trigger on the laser had not been pressed, and you had continued about your business as per usual. The point generalizes. There is nothing special about you, and nothing special about that particular time. Any of us *could* be annihilated at any of our waking moments, and this could occur without impinging on the character of the immediately preceding experiences. And this is not all. We are all familiar with the sceptical claim that 'everything could be just as it is now even if the entire universe only came into existence five minutes ago'. If this is right, then surely the universe could have come into being five *seconds* ago—or even five milliseconds—without affecting the character of our experience now. This also applies to everyone, at all times. Putting these points together, and bearing in mind the fact that these cuts could come anywhere in any stream, it is clear that the phenomenal character of any short stretch of experience *E* is logically independent of both later and earlier experiences in the same stream of consciousness: *E* could be just as it is, phenomenologically speaking, if the experiences immediately before and after it did not exist. It follows that a stream of consciousness consists of a succession of experiential phases, each of which is entirely self-contained and isolated, at least on the phenomenal level, from its immediate neighbours.

This reasoning—I will call it the *cut argument*—can seem convincing. If the conclusion to which it leads were true, successive stream-phases would not be connected by co-consciousness—merely by qualitative similarity and (perhaps) short-term memories. The DCC constraint would thus be false, the diachronic unity of consciousness would be illusory—at least beyond the confines of individual specious presents—and the project of constructing a viable account of our persistence conditions in terms of the unity and continuity we find in our streams of consciousness would be doomed. However, as we have seen in connection with the pulse and representational theories that we looked at in §3.3, there are good reasons for supposing that if our streams of consciousness did consist of discrete, phenomenally isolated phases, they could not exhibit the kind of phenomenal continuity they manifestly do exhibit! So unless our experience is very different from how it seems, which seems unlikely to say the least, the cut argument must be going wrong somewhere.

In fact, the mistake is not difficult to locate. If the cut reasoning seems plausible it is because it contains a kernel of truth. It is logically possible for a short-lived subject—a *two-second subject*, say—to have a stream of consciousness which very closely resembles the two-seconds of consciousness that you (or anyone else) has just enjoyed. Suppose you have just heard someone playing a C-major scale on a piano: *C-D-E-F-G-A-B-C* . . . .Let us also suppose that on some distant (but logically possible) world a short-lived duplicate of you comes into being, in an exactly similar room, containing a similar piano, and hears just the *D*-segment of a similarly pitched scale, before ceasing to exist. Would your ephemeral duplicate's experience exactly resemble your own? In intrinsic phenomenal respects, quite possibly. The auditory qualities of the *D*-tone you each experience might be indistinguishable; you might also both hear *D* while experiencing a short-term acoustic memory-image of a preceding *C*, along with an anticipation of hearing an *E* and a brief snippet of thought; your non-auditory perceptual experiences might also be qualitatively similar.

However, it is clearly one thing for your duplicate's stream of consciousness to resemble yours in these intrinsic respects, another for it to resemble yours in *all* respects. So far as diachronic phenomenal *relations* are concerned, your duplicate's experience cannot possibly exactly resemble yours. You hear *C*-running-into-*D*, and *D*-running-into-*E*, but since neither *C* nor *E* are experienced by your duplicate, the latter does not experience *D* as being phenomenally related to either a preceding *C* or a succeeding *E*. Your experience of *D* clearly differs from your duplicate's in respect of phenomeno-temporal relational properties. And this is a difference which matters. If the successive phases of an ordinary stream of consciousness are linked by relations of diachronic co-consciousness in the way I have argued, then putting a succession of entirely self-contained phases side by side, as it were, would not and could not yield a stream of consciousness of the kind we typically enjoy. Our streams do not consist of a succession of self-contained chunks or pulses of experience, laid end to end like a row of bricks. Or at least, if we do think of them in this way, we must not forget the cement which holds the bricks together: in addition to phenomenal connections within stream-phases, we must also recognize the phenomenal connections *between* them. The plausibility of the cut argument derives from an incomplete conception of the diachronic features of consciousness.

By way of a further illustration of this point, consider Figure 3.7, where four brief stream-segments are shown.

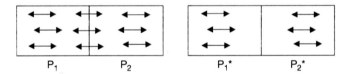

Figure 3.7 Phenomenal connections unconfined (on the left) and confined (on the right)

Thanks to the presence of the diachronic phenomenal connections linking P_1 and P_2, this pair of stream-phases forms a phenomenally continuous stretch of experience. In this instance, the depicted spatial proximity between these phases accurately reflects experiential reality. It is otherwise with respect to P_1^* and P_2^*. Given the absence of phenomenal connections between these phases, they do not constitute a stream of consciousness. In short, the cut argument presupposes that our ordinary experience is as depicted on the right, when in reality, it is as shown on the left.

It is also illuminating to consider a spatial analogue. Let the various Ps in Figure 3.7 represent momentary colour-filled expanses, rather than temporally extended sensations. Thanks to the relationships of co-consciousness linking all their constituent parts, P_1-P_2 is a single expanse of phenomenal space. Thanks to the complete *absence* of relationships of co-consciousness linking P_1^* and P_2^*, these regions do *not* form a single phenomenal expanse: despite their proximity on the page, they are entirely separate experiences. What goes for (phenomenal) space goes also for (phenomenal) time: experienced continuity requires experienced togetherness. The relationship of experienced togetherness *is* co-consciousness, synchronically and diachronically.

There is of course a sense in which this may not be obvious to the subjects involved. Let us suppose (as is perfectly possible, given the absence of phenomenal connections) that P_1^* and P_2^* belong to two distinct short-lived subjects S_1 and S_2. Depending on the precise character of their experience, it may well be that neither of these subjects has any inkling that they are as ephemeral as they in fact are. The content of S_2's experience might be qualitatively very similar to yours for the past couple of seconds; the thought 'Just another couple of minutes and I'll have that cup of coffee' might flash through S_2's mind; S_2 might remember having just had an experience with the character of P_1^*. But so far as the facts about phenomenal continuity are concerned, none of this matters. S_2 may have a strong sense of being at the leading edge of a continuous stream of consciousness that has lasted several hours, but this impression is irrelevant to whether or not this is in fact the case. Phenomenal continuity is a product of relationships of co-consciousness between successive stream-phases, not beliefs, judgements, fringe feelings, or memories (although all of the latter can contribute to what a particular instance of phenomenal continuity is like). As I noted in connection with the pulse theory, it is perfectly possible for subjects to have erroneous beliefs about their own experience, and here is a case in point. But even if the absence of diachronic phenomenal connections can go unnoticed, at least in the special case of the sort of very short-lived subjects we are currently considering, it does not follow that these connections cannot be discerned at all. In a normal stream of consciousness they can be, easily, all the time.[10]

3.6. THE ONE EXPERIENCE VIEW

Before moving on I will comment briefly on the merits (or otherwise) of an alternative way of thinking about the issue of diachronic unity. The fact that co-consciousness binds or fuses its relata into single experiential states opens up the possibility of a 'top down' approach to phenomenal unity. As noted in §2.5, Bayne and Chalmers adopt such a stance with regard to synchronic unity, and Michael Tye has recently extended the approach to diachronic unity: 'A stream of consciousness is just one temporally extended experience that represents a flow

---

[10] Most of this section is drawn from Dainton 2004: 376–8.

of things in the world. It has no shorter experiences as parts. Indeed it has no experiences as proper parts at all' (2003: 108). For Tye, the main reason why the unity of consciousness can seem so puzzling is that the issue is badly framed. It is assumed that at any one time, and over short intervals, we have a number of distinct experiences that are unified in a distinctive way, and the question is then posed: what is the nature of this distinctive unifying relationship? Once we see the situation aright, and realize that an entire stream of consciousness consists of just one experience, the problem dissolves. If streams of consciousness are not composed of experiences, there is nothing *to* unify. The alternative to this approach, he suggests, is despair or vacuity.

> Begin with the assumption that there are individual experiences somehow bundled together by a phenomenal unity relation and you will find yourself either supposing that phenomenal unity is something unique and basic about which you can say nothing except that it bundles experiences together to form a unified consciousness, or you will join Hume in confessing that the problem of the unifying principle is too hard to be solved. The latter course of action at least has the virtue of candor, but the best strategy, it seems to me, is simply to give up the assumption. (Tye 2003: 107)

The 'one experience view' as Tye calls it, has some merit. Given the way neighbouring co-streamal specious presents overlap, there is an important sense in which a stream of consciousness is indeed a single expanse or stretch of experience. On the other hand, taking an entire stream of consciousness that not only lasts for hours but has enormously varying content to be a single experience is somewhat counterintuitive, all the more so since only a tiny fraction of such a stream's contents are ever present in consciousness together. It would be rather more plausible, perhaps, to regard individual specious presents as single experiences. But even here, while it is true that the various parts of a specious present are experienced together, they also frequently contain clearly and cleanly demarcated parts—for example the visual sighting of a dog and the auditory experience of its bark—parts that it is very natural to regard as single experiences (as noted in §2.1). Tye's insistence on a single right way of individuating experiences appears rather dogmatic. Why not agree that there are a number of equally legitimate ways of carving a typical stream of consciousness into experiential parts? The 'one experience' view is legitimate for some purposes, but so too is the 'many experience' view: both can shed useful light on the phenomenal reality.

But I am not going to belabour this point, for I do not believe much of significance depends on it. For even if we were to follow Tye and accept the one experience view, so doing would not affect the fundamental problem in the slightest. Irrespective of whether we call them 'experiences' or not, our streams of consciousness typically contain many discernible *parts, regions,* or *aspects*. Some of these parts are related in a distinctive way—they are experienced together, they are phenomenally unified—and others are not. Tye himself recognizes as much.[11] The task of saying what can be said about this distinctive mode of unity thus remains, irrespective of whether we prefer to say that it is to be found within rather than between experiences. Whether we consider phenomenal unity and continuity from top-down or bottom-up, the same structures of co-consciousness are to be found, however we prefer to describe them.

3.7. STREAMAL UNITY

In §1.5 I outlined the rationale for an experience-based approach to the problem of the self. If we want a maximally credible account of our existence and persistence conditions, it would be a mistake to ignore what is without question the most compelling guide we have to our own existence and persistence: streamal unity and continuity. While our streams of consciousness continue to flow on, it is all but impossible to believe that we could either cease to exist or move on elsewhere; where the flow of our experience goes, we go. Furthermore, provided our streams of consciousness flow on, we can easily envisage surviving total ruptures in material and psychological-cum-causal continuity. All this suggested a way forward: why not try to construct an account of our persistence and existence conditions entirely in terms of phenomenal unity? The fact that our streams of consciousness seem to possess a unity of a quite distinctive, wholly phenomenal kind, suggests an account along these lines may be possible. True, there is the difficulty of dealing with gaps in consciousness—the bridge-problem—but we should not assume this to be unsolvable in advance. However, as I noted in §2.1, if we are to build an account of the self on the kinds of unity and continuity that we find in our streams of consciousness, we had best have a reasonably clear idea as to precisely what these involve. This we have now achieved, and not only this: *en route* we have disposed of a tempting but misguided conception of what the phenomenal self might be: the self as pure awareness.

The key insight we have gained is that we are on solid ground in supposing that our experience is self-unifying both at and over time. I stress again, 'self-unifying' in this context means 'unifies itself', not 'unified by some entity that stands outside or external to experience'. Our experiences at any one time are bonded into phenomenal wholes by the relationship of direct co-consciousness. The latter, I have argued, is a basic phenomenal feature, and as such cannot be analysed or reductively explained, at least while remaining on the phenomenal level. This does not mean the relationship is in the slightest elusive or mysterious.

---

[11] As is clear from passages such as this: 'In taking this view, I am not denying that, in the example of my hearing the musical scale do-re-mi, there is an experience of do-re in the first specious present and an experience of re-mi in the second. My point is that there are not different experiences: there is only one experience—an experience of do-re-mi—that has been described in different (partial) ways, an experience with different *stages* to it' (Tye 2003: 99–100, my emphasis).

In saying that experiences are linked by co-consciousness I simply mean that they are experienced together, and we all know what this 'experienced togetherness' is like. As we have seen latterly, co-consciousness operates synchronically but also diachronically. At any one moment our overall states of consciousness are unified wholes by virtue of the fact that their constituent parts are joined by co-consciousness, but the same applies over short periods of time: specious presents consist of (brief) temporal spreads of phenomenal contents that are unified by (diachronic) co-consciousness. If streams of consciousness are composed of overlapping specious presents—in the way I have argued—then they too are genuine phenomenal unities. Not because all their parts are experienced together (this is true only within the confines of particular specious presents) but because they conform to DCC: each of their successive (brief) phases is bonded to its neighbours by the relationship of co-consciousness.

It is worth stressing again that phenomenal unity has a quite distinctive feature. In both the synchronic and diachronic cases co-consciousness is *pervasive*: irrespective of how we choose to divide a temporally extended total experience into parts, each and every part is co-conscious with every other part. A small subset of these relationships are depicted in schematic form in Figure 3.8, where E_1, E_2, and E_3 are three (very) brief phases within a single specious present. Some of the co-consciousness relationships among the parts of these experiences are depicted on the left, others on the right. All parts of E_1 and E_2 are co-conscious, likewise E_2 and E_3, but so too are all parts of E_1 and E_3. Transitivity breaks down between specious presents, but *within* specious presents it holds.

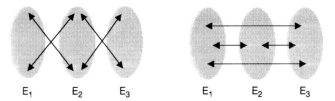

    E_1 E_2 E_3 E_1 E_2 E_3

Figure 3.8 Three brief stream-phases, revealing (in a partial way) the pervasive character of the co-consciousness relationship

Co-consciousness does not merely 'link' its relata, it binds them into a single state of unified consciousness. What is noteworthy, and for our purposes significant, is that this far-reaching unity is entirely a product of features that are internal to consciousness.

Having isolated these structures, the next task is to put them to work.

4
Powers and Subjects

4.1. BRIDGE BUILDING

Having established some secure foundations we are in a position to move on to the constructive phase of operations. I have already noted the intimate relationship between ourselves and our streams of consciousness. Since it is hard to imagine how one could become separated from one's stream of consciousness (other than by losing consciousness altogether) it is hard to see how all the experiences in a single uninterrupted stream could fail to belong to the same subject. As we saw in §1.5 this can be encapsulated in a simple principle:

The S-thesis: co-streamal experiences are consubjective.

Here as elsewhere, by 'consubjective' I mean 'belongs to the same self or subject'. If the analyses of the last two chapters are along the right lines, and the unity of consciousness both at and over time are the products of the co-consciousness relationship, we can advance a further claim:

The C-thesis: co-conscious experiences are consubjective.

The two theses are closely linked, for (as we saw in §3.4) a stream of consciousness is a collection of experiences that are directly or indirectly co-conscious—experiences are related in the latter way if they are not themselves directly co-conscious, but are linked to one another by a chain of experiences that are. The C-thesis illuminates the S-thesis by explicating precisely what is involved, at the phenomenal level, in experiences being co-streamal.

The C-thesis carries us a certain distance, but not as far as we need to go. Co-consciousness (in its direct or indirect forms) may supply us with a sufficient condition for the consubjectivity of experiences, but (on the face of it at least) it does not amount to a necessary condition. Since experiences in distinct streams separated by a gap in time are neither directly nor indirectly co-conscious, the C-thesis provides no guide as to the circumstances in which such streams belong to the same self. Hence the bridge-problem: when earlier and later streams belong to the same self, what is it that makes it so? For those who subscribe to physical or causal accounts of our persistence conditions, the bridge-problem is no problem at all—causal and physical relations (and entities) can span losses of consciousness   but the problem is clearly very real indeed for anyone committed to an experience-based approach. If the problem were not difficult enough, there is a plausible constraint that should also be borne in mind.

Solutions to the bridge-problem can be divided into two categories. Suppose S_1 and S_2 are two streams of consciousness, separated by a gap of a few hours. We might say that whereas the experiences within each of these streams are consubjective by virtue of being directly or indirectly co-consciousness, S_1 and S_2 are themselves consubjective because they causally depend on the same body or brain, or are associated with the same psychological system, where the persistence of a psychological system is measured by some form of causal continuity. These are examples of *impure* solutions: the consubjectivity of experiences within a single uninterrupted stream is determined by a single factor (in this case direct or indirect co-consciousness), but the consubjectivity of experiences in different streams is held to depend on some quite different factor. A *pure* solution to the bridge-problem will not be disjunctive in this way. Only a single unifying factor will be employed, and the consubjectivity of experiences in different streams will be explained in fundamentally the same way as that of experiences within the same stream.

Perhaps there are objects whose persistence conditions are impure. It is certainly easy enough to invent a sortal term whose diachronic identity criterion is disjunctive. A *woofwagger* is a dog minus its tail on Mondays, Wednesdays, and Fridays, and a dog's tail minus the rest of the dog on Tuesdays, Thursdays, and weekends. A woofwagger is a perfectly respectable object, or at least it is if we allow anything that has well-defined identity conditions to count as an object. But it is an object of a peculiar sort. The identity criteria of most of the objects we are familiar with (the objects for which we already have sortal concepts) are non-disjunctive. The requirements for a dog to persist do not vary from one day to the next, and the same applies to cats, mice, and trees. If we were to adopt an impure solution to the bridge-problem, we would, in effect, be saying that the persistence of subjects requires different conditions to be met at different times. I think it is fair to say that this is not how we usually think of ourselves. It seems natural to suppose that being awake and being unconscious are just different ways a subject can be; hence it seems odd to suppose that the persistence conditions of a dreamlessly sleeping subject differ from those of a conscious subject. To put it another way, when we lose consciousness we do not become a different kind of entity: an unconscious subject is exactly the same kind of entity as a conscious subject—or so most of us are inclined to think. If we were to adopt an impure solution to the bridge-problem, there would be a sense in which it would no longer be true to say this: for even if we decided to *call* conscious and unconscious subjects by the same name, 'subjects' thus construed would be compounds of more basic entities, 'conscious-subjects' and 'non-conscious-subjects', each with their own persistence conditions.

There is a second and independent reason for preferring purity. Thought experiments suggest that an experience-based account of what our survival requires will be more compelling, more believable, than any other; experiential continuity provides a surer guide to our persistence than either physical or psychological continuity. For this reason alone, a pure solution to the bridge problem, a solution relying only on co-consciousness, would simply be a better solution.

Purity in the context of the bridge-problem may be a desirable attribute, but it does make life considerably more difficult. If we rely on the C-thesis, and account for consubjectivity within streams solely in terms of co-consciousness, we must also explain the consubjectivity of disjoint streams in the same terms, but it is precisely the absence of any connecting relationship of co-consciousness between such streams which is their defining property. As for how we should proceed, the options are constrained, if not entirely determined, by the stance we take on a very fundamental issue. The doctrine that selves are fundamentally experiential beings can be—and has been—interpreted in two quite different ways. Some have found the following doctrine compelling:

The Essentially Conscious Self (ECS): a self is a thing whose essential nature it is to *be* conscious; a self is experiencing at every moment at which it exists; a self cannot lose consciousness and continue to exist.

The rationalist view of the self as an individual substance whose essential attribute is consciousness leads directly to the ECS conception, but others have found the doctrine appealing on phenomenological grounds—for example Strawson (1997, 1999a). Faced with the bridge-problem, proponents of the ECS conception have two options. They can stay close to common sense by holding that most of us have a sizeable number of distinct streams of consciousness over the course of our lives, and then provide an account of what renders streams separated by periods of unconsciousness consubjective. Or they may opt for the more radical alternative and hold that each self necessarily has just one uninterrupted stream of consciousness. Neither option is very appealing.

If we are confined to a single stream of consciousness, and people lose consciousness as often as they seem to, then our life spans will be short: none of us can expect to survive our next period of dreamless sleep. (Our bodies may waken, but they will not house or sustain the same subject of consciousness.) Proponents of the single-stream view who find this unacceptable might be tempted to follow Descartes and Leibniz, and hold that we never in fact lose consciousness during the normal course of our lives, that during periods of so-called dreamless sleep we continue to have *some* experience, usually of a low-level kind, that subsequently we cannot remember. While this cannot be rejected out of hand—sleep is far from being a well-understood phenomenon—the claim is purely speculative, and highly vulnerable to subsequent empirical discoveries.[1]

---

[1] The view is not without its contemporary advocates: 'I want to reject the assumption . . . that dreaming occurs only some of the time we are asleep. This is the "common sense" view, and it

There are also modern general anaesthetics to bear in mind, which certainly seem to entirely annihilate consciousness in a quick and effective way.

The multi-stream ECS conception is not quite so hostile to common sense. Although, as things stand, few of us equate losing consciousness with wholly ceasing to exist, this view might be acceptable if we could be sure that the past and future experiences we would ordinarily ascribe to ourselves really do belong to ourselves: a plausible solution to the bridge-problem is very much needed. However, in the absence of direct experiential relations between disjoint streams, the only obvious way of providing a solution along phenomenalist lines is by appealing to features internal to the streams in question. But what features? I have just this minute conjured up a memory-image of an experience I had yesterday, so my current stream of consciousness contains a memory-image which resembles an experience which actually occurred in an earlier stream—a stream that it is plausible to regard as belonging to me. Can we generalize from this, and hold that any pair of earlier and later streams are consubjective if and only if the later of the two contains a memory-image corresponding to some experience occurring in the earlier? Not very plausibly. Perhaps the most obvious problem is that it seems perfectly plausible to suppose that streams of consciousness can be consubjective without being so related. Suppose tomorrow I choose not to remember any experience I had today (alternatively, suppose I just find better things to do). Can we make sense of the idea that, in the envisaged conditions, these two streams have a common owner? We can indeed, very easily, and consequently it seems that apparent memories are not necessary for inter-streamal consubjectivity. (It is not for nothing that most neo-Lockeans have found Locke's own memory-based account inadequate.) Is the existence of memory-images sufficient for consubjectivity? Again, arguably not: if an exact duplicate of me as I currently am were to spring into existence on a distant world, this duplicate would have a stream of consciousness that is qualitatively (or internally) indistinguishable from mine, and hence my duplicate will have a memory-image (seemingly) of an experience I had yesterday. Does this mean my duplicate actually had those experiences? Clearly not, but it would be otherwise if the memory-based approach in its internalist guise were correct.

Although I would not want to claim that a satisfactory solution to (or evasion of) the bridge-problem is impossible under the ECS conception, it is clearly going to be an uphill struggle.[2] Happily, there are other options available to proponents of the experience-based approach. These options are made possible by a quite different conception of the experiential self:

is widely held by many, if not most, sleep scientists. The view I am going to assume is that we are always, while alive, conscious' Flanagan (2000: 68). But as Flanagan immediately goes on to concede, he himself is less than certain about the truth of his assumption: 'I don't know that it is true that we are always dreaming while asleep.'

[2] This pessimistic assessment will be confirmed in Chapter 5, when I look at some of these proposals in more detail.

The Potentially Conscious Self (PCS): a self is a thing that is *capable* of being conscious; a self has the *capacity* for consciousness at every moment at which it exists, and it possesses this capacity essentially. A self can lose consciousness provided it retains the potential to be conscious.

This doctrine has considerable *prima facie* plausibility. As is obvious, the PCS conception is implicit in how we normally view periods of unconsciousness: a subject persists during a lapse of consciousness so long as it remains *capable* of having experience. To say that the difference between sleep and death lies in the possibility of waking up seems common sense. It is important to note, however, that the relevant sense of 'possibility' here is nomological. A person is not merely asleep if it would (literally) take a miracle to wake them up. Looking at it from the other direction, a person who retains the capacity to regain consciousness *without* miraculous intervention has surely *not* yet died.

The idea that there is a connection between the concept of a subject and the notion of nomologically grounded potentialities for experience receives further support from the recognition that there is no (apparent) necessity for a subject ever to have *any* actual experience. A subject might come into, and depart from, existence without ever becoming conscious—the rather bleak example of a permanently anaesthetized foetus comes to mind. Such a subject exists and persists by virtue of possessing and continuing to possess the *ability* to have experiences, an ability that it is unable to exercise. If we assume the sleeping, the anaesthetized, and the conscious are instances of the same kind of entity in different states, their identities through time will presumably consist in the realization of the same conditions. If we make the plausible assumption that all that is essential to the existence of the subjects in these different states is their *capacity* for consciousness, it would seem as though a generic criterion of subject persistence would have to be in terms of this sort of capacity.

Further considerations point in the same direction. Recall the NRT scenarios. Intuitively, an injection of neuron-eliminating nanomachines is non-fatal provided the physical changes do not disturb one's mental capacities. More specifically, if one's *experiential* capacities are wholly unchanged—in the sense that the range of potential experiences available to one remains the same, even if the substrate of these capacities changes—it seems clear one survives the process, even if one's brain has been turned into a lump of silicates. This suggests that retaining the capacity for consciousness is sufficient for our survival. It is useful to consider a further variant in this connection: *zombifying* NRT scenarios. Here the changes wrought by the nanomachines do not affect one's behavioural dispositions, but they utterly abolish one's consciousness and one's capacity for consciousness; zombification converts a conscious being into a non-conscious entity that acts as though it is conscious, but is not. On reflection, most of us would regard such a transformation as lethal. This suggests that we believe that retaining the capacity for consciousness is necessary to our survival.

We reach much the same place from yet another direction. I have been focusing on actual streams of consciousness, but a typical self is more than the mere sum of its experiences at any one time, or so most of us believe. What is this additional 'something'? Subscribers to the PCS conception have a plausible answer: in addition to any occurrent experiences we might be enjoying at a particular time, we are also *capable* of enjoying a wide variety of other experiences. Ordinarily, at any given moment when I am conscious, only a tiny fraction of my experiential capacities are active and producing experience: I am thinking one thought, recalling a single occasion from my past, experiencing a few emotions, seeing a few colours and shapes, hearing one or two distinct sounds. But at such times I am capable of having a far wider range of experiences than this. Consequently, there is more to me (more to my self) than my current experiences: the capacities responsible for my occurrent experiences co-exist with unexercised capacities for experience, and the latter are as much *mine* as my experiences.

From this perspective the difference between being conscious and being unconscious is comparatively minor. While I am conscious the vast majority of my capacities for experience are usually dormant at any one time, when I am fully unconscious *all* my capacities for experience are dormant. Clearly, the difference between these two conditions is not great. Given that my inactive capacities belong to me rather than anyone else, the question naturally arises: what makes these capacities mine? What is it about them that is responsible for their belonging to the same self? Clearly, we need a criterion for assigning capacities for experiences to subjects. Since the vast bulk of a typical subject's experiential capacities are usually dormant, the principal function of this criterion will be to assign dormant capacities to subjects. On the plausible assumption that when subjects lose consciousness they retain their ability to have experiences, this criterion will apply to conscious and non-conscious subjects in much the same way. If such a criterion could be found, the bridge-problem would no longer be a problem at all.

The general shape of such a criterion is not too hard to discern: it is very plausible to think that what distinguishes capacities for experience which belong to the same subject from those which do not is the ability to produce unified states and streams of consciousness. However, there are different ways in which this core idea can be developed, and certain complications—of a benign kind, but complications nonetheless—which arise even in the context of quite simple minds. I will begin by taking a brief look at a simple and direct way of implementing the core idea, avoiding all complications so as to allow the basic picture to stand out in clear relief. We shall see that even this simplistic approach can be developed in different ways, depending on whether we formulate it in terms of *things which possess capacities for experience* or more directly in terms of *capacities for experience*. (I will be favouring the latter, on neo-Lockean grounds.) But while it is not without its merits or interest, this approach also has its limitations. In §4.3 I pursue a different and more revealing approach in greater depth and detail, exploring various complications and some further alternatives along the way. By the end of §4.3 the bridge-problem has been solved, and a quite general account of the persistence conditions of selves (of the PCS variety) framed in terms of capacities for experience has emerged. In §4.4 I take a step back, and look at capacities (or dispositional properties) in a general way, before focusing on more specific issues pertaining to capacities of the experiential variety.

4.2. EXPERIENCE-MACHINES AND BEYOND

Since selves may come in many shapes and forms, ideally we want an account of their existence and persistence that is as general as possible. The following concept provides a useful point of departure:

Experience Producer (EP): any object or system that has the capacity, grounded in natural law, to generate unified states or episodes of consciousness, either spontaneously, or in response to external or internal changes.

Thus characterized, an EP can come in any shape or form. Human brains may contain one or more EPs, but the same goes for dolphin brains, alien brains, and immaterial souls, if there are or could be such things. What makes something an EP is the ability to generate experiences, absolutely nothing else matters. Some EPs respond to external triggers (e.g. perceptual systems), others respond to internal triggers (e.g. systems responsible for conscious thought and mental imagery). Perhaps some EPs can respond to both internal and external influences, perhaps some are auto-activating. EPs can also vary from being severely limited in their range of outputs: some EPs may only be capable of producing a few very basic kinds of experience, others are capable of producing highly complex and varied experiences. For our purposes, given the desideratum of maximum generality, this range of possibilities is an advantage.

While identifying ourselves with EPs is an option, it is not an appealing one. First of all, and most obviously, it seems conceivable that the conscious states of what we would ordinarily take to be a single subject at a given time could be the product of two or more distinct EPs, and it would be absurd to identify a subject with what is clearly just one part of a subject. It is not inconceivable that the neural systems responsible for the auditory and visual experience of a typical human subject each individually satisfy the conditions for being an experience producer stated above; even if this is not in fact true of our auditory and visual systems, it could be true of (say) the systems which are responsible for our capacities for pain and mental imagery—and even if human EPs are in fact entirely non-modular, there could be other species of subject that are different from us in this respect.

Identifying subjects and individual EPs would also be problematic at the diachronic level. Experience producers come in different forms, and so have different persistence conditions—for example dolphin brains and immaterial souls. Given this diversity, there is no reason to suppose that all, or even most, EPs will have persistence conditions framed in experiential terms. Our own brains are a case in point. Generally speaking they possess capacities for experiences, but their continued existence depends only on physical or organic continuities, and as a consequence, they can lose their experiential capacities without their existence being threatened: it is quite possible for a human brain to survive damage which permanently obliterates its capacity for phenomenal consciousness. As this example makes clear, being an experience producer will often be a temporary and non-essential property of a material thing (or system).

Furthermore, bearing in mind the thought experiments which make the neo-Lockean approach so appealing, we want to make room, conceptually at least, for a single self to be sustained by a succession of numerically distinct experience-producing systems. Clearly, we cannot achieve this if we identify selves with individual EPs.

In light of these points a more promising option is to focus on the relationship between selves and *collections* of EPs, both at and over time. In light of the apparent inseparability of selves and their streams of consciousness, a plausible principle for assigning EPs to selves all but suggests itself. As we have already seen, the C-thesis—the claim that experiences that are co-conscious are consubjective—is very plausible. If co-conscious experiences belong to the same subject, it is natural to suppose that the same applies to collections of EPs which *have the ability* to produce co-conscious experiences, irrespective of whether that ability is being exercised. Hence we can say that a collection of EPs belongs to the same subject if and only if its members are such that (i) they are active and all the experiences they produce are co-conscious, or (ii) they are not active, but, if they were, all the experiences they produce would be co-conscious. In more succinct form:

Extended C-thesis: collections of EPs which can produce co-conscious experiences are consubjective.

The Extended C-thesis looks credible when construed as a criterion for assigning EPs to subjects at a given time, but can it serve the same function over time? It may not be immediately obvious that it can, for although co-consciousness has a diachronic dimension it is comparatively slender: only experiences within a single specious present are related by diachronic co-consciousness. In fact, this limitation does not pose an insuperable problem. We saw in §3.4 that a *stream* of consciousness can be viewed as a collection of experiences that are unified by the co-consciousness relationship, directly or indirectly. Given this, the temporal range of the Extended C-thesis can easily be increased. If all the experiences in an uninterrupted (and non-branching) stream of consciousness obviously belong to the same subject, how can it be otherwise with the EPs which produce these experiences, irrespective of how far apart they are in time? If this point is accepted just one further issue remains: is there any reason to suppose that EPs need to be active and producing experiences in order to be consubjective? There is not. We can again hold that EPs which *would* produce co-streamal experiences if they were active should also be regarded as belonging to a single subject: having the ability to feed into a single uninterrupted stream of consciousness is a plausible criterion for the consubjectivity of experiential capacities. It will be useful to express the point in a slightly more formal way, whilst also coining some new terminology:

Restricted Streamal Criterion: EPs which have the ability to contribute to a single stream of consciousness are *streamally unified*; EPs that are streamally unified are consubjective.

The rationale for this criterion seems straightforward and plausible. At any given time while I am awake only a few of the experience-producing systems in my brain are active, but the experiences they produce are phenomenally unified—they are parts of a single stream of consciousness. If some of those EPs that are not active at such times *were* active, the resulting experiences would also belong to a unified stream of consciousness; this stream of consciousness would have a different (perhaps richer) character than the stream I actually have, but all its parts would be related by co-consciousness, whether directly or indirectly. In like fashion, when I am enjoying a period of dreamless sleep none of my EPs are active, but if they were, the experiences they would produce would be streamally unified. The general idea is illustrated in Figure 4.1, which depicts a collection of EPs that are able to produce streamally unified experience. The lightly-shaded region corresponds to the range of experiences these EPs *could* produce; as can be seen, only a portion of this experiential potential is realized.

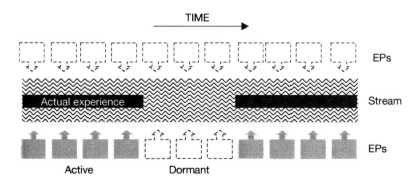

Figure 4.1 A collection of experience-machines with a distinctive feature: the ability to contribute to unified streams of consciousness

In interpreting this diagram it is important to appreciate that the lightly-shaded region corresponds with a range of different potential streams of consciousness (or stream-phases). A normal human subject may well have a large number of EPs at any one time, even when dreamlessly asleep, and these could be activated in any number of different permutations. Although most of these permutations would result in a stream of consciousness with a different character, each of the resulting streams (or stream-phases) would be composed of parts that are unified by the relationship of co-consciousness, whether directly or indirectly. This suffices to ensure that the EPs responsible for the existence of these experiences (actually or merely potentially) are consubjective also.

The Restricted Streamal Criterion may look promising, but it does not provide us with everything we are seeking. The criterion is 'restricted' by virtue of its limitation to a *single* stream of consciousness. If all subjects of experience had the ability to be conscious throughout the full duration of their lives, there would be no difficulty: the EPs of such subjects would be streamally related, they would have the capacity (whether exercised or not) to contribute to a single uninterrupted stream of consciousness. But subjects such as ourselves do not possess this ability. Call the maximum period a subject can remain conscious without interruption the 'continuous consciousness' or *CC-threshold*. The CC-threshold for the EPs of normal human beings varies, but most of us are unable to stay awake (unaided) for more than a few days at a stretch. The CC-threshold of our EPs is clearly far shorter than our typical life spans. Since EPs that are separated by more than their CC-threshold are not streamally related, such EPs are not consubjective by the lights of the Restricted Streamal Criterion.

The difficulty is real but the solution is simple. EPs that are separated by more than their CC-threshold are not directly streamally related, but they can be *indirectly* streamally related, that is they can belong to a chain of *partially overlapping* collections of directly streamally related EPs. Any two collections of streamally related EPs which partially overlap will consist of three parts, p_1, p_2, and p_3, where p_2 is the region of overlap, and p_1 and p_3 the non-overlapping parts on either side. Since p_1 and p_2 are directly streamally related they are consubjective; since the same applies to p_2 and p_3, they too are consubjective; but then, given the transitivity of consubjectivity, p_1 and p_3 will also belong to the same subject. Indirect streamal relatedness thus conveys consubjectivity beyond the confines of its direct counterpart, and in principle it can do so through a chain of any length, or any number of partially overlapping phases. We can employ this relationship in a broader criterion of consubjectivity:

Unrestricted Streamal Criterion: EPs are consubjective if and only if they are streamally unified, directly or indirectly.

By way of a more concrete illustration of the relevant relationship, suppose you are incapable of remaining conscious for more than twenty-four hours in a row.

It follows that the EPs (or EP-phases) responsible for producing your experience at noon Monday—call them E_1—are not directly streamally related to those which are responsible for producing your experience at 1pm on Tuesday—call these E_2. Nonetheless, given the various permutations of experiences you are capable of having—in these respects you are akin to any typical human—E_1 and E_2 are indirectly streamally related to one another; indeed, they are so related via a multitude of channels. Consider first collections of (directly) streamally unified EPs that extend over a period of twenty-four hours. Let's call two of these collections C_1 and C_2; whereas C_1 extends from 2am on Monday to 2am on Tuesday, C_2 extends from 2pm on Monday to 2pm on Tuesday. By virtue of the facts (i) that E_1 is included in C_1, and E_2 is included in C_2, and (ii) that C_1 and C_2 partially overlap (for a twelve-hour period), E_1 and E_2 satisfy the requirements for being indirectly streamally related. As is obvious, E_1 and E_2 are also embraced by any number of other partially overlapping collections of EPs which extend through twenty-four-hour periods. They are also included in chains whose partially overlapping links are collections of EPs which extend through less than twenty-four hours, in the manner shown in Figure 4.2.

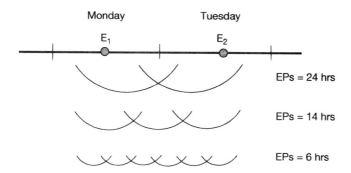

Figure 4.2 Indirect streamal relatedness

As we descend the ladder, and consider collections of EPs (or EP-phases) that are shorter and shorter in duration, more and more links are required to connect E_1 and E_2. But this is of no import: indirect streamal relatedness can convey consubjectivity through any number of such links. Since what goes for E_1 and E_2 goes for any EPs that are indirectly streamally related, it looks as though the Unrestricted Streamal Criterion gives us what we need.

Or at least, it points us in a promising direction. In its unrestricted form the Streamal Criterion is a readily comprehensible way of putting some flesh on the core idea that EPs are consubjective by virtue of their ability to generate unified states and streams of consciousness. But there are other ways of developing this idea. The alternative approach that I will be exploring and developing in some detail in the next section starts off with the unifying relationships to be found within the confines of the specious present, and builds outward from there. As will soon become apparent, by working with shorter time-scales we can avoid the complications associated with CC-thresholds. No less importantly, although adopting a 'bottom-up' approach complicates matters in some respects, it also brings several key relationships into clearer view.

Powers and things

The time has come to drop an assumption. I suggested earlier that the concept of an experience-producing object (or system) might provide a useful point of departure, and so it has proved. The concept is one with which we are familiar, for we are accustomed to thinking of experiences as being produced in or by *material things*, of one kind or another. But now we have a rough idea of what an experience-based solution to the bridge-problem might look like, this reassuring assumption can be discarded without the risk of inducing undue confusion. There are a number of reasons for adopting a somewhat different ontological framework.

All EPs have one thing in common: the nomologically grounded capacity to generate some form of experience. But since, for all we know, conscious beings may come in a very wide variety of forms, in other respects EPs might be very different from one another. Who knows what forms animal or alien brains might take? Given our current ignorance concerning the matter–consciousness relation-ship, we are not in a position to rule this possibility out, and there are certainly conceivable worlds where things are stranger still, where experience-producing objects or systems bear very little resemblance to their Earthly counterparts. We can cut through these variations and isolate what is common to all con-ceivable conscious beings, at least of the PCS variety, by defining their identity conditions in terms of what is common to all EPs. Rather than taking experience-producing *objects* as our basic ingredient, we take certain *properties* of these objects. As for the sort of property, there is only one candidate, the property common to all EPs: the capacity to generate experience. If we want an account which combines maximum generality with maximum economy—an account which abstracts from everything non-essential—then we should seek to formu-late it in terms of capacities for experience, rather than experience-producing objects.

A capacities-oriented approach can seem entirely natural as soon as the PCS conception of the self is clearly distinguished (indeed, it was tacitly introduced at the end of §4.1), but there is a further reason why neo-Lockeans should be drawn towards it. The possession of experiential capacities is not only what all (PCS) subjects have in common, but so far as their continued existence is concerned it is *all that matters*—or so our intuitions suggest. This was the upshot of the thought experiments we looked at in the opening chapter: as we saw, it is easy to envisage oneself surviving *any* change in what sustains one's mental life, provided the changes do not eradicate one's capacity to have experiences. Suppose fast-acting nanomachines dramatically alter the physical make-up of your brain in a matter of seconds. Would this transformation threaten *your* existence if your various capacities for experience remained intact? Would your existence be threatened if your experiential capacities were to be transferred to a consciousness-generating machine, or a matrix of electromagnetic fields, or a crystalline substance, or an immaterial substance?[3] Quite generally, *any* physical change seems survivable provided it is clear that the change in question does not put an end to one's capacity to have phenomenally continuous experience. The conclusion we should draw from this seems equally clear. If our intuitions suggest that it is the capacities which matter to our survival, not what houses or sustains them, then a neo-Lockean account of our persistence conditions should be framed in terms of these capacities.

Whether a neo-Lockean theory constructed along these lines will prove viable is another matter, but it is well worth trying to find out.

In assessing the viability or otherwise of an experience-based and capacities-oriented approach to the self, one set of issues that will need to be addressed concerns experiential capacities themselves. Precisely how should these be conceived? How are such powers related to their grounds (or categorical bases)? How are they to be individuated? I will be looking at some of these issues in §4.5, but will set them aside until then. I want to focus first on the question of how experiential capacities, assuming they exist, should be assigned to subjects. Although we have yet to address this question explicitly, we already have the outlines of a plausible answer to it: we can assign experiential capacities to subjects on the same basis as the things that possess such capacities. If experience-producing *objects* are consubjective in virtue of the fact that they can contribute to phenomenally unified stretches of consciousness, why shouldn't the same apply to experience producing *capacities*? Indeed, the streamal criteria outlined above apply equally well either way. It suffices to call capacities for experience *experiential powers*, and abbreviate the latter to 'EP'. The Unrestricted Streamal Criterion can now be construed as stating the conditions under which experiential powers are consubjective.

However, for the reasons already given, while the Streamal Criterion has its merits, it also has certain drawbacks. In developing a more perspicuous and more detailed account it will be useful to focus on a very simple-minded conscious being.

---

[3] Or to put the point in a less question-begging way: if some future experiences are the product of experiential capacities that are streamally related (directly or indirectly) to the experiential capacities responsible for your current experience, is it not obvious that these future experiences are *yours*? Isn't it equally obvious that the experiential capacities responsible for these experiences are also yours?

4.3. POWER STRUCTURES

Let us give our simple-minded creature a name: *Maggot*. I have no idea if real-life maggots are capable of having experiences, but since our Maggot is an imaginary creature, this doesn't matter. Maggot is so-called because he is roughly maggot-shaped, but his resemblance to real-life maggots need not be supposed to go any further. Maggot has three sensory organs—an eye, a nose, and his skin—each of which provides him with a limited range of simple sensory experiences. Moreover, at any waking moment each organ is continually active. Since the resulting sensations are co-conscious, at a time and from moment to moment, Maggot has a unified stream of consciousness. This is all Maggot has got by way of a mind.

By way of marking the switch to a capacities-oriented approach, it will prove useful to coin some fresh terminology. I will call collections of experiential powers that can produce experiences that are co-conscious *C-systems*. (Although we shall see in due course that C-systems themselves can be construed as *things*, as collections of capacities they are not ordinary material objects in the manner of EPs, as originally construed.) What does Maggot's C-system possess by way of experiential powers? Let us simplify still further by supposing that Maggot's sensory organs produce sensations of three (and only three) clearly distinct types. His visual system, V, can deliver three types of visual sensation, which we can label *yellow, orange,* and *red,* and abbreviate to v_1, v_2, and v_3 respectively. His olfactory system O can deliver three types of smell sensation: *nasty, edible,* and *delicious,* or o_1, o_2, and o_3 respectively. His temperature sense, B, can deliver three types of bodily sensation: *cold, warm,* and *hot,* or b_1, b_2, and b_3 respectively. These labels are purely for convenience—we need not suppose that the qualitative character of Maggot's experiences resembles our own. Let us further suppose that each power has its own independent triggering condition. Since Maggot has nine types of experience available to him, triggered in nine different ways, does it follow that Maggot has nine distinct experiential capacities? Not necessarily. Dispositions can be single- or multi-track. Whereas a single-track disposition has just one type of manifestation-event, triggered by a particular type of circumstance, a multi-track disposition is for a multiplicity of different types of manifestation, triggered by different sorts of circumstance. Since each of Maggot's experiential powers is grounded in a distinct neural module—or so I will suppose—it is natural to view his mind as consisting of nine single-track capacities. If, by contrast, his brain had consisted of three neural modules m_1, m_2, and m_3, responsible for his visual, olfactory, and bodily sensations respectively, it would be more natural to ascribe three multi-track powers to him. (As will become clear, nothing of great significance hangs on this issue.)

Although we now know that a total of nine different types of experience are available to Maggot, we have yet to specify which combinations of these experiences he is able to enjoy. Let us assume that Maggot's sensory modalities are such that (i) the powers belonging to each modality can only produce one type of experience at a time, and (ii) that there are no restrictions on the combinations of experiences from different modalities that can be co-conscious. Our first stipulation has the consequence that if Maggot sees *orange*, he cannot simultaneously see *yellow* or *red*; if he feels *hot*, he cannot simultaneously feel sensations of *cold* or *warm*, and so forth. I will call powers of this kind—powers that are consubjective but which cannot be active simultaneously—*opposed*. In Maggot's case, his individual visual powers—call them V_1, V_2, and V_3—are opposed, as are O_1, O_2, and O_3 and B_1, B_2, and B_3, his individual olfactory and bodily powers, respectively. However, in virtue of our second stipulation, powers in different sensory modalities are unopposed. Maggot can experience *orange* together with any single olfactory experience, any single bodily experience, or any combination of a single olfactory experience and a single bodily experience. If he feels *hot*, he cannot simultaneously feel *cold* or *warm*, but the *hot* sensation can be co-conscious with any one of his available visual sensations, any one of his available olfactory sensations, or any combination of a visual and an olfactory sensation. And similarly for other permutations.

Diachronic unity

I have (tacitly) assumed that Maggot is a single subject of experience and hence that all the above-mentioned experiential powers are consubjective. The fact that the powers in his different sensory modalities—powers such as V_1 and O_1—produce co-conscious experiences when they are active does a good deal to confirm this assumption. True, there is also the fact that some of Maggot's powers are opposed, and such powers cannot produce co-conscious experiences, but since these powers are also integral parts of a system whose other parts *do* have the ability to produce co-conscious experiences, there is clearly a case for holding that they are themselves consubjective. However, before looking in more detail at the topic of synchronic unity, and the various associated complications, I want to take a look at diachronic unity. I have (tacitly) assumed that Maggot is a *persisting* subject, and hence that his experiential powers extend some way through time. What is it about these powers which legitimates this assumption? The short answer is that each of Maggot's experiential powers can produce phenomenally continuous stretches of experience. However, to arrive at a clearer understanding of precisely what this amounts to we will need to consider the matter in more detail.

We can start by focusing on just one of Maggot's powers, V_1, a capacity for v_1-type visual experience, *yellow*. Since Maggot's streams of consciousness are structurally similar to ours (but far simpler qualitatively), they consist of overlapping total experiences, and these total experiences typically have some temporal extension. We can suppose that Maggot's specious present has a duration of half a second; this is the duration of his typical total experiences, irrespective of the modality. We can further suppose (to keep things reasonably simple) that when Maggot's experiential powers are continuously active for a period t, they produce a continuous t-length stretch of experience, and that this experience runs concurrently with the power (or powers) that produce it.[4] Now, temporarily adopting the perspective of the perdurance theorist, we can think of Maggot as a temporally extended whole, consisting of a large number of temporal parts. Since we are not interested in Maggot himself, but his C-system, and in particular V_1, we can think of the latter as a temporally extended whole. We can accordingly divide V_1 into phases of a quarter of a second; call each of these phases a *power-slice*. Consider three successive power-slices L_1, L_2, and L_3. Each of these power-slices can produce a quarter-second of v_1-type experience.

Suppose L_1 and L_2 are both active and producing experience. Since Maggot's specious present lasts for half a second, these experiences are (diachronically) co-conscious. If we assume (as seems reasonable) that powers which are producing co-conscious experiences are consubjective, we should conclude that L_1 and L_2 are consubjective. But what if L_1 and L_2 are both dormant (Maggot is dreamlessly asleep)? It matters not: these power-slices are such that if they *were* active, they *would* be producing diachronically co-conscious experiences, and in virtue of this it is plausible to regard them as consubjective. Similarly, if L_1 is dormant but L_2 is active, these powers are such that if L_1 *were* active, the experience it *would* produce would be co-conscious with the experience L_2 produces, and hence these two power-slices can be taken to be consubjective. And the same applies the other way about, that is if L_1 is active but L_2 is dormant.

I will call experiential powers that are related in the manner of L_1 and L_2 *directly potentially co-conscious*, or DPC-related. Strictly speaking, of course, it is not the experiential powers themselves that are co-conscious, but the experiences they produce or would produce, were they active. Since powers *at* a given time can also produce co-conscious experiences, we need to distinguish between synchronic DPC-relatedness and diachronic DPC-relatedness. I will usually abbreviate these to *DPC$_S$-relatedness* and *DPC$_D$-relatedness* respectively. It is the latter we are concerned with at the moment.

In taking DPC$_D$-related powers to be consubjective I am relying on an extended version of the C-thesis. If co-conscious *experiences* belong to the same subject, it seems natural to suppose that experiential *capacities* belong to the

---

[4] I will work on the assumption that there is no temporal interval between the activation of an experiential power and the occurrence of its manifestation; as will become apparent, if in some cases there is a short gap between the two, it would not affect the fundamentals: experiential powers which produce co-conscious experiences when active are consubjective even if there is a short delay between the triggering of a power and the occurrence of its manifestation.

same subject if they are either producing experiences that are co-conscious, or they would do so if they were active during the period in question. Or to put it another way, being able to produce experiences that are co-conscious is a sufficient condition for the consubjectivity of experiential capacities. The Extended C-thesis introduced in §4.2 was framed in terms of experience-producing material things but from now on I will generally be working with the capacities-oriented version. In succinct form:

Extended C-thesis: experiential capacities that can produce co-conscious experiences are consubjective.

So far as I can see, the C-thesis in this broader form has as much plausibility as the C-thesis in its original form. This is not to say the thesis is necessarily or universally true. Perhaps there are certain extreme or bizarre circumstances in which it fails—this is something we will need to investigate. But so far as ordinary circumstances are concerned—of the kind we are dealing with at present, albeit in simplified form—the Extended C-thesis seems eminently reasonable.

Bearing this in mind, we can now consider our third power-slice, L_3, which immediately follows L_2. These two power-slices are DPC_D-related and so consubjective. However, since Maggot's specious present only extends for half a second, L_1 and L_3 are not DPC_D-related: these powers do not have the ability to produce experiences that are diachronically co-conscious. But L_1 is consubjective with L_2, and L_2 is consubjective with L_3, and since consubjectivity is transitive, it follows that L_1 and L_3 are also consubjective. I will call experiential powers that are related in the manner of L_1 and L_3 *indirectly potentially co-conscious* or *IPC_D-related*. (The latter also has a synchronic counterpart, hence the need for the 'D' in the abbreviation: we are currently concerned with the relationship in its diachronic form.) More generally:

Two power-slices P_1 and P_2 are IPC_D-related if and only if they are not themselves DPC_D-related, but they belong to a chain of power-slices $[P_1 \ldots P_n]$ the adjacent members of which are DPC_D-related.

These *power-chains* can be of any length. For example, L_1-L_2-L_3-L_4-L_5 is a power-chain, and although L_1 and L_5 are not DPC_D-related (or so we can suppose) they are IPC_D-related: L_1 is DPC_D-related to L_2, L_2 is DPC_D-related to L_3, L_3 is DPC_D-related to L_4, and the latter is DPC_D-related to L_5. Since the successive links in such power-chains are DPC_D-related, and DPC_D-related powers are consubjective, it is clear that any two powers that are IPC_D-related are also consubjective, irrespective of the length of the chain separating them.

Although we have been concentrating on just one of Maggot's experiential powers, V_1, it is clear that we can account for the persistence of each of them in just the same way. O_3, say, consists of a succession of DPC_D-related power-slices for o_3-type olfactory experience. Each of these power-slices is con subjective.

It is important to note that these relationships do not depend on a subject's being awake and conscious. If an unconscious subject retains the capacity for experiences exhibiting phenomenal continuity, their C-system will consist of power-slices, and these power-slices will be DPC_D-related or IPC_D-related—as shown in Figure 4.3, where active powers are shaded and dormant ones are not.

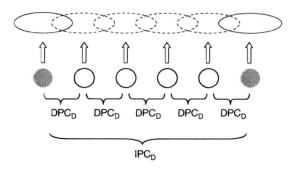

Figure 4.3 Both active and dormant powers can be DPC_D- and IPC_D-related. The dotted figures in the upper level represent the experiences which would have been produced if the powers shown on the lower level had been active rather than dormant

I have been working on the assumption that Maggot's specious present is a constant half-second long. This simplifying assumption is dispensable: the duration of the specious present may vary from subject to subject; a single subject's specious present may vary from time to time; it may even be possible for it to vary from sensory modality to sensory modality. Such variations do not affect the basic picture. As we saw in Chapter 3, a stream of consciousness consists of overlapping specious presents, that is temporally extended total experiences—and as we also saw, this overlap is necessary to secure the phenomenal continuity which is an essential feature of any stream of consciousness. Consequently, any two temporally extended total experiences T_1 and T_2 which partially overlap (i.e. overlap without wholly coinciding) will have a similar phenomenal structure. The stream-phase comprising T_1 and T_2 will consist of three sub-phases e_1, e_2, and e_3, where e_1 is the part of T_1 which does not overlap with T_2, e_3 is the part of T_2 which does not overlap with T_1, and e_2 is the region of overlap. In this structure e_1 will be co-conscious with e_2, e_2 will be co-conscious with e_3, but e_1 and e_2 will *not* be co-conscious. On the assumption that each of e_1, e_2, and e_3 is the product of a distinct power-slice, the consubjectivity of these slices is secured by either DPC_D-relatedness or IPC_D-relatedness. The same will apply no matter how brief a subject's specious present is, and irrespective of whether or how much a subject's specious present varies in extent over time. And of course IPC_D-relatedness is not confined to triplets of power-slices: it can transmit consubjectivity through chains of any length or complexity.

A second simplifying assumption has been in force: I have confined my discussion to power-slices which possess a uniform duration of a quarter of a second, a period of time which amounts to precisely half the duration of Maggot's specious present. Power-slices of this sort do exist, but it should also be recognized that experiential capacities can be divided (in thought, or perhaps in actuality also) in other ways. More specifically, power-slices do not need to be able to produce experiences of equal duration to be DPC_D-related, nor do they need to be able to produce experiences that are half the duration of their subject's specious present: to be DPC_D-related all that is required is that power-slices be able to produce experiences that are diachronically co-conscious. To illustrate, let us stipulate that (i) Maggot can enjoy visual sensations that are as short as a tenth of a second (but no shorter), and (ii) that if he experiences minimally brief visual sensations in direct succession he experiences them as diachronically co-conscious. Given these stipulations, it is clear that we could take his visual capacity V_1 to be composed of power-slices for experiences that last just one-tenth of a second. Given that his specious present is half a second in duration, it is also clear that in Maggot's case, a capacity for an experience lasting four-tenths of a second could be DPC_D-related to a capacity for experience lasting one-tenth of a second. And of course what applies in the case of V_1 applies more generally: to Maggot's other experiential powers, and the experiential powers of other subjects.

There is a further point to be made in connection with this topic, but it will help to have on hand a more general definition of DPC_D-relatedness.

We can start with a statement of the seemingly obvious: for two power-slices P_1 at t_1 and P_2 at t_2 to be DPC_D-related they must be able to contribute to a single specious present; consequently each of P_1 and P_2 must have a duration that is less than that of the relevant specious present (i.e. the specious present they would contribute to if they were active). This statement rests on two assumptions: that a t-length power-slice will produce a t-length stretch of experience if active, and that even the briefest power-slices have some finite duration. The first assumption seems entirely plausible, but what of the second?[5] There are grounds for regarding strictly momentary experiential powers with some suspicion: since (for human subjects at any rate) the briefest clearly discernible experiential features have a finite duration, is it not reasonable to suppose the same applies

---

[5] Note that this (first) assumption is distinct from the claim that experiential powers and their *triggering events* are of equal duration. This claim is not always true, at least for human subjects: in the case of brief perceptual stimuli, the resulting sensation is typically longer than the stimuli itself, for example a flash of light lasting only 1 ms can produce a visual sensation lasting 50 ms (see Pockett 2003: 59). In such cases, there is a difference between the length of time a power is active and the duration of the event which causes this period of activity, but here is no difference between the length of time the power is active and the duration of the resulting experience: the 50 ms of visual experience is the product of a visual power that is active for 50 ms. Note also that experiences of the same objective duration (e.g. 5 seconds, as measured by clock-time) can *seem* to be of very different durations, depending on the states of mind of their subjects. My 'equal duration' assumption is restricted to durations of the objective variety.

to experiential powers, at least of the kind which have a clearly distinguishable experiential output? Against this, however, it could be argued that it is still perfectly meaningful to talk about what powers at a given *instant* can or cannot do. This is a difficult issue, but we need not resolve it here. All we need to do is define DPC$_D$-relatedness in a way which is compatible with both positions. Accordingly, in the following let 't_1' and 't_2' denote either *moments* or *periods*, depending on whether our arbitrary power-slices P_1 and P_2 are instantaneous or not:

DPC$_D$-related: power-slices P_1 at t_1 and P_2 at t_2 are DPC$_D$-related if and only if either:

(i) they are both active, and all the experiences P_1 produces at or during t_1 are diachronically co-conscious with all the experiences P_2 produces at or during t_2, or

(ii) one or both are dormant, but if they were both active, all the experiences P_1 would produce at or during t_1 would be diachronically co-conscious with all the experiences P_2 would produce at or during t_2.

Although I have used the language of the perdurance view here, nothing should be read into this: DPC$_D$-relatedness for enduring powers can be defined in an analogous manner.

In cases where P_1 and P_2 are non-momentary, and the combined durations of t_1 and t_2 are equal to that of the relevant specious present, if P_1 and P_2 are both active they will produce a single uninterrupted phenomenally continuous stretch of experience; in other words, the experience(s) produced by P_1 will immediately precede (and flow into) the experience(s) produced by P_2. We can call powers with this property *succession-related*. Since Maggot's power-slices L_1, L_2, and L_3 were succession-related it would be easy to fall into thinking that DPC$_D$-related powers are invariably related in this way. In fact, this is not the case: power-slices which are of comparatively short duration compared to the specious presents to which they can contribute can be DPC$_D$-related *without* being succession-related. This is illustrated in Figure 4.4.

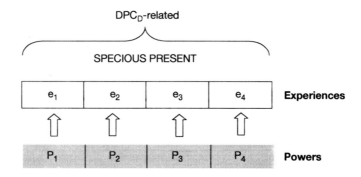

Figure 4.4 Not all DPC$_D$-related powers are succession-related

Here P_1-P_4 are power-slices which produce e_1-e_4 respectively. As can be seen, although P_2 and P_3 are succession-related, P_1 is not succession-related to P_3 or P_4, and P_2 is not succession-related to P_4. However, all four power-slices *are* DPC_D-related: they are such that if they were active, the resulting experiences would be diachronically co-conscious (as it happens, they are all active). The distinction between succession-relatedness and DPC_D-relatedness exists because experiences can be diachronically co-conscious without being immediately adjacent to one another in a single specious present. There is nothing in the least puzzling or problematic here: this result is inevitable if specious presents can house more than two minimally brief experiences. It should also be borne in mind that in the case of single persisting powers, DPC_D-related power-slices that are not themselves succession-related—such as P_1 and P_4—will generally be connected by a series of powers which are so-related.[6]

Let us take stock and return to the larger picture. I began by assuming that Maggot had a persisting experiential power, and wondered what sort of relation between the successive phases of this power would secure their con-subjectivity. Now we have our answer, DPC_D-relatedness/IPC_D-relatedness, we can see that the initial ownership assumption is not necessary. Imagine that you are looking at the world from a God's-eye perspective, with a view to detecting power-slices that are DPC_D-related or IPC_D-related. Without knowing anything about which power-slices belong to which subjects—we can suppose you are entirely ignorant about such matters—you could discern those successions of power-slices which are DPC_D- or IPC_D-related and those which are not. Despite the fact that you are entirely ignorant of Maggot's existence, his power-slices would attract your attention in virtue of their being DPC_D- and IPC_D-related. More generally, by directing your attention to experiential powers that are related in these ways, you will be able to pick out consubjective power-slices even though you lack any prior knowledge of how

[6] There is a further complication worth noting. If a human subject is presented with two stimuli in very quick succession—such that the interval between them is less than the so-called 'coincidence threshold'—the stimuli cannot be distinguished: in effect, they produce a single sensation. (In the case of auditory experience the coincidence threshold is typically 2–3msec, whereas in the case of visual experience it is around 20msec.) Stimuli that are separated by a slightly greater period of time are perceived as separate, but they do not seem to possess a determinate temporal order: subjects are unable to judge with any confidence which of the resulting sensations occurs before the other. Stimuli are only perceived as occurring in succession when the interval of time separating them is greater than the 'order threshold'—which in humans is typically around 30msec, irrespective of sensory modality (Ruhnau 1995). Should we regard power-slices that are capable of producing pairs of experiences which are distinct but which also lack a distinct temporal order as diachronically DPC_D-related? On balance I think not. The experiences in question are unambiguously co-conscious, but lacking as they do an unambiguous temporal order, they are not diachronically co-conscious in a clear and unequivocal way. Consequently, I will work on the assumption that DPC_D-relatedness holds between power-slices which can produce experiences which possess a clear phenomeno-temporal order. Slices of slightly shorter duration which produce experiences which are not so ordered are most conveniently regarded as synchronically DPC-related. I will be saying more about the latter shortly.

experiential capacities are distributed among subjects. So as seems clear, in DPC_D-relatedness and IPC_D-relatedness we have criteria for the consubjectivity of power-slices which do not presuppose anything about consubjectivity.

I have thus far adopted the perspective of the perdurance theorist: L_1, L_2, and L_3 are power-slices, each of which is numerically distinct from its neighbours, and hence V_1 consists of a succession (or sum) of numerically distinct capacities. But there is an alternative way of conceiving of a persisting power. In the case of Maggot, if we adopt the perspective of the endurance theorist, we can regard V_1 as a single enduring experiential power. We can, if we choose, view L_1, L_2, and L_3 as instances of one and the same enduring power, V_1-at-t_1, V_1-at-t_2, and V_1-at-t_3. Why is it that the latter are all instances of the same enduring power? We give the same answer as the perdurance theorist: it is because these powers are DPC_D-related or IPC_D-related. V_1-at-t_1 and V_1-at-t_2 are DPC_D-related; V_1-at-t_1 and V_1-at-t_3 are not DPC_D-related, but they are IPC_D-related—in virtue of the fact that V_1-at-t_1 is DPC_D-related to V_1-at-t_2, and the latter is DPC_D-related to V_1-at-t_3. More generally, if we have an experiential power P_1 at t_1 and a power P_2 at t_2, such that P_1 and P_2 are of the same type, then P_1 is numerically identical with P_2 if and only if they are DPC_D- or IPC_D-related. For P_1 to be IPC_D-related to P_2, they must be at either end of a power-chain, each successive member of which is DPC_D-related to its neighbours. If we define an enduring power in this way, then assuming the Extended C-thesis, such a power belongs to one and only one subject. V_1 is an enduring power, and belongs to one and the same subject: Maggot. Obviously, each of Maggot's other experiential powers could be regarded in the same way. In effect, an enduring power is a continuous capacity for diachronically co-conscious experience of a particular type, a power that is sometimes active and sometimes quiescent.

Synchronic unity: a first look

We have been looking at the conditions under which experiential powers persist, but thus far we have said little about the conditions which must obtain in order for distinct experiential powers to belong to a single subject at a given time. Remaining with our original scenario, Maggot has nine distinct powers. What is it that makes these powers consubjective? The concepts of DPC- and IPC-relatedness are highly relevant to this question too.

Consider three of these powers: V_1, O_1, and B_1. Reverting to the perdurance view, let us regard these persisting powers as a succession of power-slices, and take the labels 'V_1', 'O_1', and 'B_1' to refer to simultaneous momentary (or very brief) slices of these perduring powers. Since each of these power-slices belongs to a different sensory modality (and so generates a different type of experience) they could all be active simultaneously; and if they were active simultaneously they would produce experiences that are mutually co-conscious. Clearly, these three powers are DPC-related, but *synchronically* rather than diachronically: the experiences they would produce if active occur simultaneously rather than successively. As in the diachronic case it will be useful to have an abbreviation, so let us call such powers *DPC$_S$-related*. In a slightly more precise vein, we can say that at a given time t, any collection of power-slices are DPC$_S$-related if and only if (i) they are active and all the experiences they produce are co-conscious, or (ii) they are dormant, but if they were active all the experiences they would produce would be co-conscious. (We shall see shortly that this preliminary definition can be refined in various ways, but for present purposes these simple formulations will suffice.) Relying on the C-thesis in its extended form, we can then say that DPC$_S$-related powers are consubjective.

What applies to power-slices also applies to experiential powers viewed as things that endure rather than perdure. Instead of regarding V_1 as composed of a succession of numerically distinct power-slices, each capable of producing a v_1-type experience, we could regard V_1 as a single enduring power. Let us call this enduring power $\mathbf{V_1}$. We can view O_1 and B_1 as enduring powers too, and label them $\mathbf{O_1}$ and $\mathbf{B_1}$. What makes different enduring powers consubjective at any one time? The answer once again is the co-consciousness of their actual or potential manifestations, or DPC$_S$-relatedness. We can then say that enduring powers at any given time are consubjective if and only if they are DPC$_S$-related. Since $\mathbf{V_1}$, $\mathbf{O_1}$, are $\mathbf{B_1}$ *are* related in this manner, they are clearly consubjective by the lights of the Extended C-thesis.

Even at this early stage we are in a position to provide a quite general criterion for the consubjectivity of experiential powers. Two or more persisting powers of equal duration and which occupy the same temporal interval are consubjective if throughout this interval they are either active and producing co-conscious experience, or would do so if they were active at any given moment. But enduring powers need not coincide in this manner to be consubjective; subjects can gain and lose experiential capabilities. To accommodate the possibility of temporally non-coinciding but *overlapping* persisting powers, we need simply hold that any such powers are consubjective only if they are DPC$_S$-related throughout the interval during which they overlap. Putting these points together, and coining some new terminology:

(i) Two or more persisting powers are **concurrence-related** if and only if (a) they temporally coincide, and (b) are DPC$_S$-related throughout their careers.

(ii) Two or more persisting powers are **directly overlap-related** if and only if (a) their careers partially overlap in time, and (b) they are DPC$_S$-related throughout their period(s) of overlap.

(iii) Two or more powers are **indirectly overlap-related** if and only if they are neither concurrence-related nor directly overlap-related, but connected by a chain of powers that are related in one or other of these ways.

(iv) Experiential powers are consubjective if and only they are either concurrence-related or overlap-related, directly or indirectly.

The way these definitions are intended to operate is illustrated in Figure 4.5 As can be seen, the central cluster of four persisting powers—named 'B' in the diagram—are concurrence-related. (Note: only a few of the actually occurring DPC_S-relationships are indicated.) Persisting power A is not concurrence-related to B, but the two are directly overlap-related, and given clause (iv), this suffices to render A and B consubjective. The same applies for B and C. Powers A and C are neither concurrence-related nor directly overlap-related, but they are indirectly overlap-related to each other, via B, and given (iv) this is enough to make them consubjective.

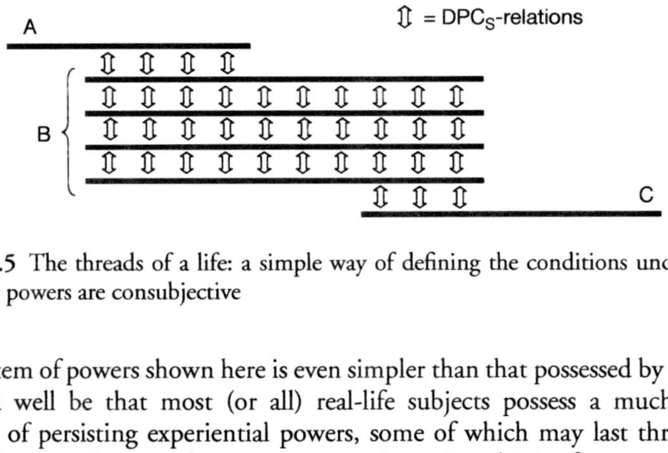

Figure 4.5 The threads of a life: a simple way of defining the conditions under which *persisting* powers are consubjective

The system of powers shown here is even simpler than that possessed by Maggot; it could well be that most (or all) real-life subjects possess a much greater number of persisting experiential powers, some of which may last throughout their existence, whereas other are more transitory. But this is of no consequence, for there is no limit to the number of different powers which can be related in the manner described. The career of a subject is akin to a rope or cord, made of a few strands or many, some long, some short, some overlapping, some not—but bonded together throughout its entire length. The threads of life are persisting experiential powers; the binding agent is synchronic DPC-relatedness.

Synchronic unity: a closer look

The position we have arrived at is simple, readily intelligible, and intuitively appealing. It seems we can define the conditions under which experiential powers are consubjective in terms of a small handful of closely linked relationships. What more could we want or need? However, while the account just outlined has several significant virtues, it also conceals a number of significant complications. In bringing these out it will be useful to look at things from a somewhat different angle. The resulting change of perspective has a further benefit: it opens up a way of specifying the conditions under which subjects persist that in some respects is more natural (or at least familiar) than those we have been considering thus far.

The point of departure is taking C-systems to be *entities* or *things* of a distinctive and significant kind, with their own existence and persistence conditions. Thus construed, C-systems are similar to the EPs introduced in §4.2—both are *objects which can produce experiences*—but unlike EPs they are not ordinary material objects: a typical human brain, as usually construed, possesses capacities for experience, but that is not all it is. Since C-systems are (by definition) clusters of experiential powers which when active produce co-conscious experiences, it seems plausible to think that powers which belong to a single C-system will be consubjective, both at and over time. If this is right, and if it proves possible to define the existence and persistence conditions of C-systems while appealing only to experiential facts and relations, we would have a quite general experience-based account of power consubjectivity: we could say that powers belong to the same *subject* only if they belong to the same *C-system*. One advantage of adopting this entity-oriented approach is that it offers the prospect of a phenomenalist account of what a self *is*. More on this later.

So much for a promising programme, how should it be implemented? The first issue that needs to be addressed is precisely how experiential powers need to be related at a given time if they are to constitute a C-system. In the light of our previous results, an obvious and plausible answer is that they must be DPC$_S$-related. But so as not to beg any questions, let us introduce a new and neutral term by saying that a collection of powers at a given time must be *S-related* in order to constitute a C-system. The question of whether experiential powers are S-related if and only if they are DPC$_S$-related is one we will leave open for the moment. The next question is how C-systems at earlier and later times must be related if they are to belong to the same subject. Again, we may already have the beginnings of a plausible answer. We have seen that the distinct phases of a single persisting power are consubjective only if they belong to a chain of phases, the neighbouring members of which have the ability to produce diachronically co-conscious experiences. Or in slightly more precise terms, such phases are consubjective only if they are DPC$_D$-related or IPC$_D$-related. If the latter relations allow us to define the conditions under which *single* powers persist, mightn't they do the same for *complexes* of powers? It seems reasonable to think they might.[7] Taken together these points suggest that we may be

---

[7] Of course this is not surprising, for we could, if we wished, view C-systems at particular times as *single (complex) experiential powers*: a C-system is a unified complex *of* powers, and such a complex can be viewed as a single multi-track capacity, one which produces different (experiential)

able to state the existence and persistence conditions for C-systems along the following lines:

(i) At any time t, any collection of **S-related** experiential powers constitutes a C-system.

(ii) C-systems (or phases of such) at different times are consubjective if and only if they are either **DPC$_D$-related** or**IPC$_D$-related**.

This picture will need some refinement and elaboration—we will, for example, have to explore precisely how DPC$_D$- and IPC$_D$-relations can apply to collections of powers, rather than individual persisting powers—but the basic framework is appealingly straightforward.

Our first task is to state in precise terms what being S-related involves and requires. Can we say that experiential powers are S-related if and only if they are DPC$_S$-related? Not without clarifying (or refining) the concept of DPC$_S$-relatedness. For while it may seem clear what synchronic DPC-relatedness involves in the case of just two experiential powers, there are (at least) two different ways in which the concept can be extended to collections of more than two powers. Here is the first:

Jointly DPC$_S$-related: the members of a collection $C[P_1 \ldots .P_n]$ are jointly DPC$_S$-related at t if and only (i) if they are all active at t, then all the experiences they produce are mutually co-conscious; (ii) if some or all the members of C are dormant, then if they were all active at t, all the experiences they produce would be mutually co-conscious.

Is this how we should construe the DPC$_S$-relation in its synchronic collective form? Experiential powers that are related in this way are obviously consubjective, but do we really want to insist that *all* of a subject's experiential powers must be able to manifest *together* in this way? No, for it is quite conceivable that a subject could have a collection of powers that are such that only some of them can be active together. To illustrate: under normal circumstances Maggot's capacities for visual, auditory and bodily experience are capable of manifesting together, but (we can suppose) when he hasn't eaten for a few hours his energy levels run low and only *two* of his sensory modalities can be active at the same time. Maggot-when-hungry can enjoy any combination of visual and olfactory experience, any combination of visual and bodily experience, and any combination of olfactory and bodily experience at a given time, but he cannot enjoy a combination of olfactory + bodily + visual experiences.

Maggot-when-hungry's experiential powers cannot all be active at the same time, but it seems wrong to say that they no longer belong to *Maggot* (or a

manifestations under different triggering circumstances. If we do opt to view C-systems as single powers, it is evident that our earlier account of power-persistence will also apply to them. However, I want to leave open the option of construing C-systems (of the sort we have, and Maggot has also) as complexes of distinct powers.

single subject) because of this. But do such powers qualify as DPC_S-related by the above definitions? In one sense they do. Even if it is in fact impossible for them all to manifest together, there are counterfactual situations in which they *do* manifest together, and in these situations the experiences they produce are co-conscious. The relevant counterfactual situations are those in which the natural laws governing the production of experience by Maggot's neural nodes no longer limit him to just two kinds of experience when his energy levels are low. However, while this is not obviously incoherent, if at all possible it would be better to dispense with the services of such strong counterfactuals—counterfactuals which will often require local suspensions of the laws of nature.

This can be accomplished by recognizing a slightly weaker form of DPC_S-relatedness, and then defining S-relatedness in terms of this weaker relationship. We can start thus:

Pairwise DPC_S-related: for any time t, any collection of powers $C[P_1, P_2 \ldots .P_n]$ is pairwise DPC_S-related if and only if the powers in every two-membered subset of C are DPC_S-related. Any two powers (p_m, p_n) are DPC_S-related at a time t if and only if either (i) they are both active at t, and all the experiences they produce at that time are mutually co-conscious, or (ii) if one or both are dormant, then if they both were active at t, all the experiences they produce would be mutually co-conscious.

So in a simple case of a three-membered collection $C[P_1, P_2, P_3]$, for C to be pairwise DPC_S-related the powers in each of the pairings (P_1, P_2), (P_1, P_3), (P_2, P_3) must be DPC_S-related, and similarly for larger collections. We can define S-relatedness as follows:

S-related: At any time t, any collection of powers $C[P_1, P_2 \ldots .P_n]$ are S-related if and only if the members of C are (i) jointly DPC_S-related and/or (ii) pairwise DPC_S-related at t.

There is a further point that requires clarification. A collection C of (more than two) powers can be pairwise DPC_S-related without being jointly DPC_S-related—this is the case if the members of C cannot all be active together—but what about the other way about? Are powers that are jointly DPC_S-related necessarily pairwise DPC_S-related? It depends on precisely how we understand 'pairwise'. If we say that the powers in C are pairwise DPC_S-related at t if and only each pairing of C's members can be activated *by themselves* at t (i.e. without any other members of C also being active at t), then powers can be jointly DPC_S-related without being pairwise DPC_S-related: a case of this kind would arise if all the members of C could *only* be active together. If we omit this stipulation, then the powers in C will count as pairwise DPC_S-related if they can all be active together—since when this occurs, each pairing is also active. I will generally work with the former construal.

Diachronic unity: a further issue

We are not yet done with synchronic unity—as we shall see, the definition of S-relatedness we have just arrived at requires further refinement and elaboration—but the preceding discussion points to an issue concerning diachronic unity that we might as well tackle straight away. Take two C-systems S_1 at t_1 and S_2 at t_2. Should we hold that these C-systems are DPC_D-related if *all* the powers in each system are able to manifest *together* to produce co-conscious experiences? If this is too strong in the synchronic case, might it not be too strong in the diachronic case also?

It might indeed. Suppose S_1 and S_2 each contain a number of powers and all of these are DPC_D-related save one: a power P_1 in S_1 that is not DPC_D-related to any power in S_2. How could this be? There might be a number of explanations, but in this instance it is the simplest: P_1 ceased to exist just prior to t_2 (due, we can suppose, to some brain damage suffered by its owner). Since subjects can gain and lose experiential powers over time, we clearly need a criterion of diachronic consubjectivity which accommodates this possibility. Such a criterion is not too hard to find.

Let us focus on two C-systems (or phases of such) S_1 at t_1 and S_2 at t_2, where C_1 and C_2 are the collections of experiential powers which compose S_1 and S_2 respectively. Consider the set of all pairs (p_i, p_j) where the first comes from C_1 and the second from C_2, and call this set P. If the powers in *every* pair in P are DPC_D-related, then C_1 and C_2 are *fully pairwise DPC_D-related*. If the powers in only *some* of the pairs in P are DPC_D-related, then C_1 and C_2 are *partially pairwise DPC_D-related*. With these definitions in place we can define DPC_D-relatedness between C-systems thus:

Two C-systems S_1 and S_2 at t_1 and t_2 are **DPC_D-related** if and only if the powers in S_1 and S_2 are pairwise DPC_D-related, fully or only partially.

This give us what we need. By allowing that C-systems need only be partially pairwise DPC_D-related to be consubjective we can accommodate the fact that subjects can lose (and gain) experiential powers over time. Of course it would be implausible in the extreme to suppose that C-systems have to be DPC_D-related in order to be consubjective, given that this relation does not extend beyond the duration of the specious present. But C-systems that are not DPC_D-related can be **IPC_D-related**, where this is understood as follows:

Two C-systems S_1 and S_2 at t_1 and t_2 are **IPC_D-related** if and only if they are not themselves DPC_D-related, but they belong to a chain of C-systems (or phases of such), the adjacent members of which are DPC_D-related.

The conditions under which C-systems at different times belong to the same subject can now be specified in a quite general way in terms of these relationships:

C-systems at different times are consubjective if and only they are either DPC_D-related or IPC_D-related.[8]

Adopting this position on diachronic unity is necessary from the point of view of general plausibility, but it does give rise to a question: just how *little* by way of pairwise DPC_D-relatedness suffices for consubjectivity? In the case outlined above it seemed clear that S_2 is consubjective with S_1 because only a single strand of DPC_D-relatedness had been severed, and (it was stipulated) numerous others remained. But what if only a few strands remained? What if only *one* strand remained?

   This question is bound up with a larger issue: just how little can a subject have by way of experiential capacities and still survive? This question can be (and has been) answered in different ways. In Chapter 8 I will be defending the view that a subject can continue to exist provided it retains *any* capacity for consciousness. If this view is correct, then even the slenderest of thread of DPC_D-relatedness is sufficient to render C-systems at different times consubjective.

Synchronic unity: opposed powers

Returning to the issue of unity-at-a-time, does the expanded definition of S-relatedness provide us with an adequate way of assigning experiential powers to C-systems? It does not: joint and pairwise DPC_S-relatedness secures the consubjectivity of many of those simultaneous powers which (intuitively) are consubjective, but not all.

   The reason for this is straightforward. As we saw earlier, Maggot has three groups of *opposed* powers: $V = (V_1, V_2, V_3)$, $O = (O_1, O_2, O_3)$, and $B = (B_1, B_2, B_3)$. The persistence of each of these powers is secured by a combination of DPC_D-relatedness and IPC_D-relatedness, in the usual way, but what secures the consubjectivity of the members of these groups at any given moment of time? To take just one example, each of Maggot's visual capacities will, when active, generate a complete visual field, filled with *yellow* or *orange* or *red*. Since Maggot has only a single visual field, only one of his visual capacities can be active at any given time. This means that V_1, V_2, and V_3 are *not* pairwise DPC_S-related: no two of them can be active at the same time and produce co-conscious experiences (and *a fortiori* they are not jointly DPC_S-related). The same applies, let us suppose, to the members of O and B. Since it would be absurd to rule out the possibility that opposed powers can be consubjective, we must appeal to something other than joint and pairwise DPC_S-relatedness to secure their consubjectivity. By virtue of what do such powers belong to a single C-system?

---

[8] A further issue connected with diachronic unity: could a C-system at an earlier time t_1 be DPC_D-related to two (or more) C-systems at a later time t_2? This depends on whether fission is possible—I will be exploring this topic in Chapter 12.

To resolve the problem it suffices to recognize two further ways in which experiential powers can be directly or indirectly co-conscious.

In Maggot's case, as for most other subjects, although opposed powers at any given time are not *directly* potentially co-conscious, they are *indirectly* potentially co-conscious, in a synchronic rather than a diachronic fashion. (In keeping with the policy adopted thus far I will refer to powers related in this way as *IPC$_S$-related*.) Maggot may not be able to see *yellow* and *red* at the same time, but he can see *yellow* while feeling *warm*, and he can feel *warm* while seeing *red*. V_1, the capacity which produces Maggot's sensations of *yellow* is thus DPC$_S$-related to B_2, the capacity which produces his sensation of *warm*. Since the latter is DPC$_S$-related to V_3, the capacity which provides Maggot with his *red* sensations, it is clear that V_1 and V_3 are IPC$_S$-related, via B_2. Maggot's other co-modal opposed powers are IPC$_S$-related in like fashion. O_1 and O_2 are not DPC$_S$-related to one another, but each is DPC$_S$-related to B_3, and so O_1 and O_2 are IPC$_S$-related. As will be clear, in Maggot's case, there is not just one channel of IPC$_S$-relatedness between any pair of opposed powers, but six. O_1 and O_2 are IPC$_S$-related by virtue of their DPC$_S$-relations to each of the three visual capacities and each of the three bodily capacities; likewise for O_1 and O_3, and O_2 and O_3. In similar fashion, B_1 and B_2 are opposed, but are IPC-related through six channels: both are DPC$_S$-related to V_1, V_2, V_3 and O_1, O_2, and O_3.[9]

We first encountered IPC-relatedness in the diachronic case, as a relationship which holds between successive powers (or power-slices) which are too far apart to contribute to a single temporally extended total experience. But we can see now that a synchronic analogue of diachronic IPC-relatedness can also connect simultaneously existing powers, powers which are opposed, for one reason or another. We can define IPC$_S$-relatedness as follows:

IPC$_S$-related: two powers (or phases of such) P_i and P_j are IPC$_S$-related at t if and only if they are not themselves DPC$_S$-related, but are linked by a chain of powers $[P_1 \ldots .P_n]$ the adjacent members of which are DPC$_S$-related at t.

This definition is similar to our earlier definition of *diachronic* IPC-relatedness, and hence it permits powers (or power-slices) to be IPC$_S$-related even if they are separated by a large number of 'links' in a chain of DPC$_S$-related powers (or power-slices). The examples we have considered so far all involved two powers P_i and P_j being IPC$_S$-related to one another by virtue of the fact that both are DPC$_S$-related to some third power, as with V_1, V_2, and O_1. But even in Maggot's mind, limited as it is, longer chains exist. To take just one example, V_1 and V_3 are IPC$_S$-related by virtue of the fact that V_1 is DPC$_S$-related to O_1, which is itself DPC$_S$-related to V_2, which in turn is DPC$_S$-related to O_2, and

---

[9] What if Maggot didn't possess a C-system with this complexity, but still possessed opposed powers? I will be dealing with this combination of attributes shortly.

the latter is DPC$_S$-related to V$_3$ (see Figure 4.6). The rational for construing IPC$_S$-relatedness in this more general manner is simple and familiar: on the assumptions that DPC$_S$-relatedness secures consubjectivity, and consubjectivity is transitive, then all the members of such a power-chain will also be consubjective.

This takes us to the second point. Just as IPC-relatedness can hold synchronically, DPC-relatedness can hold diachronically, and it can unify powers that are opposed as easily as powers that are not. Although two opposed powers, such as V$_1$ and V$_3$, cannot manifest simultaneously, they can manifest *successively*, within the confines of a single temporally extended total experience. For example, a total experience T lasting half a second could be composed of a combination of a *yellow*-type experience contributed by a V$_1$-type power, and a *red*-type experience contributed by a V$_3$-type power. Shining a strobo-scope on Maggot would be one way to exercise his visual powers in this sort of way. If the device produced a sequence of flashes lasting for a quarter of a second, spaced at quarter-second intervals, the pattern of quickly changing light intensities would cause Maggot to see a repeating pattern of a quarter-second of *red* followed by a quarter-second of *yellow* (see Figure 4.6). Since his specious present encompasses a full half-second, the opposed powers V$_1$ and V$_3$ would generate a succession of co-conscious experiences. In this manner opposed powers can be DPC$_D$-related, and the mechanism which secures the persistence of single powers also secures the synchronic consubjectivity of distinct powers.

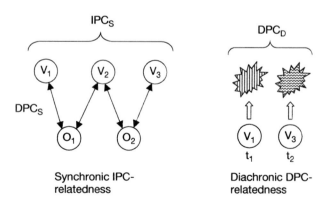

Figure 4.6 Opposed powers can be consubjective by virtue of belonging to a chain of synchronically DPC-related powers (as shown on the left), or by virtue of being able to produce experiences that are diachronically co-conscious (as shown on the right)

It would be wrong to think that only opposed powers can be IPC$_S$-related and DPC$_D$-related. Unopposed powers can also be related in both these ways.

For example, V_1 and O_1 could be activated in quick succession so as to produce a succession of diachronically co-conscious experiences, and so are DPC_D-related. V_1 and O_1 are also IPC_S-related to one another, through three channels: since each is DPC_S-related to each of B_1, B_2, and B_3. (This lower number of channels is due to the fact that V_1 and O_1 are opposed to Maggot's other visual and olfactory powers respectively.) Many persisting experiential powers are both DPC- and IPC-related, synchronically and diachronically. Opposed powers are the exception: they are not linked by DPC_S-relatedness.[10]

Where does this leave us with regard to defining the conditions under which experiential powers are S-related? If we confine ourselves to relationships which concern what is the case at a given moment of time, then we can only appeal to IPC_S-relatedness in accommodating opposed powers. We can revise the definition for S-relatedness as follows:

(SR_1): At any time t, experiential powers that are jointly or pairwise DPC_S-related at t are S-related, as are powers that are IPC_S-related at t.

We cannot appeal to DPC_D-relatedness if we confine ourselves to actual and potential relationships of co-consciousness which can obtain at a given moment, but we can if we expand our horizons and take into account what can happen over a short interval of time. Let 'Σ' stand for the minimum length of time in which two experiential powers can manifest successively; this duration can be expected to vary from subject to subject and power to power. Let us say that a Σ-length period of time *centred at time t* is precisely what its name suggests: a

---

[10] Also worth noting in this connection is the possibility that powers at different times could be related in a manner that is at least partially analogous to synchronically opposed powers. By way of a simple example, suppose a knock on the head affects Maggot's C-system in the following way: whenever his capacity for *yellow* experience is activated it disables his capacity for *orange* experience for a couple of seconds—in effect, the former temporarily *inhibits* the latter. This pattern of inhibition does not mean these two capacities are no longer DPC_D-related, but this would be the case if we further stipulated that the inhibition applies in the other temporal direction, that is that the activation of Maggot's power for *orange* experience temporarily disables his capacity for *yellow* experience. Symmetrical diachronic inhibitions of this sort need not entail that the powers so affected are no longer consubjective. Maggot's capacity for *orange* experience is DPC_S-related to several other powers that are DPC_D-related to his capacity for *yellow* experience, and vice versa. The same sort of pattern will secure consubjectivity in circumstances in any C-system possessing a modicum of complexity. More threatening is the possibility of an *across the board* inhibition, affecting all the powers in a given C-system at a given time; I will be considering this sort of situation in §10.4. What if the activation of an earlier power inhibits *two* later powers, not by rendering both inoperative, but by rendering them incapable of producing (synchronically) co-conscious experiences? In a C-system of some complexity, such as Maggot's, such powers remain consubjective, by virtue of being embedded in network of DPC_S- and DPC_D-related powers; I will be saying more about such networks shortly. In a very simple mind, consisting of just two powers, this pattern of inhibition is equivalent to a (perhaps only temporary) fission; I will be dealing with the latter in Chapter 12. (My thanks to Tim Bayne for drawing my attention to these possibilities.)

Σ-length period of time half of which occurs before t and half after. We can now say that:

Σ–*relatedness*: two experiential powers P_1 and P_2 are Σ-*related at t* if and only if they are DPC_D-related during a Σ-length period of time centred on t.

Experiential powers of all kinds can be Σ-related—and in the case of a typical C-system, generally will be—but importantly for the present purposes so too can opposed powers. Having recognized this relationship, we can incorporate it into a still broader concept of S-relatedness:

(*SR$_2$*): At any time t, experiential powers that are jointly or pairwise DPC_S-related at t are S-related, as are powers that are IPC_S-related and/or Σ-related at t.

SR_1 provides a promising-looking account of synchronic power-unity for all but the simplest of subjects. Maggot does not possess much by way of a mind, but the consubjectivity of all his experiential powers can be accounted for without appealing to anything beyond DPC_S- and IPC_S-relatedness. We need SR_2 and the Σ-relationship only if we want to accommodate subjects such as *Junior-Maggot*: the latter possesses just two experiential powers, one for a completely red visual field and one for a completely blue visual field. These opposed powers can manifest successively but not simultaneously—or so we can suppose. Since there are no other powers in this subject's C-system, we must look beyond DPC_S- or IPC_S-relatedness if we want to account for their consubjectivity. The concept of Σ-relatedness fits the bill. True, it introduces a diachronic dimension into our account of synchronic consubjectivity, but it does so in the most minimal of ways. And in the case of subjects such as Junior-Maggot there seems to be no alternative.[11]

Synchronic unity: combinatorial issues

Since the IPC_D-relation was introduced in the context of *persisting* powers, it was natural to confine it to linear successions of powers (or power-slices), but in the synchronic context there is no rationale for replicating this limitation. As well as running through *chains* of DPC_S-related powers, the IPC_S-relationship can run through (and unify) a *network* of powers, where all the nodes of the network are DPC_S-related, directly or indirectly. A simple example of such a network is shown in Figure 4.7 (where DPC_S-related powers are connected by a

[11] What of subjects who combine simplicity with brevity: for example a creature just like Junior-Maggot but who only exists for a fraction of a second, that is time enough for one (minimally brief) visual experience, but not two? Are we obliged to say that such subjects cannot possess more than one experiential power during their brief lives? No. We can say that their powers are Σ^*-**related**, meaning: *if they had existed* for a Σ-length period, their powers could have manifested successively, producing DPC_D-related experiences.

The Phenomenal Self

line, and the absence of a line indicates that the corresponding powers are not DPC$_S$-related).

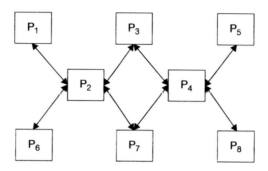

Figure 4.7 A network of IPC$_S$-related powers

In one sense our earlier definition of IPC$_S$-relatedness can accommodate this sort of case without any difficulty. Two powers are IPC$_S$-related if they are not directly DPC$_S$-related, but are linked by a chain of powers whose adjacent members are DPC$_S$-related at t. P$_1$ and P$_8$ are not DPC$_S$-related, but they are linked by chains of powers whose successive members *are* so-related: one such is P$_1$-P$_2$-P$_7$-P$_4$-P$_8$. But in another respect our current definition of IPC$_S$-relatedness is quite limited. Since it is restricted to just *two* powers—and powers that are not themselves DPC$_S$-related at that—it is ill-suited for defining in a general way the conditions under which powers belong to a network of the kind shown in Figure 4.7. Since it will prove useful to have such a definition, we need to recognize a further relationship between powers-at-a-time. The following will serve:

PC$_S$-related: a collection of powers C[P$_1$ ... P$_n$] is **PC$_S$-related** at t if and only if its members jointly compose a network all of whose nodes are DPC$_S$- or IPC$_S$-related at t.

Since all the powers in the network shown in Figure 4.7 are IPC$_S$- or DPC$_S$-related, these powers qualify as PC$_S$-related. Although many of the nodes in such systems will often in fact be IPC$_S$-related, we can define PC$_S$-relatedness solely in terms of DPC$_S$-relatedness:

PC$_S$-related: a collection of powers C[P$_1$ ... P$_n$] is **PC$_S$-related** at t if and only if its members jointly compose a *power-network* at t; the latter is an interconnected structure whose nodes are experiential powers (or power-slices), and in which the relevant linking relationship between nodes is DPC$_S$-relatedness.

Of course interconnectedness comes in different forms. Drawing on the terminology of network (or graph) theory, a power-network is *fully connected* if every node is connected (i.e. DPC$_S$-related) to every other node. Drawing on our earlier terminology, a system of this kind is *pairwise DPC$_S$-related*, and if all the relevant powers can be active at the same time, the system is *jointly DPC$_S$-related*. While the component powers in some C-systems are pairwise DPC$_S$-related, as we have seen, this is by no means universally or necessarily the case (Maggot's C-system is a case in point). Accordingly, let us stipulate that the networks constituted by PC$_S$-related powers need not be fully connected. All that is required is that each node be connected to every other node by at least one uninterrupted *path* of DPC$_S$-relatedness, in the manner of P_1 and P_8 in Figure 4.7. Let us further stipulate that there is no limit on the number of nodes such paths can encompass.

The utility of this broader and more general relationship is easily illustrated. Suppose Maggot receives a blow to the head (or his equivalent thereof) which damages some of the links between his neural nodes. As a consequence of this damage a number of his experiential powers are no longer able to produce co-conscious experiences when active. Whereas previously he was able to experience b_1 (*cold*) and o_1 (*nasty*) together, now he is unable to; likewise for v_1 (*yellow*) and o_2 (*edible*). Figure 4.8 records the full picture of devastation. As previously, powers that are not connected by a double-headed arrow are not DPC$_S$-related.

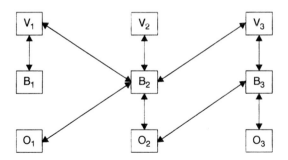

Figure 4.8 Maggot's post-accident C-system: several DPC$_S$-links have been severed

Evidently, a good many combinations of experience that were previously available to Maggot are no longer available to him—prior to his accident *all* his experiential powers were DPC$_S$-linked, with the exception of his opposed powers (i.e. $V_1/V_2/V_3$, $B_1/B_2/B_3$, $O_1/O_2/O_3$). But although the number of DPC$_S$-links has been significantly reduced, Maggot's C-system has the same number of powers as previously: all the powers shown in Figure 4.8 are components of a power-network whose parts are PC$_S$-related. If a C-system of this kind strikes us as odd it is because the vast bulk of the experiential powers of a typical (healthy) human subject are unopposed. The combinations of experience we can actually enjoy is close to what is in principle possible, given the range of

experiential powers that we possess. Our C-systems are *richly combinatorial.*
But it is surely conceivable that neural damage could result in significantly less
richly combinatorial C-systems in the human case, and there may be some
subjects whose C-systems are naturally much less combinatorial than our own.
There is no reason to suppose such C-systems are impossible. A power such
as O_1 in Figure 4.8 may only be able to manifest with *one* other power in
Maggot's C-system, but isn't this enough to render this power consubjective
with Maggot's other powers? So far as synchronic consubjectivity is concerned,
once is enough.

No less importantly, with the concept of PC$_S$-relatedness at our disposal we
can define the necessary and sufficient conditions for S-relatedness in a simpler
and more straightforward manner than previously:

S-related: a collection of powers C[P$_1$ ... P$_n$] is S-related at t if and only if all the
members of C are **PC$_S$-related at t.**

In effect, we are now saying that for powers to be S-related (and hence belong
to a single C-system) they must constitute a network of powers, where the
nodes of this network are DPC$_S$-related, directly or indirectly. The rather
sparsely interconnected system shown in Figure 4.8 satisfies this definition of
S-relatedness, but so too do the more richly interconnected systems shown in
Figure 4.9 (here the central region is fully-connected—and hence pairwise or
jointly DPC$_S$-related—the outer regions are not). Obviously, the existence of
more connections does not diminish the extent to which such a network constitutes
a single unified system of powers.

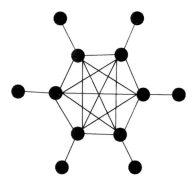

Figure 4.9 A single C-system can possess different depths of synchronic integration

What of joint and pairwise DPC$_S$-relatedness? The fact that we no longer
need these concepts to define (in a very general way) the conditions under
which experiential powers belong to a single C-system by no means renders
them redundant. C-systems have much in common, but they can also differ

in significant ways, and distinguishing joint and pairwise DPC_S-relatedness allows us to register some of these differences. The situation with Σ-relatedness is different again. If we want to assign powers-at-times to very simple subjects—subjects whose minds are as simple as Junior-Maggot's—we cannot appeal to DPC_S-relatedness in any shape or form, and so we cannot appeal to PC_S-relatedness either. Hence Σ-relatedness still has a role to play—assuming, of course, that subjects with this degree of simplicity can in fact exist (I am leaving this open at present). We can extend our definition of S-relatedness thus:

S-related: a collection of powers $C[P_1 \ldots P_n]$ is S-related at t if and only if all the members of C are PC_S-related at t and/or Σ-related at t.

The final clause captures primitive subjects, but can apply to more complex subjects too: many of our own experiential powers are PC_S-related *and* Σ-related.

Synchronic unity: transitivity

Is DPC_S-relatedness transitive? Or could there be three experiential powers, P_1, P_2, and P_3, such that they could all be active simultaneously, and produce three experiences e_1, e_2, and e_3, where e_1 is co-conscious with e_2, and e_2 is co-conscious with e_3, but e_1 is not co-conscious with e_3? Not if the co-consciousness relationship itself is transitive. If it is, then in the envisaged case e_1's being co-conscious with e_2 and e_2's being co-conscious with e_3 would entail that e_1 and e_3 are also co-conscious. As for whether co-consciousness *is* transitive, I noted in §2.5 that it is difficult to conceive how it could be otherwise, and I have been working on the assumption that it is; I shall also be offering a defence of this assumption in §8.6.

However, since the arguments I will be developing in §8.6 are perhaps less than conclusive, it is worth pausing to note that the account we have been developing is capable of accommodating failures of transitivity. If the case just envisaged could occur, then P_1 and P_2 would be DPC_S-related, P_2 and P_3 would be DPC_S-related, but P_1 and P_3 would only be IPC_S-related. Since IPC_S-relatedness suffices for consubjectivity, P_1 and P_2 would be consubjective, even though they are not DPC_S-related. Whether this is the best way of construing such situations is another matter—one I will be exploring further.

4.4. THE C-THEORY

We now have at least the beginnings of a plausible-looking account of the conditions under which both experiential powers and experiences belong to the same self or subject, both at a time and over time. The various formulations I have proposed could be improved upon, no doubt, but the general approach looks promising.[12]

While the account has gradually grown in complexity—principally to accommodate the possibility of subjects whose complement of experiential powers cannot all manifest simultaneously or successively—the various complications are no more than variations on a single simple theme. At the heart of the analysis remains the stream of consciousness and the unification *of* experience *by* experience, along with the idea that co-conscious experiences belong to the same self. However, since our concern has now shifted from accounting for the consubjectivity of actual experience to that of experiential powers, actual experience has lost its central role, having been displaced by nomologically grounded potentialities for experience. Likewise, the central unifying relation in our account is now being used in a different way. The consubjectivity of actual experiences can be accounted for in terms of the co-consciousness of actual experiences; but to account for the consubjectivity of experiential powers we need something more, and the concept of DPC-relatedness (in its various forms) meets this need. Experiences that are actually co-conscious are consubjective; experiential powers (or power-slices) which *have the ability* to produce co-conscious experiences are also consubjective, irrespective of whether they are active or dormant. We can sum up as follows.

1 A collection of experiential powers composes a C-system at t iff its members are **S-related** at t. The members of such a collection are S-related at t iff they are PC_S-related at t and/or Σ-related at t. S-related collections of powers may also be jointly or pairwise DPC_S-related at t.

2 C-systems S_1 and S_2 at t_1 and t_2 are **DPC_D-related** iff some or all of their constituent powers are pairwise DPC_D-related.

3 C-systems S_1 and S_2 at t_1 and t_2 are **IPC_D-related** iff they are parts of a chain whose adjoining members are C-systems that are DPC_D-related.

4 C-systems at earlier and later times are phases of the same persisting C-system iff they are either DPC_D-related or IPC_D-related.

5 Experiential powers are **C-related** iff they belong to the same C-system.

6 Experiential powers are **consubjective** iff they are C-related.

7 Experiences are consubjective iff they are produced by C-related experiential powers.

[12] Four-dimensionalists might find this approach worth pursuing: we say that powers belong to the same C-system iff they are PC*-related, where the latter is the *four-dimensional* analogue of the PC_S-relation, that is it applies to four-dimensional networks whose nodes are momentary (or very brief) power-slices and whose connecting relationship is DPC_S-relatedness at-a-time, and DPC_D-relatedness over time. In a more precise vein, powers are PC*-related iff they belong to a connected four-dimensional network whose nodes are all DPC_S- or IPC_S-related at any given time, and DPC_D or IPC_D-related over time. But while this approach may deliver a more economical way of formulating the conditions under which powers are consubjective, it is less neutral between the endurance and perdurance frameworks than the account I have favoured.

We can thus define the conditions under which experiential powers are consubjective in terms of a single relation, C-relatedness, which is itself (ultimately) defined in terms of DPC-relatedness and IPC-relatedness in their various synchronic and diachronic guises. The experiential powers in earlier and later C-systems are C-related, but so too are the powers in a C-system at any given time—by virtue of clause (5), C-relatedness incorporates S-relatedness.

In framing these definitions I have often glossed over the distinction between power-slices and enduring powers (and between perduring and enduring C-systems), but so far as defining the conditions under which powers are consubjective is concerned, nothing of significance hangs on whether we adopt the perdurance view or the endurance view. To accommodate certain remote possibilities the account will require certain modifications—the seemingly innocuous (7) will be scrutinized in §8.4—but little purpose would be served by introducing these now.

The synchronic unity criterion for C-systems summarized in (1) allows a C-system to have (proper) parts that are also C-systems, for example Maggot's visual system counts as a C-system, but so too does the combination of his visual and olfactory systems. Since it will be helpful to have a term which refers to the entirety of a subject's experiential capacities at a given time, let us specify that a collection of experiential powers only counts as a C-system if it is both S-related and *maximal*, that is it is *not* a proper part of any larger collection of S-related experiential powers. This specification is merely making explicit what was implicit in my earlier usage.

With these preliminaries behind us, we are in a position to formulate an ontological claim:

8 Selves (or subjects) are C-systems.

Whereas (6) amounts to no more than an account of our persistence conditions, (8) supplements this with a claim as to what a self is. Although I will generally use the term *C-theory* to refer to (6) *and* (8), it is important to note that it is quite possible to subscribe to (6) without also subscribing to (8). Accordingly, it will occasionally be useful to distinguish between the *narrow* and *broad* versions of the C-theory. The former is the doctrine that our persistence conditions are as specified in (1)–(6), the latter also embraces the ontological claim that we are nothing more than maximal systems of C-related experiential powers, as encapsulated in (8). For the time being I will leave open whether selves 'are' C-systems in the sense of being *constituted* from collections of experiential powers, or *identical* with them (I will be considering this issue in more detail in Chapter 7).

As for the bridge-problem, this has now been solved. The move to nomologically grounded potentialities for experience means that gaps between streams of consciousness are no longer in the least problematic. Two temporally separated streams of consciousness are consubjective if they are produced by consubjective experiential powers, where experiential powers are consubjective if and only if they are C-related. Actual experience results from the exercise of experiential powers whose consubjectivity consists in the co-consciousness of their potential manifestations. A particular experiential power persists through periods of quiescence in virtue of the continuous experience which would result from its activation. And as with any particular power, so with the mind of which it is part. A cycle of being conscious, unconscious, and conscious again is only one of the innumerable forms which the manifestations of the underlying set of consubjective experiential powers could have taken during that period. Or at least that is so for minds as complex as our own—Maggot's mind is not as capable in this respect.

Where do minds as complex as our own fit into the picture? I have focused on an unrealistically simple example so as to avoid unnecessary complications clouding the shape of the basic picture. Human minds bear little resemblance to Maggot's mind; perhaps a mind such as Maggot's is an impossibility. But the unrealistic simplicity of Maggot's mind does not matter. Maggot is a subject of experience (or he would be if he existed), and so are we. Our experience is usually far richer than Maggot's, but since we can regard our experience as the product of one or more experiential powers, this complexity does not alter the basic picture: our experiential powers are consubjective in virtue of being C-related. We are different from Maggot in another way: we have psychological systems and intellects. But this difference does not matter either. The bulk of our mental states and capacities are experience-involving, or experience-producing, and hence can be assigned to subjects in essentially the same way as Maggot's simple sensory capacities. More on this later.

4.5. POWERS IN GENERAL

Experiential powers or capacities lie at the heart of the C-theory, but I have yet to say anything about how these should be conceived. Although I will be returning to this topic (in Chapters 9 and 10) some preliminary remarks are in order.

Objects manifestly do possess capacities of various kinds, capacities which are sometimes manifest, but often not. Atomic bombs have the power to explode and cause massive devastation; panes of bullet-proof glass have the capacity to stop speeding bullets; magnets have the power to attract pieces of iron; iron hammers have the capacity to smash ordinary (but not bullet-proof) panes of glass. And so on. Different kinds of object have different causal powers—powers to achieve certain effects in certain circumstances—and the powers they have are correlated with the laws of nature. Our brains are objects of a highly distinctive kind, and, thanks to the laws of nature being as they are, they have a distinctive kind of power: under the right conditions they can generate a variety of conscious experiences. We also know that brains can generate more experiences than they actually do—think of all the experiences you could be having now if you weren't doing what you are currently doing. We also have every reason to believe that brains retain their experience-generating capabilities when we are unconscious. Most of us can usually be woken up fairly easily (certainly without recourse to brain surgery) and although there are physical differences between conscious and unconscious brains, they are comparatively small. We thus have every reason to believe that experiential powers exist, that they are sometimes exercised and sometimes not, and that they are as unproblematically real as other kinds of capacity.

Given that this is so, is there any difficulty with the proposal that we can trace our existence through time by reference to such powers? I cannot see that there is, although there are certain complications.

The first of these derives from the fact that the C-theory doesn't just require us to recognize that experiential capacities exist, it also requires us to recognize that such capacities can work together in a particular way. Experiential powers are DPC-related (and so consubjective) by virtue of a relationship between their effects or manifestations: they can produce experiences which are related by co-consciousness, synchronically or diachronically. This does complicate the situation, but there is nothing unusual or unique (or especially problematic) in causal powers being related in this general sort of way. Let us say that a collection of objects or properties are *manifestation-* or m-linked if, first, its members each have the capacity to produce a certain kind of effect under appropriate circumstances, and second, these effects are related in some specific manner. Consubjective experiential powers are m-linked, but so are lots of other things. Two searchlights are located on neighbouring hilltops; when switched on, their beams converge to create adjoining patches of light on the valley floor below. We could call searchlights related in this way *convergence-related*. As is evident, searchlights that are convergence-related are m-linked. But so too are their light-generating capacities: objects can be m-related, but so too can causal powers. And it is not only searchlights (or their causal powers) that can be convergence-related: so too are the big guns in an artillery battalion, targeted so that the shells will hit the same spot, or intercontinental ballistic missiles that would hit the same spot if launched. We might call radio-wave sources *interference*-related if, when activated, they will emit waves which will interfere with one another. Again, we could express the same point in terms of causal powers, and talk instead of collections of radiative *capacities* being interference-related if their manifestations would contribute to an interference pattern.

DPC-relatedness may only be one of many forms of m-linkage, but it is nonetheless distinctive: the relevant effects are phenomenal, and these effects must be linked by the co-consciousness relationship. But since experiences self-evidently can be related in this way it is difficult to see why this form of m-linkage should be any more problematic than non-phenomenal forms.

A second complication derives from a general distinction between two types of dispositional property: there are 'sure-fire' dispositions (those which are invariably activated by their trigger) and probabilistic dispositions (a match will often ignite when struck, but it will not always do so, but it nonetheless has the capacity to ignite when struck). This distinction applies to m-linked dispositions as well as to individual dispositions; it can also apply to m-linked experiential powers. Some experiential powers may be dispositions of the sure-fire variety, others may be dispositions of the probabilistic variety. Although I have thus far (tacitly) been working on the assumption that experiential powers are sure-fire dispositions, this assumption is by no means necessary. Two experiential capacities P_1 and P_2 can be DPC-related, synchronically or diachronically, even if there is only a 60 per cent chance that P_1 will produce experience in response to its standard triggering event, and only a 30 per cent chance that P_2 will do likewise, provided that the experiences they do manage to produce are co-conscious. The same applies for larger numbers of powers and different combinations of probabilities: provided they are apt to produce co-conscious experiences on those occasions when they *do* fire, such powers can be DPC_S- or DPC_D-related in a quite unambiguous manner. In a similar way, a collection of missiles can unequivocally be targeted on a particular city even if their rocket motors are less than wholly reliable, and there is only a 30–50 per cent chance that they will fire when triggered.[13]

Moving on, further and different complications flow from the fact that there are different views as to the nature of capacities and dispositions, and no consensus as to which is the most appropriate. Some of these differences derive from different conceptions of causation. Some view causation as a matter solely of *de facto* regularities among events, others believe it makes more sense to suppose that causes *necessitate* their effects. I will not attempt to adjudicate on this issue. So far as the viability of the C-theory is concerned, all that matters is that experiential capacities can legitimately be regarded as being on a par with non-experiential capacities. Provided both regularity theorists and their necessitarian opponents can view experiential capacities as being essentially akin to the explosive capacities of hydrogen bombs, and so far as I can see they can, that is sufficient for my purposes.

As for the other differences of opinion concerning the nature of dispositions, here too I will remain largely neutral. While so doing is certainly convenient, I think it is also justified. There may well be no one right way of conceiving of dispositional properties: a metaphysical account of dispositionality that is appropriate to the occupants of one possible world may be inappropriate in the context of a very different possible world; even in our world, dispositional predicates may denote very different species of property—this could

---

[13] What should we say about a probabilistic experiential power that can contribute to two distinct streams of consciousness? I will be dealing with this shortly.

be true, say, for 'electric charge' and 'fragile'. Given this, and given that we are still so ignorant about the ways in which brains succeed in producing experiences, I think it is fair to say that we are not (at present) in a position to know what the best way of conceptualizing experiential powers will turn out to be. It would certainly be unwise to be metaphysically dogmatic about the issue.

That said, the different ways of conceiving of dispositions do affect the overall tenor of the C-theory (as well as influencing how certain sorts of change should be described, as we shall see), so it would be wrong to ignore these differences completely.

According to one general conception of dispositions—for example Ryle (1949: 113)—to say that an entity possesses a disposition to behave in a certain way under certain conditions is simply to make a prediction about how the entity is likely to behave in the future, usually on the basis of how it has behaved in the past. A china vase is fragile if it will break if dropped, and on this view, that is *all* that fragility amounts to. More generally, ascribing a disposition to an object is equivalent to asserting that a collection of hypothetical statements is true of that object, statements of the form 'if . . . were to occur at *t*, then . . . would occur at *t*'. It is true that 'x is fragile' and 'x is a metre long' have the same form—both seem to involve the ascription of a property to an object—but Ryle insists that grammatical form is misleading in such cases. Unlike the predicates used to refer to categorical properties, dispositional predicates do not refer to genuine abiding properties. For a dispositional predicate to be truly applicable to an object, *all* that is required is for the relevant hypothetical statements to be true.[14]

I do not think it is altogether impossible for a subscriber to the Rylean conception of dispositions also to subscribe to the C-theory. The Rylean accepts that it is perfectly meaningful to ascribe capacities to things, and experiential capacities could be regarded as being on a par with other kinds of capacity. If we adopted this view we could still hold that subjects persist through periods of unconsciousness because certain objects continue to possess experiential capacities, where the possession of these capacities amounts to no more than certain hypothetical statements being true, statements concerning the sorts of experience which would be produced under certain circumstances.[15] However, while this may be enough for the C-theory in its narrow guise, as an account of our persistence conditions, it is by no means clear that it is enough for the C-theory in its broad form, as an account of what we are. The problem is

---

[14] Or as Mellor (2000: 765) puts it: 'all "*a* is fragile" says is that we may infer "*a* breaks" from "a drops": it does not report a state of affairs distinct from those that make "*a* drops" and "*a* breaks" true or false. So when a fragile glass *a* and a non-fragile glass *b* are not being dropped, there need be no factual difference between them.'

[15] I assume here that we are adopting a Rylean account of capacities, not a Rylean (behaviourist) conception of experience.

simple: if we construe dispositions in Ryle's way, what *is* there for a subject to *be*? The answer appears to be 'nothing'. We can suppose that a subject who falls into dreamless sleep retains their various capacities for experience, but if these capacities do not consist in real properties of anything, it is not obviously coherent or intelligible to suppose that the subject in question *consists* of these capacities.

However, the purely predictive conception of dispositions has fallen out of favour in recent years, and with good reason. As Armstrong points out (1968: 85–8), the dispositions an object has are usually a consequence of the *nature* of that object, not mere chance, and when we ascribe a disposition we usually do so with an understanding that this is the case. When a pane of bullet-proof glass stops a bullet in its tracks, its so doing is not due to a miracle, nor will it be a mere coincidence. The glass is disposed to behave in this way because of its physical composition and structure: certain physical features of the glass are *causally responsible* for the failure of the bullet to penetrate. The same applies, *mutatis mutandis*, to an atomic bomb's disposition to explode when triggered and to a hammer's disposition to shatter light bulbs. More generally, if an object x is disposed to produce an effect E in condition C, it is x's possessing some feature F that is causally responsible for the occurrence of E. This feature F is the *causal ground* or *base* of the disposition in question. This causal conception of dispositions is now widely accepted—and indeed I have (tacitly) adopted this conception throughout. Applying it to the case in hand, a schematic characterization of an arbitrary experiential power P will have the form P: (E, B, C), where 'B' is the causal basis of the power, 'C' stands for the triggering circumstances, and 'E' the type of experience that is produced when B and C are brought together in the right sort of way.

That dispositions typically have causal bases may be uncontroversial, but the precise relationship between the two is disputed. Some advocate identifying dispositions with their bases, or with their bases together with the relevant laws of nature.[16] This view has the advantage that dispositions can themselves be causally potent in an entirely straightforward way, they can be the causes of their effects or manifestations. In another respect, however, the proposed identification is disadvantageous. A substance is poisonous, for a given population, if it is likely to produce illness when ingested. Obviously, a wide range of very different substances possess this disposition. So far as humans are concerned, arsenic is poisonous, but other substances are too, for example strychnine, cyanide, deadly nightshade, and so on. Since each of these substances is poisonous in virtue of its chemical properties, and their chemical properties are different, if we identify dispositions with their causal bases we get the odd result that what seemed to be a single property—being poisonous—is in

---

16 See Armstrong (1969, 1973: 14–16), Mellor (2000). Armstrong's position has changed from the latter to the former—see his discussion in Armstrong, Martin, and Place (1996).

fact a range of very different properties. To avoid this result, Prior, Pargetter, and Jackson (1982) advocate a functionalist conception, according to which a disposition is a second-order property of *having some other property*, one that plays a particular causal role. On this view, the property of 'being poisonous' is the second-order property of having some first-order property that tends to cause illness when ingested. Arsenic, strychnine, and cyanide all share this second-order property, although the first-order property which occupies this causal role is different in each case. The functionalist approach has the advantage that possessors of the same dispositional property all have something in common, even when the causal bases of the disposition are different. It has the disadvantage that dispositions themselves appear to be causally impotent: all the causal work is done by the causal basis of the disposition, not the disposition itself.[17]

For the purposes of the C-theory it does not matter how this dispute is resolved. If we follow Armstrong, then experiential powers will be those features of their bearer which are actually capable of generating experiences (in conjunction with the relevant laws of nature). If we follow Prior, Pargetter, and Jackson, then an object will possess an experiential power if it possesses the second-order property of possessing first-order properties that are capable of generating certain kinds of experience when appropriately stimulated. Either way, experiential powers are being construed as genuine and abiding properties, and as such they can provide a solid basis for the construction of an account of what the existence and persistence of subjects requires and involves.

A second dispute concerns the source of causal powers themselves. As we have just seen, on one view causal powers are a consequence of the laws of nature acting on the categorical or qualitative properties of objects. If the relevant laws were different, objects could be disposed to behave in different ways despite being the same in all non-dispositional respects. Rubber balls might explode when kicked; rather than being brittle, china teacups could be as hard as diamond or as malleable as putty (all at room temperature). An alternative view is to regard dispositional properties as nomologically basic, and hold that it is because objects possess the dispositional properties they do that objects possessing them behave as they do. On this view the laws of nature depend, in effect, on the basic dispositional properties and the way these properties are distributed across objects with different categorical properties. The dispositions have priority; change them and the laws change too (Shoemaker 1980; Ellis and Lierse 1994; Mumford 1998: ch. 10). Upholders of the strongest forms of this doctrine claim that most, and perhaps all, seemingly categorical properties are themselves purely dispositional: the only non-dispositional properties recognized

---

[17] Mumford (1998) tries for a middle way, and holds that dispositions are functional properties that are identical with their particular instances. But the resulting position is awkward in several respects see Ryder (2004).

by Molnar (2003: §10.2) are positional properties, such as spatial location and orientation. According to yet another view, the distinction between categorical and dispositional properties is an artificial one. No property is wholly dispositional or wholly categorical; every property has both categorical and dispositional aspects (Smart 1997; Heil 2003). Here too C-theorists can, if they wish, remain above the fray. All participants of this debate agree on what matters for our purposes: that causal capacities, experiential powers included, are genuine properties.

Three grades of individuation

There is a further question we need to address: how are experiential powers to be individuated?

This question can be posed at the level of types or tokens. The latter is unproblematic. I am assuming that all experiential powers (in our universe at least) are grounded in some physical system, their *power-base*, as we can call it. If two token experiential powers existing at the same time are of the same type, to be distinct they must have different power-bases, they must be grounded in different physical things, or different parts or aspects of the same physical thing. This may not be the only way in which otherwise indistinguishable powers can be individuated, but it will serve in most instances. The question of how experiential powers should be classified into types is somewhat more involved. Suppose we have two experiential powers, $P_1 = [E_1, B_1, C_1]$ and $P_2 = [E_2, B_2, C_2]$, where as previously E, B, and C refer to experiential effects, causal bases and triggering circumstances respectively. If E_1 and E_2 are markedly different kinds of experience, then clearly P_1 and P_2 are different kinds of power. But what if E_1 and E_2 are the same kinds of experience, but C_1 and C_2 are different, that is if E_1 and E_2 can be triggered in different ways? What if E_1 and E_2 are the same types of experience, C_1 and C_2 are the same types of triggering circumstance, but P_1 and P_2 are grounded in different kinds of physical system, with the result that their power-bases, B_1 and B_2, are of different kinds? What should we say about such cases? There are three main options:

1 Two experiential powers are of the same type if and only if they produce the same kind of experience when activated.

2 Two experiential powers are of the same type if and only if (i) they produce the same kind of experience when activated, and (ii) they can be triggered in the same ways.

3 Two experiential powers are of the same type if and only if (i) they produce the same kind of experience when activated, (ii) they can be triggered in the same ways, (iii) they have the same kind of power-base.

Those drawn to the higher-order property conception of dispositions will opt for (1) or (2); those who believe with Armstrong that we should identify dispositions with their bases (and relevant laws) will opt for (3). Those of us who remain uncommitted on this question are not obliged to choose: we can simply recognize that experiential powers can be individuated in more or less fine-grained ways.

How we choose to individuate powers may not affect the viability of the C-theory but it does make a difference to how we describe the outcomes of certain transformations. Consider again a consciousness-preserving version of the NRT-procedure: the physical composition of your brain is drastically altered—it is largely siliconized, let us suppose—but your mental capabilities are entirely unaffected. How should we describe the outcome in terms of experiential capacities? Anyone who opts for (1) or (2) will say that you have numerically the same experiential powers at the end of the procedure as you did at the beginning. Anyone who subscribes to (3) will say that since the procedure involves the wholesale replacement of the causal bases of your experiential powers, it results in the wholesale replacement of the powers themselves. From the point of view of defining our persistence conditions, however, this divergence makes no difference. Provided that the NRT-procedure does not eliminate the short-term capacity of your experiential powers to produce co-conscious experiences—and for present purposes we can stipulate that it does not—then you survive the treatment, irrespective of how we prefer to describe the outcome. A succession of numerically distinct experiential powers can sustain a self in existence as easily as a collection of persisting powers.

While unproblematic in one sense, the formulations in (1), (2), and (3) are also associated with a host of difficult-to-resolve issues. Fortunately, none of these difficulties looks likely to undermine the viability of the C-theory.

So far as the relevant effects, experiences, are concerned, these too can be individuated in different ways. If we opt to individuate *narrowly*, all that counts is phenomenal character. If we opt to individuate *widely* then causal history matters too: although my Twin-Earth twin is qualitatively indistinguishable from me in all respects, when we each think 'I remember Paris' our thoughts have different contents, and so by the lights of the wide criterion are different types of experiences. The C-theory is perfectly compatible with both modes of individuation. There are other puzzles and problems. How precisely do we allocate types of experiences to experiential powers? Are my visual experiences the product of a vast number of different visual capacities—for example distinct powers for different shapes and colours? Or are they the product of a single experiential power, a massively multi-track capacity capable of generating every total visual experience I am capable of enjoying (irrespective of how complex), in response to different stimuli? Or does the truth lie somewhere between these two extremes? Analogous questions arise for the other modalities, and they are not easy to answer.

We will probably have to wait for further discoveries in cognitive neuroscience before we are in a position to pronounce with any confidence on this issue. But even if we knew a lot more about the physical underpinnings of consciousness, it could still turn out that there is no one best way of dividing up a typical human being's total experiential potential into different experiential capacities—just as there is probably no one best way of dividing the typical total *experience* into component parts. But so far as the C-theory is concerned this does not matter. Irrespective of how we answer these questions, we can still hold that what renders experiential capacities consubjective is their ability to contribute to unified streams of consciousness. Even if all my visual experiences are the product of a single multi-faceted visual capacity, and the same goes *mutatis mutandis* for my other sensory modalities, the question of how these five multi-track capacities need to be related if they are to belong to the same subject still arises, and the answer 'they need to be able to produce co-conscious experiences' remains as valid as ever. The consubjectivity of my sensory powers with my powers for mental imagery, conscious thought and emotional feelings can be explained in the same way. What if we were to regard *all* a subject's experiential powers at a given time as facets of a single multi-modal multi-track capacity? Well, the C-theory would still have a role in accounting for diachronic consubjectivity. How must neighbouring (brief) temporal phases of such a power be related if they belong to the same self? They must be able to produce (diachronically) co-conscious experiences. In fact, were we to adopt this stance, the C-theory would still have a role at the synchronic level too. A multi-track capacity is, after all, a complex dispositional property, one possessing a number of distinct *strands* or *aspects*—one for each combination of trigger and manifestation—and only those power-aspects which can produce co-conscious experience when triggered at the same time are consubjective.[18] So it seems that irrespective of how we divide up a subject's total experiential potential, the C-theory can still apply. (This said, there are certain significant subtleties here, and I will be returning to this topic in Chapter 9.)

There are also issues concerning triggering conditions. Given the complexity of our minds, spelling out the precise triggering conditions for each kind of experience we could have is not a practical possibility, and would not be even if we knew everything there was to know about how our brains work. Just consider

---

[18] If Maggot's visual capacities V_1, V_2, and V_3 were grounded in a single neural module, rather than three distinct modules, it might seem natural to regard these as aspects (or sub-powers) of a single multi-track experiential power, which could be characterized thus: $V[(c_1, v_1), (c_2, v_2), (c_3, v_3)]$—where c_1, c_2, and c_3 stand for the triggering circumstances of *yellow, orange* and *red* experience-types respectively. The three power-aspects (c_1, v_1), (c_2, v_2), and (c_3, v_3) are grounded in the same physical system, but it doesn't automatically follow that they belong to the same subject—for it is conceivable that the experiences they produce when triggered simultaneously are not co-conscious. Of course, if they *do* produce co-conscious experience when triggered, then they are consubjective. The C-theory thus finds applications at the level of power-aspects as well as experiential powers *per se*. Consequently, for most purposes, there is no harm in allowing power-aspects to be considered as experiential powers in their own right—and this is the practice I shall adopt henceforth.

the vast range of prior thoughts and experiences which might lead you to token the thought: 'Things could be better'. Even in the comparatively straightforward case of capacities for basic forms of sensory experience, triggering conditions are not easy to spell out in a full and complete fashion. To illustrate, assume my capacity to see a certain shade of blue is a single experiential capacity, with triggering conditions *C*. Since this capacity can be triggered in a variety of ways, we are faced with a choice when it comes to deciding which of these ways should be included in *C*. Should we mention only the proximate neural causes, deep in the visual centres of the brain, or should we also include reference to certain kinds of retinal activity? Or should we mention the wavelengths of light that would trigger the relevant retinal activity, or the kinds of material object which would typically reflect these wavelengths? Once again, so far as the C-theory is concerned, it does not matter. Causal effects, of all kinds, are usually the product of a complex causal field extending an indefinite way through time and space. Any number of elements in this field can be candidates for being 'the' cause of a given event, for any number of elements might be necessary and/or sufficient for the event, or simply be such as to make the event more probable, given the rest of the field. Which of these elements we identify as the cause depends on our purposes and interests. Experiential capacities are similar to other capacities in these respects. There is, however, a further and related point. Irrespective of which triggering-option we choose in this particular case, we will be obliged to state that the sorts of event mentioned in *C* will only trigger the occurrence of the relevant kind of experience under 'standard', 'normal', or 'ideal' conditions, that is my brain must be at roughly room temperature, it must not be a fraction of a second away from being crushed by a falling piano, and so on. Although, if pushed, we can spell out in more detail what the 'standard conditions' clause requires, we probably won't be able to do so in such a way as to be able to dispense with the clause altogether.[19] Given this, can we be sure that we know what experiential powers really are?

While not to be underestimated or ignored, none of these difficulties should preclude acceptance of the C-theory. We may not be able to come close to spelling out the precise triggering circumstances for many kinds of experience—in particular conscious thoughts—but this limitation does not affect the facts of the matter. It remains the case that we do have capacities for a wide range of experience, and that these capacities can be triggered in certain ways, and all the C-theory requires is that these capacities can produce co-conscious experience when active, it does not require that we be able to characterize the triggering circumstances in complete detail. Nor does it require that we be able to dispense with a reference to standard conditions in our specifications of triggering conditions. After all, the need for such a clause is the norm in dispositional contexts. A fully primed H-bomb dropped from on high will explode on impact,

[19] For further elaboration see Lewis (1997), Bird (1998, 2000), Gundersen (2000).

but only under normal conditions, in the absence of any of the innumerable and varied occurrences which would prevent the explosion, for example a fusion-inhibiting field conveniently supplied by passing extraterrestrials, the bomb's being swallowed up by a small black hole just prior to impact, and so forth. Listing all such eventualities is impossible, yet no one doubts that H-bombs possess destructive capacities.

This point is relevant to what might seem a potentially problematic sort of puzzle-case. Maggot's power for *yellow*-type experience is not currently active, nor is that of his sibling, Maggot*. Although Maggot and Maggot* are twins, they are not twins of the Siamese variety: each is an entirely separate organism, and their brains are not linked by any neural connections. Given this, the claim that Maggot's capacity for experiencing *yellow* is consubjective with all of Maggot*'s capacities for bodily and olfactory sensations might well seem absurd, especially by the light of the C-theory. But while it is true that Maggot's capacity for experiencing *yellow* is not DPC$_S$-related to any of Maggot*'s experiential capacities if we confine our attention to ordinary triggering events, the situation changes if we introduce *abnormal* triggering events into the picture. I have in mind a trigger of a complex kind which (i) causes the relevant neural circuits in Maggot's brain to start producing *yellow*-type experience, and (ii) instantaneously transfers these neural circuits to Maggot*'s brain, from which the original *yellow*-producing circuits have just been removed, and connects them up (in the normal sort of way). When Maggot's *yellow*-capacity is activated in this way, the resulting experiences are co-conscious with experiences produced in his sibling's brain. The C-theory may seem to be reduced to absurdity by possibilities of this kind. After all, what goes for the neural circuitry of Maggot and his twin also goes for your brain and mine. If triggers of this kind are possible, might it not be that for any given population of compatible subjects, every experiential power is DPC$_S$-related to every other at any given time?

It would be a mistake to draw this conclusion. For one thing, DPC-relatedness is a *nomological* capacity—powers are so-related when it is nomologically possible for them to produce co-conscious experience—but it is by no means obvious that instantaneous spatial translations of the envisaged kind are nomologically possible. This point aside, it is not only the C-theory which is threatened by the envisaged kind of deviant triggering event. Most (perhaps all) manifestation-linked capacities are similarly susceptible. Searchlights that are pointing in opposite directions (or that are located on different continents) will be convergence-related if we expand our class of triggering events to include instantaneous re-orientations (or spatial translations)—and the same applies to ballistic missiles and artillery pieces. Should we conclude that there are no facts of the matter about which ballistic missiles would converge when triggered? That would be an absurd overreaction. When we say that two particular missiles are convergence-related, what we say can be unproblematically true because we make the claim with the tacit understanding that the missiles *will only be triggered in the standard sorts of way*. And likewise for other m-linked objects and capacities, DPC-related experiential powers included. We might not be able to spell out exactly what 'standard' means in a non-circular way in this sort of context, but we are able to recognize triggering events that are significantly abnormal without any difficulty whatsoever. If the possibility of deviant triggers does not undermine the threat posed by co-targeted ballistic missiles it can scarcely do more damage to the C-theory.[20]

What of the third member of our triad, the causal bases of experiential powers? As should be plain, the C-theory itself is entirely neutral on this score. The stated conditions for power-consubjectivity work just as well in worlds where experiential powers are grounded in immaterial substances as they do in worlds where they are grounded in material substances. So far as our world is concerned, although I have been assuming that our experiential powers are materially grounded, given the depths of our current ignorance concerning the matter–consciousness relationship, we are not in a position to be able to say much about the physical pre-requisites of experience-generating potential. While this has a number of consequences, the C-theory can live with them all.

The first and most obvious consequence: we are not as yet able to specify in any detail how the experiential powers in our own brains are materially grounded. Until we know more about such matters we will not know how best to conceive of the complement of experiential powers at our disposal. (Are our powers modular in the manner of Maggot's? Are our powers for visual and bodily experience grounded in largely separate or largely overlapping neural systems?) Nor will we be in a position to begin to specify precisely what sorts of alteration in the material basis of a particular power would be fatal to that power. There can be little doubt that the siliconizing variant of the NRT-procedure obliterates all one's powers by virtue of the wholesale replacement (or obliteration) of their material bases, but suppose neural tissue transplant technology becomes available: which individual neurons, or neural systems, would have to be replaced with duplicates before one's original capacities for bodily experience had ceased to be? We have some general ideas as to which parts of the brain are involved in the production of different sorts of experience, but there is a great deal still to discover about such matters.

But while it would be useful to know more about how our brains manage to do what they do, the viability of the C-theory does not depend on it. If it were to turn out that our experiential powers are entirely non-modular, the

---

[20] I shall be returning to this topic in §10.7, where the focus will be on deviant triggers which *transform* (rather than relocate) the material bases of powers.

C-theory would still have a useful role to play: at the very least it would provide us with an account of what makes distinct temporal phases of such powers consubjective.[21] The fact that we cannot specify precisely what the material bases of our experiential capacities are does not mean these bases are lacking. Nor does it mean that we cannot make some plausible (if modest) assumptions concerning them. Even if we individuate our own experiential capacities in a fairly fine-grained way—for example a different capacity for each type of colour—it seems likely that such capacities will be grounded in thousands if not millions (or more) of individual neurons. Given this, it may well be that only some of the neurons associated with a given power will actively contribute to the production of experience at any one time. In a similar vein, in the case of a pair DPC_S-related powers, it is likely that when the powers are active simultaneously different neural configurations will be in play than when they are active independently (or singly). Is this an obstacle to holding that *just one* power is involved in such cases? Not in the least. Slight variations in the active regions of power-bases is the norm for the dispositional properties of complex interconnected systems. My computer has the capacity to play DVDs; suppose I play a particular DVD several times in succession; will precisely the same patterns of electrons flow through precisely the same micro-circuitry on each occasion? It seems unlikely: the pattern of activation will depend on which other programs my computer is running at the same time and which other tasks it is performing. Simpler devices display similar characteristics. Suppose I trigger my torch's capacity to generate light five times in quick succession (by turning it on and off); on each occasion the flow of current from the battery causes atoms in the bulb's filament to emit photons. The same atoms on each occasion? It seems unlikely. Does this variation in active power-base mean that it is wrong to say my torch has *a* capacity to generate light? Of course not. Similar considerations apply to experiential powers and their neural underpinnings.

Our failure to solve the matter–consciousness conundrum has a further and more general consequence: we are not yet in a position to know how similar to our own brains a physical system would have to be to possess experiential powers. Different stances on the matter–consciousness relationship point in different directions. Suppose David Chalmers' preferred form of property-dualism is true. On this view, experiences are non-physical particulars, and the production of experiences by material systems is governed by contingent phenomeno-physical laws. These laws are such that 'given any [physical] system that has conscious experiences, then any system that has the same fine-grained functional organization will have qualitatively identical experiences' (Chalmers 1996: 248). If Chalmers is right, experiential powers are capacities to produce

---

[21] And it can do the same for any power-aspects (or sub-capacities) which can be distinguished amid these massively multi-track capacities.

immaterial particulars that have no location in physical space, and a system's physical constitution is irrelevant to its ability to possess these capacities—all that matters is causal organization. Hence objects very unlike our brains indeed might easily be able to generate experiences. The situation would be different if other views about the matter–consciousness relationship were closer to the truth. Suppose, for example, that phenomenal properties are intrinsic *material* properties that are not recognized by current physics—variants of this doctrine have been proposed by Russell (1927), Maxwell (1978), Lockwood (1989), Strawson (1994), Unger (1999). To say that a brain has the capacity to 'produce' or 'generate' experience now means that parts of a brain can *become* conscious by acquiring physical states whose intrinsic nature is experiential. If this sort of view is right, consciousness is in no way a separate phenomenon existing over and above material objects or systems. Moreover, it may well be that objects have to be fairly similar to our brains in order to be able to possess experience-producing powers. And of course there may be other options, other pictures. But yet again, the outcome of these debates is irrelevant to the viability of the C-theory. We do not need to know how our brains manage to do what they do in order to know the conditions under which experiences and experiential capacities belong to the same self or subject. Such capacities are consubjective if and only if they are C-related.

Three modes of overlap

So much by way of an introduction to the general issue of power-individuation— we shall be returning to the topic at several points. Before moving on, a brief word on three ways in which experiential powers (or C-systems) may be able to *overlap*. Whether these different putative modes of overlap are in fact possible is debateable, but since each—in a different way—threatens to blur the boundaries between C-systems (and hence subjects), they are by no means insignificant. The first we have already encountered:

(O1) Suppose it is possible for a state of consciousness at a given time to consist of three parts or regions, e_1, e_2, and e_3, where e_1 and e_2 are co-conscious, e_2 and e_3 are co-conscious, but e_1 and e_3 are *not* co-conscious. In effect, e_1–e_3 consists of two partially overlapping total experiences. If total experiences can overlap in this way, there is no obvious reason why streams of consciousness could not do likewise. If this is possible, what should we say about the experiential powers which generate these overlapping streams? Do they belong to one subject or two? Can *subjects* partially overlap?

As I noted at the end of §4.3, whether or not C-systems (and hence possibly subjects) can overlap in this manner depends on whether total experiences can overlap. If it could be shown that the relationship of synchronic co-consciousness were transitive, then in the envisaged case where e_1 is co-conscious with e_2, and e_2 is co-conscious with e_3, then necessarily e_1 and e_3 would also be co-conscious. I will be considering this sort of situation in more detail in §8.6, where I will argue (tentatively) that synchronic co-consciousness *is* transitive, and hence that total experiences cannot (partially) overlap. Moving on to a rather different case:

(O2) Suppose it is possible for a single power P to produce at a single time *two* numerically distinct (and qualitatively identical) token experiences E_1 and E_2. What makes P one power, rather than two, is the fact that one and the same physical system (or power-base) is causally responsible for the production of both E_1 and E_2. If a single power can behave like this, there is no obvious reason why an entire C-system could not do likewise. But if C-systems *can* behave like this, we are confronted with a peculiar situation: at the experiential level we have what seems to be *two* subjects, but at the level of experiential capacities we have what seems to be just *one* subject. Can the experiential powers of two subjects *perfectly coincide* (or completely overlap) in this fashion?

I have been assuming thus far that the experiential outputs of particular powers are unified, either in the form of a single experience (all of whose parts are fully co-conscious), or several experiences all joined by co-consciousness. Call powers of this sort *uni-streamal*. (O2) poses the question of whether uni-streamality is a necessary feature: could there be *pluri-streamal* powers that are able to produce multiple outputs, where each output is a distinct state or phase or stream of consciousness in its own right? It is by no means obvious that such powers are possible. There could easily be (and probably are) powers with *entangled* physical bases, that is powers whose bases are such that they are difficult—or even impossible—to separate. Nomologically inseparable powers such as these are nonetheless distinct: they are composed of different matter, and have different (even if entangled) spatial locations. What we are now being asked to consider is whether a *single* physical power-base could have multiple experiential effects at a given time.[22] But while this may seem unlikely, given my policy of not taking a stand on the matter—consciousness relationship, I am not in a position to rule this possibility out. If pluri-streamal systems of this sort were to exist, what should we make of them? One option would be to modify the 'one stream of experience, one subject of experience' rule and hold that in such circumstances there is but one subject involved. But there is another and better option. For such cases we can modify our criterion for individuating token experiential powers. I suggested earlier that if two token experiential powers existing at the same time are of the same type, to be distinct they must have different power-bases, they

---

[22] For a given sort of triggering event, is a pluri-streamal power restricted to producing two (or more) tokens of just *one* type of experience, or could it produce tokens of two (or more) distinct types of experience? Although the latter may seem to conflict with the principle of 'same cause, same effect', given the right sort of nomological indeterminacy it may be that cases of this sort are possible. But to simplify I will work on the assumption that pluri-streamal powers, if they exist, produce distinct tokens of just one type of output on any given occasion. The proposed interpretation of this simpler case easily extends to the more complex variant.

must be grounded in different physical things (or different parts or aspects of the same physical thing). It is a simple enough modification to allow powers which cannot be distinguished in any other way to be distinct by virtue of being able to produce numerically distinct experiential *effects*. Accordingly, we can say that powers P_1 and P_2 can be numerically distinct, even if they have precisely the same physical basis, are triggered in the same circumstances, and can produce the same types of experience when triggered, provided they can produce numerically distinct token experiences. I will be defending the intelligibility of this approach in §11.4. There is one further mode of overlap that I want to consider:

(O3) We have seen that collections of probabilistic powers could belong to single C-systems in a quite unambiguous fashion. But consider a variant: suppose a single probabilistic power is able to produce at any one time only *one* token experience, but this token can occur in either of two streams of consciousness generated by (what we would otherwise take to be) distinct C-systems. To illustrate, suppose that whenever power P* is triggered there is a 30 per cent chance that the experiences it produces will be co-conscious with any experiences being produced by C-system S_1, and a 70 per cent chance that the resulting experiences will be co-conscious with any experiences being produced by C-system S_2. Given this, P* looks to be DPC$_S$-related to both S_1 and S_2; on the assumption that DPC$_S$-relatedness makes for consubjectivity this renders all the powers in each of S_1 and S_2 consubjective—in effect, they are just one C-system. But if the connection via P* is the only DPC-relation linking S_1 and S_2, the notion that they are one not two is very plausible (suppose that S_1 and S_2 are otherwise indistinguishable from your C-system and mine).

Potentially a rather worrying result to be sure, but it should be noted that other approaches to personal identity are confronted with analogous puzzles. The fact that Siamese twins can share vital organs makes life difficult for animalists, and since certain cases of dissociated identity disorder (a.k.a. multiple personality syndrome) can be construed in terms of two (or more) psychological subjects sharing some of the same psychological states, psychological theorists are confronted with an analogous difficulty. And of course it is easy to imagine cases which are even more problematic for animalists and P-theorists.

As well as presenting an intriguing puzzle, (O3) usefully brings into clear relief a further assumption that has been in play. I have spent a good deal of time discussing collections of powers that have the ability to produce co-conscious experiences. Depending on their complexity and composition, the sorts of collections we have been concerned with may well be able to produce a wide variety of experiential states at any given time t, depending on which stimuli are present at that time, but in another respect they are quite limited: whatever experiences such a collection produces at t, these experiences are all mutually co-conscious, and so form part of a *single* unified stream of consciousness. Call powers of this sort *non promiscuous*. In contrast, *promiscuous* powers—powers such as P* above—are not so restricted: they belong to collections of powers which have the ability to produce two (or more) distinct streams of consciousness at the same time. Extending our new terminology, let us say that when a promiscuous power has the ability to produce experiences that are co-conscious with those produced by another power, then the two are *promiscuously DPC$_S$-related*, or ^{P}DPC$_S$-related, irrespective of whether the second power itself is promiscuous or not. By way of an example, let us start by supposing that P_1 and P_2 are experiential powers that are not themselves S-related at t (i.e. they are neither DPC$_S$- nor IPC$_S$-related to one another at that time). Now consider two alternative scenarios: (i) P_1 and P_2 are otherwise unchanged, but each is now DPC$_S$-related to a third power P at t, (ii) P_1 and P_2 are otherwise unchanged, but each is now ^{P}DPC$_S$-related to a third power P* at t. What is the difference between these two scenarios? In (i), if all three powers are active simultaneously then the experiences they produce are all mutually co-conscious; whereas in (ii), if P_1 and P_2 are both active at t then the experiences they produce are *not* co-conscious, and if P* is also active at t, then it will produce an experience that is co-conscious with the experience produced by P_1 *or* the experience produced by P_2, but *not both*. (Now that we have recognized this new mode of connectedness, the terms in which the O3 scenario outlined is formulated are misleading: P* is *not* DPC$_S$-related to the powers in S_1 and S_2, it is ^{P}DPC$_S$-related to them.)

Returning to the question of interpretation, what can we say about the ownership of promiscuous powers? Are ^{P}DPC$_S$-related powers consubjective? Adopting the purist stance that power-systems that are connected by just one ^{P}DPC$_S$-related power should be regarded as a single C-system is implausible, at least when the C-systems involved are of some complexity. A better (more plausible) response is as follows. First, we continue to define the membership of C-systems (and hence S-relatedness) solely in terms of non-promiscuous powers, as has (tacitly) been done so far. Second, we further stipulate that promiscuous powers *can* belong to particular C-systems, but only during those times when they are active and producing experiences that are co-conscious with experiences produced by those C-systems. When non-active, promiscuous powers are of indeterminate ownership—at such times they do not belong to *any* subject. Applying this to the O3 scenario, P* belongs to S_1 during those periods when it is producing experiences that are co-conscious with experiences produced by S_1's standard complement of (non-promiscuous) powers, and similarly for S_2; when P* is dormant is belongs to neither S_1 nor S_2. The idea that the ownership of an experiential power could fluctuate in this manner can certainly seem strange, but then the sort of power we are concerned with here is itself strange, at least in comparison to the sort we possess. We will see that another response to promiscuous powers is available when further modes of discriminating between powers on the basis of their phenomenal effects are distinguished in Chapter 9.

4.6. PROJECTION AND PRODUCTION

So much by way of introduction to the C-theory. There is more to say about experiential powers, and many issues have yet to be discussed at all. But as we shall see, the various extensions and elaborations that are to come will not affect the fundamentals, and so will do nothing to diminish the distinctive character of the C-theory. Before tackling these other issues I want to take stock and address a worry.

My main aim in this chapter has been to provide a solution to the bridge-problem. The C-theory provides a solution to this problem but it also introduces a change in focus—actual experience has been joined on stage by potentialities for experience—and this change may seem problematic. We saw at the outset that there are powerful grounds for thinking that so far as our own contin-ued existence is concerned, experiential unity and continuity are of overriding importance. Recall the various imaginary cases in which streams of consciousness become detached from their subjects' bodies or psychologies, and in doing so take their subjects with them, so to speak. The claim that streams and their subjects are inseparable is very plausible indeed. But these thought experiments were con-ducted using actual streams of consciousness, not uninterrupted nomologically grounded potentialities for consciousness, of the sort we have been concerned with latterly. Given the way it defines our persistence conditions—no mention is made of bodily or causal continuities—the C-theory is compatible with our being able to leave our bodies and psychologies behind, but a question remains: can C-systems play the same role in our thinking about our persistence as actual streams of consciousness? The issue is of some significance, for someone might object:

Our ordinary thinking about our own persistence is certainly influenced by the character of our experience: it is hard seriously to doubt that a single self persists throughout the length of an uninterrupted stream of consciousness. Our persistence over comparatively short intervals of time thus seems as solid and secure as anyone might wish it to be. But many of us are inclined to suppose that our persistence over much longer periods of time—many years as opposed to a few hours, minutes or seconds—is equally solid and secure. This assumption is unwarranted. For as a moment's reflection reveals, the distinctive unity and continuity we find within our experience cannot possibly be projected beyond the confines of a single stream of consciousness.[23]

---

[23] Sidelle (2002: 280–1) puts the point thus: 'I think we mistakenly move from facts about differences in consciousness at a time to consequences about differences in consciousness through time. We focus on our present state, its real "uniqueness" and "singularity" (such that not even someone physically identical to me right now has *this* consciousness), and illegitimately extend this through time, supposing that just as "this consciousness" can only have one referent when we are thinking about the present, so it can only have one referent when we are thinking about

It is certainly true that in explaining how we persist through periods of unconsciousness the C-theory appeals to something other than actual streams of consciousness; the issue is whether this additional something can sustain us in existence in as secure and unambiguous a fashion as our actual streams. So far as I can see, there is no room for doubt on this score.

In solving the bridge-problem the C-theory appeals to what (metaphorically speaking) lies *immediately beneath* our actual streams of consciousness: those systems of experiential capacities which are causally responsible for these streams. Further, in assigning such capacities to subjects it relies solely on the co-consciousness relationship—precisely the same relationship which is responsible for the distinctive unity we find in our streams of consciousness, both at a time and from moment to moment. As we have seen, our streams of consciousness are unified by co-consciousness in its synchronic and diachronic forms, and according to the C-theory the distinguishing mark of consubjective clusters of powers is their ability to produce experiences that are co-conscious, synchronically and diachronically. So there *is* a sense in which the distinctive unity and continuity we find within our streams can extend beyond their confines. When experiential powers are dormant they are not producing any experiences, but some such powers *have the ability* to produce unified streams of consciousness—and it is these powers, and these alone, which are consubjective.

In a less abstract vein, suppose my most recent stream of experience has just come to an end; I have fallen into a dreamless sleep that will last for half an hour. Simplifying only a little, according to the C-theory what keeps me in existence after my loss of consciousness is the fact that the system of experiential capacities that was causally responsible for my waking experience continues to exist. The successive temporal phases of this system have the ability to produce diachronically co-conscious experiences, and it is this which renders the successive phases of the system consubjective, both with one another, and the phases of the C-system responsible for the experiences I had just before I lost consciousness. So long as this C-related power-system persists, I persist; the experiential powers which belong to this system clearly and unambiguously belong to me, so too do the experiences this system produces.

In a still less abstract vein, consider a variant of the thought experiment introduced at the end of Chapter 1. Rather than trying to imagine yourself moving in such a way as to leave your stream of consciousness behind, try to imagine moving in such a way that *you* go one way and your *C-system* goes another. To start with, let us suppose you travel back and forth in time (or between universes, or wherever) and you remain conscious throughout. Since the experiential powers responsible for your continuing stream of consciousness

consciousness extended through time. But this consciousness can be multiply extended into the future, and none of them will be any more "this consciousness" than any of the others.' I will be taking issue with Sidelle's final claim when I come to deal with fission and fusion in Chapter 12.

will be C-related to the powers you started with—the phenomenal continuity of your experience and the definition of C-relatedness guarantees this—then evidently you have failed to leave your C-system behind. Since a C-system *just is* a C-related collection of experiential powers, *just one* C-system has been involved throughout, the same C-system that has been responsible for everything you have experienced during the period in question. Now suppose you lose consciousness before your travels begin. Unless we further suppose that you nonetheless retain a capacity to have experiences (in some shape or form) it is no longer clear that you continue to exist, so let us make this assumption. Can we really make sense of the hypothesis that your current C-system is anything other than your original C-system? It is not easy, to say the least. If we suppose you and your C-system have gone their separate ways we are, in effect, contemplating a situation which involves *two* C-systems, one of which is C-related to the capacities responsible for the experiences you had just prior to losing consciousness (this is the C-system you have supposedly escaped from), the other of which is *not* C-related to those capacities (this is the system responsible for your current experiential potential). Now recall what C-relatedness brings: each successive phase of a C-related system has the capacity to produce experience that is diachronically co-conscious with its predecessor. Bearing this in mind, is the C-system that is not C-related to your original capacities a remotely plausible candidate for being you, given the existence of a system which *is* C-related to your original capacities? The latter is connected to your original C-system by an uninterrupted series of stages, the neighbouring members of which have the capacity to produce phenomenally continuous experience. The former is not so connected (if it were, it would be C-related to your original system, but by hypothesis it is not). In the light of this, isn't it perfectly clear that wherever *you* go—irrespective of how fast or far you travel—you cannot fail to take your C-system with you?[24]

So from the vantage point of the C-theory we do indeed begin with a particular way of thinking about our existence and persistence that is rooted in the distinctive unity and individuality characteristic of our experience at a particular moment. This unity and individuality is then projected through time, in the first instance over short intervals, and then—thanks to overlapping chains of diachronic co-consciousness, actual and potential—over far longer periods. However, as I hope is now reasonably clear, there is nothing in the least illegitimate or indiscriminate about this projection.

Granting a leading role to experiential capacities may not undermine the power or appeal of the experience-based approach, but it does shed fresh light on how we should think of ourselves. All would agree that whatever else selves or subjects are, they are *things which can have experiences*. But what does having an experience involve? As we saw in Chapter 2, according to one influential

---

[24] Could you leave your C-system behind by losing all your *capacities* for experience whilst remaining fully conscious? I will be considering this possibility (if it is such) in §8.4.

tradition selves are loci of apprehension, they are things which sense or apprehend the contents of their consciousness. I went on to argue that to the extent that this conception is based on the naïve perceptual model of consciousness, there is no reason to accept it. The C-theory moves us still further away from the conception of the self as a centre of pure apprehension. If we view ourselves as being ultimately constituted from clusters of experiential powers, we are not beings which passively witness the contents of our experiences, we are more akin to things which *make* or *generate* experiences: according to the C-theory in its ontological guise, we are enduring *potentialities* for experience. Although this view may be somewhat counterintuitive, this should not be counted against it. For as we also saw in Chapter 2, the character of our experience is such that it is not surprising that we find the bare locus conception appealing, even if it is in fact false.[25]

I began by pressing the merits of a phenomenalist approach to the self. I suggested that an account of our existence and persistence conditions rooted in purely phenomenal unity and continuity would be more compelling, more believable, than any account that is not. The C-theory fits the bill, but there is a further respect in which it is phenomenalist. It is the product of a phenomenalist *approach*, but it can also be construed as a phenomenalist account of what a self *is*. Whereas Mill maintained that material things were nothing more (or less) than enduring potentials for experience, I am suggesting that this is what we ourselves are. Phenomenalism of this variety is, I would suggest, less obviously objectionable than phenomenalism about material things.[26]

[25] This construal is not open to those who favour the direct realist view of perceptual experience. Experiential powers exist in the framework of direct realism, but (at least in the perceptual case) they will be viewed as *capacities to apprehend objects*, rather than capacities for the production of sensory experience. So far as I can see, the C-theory is compatible with both ways of thinking.

[26] Of course Mill generally talked in terms of 'possibilities for sensation', rather than 'potentials'. Interestingly, although Mill himself appealed to memory to secure the consubjectivity of distinct streams, in the Lockean manner, he sometimes came close to phenomenalism about the subjects: in *The Examination of Sir William Hamilton's Philosophy* he states that mind is 'nothing but the series of our sensations . . . as they actually occur, with the addition of infinite possibilities of feeling required for their actual realization conditions which may or may not take place'. Quoted in Hamilton (1998: 161), who usefully puts Mill's views on personal identity into context.

5
Alternatives

5.1. THE SELF IN EXPERIENCE

With the C-theory we have a solution to the bridge-problem and the beginnings of what looks to be a promising account of the self's existence and persistence conditions. But of course there are other experiential approaches, and before developing the C-theory any further it will be useful to consider some of these. So doing will not only bring out the advantages of the C-theory, it will shed further light on just what sort of account is being offered. I noted in §4.1 that the notion that selves are essentially subjects of experience can be understood in at least two different ways. According to the ECS conception, a self is a being that is *essentially* conscious, and so is always experiencing something at each moment of its existence. Opposed to this is PCS conception, the doctrine that a self is a *potentially* conscious being, and so capable of existing in both conscious and unconscious modes. I suggested that the PCS conception better corresponds with most people's common sense understanding of the kind of thing they are, and this observation led me in the direction of the C-theory. This summary dismissal did less than full justice to the ECS conception, which some philosophers at least have found very compelling. Time for a closer look.

We can start with a question: 'Are selves constituents of their conscious states?' To many contemporary ears this question will probably sound quite bizarre, but a number of ECS theorists have answered it in the affirmative. Of course, there are also ECS theorists who answer in the negative, and others who believe that *some* of the self is manifest in experience. Together these different responses give us three variants of the ECS conception:

- *Externalism:* no part or aspect of selves are to be found in their conscious states.
- *Internalism:* selves in their entirety are constituents of their conscious states.
- *Partial Internalism:* selves are partially present in their experience, but not wholly.

Traditional substance dualism can be construed as a form of Partial Inter-nalism. If selves are immaterial substances, and if experiences are *modes* of these substances—if they are akin to the colours inhering in stained glass, for example—then, arguably, something of ourselves is revealed in each of our experiences. What is revealed is *one of the ways a conscious substance can be*, one of its 'modes of being', as one might say. Since for a typical subject there will usually be many modes of being that are not revealed in any conscious episode, the self is only partially on view at any one time. The traditional Pure Ego theory is a form of Externalism. So too is the minimal form of the Ego theory, the 'bare locus view'—the doctrine that the self is a centre of pure apprehension or receptivity—that we looked at in §2.3 and §2.4. As we saw, this version of the ECS conception is problematic, and I will say no more about it here. I want instead to focus instead on some of the varieties of Internalism.

In the *Treatise* Hume opens his discussion of personal identity by announcing that 'There are some philosophers, who imagine that we are every moment intimately conscious of what we call our *self*; that we feel its existence and its continuance in existence', but famously went on to deny that *he* was aware of any such thing in his own experience, and many have subsequently agreed: all they find are particular experiences, of continually varying character. Internalists can respond to Hume along these lines: 'Scepticism with regard to the self is simply not an option: we cannot plausibly doubt that we are conscious subjects, and this is because we are aware of ourselves as such, we find our*selves* in our experience'. Here is James explaining why the doctrine can seem plausible:

If the stream as a whole is identified with the Self far more than any outward thing, *a certain portion of the stream abstracted from the rest* is so identified in an altogether peculiar degree, and is felt by all men as a sort of innermost centre within the circle, of sanctuary within the citadel, constituted by the subjective life as a whole. Compared with this element of the stream, the other parts, even of the subjective life, seem transient external possessions, of which each in turn can be disowned, whilst that which disowns them remains . . . . For this central part of the Self is felt. It may be all that Transcendentalists say it is, and all that Empiricists say it is into the bargain, but it is at any rate no *mere 'ens rationis'*, cognized only in an intellectual way, and no *mere* summation of memories or *mere* sound of a word in our ears. It is something with which we also have direct sensible acquaintance, and which is as fully present at any moment of consciousness in which it *is* present, as in a whole lifetime of such moments. (James 1952: 192–3)

In more recent times the baton has been picked up and carried forth by Strawson:

Most philosophers use the term 'subject of experience' . . . in such a way that a subject of experience can be said to exist in the absence of any experience . . . they can no longer hear the extreme naturalness of the other use, according to which there is no *subject of experience* if there is no *experience* . . . . I hope those who find this natural use of 'subject of experience' strained can accustom themselves to it. It is only a matter of terminology after all, and it is only this indubitably real phenomenon—the subject of experience considered as something that is alive and present in consciousness at any given moment of consciousness and that cannot be said to exist at all when there is no experience or consciousness—that concerns me here. (Strawson 1999a: 130)

I expect many of us have little difficulty in appreciating at least part of what these writers are saying. James is surely right in claiming that we are not naturally inclined to regard all parts of our typical streams of consciousness as being equally essential to our continued existence. We can easily imagine losing all our outer senses and continuing to exist as a thinking feeling subject. We can imagine losing all our bodily feeling (at least from the neck down) and continuing to exist, provided that we continue to think conscious thoughts and have emotional feelings. Hence anyone who agrees with James that phenomenologically speaking, conscious thoughts are a particular species of bodily sensation may well be able to make sense of his otherwise bizarre-sounding claim that *'the "Self of selves", when carefully examined, is found to consist mainly of the collection of these peculiar motions in the head or between the head and throat'* (1959: 194). Likewise, I expect most of us will agree with Strawson when he says that we often enjoy what he calls 'Self-experience' or a 'sense of the self', which he characterizes as 'the sense that people have of themselves as being, specifically, a mental presence; a mental someone; a single mental thing that is a conscious subject of experience' (1997: 407). I have something approaching Self-experience in Strawson's sense whenever I focus on my ongoing mental activities—my conscious thoughts, my conscious striving to attend to my conscious thinking—and think to myself 'Whatever else I may be, I am at least the kind of thing that can do *this* sort of thing!'

Let us agree that certain kinds of experience, at least on some occasions, do strike us as being more intimately connected with ourselves than other kinds. Call these *central experiences*. Drawing attention to the existence of this sort of experience is one thing, but how plausible is it to follow the Internalist in supposing that we are ourselves *identical* with our central experiences? Let us consider the options. There are six main contenders for literally 'self-constituting' forms of experience, each giving rise to a different identity claim and a different form of Internalism:

1 We are identical with our conscious thinking.
2 We are identical with our bodily experience, our 'somatic sense-field'.
3 We are identical with our background experiences: those parts of our overall states of consciousness to which we are not paying any sort of attention.
4 We are identical with our fringe experiences.
5 We are identical with our phenomenal space.
6 We are identical with those stretches of our streams of consciousness which include Self-experience.

We can start by briefly considering (1), a variety of Internalism with which James occasionally had some sympathy. Even if we were to agree that we can only exist when experiencing something, do we always need to be engaged in conscious thought in order to be conscious at all? True, it is notoriously difficult deliberately to bring a halt to one's inner soliloquy, but aren't there occasions when it comes to a halt of its own accord, even if only briefly?[1] Even if this were

---

[1] As James himself recognizes in another context: 'Most people probably fall several times a day into a fit of something like this: The eyes are fixed on vacancy, the sounds of the world melt into

not the case, is it not perfectly conceivable that we might stop thinking without losing consciousness altogether? Given that we would continue to have normal sensory and emotional experiences during such lapses, the claim that we would cease to exist, *qua* conscious subjects, is hard to take seriously.

While most of the other varieties of Internalism are vulnerable to this same simple objection, there are complications and additional difficulties. Let us start by looking at (2), (3), and (4), which in different ways relegate the self to the margins of consciousness.

Phenomenal hinterlands

The equating of our selves with our bodily experiences has certain undeniable advantages over (1), and several philosophers have been drawn to the doctrine. In large part this is due to the fact that Hume's rejection of Internalism rested in large part on the mutability of our experience:

> If any impression gives rise to the idea of self, that impression must continue invariably the same, thro' the whole course of our lives; since self is suppos'd to exist after that manner. But there is no impression constant and invariable. Pain and pleasure, grief and joy, passions and sensations succeed each other, and never all exist at the same time. It cannot therefore be from any of these impressions, or from any other, that the idea of self is deriv'd; and consequently there is no such idea. (Hume 1978: 251–2)

But is it really the case that *all* forms of our experience are *always* undergoing rapid change and replacement? This may often be true of conscious thought, or of visual and auditory experience, but isn't our bodily experience comparatively stable? Irrespective of whether we are paying attention to it or not, our bodily feelings—the constituents of the somatic sense-field—are a constant background presence in our consciousness. We are continually aware, even if only passively, not only that we have a body, but that our body is disposed in a particular way—that we are standing or sitting, stationary or on the move, that our limbs are disposed in a particular way. And of course, the fact that our bodily feelings are rarely attended to may explain why Hume failed to notice them.[2] The somatic version of Internalism has a further advantage. From a naïve phenomenological standpoint at any

---

confused unity, the attention is dispersed so that the whole body is felt, as it were, at once and the foreground of consciousness is filled, if by anything, by a sort of solemn sense of surrender to the empty passing of time . . . . This curious state of inhibition can for a few moments be produced at will by fixing the eyes on vacancy. Some persons can voluntarily "think of nothing"' (James 1959: 261).

[2] It was considerations such as these which led Broad to this conclusion: 'the most plausible form of this theory [Internalism] would be to identify the Central Event [and so the self] at any moment with a mass of bodily feeling. The longitudinal unity of a self through a period of time would then depend on the fact that there is a mass of bodily feeling which goes on continuously throughout this period and varies in quality not at all or very slowly' (1926: 566). See also (Broad 1923: 521–2). It should be added that Broad did not—in the end—commit himself to the somatic theory: he took the view that empirical considerations would (one day) decide the issue between

rate, the idea that we ourselves do not extend beyond the confines of the somatic sense-field has some plausibility: the objects of visual and auditory perception do not seem to be parts of ourselves, whereas our various bodily feelings clearly do.

These considerations certainly suggest Hume was wrong to be as quite as dismissive as he was of Internalism, but they fall short of establishing the truth of Internalism. Even if few of us ever actually enjoy a moment of consciousness that is entirely free of bodily experience, isn't it conceivable that we might? Imagine being administered a generalized local anaesthetic which completely obliterates all bodily experience but leaves auditory and visual experience, along with the capacity for thought, untouched. It seems absurd to suppose that one could cease to exist, *qua* conscious subject, while continuing to see, hear, and think. If the somatic sense-field could shrink to zero without our losing consciousness, we clearly cannot *be* our somatic sense-fields.

Appreciative of the force of this objection, but attracted to the notion that we are directly aware of ourselves in our ordinary experience, Evans (1970) proposes that we identify ourselves with what he calls 'unprojected consciousness', by which he means those regions of our overall state of consciousness to which we are not paying attention. This view—(3) in the list above—certainly looks more plausible than (1) or (2). Irrespective of what kind of experience we are having at any time, we generally are paying attention to only part of it, and this would presumably remain the case even if all our bodily experience were eliminated, or we ceased to engage in conscious thought. But the main advantage of the account lies elsewhere. Ryle held that anyone who tries to catch themselves in their own experience is bound to realize that 'he has failed to catch more than the flying coat-tails of that which he was pursuing. His quarry was the hunter' (Ryle 1949: 198). Evans can explain the apparent elusiveness of the self; to be more precise, he has an explanation of why the self in its guise as *subject* of experience cannot ever also and simultaneously be an *object* of consciousness. For Evans the objects of *experience* are the objects of *attention*, and consequently, if selves are identical with unprojected consciousness they cannot possibly be experienced as objects. If we attempt to turn our attention onto our selves we will simply end up paying attention to a region of our experience that we were previously ignoring, and in so doing we will cease to attend to what we were previously attending to; a new region of unprojected consciousness will thus be opened up, and the self will immediately slip into it, so evading our gaze. Evans summarizes the merits of his account thus:

The theory overcomes the paradox that the self, though discoverable in experience, is never an object of experience, and in the process removes the main prop holding up

it and the Ego theory. Other advocates of the somatic field theory include Gallie (1936–7) and Jones (1949). For further discussion see Evans (1970: ch. 5) and Shoemaker (1964: ch. 3, §8). Bermúdez (1998, chs 5 and 6) defends the claim that bodily (and visual perceptual) experience provides us with a non-conceptual form of self-consciousness; he further argues (plausibly) that these forms of self-consciousness are available to creatures that are less cognitively sophisticated than ourselves.

The Pure Ego Theory of the Self. The essence of the matter is, on my view, that the self is experiential (i.e. is composed of elements of consciousness), but is never known as an object of experience. This is one of the factors that accounts for the view that the self lies behind its experiences. It also explains why we have such a lively sense of the *presence* of the self, and why we are so nonplussed by denials of the self's existence. (Evans 1970: 150)

There could well be an important insight here. I suggested in §2.4 that part of the appeal of the awareness-content model, and hence the bare locus (or Pure Ego) conception of the self, might in part lie in the phenomenology of attention, and Evans supplies a further reason for thinking this might be so. If we have the sense—as we often do—that there is something more to our conscious selves than the contents of our consciousness, it may (in part) be because we are failing to appreciate the presence within our overall states of consciousness of what Evans calls unprojected experience. And it may be that the (in principle) impossibility of turning our attentive gaze onto this type of experience explains (in part) why so many have found the self peculiarly elusive.

But despite these merits, Evans' account is a highly implausible account of what the self is. Evans argues at some length (1970: ch. 3) that all our normal states of consciousness are divided by attention into a 'foreground' and a 'background', even states which we might normally think of as being attention-free, such as extreme forms of reverie, or 'pure sensuous consciousness'—the sort of experience one has lying on a beach doing nothing but enjoying the sun's warmth pressing down on one's skin. He may be right about this—about the character of our ordinary modes of consciousness—but I can see no reason to suppose all *possible* forms of consciousness are similarly divided. It certainly seems conceivable that a state of consciousness could be entirely attention-free—all background, as it were—and certain abnormal states may have this character: attaining such a consciousness is a goal of many meditative traditions, and many claim to have achieved this goal (see Stace 1960; Forman 1990).

Now, there is a sense in which a pure background state is 'selfless': from a subjective perspective there no longer seems to be a division between 'experiencing self' and 'objects experienced'. This much can be granted, but does it follow that just because an experience *seems* to lack a subject that it really *does* lack a subject? More to the point, I suspect few of us would regard entering such a state as existence-threatening, but if Evans were right we should! The same point can be made from the other direction. If we are identical with unprojected consciousness we should not be able to make sense of the possibility of our existing while enjoying only *projected* consciousness. But it is easy to envisage continuing to exist with a consciousness of this type. Just imagine your total state of consciousness gradually contracting down to whatever it is that you are currently focusing your attention on—for example your visual experience of the wall opposite. All through the process you ensure that your attention remains tightly focused on the same location, never letting up for a moment.

By the end of the process your consciousness may be much diminished but it is *all foreground*, it consists of nothing but *projected* experience. The notion that this process would be fatal, that you would ceases to exist, *qua* experiencing subject when the last element of unprojected experience fades from view, is surely absurd.

This last consideration is also fatal to Internalism in its version (4) guise, the claim that we are identical with our fringe experience. This account has some of the same merits as Evans'. As I noted in §2.4, fringe experience is often not explicitly noticed, yet it is a constant presence in our ordinary experience, and it may well contribute to the appeal of the naïve perceptual model of consciousness. Unlike unprojected experience, fringe experience is a possible object of attention, but by virtue of its non-sensory character it has some of that elusive character that is often attributed to the experiencing self.[3] Nonetheless, the notion that we *are* fringe experience is undermined by the ease with which we can envisage surviving the loss of our fringe experience. This is not easy to imagine clearly—fringe experience is such a ubiquitous and important part of our ordinary experience that it is difficult to imagine clearly what it would be like to have (say) just ordinary perceptual experience and conscious thought without the customary surrounding or pervading fringe. But this does not mean a fringe-free consciousness is impossible, and since the loss of the fringe would be eminently survivable—especially if experience of other kinds continued on—the notion that the self *is* the fringe looks decidedly implausible.

Self as space

What of our fifth option, the notion that selves are identical with phenomenal spaces? Stephen Priest has suggested that in spite of their significant doctrinal differences, Husserl, Sartre, and Heidegger were each committed to the idea that our experiences occur within some kind of spatial arena, a 'zone of awareness' (2000: 152). For the later Husserl this zone was the 'transcendental field of subjectivity'. For the early Sartre it was the domain of 'absolute interiority', also called an 'inside without an outside'; by the time of *Being and Nothingness* a few years later it had become 'the *nothingness*' of being-for-itself. In the non-psychologistic vocabulary of Heidegger's *Being and Time*, where talk of interiority and subjectivity is shunned, it is the *Lichtung* or clearing where the world *worlds* and being is disclosed to being. Of course, given the spatial character of our experience—a character which, as we saw in §2.2, can be characterized in more prosaic terms than these—it is scarcely surprising to find such a convergence of doctrine among phenomenologically inclined philosophers. Once the existence

---

[3] The idea that experience of this kind plays an important role in our 'sense of self' is developed in some detail, and considerable plausibility, in Damasio (2000: Part II).

of such spaces is recognized, a question naturally arises: what is the relationship between these experiential spaces and ourselves? Might it not be that each of us is *identical* with the phenomenal space within which our experiences occur? Priest finds himself drawn to just this conclusion:

Subjective space has phenomenological properties. It is phenomenologically indistinguishable from physical space as perceptually presented to oneself at its centre: unbounded, in the sense that travel seems in principle possible for ever away from its centre.

   Subjective space is Parmenidean: it is like the inside of a *sphere* with one's own being as its interior. Thoughts and experiences, including experiences of physical objects, arise and subside within it. It is the zone where being and phenomenological content coincide . . . .

   It is necessary and sufficient for my existence. It is not physical. I am or am directly acquainted with its interiority. It is hard to see how it could admit of natural generation or destruction. I conjecture that subjective space is the soul. (Priest 2000: 153)

Although Priest does not expand on this further, his proposal is suggestive and in some ways appealing. Given that we each have direct introspective access only to our own conscious states, it can seem that we live in entirely different worlds, experientially speaking. William James put it thus: 'My thought belong with my other thoughts, and your thought with your other thoughts . . . . No thought even comes into direct *sight* of a thought in another personal consciousness . . . . The breaches between such thoughts are the most absolute breaches in nature' (1952: 147). Since each phenomenal space is unbounded, and such spaces do not overlap, by identifying selves with phenomenal spaces we can not only be sure that selves are truly separate from one another, we also have an explanation as to why this is so.[4] This separation will only embrace all parts of our experience if we subscribe to the traditional Cartesian conception of phenomenal domains, rather than the Heideggerian alternative (the latter's 'clearings' are not private mental spaces), but for those of us who assume an indirect realist view of perception, this is not a problem. There are further advantages. Many of us have the sense that whatever we are, we are not identical with our experiences, we are something that *has* experiences, or that experiences are presented *to*. If we are spaces which house our experiences, this 'ownership' doctrine is satisfied in an intuitively appealing way. Last but not least, there is the supposed elusiveness of the self. Space too is elusive. We see objects in space, we see regions of emptiness between objects, but space itself cannot be seen or touched. If we *are* phenomenal spaces, it is not surprising that our selves are so hard to detect.

   It may have some appealing features but the identification of selves with phenomenal spaces begins to look problematic when scrutinized more closely, even assuming the ECS conception, and for two quite different reasons.

---

[4] Although the issue merits further investigation, I suspect Priest is right in holding that the typical human phenomenal space is unbounded, but I cannot see any reason for supposing that phenomenal spaces necessarily possess this characteristic. For subjects possessing bounded phenomenal spaces it is the non-overlapping character of such spaces that secures their separateness.

The first we have already encountered. The notion that our consciousness has the form of a three-dimensional phenomenal space is one that has a good deal of empirical support: by and large, the contents of our experience do seem to be distributed through a single three-dimensional space. But as we saw in §2.2, there are strong grounds for supposing that this is not a necessary feature of experience. There may well be phenomenal contents that are not experienced as being spatially extended or spatially related to one another, but which are nonetheless experienced together. Also, it is by no means obviously impossible for a single subject's experience at a given time to consist of *more than one* phenomenal space: recall the gymnasium example. If this were possible, Priest's proposal would obviously be problematic: can a single self have multiple souls?

As for the second difficulty, baldly stated it is this: if selves *were* phenomenal spaces, then we would have good reasons for thinking that selves do not exist! While some find this nihilistic doctrine appealing, it is clearly not what Priest has in mind, and it should only be countenanced as a last resort, when all alternatives have been tried and found wanting. To appreciate why this conclusion is difficult to avoid it is necessary to take a brief detour into the metaphysics of space *per se*.

There are two very different ways of thinking about physical space. Advocates of the so-called *substantival* conception maintain that space is a substance in its own right, one that is just as real and concrete as more familiar material things such as bricks, sticks and stones. What seem to be regions of empty space are not really empty at all: they are full of 'spatial stuff', as it were. Of course, as just noted, we cannot see or feel space, a fact which leads to the common sense view that truly empty space—regions devoid of all material fields and particles—is nothingness, pure and simple. But substantivalists maintain that the existence of space reveals itself in other ways: it is only because the spatial substance has a certain shape and structure that material objects move as they do. Wary of unnecessary ontological extravagance, advocates of the so-called *relational* conception of space beg to differ. Relationalists maintain that all the empirical facts can be fully accounted without positing a substantival space. They agree, of course, that physical things seem to be both spatially extended and separated by spatial distances. They argue, however, that we can make sense of these hard-to-deny appearances without going beyond the appearances. According to the relationists, the physical world consists of *nothing but* physical objects and the distance-relations that link them together. There is no need to suppose that expanses of empty space are filled with an invisible extended substance; for relationalists, empty space *is* nothingness, pure and simple. Of course, economizing on spatial substance leads to hidden costs elsewhere. Relationalists are obliged to recognize the reality of spatial relations, invisible and intangible connections which succeed in holding the world together. Some are doubtful of the intelligibility of such things, relationists reckon they are a price worth paying.

Since our concern is with phenomenal rather than physical space, there is no need for us to enter into this dispute further. We can, however, raise the same issue in respect of the experiential domain: is phenomenal space substantival or relational in nature? The issue is moot because it seems obvious that the spatial self-conception in the form proposed by Priest requires a substantival phenomenal space. Only then is there something for the self to *be*. For relationists, strictly speaking, space does not exist, it is not an entity in its own right—there are only spatial relations between objects (whether material or phenomenal) and in the absence of any objects there is nothing whatsoever. Obviously, identifying ourselves with a non-entity is not an appealing option. So *are* phenomenal spaces substantival, as the space-conception requires? Before addressing this question we need to consider another. How do substantival and non-substantival spaces of the phenomenal variety differ from one another?

Once posed, the answer to this question seems evident. For a *phenomenal* space to be substantival it must surely have *some* introspectively discernible qualitative phenomenal features of a recognizably spatial kind. If it were as invisible and intangible as its physical counterpart (assuming for the sake of the argument that our physical space is substantival), if it entirely lacked all experiential features, it would simply not exist *qua* phenomenon. If in the phenomenal domain there is no distinction between appearance and reality, then seeming to be non-existent and being non-existent amount to the same thing. It is not difficult to conceive of phenomenal features of the required sort. Perhaps there are beings who can see and feel substantival physical space in much the same ways as we can see and feel the ocean when swimming underwater; all the objects these beings perceive—everything they can see, touch, or hear—seems to be located in an all-pervasive medium. This perceptible plenum is a candidate for a substantival phenomenal space, as would be any phenomenal continuum with similar structural features.

Perhaps there are, or could be, beings whose experiences are located within phenomenal continuums of this sort, but our experience is not: our consciousness is remarkably *clear*. When I look up and gaze at the ceiling above me, *all* I see is the ceiling: the intervening space is entirely lacking in intrinsic qualitative features. Similarly, on a clear day there appears to be nothing whatsoever between myself and the trees I see on the horizon. Unless I move my hands quite quickly, I can feel no trace of the surrounding air—from the point of view of bodily experience I generally seem to be surrounded (and largely filled) with nothingness. The same applies to auditory experience. It is rare for our auditory sense-fields to be completely filled with sound, as is the case, say, when wearing headphones playing white noise. For the most part we hear sounds coming from some directions but not others. Think of what it is like to hear a dog barking behind you, a car passing to your left, and nothing else: although these sounds are clearly spatially related, from an auditory point of view the space between and around them is empty.

So in our case at least, phenomenal space is of the relational variety. Far from inhabiting a phenomenal *plenum* we find ourselves surrounded by a phenomenal *void*. Given that this is so, we have little option but to reject the equation of self with space proposed by Priest. For as we have already seen, for this proposal to have any appeal or plausibility, phenomenal space must be substantival rather than relational.

Self-experience

What of option (6), Strawson's preferred form of Internalism?[5] Strawson's position is intriguing in several respects, not least because his starting assumptions are in some respects similar to mine—a phenomenologically oriented approach to the self, a naturalistic view of the matter–consciousness relationship—but he ends up at a very different place. For Strawson the *problem* of the self arises in the first instance because we each have *experience* of being a self, and our experience strongly suggests—rightly or wrongly—that selves are mental entities that are distinct from anything else:

By 'Self-experience', then, I mean the experience that people have of themselves of being, specifically, a mental presence; a mental someone; a single mental something or other. Such Self-experience comes to every normal human being, in some form, in early childhood. The realization of the fact that one's thoughts are unobservable by others, the experience of the sense in which one is alone in one's head or mind, the mere awareness of oneself as thinking: these are among the very deepest facts about the character of human life. (Strawson 1999a: 104)

I think Strawson is probably right about this. I think he is also right when he says that so far as ordinary human beings are concerned, the mental self is ordinarily conceived as (i) a *subject of experience*, a conscious feeler and thinker, (ii) a *thing* in some robust sense; (iii) a *mental* thing, in some sense; (iv) a thing that is *single* at any one time, and during any unified (or hiatus-free) period of experience; (v) a *persisting* thing, a thing that continues to exist across interruptions in experience; (vi) an *agent*; and (vii) a thing that has a particular character or *personality* (1999a: 106). He then moves on to consider whether all these properties are necessary for the existence of a self, and he argues that (v), (vi), and (vii) are not. To be a subject of experience it is not necessary to last any significant length of time (the brief span of a specious present is enough), nor is it necessary to possess the capacity for action or decision making: a subject might conceivably have the impression of being nothing more than a passive witness of the passing show. Personality and character are likewise dispensable;

---

[5] Zahavi (2005) defends a line somewhat similar to Strawson's. But while there are passages where Zahavi does seem to be offering an account of what selves *are*—'Why not rather insist that the self is real if it has experiential reality and that the validity of our account of the self is to be measured by its ability to be faithful to experience, by its ability to capture and articulate (invariant) experiential structures?' (p. 128)—on other occasions he can be construed as merely arguing that all our experience is accompanied by *me*-ish quality (see §8.2 for some remarks on the latter). Since Strawson's ontological commitments are clearer, I focus on him

as we have already seen, it is not difficult to envisage surviving the loss of everything that is psychologically distinctive about ourselves. This leaves us with (i)–(iv) as the minimal, irreducible, conditions for being a self. For Strawson a self is essentially a subject of experience, a mental thing that is a single unified being at any instant and over short intervals, but which need not last longer than that.

So far so plausible, but Strawson's argument now takes a more radical turn. He focuses on the question of whether anything meets the minimal conditions for selfhood, and answers in the affirmative: he calls these entities 'SESMETs' (Subjects of Experience that are Single Mental Things). SESMETs are selves of the ECS variety, they are essentially conscious entities: 'A SESMET, then, is a subject of experience as it is present and alive in the occurrence of an experience . . . . There cannot be a SESMET without an experience, and it is arguable that there cannot be an experience without a SESMET' (Strawson 1999a: 119–20). This step taken, the question arises as to how long a typical SESMET lasts. Assuming typical human beings regularly enjoy periods of dreamless sleep, one obvious answer is several hours, the amount of time a typical person spends continuously awake each day. Strawson's answer is a few seconds. The grounds for this surprising claim are phenomenological: 'I think William James' famous metaphor of the stream of consciousness is inept . . . . I find that my fundamental experience of consciousness is one of *repeated returns into consciousness from a state of complete, if momentary, unconsciousness.* The (invariably brief) periods of true experiential continuity are usually radically disjunct from one another in this way, even when they are not radically disjunct in respect of content' (Strawson 1997: 421–2). If streams of consciousness are as Strawson describes, then given his commitment to the ECS conception, his conclusions follows: a typical self is of very short duration, a typical human life is made up of a succession of discrete SESMETS. Hence Strawson's name for his account: 'the pearl view': selves are strung through an ordinary human life like pearls along a string.

I find much of what Strawson has to say about Self-experience plausible; I often have experience with this sort of character, and on these occasions it may well be that I am a SESMET. But I see no reason to believe that I am essentially a SESMET. Strawson seems committed not only to the doctrine of the *essentially* conscious self, but to the doctrine of the *essentially self-conscious* self, and for reasons which will largely be familiar, I can see no reason to subscribe to either doctrine.[6] We are beings who *can* feel present and alive in our current experiences, but our existence is not confined to these feelings, or to those occasions when we are experiencing them. As I noted earlier in this chapter

---

[6] Or at least 'self-conscious' in the sense of having Self-experience. Strawson is careful not to commit himself to the view that selves are self-conscious in the usual sense of the term. He confines himself to observing that 'Many . . . will prefer to say that SESMETS exist only in self-conscious beings, or (even more restrictedly) only in the case of explicitly self-conscious experiences. I note this issue in order to put it aside for another time' (1999: 120).

in connection with James, there are occasions—when we drift into reverie, or similar conditions—when we are not particularly aware of ourselves *as* selves at all, but we nonetheless continue to *experience*, and so continue to *exist*. But even if it were the case that we always feel ourselves to be selves in something like Strawson's sense, how plausible is it to suppose that we must actually be experiencing such feelings in order to continue to exist? Isn't it enough that we retain the *capacity* for such feelings? To recap, the rationale for the ECS conception is along these lines:

Our experience provides us with immediate first-hand knowledge of what is involved in a self's existing from moment to moment, and this knowledge would only be possible if selves are present within—*exist* within—our experience. A self is thus a thing that *is directly experienced* in some way or other, and as such cannot exist when not experiencing or experienced. Consequently, accounts such as the C-theory—which permit selves to exist in both conscious and non-conscious modes—must be false.

The proponents of the PCS conception can respond thus:

Since a self can exist when conscious and when unconscious, experience reveals at most one aspect of what is involved in a self's existing. Our experience reveals only what it is like to be a *conscious* self, that is a self that is in the process of *having* experiences—although if the C-theory is correct, selves 'have' experiences by *producing* them. Experience can reveal no more than this, but since there is nothing that it is like to be a unconscious self, this is only to be expected.

And this seems perfectly reasonable. This general point aside, I am not convinced that proponents of essentially conscious (or self-conscious) self doctrine need to follow Strawson in supposing that ordinary human selves only last for the duration of the specious present, or thereabouts. Strawson accurately points out that our typical streams of consciousness are a mixture of continuity and discontinuity. Our conscious thought often exhibits very radical discontinuities; we may on occasion succeed in chaining together a linear sequence of conscious thoughts, but sudden starts, stops, interruptions, and digressions are probably the norm. However, these discontinuities usually take place against a relatively stable backdrop: the surrounding world is a continuous presence in our perceptual experience, likewise our bodies, which supply us with an uninterrupted flow of bodily feelings of various kinds. While Strawson recognizes this—'one is experientially in touch with a great pool of constancies and steady processes of change in one's environment including, notably, one's body' (1997: 423)—he takes the view that there is no genuine continuity here.

If there is any support for belief in the long-term continuity of the self in the nature of moment-to-moment consciousness, it is derived indirectly from other sources—the massive constancies and developmental coherencies of *content* that often link up experiences through time, and by courtesy of short-term memory, across all the jumps and breaks of flow.... If one does not reflect very hard, these constancies and steadinesses of development in the *contents* of one's consciousness may seem like fundamental characteristics of the *operations* of one's consciousness, although they are not. This in turn may support the sense of the *mental self* as something uninterrupted and continuous throughout the waking day. (Strawson 1997: 423)

Strawson does not expand on why he believes the apparent continuity of background consciousness is illusory, but I suspect it is because he subscribes to a version of the 'pulse theory' that we looked at earlier. On this view streams of consciousness are composed of discrete pulses, each the duration of a specious present, and the impression of continuity derives from a combination of qualitative similarity, short-term memory and fringe-feelings. As we saw in §3.3 and §3.5, there are good reasons for supposing that if our streams of consciousness really did have this structure, they would not even *seem* to possess the continuity they actually do. To accommodate the kind of continuity our experience seems to possess—when we listen to a passing plane, or look around a room—we need to recognize that diachronic co-consciousness operates *between* specious presents, as well as within them.

5.2. BRIDGES OF RESEMBLANCE

We saw in §4.1 that proponents of the ECS conception can hold that things are as they seem, and accept that we are conscious intermittently, or they can hold that, despite appearances, we only ever enjoy a single stream of uninterrupted consciousness. Proponents of the latter position sub-divide into conservatives and radicals. The radicals hold that our streams of consciousness last for as long as they seem to, and so urge us to recognize that our lives are far shorter than we normally believe—Strawson is a contemporary advocate of an extreme form of this position. The conservatives, by contrast, hold that our streams of consciousness last for the duration of our natural (human, organic) lives, and possibly stretch further still. This claim is by no means utterly absurd—after all, it seems at least possible that we have *some* degree of consciousness throughout a normal night's sleep. But it does bring with it the highly counterintuitive consequence that processes which *would* bring one's experience to an abrupt but seemingly only temporary halt—for example a consciousness-eradicating general anaesthetic, or being quick-frozen and then successfully thawed—are in fact impossible to survive.

Since the single-stream view is problematic in both its conservative and radical forms, it is not surprising that most ECS theorists have favoured the multi-stream option. This has the virtue of plausibility, but it does mean that a solution must be found to the problem of what distinguishes streams that belong to the same self and those which do not. One way of answering this question is to appeal to an entity of some kind. We could, for example, say that streams are consubjective only if they are generated by the same material body or brain, or belong to the same Pure Ego or immaterial substance. Neither of these options is very promising. The material option lacks generality, and will not appeal to those attracted to the neo-Lockean approach; the problem with the Ego is different: there is no reason to suppose such things exist. But there is at least one other approach available to the ECS theorist. Rather than accounting for consubjectivity in terms of something external to consciousness, we can rely solely on factors *internal* to consciousness. Of course, if we take this route we must specify *which* internal factor (or factors) does the job. One option here is to hold that a later stream is consubjective with an earlier stream if the former includes memory-like images of experiences occurring in the latter. However, as we also saw in §4.1, this proposal suffers from significant credibility problems. Since we have little difficulty in conceiving of circumstances in which streams are consubjective without being related in this way, it is implausible to suppose that (apparent) memory-links are necessary for inter-streamal consubjectivity; and since it is equally easy to envisage circumstances in which streams are linked in this way *without* being consubjective, it is equally implausible to suppose that such links are sufficient for consubjectivity. Clearly, if the internalist approach is to have any chance of success we will need to appeal to an internal feature of a rather different kind, a feature which it is to be found in all (and only) those streams of consciousness which belong to a single subject. Some have argued that *qualitative similarity* fits the bill.

The similarity approach has found favour with several philosophers. James writes: 'even when there is a time-gap the consciousness after it feels as if it belonged together with the consciousness before it, as another part of the same self'. (1952: 154). He suggested that all our states of consciousness possess a highly distinctive personal quality, a qualitative feeling that we are all on intimate terms with, and which serves to render streams consubjective:

whatever past feelings appear with those qualities must be admitted to receive the greeting of the present mental state, to be owned by it, and accepted as belonging together with it in a common self. This community of self is what the time-gap cannot break in twain, and is why a present thought, although not ignorant of the time-gap, can still regard itself as continuous with certain portions of the past. (James 1952: 155)

In more recent years variants of similarity account have been defended by Sprigge (1988) and Nathan (1997). Echoing James, Sprigge writes:

I believe that in early infancy an individual style of experiencing the world is established which will be present all along the series of moments of consciousness constituting my subsequent conscious life and can be called my personal essence. . . . The thing which is the same is not some thin abstraction, such as a numerically identical pure ego which could survive all changes in character, but rather a (more or less) distinctive style of feeling the world handed on from moment to moment in the stream of consciousness which remains generically the same though in different specific versions.' (Sprigge 1988: 44, 48)

Irrespective of how plausible these claims are—I will come back to this—the similarity theory is metaphysically revisionary to a decidedly non-trivial degree. If qualitative identity makes for numerical identity it is logically impossible for there to be an exact duplicate of you who *isn't* you. This result is difficult to believe, but it is an inevitable consequence of the approach in question. In effect, similarity theorists obliterate the distinction between qualitative and numerical identity. Rather than viewing selves as continuants, they view them as akin to (instantiated) universals. Just as it is possible for redness, construed as a universal, to be in many places at once, so too can a particular self. Some similarity theorists accept this with equanimity. Sprigge, for example: 'An ordinary continuant is a concrete universal whose instances can be expected to form one single temporal series and this is what each of us is' (1988: 47). But in the eyes of many—myself included—this radical move would only be acceptable in the absence of any viable alternatives, and in the present context, this is not the case.

But the resemblance approach is questionable for other reasons. Nathan approvingly quotes Hopkins:

I consider my selfbeing, my consciousness and feeling of myself, that taste of myself, of *I* and *me* above and in all things, which is more distinctive than the taste of ale or alum, more distinctive than the smell of walnut-leaf or camphor, and is incommunicable by any means to another man (as when I was a child I used to ask myself: What must it be like to be someone else?). (Hopkins 1959: 123)

Do our states of consciousness possess a distinctive subjective aroma of this kind? By the nature of the case, the hypothesis that they do is impossible to verify. Perhaps they do at certain times. Perhaps on occasion there is something distinctive that it is like to be me that is never replicated in anybody else's experience. But if the claim is that our successive streams of consciousness each have a distinct phenomenal essence running right through them, a unique phenomenal characteristic that is continually present through all our waking hours, then it does not strike me as very plausible. Just think, for example, of the successive occupants of a particular seat in a particular cinema, viewing the same film from the same angle; the film is a good one, and the successive viewers all find it enthralling. As they lose themselves in the onscreen action, is it not possible, or even probable, that some of these moviegoers, for brief periods, enjoy very global similar states of consciousness, states that are *not* distinguished by some unique personal essence? Since similar examples are not hard to find—what of subjects in the midst of orgasm?—if the resemblance theory of the self were true, there might be far fewer subjects of experience than there seem to be.

Perhaps I am wrong about this; perhaps we do each have a distinctive phenomenal essence. It would not matter if we did, for the proposed solution to the bridge-problem would still be problematic, and for a now-familiar reason: it seems quite conceivable that we could survive the loss of this distinctive quality. Imagine plunging into a VR-4 adventure, where you experience exactly what it is like to be somebody very different from how you actually are, somebody whose experience has an entirely different 'taste'. If the transition occurs without any interruption of phenomenal continuity, isn't it clear that you survive?

5.3. FUNDAMENTALISM

There is an alternative way for the multi-stream ECS theorist to go. Thus far I have been assuming that when an earlier and later subject are numerically identical this is in virtue of the fact that some *other* relationship holds. Perhaps this is wrong. Perhaps facts about self-identity do not hold in virtue of, or supervene upon, other kinds of fact. Perhaps diachronic identity facts, in our case at least, are primitive. If this were the case, the only connection there needs to be between an earlier and a later stream of consciousness is the simplest one of all: they belong to one and the same subject, there is nothing else to say about the matter. Call this view *fundamentalism*.[7]

On a purely intuitive level fundamentalism can seem appealing. There are a number of ways of bringing this out, here is one. Let us suppose that due to a freak quantum coincidence, you suddenly cease to exist; all the particles making up your body simply vanish into the quantum foam. (If you have an immaterial mind, this too is annihilated.) Five years later, an exact psycho-physical replica of you suddenly condenses out of the quantum foam. Call this person Enigma. There are no causal connections linking you with Enigma, nor are the pair of you linked by any form of mental or material continuity beyond mere resemblance. Might it be that Enigma *is* you, rather than a mere replica of you? Is there *some* possibility, no matter how remote, that you and Enigma are numerically identical? I suspect many of us feel a temptation to answer in the affirmative, perhaps thinking: 'Yes, this is at least a possibility. After all, if God had wanted to bring me back into existence, he surely could have; perhaps he so desired. Consequently, it is at least a logical possibility that Enigma is me, even if God does not exist.'

Although this line of thought has its attractions, these largely evaporate with a little further reflection, and an extension of our original scenario. It is uncontroversial that God (or some freak event) could bring into existence a person who is an exact replica of you (just as you were prior to your vanishing) but who is not you. Call this creation event E1. Now consider creation event

---

[7] Fundamentalism should be distinguished from the doctrine that the identity of earlier and later persons is determined by a special *property*, a haecceitas or individual essence. Like many others I am not convinced there could be (entirely non-qualitative) properties of this kind, and will simply assume as much henceforth.

E2 in which God (or some freak occurrence) brings into existence a person who exactly resembles the person in E1, but with one difference: this person *is* you. What differentiates E1 and E2? What is the crucial ingredient present in E2 but absent in E1? What does God do differently in creating the being in E2 that was not done in creating the being in E1? The fundamentalist can respond: 'In the case of E2 God makes the person he is creating *you*.' But this answer fails to satisfy. What we need is an understanding of how E1 and E2 *can* be different: how can the latter event succeed in bringing you into existence when the former event fails to, given that the two events are qualitatively indiscernible in all respects? Simply to be told that they *are* different is of no assistance, it fails to render the difference fully intelligible. The same applies to the longer answer: 'The difference lies in the fact that you bear the relationship of numerical identity to the being created in E2, but not to the being created in E1'. The alleged existence of this relationship makes no discernible difference to its relata, it does not pass through space, nor does it have any material, causal, or phenomenal characteristics. It is hard to see how such a relation can be a real ingredient of the world, it is harder still to comprehend how it can have any relevance to our lives—how it can determine who is who. In short, fundamentalism renders facts about our identity over time mysterious and unintelligible, and once this is appreciated, its initial intuitive appeal is undermined.

But not necessarily fatally. Fundamentalists have the option of responding thus: 'It's true that we cannot supply an informative explanation of how or why the identity relationship holds when it does, but why is this a problem? It is surely reasonable to suppose that *some* relationships are basic and not reducible or analysable. Why shouldn't numerical identity, as it applies to persons over time, be just such a relationship.' While this reply merits being taken seriously, fundamentalists face a further and more damning difficulty. Thus far we have been considering the most moderate form of fundamentalism. We have been assuming that the diachronic identity relation is (i) constrained by the material and mental (and in particular *phenomenal*) continuities that we ordinarily use as guides to questions of personal persistence, (ii) that it only holds between subjects at different times, and finally (iii) that when it links the earlier and later parts of discontinuous lives, the life-phases it connects (those either side of the temporal gap) are qualitatively similar, mentally and physically. There are more extreme versions of fundamentalism that do not subscribe to these assumptions, with dramatic consequences. Rejecting (iii) opens up the possibility that you and Napoleon, or Genghis Khan, are one and the same. Rejecting (ii) opens up the possibility that right now, you and I are numerically identical; worse still, everyone now living could be the same person. Rejecting (i) opens up the possibility that we are none of us the people we seem to be. I might not be the subject who started thinking this thought; the person inhabiting your body now might be the person who inhabited my body yesterday, or that of Catherine the Great 250 years ago; it is equally possible that every sentient being in the universe changes bodies every few hours—yesterday you were lizard-like creature inhabiting a planet orbiting the star Vega, the day before you were a sentient *planet* in a distant galaxy.

Now, needless to say, it is hard to believe that any of these increasingly wild scenarios are genuine logical possibilities. It is tempting to suppose that any account of our persistence conditions which entails that the more extreme scenarios are possible—those which are permitted in the absence of (i) and (ii)—is simply unacceptable. The difficulty for the fundamentalist is to explain why the proposed primitive identity relation *is* constrained in the ways required for minimal plausibility. Since (by hypothesis) the relation can hold in the absence of all ordinary continuities, it is not obvious at all why it should be constrained by them. Unless and until such an explanation is forthcoming, fundamentalism is a doctrine that is difficult to take seriously.

5.4. FOSTER'S MODAL BRIDGE

On a number of occasions John Foster has proposed a way of solving the bridge-problem which, if successful, would supply just what we have been looking for, and do so without appealing to *potentiabilia* in the manner of the C-theory. Whether Foster's bridge is ultimately up to the job is another matter.

On the question of subject-persistence, Foster's project and mine differ in that he defends a Cartesian conception of the subject as a metaphysically basic immaterial substance. I have made no such assumption, preferring instead to allow an account of the nature of the subject to develop in the course of an account of what makes experiences consubjective; I have also remained neutral on the question of whether experience is physical or non-physical. These are significant differences. However, there are also significant similarities. Although Foster believes experiences always belong to thinking substances, and are merely *states* of such substances, he appreciates the appeal of a neo-Lockean account of experiential consubjectivity. Locke may have believed that conscious states always belong to some consciousness-bearing substance, but he also regarded it as possible for co-personal experiences to be housed in a succession of distinct consciousness-sustaining substances. If this is possible, then it would be a mistake to equate subject-persistence with substance-persistence. An alternative is to sidestep substance, as it were, and define the conditions under which experiences belong to the same self in terms of relationships between experiences themselves. In adopting this approach we not obliged to abandon the doctrine that experiences are always states of substantial subjects: we can start off by assuming that every experience is a state of a temporal slice (or phase) of a consciousness-bearing substance, and then go on to define the conditions under which substance-phases are consubjective in terms of relationships between the experiences possessed by these phases. Consubjective substance-slices are those whose experiences are interrelated in certain ways. This is the line Foster pursues.[8]

Uninterrupted streams of consciousness pose Foster no difficulties. Experiences within such streams are unified by direct and indirect co-consciousness. If we assume, as Foster does, that co-conscious experiences are consubjective, then co-streamal experiences will be consubjective, and so belong to the same consciousness-bearing substance. But the bridge-problem remains. Can we also appeal to co-consciousness to account for the consubjectivity of experiences separated by gaps in consciousness? On the face of it this seems unlikely, but Foster argues that this seemingly impossible goal can be accomplished 'by putting the right interpretation on one crucial fact, that consubjective streams have what non-consubjective streams lack: the potential for being phases of a single stream' (1979: 179). He goes on to provide an initial explication of this potentiality in counterfactual terms. If A and B are two streams such that the last experience in A occurs some time before the first experience in B, then if the streams are consubjective, and A had continued with B remaining unchanged, then A would eventually have joined up with B to form a single stream; if the streams are not consubjective then no continuation of A, no matter how long, would overlap with B. Foster claims that these counterfactuals specify a condition which any satisfactory definition of inter-streamal consubjectivity must satisfy, and consequently, he formulates a general account of experiential consubjectivity in the following manner:

a *stream* of experience can be defined as any temporal sequence of successively overlapping total experiences; and a *total* stream will then be any stream which is not a portion of a larger stream. Given two total streams A and B, where A is earlier than B, and where there is a temporal interval between them, let us say that A and B are *directly joinable* if and only if there is something which ensures (whether logically or nomologically) that, with B held constant, a hypothetical continuation of A to the time when (or just after) B begins would join up with B; and let us say that two streams are *indirectly joinable* if and only if they are connected by a series of total streams whose successive members are

---

[8] See 'In *Self*-Defence' (1979), *The Case for Idealism* (1982: part 5), the penultimate chapter of *Ayer* (1985), and *The Immaterial Self* (1991: 244–61). A superficially similar account surfaces in each of these works, but the differences are such that it would be quite misleading to say each contains the same theory of subject-identity. In *The Case for Idealism* Foster defends a version of phenomenalism (with regard to the physical world as a whole, rather than just the self), and takes subjects to be mental entities whose existence and persistence are wholly irreducible; in this context Foster holds that experiential inter-relationships are only responsible for the subjective time dimension within which a subject's experiences can be viewed as unfolding. I shall focus here on the less radical position propounded in 'In *Self*-Defence' and *The Immaterial Self*, where Foster adopts a more traditional Cartesian position, adopting the view that the material and mental realms are each metaphysically fundamental, and each irreducible to the other. In *Ayer* (1985: 282) he repudiates the account of subject-persistence he earlier advocated in 'In *Self*-Defence', and consequently the version found in the recent *The Immaterial Self* differs from the earliest version, and is closer to the position advanced in *The Case for Idealism*. One aspect of this evolution in Foster's views is relevant to our present concerns, and I shall be commenting on it.

directly joinable. We can then say that two experiences are *potentially serially co-conscious* (or, for short, *potentially co-conscious*) if and only if the total streams in which they occur are either directly or indirectly joinable. (Foster 1991: 251)[9]

From here it is but a short step to a general criterion for the consubjectivity of experiences. We can say that two experiences are *consciousness-related* if and only if they are either strictly co-conscious (part of the same total experience), serially co-conscious (part of the same total stream of consciousness), or potentially co-conscious. Foster then proposes that our experiences are consubjective if and only if they are consciousness-related in the sense defined.

At first sight this is an intuitively appealing solution. If *A* and *B* are potentially joinable, it would be hard to deny that they belong to the same subject. If potential joinability is a property some temporally separated streams have, and others lack, it is natural to think that this property might be what distinguishes consubjective streams from others, those that are not consubjective. But the viability of the proposal rests upon the notion of potential joinability. Is this potential logical or nomological? What *logical* factor might ensure that stream *A* would meet stream *B*, if the latter remained the same and the former were extended? One answer is that *A* and *B* would be so related if they belonged to the same subject. Given certain assumptions, this will be the case (as we shall see), but such an account would obviously be circular. If temporally separated streams are consubjective in virtue of being potentially joinable, to say that they are potentially joinable *only* in virtue of being consubjective is to employ the very relationship we are seeking to elucidate in the elucidation itself. Foster sees this, and in 'In *Self*-Defence' he opts for the nomological alternative:

on the face of it, the potential for joining is logically grounded on the continuity of the subject: on the face of it, two streams are potentially unistreamal in virtue of being essentially consubjective and therefore, by *de re* necessity, logically guaranteed to meet if sufficiently extended. But there is an alternative, and an attractive one, namely to take the potential as resting on certain natural laws—laws statable without recourse to the concept of a subject, though constitutive of his capacity for interstreamal persistence. (Foster 1979: 179)

Unfortunately, there is a difficulty with an account along these lines. Recall the condition Foster requires the extended definition of consubjectivity to meet: 'whatever our definition . . . it must confer on consubjective streams and exclude from non-consubjective streams the potential for joining when the earlier stream is sufficiently extended' (1979: 179). Now, the idea that the earlier of two successive consubjective streams could have continued until the later stream began is quite implausible. The mind is a system whose later states are, to some extent, dependent on those which went before. This morning I woke at eight

---

[9] Foster employs different, and rather more difficult, terminology in 'In *Self*-Defence'; I have opted to use this more accessible formulation from the more recent work.

o'clock feeling no more than usually sleepy after six and a half hours sleep. No doubt I would have felt quite different had I spent the entire night awake drinking coffee; the natural laws governing my brain chemistry would have seen to that. According to Foster's theory in its nomological guise, it seems that if on waking I am the person I remember being the night before, there must be natural laws which would have ensured that the experiences I actually had on waking up would have been just as they were, even if I had spent the night without sleep. But in actual fact the reverse is the case: had I spent the night awake instead of asleep, natural laws would have *prevented* my morning experiences being as they were. The problem here is a quite general one, for given any pair of putative consubjective streams of (human) consciousness, it is unlikely that the later member of the pair would exist unchanged if the earlier member were extended to meet it. Indeed, in the majority of actual cases, it may well be nomologically *impossible* for one's earlier stream of consciousness to be extended while one's later stream remains in place. In which case, since two such streams are not potentially joinable (or co-conscious), they would not be consubjective—at least, this is the result we get if we apply Foster's criterion (in its nomological guise). Consequently, the majority of the streams of consciousness we would ordinarily take to belong to the same person are nothing of the sort. Since this is clearly an unacceptable result, we cannot take the potential for joining that consubjective streams have—and which non-consubjective streams lack—to be grounded in natural laws.

In a more recent work Foster acknowledges this difficulty, but is unconcerned by it. He considers two of his own streams of consciousness, separated by a night of dreamless sleep, and remarks:

the continuation of *A* may well have led not to a *joining up with B*, but to the latter's *replacement*—and indeed I regard this as the more likely outcome. But whatever conclusions we reach on this matter, they do not affect the validity of the example or the purpose for which we are using it. For it is entirely irrelevant whether the hypothetical situation we have to envisage, to illustrate the potential for joining, is a plausible one. The crucial point is simply that the two streams are so related in the actual world as to ensure that, *if* (however improbably) *B* had remained and *A* had been appropriately extended, they would have joined. (Foster 1991: 252)

What is the relationship between *A* and *B* which ensures this fortuitous state of affairs? The fact that these two streams are not joinable in the actual world is quite compatible with their being joinable in some other possible world. Let us suppose that the streams *A* and *B* are attached to subjects, which we can rigidly label S_A and S_B (without presupposing anything about their identity or non-identity). Consider possible world *W* in which both S_A and S_B exist, and where stream *A* (belonging to S_A) continues on to meet stream *B* (belonging to S_B). There is no reason to think such a world does not exist, for it is only the contingent psycho-physical laws that obtain in our world which stand in the way of *B*'s remaining constant should *A* be extended. When *A* joins *B* to form a single uninterrupted stream of consciousness, this stream forms, in effect, a single temporally extended experience. On the assumption that experiences are attached to subjects on a one-one basis, this experience belongs to a single subject. It follows that in *W*, S_A is identical with S_B. If this identity holds in *W*, then given the necessity of identity, it holds in every possible world in which S_A and S_B exist. It follows that $S_A = S_B$ in our world too.

This line of reasoning seems to be why Foster does not does not take the difficulty we have been focusing on very seriously in the passage quoted above. Given his view of subjects and the relationship between subjects and experiences, the fact that nomological considerations mean that streams *A* and *B* are not joinable in the actual world does not entail that they belong to different subjects; they *do* belong to the same subject if there is some possible world where they join. And we can easily envisage a world *W* where events unfold in the required manner. Suppose, for example, that after stream *A* extends through the night, it's subject takes a drug which has the twin effects of eliminating the adverse effects of remaining awake for so long, and eradicating recent memories; this not only makes it possible for stream *B* to come into existence, it also permits *A* to join with *B* to form an uninterrupted stream of consciousness. Such a drug might be nomologically impossible in our world, but there is no reason to think it logically impossible.

A natural objection at this point runs as follows. Given that it is not nomologically possible (in the actual world) for *A* and *B* to join, what makes it true that they are co-personal? Foster's answer: there is a possible world in which they *do* join. But are we really entitled to conclude that there is such a possible world? Suppose we know that *A* and *B* are consubjective, and hence that S_A is identical with S_B. It is now reasonable to suppose that there is some logically possible world *W* where S_A and S_B both exist, and where *A* continues and joins with *B*. If, on the other hand, S_A and S_B are not identical, then there is no possible world in which S_A and S_B both exist and where a continuation of S_A's experience will join with S_B's. It seems that the modal fact we are using to *account* for the fact that S_A and S_B are identical in the actual world *presupposes* this very identity. It also seems that we are only entitled to the modal fact if we stipulate in advance that S_A and S_B are identical; if they are not identical, no possible continuation of S_A's experience will merge with S_B's.

Foster's is not perturbed by this objection, because—it transpires—he has now abandoned the attempt to provide a non-circular account of what it is that makes experiences (and subject-phases) consubjective. The fact that is responsible for *A* and *B* being consubjective is simply the fact that they belong to the same subject or thinking substance; *given* that they do belong to the same subject, then there is a possible world where an extended *A* fuses with *B*. As Foster himself says:

we can see that the potential for streamal joining is grounded on consubjectivity itself. Thus, in the example of my period of dreamless sleep, it is the fact that the two streams belong to the same basic subject which ensures that, with the appropriate form or forms of continuation, they would join. Moreover, this ensuring is clearly of a *logical*, rather than a *nomological*, kind; it is a matter of what consubjectivity itself entails with respect to the unity of consciousness, rather than its contingent effects in the framework of natural law. (Foster 1991: 260)

Foster is now taking the identity of subjects to be primitive, and is content to establish that experience cannot be distributed across numerically distinct thinking substances in the deviant ways Locke and Kant thought might be possible. To summarize his reasoning, suppose streams A and B are consubjective; A belongs to a phase of thinking substance s_1 and B belongs to a phase of a thinking substance s_2. By virtue of being consubjective, these streams are joinable. If two streams are joinable they can be connected by a continuous stream of consciousness, the successive brief phases of which are co-conscious. Since any pair of co-conscious experiences are consubjective, and hence belong to the same thinking substance, it follows that A and B must also belong to the same thinking substance, and so s_1 is identical with s_2. The idea that a subject's consciousness could pass from one thinking substance to another is thus incoherent (Foster 1991: 254).

   This may well be a significant result for Cartesians, but if we want a non-circular account of the conditions under which subjects persist which is experience-based rather than substance-based, it will not do.

The proximity solution

Perhaps we can use the notion of potential joinability to solve the bridge-problem without following Foster in taking the identity of experiences to be dependent upon the identity of subjects, and the identity of subjects to be primitive. We have already seen that we cannot appeal to nomological considerations, but there is an alternative: like Foster, we could appeal to modal considerations.

   In keeping with our experience-based approach we begin by stipulating that although streams of consciousness belong to subjects, the identity of streams is not dependent upon the identity of their subjects. We might take experiences to be primitive from the point of view of individuation, or individuate them by reference to their physical bases. In any event, we do not individuate them by reference to their subjects, in the way Foster does. Now, suppose A and B are two streams we would ordinarily regard as consubjective. A might be the stream of consciousness I had yesterday, whereas B is my current stream. Is there any possible world where A continues until the time B begins, and merges seamlessly with the latter? On the face of it, there surely is such a world: all that is required is a brief suspension of the troublesome contingent features of our world which would eliminate B were A to be extended. But there is a problem too. If there is no logical barrier preventing A's joining with B, there is no logical barrier to A's joining with many *other* streams of consciousness, streams $C, D, E, \ldots$, streams in the actual world which begin after A ends, and which we would ordinarily take to belong to different people. To focus on just one case, for A to join with C would certainly be impossible in the actual world; for this joining to occur, many things might have to be different—including, probably, the laws relating experience to brains. But if there is a possible world which differs from the actual world in a way which permits a continuation of A to join with B, why should there not be a world which differs from the actual world in a manner which allows a continuation of A to join with C? And similarly for $D, E,$ and any number of other streams? This problem does not arise for Foster, since he assumes experiences owe their identity to their subjects, and then grounds the joinability of distinct streams on their consubjectivity. If we elect not to follow him in this, any two earlier and later streams of consciousness become potentially joinable, and so consubjective.

This is an absurd result, but there is a way to avoid it. We could hold A to be consubjective with B (rather than C, say), on the grounds that the possible worlds in which A is potentially co-conscious with B are 'closer' to the actual world than those in which A is potentially co-conscious with C, or any other candidate stream. That is, although in the actual world A is joinable with neither B nor C, the deviations from actual fact required to render A potentially co-conscious with B are smaller (by whatever measure of worldly proximity we adopt) than those required to render A potentially co-conscious with C. I will call this the *Proximity Solution*.

For the Proximity Solution to be viable at all, a plausible criterion of trans-world similarity, capable of doing the job required of it, would need to be devised. This is not a negligible problem, but let us suppose that such criteria could be devised. There is a potentially more damaging problem: the Proximity Solution may appear straightforwardly incoherent. In one world, call it W_1, streams A and B are joined and so consubjective. In another world, W_2, streams A and C are joined and so consubjective. Let us call the owners of these three streams S_A, S_B, and S_C. In W_1, S_A is identical with S_B and distinct from S_C. In W_2, S_A is distinct from S_B and identical with S_C. It seems that subjects who are identical in some worlds can be distinct in others, and this conflicts with the commonly held view that objects that are identical are necessarily identical, and objects that are distinct are necessarily distinct. But the problem here does not seem insuperable. The problem only arises if 'S_A', 'S_B', and 'S_C' are taken to designate the same subjects in both W_1 and W_2. Since this assignment of other-worldly referents produces (what is arguably) a contradiction, why not conclude that these labels designate numerically distinct individuals in different worlds? Let us say, as before, that in W_1, S_A is identical with S_B, but distinct from S_C. In W_2, a subject $S_A{}^*$, who is similar to but numerically distinct from S_A, is identical with someone similar to, but numerically distinct from, S_C, namely $S_C{}^*$. Also, W_2 contains a subject $S_B{}^*$ who is similar to but not identical with S_B. In saying that in W_1, S_A is identical with S_B but distinct from S_C, whereas in W_2, $S_A{}^*$ is identical with $S_C{}^*$, but distinct from $S_B{}^*$, we are talking about four different subjects: (i) $S_A \backslash S_B$, (ii) $S_A{}^* \backslash S_C{}^*$, (iii) S_C, (iv) $S_B{}^*$. Since we are currently working on the assumption that subjects owe their identity to their streams of consciousness, rather than the other way about, we have to make corresponding claims about streams. If $S_A \backslash S_B$ is distinct from $S_A * \backslash S_B{}^*$, then A and B in W_1 are numerically distinct from A^* and B^* in W_2; likewise for C and C^*.

However, there is a further difficulty, also of a broadly formal sort, that cannot be evaded so easily. Consider:

The Intrinsicness Principle: if in some actual or possible situation a certain process constitutes the persistence of a single person, then in any other actual or possible situation in which an intrinsically indistinguishable process occurs, then that process secures the persistence of a single person in that situation also.

The general idea enshrined here clearly has considerable plausibility.[10] However, substituting 'subject' for 'person', the Proximity Solution contravenes the Intrinsicness Principle. Suppose by an accepted measure of worldly proximity, stream B emerges as consubjective with stream A. It is evident that the intrinsic relationship between these two streams is not in itself sufficient to make them consubjective. They are only consubjective because no *other* stream exists in the actual world which is a better candidate for being considered consubjective with A. If such a stream existed, and (arguably) it is logically possible that it could, then A would be consubjective with it, and not B. This clearly contravenes the Intrinsicness Principle: the same process which suffices for the existence of a single subject in the actual world would not suffice for the existence of a single subject in a world in which both A and B exist, but where B is not the best candidate for being consubjective with A.

This objection is not necessarily fatal; some philosophers believe the Intrinsicness Principle should be dispensed with on other grounds: they can see no other way to handle fission cases. I will be returning to this issue later. But even if the Proximity Solution could be developed into a metaphysically acceptable way, a serious difficulty would remain: it is simply that the Solution suffers from a severe credibility problem, it can easily seem misguided in a quite fundamental way. If I go to sleep, and wake after seven hours dreamless sleep, it is natural to think I have survived because of what has actually happened (or not happened) during the past seven hours or so. According to the Proximity Solution, this is not so. I survived my night's sleep because the possible worlds where my stream of consciousness yesterday continued on and merged with my current stream of consciousness are sufficiently close to the actual world (e.g. closer than the worlds where my consciousness continued on and merged with *your* current stream). Even in these reasonably close worlds, the laws of nature governing matter and

---

[10] I have borrowed this formulation from Johnston (1989, 1992*a*).

consciousness are different from those that actually obtain. To put it mildly, the idea that our persistence through periods of unconsciousness is dependent upon merely possible events in nomologically impossible worlds does not seem very plausible.

It is also in conflict with another plausible constraint. Ideally we want an account of our persistence conditions that makes sense metaphysically, but which is also readily credible. The identity-securing connection between earlier and later selves should be such that it seems obvious to us that this connection can do the job required of it. It seems fair to say that the Proximity Solution is less than ideal in this regard: we are being asked to believe that if S_1 falls unconscious between t_1 and t_2, the connection between S_1 and S_2 which is responsible for their identity is not only not of this world, it also requires a suspension or alteration of the laws of nature. I think it fair to say that there are more intelligible connections than this one. The C-theory may appeal to experiential potentials as well as actual experiences, but the relevant potentials are all real features of this world, and from what we have seen latterly, a bridge built from real *potentiabilia* looks to be a good deal more solid than anything constructible from mere *possibilia*.

5.5. UNGER'S MATERIAL BRIDGE

In *Identity, Consciousness and Value* Peter Unger (1990) develops a detailed account of our survival conditions which he describes as 'heavily physicalist'. Despite this description, in several respects Unger's account is not very different from the C-theory. But differences there are, and significant ones.

Unger holds that a person can lose everything that is distinctive about themselves, mentally and physically, yet survive. Unger also holds that there are both mental and physical constraints on our survival, but that the physical constraints are more important. On the mental side, if I am to survive until some future time my basic mental capacities, my 'core psychology', must continue to exist—a core psychology consists of a capacity for conscious experience and rudimentary intellectual abilities. A person can undergo a good deal of change in their 'distinctive psychology'—roughly, their memories and personality traits—yet remain in existence, provided their core remains intact. On the physical side, my core psychology must have a 'physical realizer', and this too must exist continuously. An initial statement of his position, later refined, runs thus:

The person X now is one and the same as the person Y at some time in the future if, and only if. . . there is sufficiently continuous physical realization of a core psychology between the physical realizer of X's core psychology and the physical realizer of Y's core psychology (Unger 1990: 109)

The key expression here is 'sufficiently continuous physical realization', what does Unger take this to mean? Does it require sameness of brain? We saw earlier that it is hard to believe neuron replacement treatments would be fatal if they had no detrimental mental consequences. Unger considers a variety of similar scenarios and comes to the same conclusion. He suggests that most of us believe, deep down, that we could survive having our brains transformed into very different, possibly inorganic, physical objects, provided our mental capacities remain intact: 'The physical realizer need not be a contiguous object and, up to certain points, it may fail to be physically well-behaved in a great variety of ways . . . perhaps there may be an appropriate physically continuous succession of realizing entities' (1990: 109). Despite this liberality in our attitudes, Unger also holds that there are definite limits on how badly behaved a realizer can be and still be person-preserving. He argues that when we probe our deepest beliefs about our own natures using carefully selected imaginary cases, it emerges that we regard physical realizers as being akin to ships. A ship can survive the replacements of all its constituent parts, provided these replacements are fairly gradual and do not disrupt the vessel's seaworthiness. The physical realizer of a core psychology can likewise persist through the replacement (or even separation) of its parts, provided these changes do not disrupt its ability to sustain the various mental capacities that constitute a core psychology. However, just as a ship will cease to exist if its parts are changed too rapidly, so too will a physical realizer of a person's core psychology, and when a physical realizer ceases to exist, so does the person whose mental life it sustains.

Unger provides a good deal of detail about the kinds of changes and transformations that are compatible with a physical realizer continuing to exist. It turns out that in some respects, physical realizers are unlike ships. He argues, for example, that when a realizer's parts are exchanged for duplicates, these parts must be given time to become 'assimilated' into the system as a whole. Assimilation can be psychological, with the new parts contributing to mental activity, or biological, in which case the new parts interact bio-chemically with the remainder of the realizer. (Presumably, in the case of non-biological realizers, the assimilation can be mechanical, or electronic). He also argues for a causal constraint. Suppose that my body is annihilated at a certain time and place (it dissolves into the quantum foam) but is immediately replaced by an exact replica of me—as an onlooker, you think you may have observed a slight flickering, but nothing more. That this new person resembles me in any way whatsoever is due to sheer coincidence, let us suppose. Throughout this improbable sequence of events there is a spatiotemporally continuous realizer of mental capacities—the substitution of me by my replica is instantaneous, the replica appears just where I disappeared. Is this sufficient for a physically continuous realization of a core psychology? Is the replica me? No, says Unger: 'the condition of no temporal gap itself must be grounded in *real processes* that, as most naturally and relevantly described, *ensure that* there will be no interruption.' In quantum flicker cases, although there are two spatiotemporally continuous life-processes, 'there is no causal connection between those two processes, the total process consisting of them both is one that, as most naturally and relevantly described, *will allow for an interruption* in the existence of any person that might be there throughout the period . . . no process can work in so fortuitous a way if it is to involve the survival of a person' (1990: 114). So there are two people involved, not one. Physical continuity, of the sort which will keep a person in existence, is in part a causal process.

But interesting though they often are, the details of Unger's account need not concern us here. The question is whether any list of physical constraints on our persistence conditions of the kind offered by Unger could ever be credible. It is by no means obvious that it could.

The difficulty can be brought out by looking at just one example. Unger offers predictions as to the outcomes of a variety of hypothetical cases in which the cells in a person's brain are replaced by biological duplicates that are connected up with the rest of the brain in just the same ways as the originals, with no significant loss of mental functioning. If this cellular replacement is fairly gradual, with only a few cells at a time being switched, there is no difficulty: if the procedure were carried out on my brain, I would survive the procedure in a clear and unambiguous fashion. This remains the case even if the procedure is carried out quite quickly, so that at the end of a few hours I have an entirely new brain—provided the substitutions are made in a *moderately gradual* manner, the procedure remains survivable. However, if the treatment is carried out in a small number of stages, with (say) an entire quarter of my brain being removed and replaced every fifteen minutes, then I do not survive; this turnover of parts is too abrupt and too fast, with too little assimilation, to permit survival. So in this case, Unger maintains, 'as is intuitive, at the end of about an hour, or even about forty-five minutes, there is, composed of new matter, not me, but, instead, a numerically different person' (1990: 148).

Now I for one do not find this intuitive at all. Provided normal mental functioning is preserved (my consciousness flows serenely on, my psychology is undisturbed), it is not obvious *at all* that I would cease to exist in such a scenario, irrespective of what happens to my brain, or the physical realizer of my mind. Unger accepts that this will be most people's first reaction to such scenarios. He nonetheless maintains that our initial, pre-reflective, reactions to such cases are unreliable, and for a specific reason: there are certain features of these imaginary cases which distort our judgement. In particular, the fact that we are awake and conscious during the abrupt cellular replacement process is the main reason why we arrive at the *wrong* answer, that is we believe we survive the process, when in fact we do not. On the face of it this is not very plausible. It is also rather odd to find *Unger* attributing such significance to physical over phenomenal continuity. After all, he willingly accepts that so far as our personal survival is concerned, it is basic mental capacities that matter, and in particular capacities for *conscious experience*. Furthermore, and in line with this view, he holds that physical continuity is of only derivative or indirect importance: it provides for what really matters in survival, the preservation of one's core psychology, it does not matter in itself. So why does Unger takes the stance that he does?

His argument is extended and involved, but there are two main strands. First, although our responses to some imaginary scenarios do suggest that we believe radical physical discontinuity is survivable, our responses to other scenarios—quite similar scenarios in many respects—point in the opposite direction. When we become aware of this conflict, and reflect on it carefully, we soon see that our responses to the second sort of case better reflect our deepest beliefs, or so Unger proposes. I will return to this point.

Unger's second line of attack runs thus. He starts by arguing that our intuitions are influenced by some deep-seated metaphysical assumptions about the nature of conscious subjects, assumptions that are grounded in certain views as to the nature of conscious experience. We are naturally inclined to believe that experience is all-or-nothing, necessarily private and that our total states of consciousness are indivisible. Given the character of our consciousness, these propositions can easily seem to be necessary truths: 'It seems that, especially for one's own case, the absolute necessity of these truths is *revealed to one simply by reflecting on the phenomenology of one's own present experience* . . . it can also seem that these truths about it are extremely *certain*' (1990: 41, emphasis in original). Given these beliefs about the nature of experience, it is natural to conclude that *subjects* of experience have corresponding properties, that they too are absolute (a subject is all-or-none), absolutely indivisible, and absolutely separate from one another. Unger now suggests, reasonably enough, that thought experiments in which consciousness plays a prominent role are apt to bring these metaphysical assumptions into play, and that as a result the assumptions will tend to influence and even dominate our responses to the relevant scenarios. But if—as Unger argues is the case—the metaphysical assumptions are all false, and do not in fact reflect our deepest beliefs about ourselves, the result will be an inaccurate and incoherent picture of what our survival essentially involves and requires.

It is easy to see how a commitment to the six doctrines might conspire to influence our responses. In the cellular replacement scenarios in which changes at the physical level are small and gradual, the uninterrupted flow of consciousness is by far the most *salient* feature, the one which impresses itself on us as important, and this allows the six doctrines to come to the fore. If experience is necessarily private then no experience can be passed from one subject to another. It follows that since the featured stream of experience *begins* as mine it must always remain mine—it cannot be handed on or gradually transferred to any other subject—and so I persist as the owner of this stream of experience.

The absolute all-or-none character of subjects reinforces this result: it is hard to believe that one small trivial change to a brain can make the momentous and absolutely clear-cut difference between my existence and non-existence. We are thus led to conclude that I survive each small change, and so clearly and fully persist throughout the procedure.

These lines of reasoning may well be valid, but their soundness depends on whether the six doctrines are true, and Unger argues that they are false—or at least, and more importantly for present purposes, that we do not ourselves believe them to be true, not when we have reflected on the matter fully from within the framework of a naturalistic world-view. Unger's arguments for this claim are elaborate and intriguing, but whether they are ultimately persuasive is another issue, and one we need not consider here.[11] For although the six doctrines *support* the view that the imaginary processes in question are survivable, this view does not *depend* on the six doctrines. My conviction that I would continue to exist through a process which quickly replaces all my nerve cells but also allows my consciousness to flow on as per normal (phenomenologically speaking) is utterly undiminished by the thought that the six doctrines might be false. For in the envisaged circumstances it simply seems *utterly obvious* that I continue to exist throughout, and hence that the experiences in my stream of consciousness have a single owner. So far as I can judge, this obviousness has nothing to do with purported necessary truths concerning the absoluteness of subjecthood or the non-transferability of experience. The dominant consideration, by far, is the simple fact that phenomenal continuity is preserved. Consequently, even if Unger is right about the falsity of the six metaphysical doctrines, I do not believe that this would significantly strengthen the case for his desired conclusion, let alone suffice for it.

This leaves us with the first strand of Unger's argument, and the claim that the appeal of experience-oriented approaches rests on an unbalanced diet of thought experiments. Unger presents a number of relevant scenarios, for present purposes it will suffice to look briefly at just a couple.

Consider first a new variant of the rapid cell replacement procedure we have already encountered. The procedure is very quick (it is over in about an hour) and quite gradual (only one per cent of your brain is removed at any one stage). The fresh twist is that when your brain cells are removed (and destroyed), they are replaced with duplicates of Einstein's brain cells, as they were on his forty-fifth birthday; consequently, at the end of the process your brain is an exact duplicate of the newly forty-five year old Einstein's. We further suppose that you remain fully conscious throughout the process. Unger asks and

---

[11] Several of Unger's arguments rest on elaborations and extensions of fairly wild Zuboff-inspired scenarios featuring brains being divided into many scattered but radio-linked parts, yet continuing to possess the capacity to generate experiences. See Unger (1990: ch. 6) and Zuboff (1977–8, 1982, 1990).

answers the obvious question: 'Will I survive this operation? Most of us respond quite affirmatively: That conscious man will be me. Always conscious, I simply will have undergone some very remarkable, and fairly sudden, changes' (1990: 53). The process could even be viewed as an extreme form of psychological manipulation or brainwashing—with accompanying plastic surgery—and we know changes of this sort are not fatal. But now consider a further variant: suppose the procedure is carried out after a powerful anaesthetic has been administered, rendering you completely unconscious. Only after the procedure is over is consciousness restored. When you contemplate this scenario, do you think you would survive it? Unger suggests not: 'To this alternative version, most of us respond that I will *not* survive. By the end of the rapid and radical cellular changeover, the single person in this case will no more be me than he will be, say, Charlie Chaplin' (1990: 54). Why the difference in response? Unger's explanation, in essence, is that without the presence of consciousness to distract us, we are free to give proper attention to what is happening to the physical realizer of our consciousness. When we consider the magnitude and speed of the changes suffered there, it is clear—given our general beliefs about the relationship between experience and its material substrate in our universe—that the changes in question are too dramatic to be compatible with our continued personal existence. Once we realize this, we will be inclined to alter our verdict about the scenarios in which consciousness remains present throughout:

When we notice our response to this example, we confirm the suspicion that our example of much more gradual change did fool us. . . . Although it might sometimes exert great psychological influence on our judgments of personal identity, the phenomenon of continuing conscious experience, we should be convinced, has little or no weight in the truth of these judgments: When hundredths of my brain are replaced with continuing consciousness, I no more survive than when hundredths are replaced under a powerful anaesthetic, without any consciousness supported until the drug is lifted at the example's end. Although our prereflective responses to the case may favour survival, on reflection, these intuitions should be discounted. (Unger 1990: 59)

Unger has uncovered a real and interesting divergence in our responses. Physical discontinuities which seem eminently survivable for conscious subjects certainly can seem more problematic in the absence of consciousness. And they can be rendered even more problematic: in other variants, Unger invites us to imagine cellular replacements carried out on *deeply frozen* brains. When contemplating such cases, it is by no means intuitively clear that the envisaged processes are survivable. Faced with this divergence, should we follow Unger, and view actual experience as merely a distraction from what really matters?

I can see no reason for doing so. For imaginary cases to be of much use in probing our deeper convictions all relevant information must be included. Unger himself draws attention to the need for this: 'The descriptions of our examples should be reasonably rich in those details that are relevant to answering questions that we pose about the cases: Without these helpful indications, we may again be left up in the air, with no firm attitudinal basis for responding' (1990: 9). From the vantage point afforded by the C-theory, Unger's scenarios are seriously underdescribed. In those scenarios in which consciousness continues to flow, at least some of the relevant subject's experiential capacities are C-related—manifestly so—and there is every reason to suppose the remainder are C-related also. But in the case of cell-replacement procedures carried out on unconscious subjects, we are left entirely in the dark. It may be that the relevant powers retain the capacity to produce co-conscious experience, but equally, it may be that they do not—Unger does not specify. Since he does not draw the distinction between experiential capacities that are C-related and those which are not, this omission is not surprising, but it does make a difference, a highly significant one. If we suppose the capacities in question *are* C-related throughout the envisaged procedures—and hence that at any moment, or over any short interval, if the powers *were* active they would be producing co-conscious experience—then contrary to what Unger urges, there is no reason or room to doubt that the procedure is survivable. So far as their capacities for consciousness are concerned, the predicament of the subjects in question is essentially no different from that of a normal person enjoying a period of dreamless sleep. And this is the case no matter how fast or dramatic the physical changes: so long as the changes do not put an end to C-relatedness, the subject retains the capacity for experience. If we suppose the capacities are *not* C-related, then the reverse obtains. To bring about a rupture in C-relatedness a physical change must obliterate a subject's capacity for consciousness. A subject who has lost their capacity for consciousness is clearly in a very different condition from a subject who is merely dreamlessly asleep. It is by no means obvious that a change of this kind is survivable.[12]

These points connect with what I believe to be the underlying motivation behind Unger's physical continuity requirement. So far as survival is concerned, what I really care about is that some future person be me, and Unger holds that in order for a future person to be me, the latter's core psychology must be continuous with mine. The continuity is essential, for we cannot survive an interruption in our existence: 'It will never be true that someone exists, and then later does not exist, and then still later exists again. This condition of "no interruption" applies across all plausible metaphysical conceptions in which we may find a place' (1990: 113). Hence if my basic mental capacities cease to exist, so do I. But what is required for *these* particular mental capacities of mine to exist without interruption? How is the uninterrupted existence of a *particular* core psychology to be secured? It is here that the physical continuity requirement enters the picture. On the assumption that we live in

---

[12] I will be dealing with the difficult issue of the persistence of C-related powers through unusual conditions (various degrees of brain damage, etc.) in Chapter 10.

a wholly physical world, and that our mentality is wholly dependent upon material processes, Unger maintains that we can only be sure—only really believe—that some future mental capacities will really be our own, as opposed to somebody else's, if these capacities are physically continuous with our current capacities to a considerable degree. This rationale is clearly to be seen in this passage, where Unger is to be found contemplating yet another cell-replacement scenario:

> Will I survive this replacement procedure? No, I will not exist at the end. Vaguely and briefly, the reason for the failure is that too *much* relevant matter is replaced too *abruptly*. There is too large and abrupt a replacement of the matter that, most directly, realizes my core psychology. Because of this, there is *not sufficient physical continuity* of an entity that might continuously realize *my* basic mental capacities. Thus, my core psychology ceases to exist and, so too, do I (Unger 1990: 124, emphasis in the original)

What drives Unger to his physical continuity requirement is the need for a clear criterion for assigning mental capacities to subjects. He is right to insist upon such a criterion. We do want a way of distinguishing between survival and replication; we want to know the conditions under which *our own* mental capacities persist on. He is also right to insist that mere spatiotemporal continuity by itself is insufficient. What looks to be a single persisting lump of rock could conceivably be two distinct rocks: this would be the case if the original rock were instantaneously annihilated, but—thanks to some freakish coincidence—instantly replaced by an exact duplicate. What goes for rocks goes for material people. Given these various desiderata, Unger's insistence that physical continuity can only be person-preserving if it involves moment-to-moment causal dependencies and sameness of matter is perfectly understandable.

Understandable but also unnecessary. Where Unger goes astray is in assuming that when it comes to assigning inactive mental capacities to subjects, there is *only* physical continuity to go by, since there is no actual experience. If this were the case, then—in the framework of a naturalistic world-view—we might have no option but to follow the path Unger recommends. But there is an alternative. Unger has overlooked the possibility of assigning capacities to subjects on the basis of the experiences these capacities *would* produce, if active. In short, he has overlooked the possibility of assigning capacities to persons in the way the C-theory does.

By taking basic mental capacities to be consubjective if they can produce co-conscious experience, we have a criterion for power-consubjectivity which appeals only to what is directly and non-derivatively important to our survival. We are not obliged to build material continuity into our persistence conditions, a form of continuity Unger concedes has only derivative significance. This is an advantage in itself. But it also means we can avoid the counterintuitive conclusions about imaginary cases to which Unger is driven. The abrupt replacement of brain tissues, or the sorts of causal disconnection involved in quantum flicker cases, may in fact be incompatible with a continuous flow of consciousness, actual or potential. If so, they are not survivable. But if by any chance such eventualities could befall a person without disturbing their flow of consciousness, actual or potential, then that person survives. The C-theory is the more credible for being able to deliver this result.

6
Minds and Mental Integration

6.1. FROM C-SYSTEMS TO MINDS

The C-theory may have clear advantages over other experience-based approaches to the self, but its true merits will only be apparent when it has been explored in more detail. While the account elaborated in Chapter 4 provides us with a reasonably clear way of assigning experiences and experiential capacities to subjects, a number of questions remain to be answered. Is the existence of experiential powers all-or-nothing, or can it be a matter of degree? Precisely what kind of unity do C-systems possess? In its broad form the C-thesis equates selves with C-systems, but can we really make sense of the idea that we are collections of dispositional properties? Assuming that we can, how are selves thus construed related to their bodies? Can C-systems undergo fission? If so, what happens to a self that undergoes division? I will be addressing these and other issues in the remainder of the book. In this chapter the focus is on mental unity, broadly construed, and viewed from several different angles.

When introducing the C-theory I focused on the relationships holding between the experiential powers of an extremely simple-minded subject, a subject whose mind consists of nothing but a collection of capacities for simple forms of sensory experience. The C-theory supplies us with a criterion of consubjectivity for the constituents of Maggot-type minds, but in its current form it cannot do the same for complex minds such as our own, minds which possess non-experiential states and capacities. Hence the problem: how can we provide a criterion for the consubjectivity of mental items of both the experiential and non-experiential varieties while remaining true to the tenets of the experience-based approach? Being able to produce co-conscious experience may be what renders experiential capacities consubjective, but what of other kinds of mental item? The first main aim of this chapter is to explore how the C-theory can be adapted or extended to accommodate subjects possessing intellectual and psychological attributes in addition to sensory capacities.

This issue is of interest in its own right, but it also has wider implications. Given the inseparability of a self and its mental life (or capacity for such), it is tempting to think that a self just *is* a mind. If we do adopt this view, we need to supply a reasonably clear picture of what a mind is. Once again, the C-theory arguably supplies us with this for Maggot-like beings. The only mental capacities

Maggot possesses are experiential powers, and the only unifying connection of a mental kind to be found in Maggot's mind is DPC-relatedness (in its various forms). Maggot's mind is a C-system, nothing more and nothing less. But if a typical human mind also has non-experiential states and capacities—and it is very plausible to suppose this is the case—then our minds extend beyond collections of DPC-related capacities. And this makes for a potential difficulty. In its ontological guise the C-theory states that *selves are C-systems*. This claim sits easily with the doctrine that selves are minds in the case of Maggot-like minds, but it is otherwise with human minds. If there is more to our minds than DPC-related experiential capacities, we cannot simply equate our minds with C-systems, or our selves with our minds. In order to be in a position to judge just how radical a departure this is, however, we will need to have a clearer idea of the relationship between the phenomenal and non-phenomenal aspects of mind. The second main aim of this chapter is to provide this.

I start off (in §6.2) with a brief survey of the sorts of states and capacities to be found in typical human minds, and offer (what I hope) are some uncontroversial observations as to the differing extents to which these have phenomenal aspects or manifestations. In §6.3 I outline how the C-theory can be extended to embrace non-phenomenal mental items. Although this account rests largely on causal (or P-) relations, in §6.4 I argue that the autonomy of the C-theory has not been compromised. In §6.5 and §6.6 I take a different approach, and spend some time considering the issue of whether non-conscious beings (zombies) can have minds or mental states. This detour through some admittedly contentious territory brings several benefits. It sheds useful additional light on the relationship between the phenomenal and non-phenomenal aspects of mentality, and allows the C-theory to be situated in a (broadly) functional conception of the mind as a whole. It also makes it easy (or easier) to grasp a distinction between two sorts of mental subject: *phenomenal selves* and *non-phenomenal selves*. This distinction is significant in its own right, but recognizing it also helps to clarify the relationship between the two forms of mental unity and continuity, founded in C-relations and P-relations respectively; it also allows some familiar thought-experiments—for example teletransportation—to be interpreted in new and illuminating ways. In §6.7 I turn to the question of what matters in persistence, and the relative importance of C- and P-continuities. I argue that they both matter, but in different ways.

6.2. ASPECTS OF MIND

Capacities for perceptual experience, bodily sensations, conscious thought, emotional and fringe feelings, experiential memory, and mental imagery are relatively uncontroversial examples of experiential powers, and the C-theory provides a criterion for the consubjectivity of such items: roughly speaking, they belong to the same subject when they can contribute to the same stream of consciousness. What else does a typical human mind contain? Most plausible lists of candidates will include at least the following: *propositional attitudes*, beliefs, desires, intentions, hopes, wishes, and so forth, possibly including unconscious attitudes, such as repressed desires of the sort Freud postulated; *mental abilities*, such as the capacity to spell correctly, speak a language, or do mental arithmetic; *personality traits*, including likes and dislikes, tastes and values; *sub-conceptual and/or non-intentional capacities*—these might include the unconscious processes which subserve sensory perception, as well as more general forms of tacit sub-conceptual knowledge.[1] This list is crude, and also highly debatable. There may be omissions or miscategorizations. It may include too much: as the Churchlands like to point out, ways of thinking of the mind that are rooted in common sense and ordinary language may have to be revised—perhaps heavily revised—in the light of future findings from neuroscience. But since (so far as I can see) such revisions could easily be accommodated by the account of mental unity I will be developing, the list will serve as it stands.

Although we do need a criterion of co-mentality for wholly non-experiential states and capacities, it is important to note that a significant proportion of the items falling under the rubrics in our list do have experiential aspects, of one kind or another, even though they are not obviously or primarily capacities for experience. Consider the propositional attitudes. Obviously, deeply repressed Freudian attitudes (assuming they exist, which is controversial) do not have any direct experiential manifestations—if they did, they wouldn't be repressed—but what of ordinary, non-repressed, attitudes? Does believing that plastic is a polymer have a different phenomenal feel than believing that plastic is polymorphous? Not for the most part, but then most of our beliefs are usually dormant. My capacity to feel the kind of pain produced by being dropped in boiling oil has thus far never been activated, but this does not mean it is not there, and the same applies—it seems reasonable to suppose—to the bulk of my beliefs. The question that needs to be considered is whether attitude states can make a distinctive contribution to experience when they are appropriately triggered, and on some occasions at least, it seems clear that they can. Although our self-knowledge is limited, we can certainly discover a good deal about our attitudes via introspection. Whenever I *think* that plastic is a polymer, one of my beliefs is contributing to the character of my consciousness. The belief is not merely causing a particular sentence to

---

[1] Searle, for example, argues that conscious mental states only possess a determinate representational content by virtue of occurring against a 'Background' of sub-conceptual, non-intentional capacities. Searle takes as his starting point the fact that the literal meaning of any statement is compatible with any number of different interpretations. If I tell you 'Cut the grass' and you go outside and slash the lawn with a knife, I would be surprised, but does the literal meaning of the sentence I uttered rule out your interpretation? Examples of this sort can be multiplied endlessly. (1992: 175–6). As Searle notes, his doctrine of the Background is reminiscent of certain themes in Wittgenstein's later work, not to mention some of the literature devoted to connectionism.

be formed in my acoustic imagination, the belief is contributing a particular kind of understanding-experience. If understanding-experience is not necessarily verbal (as I suspect) then I can be aware that I believe that plastic is a polymer without thinking anything in words at all: there are occasions when thoughts flash wordlessly through my consciousness, exhibiting their meaning or content as they do so. It is not only beliefs that manifest themselves in understanding-experience, verbally or otherwise, every other kind of attitude can do so too. If the thought 'I hope the government falls this week' flits across my mind, its content is present in my experience, likewise for 'I fear the government will fall this week' or 'I'd better get to the shops before they close'. Once the reality of understanding-experience is appreciated, the claim that attitude-states and their specific contents can manifest themselves in consciousness seems self-evident rather than strange.

While there are strong grounds for supposing that at least some of our attitude-states sometimes manifest themselves in our consciousness in distinctive ways, it could still be argued—with considerable plausibility—that there is no *one* way, or collection of ways, in which a given attitude can manifest itself in consciousness. Just as a particular belief will influence a subject's behaviour in different ways, depending upon the other beliefs, hopes, intentions that the subject has, so too the same belief will manifest itself in *thought* in different ways, depending upon the circumstances and the other attitudes the subject has. This is not necessarily fatal to the thesis that attitudes are a species of experiential power, since it is not necessary that an experiential power have only a single type of experiential manifestation. There are multi-track dispositions, complex capacities which can produce different effects in different circumstances; perhaps attitudes belong to systems of interdependent multi-track powers of this sort. Nonetheless, the objection does suggest that tokens of the same type of attitude, in different minds, may well have widely varying phenomenal manifestations. This complicates matters considerably, and also makes plain that the relationship between the typical propositional attitudes and experience is considerably more complex than is the case with simpler sensory capacities.

What of the other candidates on our list? Some personality traits certainly have distinctive phenomenal manifestations. My proneness to melancholia in the evenings is responsible for some quite distinctive feelings, as is my tendency to be bad tempered in the mornings: there is a definite phenomenal feeling to being angry. My capacity for rudimentary mental arithmetic has phenomenal manifestations: working out sums in one's head also has a distinctive phenomenal feel. This said, it is not at all clear that many mental abilities have specific or distinctive phenomenal manifestations, and the same applies to many personality traits. Does intelligence of the problem-solving kind provide a subject with any distinctive experiential capacities? It allows a subject to respond to problems, both practical and theoretical, in ways that would not otherwise be possible, but this is different from being a direct producer of distinctive forms of consciousness.

When we work through the steps of an arithmetical calculation, deliberately following the requirements of a particular algorithm (e.g. a standard method for doing long division), we are directly aware of exercising a particular mental ability, and we also know what this ability involves. But it is not always like this. Someone might have the ability to solve crossword puzzles but be quite unaware of how they manage it—after staring at a clue for a few moments, possible solutions just occur to them, words literally come to mind. There is no awareness here of a particular ability being exercised, beyond the sense of *trying* to solve the problem. It is obviously implausible to regard this sort of ability as composed of elements which can each produce a different and distinctive range of experiences. The same applies to most other types of intelligence, many emotional capacities, and also to various personality traits, such as bravery and trustworthiness, and more generally, the processes responsible for all sorts of creative activities. We can include in the latter category the various capacities responsible for the production of thoughts, utterances and actions, for these too are largely invisible to introspection. Although a continuous sequence of thoughts passes through my mind, why is my mind occupied in *this* way *now*? I am not aware of consciously *choosing* my thoughts before I think them, or my words before I utter them, so processes going on beneath the level of consciousness must determine what I consciously think from moment to moment. These productive processes cannot be equated with my linguistic or conceptual abilities, rather they are responsible for how the latter are deployed.[2]

The conclusion I think we should draw is that the division between the phenomenal and non-phenomenal aspects of the mind is not clear-cut. Although capacities for sensory experience and simple feelings are clearly experiential powers, surrounding this phenomenal core are capacities which can directly contribute to consciousness, but which often do not have clearly distinguishable sorts of experiential manifestations they can call their own. Non-repressed propositional attitudes, many of the more complex emotions, certain character traits, and mental abilities fall into this category. Beneath or beyond the experiential core and periphery are those capacities and processes which cannot generate any distinctive forms of experience at all. The C-theory provides a criterion for the consubjectivity of the core capacities, but its applicability to peripheral states such as the attitudes is more disputable, and it clearly does not apply to those capacities which are entirely non-phenomenal. What we need, then, is a criterion of consubjectivity which clearly and unambiguously applies to each of these different components of the mind.

---

[2] A case could probably be made for including blind-sight and its analogues for the other perceptual faculties in this list. (Blindsight provides intuitive knowledge of objects in one's vicinity that one cannot see, or 'see' in the ususal sense: there is no visual experience.) A faculty of this kind can make a difference to one's thoughts and actions, but does not itself possess any distinctive experiential powers.

6.3. PSYCHO-PHENOMENAL INTEGRATION

Although in our own case, all our mental states and capacities are grounded in the same brain, co-cerebral dependence will not give us the principle of unity we are looking for. One reason for this is that it seems perfectly conceivable that a single biological (or inorganic) brain could sustain two distinct C-systems, and so two distinct subjects. In such cases, co-cerebral dependence is obviously deficient as a criterion of co-mentality: the criterion would not tell us which non-experiential mental capacities belong to which subjects. In addition, and in a more speculative vein, there is no reason (in principle) why a subject's mind need be physically localized at all. A few years from now, it may be possible to plug bio-chips into one's brain which augment one's mental capacities. Before going on holiday to a foreign land, people will plug in the module which will provide them with the capacity to understand the local language, for example Finnish. Whereas without the module, spoken Finnish is just noise, with the module, it both *sounds* quite different—the division between sentences, words, and syllables is clear—and what is being said is immediately understandable. A few years further down the road, it may be possible to buy plug-in transponders which provide the same service at a distance. Or additional services. It might be possible to augment one's memory by links to the database stored on one's home computer. In effect, the distant computer's memory is integrated into one's own; but since the computer may be some miles away, it is clear that one's mental capacities are no longer grounded in one's brain alone.

The latter example suggests the way forward. My non-phenomenal mental states and capacities need not be grounded in my brain, but they must be able to contribute to, or feed into, or influence, my consciousness, in an appropriately direct way. Broadly speaking, the criterion we are looking for is causal rather than material. My sub-intentional mental states and capacities can directly influence—and be influenced by—my experiential capacities, but not yours. The data on my home computer belongs to my memory rather than yours because the data stored there are directly accessible to my mind, but not yours. Details aside, the only issue of consequence is whether we can characterize the causal relationship between the core and the peripheral parts of minds in a more informative way. My non-phenomenal psychological states are mine because these states can influence my experiential core in a suitably direct way. What does 'suitably direct' amount to? Can we say anything more than the uninformatively circular 'the relationship is suitably direct when it is of the sort that holds between consubjective mental states'?

We can do rather better than this. A first point to note is that the mental capacities we are concerned with will usually be components of psychological *systems*. The phenomenal realm is characterized by a degree of interdependence—a point to which I will be returning—but the holistic characteristics of the psychological aspects of mentality are more familiar, and widely recognized. It is generally held, and plausibly so, that it is not possible for a subject to be able to think only one thought, or have a single belief, desire, or intention. Propositional attitudes are essentially systemic. In part this is due to their psychological character, their causal-functional role, in part it is due to their propositional content. For a belief to have a functional role at all it must be a part of a psychological system comprising other psychological states, and it must play the right sort of role within this system—beliefs have a different functional role from desires or intentions. In addition to this systemic requirement, the content of attitude-states brings with it a further dimension of interdependence or systematicity. If I can think 'Seamus is a sad dog', I have to know who Seamus is, and understand the concepts *sad* and *dog*. If I know who Seamus is, I will be able to think other thoughts about him. If I have a grasp of the concept *sad*, I will be able to think that things other than Seamus can have this property. If I know that Seamus is a dog, I will realize that there might be dogs other than Seamus. If my understanding of the concept *dog* goes beyond the simple ability to recognize dogs when I see them, I will know at least a few general facts about dogs, for example they are furry, they bark, have four legs, and wag their tails. If I know these general facts, I understand a good many other concepts—*furry, bark, four, wag, tail*—and understanding these concepts requires a good many other concepts. And so it goes on. What holds for propositional attitudes holds also for other sorts of states. My capacity to do mental arithmetic (of a limited sort) is obviously composed of a collection of interdependent sub-capacities—for handling numbers, addition, subtraction, etc. It is not clear that it would make sense to attribute a personality trait, such as quick-temperedness, to a subject who possessed nothing else by way of a personality. If our ability to interpret what we see and hear depends upon a background of sub-conceptual capacities, these too are holistic, since they constitute a general understanding of how the everyday world works. My tacit understanding of how to deal with a knife and fork is related to my tacit understanding of solid objects in general, and what counts as socially acceptable dining behaviour. My tacit understanding of solid objects is related to my background understanding of liquids, my tacit understanding of socially acceptable dining behaviour is part and parcel of my background understanding of people in general and social norms. Our sub-conceptual know-how is as holistic as our concepts and belief-system. The holistic character of the mental should not be over exaggerated; various forms of psychological disunity can occur, but the general point holds: for the most part, our minds consist of interrelated systems of mental dispositions.

The second point to note is that experiential powers (in a typical human mind) also have a causal-functional role, over and above their capacity to produce distinctive forms of experience. Experiential powers are integrated into psychological (or P-) systems. This is largely because experiences themselves have a causal-functional role. In choosing to do this rather than that, we are influenced by a combination of what we believe and want, and what we are currently perceiving. We unthinkingly take our visual experience to be a window onto the world; we see objects of familiar, and occasionally unfamiliar sorts; familiar objects are objects we can recognize; objects we can recognize are usually objects for which we have concepts, they are objects we can form beliefs and judgements about, objects we can think and talk about. We tend to believe what we see: the mere occurrence of visual experience of a certain sort will often produce a belief, desire, or judgement. This is not to say that everything we visually perceive or experience produces a belief or judgement. Our visual experience is so rich and complex that perhaps only a small part of it impacts upon our belief systems; perhaps the bulk of our experience is registered only subliminally and sub-conceptually. But while seeing is not the same as believing, there is no denying that our visual capacities are closely integrated with our broader cognitive capacities. The same applies to what we hear, touch, taste, and smell.

Putting these two points together, we can see that typical mental states are doubly unified. Experience-producing states which can produce co-conscious experience are C-related; states which belong to the same causal-functional system are P-related. The bulk of the states which clearly fall into the category of experiential powers are both C-related and P-related. The same applies to psychological states which can manifest in consciousness in a distinctive way. As for those mental states which do not have any distinctive experiential manifestations to call their own, these cannot be C-related, but they can be P-related, both to one another and to experiential cores. I have been focusing principally on the propositional attitudes, but it seems reasonable to suppose similar considerations apply to other sorts of capacities: mental abilities, emotions, character traits, and sub-intentional background states (assuming these exist). These too have their own distinctive causal-functional roles, and so can be P-related to C-systems, even if they cannot be C-related to C-systems. The web of causal-functional relations between experiential powers extends outward, beyond the phenomenal mind, through the borderline regions of the attitudes, emotions, and personality traits, and on into the non-phenomenal periphery. Causal-functional P-relations unify those parts of the mind to which C-relatedness does not extend.

I will call integrated psycho-phenomenal systems of this kind *extended C-systems* (Figure 6.1). A more familiar alternative would be 'mind'—extended C-systems *are* minds, after all—but the new coinage serves the useful purpose of making it explicit that we are construing minds in a particular way: as entities whose persistence conditions are defined in phenomenal rather than psychological terms. Can we also say that a self *is a mind*, if by 'mind' we mean 'extended C-system'? If it is conceivable for a subject which possesses an extended C-system to be reduced to a non-extended C-system—and there are grounds for thinking it is—then it would be wrong to identify subjects and extended C-systems. It would be less misleading to say that subjects *have* minds. That said, there is a further option. We could say that a subject is an extended C-system in the same way as a cat can be a kitten: 'kitten' is a phase sortal, that is a sortal concept that can apply to an object at some periods of its career but not others. If we construe 'extended C-system' as a phase sortal, we can safely say that a self can be a system of this kind.

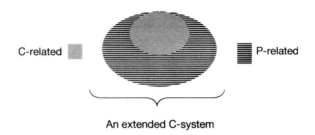

An extended C-system

Figure 6.1 A mind of the familiar kind: a phenomenal core fully integrated into a psychological system

One last point. Assuming states and capacities that are genuinely mental but non-phenomenal can in fact exist, the functional organization of an extended C-system can be many-layered. That is, there is no reason in principle why a mind should not possess multiple levels of non-phenomenal (or NP-) states, with the 'deeper' states only being able to interact with other NP-states. The uppermost level of NP-states, call it level-1, are P-related to states in the core, and hence can influence consciousness indirectly. NP-states at level-2 are P-related to the states in level-1, but cannot directly influence any core states. NP-states at level-3 are P-related to level-2 states, but cannot directly influence any state at any higher level. And so on down. There are further complications. We need not assume that the NP-states on each level are all P-related to one another—psychological unity can be a matter of degree. Nor need it be the case that different levels are permanently or clearly demarcated. The stratification of states may be dynamic and disorderly. In any event, what makes such states consubjective is still, ultimately, their causal-functional relationships with C-related experiential powers. If a particular mind has layers of NP-states, each layer is P-related to some degree with at least one higher layer, and the uppermost layer is P-related to the phenomenal core.

6.4. C-RELATIONS AND P-RELATIONS

Having given due recognition to the importance of causal-functional P-relations in a full account of mental unity, the distinctiveness of the C-theory may appear questionable. Given that the experiential powers which constitute C-systems are (usually) bound together by both C-relatedness and P-relatedness, and the fact that P-relatedness reaches parts of the mind to which C-relatedness does not extend, is it still plausible to maintain that the C- and P-theories are distinct, that they have different stories to tell about what our persistence essentially involves and requires?

It is. As we saw in §1.2, at the heart of the P-theory (of personal identity) is the notion of psychological connectedness, and psychological connections require causal dependencies. If I am psychologically connected to a future person X, some or all of X's mental states casually depend upon mine, in a suitably direct manner, for their existence and/or character. C-relatedness, by contrast, rooted as it is in the primitive relationship of co-consciousness, is phenomenal through and through. Although C-relatedness across time will usually be accompanied by causal dependencies of this sort, as we have already seen, there are conceivable circumstances in which the two come apart. Suppose a subject, Sam, is annihilated. By a freakish coincidence, a moment later (and at more or less the same place) an exact replica of him emerges from the quantum foam. Since there are no relations of causal dependency between Original Sam and New Sam the P-theorist will take them to be numerically distinct mental subjects. But for the C-theorist the lack of causal dependencies in cases such as this is quite irrelevant; all that matters is whether Original Sam's experiential powers are C-related to those of New Sam. Could these powers produce co-conscious experience? If they could, then we are dealing with a single persisting subject; if they could not, then we have two distinct subjects. The difference between the P-theory and the C-theory, as accounts of the conditions under which mental subjects persist, could not be clearer.

There are other relevant cases. If zombies have any mental states at all, they have P-systems in the absence of C-systems (I will be returning to this issue shortly). No less importantly, it may well be possible to have a C-system without a P-system. We have already encountered one such subject, in the form of Maggot. Alternatively, it may be possible for the C- and P-systems of a more sophisticated subject to come apart. It is not difficult to conceive of circumstances in which this arises. On embarking on a VR-4 trip, it will be recalled (see §1.4) one's stream of consciousness is disconnected from one's body *and* one's psychology; one's stream becomes wholly machine-sustained. How can a machine sustain a stream of consciousness? Obviously: it must possess certain experiential powers. VR-4 subjects have no mental autonomy; every part of their trip is machine-controlled, they seem to think their own thoughts, take their own decision, but this is just an illusion. Everything is pre-recorded on tape; the way one's course of experience unfolds is determined in advance. Since a VR-4 subject *seems* to take decisions and think their own thoughts, a VR-4 device must possess the capacity to generate understanding-experience—we saw above that the most direct way for propositional attitudes to manifest themselves in consciousness is via understanding-experience. A VR-4 device can mimic the purely experiential aspects of a typical human psychology down to the last detail, but this is all it does. Since the VR-4 subject is granted not the slightest degree of psychological autonomy, there is no need to 'run' a virtual psychology; it is sufficient that the phenomenal appearance of a psychology can be sustained. VR-4 devices possess experiential powers capable of generating streams of consciousness that are as rich and varied as anyone's; these experiential powers are consubjective; but their consubjectivity is entirely the produce of C-relatedness—the powers are not P-related at all.

These imaginary cases illustrate the differences between the C-theory and the P-theory, but there is a further question which they do not answer. The P-theory is essentially a causal account of both mental unity and survival. To what extent is the C-theory also a causal account? An object—a brain, say—possesses an experiential power if it can produce experience when appropriately triggered. Since the triggering event causes the brain to produce experience, experiential powers are a species of causal power, they are nomological capacities. Furthermore, experiential powers are consubjective when C-related, C-relatedness is built on the notion of DPC-relatedness, in its synchronic and diachronic forms, and the latter might be thought to be a causal relation. It is certainly a relation between causal powers, but then not all relations between causal powers are themselves causal (e.g. spatial or temporal distance). However, C-relatedness is a relation which exists between causal powers which jointly possess a distinctive causal capacity: the capacity to produce co-conscious experiences. Does this suffice to make DPC-relatedness a causal relation? In a sense it does, but it is a causal relation of a distinctive sort.

As we saw in §4.5, DPC-relatedness (in its simplest form) is a species of *manifestation* or *m-linkage*. Quite generally, objects or properties are m-linked if (i) they have the capacity to produce an effect of some kind under appropriate circumstances, and (ii) these effects are related in a certain way. DPC-related experiential powers can produce co-conscious experiences when activated, convergence-related missiles land on the same spot if launched, interference-related transmitters can produce radio-waves which interact and interfere—and so on. Experiential powers are clearly not the only items which can be m-linked, and to this extent the C-theory does not provide a unity-relation of a unique sort. This said, the C-theory is nonetheless distinctive. The relevant effects are experiences, and the relevant relationship between these effects is a purely phenomenal relationship (i.e. co-consciousness). In other cases of m-linkage, the effects are non-phenomenal, and the relationship between the effects is spatio-temporal or causal—or at least non-phenomenal. DPC-relatedness may not be the only form of m-linkage, but it is certainly a *sui generis* form.

6.5. FROM A FUNCTIONAL PERSPECTIVE

I want now to look at the relationship between the phenomenal and the psychological aspects of the mental from a somewhat different angle. Doing so sheds further useful light on the relationship between the C-theory and the P-theory, but, as will emerge, it has other benefits besides.

We have encountered a number of neuron-replacement or NRT-scenarios over the past few chapters. When I first introduced a scenario of this kind, back in §1.1, the topic of whether or not such a procedure is consciousness-preserving was sidestepped. As the nanomachines go about their business, replacing the brain cells of a typical human subject—Tom, say—with similarly sized non-biological machines, it was simply stipulated that Tom remains fully conscious and notices no changes in the character of his experience, and that he emerges psychologically and behaviourally unchanged as well. Unfortunately, in the event of NRT-treatments ever becoming a reality, we would not have the benefit of such a stipulation, and it is not difficult to predict the controversies which would develop—they have been with us for some years already.[3] No doubt many people would sign up for the treatment. Well-known media personalities would be known to have undergone NRT without any obvious adverse after-affects: so far as anyone can tell, their personalities are unaltered. Similarly, some people pondering whether or not to take the plunge themselves will know a recipient personally, and so have evidence of a more intimate and telling nature that the procedure has no discernible outward effects on personality or intellect. But there would also, inevitably, be the doubters and sceptics. Those in the latter camp would argue thus: 'Yes, we accept the fact that NRT does not result in any behavioural changes, but so what? For all we know, the procedure totally extinguishes *consciousness*. Given the elimination of the biological brain, we believe this is likely: NRT recipients are walking zombies, complicated robots with no inner life. Yes, they *say* they feel pain when they stub their toe, but this doesn't mean they really feel anything. Does a chess computer feel anything?' The sceptics would have a point. Given the unavailability of a consciousness detector, a device which can reliably detect the presence of experience when pointed at experiencing beings, how could we be sure that NRT recipients ever truly regain consciousness? Isn't there at least a *risk* that although they act normally, they are in fact utterly experienceless?

Indeed there is. It certainly seems conceivable that a procedure such as NRT could result in zombification, that is the total annihilation of experience and the capacity for experience in subjects who previously possessed both. In some conceivable world, perhaps this one, NRT turns Tom into an experienceless

---

[3] For a good overview see http://consc.net/zombies.html

being. To mark this change of condition, we can refer to Tom in his post-NRT condition as *Zombie-Tom*. Some advocates of traditional (reductive) functionalism would deny all this: they would maintain that in all possible worlds Tom and Zombie-Tom are mentally indistinguishable in all respects, on the grounds that their minds are functionally equivalent in all relevant respects. Clearly this is not the case: one is conscious, the other is not; if anything counts as a mental difference, this does. Versions of functionalism that deny this obvious difference are obviously false. However, although zombies can be used to undermine certain versions of functionalism, they can also be used to get at the kernel of truth functionalism contains. NRT has extinguished Tom's capacity for consciousness, but it has preserved as much of the causal-functional organization of Tom's mind as is compatible with the eradication of consciousness. Let this be true by stipulation: the version of NRT in the worlds we are considering is the procedure which maximizes functional similarity while extinguishing consciousness. Is the functional system which remains of a kind which constitutes a *mind*? A non-conscious purely causal-functional mind?

There are grounds for answering in the affirmative. Put yourself in the position of an agnostic: you do not know whether NRT turns an ordinary conscious person into a zombie, but you think it is at least a possibility. However, your good friend Tom turned a deaf ear to your arguments, and has undergone the treatment. After some initial uneasy moments, your friendship has resumed: you continue to enjoy Tom's company and conversation. His sense of humour is undiminished, as is his idiosyncratic mix of likes and dislikes, and you are silently relieved that his chess-playing abilities are as mediocre as ever, despite his newly siliconized brain. The debate that began before he underwent NRT has continued: Tom maintains that his experience is as rich and real as ever it was. To try and convince you, he has started to wax lyrical over the sensuous aspects of life in a somewhat tedious manner. Now, none of this convinces you that Tom is not a zombie. After all, you knew beforehand that NRT recipients behave as they always did; given Tom's character, his current behaviour was to be expected. However, although you continue to harbour doubts as to whether Tom is a conscious being, the 'new' Tom evidently has the same beliefs, ambitions, memories, intellectual abilities, and personality as the 'old' Tom. Or at least this seems a natural thing to *say*. Even if Tom *is* now a zombie, this Zombie-Tom seems to have the same *psychology* as the old Tom. This sort of case suggests that even though there is nothing it is like to be a zombie (despite their protestations to the contrary), a zombie can possess psychological states. A being which possesses psychological states possesses a *mind*.

Not everyone would agree with this. Some philosophers would argue that mentality without consciousness is a conceptual impossibility. In which case, Zombie-Tom, bereft of consciousness as he is, is a mindless being. True, he acts *as if* he is a minded being, but there is all the difference in the world between an entity behaving as it would if it did possess a mind, and its actually possessing a mind. Appearances can be deceptive.[4] This view may also seem to have a good deal to recommend it. Although psychological states are dispositional and often latent, as we have seen, most psychological states can and do impact on consciousness. Since Zombie-Tom can never be conscious of anything, he can never be conscious of his memories and what they are about. He can never be conscious of what his beliefs and intentions are: in the absence of understanding-experience, there is no experience of the *content* of psychological states. Does it really make sense to think a being such as this can possess contentful psychological states? It might seem not. Yet think again of your conversations with Tom, the knowledge he seems to have, the memories he seems to have, his ability to guess your moods, his tact and understanding. Even if Tom is a zombie, is it not obvious that he has an accurate representation of his environment at his disposal? Is it not obvious that he has a mind?

The predicament is a difficult one, in that both these points of view have something to recommend them. We can begin to clarify the situation by getting clearer as to extent to which Tom and Zombie-Tom are similar from a purely casual-functional perspective. We are currently working under the stipulation that when NRT zombifies people, it preserves as much causal-functional structure as is compatible with the eradication of consciousness. What does 'as much' amount to?

For any given type of mental item we can distinguish between two ways of specifying its functional role. Let m denote a mental state or item of a certain kind in an ordinary mind M. It does not matter what kind of item m is; it might be a certain kind of experience, a belief with a certain content, an emotion, a memory—it doesn't matter. A *full* specification of m's functional role will omit nothing, it will include a specification of the ways m is typically brought into being, the various phenomenal characteristics it has (or can give rise to), the ways m causally influences other mental states (and their phenomenal characteristics if they have any), the role m plays in reasoning and the ways it contributes to the initiation of behaviour, and so on. There is also a *non-phenomenal* or NP-specification of m's role. This will include everything that is in the full specification except the role m plays in its possessor's consciousness. The NP-specification might omit a great deal: since m belongs to an ordinary (non-zombie) mind, it might be causally influenced by other mental states possessing phenomenal characteristics, it might possess phenomenal characteristics of its own, it might be able to influence other states which either possess or produce phenomenal characteristics. But the experiential aspects of the role m possesses in an ordinary mind are all entirely excluded from the NP-specification. We can use the distinction between full and NP-specifications to distinguish two ways a mind as a whole can be characterized. A mind M can be characterized by describing all its various mental states, at a given moment of time, or over a certain interval

---

[4] See for example Strawson (1994*a*) chapters 6 and 7, and Searle (1992) chapters 3 and 7.

of time. To coin some more terminology, a *complete characterization* provides a full characterization of all *M*'s states, whereas an *NP-characterization* also mentions all *M*'s states at the relevant time, but provides only NP-specifications of them.

We can now bring these distinctions to bear on the zombie case. However, at this point it will prove useful to vary the scenario somewhat. Instead of Zombie-Tom being Tom as he is after receiving NRT, imagine that Zombie-Tom is Tom's counterpart on zombie Twin-Earth (a so-called *zombie world* where everyone is a zombie). To the extent that it is possible, given that one is conscious and the other not, Tom and Zombie-Tom live exactly similar lives, in exactly similar environments. Given these stipulations, an NP-characterization of Tom's mind will be drastically inadequate, since it will omit all mention of the phenomenal aspects of his various mental states. But an NP-characterization of Zombie-Tom's mind will omit nothing. Since all of Zombie-Tom's mental states are wholly non-experiential, there is nothing for NP-specifications to miss. However, while Tom's mind is a very different thing from Zombie-Tom's mind, there is a sense in which they are exactly similar. For every occurrent and dispositional mental state Tom has at a given time, there is a corresponding state belonging to Zombie-Tom. If Tom has a state m at t, Zombie-Tom has a state m^* at t, and m and m^* will have exactly the same NP-specifications. So, for example, if Tom is currently examining a Persian carpet, his visual experience will be rich and varied. Zombie-Tom will also be examining an exactly similar Persian carpet. Although he is entirely lacking in phenomenal consciousness, he will be able to describe the carpet in just the ways Tom can. Every shade or colour that Tom can discern in the carpet, Zombie-Tom can discern too. If Tom pauses for a moment to engage in little phenomenology and makes some judgements about the character of his experience, Zombie-Tom will do exactly the same thing. At one point Zombie-Tom wonders aloud 'Would I get an experience with such a vibrant kind of redness if the carpet were to be displayed horizontally rather than vertically?' When Tom asks himself the same question (which of course he does), he is having visual experiences which possess phenomenal characteristics. But since Zombie-Tom does not have any perceptual states with phenomenal characteristics, what is he talking about? Provided we assume that Zombie-Tom can talk about anything at all—and given his behaviour, this certainly seems reasonable—it is reasonable to suppose that he can talk about his internal states too. If so, then in this instance he is referring to a non-phenomenal state that looking at the carpet has produced in his visual system, a state that he uses the words 'vibrant red' to describe. Although this state has no phenomenal characteristics, we might find it natural to call it 'an experience', after all, Zombie-Tom certainly would. To mark the difference, however, we can call it a *non-phenomenal* or NP-experience. For any experience Tom has, Zombie-Tom has a corresponding NP-experience. Naturally, NP-specifications of the functional role of ordinary experiences and NP-experiences will exactly match. Similarly, for every belief that Tom has, Zombie-Tom has a corresponding NP-belief. An ordinary belief can manifest itself in understanding-experience, NP-beliefs cannot. There is, however, a non-phenomenal equivalent of understanding-experience: occurrent states within Zombie-Tom's mind whose functional roles—as measured by NP-specifications—are exactly similar to their counterparts in a conscious mind. What holds for belief holds too for every other kind of psychological state and ability. These all have non-phenomenal analogues in a zombie-mind.

The question now arises, are Zombie-Tom's NP-states really *mental* states at all? One thing seems clear: NP-experiences are not really *experiences*. The very idea of a non-phenomenal *pain* is an absurdity. A state is only a candidate for being pain if there is something (unpleasant) that it would feel like to have that state. Sensations are essentially things which possess a phenomenal character, something quite specific that it is like to have or undergo them. Since Zombie-Tom's NP-sensations are wholly lacking in phenomenal character, they are clearly only sensation-analogues, rather than the real thing. Similar remarks can be made about every kind of sensory experience. Zombie-Tom can 'see' things, in the sense that his eyes furnish his brain with representations of his environment, and the NP-specifications of the functional role of these representations is exactly the same as the NP-specifications of Tom's visual experiences. But there is little temptation to regard Zombie-Tom's visual NP-experiences as genuine visual experiences. As with pain, visual NP-experiences are states which are merely analogous to visual experiences in certain non-phenomenal causal-functional respects. The same applies to every form of experience, ranging from auditory and bodily experience to understanding-experience.

While all this seems relatively clear-cut, the situation is different in the case of propositional attitudes, memories, certain (of the more sophisticated) sorts of emotion, personality traits, and mental abilities. It is considerably more tempting to suppose that he really does have these, rather than mere functional analogues of them. Zombie-Tom certainly has a memory, although of course a non-phenomenal one. He certainly seems intelligent: he can produce creative solutions to all manner of problems, he can understand language, and can carry a conversation as well as most (although of course he has no understanding-*experience*). He also possesses a full complement of states with the same NP-specification as Tom's propositional attitudes. Consider Zombie-Tom's NP-beliefs about Paris. These will influence his behaviour in exactly the same way as Tom's attitudes concerning Paris. Any factual question about Paris that Tom is able to answer, Zombie-Tom can answer too. They will both profess to the same likes and dislikes about the city; when they visit it, they will seek out the same hotels and bistros, walk the same favourite streets, eat the same food, order the same wines. Of course, given that Zombie-Tom lives on Twin-Earth, if his NP-beliefs are about anywhere they are about twin-Paris, rather than Paris-Earth. But it is quite natural to suppose his NP-beliefs really are *about* twin-Paris. When he arranges to meet with friends in Paris, it is to twin-Paris that he goes. Many of his attitudes and memories about the city were formed in response to the NP-experiences he had during his visits there. The fact that his NP-states seem to have representational content that is *about* twin-Paris makes one more inclined to regard these states as genuine propositional attitudes, even though they cannot give rise to understanding-experience, or interact with states possessing phenomenal character in the way ordinary propositional attitudes can.

We can put some order into this situation by acknowledging once more—but now from a superior vantage point—that mental states vary in the degree to which they are bound up with the phenomenal. At one extreme there are sensory experiences and bodily feelings, and the experiential capacities which generate them: phenomenal character is central to our conception of this sort of mental item. Such experiences typically do possess a functional role as well. In some cases, their functional role may be necessary to them—this might be true of pain. But when we isolate the non-phenomenal aspects of this role, it is clear that a state's possessing this role does not qualify it to be an experience; having a non-phenomenal functional role is not sufficient for being an experience. Zombie-Tom's NP-experiences are not really experiences, even though (by definition) they possess the same non-phenomenal roles as Tom's experiences. The same applies, *mutatis mutandis*, for experiential capacities. At the other extreme, there are mental abilities. Phenomenal character is far from being central to our conception of these. The ability to play chess, categorize physical objects, solve problems: it is not necessary to be conscious to do these things. The same holds for various sorts of memory. It is because experience is only peripheral to our conception of these various abilities that we are strongly inclined to think Zombie-Tom has retained many of Tom's mental abilities. NP-mental abilities do differ from their ordinary counterparts in many ways. There is something that it is like to consciously work through a problem, to remember a fact or face; although Zombie-Tom can recognize and discriminate between the things he perceives, he does not do so on the basis of their phenomenal appearances, as we do. Nonetheless, these differences do not seem essential. Hence, in the case of many mental abilities, there is a strong inclination to view the NP-counterparts as the real thing. Somewhere between these two extremes lie the propositional attitudes. There is often something that it is like to want something, or to intend to do something, and there is also something it is like to understand the contents of our beliefs, hopes, and fears. But it is plausible to suppose that a typical attitude has two essential features: a propositional or representational content, and the functional role this content plays. It can plausibly be argued that systems entirely lacking in phenomenal character can nonetheless be contentful representations. (Imagine being on the run from a dangerous assassin intent on your murder, who also happens to be a zombie—after barely surviving a succession of near misses, after lengthy chases on foot and by road through intricate cityscapes, as the bullets continue to rain down, the claim that your pursuer is functioning without an onboard representation of you and your environment would ring rather hollow.) It could further be argued that the essential aspects of an attitude's role are non-phenomenal. Propositional attitudes are used to explain people's behaviour: people act as they do because of their beliefs, wants, intentions, hopes, fears, and so forth. Zombie-Tom's various NP-attitudes, acting in concert, explain his actions. He bets on United to win because he thinks the odds are that they will, and because he needs some money quickly to buy the motorcycle he wants. The fact that these beliefs and wants are non-phenomenal does not reduce their explanatory or diagnostic utility. So it could be said that in our conception of what an attitude state is, the capacity to play this kind of explanatory role is of primary importance, to such an extent that their purely phenomenal aspects are of peripheral significance. Even if this is too strong, it seems plausible that NP-attitudes have a good deal of what it takes to be a real attitude state.[5]

Even these relatively crude distinctions allow us to place the traditional causal-functional theory of mind in clearer perspective. In one sense, the doctrine that a mental state of a given type is a state which plays a certain functional role, and that this is all there is to being a state of this type, is trivially true. The *full* specification of a state's role, in the sense introduced above, includes everything there is to say about both its phenomenal and non-phenomenal characteristics and role; it is plausible to suppose that there is nothing more to say. If, however, we interpret 'functional role' to mean what is specified by a complete NP-characterization of a state, the situation is quite different. Let us call the doctrine that there is nothing more to mental states than what is captured in NP-characterizations 'NP-functionalism'. NP-functionalism can completely characterize zombie-minds. But let us focus on ordinary conscious minds. If all ordinary mental states have some phenomenal aspects, that is they have the capacity to contribute to their subject's consciousness in some way or other, directly or indirectly, then no NP-specification will be exhaustive or complete. With the possible exception of certain sub-conscious mental abilities, NP-functionalism cannot claim to provide a complete characterization of any mental state-type, let alone an entire mind. But this is not the end of the matter. Even if NP-characterizations of ordinary mental states are never complete, they do not always fall short by the same distance. In the case of sensory experiences, they fall a long way short: NP-specifications ignore the phenomenal altogether. But for those types of mental item whose phenomenal role or aspect is less

---

[5] This way of looking at the attitudes is fairly standard; e.g. see Guttenplan (1994: 6–27). The situation with regard to emotions is particularly complex, partly because emotions differ amongst themselves (compare terror, shame, love, indignation, envy) and partly because some theorists view emotions as species of feeling, others ('cognitive accounts') regard them as being more akin to propositional attitudes (many emotions have intentional objects, e.g. 'I am envious of X's new F'). For present purposes it suffices to note that the greater the feeling-component in an emotion, the greater the distance between it and its NP-counterpart. It goes without saying that NP- (or non-phenomenal) states and characterizations are quite independant of the *NP-* (or naïve perceptual) *model of consciousness* we encountered in Chapter 2.

central to their being the kind of state they are, NP-specifications omit much less. In the case of certain mental abilities, NP-specifications may diverge only slightly from full specifications. In the case of the propositional attitudes and emotions, the situation is more muddied: a lot is left out, but a lot is included. NP-specifications may not be the whole story about any (non-zombie) mind or mental state. But they provide *some* of the story, and in some cases, most of it.

6.6. NON-PHENOMENAL SELVES

So these various distinctions provide us with a clearer view of the relationship between the phenomenal and non-phenomenal aspects of mind. They also allow us to situate the C-theory in the context of a functional role conception of the mind—provided, at least, that we construe 'functional' in the fullest of senses. If the C-theory is correct, then our existence and persistence conditions can be specified in terms of the functional role of a certain kind of mental state. The relevant states are dispositional, and their functional role includes a phenomenal element: such states are able—either singly, or in conjunction with other states—to produce one or more forms of experience. In a normal human mind, the functional role of such states is not restricted to the phenomenal. A typical experiential capacity is causally integrated into a psychological system, some of the constituents which are entirely non-phenomenal in nature—these are the extended C-systems we encountered earlier. But despite its importance in other respects, the NP-roles of our experiential powers is entirely irrelevant to our persistence conditions: the latter can be specified in wholly phenomenal terms.

Although our excursion through the disputed but intriguing terrain of zom-biehood has clarified some issues, it has brought other questions to the fore, questions which have yet to be answered. Here are two: Does Zombie-Tom really have a mind or not? Is he really a self or subject?

So far as the first of these questions is concerned, I suspect the best answer is that there is no clear-cut answer. Although he does not have a *conscious* mind (where 'conscious' = 'phenomenal'), he does have states with the same NP-specifications as Tom's mental states. We could certainly say he has an *NP-mind*, but this scarcely helps. What matters is whether NP-states are genuinely *mental* states. And as on this question I expect most people's intuitions are divided, but since the meaning of our mental terms is divided between the phenomenal and NP-functional, this is scarcely surprising. Some might be inclined to think Zombie-Tom's NP-experiences are not mental, whereas his NP-attitudes and abilities are. But this is arguably an unstable position: if states or capacities entirely lacking in phenomenal features (actual or potential) can be counted as *mental* in virtue of their causal-functional role, why not count NP-experiences to be mental too? After all, Zombie-Tom's NP-experiences have a causal-functional role that is analogous to the roles of ordinary experiences.

However, a case for denying mentality to *all* NP-states can be made out along these lines:

The distinction between the mental and the non-mental is an ontological distinction of the most profound kind. In this it is akin to the distinction between the abstract and the concrete. A system of NP-states is nothing but a complex information processing system. A complex zombie mind occupies a higher position in the ranks of information processing systems than a pocket calculator, just as the latter occupies a higher position than the humble thermostat. But the difference here is one of degree. Thermostats and zombie minds are both physical *machines*. All that separates a zombie mind from a thermostat or a lump of rock is mechanical complexity. The distinction between the mental and the non-mental is not of this kind. There is no fundamental ontological division between more or less complex physical machines. There is, however, a basic ontological distinction between the conscious and the non-conscious, between experiential states and properties and non-experiential states and properties. This suggests that we should make the phenomenal the mark of the mental. In which case, NP-states are not genuinely mental, and a zombie, no matter how sophisticated, is a mindless being.

This general line of argument is one some people find compelling. Others are not convinced. A reply might run thus:

Suppose it were the case that jellyfish have a simple form of consciousness. They are sensitive to small changes in ambient sea temperature; these differences result in feelings of warmth and coolness. What is so remarkable about the existence of these simple sensations? The information processing carried out in a zombie-mind requires a physical complexity (call it *mechanical* if you like) of an astonishingly high order. Viewed purely as a machine, the average mammalian brain is an awe-inspiring engineering achievement. The distinction between complex and non-complex cognitive machinery is of far greater significance than the distinction between the experiential and non-experiential. Isn't experienceless Zombie-Tom a more remarkable being than the experiencing jellyfish? Just look at the differences in what each can *do*!

Each of these positions has its merits, and I will not try to decide between them. So far as I can see, appreciating the similarities and differences between conscious minds and zombie-minds is more important than reaching a decision as to whether zombies *really* have minds. Likewise for ordinary mental states and their NP-counterparts: as long as we fully appreciate the extent to which the NP-states differ from ordinary mental states, the question of whether or not we apply the adjective 'mental' to them is of comparatively little significance.

The issue of whether Zombie-Tom is really a self can be approached in a similar way. Taken singly and also in combination, the two forms of mentality (or pseudo-mentality) yield three types of self.

(i) *Non-phenomenal selves*: their mental (or quasi-mental) states are entirely non-phenomenal, hence they have entirely NP-minds.

   (ii) *Psycho-phenomenal selves*: their mental states and capacities generally have both phenomenal and psychological roles.

  (iii) *Purely phenomenal selves*: their mental lives are purely experiential, their minds are composed exclusively of experiential powers; they have no operative psychological or cognitive systems.

We have already encountered examples of each of these. Zombie-Tom is self-evidently a non-phenomenal self, Maggot is a self of the purely phenomenal variety, whereas you and I, along with other typical humans, are psycho-phenomenal selves. To put it another way, whereas you and I have extended C-systems, Maggot has a C-system of the Non-extended variety, and Zombie-Tom has no C-system whatsoever. (Or, if you prefer, Zombie-Tom has an *NP-C*-system, but a C-system of this kind cannot sustain a self of the phenomenal variety.)

The notion that there could be a self or subject of the NP-variety may seem odd, at least on first encountering the notion. And it is certainly the case (by definition) that subjects of this kind are not subjects of experience (save of the extremely ersatz NP-variety). But perhaps this does not matter, or should not be allowed to matter. For the reasons outlined above, there is a case for supposing that Zombie-Tom and others like him are *psychological* subjects, even though all their psychological states are of the NP-variety. In one important respect zombies enjoy selfhood—in another they do not. Recognizing the similarities and differences between ordinary and NP-selves is ultimately more important than resolving the issue of whether entities of the latter kind really are selves.

These distinctions shed further useful light onto some relevant thought experiments. Although a typical human life is characterized by both experiential and psychological continuities, the fact that we can easily envisage surviving disruptions in psychological continuity, provided there is no similar rupture in phenomenal continuity (whether actual or potential) implies that we do not regard P-continuity as being necessary for our own continued existence. The quantum-replacement and VR-4 scenarios rehearsed in §6.4 illustrate this point as well as any. Similarly, although we are ordinarily subjects of the psycho-phenomenal kind, the fact that we can so easily imagine continuing to exist *without* a psychology, provided our streams of consciousness flow on—as in VR-4 adventures—implies that we are not essentially subjects of this kind. Hence, if we are essentially anything, we are essentially subjects of the purely phenomenal kind. Ordinarily we possess a C-system of the extended variety, but we could conceivably be reduced to a C-system of the non-extended kind. Life in the absence of a psychology is a diminished life, but it is *a life*—a way in which we could continue to exist, albeit in diminished form—or so our intuitions with regard to the VR-4 scenarios (and Nozick's experience-machine) strongly suggest. This verdict is further confirmed by the prospect of imminent zombification. A consciousness eradicating NRT-procedure is not something *we ourselves* could survive, even though the being who emerges will possess our psychology (albeit in

NP-form) and will be indistinguishable from us in both behaviour and outward appearance. When the lights go permanently out—when we permanently lose consciousness and the capacity for it—we cease to exist.

These distinctions also make possible (or at least conceivable) an unfamiliar kind of bifurcation. It is not difficult to devise scenarios, admittedly of the far-fetched variety, in which the two components of ordinary psycho-phenomenal selfhood diverge. Here is one such.

We help ourselves to two *mind-machines*, X and Y, of very different types. X is an experience-machine, capable of sustaining a stream of consciousness with the aide of VR-4 technology. Y is a zombified human brain, which has also had its original psychology wiped. Two additional devices are also used: a 'C-diverter' and a 'P-diverter'. These are put to work at the same time. The C-diverter transfers your stream of consciousness into the X-machine, where it then comes under the control of the VR-4 program: your stream of consciousness flows seamlessly into a machine-generated virtual environment, where you spend your time happily engaged in underwater exploration. This is all the C-diverter does. The P-diverter transfers your psychology into the Y-machine, where it becomes functional, albeit in NP-form: a zombified version of your earlier self now inhabits the Y-machine. The outcome of this double-exchange (also depicted in Figure 6.2) is evident: an integrated psycho-phenomenal subject—you, prior to the procedure—has been split into its phenomenal and NP-psychological constituents.

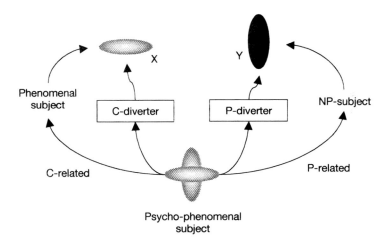

Figure 6.2 A novel form of fission: mind-machines split a normal subject into phenomenal and non-phenomenal parts

As for what happens to the original subject, the answer seems clear. You are reduced to the condition of a purely phenomenal subject, and continue to exist—in this case, enjoying an underwater adventure—sustained by the experiential powers of the X-machine. As for the Y-machine, *you* do not move into it. If we suppose the Y-machine is hooked up to a human body in the normal ways, the resulting 'person' (an NP-subject) will inherit your behavioural dispositions, and so act as though it were you. But since you cannot exist as a zombie, this being cannot be you.

The case of teleportation is rather different. We saw in §1.3 that in some contexts, teleportation of the purely informational variety—where your body and brain are scanned, destroyed, and replicated elsewhere using new materials—can appear to be person-preserving. Since informational teleportation ruptures C-relatedness this result is problematic from the perspective of the C-theory. But as we also saw, when what is essentially the same procedure is presented in a different way, it seems evident that the procedure in question is far from being person-preserving (recall the bacon-slicer scenario). We are now in a better position to appreciate why this divergence of responses occurs. When you undergo informational teleportation the replica who emerges on Mars (let us suppose) is in all intrinsic respects a normal human being. Consequently, this newly created subject is of the psycho-phenomenal kind, and so at least a candidate for being you. Moreover, since it is fully P-related to you, this subject possesses a direct and unique copy of your psychology—a psychology that is not of the NP-variety. Given the presence of this far from non-negligible mental connection, it is not surprising that the claim that the replica *is* you can be made to seem quite plausible. If psychological continuity is the only form of mental continuity that is mentioned or given prominence when presenting the scenario—as is often the case in the philosophical literature—it might easily seem very plausible to suppose that the process is fully self- or person-preserving. However, as is now clear, psychological continuity is but one component of full mental continuity. There is also phenomenal continuity, sustained by C-related experiential capacities. And so far as our continued existence is concerned, this is the continuity which counts. P-continuity by itself is all that is required for preservation of NP-subjects, it is neither necessary nor sufficient for the preservation of phenomenal selves. It is otherwise with C-relatedness.

6.7. WHAT MATTERS

Concerning teleportation Parfit writes: 'my relation to my Replica contains what fundamentally matters. This relation is about as good as ordinary survival. . . . It would therefore be irrational to pay much more for a conventional spaceship journey' (1984: 287). Parfit can say this because he is of the view that what fundamentally matters, when it comes to our own persistence, is 'Relation R', that is psychological continuity and/or connectedness (1984: 216). Given this view, it is not surprising that Parfit adopts the position that he does. But as we have just seen, if teleportation fails to preserve C-relatedness, it manifestly does *not* preserve everything that matters with regard to the continued existence of phenomenal selves, for it fails to preserve the continuous potentiality for experience that is constitutive of the persistence of such selves. In the light of this, paying extra for the conventional spaceship journey is not only not irrational, it might be a good idea.

However, the situation is not quite so straightforward. In response, Parfit could argue like this:

No, paying the extra would be irrational, even if you believed that teleportation would rupture C-relatedness. It is vital to distinguish two senses of 'what matters'. On the one hand, there are the relationships between earlier and later persons that are required for personal identity, and on the other, there are the relationships we *care* about, the relationships which we value. Even if teleportation fails to preserve numerical identity, it does preserve everything of real significance. This is because what matters in the latter sense is P-relatedness, psychological continuity and connectedness, and as you concede, this is not threatened by teleportation.

To simplify, from now on I will follow recent practice and use 'what matters' in the second sense, to refer to what we value and care about in our persistence. The claim that identity and what matters (in this sense) can come apart is a familiar theme in the recent personal identity literature. Parfit's argument for the claim is largely based on an interpretation of what would happen to a person if they were to undergo fission (1971, 1984), an argument I will be considering (and rejecting) in Chapter 12. More recently it has been put to use in the defence of animalism. As we saw in Chapter 1, despite its initial appeal, the claim that we are each identical with a particular human animal looks very implausible in the light of certain imaginary cases. Recall the CRT-procedure, which would transform you from a living animal into a non-living machine without impinging in the slightest on your consciousness, psychology, or outward physical appearance. It is hard to believe that this cell-replacement procedure would put an end to your existence, but if animalism were true it would: if you are an animal, and no animal survives the process, then you do not survive either. However, as Olson argues (1997: ch. 3), although most of us would treat the person who emerges from such a procedure just as though they were the original, and this course of action might be perfectly reasonable, we need not draw the conclusion from this that numerical identity has been preserved. It would be reasonable to regard the CRT-procedure as being as good as ordinary survival, for all practical and prudential purposes, if it preserves everything that matters from the practical and prudential perspectives. Perhaps what matters in the latter ways is not numerical identity, but the preservation of various forms of mental continuity, all of which are preserved by the CRT-procedure. In this way the animalist can explain why we respond as we do to the scenarios in question. When we ask ourselves

'Would such-and-such a transformation change the way I feel about the person involved?', it could easily be that rather than discovering anything about the real nature persons, we are simply unmasking which of the various life-continuities that normally accompany numerical identity has greatest practical and emotional significance. Hence such enquiries may in large part be practical or ethical in orientation, rather than metaphysical.

As Olson concedes, this reasoning in itself does not establish that animalism is true, but it does give rise to some pertinent questions.[6] To what extent are the relationships which, according to the C-theory are of metaphysical significance, also of practical and prudential significance? C-relatedness may be of interest from the perspective of a purely metaphysical inquiry into the phenomenal self, but does it matter in any other way? Also and more specifically, bearing in mind the neo-Parfittian argument outlined above, we need to consider whether C-relatedness or P-relatedness matters most, and in what respects.

We can make a start by stating the obvious. So far as the persistence of ourselves and those closest to us is concerned, what most of us want is a package deal. I want to continue to exist, certainly, but that is not all that matters to me: I have very definite preferences as to the *way* I exist. Other things being equal I would opt for more health rather than less; I would prefer that my ambitions come to fruition rather than fail, that my desires are realized rather than not, and so on. I want similar things for those I most care about: yes I want them to continue in existence, but I would much prefer it if they did so in particular ways. In a nutshell, identity matters, but it is not all that matters.

To register this fact, Unger distinguishes two senses of what matters in survival (1990: 93–4). According to what Unger calls mattering in the *desirability* sense, what is of importance in survival is whatever it is that makes remaining in existence something worth having, something preferable to ceasing to exist. What people value about their lives will vary, but there will likely be some constant factors: a healthy, presentable body, the preservation of the bulk of one's memories, basic personality and intellectual powers, and so forth. Unger contrasts this with what he calls mattering in the *prudential* way. At issue here is a person's ego-centric concern with their own future well-being. I have a special concern with my future self's welfare, a concern which is largely independent of what my future self is like, of how similar to my present self he is. If I will exist at some future time, it is rational for me to care about my future self, even if this self will have the sort of life I would prefer *not* to have. For instance, it seems reasonable for me to fear, and seek to prevent, my future self's suffering great pain, no matter what my future self is like, even if he is very different from me both psychologically and physically. After all, any pain felt by my future

⁶ Olson's case for animalism rests, to a large extent, on various arguments which purport to establish that mentalistic approaches are metaphysically inadequate. I will be addressing his central argument in Chapter 7.

self is pain *I* will feel. These two senses of 'what matters' can come apart. If a severe accident were to deprive me of almost all of my memories and mental abilities, and left me hideously disfigured physically, I would be left with little or nothing of what matters in the desirability sense. Yet everything that matters in the prudential sense could be preserved. My post-accident life is one I might prefer not to have at all, but it is still my life, and it makes sense for me to dread myself being reduced to such a condition, and be concerned about the pain my injuries might continue to cause me.

Another way of marking the distinction is by distinguishing concerns which are bound up with the fates of particular *entities*, and concerns with the distinctive *attributes* of these entities. As the example of the accident shows, these can come apart. The fact that I no longer possess many of the mental or physical attributes which are distinctive of my present self does not prevent my being very much concerned about the well-being of my very different post-accident self. The primitive ego-centric concern I have for the particular entity I am is irreducible to the importance I attach to my distinctive characteristics. The latter play a vital role in determining how desirable my future life might be, but they do not determine, in themselves, whether or not I will have a future life. This entity-attribute duality also plays a significant role in our attitudes and feelings towards others. Although much of what we value in a person is tied to what is distinctive about them—their appearance, personality, and style—some attachments go further and deeper. Most of us are capable of becoming emotionally attached and morally committed to people in ways that are largely independent of their distinctive attributes. Perhaps the most vivid illustration of this is the feelings of parents towards their children, where a strong emotional attachment pre-dates the formation of any personality whatsoever, and is largely independent of physical appearance too. But more generally, bonds of strong friendship or love for a person which are founded, in part at least, on the basis of an affinity between personalities or physical attraction, do not necessarily end when, through some misfortune or other, this foundation is no longer there. Provided some basic level of mental functioning persists on, we tend to think the person too persists on, albeit in a tragically diminished condition. So long as a spark of mental life remains, we can make sense of the idea that the person too remains; if this spark can be rekindled, so much the better; if it expires altogether we can be certain the person too has ceased to be.

Keeping these points in mind we can turn to the question of the comparative significance of P- and C-relatedness. Two things at least are quite obvious. It is clear that psychological continuity matters a great deal with regard to what is desirable in survival. Most of us want to retain our memories, personality traits and intellectual abilities; we do not necessarily desire total *stasis* with regard to these attributes, but we would prefer any changes to develop out of our current psychology in the usual sorts of way. It is equally clear that the preservation of C-relatedness does not guarantee the preservation of everything (or even most) of what matters in this sense. According to the C-theory, you are identical with a future self or subject if you are connected to the latter by an uninterrupted potentiality for experience; there is no restriction on the sorts of experience this future self can have, or their physical or psychological traits. Hence as far as the C-theory is concerned, there is no assurance whatsoever that your future life will be one you would even remotely like to have. Since most of us can envisage ourselves existing in a radically transformed state, for better or for worse, the flexibility of the C-theory in this regard is an advantage.

So far so obvious. But there is a further question: just how much of what matters in the prudential sense is due to C-relatedness, and how much to P-relatedness? The answers, I suggest, are 'everything' and 'nothing' respectively.

A strong case can be made for supposing that C-relatedness is all but inseparable from the primitive ego-centric concern we have with our own future selves and their experiences. Since the relevant considerations should by now be familiar, I will be brief. Suppose you know that at noon today, just an hour or so from now, someone will be in terrible pain; suppose you also know that an uninterrupted (and non-branching) stream of consciousness will connect this pain with your current experience. How could the pain fail to belong to you? How could any experience that lies directly downstream *in your current stream of consciousness* possibly belong to anybody else but you? To avoid encountering this future pain you would have to leave or escape from your current stream of consciousness, but how could you possibly do that? The idea seems absurd. As we saw in §4.6, C-relatedness also carries self-interested concern across periods of unconsciousness in an equally secure manner. When we fall into dreamless sleep we retain the capacity for consciousness (if we didn't we would be dead), and this capacity typically resides in a number of dormant experiential capacities, capacities which would—if active—contribute to a single unified stream of consciousness. The experiences I had just prior to falling asleep were the product of a particular C-system, and this same C-system persists through the period during which I am unconscious and is responsible for the first experiences I have upon regaining consciousness. Sameness of C-system over time is secured by direct diachronic co-consciousness: adjacent temporal phases of a C-system have the ability to produce temporally extended experiences whose successive parts are co-conscious. The notion that a subject could in some manner escape from its C-system seems as bizarre as the notion that it could escape from its stream of consciousness. Since a C-system just is a (usually complex) capacity for consciousness, so long as a subject retains the capacity to have experiences it necessarily retains its C-system, and so where subjects go their C-systems go.[7]

---

[7] As I mentioned in Chapter 4 in a similar context, there are two special cases that I will be dealing in more detail later on. One way a self could become separated from its C-system is by losing all its *capacities* for experience, but continuing to exist as a 'mere' stream of consciousness. If this is possible—and I will be suggesting in Chapter 8 that it might be—it doesn't amount to a case in which a C-system and a self come apart, with each continuing to exist in the other's absence—what we have, rather, is a self continuing to exist after its C-system (as normally construed) has perished; I

What of P-relatedness? The situation is altogether different. Under ordinary circumstances P- and C-relatedness go together (along with material continuity), and they can only come apart in rather unusual circumstances. There are two basic types of case to consider: in one P-continuity extends beyond C-relatedness, in the other it branches off from it. As soon becomes apparent, in neither case does it carry entity-oriented ego-centric concern with it.

Informational teleportation is an instance of the first mode of separation. My body and brain are scanned and destroyed; the information from the scan is stored—in a pile of DVD disks, say—and at some future time these data are used to construct a replica of me. As we have already seen, the claim that this future person is me is not in the least compelling: it is very easy to believe that the person in question is somebody else—an accurate copy of me but nothing more. If I am informed that this future person will suffer great pain, it seems entirely plausible to suppose that this pain will be suffered by someone else entirely, someone who is very definitely not me. In this sort of case at least, P-relatedness secures little or nothing of what matters in the purely prudential sense. And we now have a reasonable explanation as to why this should be so: C-relatedness preserves what prudentially matters in a clear and unambiguous way, and the envisaged process clearly fails to preserve C-relatedness. When my body and brain are destroyed, so too are my experiential capacities—utterly and completely—and *qua* phenomenal self I am annihilated. It is not surprising that my ego-centric concern cannot extend beyond this terminus to my P-related successor.

The second way in which a future self could be P- but not C-related to my present self is even more clear-cut. A variant of the teleportation scenario illustrates the relevant mode of branching. As previously I am scanned, and the resulting data are used to construct a replica of me. But this time the scan is of the non-destructive variety: not a cell of my body is harmed, I remain conscious throughout, and carry on with my life afterwards as if nothing had happened. When subsequently I contemplate any pain that my replica might be suffering, it seems very clear that this pain is being felt by somebody else entirely. Similar reflections conducted prior to the scanning yield the same result: it seems obvious that the replica will be someone else, that *I* will not be having its experiences. When C-relatedness and psychological continuity branch in this manner, entity-oriented prudential concern goes only one way: with C-relatedness.

While this seems undeniable it might be objected: 'Yes, but your scenario is blatantly biased against P-continuity. You are supposing, in effect, that P-continuity branches, and that one branch is accompanied by uninterrupted

will be suggesting that the concept of a C-system can be extended to cover this eventuality. The case of fission is different again. Might this be a way for selves and C-systems to go their separate ways? Perhaps on some interpretations, but I will be arguing in Chapter 12 that selves and C-systems remain locked together during fission.

physical and experiential continuity, whereas the other is not. Given this asymmetry, it is to be expected that our prudential concern follows one branch but not the other.' A fair point, but so far as I can see, eliminating the asymmetry changes nothing.

Let us return to the destructive mode of scanning, and again make use of the C-diverter introduced in the previous section. Your body is scanned, destroyed, and a few hours later the resulting mass of data is used to construct a replica of you. Just prior to the scan, the C-diverter lifts your stream of consciousness from your brain, and transfers it to a VR-4 device, where a new (apparent) psychology is imposed, and you begin a new (apparent) career as the captain of a nineteenth-century Icelandic whaling ship. The asymmetry has now been eliminated. Your body has been destroyed, and your phenomenal successor (as we might call it) is no longer psychologically continuous with your pre-scan self. But if you ask yourself, 'Where do I go? Which future experiences will be experienced by me?' the answer seems as clear as before: the experiences being generated in the VR-4 device lie in *your* experiential future—they are connected to your present experience by an unbroken chain of actual and potential co-consciousness—those had by the P-continuous duplicate do not. As usual, in outlining the VR-4 scenario I have question-beggingly assumed that 'you' go with your stream of consciousness—but again, given that your stream of consciousness is uninterrupted, that the transition to the VR-4 device is smooth, and involves not the slightest rupture in moment-to-moment phenomenal continuity, this stipulation seems entirely warranted.

Variants of these scenarios which provide the C-theory with even sterner tests are not difficult to devise. Suppose, as previously, that you are replicated via destructive scanning. Let us further suppose that just prior to the destruction of your body your stream of consciousness is transferred into a VR-4 device, and that, as previously, your consciousness is informed by a new psychology. This time around the new psychology is that of an entirely unexceptional mouse, and the virtual adventures you are supplied with in this condition are of the kind an unexceptional mouse might have. Once again there are two candidates for being you. On the one hand we have a P-related physical replica of you (as you were at the scanning); on the other we have a machine-sustained stream of mouse-like consciousness. Does this extensive psychological alteration and diminishment prevent your prudential concern tracking phenomenal continuity, rather than its psychological counterpart? I doubt it, and why should it? As previously, given that the mouse-ish consciousness is linked to your original (pre-scan, pre-transfer) stream of consciousness by an uninterrupted (and non-branching) phenomenal flow, isn't it clear as can be that the mouse-ish experiences lie in your own experiential future?[8]

---

[8] To make the case more compelling still consider a 'reduction–restoration' variant: your stream of consciousness is reduced to a mouse-like condition, but some time later it is restored to a normal

We can stack the deck against the C-theory in yet another way. Suppose your stream of consciousness is transferred into a VR-4 device, and has a new psychology imposed upon it (in light of the preceding we need not dwell on the details of what *kind* of psychology). Suppose your body is *not* destroyed, but a new stream of consciousness (mine, say) is transferred to your brain with the aid of a streamal diverter; your original psychology comes to inform this stream. Once again we have two candidates for being you. Once again, one of them is a machine-sustained consciousness, but this time around the second candidate is a human being who is both physically *and* psychologically continuous with your pre-transfer self. But is there any room for real doubt about what happens to *you*? When *I* contemplate this scenario it seems plain where I end up: in your body, sustained by your brain. When you contemplate this scenario—focusing on the uninterrupted flow of your consciousness from your original body into the VR-4 sustained virtual environment, isn't it clear where *you* end up?[9]

If I am right in suggesting that P-continuity in the absence of C-relatedness has little or no prudential importance, it does not follow that it has no significance whatsoever. Far from it. For as I pointed out in §6.6, P-continuity all by itself amounts to a genuine mental connection—albeit of the non-phenomenal variety—between earlier and later subjects. Were any of us ever to have purely psychological successors—generated after a non-destructive scanning process—then we would be related to these offspring in a uniquely intimate way, and as a consequence our relationship to them would be of a quite distinctive kind.[10] But intimacy does not make for identity, and the kind of concern we might have for our purely psychological offspring would be quite unlike the sort of concern we have for ourselves. Producing such offspring could well be an effective way of ensuring that one's cherished projects are completed after one's death—but it would not be a way of cheating or evading death itself.

That said, there is of course no way of predicting with any confidence the ways our feelings may change in the light of future social, intellectual, and technological developments. Our patterns of concern could change if psychological replication technology were ever to become commonplace; we might start to feel differently

---

human level; we can throw in normal embodiment too. In this case it can seem even more evident that you go with C-relatedness rather than P-relatedness (yes, there's a P-related duplicate here also). If you can survive with the diminished stream of consciousness in this case, why not the previous one?

[9] Some philosophers—e.g. Ardon Lyon (1980), Nozick (1981)—have argued that in cases where the continuities which characterize an ordinary life diverge in an asymmetrical manner, the original person goes with *most* of the continuities. As will be clear, I disagree. Once the existence and importance of phenomenal continuity and C-relatedness are recognized, this majoritarian approach loses its appeal. Closest-continuer theories *can* seem appealing, but only when C-relatedness is left out of the picture. In a related vein, as I noted in §1.5, Williams' cases only seem ambiguous because no mention is made of phenomenal continuity; when this lacuna is filled, all ambiguities vanish.

[10] See Brin (2003) for an occasionally intriguing exploration of some ways in which this type of relationship might develop

about the relative importance of psychological and phenomenal continuities. Our entity-oriented prudential self-concern might become evenly split between C- and P-relatedness; it might even transfer entirely to the latter. But equally, it might not.[11] In any event, as things stand at present, so far as our current attitudes and values are concerned—and it is these I am interested in here—it seems clear where our allegiances lie. Identity may not be all that matters to us, but it does matter. We have a distinctive type of identity-related concern, a concern that remains unwaveringly locked onto particular selves through all the changes and vicissitudes selves can undergo. This concern can easily diverge from P-relatedness, but from C-relatedness it is inseparable. This is surely not a coincidence.

To return to our starting question—the extent to which teleportation preserves what matters—we now have our answer. Modes of teleportation which transmit psychological continuity but rupture C-relatedness preserve little or nothing of what matters in a prudential sense. To the extent that psychological continuity in the absence of C-relatedness is a genuine mental connection, this sort of teleportation does not annihilate you completely—something *of* you will remain in existence—but the possessor of this something is most definitely *not you*. In view of this, paying a little extra for a more traditional form of transportation might be worthwhile.[12]

---

[11] Devising plausible-seeming science fiction scenarios where people have come to regard P-continuity as all that matters (in the desirability *and* prudential senses) isn't difficult. Imagine a society in the not-too distant future where most children are teleported to school every day—the measure was introduced by the government as a way of reducing school-run traffic congestion. The teleportation system is purely informational, and ruptures C-relatedness. Under such circumstances, after the system had been in place for a generation or so, wouldn't everyone regard P-continuity as fully person-preserving? Well, they probably would *if* the system were ever successfully introduced—but how likely is it that any government could introduce a 'transport' system which could (very plausibly) be construed as invariably lethal? Our current patterns of concern may well be very resilient. See Egan (1997) for an interestingly different take on this topic.

[12] We aren't yet quite done with teleportation—see §10.8 for some further thoughts.

7
Embodiment

7.1. A BLURRING

I want now to take a closer look at a topic that I have thus far largely overlooked: the relationship between selves and their bodies. Under what circumstances is it appropriate to say that a self *has* a body? Disembodied selves are possible (e.g. vat-brains), but subjects such as ourselves are evidently embodied. What does embodiment amount to and require? Once we have answered this question we can ask another: Is having a body tantamount to *being* a body? Some philosophers have alleged that it makes no sense to suppose an embodied subject is an entity other than their body. Looking at the reasoning behind this claim will take us into the proximity of a dense thicket of metaphysical issues. In finding our way through—or around—this jungle, a clear understanding of embodiment will be useful. As a preliminary, I will pause briefly to mention a related but distinct aspect of the mind–body relationship.

Another variant of the NRT-scenario will serve to bring out the point I have in mind. As usual, the NRT injection siliconizes your brain, and it does so while preserving your experiential capacities and your psychology. When you wake up, everything is much as it was before: you can see, hear, touch, taste, and smell, you have a full range of bodily sensations, you can move at will, your gait, agility, and dexterity are unaltered, you can tie your shoelaces as easily as you ever could. The process seems to be a success. It is a few hours before you notice that something is amiss. At a partly later that evening, you celebrate the happy outcome, and you drink heartily, perhaps more than you should; gradually, it dawns on you that the alcohol is not having its usual effect. After two hours of downing sizeable gins, and a couple of cocktails to boot, you do not feel in the least intoxicated; you might have been drinking milk all evening. Somewhat perturbed, you seek out the nano-surgeon who supervised your operation. 'Didn't you read the small-print?', he asks. 'One of the side-effects of NRT is a change in internal brain chemistry, as you would expect. Alcohol doesn't interact with silicon neurons. Drink as much as you like, you'll never get drunk. Unfortunately, the stuff can still damage your liver, so don't overdo it too much!' You find the prospect of a lifetime of enforced sobriety a sombre one, but not (yet at least) an unbearable one. Over the next few days, you notice some further differences. You go running a couple of times a week; although you get breathless as before, you feel nothing of the 'exercise high'; your mood is not altered in the slightest. You still feel sexual impulses, but their phenomenal quality is subtly altered. You still feel hunger as a sensation in the pit of the stomach, but there is no accompanying feeling of light-headedness. Overall, your moods and emotions, the affective side of your mental life, is flatter, more even, than before.

In a manner of speaking, this example illustrates the relationship of heart and mind. This is more than a metaphor, for the example illustrates the influence of *blood*, or at least body-chemistry, on our brains, and hence on our minds. Perhaps this is an oversimplification, but there is no denying that physical changes in our bodies, such as those produced by exercise (and subsequent exhaustion) or the absorption of intoxicants (or just plain wholesome food), can significantly influence the character of our conscious mental life; and many of these bodily changes affect the brain by altering our body-chemistry. It is easy to imagine creatures whose brains and minds are not at the mercy of their body-chemistry, but we are not like this. What we do with (or to) our bodies makes a difference to our minds. It is an oversimplification to speak of 'bodily' induced alterations to blood chemistry in this context, since many mood-altering chemicals are introduced into our blood supply by the brain itself, in response to what we think and perceive ('That really is an angry bull bearing down on me, not just a friendly cow!'). But this only serves to confirm the extent to which the character of our mental life can be influenced by bio-chemical factors.

Since our minds are grounded in physical systems, none of this is surprising. But the recognition of the importance of body-chemistry (oversimplifying again) complicates the relationship between body and mind. I have taken a 'mind' to consist of a combination of experiential and psychological capacities. Although I have assumed that experiential powers are usually triggered by physical changes in or at the periphery of the systems which constitute their power-bases, I have also assumed that these physical changes are brought about either by other mental occurrences, or incoming stimuli from the sensory organs. The explicit recognition of the importance of bodily chemistry complicates this picture.

Should we regard our sensitivity to changes in bodily chemistry as another experiential power, and so incorporate this sensitivity into our understanding of what our own C-systems comprise? Or should we regard it as a non-mental attribute, a simple consequence of the fact that our C-systems are physically grounded, and hence inevitably sensitive to a certain range of physical interactions? Perhaps the best course is to accept a certain blurring of boundaries. There is clearly a sense in which the desensitizing NRT-process reduces your range of experiential capacities; there are some moods and sensations you can no longer have, for example certain feelings of euphoria are no longer available to you. So to an extent the NRT-process reduces your experiential capacities, even if only to a relatively slight degree. On the other hand, the desensitizing process could be regarded as reducing the number of ways some of your mental powers can be impeded or impaired. Thanks to the siliconization procedure, alcohol and hunger no longer adversely affect your ability to think and remember clearly. Your mental abilities have been liberated from some of the consequences of their physical grounding. But then again, you can no longer employ certain useful cognitive stimuli, so perhaps your cognitive capacities have been diminished after all.

What we see here is a general pattern of dependency: our mental capacities, experiential and cognitive, are deeply entangled with their physical bases. As a result of this entanglement, changes to the physical basis of our minds alter both the range of mental capacities we have, and the way in which these capacities can be exercised. It will not always be useful to draw a clear distinction between cases in which a physical change in a power-base affects the existence or persistence of a given mental capacity, and cases in which such a change affects the way in which the capacity can be exercised, where the latter include the circumstances which trigger the power, and the consequences of triggering it. But there is nothing very surprising here.

I have been talking of the influence of *body* on mind. In a way this is misleading: the influence of the body is real enough, but it is also indirect and only contingent. Changes in bodily chemistry only affect our mentality if they reach (and affect) our brains. If my brain were removed from my body and envatted, I could conceivably be supplied with a virtual sensory world—and a virtual body—by the appropriate stimulation of my sensory nerve-endings; I could be made to feel hungry or drunk by appropriate alterations to the supply of blood that is being artificially pumped through my brain. It is not necessary to be embodied to experience the normal consequences of embodiment.

7.2. FOUR GRADES OF EMBODIMENT

We have been considering a contingent consequence of embodiment. Let us move on to consider embodiment proper. What does it take for a subject of experience to have a body? I have been assuming that conscious subjects can take all manner of physical shapes and forms. While this may well be true, the only embodied subjects we know of have organic bodies broadly similar to our own. So to simplify the discussion I shall restrict my attention to embodiment of the kind we are familiar with: I will be concerned for the most part with human subjects, human bodies, and human brains. There may well be other ways to be embodied, but this is not the place to speculate as to what these may be. In any event, the restricted approach I will be pursuing yields some general principles, and these may well have broader relevance.

To start with, we can make matters more precise by distinguishing four grades or depths of embodiment. A subject is embodied in one sense if its mind—composed of its C- and P-systems—is physically grounded. Call this *minimal embodiment*. A subject is *phenomenally embodied* if it seems to the subject, phenomenologically, that it has a body. A subject is *effectively embodied* if it is phenomenally embodied and, in addition, its mind is connected to a body in the right sorts of way—quite what these ways are is a question I will be addressing. Finally, a subject is *maximally embodied* if it is both minimally and effectively embodied. The rationale for distinguishing effective from maximal embodiment will become plain shortly.

I have already said a little about minimal embodiment in my remarks (in Chapter 4) on the relationship between C-systems and their material bases. To reiterate: assuming moderate naturalism, all subjects in our universe are minimally embodied. From this alone, however, it does not follow that a subject's mental capacities at or over time are necessarily grounded in (what we would ordinarily take to be) a single physical object. Focusing on the synchronic case, it is at least conceivable that C-related experiential powers could be grounded in a number of different brains (powers could be C-related at a distance); it is equally conceivable that experiential powers grounded in the same brain could fail to be C-related.[1] In the former case, a number of distinct brains sustain a single subject, in the latter case, a single brain sustains a number of distinct subjects. What holds for brains holds for any physical object or objects which are subject-sustaining. Some philosophers believe, as did Descartes, that the entire physical universe consists of a single physical object, and while not endorsing this view, contemporary physics has not ruled it out. It is at least conceivable that our universe, when viewed from the most ontologically perspicuous perspective, consists of a single four-dimensional spatio-temporal field. If this were the case, all ordinary things—even things as seemingly substantial (and hence object-like) as elephants and stars—would be no more than complex patterns of perturbation that swell and quickly fade; they would be akin to the ripples created by a gnat as it struggles vainly to escape the ocean into which it has fallen. The only genuine object would be the universe-wide field itself. If the universe were like this, all experiential capacities would be possessed by a single physical object. Your experiential capacities and mine would both be aspects of the overall experiential capacity of the universe itself. Would such a universe contain only a single conscious subject? Would you and I be one and the same conscious subject? There is no reason to think so. Such a universe contains untold billions of experiential powers; some but not all of these powers are grouped into consubjective ensembles: some powers are C-related, some are not.

---

[1] In saying this I am relying on a common sense understanding of what counts as a physical object (hence gerrymandered constructs from widely scattered parts *are not* physical objects), and allowing any such object which possesses experiential capacities to count as a brain. Anyone who objects to this use of 'brain' can reformulate these claims in terms of 'unified physical systems' or somesuch.

Returning to a more mundane level, given my simplifying assumptions, we can take it that a minimally embodied human subject is a subject whose mental life is sustained by a brain. In fact, even this is something of an oversimplification because an ordinary organic brain could possess parts with no direct relevance to mentality. If a bang on the head damages those parts of my brain which control my digestive processes, I may die quite quickly due to starvation, but there is a clear sense in which my mind might be quite unimpaired: my experiential capacities remain intact, there is no loss of psychological functionality.[2] This point will not be significant in what follows.

My main concern here will be with *effective* embodiment. Both the adjectival and adverbial senses of 'effective' are relevant here. A subject is effectively embodied if, as a matter of actual fact, it has a body, that is if it has a body in the way you or I have a body (or believe we do). If a subject really has a body in this sense, the relationship is an effective one: we are sensitive to changes in our body, we can (to a certain extent) control what our bodies do. We shall see that to be effectively embodied it is not sufficient to have a body that one can call one's own; it is necessary to be related to that body in certain distinctive ways. I will call these distinctive ways *E-relations*; a subject is effectively embodied when E-related to a particular body. I distinguish between effective and maximal embodiment because I do not want to rule out the possibility of immaterial subjects being effectively embodied (in the way Descartes envisaged). It would be very odd to suppose that an immaterial subject is as deeply embodied as a subject whose mind is physically constituted.

Moving on, a subject could be *phenomenally* embodied without being embodied in any other way. An immaterial soul could, quite conceivably, have a stream of consciousness that is qualitatively just like yours or mine without being related to the physical world in any way whatsoever. Despite this, from a purely phenomenological point of view, this soul would be just as embodied as you or I. If Berkeley is right, we are all in this condition: the only bodies we have are purely phenomenal.[3]

If we want to understand what is involved in effective embodiment, a useful, probably indispensable, first step is reaching a reasonably clear understanding of what phenomenal embodiment involves. We need not probe all the subtleties of phenomenal embodiment in any detail; the main structural features are all that matter for our purposes.

[2] This example may be a bad one. There is a hypothesis that our digestive systems have their own brains, in the sense of systems of cells which perform information processing; these systems are located in the gut rather than the head. If this is the case, it reinforces the point that not all of a human nervous system (interpreted in a wide way, so as to include gut-brains) is relevant to human mentality.

[3] Berkeley might not have agreed with this way of describing his position: given his phenomenalist account of matter, he might have insisted that most phenomenal bodies are also physical bodies. In line with moderate naturalism, I am assuming that Berkeley was wrong about matter.

7.3. PHENOMENAL EMBODIMENT

What are these structural features? What features of our experience must be present if we are to feel normally embodied? There must, of course, *be* a body, or at least the appearance of one: the relevant type of body is the *phenomenal body*, as we can call it. Let's start with this.

Obviously, to have any phenomenological reality one's phenomenal body must itself be a phenomenon, it must feature in one's experience in one way or another. In fact, it must feature in one's experience in certain quite specific ways. Imagine having an out-of-body experience: you suddenly find yourself looking down on a sleeping body from the vantage point of the ceiling; you have no bodily sensations, just your visual experience and your thoughts. As you pay closer attention to the body below, the realization dawns that it is your own body that you are looking at. This is one way for one's body to figure in one's experience, but clearly it is not the right way: from a phenomenological point of view you are no longer embodied at all!

This example suggests a way to proceed: perhaps we can isolate the main features of phenomenal embodiment by imagining what it would be like to be *differently* embodied. In what respects would a subject's experience have to change for them to lose the sense they have that they have a body? The out-of-body scenario is suggestive, but in exploring this issue it will be useful to have a more detailed scenario.

Suppose last night on falling asleep you were given an injection of nanomachines. These do not siliconize your brain, but they do engage in some drastic neural surgery: they sever every neural connection between your body and brain that is not needed for autonomic bodily functions (so your brain keeps your body breathing, and your heart beating, and so on). You regain consciousness at the usual sort of time tomorrow morning. You wake up—but to what? Your stream of consciousness will be entirely lacking in sensory input: no visual experience, no auditory experience, no tastes or smells, no bodily sensations of any kind. You have a stream of *thought*, but this thinking takes place, as it were, in a dark and silent place, a non-spatial void. You can still remember what it was like to have a body, to feel bodily sensations, to move, to see and touch the things about you, but these memories only bring home to you how different things are now; they intensify your sense of loss and diminishment. Given the extent of these various absences, it is reasonable to predict that you will *feel* entirely *dis*-embodied. You may suspect that you have suffered some kind of brain-damage; perhaps more likely, you will conclude that you have died while asleep, and that some kind of disembodied after-life is real after all. In other words, you will very likely *believe* yourself to be disembodied. Perhaps you *really are* disembodied, and you no longer *have* a body in the sense of this word that is most relevant to the question of embodiment: perhaps you are no longer effectively embodied. Whether this is so or not is a question to which I shall be returning. What is clear is that you are no longer *phenomenally* embodied; it no longer seems to you that you have a body, even when you are fully conscious.

We can now work in reverse: a further injection of nanomachines has the effect of gradually restoring the connections between your body and brain. You start by getting your sight and hearing back. All at once, you are transported back from the darkness and silence of the non-spatial void; there is light and sound, you can see and hear the doctors anxiously peering over you. This would be an immense relief, you would immediately seem to have a spatial location once again: your thinking would seem to be taking place somewhere in physical space: at the place that it seems to you that you are looking out at the world from. At this point, although you would feel yourself to be spatially located, would you feel yourself to be embodied? I suspect not, for the only sensory experience you currently have is audio-visual. You can remember what it is like to have a body, you can remember the general shape of your body, but since you do not have any bodily sensations of any kind, it would still seem to you that your body is itself still missing, still *gone*, departed, having left behind memories and nothing more. The situation improves somewhat when you regain the power of movement. The doctor monitoring your brain-waves tells you that you should now be able to move your limbs. This comes as a surprise, for as yet you have no bodily sensations. However, you decide to put it to the test and decide to sit up. To your surprise, you find yourself moving. You do not *feel* your body moving, but you deduce that it is from the way your visual experience changes. By way of analogy, imagine the images on a TV screen produced by a hand-held video camera being handled by an inexperienced or drunken operator. Since you still cannot feel your body in any way, it is surprisingly hard to control your movements; the only sensory feedback you have about your movements is visual, and this proves to be less useful than might have been thought. But once you have managed to get yourself into a stable sitting-up position, you see your body stretched out beneath and in front of you; if you try to wiggle your toes, you feel nothing, but you can see them move; you can look about the room more or less as you like. This is comforting: it is clear that your body still exists, and is intact and in working order, after a fashion; this is certainly something. But you still have no bodily experience, so you do not feel as though you are fully *present* inside your body, your body does not feel fully *yours*. You raise your arms in front of your eyes, and clasp your hands together firmly, squeezing and wringing them this way and that, but you feel nothing: no sense of muscles moving, no sense of friction or pressure.

The effect of this is disturbing. You have experienced something akin to it several times before. On occasions you have woken up to find yourself lying on an unfamiliar object, a podgy soft thing with a hard centre; usually, in a sleepy sort of way, you try to throw the thing out of bed, only to find that it firmly attached: it is your own arm, numbed by several hours of your body's weight pressing down on it. This is how your entire body currently feels, numb through and through, from top to bottom, as though a local anaesthetic has been applied generally. Fortunately, as you are trying to relate these thoughts to the rather bored doctors (your speech is not very clear), bodily sensation starts to return. At first, you feel a thawing in the head, the numbness is gradually replaced with a tingling; you soon find that you can stretch and move the tingling by exercising your cheeks; the tingling fades, and your face feels normal, *your head has come back*. Or so it feels. You now feel as though you are nothing but a head, a head that is floating in empty space a couple of feet above a bed, attached to a foreign object, an object that looks like your body but feels as though it is made of lifeless putty. As the minutes pass, feeling gradually spreads from your head down to your neck and chest, out along your arms into your fingers, and finally down to your feet and toes. As the thawing proceeds, you feel as though your body is gradually being returned to you, it feels as though you yourself are gradually extending and expanding through space.

This brief and fairly crude phenomenological excursion points to a number of factors that are needed to maintain the appearance of embodiment.

1 *Sensory-links* We perceive the world through our bodily sense-organs. Our senses of sight, hearing, smell, touch, and taste all depend on bodily organs of one kind or another.

2 *Action-links* We can control our bodies; our bodies move in accord with our evolving psychological condition. As a result, we have the impression that our bodies do what we want them to do; at least for the most part, for our bodies do not always respond to our wishes. This is not to say that we always or usually consciously will our bodies to move in this way or that. That is not how it works or feels. For the most part our bodily movements are the product of 'decisions' made sub-consciously. If I am sitting reading, I might find myself reaching across to put the light on; I may not have consciously realized how dark it was getting, I may not have consciously decided to turn on the light, but my turning on the light is clearly an action I am performing. To take another example, think of carrying on a conversation. We rarely consciously deliberate about what we will say next; we often just find ourselves saying something. It can seem as though our bodies do our talking for us—but we would soon notice if our bodies started saying things we didn't want to say.

3 *Corporeal form* By this I mean the phenomenal body-image or bodily sense-field, in the most inclusive sense. A diverse range of different bodily experiences is relevant here. There are localized bodily sensations, such as aches and pains, tickles and itches; less localized sensations of warmth, cold, and wetness. Then there are general bodily feelings such as nausea, bodily-fatigue, and bodily-vitality. There are also the experiences relating to our sense of proprioception, that is the feelings we have when our limbs are disposed in a certain manner,

or moving in a certain way. (This is not to say that proprioceptive awareness is wholly sensory, but it is to an extent.) Then there is our general sense of balance: we do not need to use our eyes to tell us if we are upside down or spinning around; there is a distinctive bodily-feel to certain bodily orientations and certain types of movement. Taken together, our various bodily experiences give us the impression that we ourselves extend through a certain volume of space, the boundary of which is fixed by our skins; they thus provide us with a corporeal form. Our thoughts and emotions, our memories and imaginings, our 'inner' consciousness in its entirety, seems to be located within our corporeal form. By virtue of having a corporeal form, we feel we know something of the intrinsic character of what occupies a certain volume of space, that which is filled by our bodies.[4] Since bodily experience can be regarded as a distinctive kind of perceptual awareness, it could regarded as another sensory link. But since—as we have just seen—this form of awareness plays a special role in maintaining the appearance of full-blooded embodiment, it seems appropriate to give it a label of its own. Not surprisingly, bodily experience plays a crucial role in the phenomenology of embodiment: if we were to lose sight, hearing, taste, and smell, all the usual sensory-links, we could still feel embodied, provided our bodily experience remained; likewise for the loss of action-links: a totally paralysed person will still feel embodied provided they continue to have bodily experience. A disembodied soul would *feel* as though it were embodied, provided it had a corporeal form, even if it had no other kind of experience.

Needless to say, these three ingredients are usually integrated. We are action-linked and sense-linked to the (phenomenal) body through which our corporeal field extends. We perceive the world through sensory organs in a body we can move at will; in moving about without bumping into things (too often), we rely on feedback from sensory-links and our corporeal fields—especially relevant here is proprioception. I will refer to these different ways of being related to a body as *phenomeno-functional connections*.

7.4. EFFECTIVE EMBODIMENT

How does effective embodiment differ from phenomenal embodiment? At one level there is no difference at all: by definition the two conditions are phenomenally indistinguishable. But at another level there is all the difference in the world: to be effectively embodied, a self must actually have a physical body,

---

[4] Of course, those who subscribe to the indirect realist (or projectivist) view of perception will hold that our bodily sense-fields do not really extend beyond our brains—but they certainly seem to.

rather than merely hallucinate that they have one. The question is, in what way must a self 'have' a physical body to be effectively embodied in it?

Our brief look at phenomenal embodiment suggests one answer, namely that an effectively embodied subject must be related to its physical body in the same way as a phenomenally embodied subject is related to its phenomenal body. There must be something right about this answer, but it cannot be the whole story. The phenomeno-functional relations we have been considering all consist of patterns to be found within streams of consciousness, and consequently all it takes for a self to be phenomenally embodied is for its stream of consciousness to have a certain character. What we are now looking for are relations which exist between subjects and the physical objects that are their bodies; these relations cannot be purely phenomenal. What sort of relations can exist between a self and a physical body? The answer, obviously, are relations of a physical and causal sort. On the assumption that our minds are sustained by our brains, the relevant relations are those which hold between bodies and brains, and we know a good deal about these. My brain is lodged within my skull; there are neural connections between my brain and various bodily parts; blood from my body is pumped round my brain and out again. Call these various brain-body links *organic* connections, or *O-relations*. Thanks to these O-relations, my mind is related to my physical body in ways which match the phenomeno-functional relations described above. The sensory-links are in place: I perceive the world through my body's sense organs. The action-links are in place: my body responds to my will. Most importantly, my (wholly phenomenal) corporeal form coincides with my physical form, and is sensitive to it. The region of physical space which my corporeal form seems to fill is that which is occupied by my physical body; changes in my physical body are reflected in my corporeal form; how my body *feels* corresponds with how my body *is*. Just as my visual and auditory experience is causally sensitive to changes in my eyes and ears, my bodily experience—in all manner of ways—is causally sensitive to changes in my body;.

So, as a consequence of its being O-related to my body, my brain sustains a mind which is related to my body in *causal-functional* ways which exactly correspond to the *phenomeno-functional* relations required for phenomenal embodiment. Call these causal-functional relations F-relations.

The traditional substance-dualist will regard F-relations as sufficient for being effectively or E-related to a body. Since the dualist regards the mind as an immaterial substance, the only way a mind *can* be related to a body is through the kinds of causal relations which go to make up F-relatedness.[5] For the dualist, F-relatedness is necessary and sufficient for E-relatedness. However, if we assume that our minds are physically based, there are the organic O-relations to consider. Might it be the case that for subjects such as ourselves to be effectively embodied, our brains must be O-related to our bodies? There are three positions to consider:

[5] See, for example, Foster (1991: 261–5).

1 F-relatedness is necessary and sufficient for E-relatedness.

2 O-relatedness is necessary and sufficient for E-relatedness.

3 Neither F-relatedness nor O-relatedness is by itself sufficient for E-relatedness; however, each is necessary for E-relatedness, and jointly they are sufficient for E-relatedness.

It should be obvious by now, (2) does not have much plausibility. Recall the example in which all the links between your body and brain were cut, save those necessary to maintain basic bodily functions. Did you not *lose* your body when this occurred? Although you remained minimally embodied, since your mental life continued to be sustained by your brain, it would be implausible to maintain that you continued to be *effectively* embodied. For all practical purposes, your brain could have been envatted and your body destroyed—you would have been none the wiser. But does the severing of the neural connections required for the sensory- and action-links suffice to disconnect your body and brain at a biological level? Clearly not: from a biological perspective, your brain and body form parts of a single integrated organism (your brain is still controlling your body's basic functioning). This suggests that F-relatedness is at least necessary for E-relatedness, and that O-relatedness alone is not sufficient for E-relatedness.

However, while F-connections might be necessary for effective embodiment, it might be thought that they are not sufficient. Perhaps causal-functional links have to be supplemented by organic links for a subject to be *fully* and effectively embodied. It might be thought that *having* a body requires one to *inhabit* that body, and that to inhabit a body one must be located *within it*. In other words, to be fully and effectively embodied, one's brain must be within one's body, and connected to it in ways which secure some degree of F-relatedness. This position, (3), undoubtedly has some initial intuitive plausibility. However, this plausibility evaporates on contact with a few further imaginary scenarios.

Nerve-stretching

Consider the scenario Dennett describes in his well-known paper 'Where Am I?' (1982). For reasons we do not need to enter into, Dennett's brain has been removed and envatted. However, the neural connections between his brain and body have been *stretched* rather than severed. Prior to the removal of his brain, the nerves connecting body and brain were cut and spliced with tiny radio transceivers. Thanks to this splicing, communication between body and brain is scarcely impaired at all, especially over short distances. We can assume also that the Neural Engineers overseeing the envatting have ensured that the device sustaining Dennett's brain is constantly monitoring his body chemistry, and makes suitable adjustments to the blood-supply being pumped through his brain.

When Dennett first wakes up after the completion of the operation, nothing feels amiss. The vat containing the brain is some distance away, in a different building, but it does not feel this way; everything feels perfectly normal; everything *looks* normal (save for the antennae protruding from his head). So far as Dennett can tell, relying only on how things look and feel, his thinking is going on in his head, as per usual. The strangeness of the predicament is only fully brought home when Dennett is taken to the lab and shown his brain. Being a philosopher of unswerving physicalist conviction, he thinks: Shouldn't I be thinking 'Here I am, suspended in a vat of bubbling fluids, being stared at by my own eyes'; but try as he might, this thought carries no conviction whatsoever. Although intellectually convinced that the tokening of his thoughts is occurring in his brain, as he looks down on his brain, it seems for all the world that he is where he seems to be: in his body, looking down at a brain.

This case has several interesting aspects. It could be taken to demonstrate the possibility of a person whose perceptual faculties are working perfectly suffering a delusion as to their whereabouts: Dennett is really in the vat, but it seems to him that he is in his body. I suspect there is a sense in which this is correct. If Dennett's body is suddenly annihilated (as happens later on in his story), Dennett himself would not be annihilated. When the links between body and brain are cut he has the impression that he is *now* back in his brain; he seems to have undergone an almost instantaneous movement from the place where his body was just prior to its destruction, to the lab where his envatted brain is to be found. Nonetheless, there is also a sense in which the delusional interpretation is an oversimplification. To see this, we need only pose the question: 'As Dennett looks at his envatted brain, is he an embodied mind? Does Dennett still have a body?' The answer, as I think is clear, is that he does. Dennett is not just a brain, he has a body—indeed, he has the same body as he had prior to the operation. To start with, the sensory-links are in place. He perceives the world through his body's sensory organs. More importantly, it *feels* to him that he is where his body is. He does not merely see the world from the perspective of his body, he feels as though he himself is occupying the same space as his body: so far as he is concerned, his corporeal form, and the associated field of bodily experience, seems exactly to coincide with his physical body. Then there are the action-links. Dennett's body is fully under his control (to the extent that anyone's body ever is). When you cut his finger, Dennett will react in just the ways you or I would. He will say 'Ouch!'—he will not just *think* this, but *say* it, out loud. This body-involving action is not something he will do voluntarily, it will be quite spontaneous. Similarly for when he instinctively puts his finger into his mouth—before taking it out again after realizing that this isn't perhaps a good idea. In acting like this, it will not seem to Dennett that he is commanding his body by remote-control; there will seem to be no greater distance between him and his body than there seems to be between you and your body.

This case forcefully suggests that F-relations alone are sufficient for effective embodiment. This conclusion is reinforced by a further variant of the nerve-stretching scenario. Our playful Neural Engineers played a trick on you and I at birth. Your brain was transplanted into my body, and my brain into your body. However, transceivers were fitted as our brains were removed. The nerves connecting your body and brain were not severed, but stretched. So although your brain is currently residing in my body, and has been doing so for a good many years, your brain has remained in constant contact with your body; there are no neural links connecting your brain with my body. All my body does is carry your brain about and supply it with blood and other nutrients. Even this relationship is mediated: before entering your brain, the chemical composition of my blood is adjusted so that it reflects the composition of the blood flowing in your body's veins. If a general anaesthetic is administered to your body, the brain in my body quickly falls unconscious. But no one watching me would notice the fact: I (or my body) continues to behave as if nothing has happened. This is to be expected. My brain—located in your body—is also in at-a-distance contact with my body. So although the brain inside my *head* has been rendered unconscious, the *brain controlling my bodily movements* is unaffected. Since neither of us has ever been informed about any of this, we are each deluded enough to suppose that our brains are where they seem to be, that *we* are where we seem to be. I assume that my brain is within my body, that is *here* or hereabouts, and you assume that your brain is within your body, *there* (wherever 'there' might be). Although we are wrong about this, are we misguided as to which body belongs to whom? My brain is within your body, but does this make your body mine? Does the fact that your brain is located within my skull suffice to make this body yours? If the sense of 'belongs' we are concerned with is that of the ownership which comes through effective embodiment, the answer seems clear: things are as they seem to be. We each have the body we have become accustomed to thinking we have. Because of this, we are not as deluded as to our whereabouts as we initially seemed to be. We are each mistaken as to the location of our brains, but we are right about the location of our bodies: they are where they seem to be.

These scenarios suggest that nothing more than F-relations are needed for effective embodiment. For as now seems clear, although the nerve-stretching procedure has ruptured the O-relations between our brains and our bodies, and our brains are not even contained within our bodies, we nonetheless have bodies, we are as *effectively* embodied as a person could be.

Perhaps not everyone will be convinced. An objection to the conclusion I am drawing from these examples might run as follows. Consider again the initial Dennett-scenario.

Dennett isn't really embodied in this case, it merely seems to him that he is. There is no denying that nerve-stretching preserves F-relatedness, and consequently produces a wholly realistic appearance of being effectively embodied. But appearances can be deceptive, and this is a case in point. For consider: if I were to pass a billion watts of electrical power through Dennett's body, it would vanish in a puff of smoke, but would Dennett himself be affected? No, not in the least; he would simply be deprived of the illusion of being embodied. That illusion is all it ever was is demonstrated by the fact that destroying Dennett's body doesn't destroy Dennett. If Dennett really were fully and effectively embodied, destroying his body would be a way to destroy him.

I do not think this objection carries much force. Suppose Dennett does not realize the envatted brain he is looking at is his own, and so does not realize his brain is not inside his body. He is certainly the victim of a illusion. But what manner of illusion? Is the impression he has of *being embodied* illusory? Or is he merely deluded as to the *location of his brain*? I suggest the latter. Now, it is true that people cannot usually survive the complete destruction of their bodies. This is a simple consequence of the fact that they carry their brains around with them inside their skulls. It would be a simple enough task to arrange matters such that Dennett's brain is immediately destroyed if his body is destroyed. We could fit a small explosive device under his brain that will explode upon receiving certain signals from transceivers located in his body; these signals are only sent if his body suffers irreparable damage (they are very fast-acting devices). The survival of Dennett's brain is now dependent upon the survival of his body; destroy his body and you destroy his brain. The point to consider is whether arranging matters in this way increases the depth of his embodiment. I cannot see that it does. Take another example. Suppose a device is devised which generates a small impenetrable force-field, large enough to protect the wearer's brain. If a device of this sort is attached to your brain, it will be activated if any serious damage is done to your body; it not only protects your brain from damage, it 'freezes' it in an instant, and so keeps it healthy until it can be envatted or re-embodied. Would the fitting of such a device make you feel any less embodied? If you were fully convinced of the device's reliability, it might lead you to feel less concerned about your body's welfare, but I doubt whether you would feel any less effectively embodied.

If we take F-relatedness as both necessary and sufficient for effective embodiment, as I think we ought, it is clear that embodiment of this sort can be a matter of degree. There are various components to F-relatedness: sensory-links, action-links, and corporeal form. Since each of these components has several strands there are many different ways in which F-relatedness can depart from the norm. One or more sensory-links could be severed; one or more action-links could be impaired; one's corporeal form could shrink (think of the situation described above, when only the head had 'thawed'), or one's corporeal form could remain intact, but the causal-functional links to one's body be impaired or eliminated. I have suggested that corporeal form is the most important element of F-relatedness; perhaps bodily experience—caused by changes in one's body—is sufficient for effective embodiment all by itself. But since this mode of connectedness comes in degrees, so too does E-relatedness.

7.5. BOUNDARY DISPUTES

We now have an idea of what relationships must hold between a subject and a body for the latter to have or own the former. A particular subject *has* a body *B* if it is effectively embodied in *B*, and effective embodiment requires F-relatedness; to be effectively embodied in *B* a subject does not need to be spatially located within *B*, the F-relations suffice. In arguing for the latter conclusion I tacitly adopted a certain stance on the synchronic boundaries of the self. I assumed that the spatial boundaries of a self at a given moment in time do not extend beyond the confines of the physical system or systems in which its mental (and particularly experiential) capacities are directly grounded. In the case of human selves, the relevant systems are of course brains, or certain regions of brains. This *minimalist* position (as I shall call it) certainly sits well with the doctrine that we are essentially our minds, and the C-thesis in its ontological guise—the doctrine that we *are* C-systems—is minimalist in this respect. Nonetheless, there are neo-Lockeans who subscribe to the *maximalist* doctrine (as I shall call it) that our synchronic spatial boundaries coincide with those of our *whole bodies*, even though our persistence conditions are entirely mentalistic. Maximalism certainly has common sense on its side: most of us regard our limbs and bodily organs to be parts of ourselves; we are accustomed to thinking of our skins as the boundaries between ourselves and the rest of the world. In ordinary life few of us distinguish between touching a *person* and touching a *person's body*.

If maximalism is metaphysically viable, then a maximalist version of the C-theory would be perfectly possible. However, while maximalism is perfectly defensible, minimalism is somewhat *more* defensible: it is viable in a wider range of metaphysical frameworks. And since I am trying to remain as neutral as possible on general metaphysical issues, minimalism is thus a more appealing option. The advantages of the minimalist path will emerge as we proceed. Let us begin by taking a look at the problems faced by maximalists.

The notion that I coincide with my body, but am also distinct or separable from it, can seem quite natural. With a little further reflection it can also seem quite odd. If I coincide with my body, then—assuming a naturalistic standpoint—I am presumably a material entity. But if I am a material entity, then given that my body is also a material body, we have two material entities occupying the same volume of space at the same time. Isn't this impossible? Not necessarily. The more general issue of whether distinct material things can coincide by having the same spatial location and the same material parts at a given time is controversial: *pluralists* think material coincidence of this sort is perfectly possible, *monists* disagree. The monist looks at a plastic cup and sees just one object: the cup, which is also the piece of plastic, and also the collection of molecules which compose the cup (and the piece). The pluralist looks at the same cup and sees several numerically distinct objects: the cup, a piece of plastic, a collection of molecules.[6] The relevance to the issue in hand is obvious. Contemporary neo-Lockeans who are drawn to the maximalist position—such as Shoemaker (1984), Garrett (1998), Baker (2000), and Tye (2003)—hold that the relationship between persons and their bodies is simply a special case of the far more general phenomenon of material objects coinciding yet remaining numerically distinct. In its contemporary form, maximalism thus rests on pluralism. As for the plausibility of pluralism, a plausible case can easily be made.

To take a well-known example, consider *Lumpl* and *Goliath*.[7] Goliath is a statue, and Lumpl is the lump of clay which Goliath is made out of (we can treat both 'Lumpl' and 'Goliath' as proper names, since we can name lumps of clay if we so choose). As it happens, Goliath and Lumpl come into existence at exactly the same time, and both cease to exist at exactly the same time. However, as is obvious, statues and lumps of clay are different sorts of object, and have different identity criteria. Without going into too many details, lumps of clay can survive radical changes in their shape, but cannot lose any (or many) of their constituent parts; statues, by contrast, can lose some significant parts—for example an arm or a leg—but cannot survive radical shape change. In virtue of this, there are circumstances in which Lumpl would cease to exist but not Goliath. Perhaps Goliath is very heavy, and is threatening to damage the floorboards, so its owner removes some clay from Goliath's interior. Lumpl no longer exists—it cannot survive the loss of any parts—but Goliath can and does. There are also circumstances in which Goliath would cease to exist but not Lumpl. Shortly after completing Goliath the artist might (in a fit of temper) have squeezed the not-yet-set piece of clay into a ball; provided that no bits of clay drop off during the squeezing, Lumpl survives, but Goliath clearly does not. Now, if Lumpl and Goliath *were* one and the same object, one of them could not cease to exist without the other doing so too. Since each *could* survive in the absence of the other, they cannot be one and the same thing. The point can be made in terms of Leibniz' Law. Identicals are indiscernible, they have the same properties. Lumpl was not squeezed into a ball, but this might have happened. So the modal property *might have been squeezed into a ball without being destroyed* is possessed by Lumpl but not by Goliath. Given this difference, Leibniz's Law (of the indiscernibility of identicals) prevents our taking Goliath to be identical with Lumpl: two objects cannot be

---

[6] A good many influential relevant papers are found in Rea (1997). For an informal (but partisan) survey of the options, see Lowe (2003). I have borrowed the monist/pluralist labels from Fine (2003).

[7] See Gibbard (1975)—although, actually, Gibbard used this example to criticize the argument which follows, but more on this later. Recent interest in this line of argument dates back to Wiggins (1968).

identical if they possess different properties. Moreover, if we did take Goliath to be identical with Lumpl, there would be other consequences. The identity of Lumpl and Goliath can only be a contingent matter, since Lumpl could have existed without being moulded into Goliath. And if we accept that Lumpl is only contingently identical with Goliath, we cannot take 'Lumpl' and 'Goliath' to be rigid designators, since identities formulated using rigid designators are necessary.[8]

There are, then, grounds for holding that Lumpl and Goliath are numerically distinct objects. But it is also important not to lose sight of the fact that they are very intimately related. Objects which materially coincide are clearly not 'separately existing' entities. Pluralists appreciate this. They point out that we can accept Lumpl's non-identity with Goliath while also accepting that Lumpl *is* Goliath. We can say the latter provided what we mean by 'is' here is not 'is numerically identical with' but 'is constituted from the same matter as', or somesuch. Goliath is *constituted* from a certain lump of clay (Lumpl, in fact), but is not *identical* with that lump (Wiggins 1968; Johnston 1992*b*).

All this suggests that it is legitimate to suppose that a portion of matter can constitute two (or more) distinct objects at a given time, provided that the matter falls under two (or more) different sortal concepts—such as *statue* and *lump of clay*. Since analogous considerations apply to all manner of physical things and their constituent parts, why not also to persons (or subjects) and their bodies? My existence may in fact coincide with that of a single human organism, but there are conceivable circumstances in which it does not. An injection of nanomachines might eliminate my capacity for consciousness, and so put an end to me, but wreak only minimal changes on my body and brain: a living organism continues on, but no longer sustains a conscious subject. This sort of example suggests that a living organism and a subject can no more be identical than a statue and a lump of clay, even if they in fact coincide throughout their respective careers. If I am not identical with the living organism which sustains my mind and mental life, what is my relationship with this organism? The pluralist treatment of the Lumpl–Goliath case suggests an answer which has a good deal of appeal for maximalists: I am distinct from the organism which sustains my mental capacities, but I share my matter with this organism—I am *constituted* by this organism—but I am not *identical* with it.

---

[8] Suppose N is a rigid designator, and in the actual world refers to O. In virtue of its rigidity, N refers to O in all possible worlds in which O exists, and to nothing otherwise. If 'Goliath' and 'Lumpl' are both rigid-designators, and if in the actual world Goliath = Lumpl, then there is no possible world in which Goliath ≠ Lumpl, since in any world in which 'Goliath' refers to anything, it refers to the same object as it refers to in the actual world, namely Lumpl, and in any world in which 'Lumpl' refers to anything, it refers to Goliath. Since there is no world where Lumpl ≠ Goliath, the latter is a necessary truth.

Overpopulation worries

Its current popularity notwithstanding, the pluralist approach is not without its difficulties, and may well be particularly problematic in the context of persons and their bodies. I have in mind an objection that has been forcefully pressed by Snowdon (1990) and Olson (1997, 2003), amongst others. It goes by various names, I will call it the 'Too Many Subjects' objection.[9] Let us suppose that the pluralists are right and you are not the same thing as a human animal, even though you coincide with one. It goes without saying that as a person or self, you are a mental subject, and as such you have a range of psychological and experiential capacities. But what of the animal with which you share your matter? This animal may not be you, but it is an *exact physical duplicate of you*. Given the naturalistic framework that we are currently working within, an exact physical duplicate of you cannot fail to have the same mental capacities as you—especially if this duplicate spatially coincides with you, and so has been interacting with the same objects. If the animal with which you coincide has the same mental capacities as you, then it too possesses a mind—a mind that is just like yours in all respects. Since we are assuming you and the animal are distinct things, the animal's mind must also be distinct from your mind, and likewise for the animal's mental life. If the animal has a mind, if it has a conscious mental life (or the capacity for it), then it too must be a mental subject, a self. We thus have two selves where there seemed to be only one. Surely this is absurd.

Snowdon develops the point further, and anticipates some objections. After pointing out that we have every reason to suppose animals could possess the mental capacities distinctive of personhood, he invites us to consider a particular animal, a human being (H), who says 'I am an animal', on some occasion O. There is, suggests Snowdon, a prima facie case for taking H to be speaking a truth:

cannot animals ever think about themselves? cannot animals use the first-person pronoun? The answer has surely to be that they can; surely some animals could and have evolved with that capacity. Now, if it is agreed that animals can, then surely H (this animal) is one such. But if H can talk of itself using 'I', then it seems that the remarks made at O through the mouth of H are such remarks. Clearly there could not be any better candidate for such a case. (What must the animal H do to speak about itself which it did not do then?) If, however, that remark was a case where an animal spoke of

---

[9] Also see Ayers (1991: 285) and Berglund (1995: 154–7)—the latter dubs it the 'Two Lives Argument'. Zimmerman (2003) refers to the 'Too Many Minds' Objection—as does Shoemaker (2003*b*)—but Zimmerman further distinguishes the 'too many thinkers' problem and the 'too many thoughts' problem. As Zimmerman also observes, the basic difficulty was first noted by Chisholm. My preference for talking in terms of multiple subjects—rather than multiple thoughts (or experiences)—is a consequence of my opting to individuate subjects by reference to experiences and experiential powers, rather than vice-versa.

itself, and what it said was 'I am an animal', then that must rank as a truth. (Snowdon 1990: 91)

This situation presents the pluralist with an embarrassing dilemma. Since H looks to satisfy the conditions for being a mental subject, we must accept that there are two mental subjects present where there seems to be only one: the animal-subject H, and the non-animal-subject P. To avoid this absurd result, the pluralist could modify the criteria for self- or personhood in such a way as to rule out the animal subject. But how? H is a conscious being equipped with reason and reflection, memory and personality. If H is not a person, what is? Other routes through the horns of this dilemma are available, but as Snowdon shows, none seem very inviting. Perhaps H's statement 'I am an animal' should be interpreted as 'I am currently sharing my matter with an animal', or 'I am currently constituted by an animal'. This interpretation evades the problem, but it fails to solve it: the claim is that 'I am an animal', uttered by H, is a plausible truth when interpreted as an identity statement, and this claim is not undermined by putting a different meaning into H's words. The pluralist might try this route: 'If a *mouth* were to say "I am a mouth" we would see the truth in the remark, but would not conclude that "I" here refers to a person, for a mouth cannot be a person. So why conclude that H is a person?' But as Snowdon points out, this analogy is imperfect: we are not in the habit of ascribing beliefs, hopes, plans, values, and experiences to mouths, but we do to animals, at least of the human sort. In desperation the pluralist might try this: 'Why not say that "I am an animal" is both true and false: it is true of the animal here, but false of the person here.' It is hard to see how this helps: we are still conceding that H is a person, so there are still two people involved. We might try to reduce the implausibility of this by distinguishing between different kinds of person: animal-subjects and pure- or Lockean-subjects. H is an animal-subject, P is a pure-subject. But this doesn't help much either. We are still confronted with two subjects in the same body, (seemingly) sharing the same thoughts. If I were to think 'I am a pure Lockean subject', I would be thinking something which is true of the pure subject currently inhabiting my body, but false of the animal subject. The problem is, how do I know what 'I' refers to: am *I* the animal-person or the pure-person? Since we are both thinking the same token thoughts and undergoing the some token experiences, all our uses of 'I' have a dual reference, so it seems the same thought is simultaneously true and false.[10]

---

[10] Olson pursues a similar line: 'Because the human animal connected with you is a perfect duplicate of you, it is conscious and intelligent if you are conscious intelligent. Whatever makes it the case that you think and act rationally would seem to make it the case that the animal thinks and acts rationally as well . . . . If you believe you are a person, the animal connected with you thinks it is a person as well. It thinks so for the same reasons that you think so; it has the same evidence as you have . . . . But if it is so easy to believe that one is a person and be wrong, how do you know that you aren't mistaken about this? How do you know you're not the animal rather than the person?' (Olson 1997: 106– 7).

There is no need to go on. The Too Many Subjects objection is clearly a serious hurdle standing in the way of the maximalist approach to the self–body relationship. The severity of the problem stems in large part from the fact that living animals are such outstanding candidates for being regarded as genuine objects, or substances. By way of a contrast, consider the collection of molecules which compose your body at a given time t; call this collection C. Although this collection composes a living animal at t, arguably it is not identical with any living animal by virtue of the distinctive and different persistence conditions of collections and animals: the latter can survive changes in their constituents, the former cannot. So does the fact that C exists at t pose a problem for the pluralist? Given that you and C are physically indistinguishable at t, if you have mental capacities at t mustn't C have them as well? And if C has the same sorts of mental capacities as you, mustn't C be a person or self too? In this instance pluralists can respond thus:

Whatever else subjects may be, they are genuine substances; among the distinguishing features of genuine substances is the ability to persist through change; compound material substances can change their constituent parts. Since collections (by definition) cannot survive such changes, they are not genuine material substances. In which case C is not a self or subject, and there is no menace of overpopulation.

This sort of argument will only appeal to those who subscribe to some version of the traditional substance-oriented ontology, but many pluralists (such as Lowe, Oderberg, and Wiggins) fall into this category. More of a problem is that this response is entirely ineffective against the Too Many Subjects objection: unlike collections or aggregates, *animals* have all the hallmarks of being genuine material substances. The menace of overpopulation is consequently very real indeed.

Responses

Is the combination of pluralism and maximalism doomed? Not necessarily. There are at least two ways in which the maximalist can stave off the absurdity of coincidence-induced overpopulation. One would be to argue, persuasively, that in cases where an animal and a subject coincide, the subject's mental properties are *confined to the subject*, and not shared or possessed by the animal. Another route would be to argue that although coinciding animals and subjects both possess mental capacities, they do not possess them in the same way, and further, that this difference in mode of possession is of such a kind as to alleviate the menace of overpopulation. Both strategies have found advocates.

Olson remarks: 'if you can refer to yourself by saying "I", the animal too should be able to refer to itself by saying that word. How could its merely having the wrong persistence conditions, which is all that makes the animal different from you, prevent it from thinking about and referring to itself' (1997: 106). In reply, the pluralist can maintain that it *only makes sense* to ascribe certain ranges of properties to objects which possess the right kind of persistence conditions. Shoemaker takes precisely this line and argues that organisms (and human animals in particular) have the wrong kind of persistence conditions to be subjects of mental states: 'Mental states being what they are, being a subject of mental states necessarily goes with having the persistence conditions that allow them to have their characteristic functional roles and cognitive dynamics' (1999: 304). If this position could be sustained within the context of the C-theory the pluralist would be out of the woods. But I have my doubts.

Irrespective of its merits on its own terms, Shoemaker's argument hinges on the peculiarities of *psychological* states, the fact that it is part of the essence of such states—part of their causal-functional role—to impact in certain characteristic ways upon future psychological states. Although a plausible case can be made for holding that such states can only exist as parts of psychological systems, and that the persistence conditions of the latter are psychological (i.e. causal-functional) rather than organic or biological, this would be of interest to those inclined to subscribe to the P-theory—in the context of the C-theory it looks to be largely irrelevant. So far as the existence of many *experiential* capacities is concerned, what matters is the here and now. What reason do we have for supposing that animals (or animal brains) cannot possess experiential capacities simply because their persistence conditions are organic rather than experiential? How could a fact like this impact upon a creature's capacity to experience pain? It is certainly true that animals can survive the loss of their experiential capacities, and it may well be true that experiential capacities can be transferred between animals (e.g. by way of cerebral transplants), but it is difficult to see why this should stand in the way of animals possessing such capacities under normal circumstances: does the possibility of lung transplants mean animals lack the capacity to breathe? If at a given time (or over a short interval) an animal's brain is such that it will produce certain types of experience when appropriately stimulated—or if it is actually in the process of producing experience—it is difficult to see how the animal (or its brain) could possibly fail to possess the corresponding experiential capacities.

But there is another option. The pluralist can accept that animals do possess experiential capacities, but do not do so in the same way as subjects of experience which share their matter. Baker has developed a position along these lines in some detail (1999, 2000, 2002). She holds that in the case of persons and their associated animals, the properties characteristic of persons *are* possessed by the animal, but only in a derivative way: the animal 'borrows' the relevant mental properties from the person by virtue of the fact that it constitutes the person; the animal only possesses its mental capacities *because* it constitutes a person, whereas the person possesses them directly and non-derivatively. She holds that such 'borrowing' is a standard feature of constitution, and is usually a two-way affair. In the case of Lumpl and Goliath, the statue borrows its shape, mass, and molecular constitution from Lumpl, whereas Lumpl borrows its aesthetic and monetary value from Goliath. More generally, if we say that x and y have 'constitution-relations' if and only if either x constitutes y or y constitutes x, then 'H is a borrowed property of x at t if x's having H at t derives exclusively from x's being constitutionally related at t to something that has H independently at t' (Baker 1999: 152). In more concrete terms, Lumpl has a particular shape S at t—the same shape as the statue Goliath—but it has this shape independently of its constitution-relations. Why? Because it is possible that Lumpl could have had shape S at t without constituting Goliath: for example if instead of being deliberately moulded into S by an artist, it had been accidentally pushed into this shape as a consequence of a child's random manipulations. Hence Lumpl does not need to constitute something else in order to have S. The fact that Lumpl has the property of being S-shaped independently of what it constitutes means that it possesses this property in a non-derivative way, or so Baker argues. What of Goliath? Does *it* possess S independently of its constitution-relations? Arguably not: Goliath can *only* have the property of being S-shaped if it is constituted by something else—a portion of matter—that is S-shaped. Furthermore, as we have seen, although the matter that constitutes Goliath *is* S-shaped, it need not have been. Put these points together and we can state in a more formal way what is involved in a case of an object x 'borrowing' a property from an object y at some time t: (i) it is not the case x has H at t independently of x's constitution relations to y at t, and (ii) y has H at t independently of y's constitution relations to x at t (Baker 1999: 154).

How does this apply in the case of subjects (as we are currently conceiving them) and animals? If at a particular time t the animal borrows its mental properties from the subject it constitutes, then (i) the animal's possession of these properties must be dependent on its constitution relations to the subject it constitutes, and (ii) the subject's possession of these properties must be independent of its constitution relations with the animal. Are these conditions met? A case can be made for saying that they are. The animal certainly would not have the experiential capacities it does at t if it didn't possess a C-system. And if (in line with the C-theory) the existence of a C-system is necessary and sufficient for the existence of a subject, then the animal's possession of its experiential capacities could be said to depend upon its constituting a subject. In which case (i) looks to be satisfied. As for (ii), arguably there are conceivable circumstances in which a given subject could exist at t without being constituted by any animal. Drastic and destructive surgical procedures might have this consequence, procedures which reduce a normal human being to an artificially maintained mass of neural tissues; more radical still are the NRT-procedures which eliminate the biological substrate of mentality. If such procedures are possible, then it is plausible to suppose that a subject's possession of its mental capacities is independent of its constitution relation with the animal which actually sustains them.

With further work a version of pluralism along these lines might prove to be a coherent option.[11] Even so, there is no denying that accepting Baker's proposal certainly involves treading an extremely fine line. On the one hand she stresses that an object that borrows a property *really has that property* (1999: 160). This might easily seem problematic, for if the animal which constitutes me really has the complete complement of my mental capacities, how can it fail to be a person or self? The Too Many Subjects objection bites once more. By way of an antidote, Baker insists that 'if *x* borrows *H* from *y*, there are not two independent instances of *H*: if *x* borrows *H*, then *x*'s having *H* is entirely a matter of *x*'s having constitution-relations to something that has *H* non-derivatively' (*ibid.*). Extending this proposal to the case in hand yields something along the following lines. Any animal which constitutes a subject really has experiential capacities, but these capacities are numerically identical with those which belong to the subject; since there is only a single C-system, and assuming that subjects are individuated by reference to C-systems, rather than vice-versa, then there is only a single subject involved. Since it is the subject rather than the animal that possesses mental capacities in a non-derivative way, there is only one *genuine* or *basic* subject present. The animal qualifies for subjecthood, but only in a derivative way, by virtue of the fact that it happens to constitute a genuine subject at the time in question. The animal not only borrows its mental capacities from the subject, it also borrows *its status as a subject*, and as such, it does not constitute a second subject in addition to the first.

This appeal to the notion of derivative property-possession—at least in this form—will not convince everyone. It is not difficult to envisage the sort of reply which Animalists will make: 'You step on your cat's paw, it yelps in pain: isn't it obvious that it is the *animal* that is feeling pain? Isn't it equally obvious that the animal is feeling this pain in a direct and non-derivative way? What else *but the animal* evolved the capacity to feel pain?'[12] And at an intuitive

---

[11] For Baker the essential or defining characteristic of persons is the capacity to enjoy a first-person perspective (which she equates with a strong form of self-consciousness: 'one must be able to conceive of oneself as having a perspective, or a subjective point of view' (2002: 64)). Since it is plausible to suppose that entities that don't have this capacity can nonetheless have mental states (such as pain), her general position on constitution commits her to an unusual view of the ownership of mental states and capacities: 'Any mental property of mine whose exemplification requires a first-person perspective is one that I have non-derivatively, if I have it at all. Any mental property of mine that dogs or chimpanzees (organisms that do not constitute persons) could have is one that I have derivatively' (2002: 104). Adopting the C-theory avoids this counterintuitive dual ownership. If the defining feature of persons (or subjects) is the capacity to have experiences, then human subjects can possess pains and other basic forms of experience in just the same (non-derivative) manner as chimpanzees and dogs.

[12] Olson objects thus: 'Can my body think first-person thoughts, or not? It can in a sense, Baker says, but not in the sense that I can. Well, insofar as it can, it's a thinking being numerically different from me. Insofar as it can't, I want to be told why it can't. Nothing is gained. If anything, saying that my body thinks only insofar as it relates to something numerically different from it that thinks would seem to be a way of saying that it doesn't think, for thinking is not a relational property' (2001: 429).

level this is quite compelling. Of course this is not a decisive consideration. We should not lose sight of the powerful considerations which suggest that numerically distinct objects *can* coincide, and it may well be that no solution to the conundrums of material coincidence will be entirely congenial from the standpoint of common sense.

That said, it seems fair to say the case for pluralism (and hence maximalism) is not as strong as it could be. Baker does provide us with a rationale for distinguishing the ways in which animals and subjects possess mental capacities. But even if we grant that animals do in fact only possess experiential capacities in the derivative way Baker proposes, it is not perhaps sufficiently obvious why possessing experiential capacities in this way is incompatible with being a subject. A response to the Too Many Subjects objection which makes it absolutely clear why the animal is not a subject that exists *in addition to* the neo-Lockean subject would be a more compelling and credible solution. Given the current state of play, it is by no means evident that such a solution is available within the framework of assumptions common to both maximalists and pluralists.

7.6. MONIST ALTERNATIVES

Maximalism may be problematic when combined with pluralism, but it is far less so when combined with monism. Where a pluralist sees an animal *and* a subject, the maximalist monist sees just one object. Monists are consequently not troubled in the slightest by the Too Many Subjects problem. The troubles with monism stem from another source. In order to circumvent the considerations which make pluralism seem plausible in the first place, monists are obliged to adopt measures which are metaphysically revisionary in one way or another. There are a good many variants of monism; I will focus here on just a couple.

A form of monism which invokes a minimal of metaphysical machinery is the approach ingeniously developed over a serious of papers by Michael Burke (1994, 1996, 1997). Unable to see how materially coinciding objects could really be distinct, Burke finds pluralism absurd. In its stead he offers a monistic theory which conforms to the principle of 'one object to a place'. According to Burke's theory, sortal concepts are hierarchical, and objects falling under higher sortals *displace* those beneath when coincidence threatens. So when a sculptor fashions a lump of clay into the form of a statue, the lump instantly (and conveniently) ceases to exist: 'statue' being a higher-level sortal than 'lump'. Similarly, if the particles constituting a living organism become so configured that they *also* constitute a person, the organism immediately ceases to exist: 'person' occupies a higher rank in the sortal hierarchy than 'organism'.

While there is no denying that this is an elegant solution to the overpopulation problem, it does have consequences which many find problematic. Can a lump of clay really be annihilated simply by changing its shape? Is the acquisition of mental capacities *fatal* to an animal? Can the loss of such capacities be sufficient to bring an animal into existence?

There is more to be said on this, but I want to focus here on another version of monism, one which is in some respects less counterintuitive than Burke's. Let us return to the Lumpl and Goliath case. Although the lump and the statue are physically indistinguishable, and exist at the same place at the same time, holding that there is just one object present seemed not to be an option. In virtue of the fact that the objects are of different kinds, and have different persistence conditions, each has properties the other lacks—Lumpl but not Goliath could survive being squeezed into a ball, Goliath but not Lumpl could survive the loss of a few parts—and so given Leibniz's Law, we have no option but to conclude that Lumpl and Goliath are distinct. Moreover, if we did take Goliath to be identical with Lumpl, there would be other consequences: if they are identical, they are presumably only contingently so, since Lumpl could have existed without being moulded into Goliath, and if we accept that Lumpl is only contingently identical with Goliath, we cannot take 'Lumpl' and 'Goliath' to be rigid designators, at least if we assume that identities formulated using rigid designators are necessary.

Leaving these latter obstacles (if such they be) to one side for the moment, let us focus on the problem posed by Leibniz's Law. A strategy for circumventing this is to hold that sentences which consist of a modal predicate being ascribed to a singular term, such as ' . . . might have been squeezed into a ball without being destroyed' are referentially opaque. That is, in the manner of propositional attitude contexts, such contexts do not permit the substitution of co-referring singular terms *salva veritate*. The reasoning behind this proposal runs thus. It is uncontroversial that Leibniz's Law is false unless we restrict the sort of properties for which it applies. If identicals are indiscernible, then if $a = b$, then everything true of a is true of b. This yields a substitution principle: if 'a is F' is true, then 'b is F' is also true. So far so good, but in some situations substitutivity fails: from 'S believes a is F' we cannot conclude 'S believes b is F', where $a = b$. Lois Lane can believe that Superman is super-strong without believing that Clark Kent is super-strong, even though Superman and Kent are numerically identical. Despite their identity, it is clear that Superman and Kent differ in at least one property: that of being believed to be super-strong by Lois Lane. Should we conclude that Leibniz's Law is false? No, there is a better and more plausible diagnosis of what is going on in such cases. Leibniz's Law is valid, but only for *genuine* properties of an object, where the mark of a genuine property is that it applies to an object irrespective of how that object is referred to. The predicate 'S believes . . . is F' fails to denote a genuine property in this sense. Now, with respect to predicates such as ' . . . might have had F', if these too only apply to an object relative to a particular way of referring to that object, then they will not be included in the class of properties for which identity can reasonably be thought to imply indiscernibility.

Lewis, Gibbard, and Noonan are among the recent proponents of the idea that modal predicates are indeed like this, and that in consequence modal discernibility does not imply numerical distinctness.[13] Their underlying idea is fairly straightforward. In Fregean terms, it relies on the idea that singular terms have a sense as well as a reference, and the sense helps determine the reference, both in the actual world and in other possible worlds. Although the names 'Lumpl' and 'Goliath' refer to the same entity, they have different senses, and these differences in a sense involve each name being associated with a different sortal concept. 'Lumpl' is associated with the *lump of clay* sortal, whereas 'Goliath' is associated with the *statue* sortal. Just as different sortal concepts determine different persistence conditions for objects falling under them, they also determine different conditions for tracing objects (or their counterparts) across possible worlds: the sorts of changes a lump of clay could survive are different from those a statue could survive. Consequently, although Lumpl is the same object as Goliath, it is not surprising that they exist in different possible worlds, since 'Lumpl' and 'Goliath' are associated with different principles for tracing their referents through time and space *and* across worlds. So, although Lumpl and Goliath are the same object, in thinking of this object as *Goliath* we are thinking of it under one sort of (sortal) representation, and under a different sort of (sortal) representation when we think of it as *Lumpl*.

This gives us an explanation of why it is that the sort of modal contexts we are concerned with are referentially opaque. If we want to know whether the predicate 'might have been squeezed into a ball without being destroyed' applies to an object, the answer will depend on how we think of the object, more specifically, on *the sort* of object we think we are dealing with. So given that different proper names can be associated with different sortals, and different sortals determine different trans-world tracing principles, there is no guarantee that we can substitute co-referring names into the sentence-form ' . . . might have been squeezed into a ball without being destroyed' and end up with sentences with the same truth value. Likewise for other predicates of the same kind, attributing modal properties to objects. On this view, modal predicates do not apply to *things* directly, but only to things as represented or conceived in some way or other. There is a further significant consequence. If objects picked out by co-referring names can possess different modal properties, such objects can exist in different possible worlds. If objects such as Lumpl and Goliath are numerically identical in this world but not in others, then clearly their identity is contingent rather than necessary.[14]

---

[13] Gibbard (1975), Lewis (1971, 1986: 248–63). See also Noonan (1991, 1993), who traces the general line of argument back to Abelard. Perdurance theorists, it should be noted, can handle cases of partial coincidence in a more direct manner: if Lumpl outlives Goliath, they are distinct simply by virtue of the fact that they each consist of a distinct (but partly overlapping) collection of temporal parts. But this solution is not available in cases of total coincidence—when Lumpl and Goliath coincide throughout their respective careers—and perdurantists typically appeal to the Abelardian approach to deal with this sort of case: different sortal concepts determine different ways of tracing *object-stages* (or *phases*) across worlds.

[14] If whether or not a modal predicate applies to an object depends on how that object is referred to, the so-called 'Barcan Proof' for the necessity of identities fails. This proof relies on Leibniz's

There are different ways of developing this approach, and correspondingly different accounts of names and modal semantics.[15] I shall make no attempt to evaluate these different accounts here. For present purposes what matters is that the option exists of taking objects with different identity conditions, and hence objects which are modally discernible, to be identical, even if only contingently so. If subjects of experience and the animals which sustain their mental capacities fall into this category, the option exists of taking animals and subjects whose lives coincide to be identical, albeit only contingently so. And the same applies, of course, to subjects whose mental capacities are sustained in other ways, for example conscious machines.

That this option is not without significant costs of its own goes without saying. The notion that one cannot ascribe predicates to objects directly, but only via some mode of representation, is not one that everyone will find congenial. Not everyone will be willing to accept that objects *can* be contingently identical.[16] As we have seen, alternatives do exist for those who find these costs too high to bear. The contingent identity approach will have most appeal for maximalists who find it intelligible to suppose that subjects and the organism which sustains their mental life could go their separate ways, but who also find it implausible to withhold from human animals the mental capacities that are constitutive of subjecthood.

7.7. MINIMALISM AND POSSESSION

According to the views we have been considering, selves and their bodies are coextensive: they are both composed of the same matter, they occupy the same volume of space. While the C-theory in its narrow guise can be developed along maximalist

Law, and runs thus: every object is necessarily identical with itself (we assume); if a is identical with b, then from Leibniz's Law, a must have all the properties b has, including that of being necessarily identical with b. But clearly, this only works if ' . . . is necessarily identical with b' is a predicate which applies to an object irrespective of how the object is referred to. And this is precisely what is denied by those who hold that modal predicates do not apply directly to things, but only to things under one name or another, together with the accompanying (sortal) ways of thinking of the names' bearer.

[15] Lewis holds that different names can invoke different counterpart relations even when they are co-referential. A sentence like 'Lumpl might have been squeezed into a ball without being destroyed' is true if in some world there is a counterpart of Lumpl which does survive this treatment. If the names 'Lumpl' and 'Goliath' are associated with different sets of counterparts, then Goliath may well not have a counterpart which could survive being squeezed into a ball, although Lumpl has. Gibbard suggests an alternative framework—a variant of one of Carnap's modal systems—which is compatible with trans-world identities.

[16] For further problems with the view, of a different kind, see Fine (2003). A different approach, which for present purposes yields a similar result, is to hold that identity is *temporary*: objects can be identical at some times but not others. See Gallois (1998) for an impressively detailed development of this position. Although this approach does have considerable puzzle-solving potential—fission and fusion are easily accommodated too—it is also heavily revisionary: is temporary identity really *identity*? See Lowe (2000) for more on this.

lines, the theory in its ontological guise makes a different claim: selves or subjects *are identical with C-systems*. On this minimalist view typical human selves are far from being co-extensive with their bodies, they are merely parts or properties of their bodies. The C-theory thus sidesteps the difficulties associated with material coincidence. Most significantly, if we do not coincide with our bodies, the Too Many Subjects objection, at least in its standard form, finds no grip.

Adopting minimalism is compatible with also accepting that in thinking and speaking about ourselves—in using 'I'—we often intend to refer to our bodily selves as well as our selves *per se*. To make sense of this we need simply suppose that the intended reference of 'I' can expand or contract, depending on circumstance. Just as we can use 'here' to refer to where we are standing, or the room we are in, or the solar system, depending on context, we can use 'I' to refer to our selves, or to the human animals in which our selves (or C-systems) are embedded. If someone says 'I look good in red' they are using 'I' in the broader, more encompassing way. If they say 'I am looking forward to knowing what it's like to undergo a full body-swap' they are using the same term in the narrow way. Strawson makes the point like this:

'I' is not univocal, and can refer to two different things. Or rather, its referential reach can expand outwards in a certain way, so that it can refer to more or less. The same is true of 'here' and 'now', but the phrase 'the castle' provides a better analogy for 'I', given the present concern with objects. Sometimes 'the castle' is used to refer to the castle proper, sometimes it is used to refer to the ensemble of the castle and the grounds and buildings located within its outer walls. Similarly, when I think and talk about myself, my reference sometimes extends only to the SESMET that I then am, and sometimes it extends further out, to the human being that I am. The castle proper is not the same thing as the castle in the broad sense, but it is a (proper) part of the castle in the broad sense.

The same is true in the case of a SESMET and a human being . . . the relationship between S [the self or SESMET] and Louis the human being (an object with, say, a seventy-year old existence) is a straightforward part–whole relation, like the relation between Louis and one of his toes—or the relation between a morning glory plant and one of its flowers, or between Louis and one of his pimples. (Strawson 1999*a*: 131)

Strawson's 'SESMETS' are short-lived bursts of experience, that (he believes) are identical with certain goings-on within the brain, rather than C-systems, but what he says applies equally well to the latter. We have here the outlines at least of a plausible account of how selves (conceived as C-systems) might think of themselves in relation to their bodies. The earlier account of embodiment and F-relatedness provides another element of this account. Like castles, the constituent parts of an embodied self can be spatially scattered.

But in the light of the preceding two sections it is clear that a further question needs to be addressed. Animalists will surely respond thus:

You say you are merely *a part* of a human animal. Fine. But what of the animal itself, considered as a whole? It possesses precisely the same experiential and psychological capacities as you do, and hence satisfies the conditions for being a self or subject. If the animal is a subject, and you are a subject, and you are not the same subject as the animal, then we have two subjects where there seems only to be one. Moreover, how do you know which of these two subjects *you* are? Or are you claiming that animals are incapable of thought and experience?

If we view (human) selves as merely parts of (human) animals, rather than co-extensive with them, this objection loses much of its force. On the assumption that I am the C-system responsible for my current experience, then evidently I am not the same thing as the animal which contains this system. Quite generally, a proper part is numerically distinct from its whole. But if it is me, in the form of a mental subject, that has a mind, then are we not, in effect, denying that animals *can* have minds, or possess capacities for thought and experience? Acknowledging that the reference of 'I' can expand or contract in the way described by Strawson allows us to make sense of the idea that subjects can appropriate and *fill* their bodies. But if it is the subject that is doing all the thinking and feeling we still look to be denying the capacities for thought and experience to animals *per se*. And isn't this rather implausible?

It is indeed. But only if the denial is interpreted in a particular way. To make better sense of the situation we can distinguish *primary property possession* from *secondary property possession*. An object has a property in the secondary way if it possesses it by virtue of having a (proper) part which possesses it in the primary way. An object is a primary property possessor if it is the whole object, rather than any of its (proper) parts, that has the property. Something like this distinction is a tacit feature of common sense. If I were to tell you 'My car can play DVDs now', you would not take me to be saying that *my entire car* has been converted into a DVD player. Rather, given your knowledge of the typical relationships between cars and entertainment systems, you would take me to mean that I had replaced the old CD-radio player with a new-fangled DVD player (you might also wonder how I would manage to drive and watch movies at the same time). The average car possesses the capacity to play music in a secondary way, the primary possessor of this property is the small box of electronics lurking in or beneath the dashboard. Similar remarks apply in the case of 'My new cooker can tell the time' or 'Thanks to the upgrade, my computer is faster than it was before'—it is not the cooker as a whole that can tell the time, but the small clock mounted in its fascia, it is not the computer as a whole that's faster, just the CPU chip and the computational processes it drives.[17]

In like fashion, the C-theorist can say 'Yes, of course human animals can possess mental capacities, but they possess them in a *secondary* way, by virtue of possessing a part—a C-system—which possesses them in a primary way.' Animals possess experiential and psychological capacities in the same way as they possess the capacity to digest food or metabolize alcohol: by possessing parts

[17] As noted in Dainton (1998), and also Persson (1999, 2004).

(digestive systems, livers) which are the primary possessors of the properties in question. No one thinks there is a 'Too Many Metabolizers' problem with regard to human animals—and rightly, and for obvious reasons. Precisely analogous considerations, I suggest, undermine the Too Many Subjects problem in the context of minimalism. We can recognize that both animals and C-systems are subjects without any risk of overpopulation provided we also recognize that whereas C-systems are subjects in a primary way, animals are subjects in a secondary way.

The viability of this approach does depend on the assumption that C-systems are genuine objects in their own right, just like more familiar animal-parts such as hearts or livers (although of course the persistence-conditions of the latter are framed in biological rather than phenomenal terms). I will simply assume this for now; I will return to the ontological status of C-systems in Chapter 11. The approach is also similar in some respects to one we considered earlier: Baker's response to the overpopulation problem also relies on a distinction between two ways of possessing properties. But the differences between the two approaches are significant. Baker's distinction between derivative and non-derivative property possession applies to objects which materially *coincide*. Secondary property possessors do not coincide with primary possessors, they *contain* or *include* them. Also, as was noted earlier, accepting Baker's proposal means treading a very fine line. According to Baker animals *really do* possess the same mental states and properties as persons (or subjects), albeit in a derivative way. While taking this step is needed for the proposal to be at all plausible—it is by no means obvious how things which materially coincide can differ in their intrinsic properties—it also makes for a problem: if animals really do possess the same range of mental states and capacities as subjects, why aren't they also subjects in their own right, *rival* subjects which exist in addition to those recognized by the neo-Lockean? When primary possessors are proper parts of secondary possessors, the risk of rivalry is eliminated, and the relationship between the two is entirely transparent. In the case of animals and their brains, for instance, it is perfectly clear that the whole animal (including its brain) is not a thinking thing which exists *in addition to*, or over and above, its brain. In like fashion, when we attribute the property of personhood to animals on the understanding that animals only have this by virtue of the fact that they include parts which directly sustain the relevant mental capacities, there is no risk of overpopulation, it is clear that there is only one person or self involved.

Not all instances of secondary property possession are a like. Many in-car DVD players are discrete units that can easily be removed, and transferred from one vehicle to another. Human brains, and human C-systems, are significantly less modular. Of course, this may change as medical technology advances, and as we saw earlier in connection with cell replacement procedures, a C-system could conceivably leave a body behind (in a manner of speaking) without being separated from it. Also, as we have seen in this chapter, on a more general level subjects can be fully embodied without being in direct physical contact with their bodies—it is F-relations that matter, not spatial proximity or containment. But even if it were to turn out that human C-systems are inseparable from their immediate biological environment, it matters not. What distinguishes primary and secondary property possession is *redundancy*, not *removability*. Suppose your car's DVD player were welded to your vehicle's chassis in such a way that it could not be removed without destroying it. This change does not affect the fundamentals: it remains the case that your car can play DVDs by virtue of having a proper part that is capable of so doing. Since the vast bulk of your car is entirely redundant so far as the ability to play DVDs is concerned—and could be trimmed away without loss, in this respect—it clearly is not your car *as a whole* that possesses the relevant property. In a similar way, if C-systems and human animals were to prove inseparable, it would remain the case that the animal possesses mental capacities only by virtue of possessing a proper part that is their primary possessor.

Animal-based subjects vary in the degree of redundancy their bodies display with regard to mentality. Adjusting for the difference in overall body sizes, human brains tend to be bigger than rat brains, and so—assuming rats are conscious subjects—rat bodies possess more redundancy than their human counterparts. At the other extreme are creatures that are nearly all brain. We are not acquainted with any such beasts, but they may well exist. Parfit is fond of mentioning The Mekon in this connection. Of a more recent provenance, but in the same vein, are the Brain Bugs featured in Paul Verhoeven's movie-version of Heinlein's *Starship Troopers*: save for a small mouth and a cluster of small eyes, a Brain Bug is brain and nothing but. Even in these cases, unless every part and aspect of the brains of such creatures is relevant to the production of experience, and if their brains are anything like our own this will not be the case, there will still be redundancy, and so the animal will still only possess its mental capacities in a secondary way. With C-systems it is different. Since a C-system is *nothing but* a system of experiential capacities—and an extended C-system a system of integrated experiential and psychological capacities—there is no loose flesh here at all. C-systems are manifestly the primary possessors of the properties that are constitutive of selfhood. Speaking figuratively, there is *no gap* whatsoever between you and your C-system; hence there is a sense in which nothing can be closer to a subject than its C-system.

Complications

So far so good, but a further—and now familiar—issue looms. A typical C-system is a complex entity, comprising various integrated experiential powers. What is the relationship between a C-system and its constituent parts? How is a C-system related to the experiential capacities which comprise it at any given time? If we want to identify ourselves with C-systems we should at least pause before identifying ourselves with our constituents.

Let us use the term 'C-aggregate' to refer to the experiential powers that constitute a C-system at a given time. A C-aggregate will consist of a maximal collection of C-related experiential capacities. We further stipulate that all the constituents of a C-aggregate are essential to it, and so a given C-aggregate cannot survive the loss or gain of any experiential capacities. Now, although each of us has a particular complement of experiential powers at a given time, if our lives had gone differently we could easily have had a different complement. If a roof tile had hit my head yesterday (rather than narrowly missing) I might today lack any capacities for visual experience. Myriad similar contingencies afflict us all. If we are the kind of thing that could have had different experiential capacities than we actually do, then clearly we cannot be numerically identical with the C-aggregates with which we share our experiential powers at any given time. But if we are not identical with these C-aggregates we must be distinct from them; and if we are distinct from them, given that they satisfy the synchronic conditions for subject-hood just as well as we do, it seems they too must be subjects. The overpopulation problem is with us once more.

C-systems may not coincide with entire animals, but they do coincide with C-aggregates. Consequently, in this case at least we cannot appeal to the distinction between primary and secondary property possession to circumvent the threat of overpopulation. Given this, the various options we considered earlier in connection with maximalism become relevant. Monists will have no difficulty with the relationship between C-systems and C-aggregates. Followers of Burke will hold that a collection or aggregate of experiential capacities ceases to exist (as a genuine object) when it comes to form a C-system. Those who favour contingent identities and multiple counterpart relationships can hold that C-aggregates and C-systems are numerically identical, despite their differing modal properties. On the face of it, the situation with regard to pluralism is equally straightforward. Pluralists can hold that the relationship between C-aggregates and C-systems is one of constitution, with the former constituting the latter. To circumvent the residual threat of overpopulation, pluralists have the option of following Baker, and holding that C-aggregates do not possess mental capacities in the right sort of way to be counted as genuine subjects. Alternatively, and perhaps more plausibly, they can take the line that C-aggregates are not the right kind of object to be genuine subjects. If subjects are *substances*, and substances (at least of the compound variety) can gain and lose component parts, then C-aggregates are not substances, and so cannot be subjects. In the context of maximalism, where the coinciding entities were whole animals and neo-Lockean persons, this line had little (and probably no) plausibility: animals are clearly substances. But the situation is transformed by the switch to minimalism. It is by no means entirely implausible to suppose that *aggregates* or *collections* are not on an ontological par with genuine substances, at least for those who favour a substance-oriented ontology. Of course for this line to be viable it must be reasonable to regard C-systems as substances. I will be arguing that so regarding them *is* viable (and reasonable) in Chapter 11.

It is worth noting here that C-theorists who adopt the latter solution are following a path similar to one taken by some animalists. Let us suppose that you are an animal, and let an *A-aggregate* be the collection of atoms that constitute you at a given time. What is the relationship between you and one of your A-aggregates at a given time t? It cannot be identity, for like any animal you could easily have been composed of a different collection of atoms at t—a different choice of evening meal the night before would do the trick—so you and your A-aggregate must be distinct. But a familiar overpopulation problem now looms. Doesn't your A-aggregate satisfy the synchronic conditions for being an animal? It does indeed. So why do most animalists see no threat here? It is because they view animals as *substances*. Like any compound substance, an animal substance can gain and lose parts; since an A-aggregate cannot gain and lose parts it is not a substance, and so cannot be an animal. The menace of overpopulation is thus avoided. It goes without saying that relying in this manner on the distinction between substances and non-substances will not appeal to philosophers of all persuasions. Nonetheless, bearing in mind the animalist allegation that neo-Lockean accounts are fatally undermined by overpopulation problems, the fact that when it comes to aggregate-based overpopulation worries the C-theorist and the animalist are in much the same position is of some significance—assuming, of course, that a case can be made for regarding C-systems as substances.[18]

It may be that C-theorists are in an even better position with regard to this issue. As will emerge in Chapter 9, there are grounds for thinking that many C-systems are not in fact compound objects in the usual sense, that is to say that they are not wholes composed of constituents parts which could enjoy a separate existence, or an existence in a different whole. If, as I shall argue is the case, experiential capacities are often so closely interdependent that C-systems can reasonably be regarded as metaphysically simple entities, the issue of the relationship between such C-systems and collections of their constituents does not arise. How could it, if the relevant C-systems do not have constituent parts in the relevant sense of the term? Adopting this view of C-systems is a legitimate option, but it also comes with certain costs, and there are complications, as we shall see.

Moving on, a question I have not yet addressed is the precise relationship between subjects, construed as C-systems, and what earlier I called 'minimal bodies', that is the physical systems (or power-bases) which directly possess the

---

[18] Van Inwagen (1990), of course, denies there are any compound substances *other* than organisms. While Olson (1997) subscribes to a substance-oriented ontology, in his (2007) he acknowledges that animalists are also vulnerable to overpopulation problems (competitors include heads and lumps of flesh), and suggests there may be no satisfactory solution to the problem (for anyone).

experiential capacities which jointly constitute a given C-system. This question can be answered very quickly indeed. The relationship is not that of part-hood or coincidence, but property possession or instantiation, where the relevant properties are dispositional. A C-system is related to the physical system which directly sustains it in the same way as any system of dispositional properties is related to what sustains it. There is no difference between the way a neural system has a capacity to generate experience and the way a mirror has the capacity to reflect light, or a torch the capacity to produce light.

The general way of thinking of animals, both human and non-human, that I am recommending is open to a different objection. Assuming that animals evolved through natural selection, their mental capacities are presumably as much of a product of selection as their physical characteristics. Does this fact not mean it is absurd to ascribe the mental capacities of an animal to an entity that is in *any* way distinct from the animal itself? Surely the mental capacities characteristic of a given species evolved because they proved useful to typical members of the species, particular animals, rather than anything distinct from the animals?

This objection is without real force. Yes, mental capacities evolved through a combination of genetic mutation and competitive selection. Yes, mental capacities proved beneficial, in the evolutionary sense, to the animals which possessed them: the survival prospects of the relevant genes increased. But these facts are compatible with recognizing that the *owners* of these mental capacities are entities distinct from any animal, and are related to them as part to whole. As animals evolved experiential capacities, subjects of experience appeared on the scene. Since these subjects are distinct from the animals that sustain them, the animals, in a sense, become *possessed* by conscious beings. However, since these conscious beings were effectively embodied, their mental capacities were naturally at the service of the animals which housed them, and this fact also has an evolutionary explanation. The distinctive innate psychological characteristics of subjects are themselves the product of natural selection. So, needless to say, selection will favour subjects who are innately disposed to act in a way which maximizes the evolutionary fitness of the animals they possess—again 'fitness' in this sense is measured in terms of the likelihood of an animal successfully reproducing and so passing some of its genes on to the next generation.

A further question now arises. Given that we are programmed, as it were, to want our bodies to survive, why is it that we can conceive of ourselves as surviving without our bodies? How could it come about that most of us would willingly sacrifice our bodies if our minds could continue to exist in a differently embodied state? Why is our self-interested concern in our own survival so biased in favour of the mental, rather than the bio-physical? Well, one explanation runs like this. We have a strong concern to carry on living, to avoid death, a concern that is innate and which evolved through natural selection. But life, for a conscious being is *not* obviously or primarily a matter of the continuation of biological activity, but the continuation of consciousness and the capacity for consciousness. Our most basic desire to survive is thus focused on *life as a conscious being*, rather than *life as a biological being*. It is therefore hardly surprising that our desire to go on living takes the form that it does: on reflection, it is clear to us that if our consciousness continues on, we continue to exist, we remain alive (in the relevant sense of *continuing to exist*), irrespective of where or whether our consciousness is physically grounded.

8

Simple Selves

8.1. SIMPLICITY AND ISOLATION

The typical adult human has a wide range of experiential and cognitive capacities, and most of us enjoy a correspondingly rich and varied conscious mental life. But not all subjects are so fortunate. Subjects with much simpler minds than our own are almost certainly possible, and subjects of this kind will have conscious lives that are considerably less rich and varied than our own. Beings which possess the capacity for only a few *very* basic forms of consciousness I shall call *simple subjects*.

Simplicity is a matter of degree. Just as some subjects are simpler than ourselves, there may be subjects whose conscious lives are far richer and more varied than anything we are familiar with, subjects who could legitimately regard human streams of consciousness as simple in comparison to their own. The question I want to focus on here is just how simple a subject could possibly be. In the framework of the C-theory, the answer to this depends on the answer to another question: how simple can a nomologically grounded potentiality for experience be? If we assume that there can be an experiential power for every type of experience—which seems a reasonable assumption—then we can address this question by considering how simple a stream of consciousness could be. Is there a threshold of simplicity below which no stream of consciousness can pass?

In broaching these issues we are inevitably hampered by our general ignorance concerning the relationship between consciousness and the physical world. We know human beings can vary enormously in the kinds of mentality they possess, and most of us believe organisms much simpler than human beings are conscious, but we do not know how much simpler an organism can be and still be conscious; nor do we know at which point during the evolution of life on Earth consciousness first appeared, or along which phylogenetic branch. We are similarly ignorant about the possibility or otherwise of non-biological forms of conscious life. Could an entity that is radically different from us physically still be a conscious subject? Perhaps we will learn the answer to these questions one day. In the meantime we have no option but to confine ourselves to speculations grounded in a combination of phenomenological considerations and our very general beliefs about the relationship between the physical and the phenomenal. The results of such an inquiry will be tentative at best, but given the limitations of our current knowledge this may well be the best we can hope to achieve at present.

A couple of preliminary points. So far as mentality is concerned, simplicity may be a matter of degree, but it also comes in different forms. Could a being with very limited experiential capacities be equipped with a highly sophisticated cognitive system? This is an intriguing question, but for present purposes I will ignore it and focus on subjects that are limited in both respects: the simple subjects we will be dealing with should be thought of as simple *minded* in every sense of the term. Of course this raises another question: just how simple can the cognitive system of a subject of experience be? There are grounds for thinking that the answer to this question is: very simple indeed. If (as most of us believe) creatures as diverse as horses, dogs, rats, and human infants are capable of having experiences, then clearly little and quite possibly nothing by way of reasoning ability is required for consciousness *per se*, and the same goes for linguistic and conceptual abilities. Creatures with an extremely low level of intellect will be incapable of forming any sort of conception of themselves—and so lack *self*-consciousness to any significant degree—but they could nonetheless experience sensations of warmth, cold, light, darkness, pain, pleasure, or sensations quite different from any of these (i.e. different from anything we humans are acquainted with). Or so I think it reasonable to believe, and will assume in what follows.[1]

This assumption has a consequence that is worth making explicit. The sensations of a creature which possesses little or nothing by way of a cognitive system will inevitably lack any significant cognitive content, and consequently need not be thought of as *representing* anything. To illustrate, consider the case of a worm whose body is covered with light-sensitive cells; if light is shone on this worm it wriggles about, and continues to wriggle until it moves into shade; the wriggling-behaviour is triggered by sensations the worm feels when its light-sensitive cells are activated—these vary in intensity depending on the strength of the stimulus. Now, although the worm's behaviour could easily be interpreted by us as resulting from beliefs, intentions, and desires appropriate to the observed behaviour, it is in fact (we can suppose) the consequence of a brute stimulus-response mechanism. The worm's cognitive system is so primitive

---

[1] As with so much in this area, this assumption is controversial. To mention just one instance of a different view, Tye (1997) argues (roughly) that only creatures that are able to form beliefs in response to their experiences can have experiences; he further argues that while fish and honeybees satisfy this criterion—and so may be regarded as conscious—carnivorous plants do not. While plausible on its own terms, Tye's verdict stems from his PANIC theory of what makes a state phenomenal (again roughly, it must have a certain kind of representational content, and be poised to impact upon a subject's cognitive system). Given this reductive view of the phenomenal, Tye's position is understandable. But for anyone who adopts a non-reductive view of the phenomenal the situation looks very different. If intrinsic character is all that matters when it comes to distinguishing phenomenal from non-phenomenal states—as I am assuming throughout—then it is by no means obvious that experiences must be able to impact upon cognitive systems in certain ways in order to exist at all.

that it has no internal representation of its environment, nothing approaching a conception of itself as a thing distinct from its environment. Despite this, it can and does feel simple sensations. Since these sensations lack any representational content, what content they do have is purely qualitative. (So perhaps creatures such as Maggot are possible after all.)

With these preliminaries out of the way we can take a further step in the direction of maximal simplicity by addressing this question: If there could be creatures with the capacity for only a few types of basic sensation, could there be a creature with an even more primitive mind, possessing the capacity for only a *single* kind of simple sensation? We are now encroaching on territory already explored by Hume: 'We can conceive a thinking being to have either many or a few perceptions. Suppose the mind to be reduc'd even below the life of an oyster. Suppose it to have only one perception, as of thirst or hunger. Consider it in that situation' (1978: 634). If such a creature were possible, its mental life would consist of a stream of *very* simple consciousness. In the most extreme version of the scenario, the creature only enjoys a single brief *burst* of sensation, for example a fleeting pain—for the creature could be killed shortly after being born.

I shall refer to the claim that simple solitary experiences (and the corresponding experiential powers) are in fact possible as the *Isolation Thesis*. The notion that a conscious mental life could take such a simple form—that, *in extremis* an entire universe could consist of nothing but an isolated sensation of pain or hunger (or the capacity for such)—may well seem strange, perhaps absurd. But strangeness is one thing, impossibility another.[2] It may be that the Isolation Thesis *is* false, but have we any good reason for thinking it is?

8.2. ISOLATION: STRANDS OF A DEFENCE

A familiar doctrine which may seem to run counter to the Isolation Thesis runs as follows. For a pain-sensation to exist there has to be a subject whose pain it is, a subject who is there to sense or feel the pain. And what goes for pain goes for all other experiences. If this is right, then it is unintelligible to suppose there could be a universe that contained a single sensation of pain and absolutely nothing else: at the very least a *subject* must also exist, a subject who feels the pain in question. Frege, a philosopher not best-known for metaphysical speculations about experience, put the point nicely:

The field and the frogs in it, the sun which shines on them are there whether I look at them or not, but the sense impression I have of green exists only because of me, I am its bearer. It seems absurd to us that a pain, a mood, a wish, should rove about the world

---

[2] Such a universe need not be devoid of matter. If experiences are themselves material, then a universe comprising a single sensation will contain a (probably small) quantity of matter too, the matter composing the sensation.

without a bearer, independently. An experience is impossible without an experient. The inner world presupposes the person whose inner world it is. (Frege 1967: 27)

I am not of course in the business of denying that there are such things as subjects of experience. But, from the vantage point of the C-theory, subjects are simply collections of experiential powers, and if simple subjects are possible, then a subject can exist in the form of a nothing more than a capacity for a single simple form of experience. This possibility could be regarded as problematic for very general metaphysical reasons—I will be commenting on this in Chapter 11—but it might also be spurned on grounds of general plausibility: the idea that subjects such as *you or I* could be reduced to such a minimal form may seem absurd. Given this, the possibility of minimal subjects is potentially in tension with the claim that the C-theory provides a believable account of our own persistence conditions. I will be dealing with this issue in §8.3. To start with I want to consider certain other respects in which the notion of a minimal subject might seem problematic.

Someone might argue thus: 'Experiences certainly need an experienc*er*, but I can't see how this principle can be accommodated in the case of minimal subjects. If we were to try to reduce a subject to the supposed minimal condition the experiencer would have vanished from the scene long before we succeeded: there just *wouldn't be enough left* to constitute a subject.' If this complaint has some intuitive appeal (and I think it does), this may well be due to an assumption concerning the phenomenology of experiencing: it can seem natural to think that whenever a pain is felt by a subject there is always (and necessarily) more going on *at the experiential level* in the subject's consciousness than the mere occurrence of the pain-sensation. If so, then clearly for a pain to be experienced by a subject the pain must exist within a more encompassing experiential state. Why does this assumption seem intuitively appealing? Because contrary to what Hume may have thought, it is not at all easy to conceive of entirely isolated sensations—or at least, it isn't if by 'conceive' we mean 'imagine'. Generally speaking, when we try to imagine such things—for example an entire universe consisting of nothing but a single twinge of pain or hunger—we usually end up imagining rather *more* than a single sensation. We then take this surplus to be indicative of (or even constitute) the presence of a subject, or at the very least of a more encompassing stream of consciousness.

However, as I hope to make clear, this imaginative limitation is understandable, and once understood, largely irrelevant to the truth or falsity of the Isolation Thesis. Although the point I have in mind is a simple one, it takes a little stage-setting.

Whenever I focus my attention on a pain I am currently feeling (or any other kind of experience for that matter), I usually do so against the backdrop of various other forms of consciousness: a range of bodily experience, tactile sensations, visual and auditory experience, intentional or willed bodily movements, conscious thinking, fringe feelings, visual images, memories, emotions, and so forth. It will be useful to have a term for the regions of our overall consciousness which we are not paying attention to at any given time: call it the *phenomenal background*. This background has a number of components, but for present purposes it will suffice to distinguish two: the *worldly* and the *inner*.[3] The former consists of what we unthinkingly take to be the surrounding world, or those parts of it that we can touch, see, and hear. The latter consists of bodily experience, thoughts, memories, imaginings, and emotions: those aspects of our overall experience which we naturally take to be *experience*, even from the standpoint of the natural attitude of naïve realism.

Both components of the phenomenal background have a familiar feel (for want of a better term) and this is a significant feature of the background (not least because it helps explain why its existence and significance are so easily overlooked). The outer component is the environment we encounter in the course of our ordinary lives and, as is obvious, we normally find ourselves in the midst of a world that is largely familiar. If I wake up in a strange and unfamiliar room, unless the room is very strange indeed, I will be surrounded by things of a comfortingly familiar *type* (e.g. walls, a ceiling, a floor, a few items of furniture). The familiar feel of the inner phenomenal background is perhaps rather more elusive, but just as real. The latter can reasonably be construed as contributing to (and perhaps constituting) the feeling of what it is typically like to be *me* (or *you*). To appreciate the rationale behind this claim, let us again suppose that I have just woken up to find myself (unexpectedly) in strange and unfamiliar surroundings. Needless to say, I would feel alarmed, puzzled, worried, far more so than usual. But although in this case the worldly component of the phenomenal background is unexpected, and my emotions would reflect this, these feelings and perceptions would occur in the midst of an inner background that is very familiar indeed: *what it feels like to be me* (what I feel like *as* I think, worry, experience panic) is much as per usual. Does the inner background consist of a single kind of experience, a particular sensation or feeling? Probably not. Although (in my own case, at least) the inner background is quite stable from one occasion to another, I can see no reason to take this stability as indicative of a single special type of experience, something over and above the changing stream of thought, perception, volition, emotion, memory, bodily sensation, and so on. For consider: would the inner background remain the same in the absence of these more particular modes of consciousness? What would it feel like to remain conscious, but not conscious of any thought, mood, perception, or bodily sensation whatsoever? Would there be anything left at all? It is hard to see what. It is far more plausible to think of the ambient

[3] In Dainton (2000 §2.2) I discuss the phenomenal background in a little more detail, and consider how we go about exploring those regions of our consciousness which we are not attentively aware of.

'sense of self' as a joint product of memory, recognition, and specific forms of consciousness—and as we saw in §2.4, fringe feelings are particularly important in this connection.

Both the existence of the phenomenal background and our tendency to overlook it are relevant to the imaginability (or otherwise) of isolated sensations. The inner component of the phenomenal background is so pervasive in our conscious lives that it automatically accompanies, and is incorporated into, a good deal of what we imagine. This is especially true whenever we deliberately try to imagine what a particular kind of experience would be like. Since we are rarely explicitly aware of the phenomenal background, especially the inner component, we do not make any attempt to exclude it from our imaginings. So, for example, if I try to imagine what an unusual flavour of ice-cream would taste like, I automatically conceive a taste-sensation occurring against the familiar background state of my stream of consciousness; I am not explicitly aware of inserting this additional ingredient into what I imagine, but it is inserted nonetheless. Moreover, it would be fruitless to try excluding this additional ingredient: I cannot alter or exclude the inner background at will—I cannot just *decide* that it will feel different to be me. (Perhaps there are drugs that would produce significant alterations, but the resulting alterations would not then be under my direct control.) As a consequence, whatever form of experience I try to imagine will generally be accompanied by a phenomenal background, and there is little I can do about this—short of rendering myself unconscious and unable to imagine anything at all. More generally, it seems plausible to suppose that it is all but impossible for us to exclude the phenomenal background from attempts to imaginatively recreate the character of an experience.

If this is right then we have the beginnings of an explanation of why a solitary pain can seem so unimaginably odd. It seems so odd because it is all but impossible for us to imagine such a thing. But clearly, this inability is to a large extent a direct consequence of our minds being as they are: since our consciousness is ordinarily unified, the products of our imaginations are co-conscious with the rest of our contemporaneous experience, the ambient sense of self included. Consequently, our inability to imagine an 'ownerless' pain-sensation need not be put down to the impossibility of such a sensation. If isolated sensations were possible, we would still be unable to imagine them.

These considerations assist with a related issue. At the start of this chapter I suggested that subjects with rudimentary (or non-existent) intellects would lack any significant form of *self*-consciousness. This claim is by no means uncontroversial. There are philosophers—philosophers whose general conception of consciousness is in other respects quite plausible—who hold that *all* forms of experience are necessarily accompanied by a particular form of self-consciousness. The form of self-consciousness they have in mind is not the high-level cognitive variety—the sort deployed in 'I'-thoughts and the like—but rather a 'minimal' or 'non-reflexive' variety, one that can easily be conceived as being able to exist independently of linguistic or conceptual capacities. In a recent elaboration and defence of this doctrine, Zahavi begins with the plausible observation that in order for there to be something that it is like for a subject to have an experience, the subject must have some form of access to the experience; he further maintains that while different sorts of experience have different phenomenal characteristics (compare the smell of mint with the seeing of a sunset) there are also certain features that all experiences share:

> One commonality is the quality of *mineness*, the fact that experiences are characterized by first-personal givenness. That is, the experience is given (at least tacitly) as *my* experience, as an experience *I* am undergoing or living through. . . . phenomenal consciousness must be interpreted precisely as entailing a minimal or thin form of self-awareness. On this account, any experience that lacks self-awareness is nonconscious. (Zahavi 2005: 16)

This link between experience and self-awareness was, he suggests, recognized by all the classical phenomenologists, for example Brentano, Husserl, Sartre, and Henry. Zahavi may well be right about this, but what are we to make of the claim itself? Do all experiences come stamped with a *me*ish quality?

The first point to note is that even if this claim were true, it would not in itself mean that the Isolation Thesis is false; all it would mean is that even the most solitary of sensations would have the quality of *mineness*.[4] As it happens I can see no reason to accept the various claims Zahavi makes on behalf of minimal self-consciousness. There is certainly no obvious need to posit a quality of *mineness* to explain how it is that we are always aware of our own experiences. According to the one-level Simple Conception, experiences are intrinsically conscious items, and as such automatically contribute to the overall character of their subject's consciousness at the time of their occurrence; experiences do not need any further assistance to enter our awareness in this minimal sense. (As noted in §2.5, experiences can in this respect be regarded as *self-intimating*.) After rightly observing that we are not usually in any doubt as to who the subject of our own experiences is, Zahavi suggests: 'Whether a certain experience is experienced as mine or not, however, depends not on something apart from the experience, but precisely on the givenness of the experience' (2005: 124). But do we need *mineness* to explain whether an experience is experienced as mine? Again, it is not obvious that we do. If an experience is *co-conscious* with my other experiences does it not clearly and unambiguously belong to me? What else is required? These points aside, Zahavi's main phenomenological claim—that when we have an experience, we have the sense that the experience is *something that we ourselves are*

---

[4] Zahavi certainly seems willing to countenance the possibility of simple subjects and simple modes of consciousness. He argues that the pre-reflective sense of *mineness* can also be equated with a minimal or core sense of *self*, and writes: 'As for the question of where to draw the line, i.e., whether it also makes sense to ascribe a sense of self to lower organisms such as birds, amphibians, fish, beetles, worms, etc., this is a question I will leave for others to decide. All I will say is that *if* a certain organism is in possession of phenomenal consciousness, *then* it must also be in possession of both a primitive form of self-consciousness and a core self' (2005: 235–6).

living through or undergoing—is by no means an implausible one, but is it best explained in terms of a primitive quality of *mineness*? An alternative (and more economical) explanation runs thus. Any sense I have that a typical experience is *experienced by a subject* when it occurs is due to the fact that this experience is co-conscious with certain other experiences, namely those comprising the inner component of the phenomenal background. The inner background largely constitutes *what it feels like to be me*, or so I have just argued. If so, then when the inner background is present, so too am *I*, phenomenologically speaking. Consequently, any experience which is co-conscious with the inner background will seem as though it is occurring to a subject (= me).

If this analysis is broadly correct there are two consequences of some significance. First, we can account for the phenomenology of *mineness* without positing any primitive 'ownership' quality. Second, the doctrine that there cannot be an experience that lacks *mineness* is largely undermined. If the sense that a pain sensation (say) is something that is owned—or something that its owner is undergoing—depends on the presence of the inner phenomenal background, and if the latter is itself a composite of various other kinds of experience (bodily, fringe feeling, mood, etc.), then there is no obvious obstacle to our supposing that an intrinsically similar pain sensation could exist in the absence of the inner background. Do we have any reason for supposing the combination of specific forms of experience which are jointly responsible for a typical inner phenomenal background form an unmodifiable and inseparable ensemble? I can see no such reason. Bodily sense-fields can vary in size and quality; fringe feelings can come and go, likewise moods. If the inner background can change and shrink, why can't it vanish altogether? The possibility of isolated and *phenomenologically ownerless* (or impersonal-seeming) experiences is thus difficult to rule out.[5] Parfit advocates a reductionist view of what we are: the existence of a self requires nothing more than the existence of a brain and a body and a collection of interrelated physical and mental events. Even if this form of reductionism were mistaken, a reductionist view of our *sense of self* might still be correct. According to the latter, our sense of self is not the product of a single simple form of experience, but rather the joint product of several different sorts of (quite ordinary) experiences.

Moving on, there is another and quite different explanation of why the Isolation Thesis strikes can seem obviously absurd: an allegiance to the act-object (or naïve perceptual, or bare locus) conception of consciousness. If particular experiences, such as sensations of pain, are the objects of a centre of pure awareness, and are only conscious in virtue of so being, then there obviously

---

[5] Kriegel (2004) argues that all forms of consciousness involve 'intransitive self-consciousness' which he equates with *peripheral self-awareness*. In effect, he maintains that we are always tacitly aware of ourselves as experiencing (what I call) the phenomenal background. I am not sure the latter claim is true, but in any event, these considerations concerning the role of the inner background suggest that even if we are normally peripherally self-aware in Kriegel's sense, there may be abnormal states of consciousness from which this awareness is absent.

could not be a pain unless there were also a centre of awareness. Take the centre of awareness out of the picture and there is no longer any possibility of consciousness, and so no possibility of pain (since pain-states are essentially conscious). However, since we have already found reason to reject the act-object model, little more needs to be said on this point. On the one hand, we can scarcely take the pure centre of awareness out of the picture, because there is no such thing—the very idea of such a thing is misconceived. And on the other hand, once we accept that sensations are intrinsically conscious (and I have argued that this is how we should think of them), there is no need to bring anything else into the picture. If a pain-sensation is inherently conscious, it is complete *as* an experience in its own right; whether or not it is the object of a higher-level pure awareness is neither here nor there.

It could be argued that the Isolation Thesis cannot be true because it is a conceptual truth that every experience must have a subject. The Isolation Thesis is incoherent because it is in conflict with the concept *experience*. There are two responses to this. Perhaps it is true that our concept of experience requires every experience to have an owner. But what if a simple, isolated, experiential power *is* a subject? A capacity for experience is something over and above any experiences the capacity produces. Perhaps this is enough to render talk of 'ownership' meaningful. We can take a further step in the same direction. What if there could be extremely aetiolated subjects consisting of *nothing but* experience? In this limiting case, a stream of consciousness would be identical with the subject who owns it. Even a very simple stream of consciousness would have a subject. (I will be exploring this radical possibility shortly—in §8.4.)

Alternatively, by way of a second line of response, we might question the relevant conceptual truth. We can imagine a race of people—call them *the Humeans*—who think and talk about their experience in much the same way we do, with one exception: the Isolation Thesis does not strike them as strange at all. It may seem absurd to us that a pain, a mood, a wish, could rove about the world without a bearer, but not to these people, who work with what Parfit calls an *impersonal* conception of reality. Do the Humeans mean by 'experience' what we mean? It is hard to tell, and it does not matter. If the Humeans' concept of experience is different, we can coin a new word to translate it: experience*. Experiences may have to have subjects, but experiences* do not. We can now reformulate the Isolation Thesis in terms of the new concept: there could be a creature with a simple mind capable of only a single simple kind of experience*. We have both experiences and experiences*: in our case, the two concepts refer to the same items. If there are possible worlds where there are such simple subjects, then in these worlds there are experiences* but no experiences. The question is whether there are such worlds, and the conceptual link between 'experience' and 'subject' is irrelevant to this question.

These points do not in themselves establish the possibility of solitary sensations, but taken together they go some way to undermining the claim that their impossibility is in any way an obvious truth. Since it does seem plausible to think that minds much simpler than our own might exist, I can see no reason not to go one step further and at least take seriously the possibility that there might be minds so simple that they can only generate a single kind of simple experience. Perhaps the laws of nature in our universe forbid such things—but perhaps they do not (we don't yet know). In any event, this is irrelevant to the issue of whether such simple minds are logically possible.

One last point. If simple subjects are possible, is there any minimum period of time a subject need exist to be properly counted as a subject? How brief a life could a *maximally short-lived* subject enjoy? The answer, I think, is: very brief indeed. Consider your own existence over the past hour. Your life during this interval consisted of a series of mental and physical happenings. If an indistinguishable series of happenings were to exist all by itself—they just appear out of thin air—it is clear that this half-hour series would also constitute a subject. This comparatively short-lived subject would suffer the delusion of having a past it did not have, and doubtless have expectations of a future it will not live to see, but being deluded is not a barrier to being a subject (only subjects *can* be deluded in these ways). If a half-hour subject is possible, then why not a quarter-hour subject, or a one-minute subject? It is hard to see why brevity should be a barrier to subjecthood. A very short life is not much of a life, and in extreme cases not a life that is liable to be noticed by anyone else, but it is a life all the same. However, in the context of the C-theory there is a limit on how short subject's life can be: if strictly durationless experience is impossible, and I am inclined to think it is, then a strictly momentary subject is impossible too. No subject can have a life-span shorter than the shortest possible experience.[6]

8.3. REDUCTIO?

These various strands of argument just outlined all point in the same direction. The claim that extremely simple forms of experience might exist all on their own, independantly of anything resembling a more encompassing mind (as the term is usually construed) can seem absurd, and the same applies with regard to the corresponding (simple) capacities for experience. But when the issue is examined more closely, the air of absurdity quickly dissipates.

The possibility or otherwise of simple subjects is relevant to the larger scheme of things: to the question of the kind of thing subjects are, and the kind of thing we are. An isolated experiential power capable of producing a solitary sensation is not *just* an experiential power, it is a subject in its own right, a very simple subject. Or at least, this is the case if we accept the C-theory in its broad guise, which

---

[6] See Zimmerman (1999) for a more wide ranging discussion of short-lived subjects.

equates subject persistence with persisting experiential potential. Furthermore, if simple subjects are possible it may also be possible that human subjects could be reduced to this level—it depends on how little a human brain could possess by way of experiential capacity. In any event, accepting the C-theory in an unrestricted form means accepting that if one's current stream of consciousness were smoothly reduced to a single enduring sensation, and one's capacity for consciousness were reduced in a corresponding manner (e.g. as a result of rapidly progressive brain degeneration), then one would still be in existence.

Although this conclusion might strike some as absurd, as a *reductio* of the C-theory rather than a possible mode of human existence, it is also a direct consequence of the doctrine that a conscious subject cannot cease to exist while it remains conscious, or retains the capacity for consciousness—or to put it a slightly different way, that we cannot cease to exist (*qua* conscious subjects) while our streams of consciousness flow on. This thesis underpins the C-theory, and as we have seen, it has a good deal of intuitive appeal. Is there any reason for thinking that a stream has to have a certain degree of complexity or sophistication in order to carry its original subject with it? Not if the only essential property of a subject is its capacity to have experiences. Isn't this a plausible conception of what a subject is? It is indeed, and there is also a point of principle to bear in mind. The C-thesis states that experiences that are co-conscious have the same subject. Since the envisaged (diminishing) stream of consciousness is a *stream* of consciousness, it must exhibit phenomenal continuity throughout its length. Assuming the overlap model, this stream consists of a succession of overlapping specious presents, and this means that its neighbouring brief phases are diachronically co-conscious. Given that they are related in this way, how can they fail to be consubjective?

The idea that we would not survive the transition to minimal subjecthood is problematic for a further reason: just where should we draw the line? Imagine your own stream of consciousness flowing smoothly on, but becoming increasingly simple as your brain degenerates. Now imagine drawing a borderline at some point along this spectrum of increasing simplicity. On one side of this border you exist, on the other you do not. When your stream of declining consciousness hits the threshold of fatal simplicity, it continues to flow on, albeit in a very slightly diminished form, but it leaves you behind. This is surely hard to believe. If you survived *that* far, what prevents you surviving an instant longer? While we could simply stipulate that a subject fails to survive beyond a certain point, the stipulation would not only be completely arbitrary, it would lack any obvious rationale. A single grain of sand clearly does not make a heap, so there is a reason for thinking that removing grains from a heap one by one eventually leads to a significant change, even if this change does not occur all at once. Stipulating that a heap must contain *n* grains (appropriately organized) thus has some rationale, even if the actual value for *n* is an arbitrary stipulation—for example we could equally well have chosen *n* plus or minus 1. But it is by no means self-evident that a capacity for a very simple form of consciousness fails to constitute a subject of experience. This is why, in the case of an increasingly simple stream of consciousness, selecting a cut-off point could be viewed as not only arbitrary, but as entirely unmotivated.

This conclusion can be resisted. It is certainly possible to distinguish between different types of conscious being on the basis of their mental capacities. For example we could draw a distinction between *Lockean* and *sub-Lockean* subjects: the former are conscious beings with a capacity for self-consciousness—they can think of themselves *as* persisting conscious intelligences—whereas sub-Lockean subjects are conscious beings who lack the intellectual sophistication to think of themselves in this way. We could then identify ourselves with subjects of the Lockean variety. Peter Unger advocates something along these lines. Although Unger holds that a persisting and uninterrupted capacity for consciousness is necessary to our survival, he also maintains that it is not sufficient. Commenting on an imaginary case involving the progressive elimination of neural tissues, he writes:

Whether or not the continuous realization of a capacity for consciousness is necessary for my existence, it is far from being sufficient. . . . If too many cells gradually are taken away, then my reasoning ability gradually will fall to what are disastrously low levels, disastrous, that is, for my survival. When there is only a part of my brain left that, in addition to conscious experience, realizes only the reasoning ability of a *typical dog*, then *I* will no longer exist. There may then be a subject of experience in the situation, all right, a subject that is then and there even having conscious experience, but that will be a numerically different subject. As far as any non-conventional matters are concerned, the example's original subject of experience, me, will have gradually faded out of existence. A personal subject of experience will gradually have faded into, and will gradually have been replaced by, a very markedly sub-personal subject of experience. (Unger 1990: 195–6)

Unger suggests that the degree of psychological sophistication which demarcates personal from sub-personal subjects may well be highly and ineliminably vague, but certainly includes a capacity to reason in a rudimentary way, and a capacity to form some simple intentions. This position may seem an attractive compromise. The idea that we might survive as subjects possessing nothing whatsoever by way of psychological sophistication can easily seem far-fetched, whereas the Lockean claim that to survive we need a good deal of psychological sophistication can easily seem too strict. We could, if we wanted, incorporate Unger's psychological constraint (or some variant of it) into the C-theory. If we did so, the C-theory in its original (and unrestricted form) could be construed as providing us with the persistence conditions of sub-personal subjects. The persistence of personal subjects could be spelt out along these lines: for a personal subject *S* to survive, *S*'s experiential capacities must continue to exist (appealing here to C-relatedness), and these capacities must be part of a psychological system which provide *S* with the capacity to form simple intentions and engage in rudimentary reasoning. As for the C-thesis, if we were to follow Unger we could still subscribe to the claims that experiences invariably have subjects, and that co-conscious experiences are invariably consubjective: all we need do is add the stipulation that the subject of an experience can be of the personal kind *or* the sub-personal kind.[7]

If we believed ourselves to be essentially personal subjects, a restricted C-theory could easily provide a viable account of our survival conditions. But it is not at all clear that we *do* believe ourselves to be essentially personal subjects. The concept of a simple subject may be somewhat fanciful, but one need not suppose there are or could be such things to find it plausible that one will remain in existence for as long one's current stream of consciousness continues to flow on, even if that consciousness is somewhat simpler than what one is accustomed to, and even if it is not accompanied by a psychological system with anything approaching the complexity required for rudimentary reasoning and the forming of intentions. We saw in §5.5 that although Unger is well aware that the continuity of consciousness can easily seem all-important when we contemplate the sorts of changes we could survive, he is also of the view that this appearance is deceptive. However, as we also saw, his arguments for this view are problematic in several respects. A consideration of a somewhat different kind also counts against Unger. I think it very likely that many of us would find ourselves tempted by the offer of VR-4 excursions which provide one with the sort of experience a non-human creature might have. It would be interesting to know what it is like to be a dolphin, or a bat, or a dog. If one's stream of consciousness gradually altered in character, ending up as dog-like in all phenomenological respects, provided full phenomenal continuity is preserved, is it not clear that the doggish experiences are one's own? Needless to say, one would be unlikely to make use of an experience-machine to sample a dog's life if the trip were one-way. Few of us would willingly exchange our real lives for a virtual life, fewer still would exchange their current life for a dog's virtual life. But in cases where the trip is temporary, it seems clear that the experience-machine not only keeps one in existence, it provides one with experiences. Survival in the absence of the kind of psychology Unger regards as necessary for our survival thus seems eminently possible. And if by some chance the trip does become a one-way affair—an accident destroys one's body and psychology—the essentials of the situation are unchanged. Provided the experience-machine is not turned off, one's stream of consciousness will continue on, in a dog-like manner.

One final thought: if one could survive with the experiential capacities of a dog, why not those of a bird? Why not those of a worm or maggot? Why not those of a simple subject?

---

[7] How should we describe a declining or degenerating C-system which at the outset sustains a personal subject but ends up only sustaining a sub-personal subject? This poses a difficulty for Unger's position, but probably not an insuperable one. Rather than talking of two types of subject who exist in alternation, it might be better to regard 'personal subject' as a phase sortal, corresponding to a particular *way* a subject can be. We could then say that a single subject is present throughout the process of decline, although only some phases of this subject's life belong to (or constitute) the life of a person.

8.4. MINIMAL SUBJECTS

Simple subjects have simple conscious lives, but their consciousness is the product of a persisting experiential capacity. Might there be streams of consciousness that are not products of experiential powers? It depends on whether the following sort of scenario is metaphysically possible.

Suppose that six minutes ago God annihilated the entire physical world; exactly five minutes later he brought it back. The re-born physical world is just the way the original world would have been five minutes later: clocks have moved on five minutes, as have conversations and broadcasts, cakes in ovens have risen a little more, moving vehicles re-appear where they would have been five minutes later, and so on. Let us further suppose that during the five-minute hiatus the world was not completely empty. God ensured that each subject's stream of consciousness continued on, in just the way it would have done (with respect to phenomenological character) if the physical world had gone on as usual—for the sake of clarity and simplicity, let us suppose that every subject was awake and conscious when God intervenes, and their stream of consciousness continues throughout the five minutes (no deaths occur). Throughout the five minute period, God was the direct cause of our continuing experiences. When the five minutes were up, our streams of consciousness continued on their way, but now sustained by our brains in the usual manner. We might call this case *the five minute Cartesian nightmare*. But this label would be misleading; there is really nothing nightmarish about it, since we do not notice the world's sudden departure—for us, it is as if nothing out of the ordinary had happened at all. We can remember the experiences we had during the five minutes world-gap as well (or as badly) as we can usually remember our past five minutes. And crucially, complete experiential continuity is retained throughout: streams of consciousness flow seamlessly across the changes in their causal grounds, and these changes are invisible to introspection.

Questions have been begged in the way I have described this case.[8] If phenomenal states are themselves material in nature, then at least some matter survives the obliteration of the physical universe. I spoke of 'our' consciousness continuing on across the worldless chasm. Why should *we* remain when the entire physical world departs, taking with it the objects (our brains) which are the causal grounds of our capacities for consciousness? Given the axioms of the experiential approach, the answer may seem obvious. The C-theory is built on the C-thesis, the contention that co-conscious experience is consubjective. When the physical world is suddenly annihilated, the last moments of your brain-based consciousness are co-conscious with the first moments of a non-brain-based

---

[8] The case is taken (almost verbatim) from Dainton (1996), but is put to a different use here.

stream, and five minutes later, the last moments of the latter stream are co-conscious with the first moments of the stream sustained by the newly created replica of your old body. These phenomenal links ensure that there is only one uninterrupted stream of consciousness here—your original stream merges with the divinely sustained stream, a stream with all the character and richness of everyday consciousness, and continues on to be sustained by a replica of your original body. If we accept that co-conscious, and derivatively, co-streamal, experiences are consubjective, then the experiences which comprise the divinely sustained continuation of your original stream are certainly *yours*. The whole point of the experience-based approach is that nothing is more compelling than co-consciousness when it comes to allocating experiences to subjects.

So, the experiences in the divinely sustained stream are yours. But there is a further begged-question: do *you* exist during the five-minute period? Is there, during this five-minute period, a self or subject of experience who is a candidate for being you? There is a stream of consciousness that belongs to you, but do you, as a subject of experience, exist for the duration of this stream, or do you merely lay claim to these experiences from a temporal distance, as it were, while enjoying an intermittent existence? There are several reasons for preferring the continuous existence option. We avoid the complications of intermittent existence; we avoid having to say that there can be experiences which can occur without a subject being present at the time. More importantly, the no-subject option is highly implausible from a phenomenological perspective. Suppose that now, as you read this, we are in the midst of a five-minute period during which the physical world does not exist, and your current stream of consciousness is divinely sustained. Do you not exist as you read this? The idea seems absurd, and is all the more unacceptable from the experiential perspective we have adopted. It is true that these attenuated subjects do not possess anything resembling a normal psychology. In saying that a minimal subject is 'nothing over and above' a stream of consciousness, I mean just that. Our own streams of consciousness depend for their character on our memories, beliefs, mental abilities, etc., but minimal subjects have none of these. But as I suggested when discussing the virtual lives of VR-4 subjects, a psychology does not seem necessary to survival: the illusion of thinking and understanding is not as good or desirable as the real thing, but the illusion can be phenomenologically indistinguishable from the real thing. So we should accept that during the five-minute world-gap, you remain in existence. This means accepting that a subject can exist as nothing over and above a stream of consciousness. I shall call these attenuated entities *minimal subjects*. A minimal subject is a stream of consciousness, no matter how brief, and *nothing more*.

In the imaginary case we have been considering, since God is actively sustaining our streams of consciousness, it could be objected that we have not been reduced to minimal subjects—our experiences are the direct products of God's experiential capacities. This objection is not very threatening. Our experiences are created by God, they are not experienced by God; our experiences are the products of divine power, but the capacity to create experience at will is different from a causal potentiality grounded in natural law. But I shall not dwell on this point since there are alternative cases that are free from any ambiguity. Suppose it is just a brute fact that our streams of consciousness continue for the five minutes during which the physical world is absent. Here, our continued experience is not the product of any potentialities of any kind, it *just is*, and as a consequence we persist, temporarily reduced to minimal subjects.

The concept of a minimal subject is distinct from the concept of a simple subject. A simple subject can enjoy a very restricted range of experience, a minimal subject can have experience as rich as ours (or richer). The difference is that a simple subject's experience is the product of experiential powers, a minimal subject's is not. By combining the two notions we arrive at a limit condition on subjecthood. A subject which is both maximally simple and minimal is in as diminished a condition as a subject can attain. Where does the notion of a minimal subject stand in relation to the Isolation Thesis? Well, a subject which is both maximally simple and minimal is nothing more than a single experience, an experience that is not the product of a nomologically grounded potentiality. If such an experience could exist, the Isolation Thesis would clearly be vindicated. But since this experience can also be regarded as constituting a subject, it is not clear what Hume himself would say about the matter—more on this shortly.

8.5. A MINIMAL MODIFICATION, AND A MORAL

If we are prepared to recognize the bare metaphysical possibility of minimal subjects, how can we reconcile this possibility with the C-theory? According to the C-theory a subject is essentially a continuous potential for consciousness. We cannot regard a minimal subject in this way. I will call experiences that are the product of experiential capacities *power-produced*. In outlining the C-theory I assumed that all experience is power-produced in order to keep things relatively simple. Our experience is, I take it, power-produced, as are the experiences of most of the other subjects in our universe. Even subjects who live out their lives hooked up to a VR-4 device enjoy power-produced experience (the relevant capacities are grounded in a programmable machine rather than a brain, but this is of no import). Only the bizarre type of circumstance we have just considered will sustain truly minimal subjects. Given this, it seemed pointless to elaborate further an already complicated picture to accommodate a possibility as remote as that of minimal subjects. As it happens, accommodating this possibility requires only a minor modification to the C-theory as it currently stands. The following formulations provide us with what we need:

1 A collection of experiential powers composes a C-system at t iff its members are **S-related** at t.

2 C-systems at earlier and later times are phases of the same persisting C-system iff they are either DPC_D-related or IPC_D-related.

3 Experiential powers are **C-related** iff they belong to the same C-system.

4 Experiences which are directly or indirectly co-conscious are C-related, whether power-produced or not.

5 For any experiential power P and any non-power-produced experience E, if E would be co-conscious with the experience that P would produce were it active, then E and P are C-related.

6 Experiential powers and experiences are consubjective if and only if they are C-related.

7 C-systems are maximal collections of C-related experiential powers *or* non-power-produced experiences.

8 Selves (or subjects) are C-systems.

The essentials of the original (see §4.4) are condensed into (1)–(3) of the revised formulation. The fourth clause extends the notion of C-relatedness to all co-streamal experiences: experiences in an uninterrupted stream of consciousness are C-related, irrespective of whether or not they are power-produced. Suppose an experiential power P is active and producing experience of type e. Further suppose that P ceases to produce experience when the world vanishes—as in our example—but the last e-type experience P produces is co-conscious with the first experience of a non-power-produced stream of f-type experience. Clause (4) now ensures that the power-produced e-type experience is C-related to the stream of non-power-produced f-type experience. But what if P is dormant and so not producing experience? Can it be consubjective with a non-power-produced experience? Of course it can: provided that if P were active it would produce experience that is co-conscious with the non-power-produced experience in question. Hence the need for clause (5).

Although C-relatedness now applies to experiences as well as experiential powers, the only binding agent in play is co-consciousness, and so we are remaining true to the spirit of the original. Going back to the five-minute Cartesian nightmare, we can now say not only that you persist throughout the five minute world-gap (by being reduced for its duration to a minimal subject), but that your experience is C-related throughout, as are your experiential powers, save for the period during which you persist without any. The new clause (7) extends the definition of a C-system so as to accommodate this possibility: a phenomenally continuous stream of non-power-produced experience is a C-system—and thus a self, according to clause (8). In §4.1 I suggested that ideally we want an account of our persistence conditions that is pure or non-disjunctive.

The proposed alteration to the C-theory does render it disjunctive, but not in a damaging way. Minimal and ordinary subjects are not two entirely different kinds of thing, they are simply different ways for a subject of experience to be.

I should stress that I am not claiming that minimal subjects are real metaphysical possibilities. As already noted, if states of consciousness are identical with physical phenomena, then for a minimal subject to exist certain physical phenomena will also exist; if states of consciousness are states of non-physical substances, then a minimal subject requires the existence of non-physical substance. In either of these cases, it could easily be that in the world-gap scenario something in addition to experience exists: perhaps the material systems that possess phenomenal characteristics also, and necessarily, possess non-phenomenal properties; the same might apply in the immaterial case. The question of *how little* has to exist for a stream of consciousness to exist depends on how we answer questions about the nature of consciousness that at present we have little or no idea how to answer. A minimal subject would be a very strange phenomenon, but so far as its mentality is concerned, it would not differ in any essential ways from that of the VR-4 subjects we have already considered. And as I noted earlier, a virtual life of the sort VR-4 subjects have is not much of a life, it is a kind of life we might prefer not to have, no matter how enjoyable and rewarding it could be, subjectively, but a virtual life is nonetheless a *life*, it is a way to go on existing, and it is a way to go on existing as an experiencing mental subject.

So the important point is that since a minimal subject's conscious mental life could be indistinguishable from our own, in all phenomenological respects, there is every reason to regard such an entity *as* a subject. (Of course, if a minimal subject's experience were indistinguishable from our own, it would be completely unaware of its mentally and metaphysically aetiolated condition). There is also at least one significant consequence of taking the possibility of minimal selves seriously. When discussing the Isolation Thesis, I suggested that the conceptual objection—'our concept of *experience* requires all experiences to have an owner'—would have no teeth if even simple solitary experiences, could (in the limit case) *be* subjects. When Descartes found he could doubt the existence of everything save his own self, Lichtenberg famously remarked that he was not entitled to even this much. If everything is illusion, perhaps the existence of the self is an illusion too; perhaps all that exists is the stream of consciousness that contains these very thoughts. For, in a Humean spirit, we can ask: what evidence do we find in consciousness itself for the conclusion that consciousness belongs to a substantial subject? We can now reply, in accord more with the letter of Descartes than the spirit, that consciousness alone can constitute a subject, even if only a minimal subject. If a world were Humean, and contained nothing but experience, it would (*contra* Hume) also contain subjects. Lichtenberg was wrong: the existence of a stream of consciousness *does* justify the postulation of a subject, even if only a minimal subject, and so—in a sense—Descartes was right all along. If we are conscious we can be certain that we exist, as subjects. What we cannot be certain about is what *kind* of subject we are.[9]

8.6. WEAK UNITY

Before moving on I want to look at another issue that is relevant to the simplicity of the self, but in a rather different way to those we have been concerned with thus far. Recalling the terminology introduced in §2.5, let us say that a state of consciousness at a given time is *strongly unified* only and only if every part of it is co-conscious with every other part, and *weakly unified* if this is not the case. (Or to be more precise a state S is weakly unified if every part of S is co-conscious with some other part in S, but there are also parts of S that are not co-conscious with one another.) Whether or not a weakly unified consciousness is possible or not is intimately bound up with the nature of co-consciousness. Focusing on the simplest of cases, if synchronic co-consciousness is a transitive relationship then for any three experiences e_1, e_2, and e_3, irrespective of their type or owner, if e_1 and e_2 are co-conscious and e_2 and e_3 are co-conscious, then necessarily e_1 and e_3 will be co-conscious as well—in which case weak unity is impossible. But if co-consciousness is not a transitive relationship, then it would be possible for e_1 and e_3 *not* to be co-conscious with one another, despite the fact that e_1 is co-conscious with e_2 and e_2 is co-conscious with e_3. A weakly unified state of this sort can be described in different ways. We could say that it involves two partially overlapping states of consciousness S_1 and S_2, composed of (e_1, e_2) and (e_2, e_3) respectively. Alternatively, we could say that there is a single state of consciousness all of whose parts are either directly or indirectly co-conscious. It is not obvious that much hangs on this terminological decision. The single-state option does full justice to the fact that we are dealing here with a single uninterrupted *expanse* of consciousness, in which full unity obtains locally if not globally, whereas the two-state option allows us to retain the appealing notion that all the contents of a single state of consciousness are *presented together*, as a unity.

Although at first sight this issue may seem somewhat abstruse, it is of more than narrow technical interest. If weak unity were possible the C-thesis would be unthreatened: the claim that co-conscious experiences are consubjective remains as compelling as ever. What would be undermined, however, is a close relative

---

[9] Minimal subjects can be of use in other metaphysical domains. Panpsychism is on the verge of becoming (once again) a respectable position on the matter–consciousness relationship—see Strawson *et al.* (2006). If even elementary material things (electrons, strings, etc.) have simple forms of experience, what sort of *subject* can these experiences have? For those who insist that there cannot be experienc*es* without experienc*ers* there is a real problem here. Allowing that (at the limit) experiences can *be* subjects eliminates the problem.

of the C-thesis, namely its time-indexed converse, which can be formulated as follows:

$C^{\#}$-thesis: at any time t, experiences that are consubjective are (mutually) co-conscious.

Without the temporal restriction the $C^{\#}$-thesis is obviously false, since plenty of experiences belong to the same subject but are not co-conscious with one another—the experiences you had five minutes, five hours or five years ago, for example. With the temporal restriction in place, however, the $C^{\#}$-thesis has a good deal of appeal. It is certainly plausible to think that all our own experiences at any one time form a fully unified ensemble—certainly nothing in our ordinary experience suggests otherwise. Indeed, it is by no means obvious what a subject's experience would have to be like in order to give them the impression that their consciousness is only partially unified. For on the plausible assumption that experiences that are objects of a single act of attention are necessarily co-conscious, if weakly unified states are possible they will not be discernible (as wholes) to any single act of attentive introspection. But perhaps it would be wrong to conclude that a form of consciousness cannot exist solely because it cannot be introspected. In any event, if the $C^{\#}$-thesis should turn out to be false, there is a weaker principle constraining the relationship between subjects and experiences which also has a good deal of plausibility:

$C^{\#\#}$-thesis: at any time t, experiences that are consubjective are co-conscious, directly or indirectly.

As previously, experiences are indirectly co-conscious if they are linked by an chain of directly co-conscious experiences.

Whatever its merits, this weaker principle does have consequences, not least of which is a loss of necessary simplicity with respect to the structure of a subject's consciousness at any given moment. The $C^{\#}$-thesis entails strong unity, the weaker $C^{\#\#}$-thesis does not, and once the door of possible partial unity is open, there is no obvious reason to rule out the possibility of some very strange experiential structures, a couple of which are depicted in Figure 8.1. In these diagrams the circles represent fully unified experiential states.

Figure 8.1 If partial unity is possible, so too are peculiar experiential structures

Even if we confine our attention to less fanciful instances, there are potential puzzle cases. In cases of very mild disunity, of the sort depicted in Figure 8.2a it seems more plausible than not to suppose that all the experiences involved belong to the same subject. The situation is not so self-evident in cases of more extreme disassociation, of the sort shown in Figure 8.2b.

Figure 8.2(a). Mild disunity

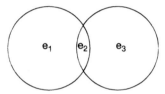

Figure 8.2(b). Extreme disassociation

To make matters more concrete, suppose the left- and right-hand circles represent temporal cross-sections of streams of consciousness very similar to yours or mine, and the region of overlap (e_2) consists of a comparatively insignificant bodily sensation—the feelings associated with the sole of a foot, say. Since we are supposing that the streams in question, with the exception of the small overlap, are typically human in character, it might seem self-evident that each belongs to a different subject. Given the region of overlap, these hypothetical subjects—call them S_1 and S_2—are not wholly distinct, they (or their C-systems, which comes to much the same thing) have a common part. But since this part is comparatively minor, is it reasonable to allow its existence to stand in the way of our recognizing what seem clearly to be two experiential subjects as such? Taking this step may seem reasonable, but there are significant costs.

We could accept the possibility of partially overlapping subjects without abandoning the C-thesis, but we would have to abandon the doctrine that consubjectivity is a transitive relationship, at least in the synchronic case—in the envisaged scenario a first experience is consubjective with a second, and the second with a third, without the first and third being consubjective. Needless to say, this is not a step to be taken lightly. We would also have to give up the principle that a single experience necessarily belongs to just one subject: as shown in Figure 8.2b, e_2 belongs to both S_1 and S_2. Alternatively, we could uphold the transitivity of consubjectivity and maintain that partially overlapping subjects such as S_1 and S_2 are numerically identical. However, while this step simplifies the situation metaphysically speaking, it does leave open the possibility that our ordinary patterns of self-concern and self-identity can come apart. Depending on the precise details of the scenario, and the degree of overlap, it might make sense for others to treat S_1 and S_2 as though they were different subjects, and it might make sense for S_1 and S_2 to think of themselves as different subjects—after all, if e_3 contains a severe pain, it will not be co-conscious with (and so *experienced* by or in) the unified consciousness of S_1.

As for whether a weakly unified consciousness is a genuine possibility, there are considerations which point in different directions. In the eyes of some philosophers, experiments carried out on split-brain patients suggest that weak unity is a real phenomenon, not merely a possible one. If this is right then synchronic co-consciousness is non-transitive. But as I indicated in §2.5, there are considerations of a purely phenomenological kind which suggest that this form of co-consciousness cannot fail to be transitive. I will start with the case for weak unity.

The relevant evidence from split-brain cases is reasonably familiar, at least in outline. The surgical procedure known as cerebral commissurotomy involves cutting the nerves which connect the two cerebral hemispheres; most of these nerves are contained in the corpus callosum; the neural links between each half of the cortex and the lower regions of the brain are left intact, and the lower brain itself is not divided. Despite the fact that a functioning lower brain is essential for conscious mental life, there is some evidence that the right and left halves of a divided cortex each sustain a separate mental life: experiments have shown that information passed only to the right hemisphere (via the left-hand side of the visual field) is not available to the left hemisphere, and vice-versa. If completely severing the inter-hemispheric connections led to the creation of two completely separate and independent streams of consciousness, interpreting these results would pose no difficulty: dividing the cortex would produce two subjects of experience out of one (assuming the C-theory). The two resulting streams of consciousness would, of course, depend on a common lower brain, but this would not matter provided the resultant states of consciousness were non-overlapping; under these conditions there would be two distinct C-systems, and hence two distinct subjects. (The situation would be analogous to a pair of Siamese twins sharing more vital bodily organs than is usually the case.) However, commissurotomy does not lead to such a clear-cut result. It is only under carefully controlled circumstances that the right and left hemispheres show signs of housing entirely separate minds; for the most part a split-brain patient behaves quite normally. This has led some commentators to suggest that split-brain patients for the most part enjoy a fully unified consciousness, suffering a partial loss of mental integration only under the highly contrived circumstances devised by psychologists investigating their condition.[10] No less significantly, there are test results which suggest that the minds associated with each hemisphere might share basic emotional feelings, such as sexual arousal, feelings that are closely linked to areas of the lower brain, areas which are not divided.

This combination of findings makes it difficult to sustain the thesis that commissurotomy produces two wholly and permanently separate centres of consciousness, but it is also difficult to believe that the patients' consciousness is altogether unchanged. Lockwood (1989, ch. 6) argues that we if find the split-brain data baffling it is because we naturally assume that the unity of consciousness is all-or-nothing. If we are prepared to admit that weak unity is possible, we can easily accommodate the evidence of shared sensations: the subject or subjects in question have states of consciousness which partially overlap. If we are prepared to admit the possibility that the degree of overlap might be different at different times, we can accommodate the evidence that split-brain patients enjoy varying degrees of mental integration. Under normal circumstances the disunity is typically minimal, but under experimental conditions, when quite different stimuli are supplied to each hemisphere, the disunity increases.

Lockwood reinforces the case for partial unity with a thought experiment. We are asked to imagine a very gradual commissurotomy being carried out on a patient who remains fully conscious throughout. If we suppose first that weak unity is impossible, and secondly that by the end of the procedure two wholly distinct streams of consciousness exist, then assuming only a single stream is present at the outset, it is evident that the transition from one stream to two must happen all at once. While this may not be an impossibility, how plausible is it to think that slicing through just a few neurons—the procedure is being carried out very gradually, don't forget—could be responsible for such a massive and abrupt change? If we are prepared to admit the possibility of varying degrees of weak unity, the situation is very different. We can now suppose that the subject's consciousness becomes progressively more disunified as more and more neurons are cut, until in the end there are two completely separate streams.

While Lockwood's arguments have considerable force, they are a good deal less than conclusive. The evidence which suggests that right- and left-hemisphere subjects (assuming they exist) can be aware of the same experiences is susceptible to a different interpretation. Rather than a single token experience being involved, perhaps each subject has a qualitatively similar but numerically distinct token experience—perhaps there is phenomenal duplication rather than overlap. Alternatively, perhaps there is just one subject present, a subject with a fully unified consciousness but a fragmented psychology. The behaviour which is suggestive of phenomenal disunity could instead be the product of a less than normally integrated psychology—case studies of multiple-personality syndrome suggest that such psychologies are possible. In a similar vein, the evidence which

---

[10] For arguments supporting this interpretation see Marks (1980) and Wilkes (1988: ch. 5).

Lockwood uses to support the hypothesis of varying degrees of phenomenal integration can equally well support the alternative hypothesis of varying degrees of *psychological* integration, variations which again take place against the backdrop of a fully unified consciousness. These are difficult issues, and there is a great deal more to be said about the interpretation of the relevant neuropsychological evidence. But so far as I can see there would be little point in going into these issues in more depth here, for it is widely accepted that we currently have insufficient data to settle which of these competing hypotheses is closer to the truth. Lockwood's thought experiment is also less than decisive, and for a similar reason. Given that we are still so ignorant about the mechanisms underlying the production of consciousness, we are certainly not in a position to rule out the abrupt change hypothesis. Perhaps eliminating just a few brain cells in the corpus callosum *would* result in the immediate creation of two entirely separate phenomenal fields. I cannot see that we have any reason to think this hypothesis is any less probable than the gradual change hypothesis that Lockwood prefers.

What of the phenomenological considerations? These too may be inconclusive, but they are far from negligible. As even those sympathetic to the possibility of weak unity concede, the notion that a state of consciousness could ever be anything less than fully unified is a hard one to take seriously.[11] How at a given time could I possibly be aware of e_1 and e_2 occurring together, and also being aware of e_2 and e_3 occurring together, without also being aware of e_1 and e_3 occurring together? If weak unity is a genuine possibility, why should it seem so obviously impossible? Part of the answer lies in the fact that we cannot *imagine* what it would be like to have a consciousness of this kind. (Try as I might, I for one cannot even get *close*.) But it would be unwise to place any great weight on this. First because not everything that is possible is humanly imaginable, but secondly and more importantly in this connection, as I noted earlier, our 'imaginative space' (for want of a better expression) is itself a fully unified phenomenal field. Any experiences that we imagine at a given time are invariably presented together (and hence as co-conscious) in our imaginations. Given this limitation it would clearly be wrong to conclude that weak unity is impossible simply because we are unable to conjure up the relevant kind of experiential configuration in our imaginations. However, the feeling that there is something profoundly unintelligible or problematic about the notion of a weakly unified consciousness may well have a second and deeper source: an insight into the *kind of unity* produced by the co-consciousness relationship, an insight afforded to us by our first-hand acquaintance with the relationship in question.

---

[11] e.g., Lockwood: 'I must confess, however, that, in spite of having defended it in print, I am still by no means wholly persuaded that the concept of a merely weakly unified consciousness really does make sense' (1994: 95). More recently, and in the opposite camp, Bayne and Chalmers have expressed similar doubts (2003, §5).

Arriving at a clear articulation of this insight is a delicate matter—it is not always easy to put experience into words—so the formulations which follow could no doubt be improved upon.

Using partially overlapping circles to represent a weakly unified state is convenient but it may also be misleading. To state the obvious, spatially extended entities can partly overlap only if they do not wholly coincide; a pair of objects which occupy precisely the same region of space overlap completely. In the case of ordinary three-dimensional material objects, difference of spatial location is a necessary pre-requisite for being connected by familiar non-transitive relationships. One such is 'being linked by a chain': the bicycle can be chained to the lamp post, and the lamp post chained to truck without the bicycle also being chained to the truck. In the phenomenal realm also, experiences that are co-conscious at a given time typically occupy different locations in phenomenal space. Since experiences separated in this sort of way do not appear to be wholly coincident, and bearing in mind the physical analogy, it might seem perfectly intelligible for such experiences to be linked by a non-transitive type of (phenomenal) connection. But this is to overlook the distinctiveness of the co-consciousness relationship: there is in fact a very real sense in which the various parts of a spatially extended spread of experience *do* coincide completely.

To appreciate how this can be it will help if we remind ourselves of some of the distinctive features of the co-consciousness relationship. First of all, it is a direct and unmediated connection between experiences and their parts. Co-consciousness is the relationship of *experienced togetherness*. Although it has no discernible features of its own—in this respect it is quite unlike physi-cal links such as chains or lengths of string—we know perfectly well what it is like for experiences to be unified by the co-consciousness relationship. Also, as I noted in §2.5 and §3.5, co-consciousness is a pervasive relation-ship, one which directly connects each part and aspect of a total experience to every other part and aspect, irrespective of how we divide the total expe-rience into parts. Not only is every part of a total experience co-conscious with every other part, it is co-conscious to precisely the same degree: co-consciousness does not come in different grades or strengths, experiences are either co-conscious or they are not.[12] These points taken together lead us to the conclusion that each part of a co-conscious collection of experiences is in direct *and equal* phenomenal contact with every other part. This applies even when the members of the collection extend through phenomenal space. The independence of phenomeno-spatial relatedness and co-consciousness is

---

[12] Or so it seems reasonable to think, assuming as I do here, that there cannot be 'vague experiences', in the sense of entities for which it is neither true nor false to say that they are experiential in kind—there can of course be experiences whose kind is unclear. See Dainton (2000: 89) for more on this.

easily appreciated, for it is easy to conceive of a pair of experiences remaining
as co-conscious with one another as ever despite the fact that their spatial
relationship with one another becomes progressively weaker or more confused—or even vanishes altogether, as in the more extreme cases we considered
in §2.2.

In virtue of this additional mode of connectedness and unity—one that is
always present, but easily overlooked—there is a sense in which co-conscious
collections of experiences are akin to geometrical points, or singularities, for
like the latter they do not have parts that are not in direct mutual contact.
Phenomenologically speaking, irrespective of how they are related in other
ways, experiences that are both co-conscious and simultaneous are at *zero
distance* from one another: they are as close to one another as it is possible
for experiences to be. This two-sided character is depicted in Figure 8.3,
where the double-headed arrows represent relationships of co-consciousness.
What goes for this phenomenal expanse applies to *all* collections of mutually
co-conscious experiences at a given time: irrespective of their complexity and
spatial organization, such collections are also simple and singular. Although
Figure 8.3 makes this point reasonably well, in some respects it is misleading.
First, the relationships of co-consciousness do not extend through a higher-order
spatial dimension, they are direct, unmediated connections between phenomenal
items; second, *all* parts of a total experience are related to one another by
co-consciousness, not just a few.

Phenomenal singularity

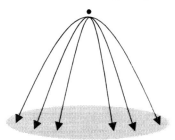

Phenomenal expanse

Figure 8.3 The consequences of co-consciousness: each part of the phenomenal expanse
is phenomenally connected to every other part

Returning to our earlier example, we can now see that even if e_1 and e_2 are
separated by some distance in phenomenal space, by virtue of being co-conscious
there is also a sense in which they entirely coincide, since all of their parts are in
direct and distance-free phenomenal contact with one another. Given that the

co-conscious ensemble (e_1/e_2) has this dimensionless aspect, the hypothesis that e_3 could be co-conscious with e_2 but not e_1 is as absurd as supposing that a line could be in contact with only a part of a geometrical point: e_1 and e_2 are different aspects of a single conscious state, aspects that are *so* intimately related that it is impossible to be in phenomenal contact with one without also being in contact with the other. In effect, given the distinctive way in which co-consciousness compounds its relata, the fact that co-consciousness is a *symmetrical* relationship is in itself sufficient to ensure its transitivity.

Of course, this only applies in the case of synchronic co-consciousness. We know that in its diachronic form co-consciousness is not transitive. If $E_1 = (e_1 - e_2)$ and $E_2 = (e_2 - e_3)$ are two temporally extended total experiences, although their respective constituents are fully and mutually co-conscious, it is perfectly possible for e_1 and e_3 not to be co-conscious. As we saw in Chapter 3, this inter-experiential structure is characteristic of streams of consciousness that last any significant length of time. The fact that all forms of co-consciousness are not transitive might seem to undermine the case for transitivity in the synchronic case, but arguably the reverse is true. When we try to envisage breakdowns in transitivity in the synchronic case we are imposing an experiential structure of a kind that ordinarily exists among contents spread over an interval of time onto contents that are fully simultaneous and experienced as such. Might it not be that the structure in question can only exist in the diachronic case, where contents are separated in a way that momentary (or extremely brief) simultaneous contents are not? Might it not be that breakdowns in the transitivity of co-consciousness are characteristic of phenomenal temporality, that the *only* way in which co-consciousness can fail to be transitive is in the case of contents spread through time? It seems not unreasonable to conclude that this is indeed the case. After all, we all know exactly what it is like for transitivity to break down in the temporal case: we all know what it is like for contents to *pass through* consciousness, with the experienced passage of time. The arrival of new contents within the brief span of the phenomenal present is accompanied by the displacement of their predecessors: recall the manner in which the temporally extended experience (*Do-Re*) is transformed into (*Re-Mi*) and then (*Mi-Fa*). This sort of phenomenal process manifestly cannot occur in the synchronic case. Given that phenomenal passage *consists of* the relentless tearing apart of strong phenomenal unity, it would be surprising if consciousness at any given moment were anything other than strongly unified.

I would not claim that these considerations are decisive. When it comes to characterizing any aspect of our experience, co-consciousness included, mistakes and confusions are possible. Nonetheless, it would be wrong to conclude that we have no insight at all into these matters: we know *something* about the nature of the co-consciousness relationship simply because we know what it is like to have experiences that are so-related. Since the unique perspective on the relationship in question strongly suggests that it is necessarily transitive, and the considerations from split-brain cases are less than decisive, there is a reasonably strong case for rejecting the possibility of a weakly unified consciousness, and the complex modes of self-hood that would otherwise be possible. Hence there is a further sense in which selves may be simple things.

9
Holism

In considering the merits or otherwise of identifying ourselves with C-systems, it would help if we had a clearer idea of the kind of objects these systems are. We know that C-systems are composed of C-related experiential powers, and that C-related experiential powers are distinguished by virtue of their ability to produce co-conscious experiences (directly or indirectly). What we do not as yet know is precisely what kind of unity (or unities) C-related powers possess. There are different answers this question, depending upon whether we consider C-systems from a phenomenal, physical, or causal perspective. My focus here will be mainly on the kinds of unity which obtain among experiential powers solely in virtue of their being C-related, a question we have not considered hitherto. I will be particularly interested in trying to identify and elucidate the various ways in which C-related powers are interdependent. As will emerge, this is an intricate and difficult issue—and even though this chapter is a long one there are aspects of it that receive only a cursory treatment in what follows. But the difficulties are worthy of our engagement. For if the main line of argument I will be developing proves to be along the right lines, the ontological implications will be far from negligible.

By way of setting the stage, adopt for a moment the perspective of a psychological continuity theorist. If we were to suppose that a subject essentially consists of a collection of P-interrelated states, what could we say about the sort of thing a subject is? Since subjects typically have a large number of different psychological states, they have distinguishable mental constituents, and so in this sense at least are composite beings. Are these constituent parts the sort of item which could enjoy an independent existence? Many would say not. It is widely accepted that a belief state could not exist in isolation, since in order for a state to *be* a belief state it has to be an integral part of a psychological system—it has to be able perform the distinctive role of a belief state, and this role essentially involves the ability to interact with other psychological states—other beliefs, desires, intentions, and suchlike. And what goes for beliefs also goes for many other sorts of psychological state: they too can only exist as constituents of psychological systems. This is not to say that a given psychological state has to be a part of a particular P-system, or a P-system of a particular type. It could be that my belief that Paris is the French capital would continue to exist if I lost a large portion of my personal memories, or underwent a massive psychological transformation of some other sort—for example I come to believe that I am Napoleon. But the point remains. It is plausible to think that many kinds of psychological state are essentially *systemic*: they can only exist in systems of a certain sort.

There is a second source of interdependency among psychological states. Tom and Sam may both be acquainted with Seamus, and so both would assent to the statement 'Seamus is a dog'. Tom adores dogs, believes they are conscious beings who in many ways are like human beings, but knows very little about them beyond this. Sam, on the other hand, hates dogs, believes that all non-human animals are entirely lacking in consciousness, but knows a great deal about them: he studied veterinary science for several years, until he read Descartes and developed his current views about animal mentality. Although both Tom and Sam believe that Seamus is a dog, do they understand this proposition in the same way? It is not obvious that they do, for they obviously have very different understandings of what a dog is. For present purposes, whether we put this down to a difference in their concept of a dog, or a difference in their beliefs about dogs does not matter. The point is that the psychological role played by the belief in question in their respective P-systems is quite different, irrespective of whether we explain this in terms of their possessing different dog-concepts, or the same dog-concept but different associated beliefs. To put the point in a slightly different way, the *psychological character* of P-states—which I am assuming can be largely if not completely specified in terms of causal/functional (or inferential) role—is to some degree holistic: the precise psychological character of one P-state depends, to some degree, on the precise psychological character of other states in the same P-system.

If the constituents of P-systems are systemic and holistic in the ways just indicated, then P-systems are unified in quite deep ways. P-systems may be composite entities, but they are composites of a distinctive kind: in certain respects they are very unlike bundles of twigs held together by a piece of string, or a wall of bricks held together by cement. For although bundles and walls are composed of parts that are bound together, their parts also enjoy a certain independence with respect to their respective wholes: any given twig in a given bundle could as easily exist (largely unchanged) in another bundle or all by itself, and the same applies to the bricks in a wall. It is otherwise with the constituents of P-systems. And some P-theorists—for example Shoemaker (1997)—are very much alert to this point.

Since many experiential powers are themselves P-states—they have a psychological role in a broader mental economy—they will be unified in this two-fold manner also. But P-relatedness is distinct from C-relatedness. Is C-relatedness responsible for further interdependencies, interdependencies that are rooted in the phenomenal realm? There are grounds for thinking that it is, for some subjects if not all. I have argued that very simple subjects may be possible, subjects capable of only a single basic type of experience. If this is right then some sorts of experiential powers are not essentially systemic—or are only weakly so—and so are different from typical P-capacities. But as soon as we consider even slightly more complex (and hence realistic) subjects, some distinctive interdependencies quickly emerge. In fact, the interdependencies between experiential powers are analogous to those which characterize P-systems: interdependencies of character and systematicity.

The route to this conclusion comprises several stages. To set the scene I start off by taking a brief look at a variety of potential sources of interdependencies among experiential powers. I then focus on the potential source I am particularly interested in: power-interdependencies rooted in interdependencies among experiences. Since the only thing experiential powers necessarily have in common is the capacity to produce experience, forms of power-interdependency that are generated by experiential interdependencies can, in principle, extend to powers that are in other respects as different as can be. But obviously, the precise extent of power-interdependencies generated in this way will depend on the nature and extent of experiential interdependencies. Hence in §9.3 I turn my attention to the topic of phenomenal interdependence: the ways in which experiential wholes impact upon the phenomenal character of their parts. In the course of this detour through some difficult terrain, several types of phenomenal interdependence are distinguished. It is only in §9.6 and §9.7 that experiential powers once again occupy centre-stage, as I apply the results gleaned from the exploration of experiential interdependencies to the issue of interdependencies among experience-producing capacities.

9.2. INTERDEPENDENT POTENTIALS

We saw in §4.6 that the most discriminating criterion for power-individuation comprises three components: (i) material base; (ii) triggering circumstances; (iii) phenomenal effects. Each of these can be specified in more or less detailed ways, and each also has the potential to generate interdependencies among consubjective powers. (There are ways in which powers that are *not* consubjective can be interdependent, but apart from one brief mention, I will be ignoring these here.) Let us consider them in turn.

It is debatable whether powers in general, and experiential powers in particular, necessarily have bases or grounds; it is also debatable whether all experiential powers necessarily have *material* bases, but let us confine ourselves to those that do. There is a great deal that we do not know about how our brains generate our experiences, but given what we do know about the complexity and interconnectedness of the neural circuitry of our brains, it may well be that many of the neural systems responsible for our experiential capacities are heavily integrated. It probably isn't easy to surgically isolate and remove, say, a brain's capacity for conscious thought or mental imagery while leaving behind its capacity for sensory experience. The neural structures responsible for many kinds of experience could easily be profoundly entangled, or even overlapping—perhaps to different extents for different types of experience. I will call powers whose grounds are physically related in these sorts of way *base-integrated.*

The precise extent to which our experiential powers are base-integrated is an empirical matter, and I will not speculate here about what future developments in neuroscience may discover.[1] I will make only a couple of general observations. The first is that base-integration is a widespread phenomenon, and by no means is it confined to mental capacities. It is not uncommon, after all, for the causal powers of complex physical systems to be difficult to prise apart—just try separating your computer's capacity to run word processing software from its capacity to run graphics software. Secondly, and more importantly for present purposes, there is a sense in which the dependencies resulting from base-integration are typically not very deep: the items so related could exist, essentially unaltered, without being so related. This is obviously so for cases of physical entanglement. Think of a key on a keychain. Although these two objects cannot easily be separated—pulling alone doesn't do it—this is not enough to render them interdependent in any strong sense, for it is possible (in principle anyway) to destroy the key without affecting the chain in the slightest, and vice-versa. In analogous fashion, from the mere fact that the neural systems in a single brain responsible for different kinds of experience are entangled in a way which precludes their non-destructive separation we cannot conclude that the systems are interdependent in any further or deeper way: a suitably skilled surgeon might be able to destroy some of these systems without affecting the others. Similar considerations apply to cases of overlap. Suppose the neural systems responsible for auditory and visual experience in some creatures' brains share an indivisible common component. Could we conclude that auditory and visual experiential capacities in these creatures are interdependent in any significant sense? Not if destroying the non-overlapping part of the visual system eliminated the capacity for visual experience without affecting the auditory system, and vice-versa. Is there any reason to think this sort of selective elimination would have more far-reaching effects? The bare fact of base-integration provides no such reason.[2]

---

[1] Nor will I speculate on whether or not it is possible for a subject to have experiential powers that are not base-integrated at all, intriguing though such speculations are (e.g. Zuboff 1982).

[2] Powers for similar kinds of experience whose physical bases overlap are naturally construed as aspects (or sub-powers) of multi-track dispositions—in the sense introduced in §4.5. But since it is not obvious that base-integration has any automatic implications for the sorts of interdependencies I will be concerned with in this chapter, and to avoid needless complication, here (as elsewhere) I take 'experiential power' to refer both to single-track experiential capacities and particular aspects of multi-track capacities.

Triggering conditions can also give rise to interdependencies, both in principle and in practice. I am fortunate in that my capacity for blue visual experience and my capacity for feeling nauseous have independent triggering conditions—if it were otherwise I would be less pleased by the prospect of fine weather tomorrow than I actually am. For easily understandable reasons, natural selection has ensured that most of our experiential capacities have distinct triggering conditions. The capacity to see red has advantages in many walks of life; these advantages are drastically reduced if the capacity for red-type experience is also triggered by the presence of blue objects, or the smell of warm grass, or the sound of a bird-cry. That said, it is perfectly conceivable that it should be otherwise. There may be some unfortunate subjects whose capacity for feeling nauseous *is* triggered by precisely the same circumstances as their capacity for seeing blue. In such cases the relevant powers are interdependent by virtue of having a common trigger. A condition similar to this imaginary one is to be found among synaesthetes: there are subjects whose capacity for blue-type experience is triggered both by their looking at things that are blue, or by hearing a tone of a certain pitch (Ramachandran and Hubbard, 2001). More far-fetched, but no less easily conceivable, are trigger-induced interdependencies among experiential powers that belong to different subjects. A devious neuroscientist could, for example, fit radio transceivers into your brain and mine, the effect of which is to ensure that you feel a pleasurable sensation whenever I feel a painful sensation. In virtue of this connection, the relevant powers no longer enjoy the independence they once did: events which will trigger my pain-power will also trigger your pleasure-power, so to speak.

Although there is clearly more to be said about power interdependencies of this kind, I will not pursue the matter further. As with the interdependencies arising through base-integration, interdependencies arising from the possession of common triggering circumstances are fairly commonplace among ordinary physical capacities: trigger your car's capacity for self-powered motion and you will also trigger its capacity for noise and smoke production—similar examples are easy to find. Also, as with base-integration, interdependencies due to common triggering conditions typically do not run deep. If your brain and mine come to be linked in the way just envisaged, your capacity for feeling pleasure and my capacity for feeling pain are no longer entirely independent, but nor are they interdependent in any significant sense. The fact that you have a pleasurable sensation whenever I have a toothache does not affect the intrinsic character of my pain. And if the link were severed, my pain capacities would be entirely unaltered.

A potentially more significant source of power interdependency flows from the third element of our tri-partite criterion of power-individuation: phenomenal *effects*, the experiences produced when experiential powers are triggered. I say 'potentially' for a reason. As is well-known, Hume subscribed to an atomistic conception of experiences. He held that experiences are 'separate existences', by which he meant (in part) that the phenomenal characteristics of experiences are entirely unaffected by the experiences with which they are co-conscious. Take any two co-conscious experiences E_1 and E_2; according to Hume, E_1 could exist just as it is in the absence of E_2, and vice-versa. Clearly, if this Humean doctrine were true, there would be little or no scope for effect-driven interdependencies among experiential powers. But if experience is *not* in fact atomistic—if the character of at least some experiences *is* affected in some way by virtue of their being co-conscious with other experiences—then the situation will be very different. Since I think the Humean conception of experience is mistaken—for reasons which will be explained in due course—it is this source of interdependency that I will be concentrating on.

In broad outline at least, the route from experiential interdependencies to power interdependencies is straightforward. Let us say that a power's *experiential potential* (or *e-potential*) is the full range of experiences that it can produce under normal conditions. Let us also say that an experience's *phenomenal context* consists of the various other experiences with which it is co-conscious. Now suppose that the phenomenal character of any experience is affected or influenced in some way by the phenomenal context it finds itself in. (This may not seem in the least plausible, but just suppose.) If context does impact on character in this manner then the precise e-potential of any power P will itself depend on the other powers to which P is C-related, synchronically or diachronically. Why? Because at least some of the latter powers will be DPC_S- or DPC_D-related to P, and hence able to produce experiences that are co-conscious with the experiences that P can produce, and so impact on the character of the experiences P can produce. If the experiential potential of P can be influenced in this way, P's experiential potential is clearly bound up with the experiential potentials of the other powers to which it is DPC-related.

By way of a concrete (but simplistic, and in some ways unrealistic) illustration, consider again our earlier example of a simple subject: Maggot. Varying the original scenario slightly, let us suppose that objects which look *yellow* to Maggot when he feels *cold* or *warm*, appear to have a subtly different colour—*yellow**—when he is feeling *hot*. Let us further suppose that this alteration is due to interactions at the phenomenal level. (At this early stage we will not inquire further into how or why such an interaction can take place.) Precisely how we describe this situation depends on how finely we individuate experiential powers. To keep things as simple as possible, let us individuate in a fairly liberal manner and allow a single power to produce a range of experiential outputs. Accordingly, we can hold that Maggot's *yellow* and *yellow** experiences are both produced by a single power, V_1, which varies its output as a function of which other powers in Maggot's C-system are currently active and producing experience. The e-potential of one of Maggot's visual capacities is thus dependent on one of his capacities for bodily sensations: the precise character of the experiences produced by V_1 when it is active differs depending on which other powers are active at the same time. To coin some further terminology, Maggot's capacity for yellow-type experience is *output-dependent* on one of his powers for bodily sensations. More generally, for any two DPC$_S$- or DPC$_D$-related experiential powers P_1 and P_2, P_1 is output-dependent on P_2 if the phenomenal character of the experiences produced by P_1 differs in some way depending on whether P_2 is active or not.[3]

There are a few further complications, one of which it will be useful to deal with right away. Output-dependence comes in weaker and stronger forms. Although these hold synchronically and diachronically, to simplify I will focus on the synchronic case. Let P_1 and P_2 be two DPC$_S$-related experiential powers at a given time t, and $E(P_1)$ denote whatever experience P_1 produces at t, and $E(P_2)$ denote the experience P_2 produces at t if it is active. We can draw the following distinctions:

1 P_1 is *output-independent* with regard to P_2 if the character of $E(P_1)$ is the same irrespective of whether P_2 is active or not.

2 P_1 is *weakly output-dependent* on P_2 if the phenomenal character of $E(P_1)$ is different depending on whether P_2 is active or not, but an experience with the character that $E(P_1)$ has when P_2 is active could exist in a different type of phenomenal context.

3 P_1 is *strongly output-dependent* on P_2 if P_2's being active would result in $E(P_1)$'s possessing a character it could *only* possess by virtue of being co-conscious

---

[3] What if we individuate in a more fine-grained way, and construe *yellow* and *yellow** as the product of two distinct powers, V_1 and V_1*? On this view, a given external triggering event, call it T, will result in the activation of V_1 if Maggot isn't feeling hot at the relevant time, and V_1* if he is. Does it still make sense to think that experiential powers can be output-dependent? If powers can only produce *one* type of experiential output then how can it make sense to suppose that powers can produce different outputs in different circumstances? When experiential powers are construed in this fine-grained way, interdependencies remain, but they need to be differently described. It is true that we no longer have a single power varying its output depending on which other powers are co-active. We do, however, have a situation in which the experiences Maggot enjoys in response to a given stimulus varies as a function of the other powers in his C-system that are active at the time in question. More specifically, the *collection* of powers V_1, V_1*, and B_2 are interdependent: in response to a T-type trigger this system will produce *yellow**-type experience if B_2 is currently active, and *yellow*-type experience if it is not. Although this way of construing matters may in some cases be quite valid, I will generally work with the more liberal mode of power-individuation. The rationale for this choice will emerge in due course: see §9.6 where the distinction (yet to be drawn) between 'local' and 'global' features of experience allows interdependencies among powers to be characterized in a rather different way, a way which renders the liberal interpretation of e-potentials very natural. (Staying with the present way of looking at things, yet another alternative is to construe the interdependencies solely in terms of differences in triggering circumstances. Assuming as previously that V_1 can produce both *yellow* and *yellow**, we could—if we thought it convenient—include the presence or absence of bodily experience (and the corresponding power activity) into V_1's triggering conditions. Accordingly, we could reserve the label T_1 for the circumstances which cause Maggot's C-system to produce *yellow* and use T_2 to refer to the circumstances which result in the production of *yellow**. The sole difference between T_1 and T_2 is that if the former obtains Maggot's powers for bodily experience is dormant, where as if the latter obtains it is not. But once again, this alternative way of describing the situation leaves the essentials unaltered: Maggot's C-system is such that the sorts of experience it produces at any given time is sensitive to which *other* experiences it is currently producing.)

with either $E(P_2)$ itself, or an experience with the same qualitative character as $E(P_2)$. If the latter obtains then we have an instance of *strong type-specific output-dependence*, whereas if the former obtains we have an instance of *strong token-specific output-dependence*.

If the outputs of some experiential powers have the same character irrespective of what other experiences they happen to be co-conscious with, then such powers will be output-independent with respect to their C-system (unless of course some further source of power-interdependency exists). Perhaps such powers are possible (or even common), but let us focus on output-dependency. By way of an example of weak output-dependency, suppose that your visual and auditory centres are linked in such a way that your ceiling looks a darker shade of yellow whenever you can hear the sound of passing traffic.[4] The relevant visual and auditory capacities are clearly connected, but only in a comparatively shallow manner: it is perfectly possible for you to experience the darker shade of yellow in the absence of traffic noise—all you need do is reduce the amount of light entering the room. Strong output-dependence is very different. If P_1 is strongly output-dependent on P_2, then when both powers are active the experience produced by P_1 is not only different in character from the experience this power would have produced if P_2 had been dormant, the experience produced by P_1 has a character that it *could not have had* in the absence of the experience produced by P_2. Hence a power with the e-potential of P_1 *could only exist* in a C-system which includes P_2 (or a power just like it, in the case of type-specific output-dependence). Whether or not powers can be output-dependent in this way is another matter. It may seem implausible to suppose that it is possible for powers to be strongly output-dependent in the type-specific way, and even more implausible to suppose that strong token-specific dependencies could exist. But let us not prejudge matters at this early stage. What is beyond any doubt is that *if* it is generally the case that DPC-related powers are output-dependent in the strong sense, then C-systems—and hence selves—would be entities that are unified in a very deep way indeed.

A few more differences and distinctions are worth noting. Output-dependence (in whatever form) can, in principle, be a one-way affair: the manifestations of a power P_1 could be affected—in some way or other—by those of P_2, while those of P_2 are entirely unaffected by the manifestations of P_1. Where the dependency runs in both directions we can speak of *inter*dependence. Dependencies that are effect-driven can hold between more than two powers: we can say that a collection of powers is *fully* output-dependent if each of its members is output-dependent on each of the remaining members, and that a collection of powers is *partially* output-dependent if each of its members is output-dependent on at least one

---

[4] We have already encountered one example of weakly interdependent powers—there is no reason for thinking Maggot's yellow*-type experience could not exist in different phenomenal contexts but it may be more profitable to focus on an example that is rather closer to home.

other; full and partial interrelatedness can be defined along the same lines. Lastly, whereas some instances of output-dependence are contingent, others may be necessary—either nomologically or metaphysically. While cases of contingent interdependence are of some interest in their own right, they shed no light on the essential nature of C-systems, and hence selves and subjects of experience. Since most instances of contingent interdependence will be species-specific—or at least less than universal—it could hardly be otherwise. For our purposes it is the metaphysically necessary interdependencies that matter most.

9.3. PHENOMENAL INTERDEPENDENCE

Whether or not there exist any kind of effect-driven interdependencies among experiential powers depends on whether, and in what ways, experiences occurring in the same unified states of consciousness are interdependent. Are there any such interdependencies? It is this issue I want to turn to now. On a number of occasions I have suggested that co-consciousness creates a quite distinctive form of unity, and given some indications as to why this is so, but it is time to investigate this unity and its consequences in greater detail. I will start by drawing some relevant distinctions—most of which echo those just drawn in connection with output-relatedness—and then move on to consider how these apply to some simple (but not maximally simple) subjects.

A total experience, it will be recalled, is an experience whose parts are all mutually co-conscious, and which is not itself a proper part of any larger experience whose parts are all mutually co-conscious. A typical human total experience is highly complex, and can be divided into parts in any number of ways. For any such division we can put the question: how is the phenomenal character of the parts affected by the whole to which they belong? To make matters more concrete, consider the very simple case shown in Figure 9.1. This total experience, E, consists of a single auditory sensation a_1 and a single visual sensation v_1, and as such naturally divides into two parts.

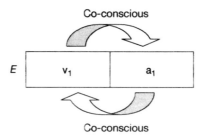

Figure 9.1 A simple total experience

We can now ask questions such as these. How is the phenomenal character of v_1 affected by the fact that it is co-conscious with a_1? Would the phenomenal character of a_1 be different if it were *not* co-conscious with v_1? If so, how? Would the phenomenal character of a_1 be any different if it were experienced in isolation, all by itself?

I will call the general doctrine that the character of an experience is in some manner influenced or affected by the other experiences with which it is co-conscious *phenomenal* or ϕ-*holism*. Further sub-varieties of this sort of holism can be distinguished. For example, ϕ-holism could apply to some types of experience, but not others; or it could apply to all kinds of experience. Call the latter *complete ϕ-holism* and the former *partial ϕ-holism*. Irrespective of whether it is complete or partial, ϕ-holism could obtain *necessarily* or merely *contingently*.

We can further distinguish *type* ϕ-holism from *token* ϕ-holism. If type ϕ-holism applies to E and its parts, then although the phenomenal character of v_1 is (in some as yet unspecified but non-fatal way) affected by being co-conscious with a_1, the character of v_1 would be just the same if it were co-conscious with a numerically distinct token experience of the same phenomenal type as a_1, rather than a_1 itself. If token ϕ-holism obtains, however, then in order for v_1 to have the character it does it must be co-conscious with a_1 itself. To make matters more explicit, and to introduce some terminology which will prove useful later on, let us say that $a_1{}^*$ is a *phenomenal counterpart* of a_1 if it is an experience that is qualitatively indistinguishable from a_1 in all intrinsic respects, but numerically distinct from it by virtue of having a different material basis (e.g. it is grounded in a different region of its owner's brain). If type ϕ-holism obtains, whether essentially or contingently, then v_1 can only exist if co-conscious with an experience of the same character as a_1, but it matters not whether it is a_1 or one of its phenomenal counterparts. By contrast, if token ϕ-holism obtains, then v_1 can only exist if it is co-conscious with a_1 itself. The same applies, of course, with regard to the influence of v_1 on the character of a_1.

9.4. ORGANIZATION AND INTERFERENCE

The need for these distinctions may not be obvious, for it is by no means self-evident that any form of ϕ-holism applies to our experiences and their parts. To take an extreme (but utterly commonplace) sort of case, suppose you are watching a televised concert; as you do so, at each moment you are enjoying (or suffering) auditory and visual experiences of a quite specific character. Now envisage a counterfactual scenario in which the small painting on the wall behind the television is located a few millimetres to the left of where it actually is. Since the painting is in full view, your overall visual experience in this situation is of course slightly different. So far as the issue of holism is concerned, however, what matters is whether the alteration in the part of your visual field where the painting is to be found would affect the other parts. Would the visual appearance of what you see onscreen be affected by the picture's slight change of location? It seems unlikely. Indeed, it seems quite conceivable that the television screen would look just the same even if the painting were altogether absent (providing the lighting is right). The inter-modal case appears even more hostile to any form of holism. It seems unlikely, for example, that the character of your auditory experience would be in any way affected by the slight difference in your visual experience resulting from the different location of the painting. And the same applies to sensory experiences in the other modalities, to your conscious thoughts, emotions, and to the entire range of bodily experiences you have at the time in question.

It is fair to say that ϕ-holism is not an altogether obvious feature of our ordinary streams of consciousness. Nonetheless, it would be a mistake to adopt an overly atomistic conception of experience. Experiential parts do have a considerable degree of independence from their wholes, but there are also dependencies, some more subtle than others, that it would be wrong to ignore.

To start with an obvious point, total experiences are not just collections of experiential parts, they are collections *organized* in a particular way. By way of a simple example, Figure 9.2 shows two complete visual fields, F_1 and F_2, whose overall characters are very different, despite the fact that—in one sense at least—the contents are precisely the same.

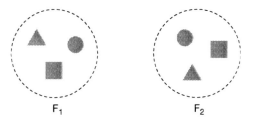

Figure 9.2 Two complete but different visual fields

In specifying the character of even a moderately complex experience, it is not sufficient just to specify the phenomenal character of its constituent parts, it is also necessary to specify their phenomenal organization, and in order to do this we will need to specify just how the relevant experiential parts are related to one another, as well as what they are like in themselves. In the case of simultaneous experiences, spatial organization predominates, but when we broaden our horizons to take in temporally extended experience—or entire streams of consciousness—temporal organization also enters the picture. The experience of *do-re-mi* is very different from that of *re-mi-do*.

The fact that the same parts can be organized into wholes in different ways illustrates one significant respect in which a whole is more than the mere sum of its parts. But organization, at least of the spatiotemporal variety, does not always or invariably generate interdependencies among the parts of wholes. The intrinsic physical properties of a cup and saucer are not significantly affected by their relative positions on the table-top: it makes little or no difference whether the cup is to the right or left of the saucer, or whether the cup is on the saucer or the saucer is on the cup. The same applies in the phenomenal domain. Looking again at Figure 9.2, so far as their intrinsic phenomenal features are concerned, the triangle-shapes in F_1 and F_2 are virtually indistinguishable, despite the differences in their phenomeno-spatial relations. In real life, if I were to hold a plastic triangle-shape in front of my eyes, and move it slowly from right to left, it probably would change in appearance to a quite noticeable extent; but this will be mainly due to its being viewed from different angles, and consequent changes in lighting, rather than changes in the phenomenal distance-relations connecting the triangle with the other objects appearing in my visual field. Like their physical counterparts, phenomenal distance relations seem to be of the 'external' variety: the ways in which a phenomenal object is spatially related to other phenomenal objects in the same overall field of consciousness does not impinge on its internal or intrinsic features.

Are there any instances in which phenomenal context impinges on the intrinsic character of phenomenal parts? There are indeed. Paradoxically, perhaps the most obvious form of phenomenal interdependence is the least common. Consider the familiar Müller–Lyer illusion. This consists of two horizontal lines that are of equal length on the page, but thanks to the presence of the attached forwards- and backwards-pointing fins, one of these lines looks longer than the other. Since the presence of the fins affects the phenomenal character of the horizontals—remove them and the lines appear to be of the same length—what we have here is a clear-cut case of phenomenal interdependence: the character of an experiential part is dependent upon the character of its whole, that is with the other experiences with which it is co-conscious. Rather more dramatic is the 'rotating disk' illusion, shown in Figure 9.3. When the circular patterns are viewed in isolation they appear perfectly motionless; put several together and things change.[5]

This kind of phenomenal interdependence is almost certainly of the contingent variety—it is due to the peculiarities of our visual systems, and the ways in which they process raw sensory data. In some instances the peculiarities may well be, in part, acquired rather than innate: there is some evidence that people who grow up in environments where right-angled corners are not commonplace are less susceptible to the Müller–Lyer. Let us call this sort of localized and contingent inter-experiential interdependence *phenomenal interference*. Other well-known visual illusions are also instances of phenomenal interference, but

---

[5] Otherwise known as an Optimized Fraser–Wilcox illusion (Kitaoka 2006). The black-and-white version in Figure 9.3 works best under a bright light source; for far more dramatic variant see http://www.ritsumei.ac.jp/~akitaoka/rotsnake.gif

Figure 9.3 The rotating disk illusion

there are also inter-modal cases too. The 'ventriloquism' effect is perhaps the most vivid. In the special case of speech perception, there are circumstances in which our brains prefer to believe our eyes rather than our ears: if we hear the sound of speech, and see a mouth moving, we tend to hear the sound coming from the mouth, even if it is in fact coming from a different source—in the absence of the visual stimuli our brains believe our ears, and we hear the sound-source as located where it actually is located.

The Müller–Lyer and rotating disk illusions are both instances of what can aptly be called *weak* phenomenal interference. Focusing on the latter, it would easily be possible to produce an experience of a *single* rotating disk that is visually indistinguishable from any of those in Figure 9.3: it would suffice to mechanically rotate the image at the right speed. Generalizing, in cases of weak interference, although the character of certain phenomenal objects is influenced by their phenomenal context, objects with a very similar character could be experienced in phenomenal wholes that are otherwise very different. In cases of *strong* phenomenal interference, by contrast, the influence of the whole in the part is of a more profound kind, so much so that the part in question could only exist in wholes of a similar kind to that in which they are actually found. Cases of phenomenal interference that are uncontrovertibly of the strong variety are not easily found. In the visual realm some of the more promising candidates involve subtle interactions of shape on their surroundings. It is not obvious that 'subjective contours' of the kind found in Kanisza's triangle could exist in markedly different phenomenal contexts—see Figure 9.4. Likewise for the more minimalist version shown in Figure 9.5.

Figure 9.4 Kanisza's triangle

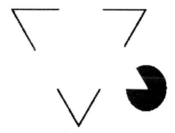

Figure 9.5 Kanisza's triangle—minimalist version

Phenomenal interference is a striking form of phenomenal interdependence, even in its weak guise, but it is also fairly rare. Generally speaking, the different parts of our states of consciousness do not interfere with one another in this sort of way—if they did, the effects we have been considering would not be as well-known as they are. Also, it seems plausible to suppose that all forms of phenomenal interference are due solely to the peculiarities of our experience-producing systems, and consequently the resulting ϕ-holism is merely contingent. As we shall now see, there is a more far-reaching and deep-seated form of phenomenal interdependence, this time of the necessary variety.

9.5. C-HOLISM

To provide a complete description of the overall phenomenal character of a complex total experience it is not enough merely to specify what each (proper) part is like in itself, we must also specify how the various parts are related to one another. The most obvious and familiar relationships between experiential parts are spatial and temporal. As we have already noted, it seems unlikely that these relationships (in and of themselves) give rise to any significant forms of ϕ-holism. On the face of it at least, spatial and temporal relations in the phenomenal domain seem akin to their physical kin in that both are relations of the external variety; generally speaking, the intrinsic character of items thus related is unaffected by the fact that they are so related. However, there is another phenomenal relationship, one which connects all parts of every total experience, which is arguably a relation of an *internal* variety: its nature is such that it necessarily makes a qualitative difference to its relata. The relation in question is co-consciousness, the very relation which binds experiential parts into experiential wholes.

Consider again the simple audio-visual experience, $E = v_1 \backslash a_1$ shown in Figure 9.1. To keep things as simple as possible, let it be stipulated that the subject of E is experiencing nothing in addition to v_1 and a_1 at the time in question; and for the sake of convenience, let us use 'F' and 'G' to refer to the (purely visual) phenomenal character of v_1 and the (purely auditory) phenomenal character of a_1 respectively. Now, if v_1 were a complete total experience in its own right—and so not experienced with a_1—then an exhaustive specification of its phenomenal character, a specification which fully captures what it is like to have v_1—would be entirely straightforward: *F-type*, end of story. Similarly, if a_1 were experienced all by itself, a complete specification of its phenomenal character would be: *G-type*, end of story. But neither a_1 nor v_1 are in fact total experiences in their own right, they are co-conscious with one another. This makes a difference, and since co-consciousness is *experienced togetherness*, the difference is of a phenomenal kind. The question now arises as to how best to characterize this phenomenal difference.

Some of our earlier results are relevant here. According to the Simple Conception of experience, defended in Chapter 3, co-consciousness is a symmetrical phenomenal relationship of a basic kind that exists between experiences themselves. It is not imposed from on high by some separate act of pure awareness, nor does it depend on the relevant contents being introspected or introspectible. Although the consequences of co-consciousness are readily introspectible—we all know what it is like for two experiences to be related in this way—the relationship of co-consciousness is not an additional ingredient in experience, an ingredient possessing its own distinctive phenomenal features. (Co-consciousness is not itself an experience, it is a way experiences can be related.) Since we have stipulated that there is nothing else going on in the consciousness of the subject of v_1 and a_1, and given the symmetrical character of the co-consciousness relationship, it seems clear that the phenomenal feature we are seeking to characterize—the phenomenal consequence of the co-consciousness of v_1 and a_1—must reside entirely in v_1 and a_1 themselves. There is simply no alternative. And this in turn means that the phenomenal character of both v_1 and a_1 must each in some manner be altered or affected by the fact that they are co-conscious with one another.

In trying to characterize this influence there is a further consideration to bear in mind. The phenomenal characteristics of v_1 and a_1 may be influenced in some way by their being co-conscious with one another, but they are by no means wholly transformed thereby. The blue wall to my right looks much the same irrespective of whether I am listening to music or not, and the music sounds much the same irrespective of whether I am looking at the blue wall or the white ceiling—or have my eyes closed. Generally speaking, as was noted in connection with phenomenal interference, the intrinsic properties (or what are commonly recognized as such) of a typical experience are largely unaffected by the broader phenomenal context it might find itself in. To accommodate this fact, if we want to register the distinctive way in which co-consciousness impinges upon its relata, we need to distinguish between two general types of phenomenal character (or property). The distinction we need is between what I will call the *local* and *global* features of an experience. The local features of an experience are its intrinsic features, as ordinarily construed: v_1 and a_1 are of local types F and G respectively. A typical experience's local phenomenal properties are largely unaffected by its broader phenomenal context. The global features of an experience, by contrast, are the additional phenomenal characteristics it acquires solely in virtue of being co-conscious with the other parts of the total experience(s) to which it belongs. I will call these global features *C-properties*.

As for how the C-properties of any particular experience should themselves be conceived, there are three main options. The first is entirely undiscriminating. In the case of v_1, by virtue of being co-conscious with a_1 we say that it acquires the C-property of 'being co-conscious with *some other experience*'. In schematic form, and bringing a_1 into the picture:

$$v_1 : C[\mathbf{F}\backslash x] \tag{1}$$
$$a_1 : C[\mathbf{G}\backslash x] \tag{2}$$

Here, '$C[i, j]$' means 'i is co-conscious with j', the backslash indicates simultaneity, and boldface is used to pick out the local type of the experience we are trying to describe. Hence (1) states that v_1 is an experience of local type F that is simultaneous and co-conscious with some other unspecified experience x, and (2) states that a_1 is an experience of local type G that is co-conscious and simultaneous with an unspecified experience x.

These characterizations will not suffice. Co-consciousness is a relationship which makes a phenomenal difference (it couldn't be otherwise, given that co-consciousness is *experienced togetherness*) and as just noted, this difference must reside in the experiences that are so related. As soon as we try to spell out the precise character of this difference—of the experiential consequences of co-consciousness—the inadequacies of non-specific C-properties such as (1) and (2) soon become plain.

Co-consciousness is a pervasive relationship; it does not merely connect experiences at the edges, as it were, rather, each and every part of any total experience—irrespective of how it is divided into parts—is directly and immediately co-conscious with each and every other part (see §3.5 and §8.6). To put it another way, every part of every total experience is phenomenally bonded with every other part of the same total experience; to put it less metaphorically, every part of a total experience is *experienced together* with every other part. The phenomenological character (or consequence) of experienced togetherness is such that, quite general-ly, when two experiences are connected in this way it is very plausible to think that a truly complete characterization of the experiential character of each must register the fact that it is co-conscious with the other. To illustrate, suppose you are staring at a plain white wall, and while you are doing so you hear a fly buzzing round the room. Now consider what an exhaustive description of the phenomenal features of your visual experience would include. Such a description would obviously mention a sizeable expanse of phenomenal white, but it would be incomplete if that is all that it included: after all, you are experiencing a white expanse *that is co-conscious with a (somewhat irritating) buzzing sound,* and a characterization which omitted this fact would not reflect what your visual experience is actually like. Or rather, it would capture the intrinsic visual features of your experience, but not its relational (or global) phenomenal features. Since it is undeniable that your visual experience has this relational property, it also seems plain that a full and accurate description of its character must register this. What would a complete description of the relational phenomenal features of your visual experience include? At the very least it would register that each and every part of the white phenomenal expanse is co-conscious with *a buzzing sound.* And of course the same applies in the other direction. A full description of your auditory experience, one that did justice to *all* its phenomenal properties, intrinsic and relational, would mention the fact that the buzzing sound is experienced together with (each part of) a white expanse. In fact, since your experience is unlikely to be confined to the auditory and the visual—you probably have some bodily feelings, thoughts, emotions—a complete description of the relational properties of the two experiences we have been focusing on would probably be a good deal more complex. But the artifi-cially simplified example serves to make the point. It seems clear that non-specific characterizations such as (1) and (2) fail to capture the phenomenal feature we are seeking to describe: they are adequate at the local or intrinsic level, but they fail to do full justice to the global features of our experience. Since these same con-siderations apply irrespective of the number of experiences we are dealing with, it follows that a full description of the global properties of any experience must in some manner register all the other experiences with which it is co-conscious.

If this is right then although co-consciousness is a relation, it is not an *external* relation in the usual sense of the term: it is not a relation which leaves the nature of its relata untouched. When a collection of experiences are related to one another in this way, a full description of the phenomenal features of each experience—that is a description which *fully captures what it is like to have that experience*—will mention (in some manner) all the other experiences with which it is co-conscious. Accordingly, if we think of the 'intrinsic' properties of an experience as being exhausted by what the experience is like, then we should also recognize that the intrinsic properties of experiences that belong to co-conscious ensembles have a relational aspect. (Describing matters thus may sound a little odd, but it is what the phenomenal facts seem to require.)

Bearing all this in mind, how should we characterize the global C-properties of an experience? There are now only two obvious ways forward, and both have implications with regard to ϕ-holism. We can say that a complete description of what it is like to experience v_1 must mention the fact that v_1 is co-conscious with a_1; alternatively, we can say that a complete description of v_1 must mention the fact that v_1 is co-conscious with an experience that has the same local phenomenal characteristics as a_1. In schematic terms, the first option amounts to exchanging (1) and (2) for the formulations below:

$$v_1 : C[F(\mathbf{v_1})\backslash G(a_1)] \tag{3}$$
$$a_1 : C[F(v_1)\backslash G(\mathbf{a_1})] \tag{4}$$

Using the same conventions as previously, (3) states that v_1 is an F-type experience that is simultaneous and co-conscious with a_1, a G-type experience. Expression (4) states that a_1 is a G-type experience that is simultaneous and co-conscious with v_1, an F-type experience. The same characterizations can be expressed in a more succinct way thus:

$$v_1 : C[F\backslash a_1] \tag{3*}$$
$$a_1 : C[G\backslash v_1] \tag{4*}$$

Here the qualitative types of a_1 (in (3*)) and v_1 (in (4*)) are not made explicit, which has the advantage of bringing to the fore the fact that C-properties of this kind are relations between token experiences. For obvious reasons I will call this sort of C-property *strong* or *token-specific*.

The second approach relies only upon *weak*, or *type-specific* C-properties. These can be characterized in schematic terms thus:

$$v_1 : C[F\backslash Gx] \tag{5}$$
$$a_1 : C[G\backslash Fx] \tag{6}$$

Here, (5) states that v_1 is an F-type experience that is simultaneous and co-conscious with some G-type experience, and (6) states that a_1 is a G-type experience that is simultaneous and co-conscious with some F-type experience. Weak C-properties are confined to the purely qualitative aspects of an experience's global character.

We need not feel obliged to decide between these options, for there is something to be said for each. Weak C-properties are phenomenal properties in the most familiar sense: they are individuated entirely in terms of what it is like to have an experience with the property in question. If we envisage a situation in which v_1 is a part of a total experience $E^* = [v_1 \backslash a_1{}^*]$, where $a_1{}^*$ is a phenomenal counterpart of a_1 (i.e. $a_1{}^*$ and a_1 are qualitatively alike but they are distinct by virtue of having different material bases), there would be no difference in the introspectively distinguishable phenomenal features of the v_1-experience in the two cases. How could there be? By definition, a phenomenal counterpart of $a_1{}^*$ is phenomenologically indistinguishable from a_1. Strong C-properties are more discriminating. Since they are token-specific, the C-properties [. . . is co-conscious with a_1] and [. . . is co-conscious with $a_1{}^*$] are distinct, even though their introspectible features are precisely the same.

The idea that *phenomenal* properties could be distinct despite seeming exactly the same might seem absurd. In fact it is not, for in recognizing this possibility we are simply adopting a broader (or more discriminating) way of individuating phenomenal properties. Echoing Putnam's well-known distinction concerning propositional content, we can distinguish between *broad* and *narrow* schemes of individuation. When phenomenal properties are narrowly construed, the only features relevant to their identity are those which can be discerned in experience; when they are broadly construed, certain *relational* properties also become relevant to their identity. In the case of strong C-properties, the relational properties are entirely phenomenal: in the case of E, v_1 is co-conscious with a_1, in the case of E^*, by contrast, v_1 is co-conscious with the numerically distinct experience $a_1{}^*$. Given the fact that there is no more intimate way for experiences to be related to one another than by co-consciousness — recall the way each and every part of such experiences are experienced together — it is by no means obviously absurd to allow phenomenal relations of this broader sort to impact upon the identity conditions of experiences. If it is legitimate to individuate propositional attitudes or perceptual experiences in terms of the *physical* environments of their subjects, why can't we not individuate experiences in terms of their *phenomenal* environments? We are not obliged to individuate experiences in this way, but it is an option. Moreover, it is an option that looks to be well-founded, firmly rooted as it is in the phenomenal facts.

If we do elect to individuate experiences by reference to their precise phenomenal character, along with time of occurrence and material basis, then we have no reason to exclude C-properties, whether construed in type-specific or token-specific ways, from the features that are considered essential to a particular experience being the experience it is. If we regard C-properties as being on a par with other phenomenal properties—and there is every reason to do so, especially so in the case of weak C-properties—then a new source of phenomenal inter-dependence and ϕ-holism opens up. For obvious reasons I will call it *C-holism*. In the case of $E = [v_1 \backslash a_1]$ and its parts, if we individuate in terms of weak C-properties, then v_1 can only exist as part of an experiential whole of the same (narrow) type as E, that is, it can only exist if co-conscious with a G-type auditory experience, and the same applies, *mutatis mutandis*, for a_1. If we individuate in terms of strong C-properties then both v_1 and a_1 can only exist in each other's company. This has the consequence that our earlier example of $E^* = [v_1 \backslash a_1{}^*]$ was misdescribed. From the token-specific standpoint it simply makes no sense to suppose that v_1 can exist in both E and E^*. An experience of the same local type as v_1 can exist in E^*, but this experience can only be a phenomenal counterpart of v_1, it cannot be v_1 itself.

C-holism of the weak type-specific variety yields a far from negligible variety of ϕ-holism: the proper parts of any total experience can only exist in experiential wholes of the same overall character (construed narrowly) as the whole to which they actually belong. C-holism of the strong token-specific variety amounts to something more. Under this mode of individuation it makes no sense to suppose that the proper parts of a total experience could exist in different company. The upshot of this is significant. Experiential parts are (logically) inseparable from their wholes, and consequently total experiences are metaphysically simple entities: they have no parts which can enjoy an independent existence, an existence outside the whole they happen to find themselves in.

I have been concentrating on a single unrealistically simple example, but what goes for $[v_1/a_1]$ also goes for more complex total experiences. C-holism (in either form) is ubiquitous. Since it is generated solely by relationships of co-consciousness, it affects all parts of all total experiences, irrespective of how these totals are divided into parts. In the terms introduced earlier, it is a ϕ-holism of the complete and necessary variety.

Strong holism requires strong (token-specific) C-properties, and while prop-erties of this sort may be unfamiliar, a case for individuating experiences in this way can certainly be made, as we have seen. However, some peo-ple might still be reluctant to regard C-properties in this guise as essential to the identity of experiences, and there may be others who are reluctant to draw upon anything beyond phenomenal character (narrowly construed) when distinguishing between types of experience. For anyone in either of these camps there is another route to strong C-holism that should not be overlooked. So as to presuppose as little as possible about the ways in which subjects and experiences are related, from the outset I have worked with a variant of the standard tripartite criterion for the individuation of token experiences. According to the latter the identity of a token experience is deter-mined by its precise character, time of occurrence and *subject*, whereas I have been assuming that it is determined by precise character, time of occurrence, and *material basis.* In the context of the modified criterion, token-specific C-properties are required to generate token-specific C-holism. But in the context of the standard criterion *type-specific* C-properties suffice for token-specific C-holism.

The route to this result is straightforward. Returning to our simple example of $E = [v_1/a_1]$, if we leave strong C-properties out of the picture, and individuate by reference to character, time, and material basis, then it is perfectly possible for the token experience v_1 to be co-conscious with a_1^*, a phenomenal counterpart of a_1 — that is, an experience that has the same (narrow) character and time of occurrence as a_1, but is distinct from it by virtue of having a different material basis. How would things look if we decided to individuate token phenomenal states in terms of time, character, and *subject*? The answer is: very different indeed. On the plausible assumption that co-conscious experiences have the same subject, the hypothesis that a_1 and a_1^* are numerically distinct is no longer tenable. The fact that a_1 and a_1^* occur at the same time, have the same (narrow) phenomenal character *and the same subject* entails that they are numerically identical. Consequently, we need only take the *type*-specific C-property '. . . is co-conscious with a G-type experience' to be an essential part of v_1's phenomenal character to obtain the result that v_1 cannot exist in the absence of the *token* experience a_1. If v_1 necessarily has this C-property, then it is necessarily co-conscious with a_1, since any G-type auditory experience that occurs at this time, and is co-conscious (and hence consubjective) with v_1 will necessarily be numerically identical with a_1. And the same applies the other way around. On the assumption that the type-specific property '. . . is co-conscious with an F-type visual experience' is essential to a_1, then a_1 could only exist if co-conscious with v_1 — and for the same reason: any putative phenomenal counterpart of v_1 *is* v_1. Provided, that is, that we individuate in terms of subject, time, and character. Strong holism is thus more easily achievable than one might think—and the implications are potentially quite significant, as will emerge. But let us press on.

Thus far I have confined my attention to the synchronic case, but C-holism also applies diachronically. Simultaneous experiences are co-conscious, but so too are the earlier and later phases of specious presents, and—as we saw in Chapter 3—a stream of consciousness consists of overlapping specious presents. For present purposes it will suffice to look at just a couple of simple examples of the diachronic workings of C-holism. To start off, a very simple case indeed:

$$S_1 = [a_1 - a_2 - a_3] \qquad\qquad (7)$$

Here, S_1 is a simple stream of consciousness, consisting of a succession of three auditory sensations, a_1, a_2, a_3, of types C, D, E respectively, which unfold over two overlapping specious presents, thus: $[a_1 - a_2]$, $[a_2 - a_3]$. Concentrating on the middle experience, a_2, we can specify its C-properties in token- and type-specific ways thus:

$$a_2 : C[a_1 - \mathbf{a_2} - a_3] \tag{8}$$
$$a_2 : C[C - \mathbf{D} - E] \tag{9}$$

Here (8) tells us that a_2 is co-conscious with the preceding a_1 and the succeeding a_3. (To avoid clutter I use an even more succinct notation for the token specific characterizations—in a fully detailed characterization the type of each token would be included.) All the type-specific (9) tells us that a_2 is a D-type experience that is co-conscious with both a preceding C-type experience and an E-type experience which follows it. Alternatively, if we wanted to make explicit the way this short stretch of consciousness divides into specious presents, we could employ the slightly more cumbersome formulations below:

$$a_2 : C[a_1 - \mathbf{a_2}, \mathbf{a_2} - a_3] \tag{10}$$
$$a_2 : C[C - \mathbf{D}, \mathbf{D} - E] \tag{11}$$

As each of these formulations makes clear, our target experience a_2 is a constituent of two partially overlapping specious presents.

Moving on to a slightly more realistic example, expression (12) represents a short stretch of experience consisting of a succession of concurrent auditory, visual, and gustatory experiences. Experiences in the same vertical column are simultaneous, succession is indicated as in the previous example.

$$S_2 = \begin{matrix} a_1 - a_2 - a_3 \\ v_1 - v_2 - v_3 \\ g_1 - g_2 - g_3 \end{matrix} \tag{12}$$

Focusing on the experiences in the middle row we can represent their token-specific C-properties thus:

$$a_2 : \begin{matrix} a_1 - \mathbf{a_2} - a_3 \\ v_1 - v_2 - v_3 \\ g_1 - g_2 - g_3 \end{matrix} \quad v_2 : \begin{matrix} a_1 - a_2 - a_3 \\ v_1 - \mathbf{v_2} - v_3 \\ g_1 - g_2 - g_3 \end{matrix} \quad g_2 : \begin{matrix} a_1 - a_2 - a_3 \\ v_1 - v_2 - v_3 \\ g_1 - \mathbf{g_2} - g_3 \end{matrix} \tag{13}$$

Of interest here is the manner in which the overall character of an entire total experience is reflected in each of its parts. As can be seen, the experiences that are simultaneous with a_2—namely v_2/g_2—contribute to the latter's global character, as do the three simultaneous experiences which precede a_2 (i.e. $a_1/v_1/g_1$), and the three simultaneous experiences which immediately follow it (i.e. $a_3/v_3/g_3$). As can also be seen, the C-properties of v_2 and g_2 are strikingly similar. Since all parts of a total experience are mutually co-conscious, it is to be expected that the character of the whole should be reflected in the (global) properties of its parts in just this way. For the sake of brevity I have omitted the weak, type-specific characterization here, but similar remarks would apply.[6]

In the diachronic case there is an interesting difference between the longer-term holistic implications of strong and weak global C-properties. Returning to the stream-segment $S_1 = [a_1 - a_2 - a_3]$ consider this counterfactual variant:

$$S_1{}^* = [a_1{}^* - a_2 - a_3] \qquad (14)$$

Here $S_1{}^*$ is indistinguishable from S_1 save for the fact that a_1 in the latter has been replaced with a phenomenal counterpart in the former. How does this difference register on how this segment should be described? Since a_1 and $a_1{}^*$ are phenomenally indistinguishable there is no impact at the level of type-specific C-properties. In both cases the characterization $[C-D-E]$ captures all the relevant phenomenal facts. But a difference does emerge when strong, token-specific C-properties enter the picture. Expressions (15) and (16) provide a first-approximation of the token-specific C-properties of a_2 in S_1 and $S_1{}^*$ respectively:

$$a_2 : C[a_1 - \mathbf{a_2} - a_3] \qquad (15)$$
$$a_2 : C[a_1{}^* - \mathbf{a_2} - a_3] \qquad (16)$$

Obviously there is a difference. If we adopt the policy of allowing differences in token-specific C-properties to impact on experiential identities, we must regard a_2 in (15) as being numerically distinct from a_2 in (16); we can register this by re-labelling the latter '$a_2\#$'. There is nothing at all peculiar here, this difference is a straightforward consequence of strong C-holism: $a_2\#$ may have the same material basis and qualitative character as a_2, but it is co-conscious with $a_1{}^*$ rather than a_1, and the latter are numerically distinct. Now consider the token-specific C-properties of the third and final experience in our stream-segment:

$$a_3 : C[a_1 - a_2 - \mathbf{a_3}] \qquad (17)$$
$$a_3 : C[a_1{}^* - a_2\# - \mathbf{a_3}] \qquad (18)$$

Since a_3 in S_1 is co-conscious with the preceding experience a_2, whereas a_3 in $S_1{}^*$ is co-conscious with the preceding $a_2\#$, we must again conclude that a_3 in S_1

---

[6] For a fuller treatment of C-holism see Dainton (2000, ch. 9)—the notation I have been using here is somewhat different (and simpler) than the notation used there.

is numerically distinct from a_3 in S_1^*; to mark this difference we can re-label the latter '$a_3\#$'. In line with this (18) should read:

$$a_3 : C[a_1^* - a_2\# - \mathbf{a_3}\#] \tag{19}$$

What may seem peculiar here is the way in which the identity of $a_3\#$ has been influenced by the substitution of a_1 for a_1^*, when $a_3\#$ is not itself co-conscious with a_1^*. And of course the influence of a_1^* need not stop there: if S_1^* is part of a longer stream of consciousness, it will impact on the identity of every experience in this stream. While this may seem odd, even bizarre, it is the direct consequence of allowing token-specific relational properties (of a phenomenal sort) to figure among the identity (and hence existence) conditions of experiences.

For those who find themselves in the awkward position of being quite willing to recognize token-specific C-properties, but reluctant to accept that these can exert an influence beyond the range of direct co-consciousness, there is a further option. We can distinguish *unrestricted strong C-holism* from *restricted strong C-holism*, which we can abbreviate to 'USH' and 'RSH' respectively. RSH does not allow the impact of token-specific holism to extend beyond the reach of the (direct) co-consciousness relationship; USH makes no such restriction. In more concrete terms, the proponent of USH accepts that in the counterfactual situation in which a_1^* replaces a_1, this substitution results in $a_2\#$ and $a_3\#$ existing in place of a_2 and a_3, whereas the advocate of RSH accepts that $a_2\#$ would exist in this situation, but denies $a_3\#$ would supplant a_3—and similarly for more complex situations involving greater numbers of experiences. In defence of their position the advocate of RSH can say: 'I'm willing to discriminate between token experiences in an extremely fine-grained way—I am, after all, an advocate of strong C-holism. But it's one thing to accept that the identity of a token experiences is sensitive to the identity of other token experiences with which it is directly co-conscious, it's quite another thing to accept that it is also sensitive to the identities of experiences it is *not* connected to by the co-consciousness relationship.' Clearly, there is something to be said for this more moderate position. In the envisaged scenario a_1 and a_1^* have different material bases (this is why they are numerically distinct); a_2 and $a_2\#$ (if it were to exist) have precisely the same material basis, they differ only in their relational properties, with a_2 being co-conscious with a_1 and $a_2\#$ with a_1^*. Given that a_2 and $a_2\#$ are indistinguishable in so many respects, what rationale is there for holding that the (purely relational) difference between them could impact upon the identity of an experience in a_3's position? The proponent of USH could respond: 'All I am doing is following the logic of token-specific holism through to its conclusion. Given that a_2 and $a_2\#$ *are* numerically distinct then—given token-holism—this difference will impact on the identities of any and all experiences with which they are co-conscious.' And there is something to be said for this too. Anyone inclined to individuate experiences in as discriminating a fashion as possible *does* have the option of adopting USH. They must also accept, however, that the latter does have some rather counterintuitive consequences.

Details aside, the general line of argument which leads to the recognition of the various forms of ϕ-holism rooted in C-properties may seem dubious. I have in mind an objection such as this:

The general case for C-holism rests on an unusually strict criterion for individuating token experiences. You maintain that the identity of an experience depends on the totality of its phenomenal relations to other experiences. Is there anything to prevent my adopting an analogous criterion for material objects? There is, after all, a case for saying that a truly complete physical description of an ordinary material object would mention its relational properties as well as its intrinsic properties. So it seems there is nothing to prevent my holding that the precise physical character of my pen, or even its identity, is determined by the totality of distance relationships it has to other material objects in our universe throughout its career. Extending the policy to all material objects leads to a universe-wide physical holism: the character (or identity) of every object essentially depends on the location of every other object; if any object were differently located, even by a few inches, every other object in the universe would have a different character—or would not exist at all, if we adopt the most stringent identity criterion. This seems quite absurd. But if it is absurd in connection with material objects, why is it less absurd in the phenomenal realm?

The two cases are indeed analogous, but only up to a point. Our normal practice in the material case is to individuate objects in terms of their intrinsic properties—shape, size, mass, etc.—together with their causal powers. In short, a physical object's *kind* is determined by how it is in itself and what it can do. Consequently, incorporating distance relations into the identity criteria for physical things would be a significant change in our usual practice—it would constitute a significant change in our *concept* of a typical material object. It is otherwise in the phenomenal case. Here the standard practice is to classify types of experiences primarily by reference to *what they are like*. The case for accepting the existence of C-properties rests on the claim that the phenomenal character of any experience is altered by its being joined to other experiences by the co-consciousness relationship. Not just altered, but altered in such a way that a complete description of the experience's subjective character will mention all the experiences with which it is co-conscious, in either type- or token-specific ways. The considerations which lead to a far-reaching holism in the phenomenal realm thus flow directly from our ordinary (philosophical) way of thinking about experiences. It is quite different for the analogous reasoning in the physical case. Hence, from the vantage point of our ordinary methods of individuation, to adopt the policy which yields holism for material things would be revisionary in the extreme, whereas taking the analogous step in the phenomenal realm is not revisionary at all.

However, we not yet quite done. The objection could be continued thus:

Suppose we lived in a Newtonian universe, where gravity is an action-at-a-distance force. The pattern of forces acting on a given body is determined by the totality of other objects in the universe. In this case material bodies *are* affected by the rest of the universe. Would we be inclined in such circumstances to individuate bodies by reference to all the other bodies in the universe? Of course not.

The analogy is still far from perfect. While it is true that in the envisaged Newtonian scenario each object makes a physical difference to every other object, the pattern of forces impinging on a given object could be replicated by another arrangement of objects, objects of different masses at different distances. In cases of this kind patterns of force and their at-a-distance causes are not correlated in a unique one-to-one way, and a complete physical description of any given material body—a description which fully captures all those properties we would normally consider to be possessed by the object—need mention only the forces acting upon it; no mention need be made of the objects responsible for the forces. The situation in the phenomenal case could not be more different. For as we have seen, when two experiences are directly co-conscious a complete description of either—a description which does full justice to what it is like to have that experience—must embrace the other. Co-consciousness brings its relata *together* in a way that mutual (gravitational-style) attraction does not.[7]

9.6. FROM C-HOLISM TO POWER HOLISM

Enough has been said—for present purposes at least—on the topic of interdependencies among experiences. I want to return now to the issue of interdependencies among experiential powers, focusing first on the implications in this regard of C-holism. The interdependencies among experiences that are created by the existence of global properties transfer down to the level of powers—more specifically, to those powers that are DPC-related. As a consequence, such powers are strongly output-interdependent, in the sense introduced in §9.2.

As usual a simple example will help bring the essentials to the fore. Suppose you have been gazing at your plain white wall for a few minutes in complete silence; all of a sudden a dull droning sound becomes audible, but you continue to gaze at the wall while listening to this new sound. Over this short period it is natural to suppose that a single visual experiential capacity is active throughout, a capacity that (in this instance) is generating a white visual expanse; initially the output of this power is unaccompanied by any auditory experiences, but this changes when the droning begins to be heard: from this point on the output of the visual power is co-conscious with an auditory experiential output. How

---

[7] What of quantum entanglement? Perhaps a complete physical description of a particle *should* include reference to any other particles it is entangled with. But since this very special sort of connection is confined to the micro-realm and does not extend (in any obvious way) to ordinary macroscopic material things, its existence does not undermine the case for excluding relational properties from the identity conditions of ordinary material things.

precisely should we describe this sort of situation? Does the output of the visual power *change* when the auditory power becomes active? When the output of the visual power is co-conscious with the output of the auditory power, does it acquire a character it would (or could not) otherwise possess?[8] It is not difficult to see that C-holism implies precisely this.

Returning to the starkly simplistic schematic example we have already employed, let us suppose that P_1 is a power for F-type visual experience and P_2 is a power for G-type auditory experience, and that these two powers are synchronically DPC-related. (As previously, we leave other powers out of the picture.) If P_1 is active all by itself, it will produce an F-type experience, and no global complications ensure. But if, on the other hand, P_1 is active simultaneously with P_2, then the experiences these two powers produce are mutually co-conscious, and so C-properties enter the fray. We can focus on a single time t, when both powers are active, and P_1 is producing a token visual experience v_1, and P_2 is producing a token auditory experience a_1. Since the powers are DPC_S-related, v_1 and a_1 are co-conscious. In virtue of this fact, for the reasons set out in §9.5, an exhaustive characterization of the phenomenal features of v_1 will not stop at 'F-type visual experience', it will also include the global C-properties of this experience. Accordingly, in terms of type-specific C-properties, in the envisaged circumstance P_1 will produce—or more accurately, *contribute to the production of*—an experience with local character F, and global character [F\G]. Clearly, P_1's total experience-generating potential is not confined to F-type experience *simpliciter*, it also has a global (or relational) dimension, and we need to register this fact in some manner.

A natural way to do this runs as follows. Extending our existing terminology, we can say that P_1's *local e-potential* is for F-type experience, whereas its (type-specific) *global e-potential* is [F\G], or 'for F-type experience that is co-conscious with a G-type experience'. Now, for P_1 to have this global e-potential it must be able to join with a power for G-type experience in producing co-conscious F/G-type experience. In other words, P_1 must be DPC_S-related to a power for

---

[8] As the latter formulation usefully illustrates, the issue of power-interdependence is independent of the 'same power throughout' assumption. We have no reason to think that the neural systems our brains use to generate visual experience differ dramatically depending on whether any of our auditory capacities (or capacities for bodily experience, olfactory experience, etc.) are also active, but if this *were* the case, the issue of whether the relevant capacities are output-interdependent still arises. But to complicate matters as little as possible I will generally continue to work on the assumption that a single experiential power can be active both by itself and in combination with other powers to which it is DPC-related. There is a further issue here: how is the 'same power throughout' assumption to be reconciled with the doctrine (which I am also assuming) that in our universe experiential powers are to be individuated (in part) by reference to their material bases? When my visual system starts to produce a yellow expanse that is co-conscious with an auditory experience won't additional neural systems come into play? This does seem likely, but for the reasons outlined in §4.5, it is plausible to suppose a degree of variation in (the active part of) a power-base falls within the confines of what is compatible for a single power's remaining intact in such cases (recall the case of the DVD player).

G-type experience. And the same applies, *mutatis mutandis*, to P_2. The latter can produce experiences with local character G, and it can contribute to the production of experiences with global character $[F\backslash G]$, and it would not and could not have this global e-potential were it not DPC$_S$-related to a power for F-type experience. The situation is much the same if we move from type- to token-specific C-properties. Still using the conventions of the previous section, the global character of the experience which can be attributed to P_1 will be $[v_1 \backslash a_1]$, and that of P_2 will be $[v_1 \backslash a_1]$. Again, it is clearly the case that for each of these powers to be able to contribute to the production of experiences possessing this (token-specific) global character it must be DPC$_S$-related to the other. It is also clear that the token-specific global e-potentials of these two powers are inseparably tied together: neither could exist in the absence of the other.[9]

In describing matters thus I have assumed that P_1 and P_2 alone are causally responsible for the production of experiences of type $[F/G]$. Is there no other option? Might there not be three distinctive sorts of power involved in this case: one for tokens of F-type experience, one for tokens of G-type experience, and one for tokens of the co-consciousness relationship which connects the two? This would be the obvious way of viewing the situation if the co-consciousness relationship were a feature of experience possessing its own phenomenal features, but as we have already seen, there is no reason to think this is the case. When phenomenal contents are co-conscious they are experienced *together*, but (phenomenologically speaking, at least) this togetherness is a primitive mode of unity: we are not aware of any additional glue-like entity connecting (or coming between) the contents experienced as unified. Hence to accommodate the relevant facts we need only posit (i) a capacity for F-type experience; (ii) a capacity for G-type experience; and (iii) a capacity for co-conscious fusions of F- and G-type experiences. If we further assume (as seems plausible for our own case) that the capacities responsible for (i) and (ii) are also at work in (iii), it is natural to describe the situation in the way already outlined, in terms of capacities with local and global e-potentials.

If this analysis is along the right lines it would clearly be a mistake to suppose that P_1 and P_2 are output-independent powers. Indeed, not only are such powers interdependent, they are interdependent in a deep way: these powers are not merely output-interdependent, they are *strongly* output-interdependent. P_2's being active not only impacts on the character of the experience produced by P_1, the difference it makes is one that could *only* have been produced by P_2, or by a power capable of producing a qualitatively identical output—depending on whether we are dealing in token- or type-specific C-properties. And what goes

[9] When I introduced power-interdependencies in §9.2 I assumed each power had a range of different *local* outputs (e.g. Maggot's *yellow* and *yellow**). Now that we have recognized the distinction between local and global phenomenal properties we can see that a power for a single local type of experience (e.g. yellow) can have varying global phenomenal properties, depending on which other DPC-related powers are active with it.

for P_1 and P_2 applies to the members of *any* collection of DPC-related powers, and for the same reason: experiential powers are DPC-related (synchronically or diachronically) if they can produce co-conscious experience; if two or more experiences are co-conscious their respective C-properties reflect this fact (in either type- or token-specific ways), and since these C-properties will necessarily be reflected in the global e-potentials of the relevant experiential capacities, the latter will themselves be interdependent (in either type- or token-specific ways). This interdependence is of the full rather than the partial variety, and it is in no way a contingent matter: it applies to all DPC-related power-systems, and all subjects—save the very simplest—irrespective of their differences in other respects. From the type-specific perspective, the global e-potential of each power in a DPC-related system is determined by the kinds of experience the other members of the system can produce, whereas from the token specific perspective, the global e-potential of each power depends on the particular collection of token powers to which it is DPC-related.[10]

So much for the basic picture. The essentials remain the same, but things rapidly become more complicated when dealing with more complex C-systems. Suppose we vary our two-power scenario just a little by introducing a third experiential power, P_3 for H-type auditory experience; we can further suppose that this power is part of a C-system that also includes P_1 and P_2—or at least, powers that are as similar to these as it is possible to be. Focusing just on P_1, previously its e-potential was confined to just two possibilities: it could be (i) active by itself, and produce just an F-type experience; or (ii) be active and contribute to the production of an experience with (weak) global character $[F\backslash G]$. But now, thanks to the arrival of P_3, two new possibilities have opened up. P_1 could be active with P_3, and thus contributing to the production of an experience with (weak) global character $[F\backslash H]$; alternatively, it could be active with both P_1 and P_2, and thus contributing to the production of an experience

---

[10] Someone might object: 'But what if we adopt a different way of individuating powers? In the case just considered we say that *three* numerically distinct powers are involved: P_1, a capacity for solitary F-type experience; P_2, a capacity for solitary G-type experiences; and P_3, a capacity for compound experiences with the character $[F/G]$. More generally, we assign a completely different and distinct power to every distinct permutation of experiences. Hasn't all trace of interdependence *between* powers now vanished?' It has indeed, and not surprisingly, given that distinct powers can no longer be active together in producing co-conscious experiences. The envisaged way of individuating powers is not very economical, to say the least. Nor is it the natural way to go, given the assumption (currently in force) that in such cases the same physical power-bases are responsible for the F- and G-type experiences, irrespective of whether these occur in isolation or together as constituents of $[F/G]$-compounds. In any event, if we do accept the proposed mode of individuation as legitimate, it is important to recognize that interdependencies nonetheless remain. These interdependencies can no longer be construed as obtaining amongst distinct experiential powers, rather, they exist at the level of what we might call *power-elements*, i.e., distinguishable parts or aspects of a power. In the case of P_3 we can distinguish two distinct experience-generating elements: PE_1, a capacity for experience of local type F, and PE_2, a capacity for experience of local type G; each of these elements can be active independently of the other, but when active together they produce co-conscious experiences (of type F/G).

with (weak) global character [F\G\H]. The same applies, *mutatis mutandis*, to P_2 and P_3. Full descriptions—type-specific on the left, token-specific on the right—of the e-potentials of all three powers are given below:

P_1^* : {[F], [F\G], [F\H], [F\G\H]}{[v_1], [v_1\$a_1$], [$v_1$\$a_2$], [$v_1$\$a_1$\$a_2$]}

P_2^* : {[G], [G\F], [G\H], [G\F\H]}{[a_1], [a_1\$v_1$], [$a_1$\$a_2$], [$a_1$\$v_1$\$a_2$]}

P_3 : {[H], [H\F], [H\G], [H\F\G]}{[a_2], [a_2\$v_1$], [$a_2$\$a_1$], [$a_2$\$v_1$\$a_1$]}

The asterisks affixed to P_1 and P_2 are there for a reason. Although P_1 and P_1^* have the same local e-potential—F-type—their global e-potentials are quite different. Compare the specifications provided above for P_1^* with those for our original P_1:

$$P_1 : \{[F], [F, G]\} \qquad \{[v_1], [v_1 \backslash a_1]\}$$

The differences between the two may only exist at the global level, but it would be negligent to fail to register them. Should we regard P_1 and P_1^* as the same power, or as different powers? There is something to be said for each option. Both P_1 and P_1^* produce experience of the same local type when activated; if we further suppose (or stipulate) that P_1's capacity for F-type experience resides not only in the same brain, but the same (or similar) neural systems as P_1^*'s capacity for F-type experience—an assumption I have been making thus far—then one might well be inclined to regard them as same power. But the fact that P_1^* can produce experiences with a wider range of global properties than P_1 could equally incline one to the view that they should be regarded as numerically distinct powers, notwithstanding the features they have in common. Those who prefer maximally discriminating modes of individuation will certainly be so inclined.

If we do choose to hold exact global e-potentials as relevant to the identity (and so existence conditions) of experiential powers, the consequences are quite dramatic. It immediately follows, as we have just seen, that P_1 and P_1^* are numerically distinct powers, and the same goes for P_2 and P_2^*. We are also confronted with two far-reaching forms of power-holism. From the type-specific perspective, P_1 can only exist if DPC_S-related to a power for G-type experience and P_1^* can only exist if DPC_S-related to a power for G-type experience and a power for H-type experience—for if these powers were not so related, they would not have the global e-potentials that we are now taking as essential to their identities. Moving to the token-specific perspective deepens the interdependencies. If we regard broad C-properties as essential to the identities of experiences and the capacities that produce them, then P_1^* can only exist if DPC_S-related to P_2^* and P_3, and the same applies, *mutatis mutandis*, for P_2^* and P_3. These three token powers are thus as interdependent as it is possible to be: each can only exist in the company of the others. And consequently, since the

C-system comprising these powers is not composed of parts which could enjoy a separate existence, it is—in effect—a metaphysically simple object.

Issues of integration

C-systems can differ in regard to the number of constituent powers they possess at a given time, but as we saw in §4.3, it is also possible for C-systems to have different depths of synchronic integration. In the most straightforward of cases all the experiential powers in a system will be mutually DPC_S-related. The powers in such systems are interdependent in the ways just outlined, and the same applies to systems whose constituent powers are all pairwise DPC_S-related, even if the powers are not all capable of manifesting simultaneously. But what of C-systems of the sort depicted in Figures 4.7, 4.8, and 4.9? C-systems such as these are not composed of powers that are jointly or pairwise DPC_S-related, rather, they compose power *networks* whose nodes are DPC_S-related or IPC_S-related (i.e. *indirectly* DPC_S-related). For present purposes it will suffice to consider a single simple case, of the kind depicted in Figure 9.6. As can be seen, although each of $P_1 - P_4$ are DPC_S-related to P_5, it is also the case that $P_1 - P_4$ are only IPC_S-related to one another.

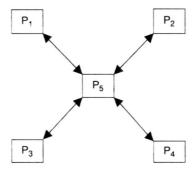

Figure 9.6 A C-system with less than maximal synchronic integration

Individuating powers in terms of type-specific C-properties yields significant, but far from complete, interdependencies here. Each of $P_1 - P_4$ can only exist if DPC_S-related to a power with a local e-potential indistinguishable from that of P_5, whereas P_5 itself can only exist if DPC_S-related to powers with local e-potentials that are indistinguishable from P_1, P_2, P_3, and P_4. However, the interdependencies go no further or deeper: since none of $P_1 - P_4$ is DPC_S-related to any of the others, there is no obstacle to any of them existing in the absence of the others.

What if we individuate powers in terms of token-specific C-properties? Here the situation is complicated by the distinction drawn in the previous section between *restricted* and *unrestricted* token-specific C-holism, RSH and USH. It will be recalled that proponents of RSH hold that the impact of token-specific C-holism is confined to experiences that are directly co-conscious, proponents of USH impose no such restriction, and allow it to be transmitted through chains of experiences that are only indirectly co-conscious. This distinction may have been introduced in the diachronic context, but it applies equally well in the synchronic case. If we opt for USH, the situation with regard to the $P_1 - P_5$ system is clear and unambiguous. The USH theorist will hold that token–token interdependencies can be transmitted throughout a power-network by the IPC_S relationship. Consequently, even though P_1, P_2, P_3, and P_4, are not DPC_S-related (and so cannot produce co-conscious experiences when activated simultaneously) they are nonetheless essentially interdependent. And since the same applies for more complex systems, the USH theorist will view any PC_S-related network as a simple substance. (As will be recalled from §4.3, a PC_S-related network is one whose nodes are DPC_S-related or IPC_S-related.)

Those who adopt the more moderate RSH will regard only those powers that are DPC_S-related as existentially interdependent. Applying this to the C-system currently under consideration yields an intriguing result: this system divides into four partially overlapping sub-networks— $[P]_1 - P_5]$, $[P_2 - P_5]$, $[P_3 - P_5]$, $[P_4, P_5]$—each of which constitutes an interdependent pairing of powers. Since RSH is a form of token-specific C-holism each of these sub-networks is composed of parts which could not exist independently, and so each is a metaphysically simple entity. The idea that simple entities could partially overlap in this manner is certainly an unfamiliar one, but this in itself does not mean it is unintelligible. It *would* be absurd to suppose that two dimensionless geometrical points could partially overlap, but the power-clusters we are considering are not point-like, each has distinguishable parts. However, there someone might object: 'Isn't it absurd to hold that (i) P_1 and P_5 are such that each can only exist with the other, (ii) P_2 and P_5 are such that each can only exist with the other, and also hold that (iii) P_1 and P_2 are such that they *could* each exist *without* the other?' At first view it might well seem so, but the RSH theorist has the resources to accommodate precisely this sort of situation. Consider first a counterfactual scenario in which P_1 is replaced with a phenomenal counterpart P_1*; in this situation (and recalling the discussion of the previous section) the RSH theorist will hold that rather than being co-conscious with P_5, P_1* is co-conscious with the otherwise indistinguishable P_5*; the RSH theorist will *also* hold that the difference between P_5 and P_5* is not such as to impact upon the identity of any other experiences with which this experience is co-conscious—hence P_2 survives in this scenario. In analogous fashion, were P_2 to be replaced by a phenomenal counterpart P_2*, we would have P_5** rather than P_5, but again, this difference would not impact upon the identity of P_1. The RSH theorist can thus agree that P_1 and P_5 are existentially interdependent, and likewise P_2 and P_5, but also hold (consistently) that the non-existence of P_1 does not entail the non-existence of P_2, and vice-versa.

Diachronic considerations

We have been considering power-interdependencies from the synchronic stand-point, but since experiential powers can be DPC-related diachronically as well as synchronically, the global characteristics produced by experienced continuity and succession need to be taken into consideration too. In a full description of the global characteristics of the experiences a power can produce, the various kinds of temporally extended total experiences to which a power can contribute will be relevant. To illustrate how this works out in a simple case, we can return to Maggot's basic complement of experiential powers. Take his olfactory power (O_1) for the sensation with the local characteristic *nasty*. At any given time, O_1 can be active and produce an experience that is co-conscious with any one of Maggot's visual powers, and any one of his powers for bodily sensations. So to describe O_1's synchronic global e-potential we will need to mention the local characters of a total of six other types of experience (those produced by powers V_1, V_2, V_3, B_1, B_2, B_3). The two remaining olfactory powers, O_2 and O_3 are not included in this specification since they are opposed to O_1, and cannot be active at the same time. How do things stand when we introduce the diachronic dimension? Relevant to O_1's diachronic global e-potential at any given time are all those powers which it can cooperate with to produce a single specious present. Evidently, the relevant powers are those which are DPC_D-related to O_1. These include Maggot's three visual and three bodily powers, but also include his other two olfactory powers, O_2 and O_3. The latter cannot be active simultaneously with O_1, but they can be active just before or just after a triggering of the latter, and so contribute to a single temporally extended total experience. (In the terminology of §4.3 such powers are Σ-*related*.) Hence we can see that a full description of the O_1's global e-potential for the time in question, a specification which included diachronic factors as well as synchronic, would mention the local characteristics of a total of nine different experiences and their corresponding powers. Since the same will apply to each of his other powers, it is evident that all nine powers are interdependent.

As previously, the precise mode of interdependence will depend on whether we opt to individuate powers in type- or token-specific ways. For those who acknowledge token-specific forms of C-holism, the distinction between USH and RSH is once again relevant. As in the synchronic case, the proponent of USH will allow token–token interdependencies to run through chains of powers that are only IPC-related. Of course there is a difference: since we are now considering the diachronic case, it is powers that are IPC_D-*related* that are at issue. Since powers that are widely separated in time can be IPC_D-related, USH has the consequence that (counterfactual) alterations in the power-complement of a subject at one time can impact on powers that are hours or years distant. This counterintuitive result can be avoided by adopting USH, which in the diachronic case confines interdependencies to the span of the specious present. It is worth noting that the option also exists of retaining USH for the synchronic case, but applying RSH in the diachronic case.

These complications aside, it seems that acknowledging the diachronic dimension of experience does not introduce new *forms* of power-interdependence, but it can (and usually does) increase the *quantity* of interdependencies, in the manner just illustrated. And of course, what goes for Maggot will go for more complex subjects.

This increased connectedness is not without its broader metaphysical implications. As we have just seen in the context of synchronic unity, some C-systems are more unified than others. In the case of the network composed of $P_1 - P_5$, the four outlying powers P_1, P_2, P_3, and P_4 are not DPC_S-related to one another, and consequently these powers are immune to the weaker (and arguably more plausible) forms of global C-holism; only USH delivers pervasive interdependencies in cases such as this. However, as soon as we consider matters from the diachronic perspective, the situation changes considerably. $P_1 - P_4$ cannot produce experience simultaneously, but they may well be able to *successively*, within the confines of a single specious present. If we suppose $P_1 - P_4$ are all pairwise DPC_D-related—an assumption which is by no means implausible—then the type-specific and RSH-generated interdependencies enter the picture once again. This applies quite generally to powers which are Σ-related. Hence the more modest (and least objectionable) forms of output-interdependence can extend even to subjects whose C-systems are less than maximally integrated at any given time. This has some relevance to our own case. The experiential powers of typical human subjects are moderately well-integrated, even if not maximally so. The range of visual experiences I am able to enjoy at a given time is not at the mercy of the sort of auditory experience I am having, or what I am consciously thinking, or feeling. Generally speaking, any capacity in one experiential modality can be exercised simultaneously with any capacity in a different modality. Powers in different modes can be opposed—my capacity for a completely red visual field cannot be exercised simultaneously with my capacity for a completely blue visual field—but such powers are normally Σ-related. Given this, it seems likely that all our powers are interdependent in type- and/or token-specific ways. If so, then for subjects such as ourselves simplicity does not require the extremes of USH.

Recognizing the interdependencies among powers induced by inter-experiential interdependencies permits a new interpretation of a special case. In §4.5 we encountered promiscuous powers, that is experiential capacities of the probabilistic variety that are able to contribute to the unified states of consciousness produced by two or more otherwise distinct C-systems. I suggested that in the case of a promiscuous power P^* that is ^PDPCS-related to two systems S1 and S2, P^* should be regarded as a part of S1 when it is contributing to a stream of consciousness produced by S1, as a part of S2 when it is contributing to a stream of consciousness produced by S2, and as belonging to neither when it is dormant. The recognition of C-holism casts new light on the situation. Suppose first that S1 and S2 have somewhat different complements of constituent experiential powers, and hence different e-potentials. This entails that the type-specific global e-potential of P* in conjunction with S1 will be different from that P* in conjunction with S2: for when P* is co-active with powers in S1 it is able to contribute to a range of total experiences which differs from the range it can produce when active with powers in S2. In virtue of this we now have the option of holding that the power we have thus far been calling 'P*' is really two distinct powers—which we can label P*1 and P*2. For even if the latter have a common material basis, we can take them to be distinct by virtue of the diversity of experiential effects they can produce.[11] Of course this option is not available if S1 and S2 can produce qualitatively indistinguishable ranges of experience. The situation changes again if we recognize token-specific C-holism. P*1 and P*2 can now be regarded as possessing distinct global e-potentials by virtue of the fact that the experiences produced by the powers in S1 are numerically distinct from their qualitatively indistinguishable S2-produced counterparts.

These considerations may seem rather abstruse, but it would be a mistake to allow the complications considered latterly to obscure the simplicity of the underlying picture. An experience's local character consists of the intrinsic features of the experience considered in abstraction from its experiential context, and the local e-potential of a power is a function of the local character of the kind of experience it can produce, considered in abstraction from the various phenomenal contexts these products might find themselves in. However, whereas the global character of an *experience* reflects the local characters of all the experiences with which it is actually co-conscious, the global e-potential of an experiential *power* is a function of the all different total experiences to which it *can* contribute; the global character of an experience is defined by actual inter-experiential relationships, but the global e-potential of a power goes beyond this. As for the total experiences to which a given power can actually contribute, this will depend on the other powers to which it is DPC_S- and/or DPC_D-related. The network of DPC-relations a power finds itself in determines its global e-potential. It is equally important not to lose sight of the fact that these considerations have a significant corollary. The different forms of power-holism deriving from C-holism have implications for the kind of unity C-systems possess, and hence the kind of things selves or subjects are. The picture which has emerged is by no means entirely straightforward. The different forms of C-holism generate different degrees of interdependence, and different C-systems can have different degrees of integration. If we opt to individuate in the token-specific way, systems of DPC-related experiential powers no longer possess any logically detachable parts,

---

[11] This is in line with the treatment of pluri-streamal powers in §4.5.

they are metaphysically simple objects. If we adopt the USH, the same applies to powers that are only IPC-related. But even if we only recognize type-specific C-properties, there is no denying that the e-potentials of DPC-related powers are interdependent to a significant degree—and if we individuate experiences in terms of time, character, and subject (rather than material basis) such powers lose their logical independence altogether.

Of course, someone might object: 'This is all very well, but these metaphysical consequences all depend upon adopting a particular—and extremely stringent—policy on the individuation of experiential powers.' And this is certainly true. Opting to individuate experiential powers in terms of their precise global e-potential renders them fragile in the extreme; the loss or alteration in the local e-potential of any part of a DPC-related system of powers immediately impacts upon—immediately eliminates—the remainder of the system, irrespective of whether we opt for the type- or token-specific schemes. The style of 'elimination' involved is of the bloodless variety: the new powers which instantly come into being resemble their predecessors almost exactly, and will often have exactly the same local e-potential and very similar material bases. For most practical purposes individuating in terms of local e-potential suits very well; this policy allows us to think of powers as persisting through alterations in their global e-potential, and in some respects this is no doubt a more natural way to think of them. If I were to become blind, and so lose all my visual powers, the global e-potential of all my remaining experiential powers would be different, even if their local e-potential were completely unchanged. It would be odd, in these circumstances, to say that my capacities for bodily and auditory experience had been eliminated and replaced by numerically different powers. Individuating by reference to local e-potential does not oblige us to say this.

But the practical benefits of less-discriminating modes of individuation do not affect the realities of the situation. Being co-conscious *does* impact on the character of experiences that are so related (even if their local features are unaffected), and this in turn means that the e-potentials of experiential powers that are DPC-related, synchronically or diachronically, are influenced by their being so related. Returning to our opening example, if P_1 and P_2 are powers for F- and G-type experiences respectively, and are DPC$_S$-related, included in the global e-potential of both powers is the capacity for an experience with global character [F\G]. Neither power could have this e-potential in isolation, and the same applies to the token-specific counterpart [$v_1 \backslash a_1$]. Although variations in global e-potential need not be taken to not affect the identity of the powers which carry it, the existence of global e-potential still makes a significant difference to the way DPC-related powers are connected: their experiential potentials are interdependent. A C-system is a composite of experiential powers, and the overall character of a C-system depends upon the types of experiential powers that belong to it; the character of an experiential power depends upon its e-potential; and the e-potential of a power depends in turn upon the precise composition of the

C-system to which it belongs. P-systems may well be unified in analogous ways, but the unity we have been concerned with here is rooted in purely phenomenal considerations. C-systems thus possess a distinctive form of unity all of their own. We could even call it an *organic* unity, despite the fact that the unity is phenomenal rather than biological, chemical, or causal.

9.7. POWER SYSTEMATICITY

C-holism at the level of experience creates a pervasive power-holism. But just as most P-systems are systemic, so too are many C-systems. If we leave C-holism out of the picture entirely, there remain forms of experience which can only plausibly be attributed to powers that are essentially integral components of power-systems.

One source of systematicity is inherited from the psychological domain. The component parts of a P-system, in particular the capacities associated with the ability to understand a language or think thoughts or entertain conscious beliefs or desires, are essentially systemic at the functional level (or so it is widely supposed). But these same cognitive capacities also have a phenomenal role—they can produce distinctive forms of experience, and more specifically, episodes of understanding-experience. Hence it seems likely that episodes of genuinely contentful conscious thoughts (or beliefs, or intentions, etc.) are the product of essentially systemic experience-producing systems. I say 'genuinely contentful' to accommodate the possibility of episodes of *seemingly* contentful conscious thought which are produced by defective (or even non-existent) cognitive systems. Perhaps not all episodes of seemingly meaningful thought really are such—and if there can be illusory thoughts, perhaps they can be the product of capacities that are not systemic in the manner of those cognitive capacities which are responsible for genuinely meaningful episodes of understanding-experience.

Needless to say there are different forms of systematicity. Let us say that a mental state is *moderately systemic* if it cannot exist in isolation—it has to belong to a mental system of some kind or other—but it is not tied to any particular kind of mental system nor any particular mental system. If a mental state is essentially bound up with a particular mental system of a particular type, let us say that it is *strongly systemic*. If a mental state is such that it can belong to a mental system, but can also exist all by itself, in isolation, let us say that it is *weakly systemic*. It may well be that all P-states with propositional content are at least moderately systemic—by their nature, beliefs, desires, intentions, and the like must exist in a psychological system of some kind or other. If the precise functional (or inferential) character of a P-state depends on the other P-states in the same cognitive system, then some such states may even be strongly systemic—at least if we individuate P-states in a very discriminating way. Since many (perhaps the majority) of P-states can also contribute to experience, these interdependencies can also be regarded as existing among certain kinds of experiential powers.

Since the relationship between consciousness and cognition is poorly understood, it is difficult to pronounce on such matters with confidence. But there is no need to venture into such troubled waters to locate instances of systematicity among experiential powers. There are grounds for supposing that the capacities responsible for even simple forms of sensory experience can be systemic too.

Recall some of the simple forms of phenomenal interference that we encountered in §9.4. In the case of the Müller–Lyer illusion, the apparent lengths of the horizontal lines is affected by the presence or absence (or orientation) of the arrow-heads. The powers responsible for such interference effects are clearly parts of an interdependent system: for whatever reason, the output of one power (the kind of experience it produces) differs depending on which other powers (in the same C-system) are active or inactive at the time. This kind of interdependency (and hence systematicity) is no doubt of the contingent variety, and not very common—in our experience at least—but it is certainly real. However, as we also saw, the interference in such cases is of the weak variety, that is the altered forms of experience (e.g. the shortened lines in the Müller–Lyer) can exist in different phenomenal contexts. Consequently the responsible powers are only weakly output-interdependent, and only moderately systemic. Most other familiar instances of interference—including the cross-modal ventriloquism effect—fall into the same category. Are there any instances of strong phenomenal interference, cases in which afflicted experiential parts can only exist in phenomenal contexts of a similar kind to that in which they are actually located? Perhaps the illusory contours to be found in Kanisza's triangle (and similar cases) are an instance of strongly context-dependent phenomenal contents. If so, then the responsible powers are strongly output-interdependent (if only in a type-specific way), and strongly systemic.

These comparatively *recherché* interference effects aside, many very ordinary varieties of sensory experience can also be regarded as being the products of interdependent powers. As noted in §9.3, quite independently of subtle interference effects, a typical phenomenal whole is distinct from the mere sum of its parts in virtue of the fact that its parts are arranged in a particular way. Taken as a whole, a visual experience of a yellow square appearing to the right of a blue circle is different in character from the experience of a yellow square appearing to the left (or above, or below) a blue circle, even if the intrinsic features of the shapes are exactly the same in the two cases. In a similar vein, the experience of *do-re-mi* is very different, taken as a whole, from the experience of *mi-re-do*. And taken as wholes, the experience of either of these successions is very different if accompanied by a sensation of intense pain, or a tickle, or the smell of rosemary, or the flavour of herring—and so on and on. The fact that a capacity for a single type of simple sensory experience (a shape of a particular colour, a tone of a particular pitch, etc.) can contribute to a vast range of different total experiences may be something we take entirely for granted, but it is also a manifestation of a far-reaching systematicity. If an experiential power possesses the capacity to contribute to a range of different phenomenal contexts (or total experiences) then it is necessarily DPC-related to a range of other powers—powers for the types of experience of which these phenomenal contexts are composed. Powers possessing rich combinatorial properties—powers with the global e-potentials of the sort we are familiar with—are thus highly systemic, and essentially so. Given that we are currently ignoring the implications of C-holism, it seems plausible to suppose that combinatorial factors only generate type-specific and (at most) moderate systematicity. For it may well be that powers which actually possess rich combinatorial possibilities could produce experience of the same (local) intrinsic type in complete isolation—weak systematicity cannot be ruled out. If we further discount strong interference effects, it seems likely that the relevant powers are only weakly output-interdependent. Nevertheless, despite these limitations, this source of interdependence is a force to be reckoned with.

While it is obvious that powers with rich combinatorial possibilities are systemic, it is somewhat less obvious that the same often applies to powers for very simple forms of experience indeed. In fact, a degree of systematicity is involved in the production of the most primitive spatial and temporal phenomenal features. To appreciate how and why, let us return to our simple subject.

Maggot has a number of different experiential powers and depending on how these are triggered his streams of consciousness can exhibit phenomeno-temporal patterns of one kind or another. Suppose his visual experience takes the form: a period of *red* followed by a period of *yellow* followed by a feeling of *cold*, where each succession occurs within a phenomenally continuous stretch of experience. This temporal pattern involves three different experiential powers, and to be capable of experiencing this temporal pattern Maggot must possess diachronically DPC-related powers of the appropriate sort. The same applies, of course, to more complex patterns featuring two or more simultaneous experiences, for example *red/warm* followed by *yellow/warm* and *orange/delicious*. These examples illustrate the way in which combinatorial possibilities and systematicity go hand in hand. Maggot does not just have capacities for experiences of specific qualitative types, he also possesses the capacity to experience these qualitative types in various combinations, and for an experiential power to be such that it can contribute to the resulting temporal patterns it must not only persist, it must persist as a component of a power-system whose component parts are diachronically DPC-related. The patterns considered so far have not been very complex, to say the least, but there are even simpler patterns, and some of these presuppose a degree of systematicity. By way of an example, consider what must be the case in order for Maggot to be able to directly experience an evenly spaced sequence of v_1-type experiences, that is brief flashes of yellow separated by brief periods of total darkness. One way of construing this experiential pattern is shown in Figure 9.7, where the dotted lines signify a complete absence of visual experience.

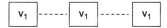

Figure 9.7 A pattern *of* experiences

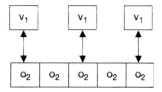

Figure 9.8 A pattern *in* experiences

If we suppose that the succession depicted in Figure 9.7 represents *everything* that Maggot experiences during the period of time in question, then it seems clear that the depicted succession of yellow-type experiences will not be experienced as such. The depicted sequence of experiences does not constitute a single stream of consciousness featuring an alternation of flashes of colour and darkness, rather it constitutes three distinct streams of consciousness, each consisting of nothing more than a brief flash of *yellow*. In effect, since Maggot entirely loses consciousness after each experience of *yellow* he does not consciously live through the periods of darkness. The situation depicted in Figure 9.8 is very different. Here too there is a succession of v_1-type (yellow) experiences, but the interval between each burst of colour is filled with o_2-type olfactory experience. Since Maggot now remains fully conscious throughout, the relevant temporal pattern—of *yellow* alternating with darkness—is instantiated in his stream of consciousness. For this temporal pattern to feature *in* his stream of consciousness, he must *have* a stream of consciousness which encompasses it, and this is precisely what is lacking in the state of affairs depicted in Figure 9.7.

The example is a simple one, but it suffices to make the point. A typical stream of (human) consciousness is a realization of a temporal pattern of some complexity, and some strands of these patterns are naturally described in terms of patterns of absence and presence. But since a total phenomeno-temporal void is not something which can be experienced—a complete absence of experience is equivalent, subjectively, to a period of complete unconsciousness—any gaps between experiences of one type must be filled by experiences of another type. Hence for a subject to be capable of experiencing intermittent sensations of the same type—for this temporal pattern to be instantiated in their stream of consciousness—they must possess powers for more than one type of sensation, and some of these powers must be active during the periods of absence.

There are spatial features in experience which also require a degree of power-systematicity. Consider Maggot's visual powers. There are three of these, and we have been supposing that each can generate a two-dimensional circular phenomenal field entirely filled with a single homogeneous colour. Focus on V_1, a capacity for a *yellow*-filled disc-shaped expanse. Hitherto I have assumed that V_1 is a simple power, with no component sub-powers. Suppose this is wrong, and that Maggot's *yellow*-type experiences are the product of three DPC-related powers, $V_{1(a)}$, $V_{1(b)}$, and $V_{1(c)}$, responsible for three different regions of Maggot's visual field, r_1, r_2, and r_3. The latter could take many forms, among which are those shown in Figures 9.9 and 9.10.

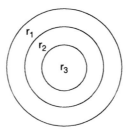

Figure 9.9 A visual field with a hole: region r_2 is blind

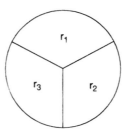

Figure 9.10 Differently holed: region r_3 is blind

Construing Maggot's e-potential for *yellow*-type sensations in either of these ways could be justified by the way his visual capacities can be disabled. Damage to specific brain regions might alter the shape of his visual field: for example it might leave a 'hole' with the shape and size of r_2 in Figure 9.9, or r_3 in Figure 9.10.

Each of r_1, r_2, and r_3 are experiences possessing their own intrinsic spatiality; they are filled-shapes of one sort or another. For these regional powers to jointly generate one of Maggot's *yellow*-type experiences—that is a complete filled circular expanse of colour—they have to be DPC-related. But DPC-relatedness alone is not sufficient: a *yellow*-type experience consists of r_1, r_2, and r_3 in a particular spatial configuration. In Figure 9.9 the power responsible for r_2 generates a ring of *yellow*, enclosed by the regions generated by r_1 and r_3; in Figure 9.10 the relevant power generates very different shapes (wedges) in a very different configuration. Clearly, if $V_{1(a)}$, $V_{1(b)}$ and $V_{1(c)}$ are to succeed in producing a *yellow*-type experience, three conditions must be satisfied: first, they must each generate experiences possessing certain (local) intrinsic spatial features, and secondly, these experiences must be mutually co-conscious, and thirdly, these experiences must be spatially related *to one another* in a quite specific way. The first condition might conceivably be satisfied by independent (non-systemic) powers, the third could not. It only makes sense to think of $V_{1(a)}$ as a power for a part of a *yellow*-type experience if we think of $V_{1(a)}$ as a component of an interdependent system of powers, powers which produce intrinsically spatial experience in specific extrinsic spatial relations.

The point generalizes. We saw in §5.1 that a distinction can be drawn between two very different types of sensory-field or space: those which take the form of a phenomenal *plenum*, and those which take the form of a phenomenal *void*. Call the latter 'V-spaces' and the former 'P-spaces'. Our visual experience typically occurs with a V-space (or we might say that our visual field *is* a V-space). When I look at the house across the street, I see it as being a certain distance away, but in between lies nothing whatsoever—since I cannot see the air (in the absence of smoke, heat-haze, etc.); phenomenally speaking, it is as if the objects I see around me are surrounded by a void. Not all phenomenal fields or spaces are necessarily of this kind. There could conceivably be a species of creature whose visual experience is limited to the seeing of green shapes moving through a homogeneous and three-dimensional blue mist. Understandably, these creatures take the blue-continuum to be empty space. While odd from our perspective, this decision is entirely reasonable: this phenomenal plenum, this P-space, is the unchanging framework within which everything else they visually perceive occurs.

Since they are phenomenal plenums, Maggot's visual fields are P-spaces. While some P-spaces are the product of a single experiential power, others will be the product of several different powers. Whenever the latter situation applies, the P-space in question can legitimately be regarded as a product of a complex of interdependent powers. The same applies to the powers responsible for phenomenal objects which exist within P-spaces, objects whose phenomeno-spatial position is determined by their location within a P-space. Let us change modality, and consider Maggot's bodily experience, whilst simultaneously expanding his sensorium. As before, Maggot's bodily experience takes the form of an all-over feeling of temperature, either *cold*, *warm*, or *hot*. The *warm*-type sensation is a homogeneous three-dimensional P-field, of a shape similar to that of Maggot's body. Focusing only on this field, we can suppose Maggot's experience is slightly richer: he can feel sharply localized feelings of pain. (On taking a gulp of icy-cold water, he feels a sharp pain sensation sliding through his interior; on crawling over

a sharp stone he feels a pain moving along the underside of his bodily P-field.)
If we suppose (as seems plausible anyway) that the only way for Maggot's pains
to have a phenomeno-spatial location is for them to be located in his bodily
P-field, then for Maggot to feel a pain that is spatially located, one or other of
the powers for his bodily P-fields must also be active. Hence we have a further
illustration of power-systematicity: Maggot's capacity for *spatially located* pain
essentially depends upon his bodily P-field powers.

What of V-spaces? The situation here is rather more complicated, as there are
different types of V-space; since a detailed survey of the various possibilities would
take us far afield, I will concentrate on the essentials. The size and shape of a
P-space—for a given subject at a given time—has more or less definite phenomenal boundaries, that is the boundaries of the phenomenal plenum which
constitutes the space. Being a phenomenal void, a V-space has no intrinsic phenomenal character, and so its shape and boundaries (again for a given subject at
a given time) are not determined in the same way. A V-space can have as definite
a shape and structure as a P-field, but these parameters are not determined by
the shape and structure of an experienced spatial medium, but by the constraints
on the sorts of experience, and the spatial relations between these experiences,
available to the subject in question. If we suppose that the structure of a non-
substantival physical space is determined by the nomologically possible locations
and movements of physical objects, we can say something analogous for a non-
substantival phenomenal space. But in the latter case, the relevant nomological
possibilities are not fixed by the physical law governing the movements of physical
bodies, but by the nomological constraints on a given subject's experience.

Consider a further variant on the Maggot scenario. Maggot is now a deep sea
dweller. He drifts—more or less aimlessly for the most part—a few feet above
the ocean floor, in total darkness. He shares the ocean depths with several species
of predatory fish, many of which are luminescent. This aquatic Maggot's visual
capacities have evolved so as to take advantage of this, and are quite different
from those of his Earth-bound cousins: this Maggot's visual field is a V-field,
it has no intrinsic phenomenal features to call its own. But Maggot is far from
being blind. If one of the luminous predators approaches, his eye detects the light
and produces a corresponding visual sensation: Maggot sees a patch of light, of a
certain shape and size, and at a certain distance and direction. Now, the structure
of the phenomenal space within which this phenomenal object appears is not
determined by anything else that Maggot is currently experiencing visually: his
visual *experience* consists of the luminous shape and nothing else. The shape of
the surrounding phenomenal space is fixed by the other experiences he is *capable*
of having. If we suppose that his eye is able to detect light from all directions,
his V-field has the form of a sphere. But it is equally possible for his vision to be
restricted to a semi-sphere, or a disc-shape.

There are many possibilities, but the important point should be plain: the
overall structure of Maggot's visual V-space is fixed by the different kinds of visual

experience he can have. Consequently, a power for a particular (local) type of experience can only exist within a wider V-type phenomenal space if it is part of a system of powers, a system capable of generating a range of phenomeno-spatially related experiences, and the precise structure of the V-space is determined by the range of experiences the system as a whole can produce. We can thus see that a capacity for even the simplest form of sensation—a single flash of colour appearing in an otherwise empty void—can be essentially systemic. All it takes is for the void to have a particular form.

9.8. SIMPLICITY

In exploring the various avenues leading to different forms of power-interdependency, I spent a good deal of time on subjects with very simple minds—subjects who are capable of only a few basic forms of sensation. This is partly because it is easier to get to grips with the various forms of interdependence in such scenarios, but it is also because I wanted to bring to the fore the fact that the interdependencies in question are due solely to *phenomenal* factors: they can arise in subjects with little or nothing by way of a psychology, in any ordinary sense of the term.

To recap. We can distinguish between interdependencies among experiential powers that are due to phenomenal factors, and those which are due to non-phenomenal factors. The non-phenomenal factors themselves divide into those which are mental and those which are non-mental. It seems likely that many of our own experiential powers are base-integrated: their physical grounds overlap or are entangled in such a way that the elimination of one power would result in the elimination of others. Powers can be interdependent in virtue of non-phenomenal *mental* factors because many powers can be individuated by reference to both their phenomenal and their psychological roles. In such cases P-relations become relevant, in that the identity of a power is determined by both the sort of experience it can produce and the causal-functional role it plays.

So far as the interdependencies that are due to purely phenomenal factors are concerned, there are three main sources.

1 If we recognize that experiences possess both local and global characteristics, then we are led to a very widespread holism. The global e-potential of any experiential power depends upon all the other powers to which it is DPC-related, in type- or token-specific ways (depending on how we opt to individuate C-properties). These forms of holism are of the complete and necessary varieties. The nature of C-properties are such that DPC-related powers are strongly output-interdependent, in either type- or token-specific ways.

2 Phenomenal interference effects (such as the Müller–Lyer) also engender interdependencies among experiential powers. But it is far from being the case

that the outputs of all DPC-related powers are related in this way, and it is plausible to think that most instances of interference are contingent rather than necessary. Most forms of phenomenal interference give rise to weak output-interdependence, but in a few instances—such as Kanisza's triangle—the relevant powers may be strongly output-interdependent.

3 The powers responsible for many forms of experience—even simple temporal and spatial patterns—are systemic and essentially so.

These interdependencies—summarized in Figure 9.11—have broader ontological implications for the sort of thing selves or subjects are. Does it make sense to think that a given mental capacity could exist in a mind of a different type, or a different mind of the same type? How these questions are answered depends on the sort of mental capacity we are concerned with, and on the way we choose to individuate them. If we confine our attention to interdependencies that are due to purely phenomenal factors, much depends upon how strictly we individuate powers. Suppose we elected to individuate experiential powers in terms of their exact local and global e-potentials, and do so in a token-specific way. This strict policy on individuation yields power-holism of the strongest type: complete, necessary, and token-specific. C-systems, and hence subjects, or their essential cores, would be metaphysically simple entities, in the sense that they lack logically separable parts. We could extend the scope of this simplicity by adopting the same policy with respect to the psychological states and their causal-functional roles. A subject could wax and wane, their mental powers could vary over time, but their minds could not lose or gain parts.

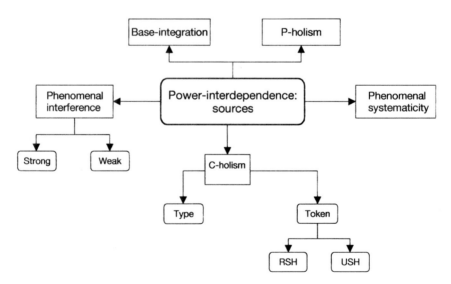

Figure 9.11 A taxonomy of interdependencies

While this result may have a certain appeal, it also rests upon an particularly stringent policy on individuation. This policy is by no means arbitrary—it is rooted in real inter-experiential relations, whether actual or merely potential—but neither is it obligatory. A looser (and for practical purposes, more convenient) policy yields a correspondingly weaker sort of holism. We could, for example, adopt a type-specific rather than a token-specific scheme, and also permit the system-dependent properties of a given mental capacity (in particular global e-potential) to vary to a considerable degree without threatening the power's survival. By adopting this more liberal position, the change or loss of some capacities does not threaten the remainder, for example there are situations in which I lose my auditory powers but my visual powers remain intact. Also, if some of my powers were replaced by phenomenal counterparts, this would not affect the identity of the powers which remain. If our minds can gain and lose (or change) parts in either of these ways, without the existence of the remaining powers being threatened, then our minds are not metaphysically simple objects, they are composed of parts which are logically detachable from one another, and in this respect they are quite unlike traditional Cartesian Egos.

However, while the less stringent regime certainly yields a weaker form of holism—liberalism entails a loss of simplicity—there is also a sense in which all the phenomenal facts remain the same, we are simply adopting a different way of describing them. These facts are the real interdependencies. The global e-potential of an experiential power is still dependent upon the other powers in the same C-system; the capacities for even simple forms of experience are essentially systemic. Recognizing the reality of these interdependencies is at least as important as fastening on to a particular way of describing them.

That said, even if adopting the more stringent scheme is not a forced option, it is one that some may be tempted to adopt on more general metaphysical grounds. In §7.7 I argued that the minimalist conception of embodiment has advantages over the maximalist alternative. In particular, by adopting minimalism the neo-Lockean can respond to the 'too many subjects' objection in a more plausible way than would otherwise be possible. But as I also noted, the risk of overpopulation is not entirely avoided, for there remains the issue of the relationship between C-systems and the C-aggregates which exactly coincide with them at any given time. Both sorts of entity are composed of experiential powers, but whereas C-systems can gain and lose experiential powers, C-aggregates (by definition) cannot. Those who adopt some form of the perdurantist conception of persistence can deal with this sort of issue without too much difficulty, but endurantists are in a more awkward position. Holding that C-systems are constituted from C-aggregates is one option, but it is by no means problem-free. A second option is to hold that only C-systems are genuine substances, and so candidates for being subjects. But while this may appeal to those who subscribe to substance-oriented ontologies, not everyone does. Hence the potential interest of the third option opened up by the existence of C-holism and the consequent power-holism. By individuating experiential powers in as fine-grained a way as possible, we obtain the result that many C-systems are metaphysically simple objects. Since such systems do not possess constituent parts, the issue of how such wholes are related to their parts does not arise.

It is true that, as I have presented this issue, the strongest form of holism requires that C-properties be individuated in token-specific ways, and it may well be that not everyone will be persuaded of the legitimacy of distinguishing between subjectively indistinguishable phenomenal properties on the basis of their phenomenal environments. However, as I noted in §9.5, anyone who opts for the more familiar tri-partite criterion of *subject*, *time*, and *character* when it comes to individuating token experiences only needs type-specific C-properties to avail themselves of the strong form of holism. It is also true that the most far-reaching form of token-holism—USH—is required to secure the simplicity of subjects whose experiential capacities are not as synchronically integrated as they might be. However, as we have also seen, the experiential powers of the typical human subject are integrated to quite a high degree, and any residual powers which are not DPC_S-related will usually be Σ-related. In our own case, simplicity is obtainable without recourse to the most drastic form of token-specific holism.

One thing is absolutely clear. So far as part–whole relations are concerned, there is a world of difference between a typical C-system and a typical compound material object. The constituents of most medium-sized physical objects are not essentially systemic, and generally speaking the intrinsic physical characteristics of their constituent parts are not significantly altered or affected by the whole they belong to. Many mental capacities *are* essentially systemic, and their mental characteristics are affected by the sort of whole they belong to. Since this applies to experiential capacities to at least as great an extent as it applies to psychological states, the implications are obvious: the C-theory may be a bundle theory of the mind (or self), but the bundles it trades in are of a very distinctive kind. Our minds may not be metaphysically simple in a simple or straightforward sense, but their parts are profoundly interdependent. And this amounts to something akin to simplicity, at the very least.

10
Modes of Incapacitation

10.1. ABSOLUTENESS

If you were to suffer the misfortune of being instantly annihilated by a fast-falling meteorite your existence would come to a sudden and abrupt end. But not all lives terminate in such an unambiguous manner, far from it. Many afflictions result in a gradual and progressive decline in mental and physical capabilities. In some cases it might seem as though the afflicted subject gradually *fades away* over an extended period of time, rather than abruptly ceasing to exist at a particular moment. Of course, quite what we should make of such cases depends on the particular conception of the self that we adopt. My main aim in this chapter is to explore the implications of the C-theory for the sharpness of our temporal boundaries.

Irrespective of where the truth of the matter lies, the notion that our own existence and persistence is absolute—in the sense of being all-or-nothing, not in the least a matter of degree—can seem quite plausible, especially when we consider the issue from the experiential perspective. Provided my present stream of consciousness continues to flow on without interruption it seems clear that *I* continue to exist in a perfectly determinate manner, irrespective of what happens to my body and brain. Do interruptions in consciousness make it easier to believe that it could be indeterminate whether some future subject is oneself or somebody else? Not necessarily: the notion that it could be indeterminate whether some future *experience* belongs to me or somebody else can easily seem absurd, irrespective of what transformations I might undergo, even if the transformations take place when I am unconscious. If the ownership of experiences is always and necessarily a fully determinate matter, how could it be otherwise with the persistence and existence of subjects?

Considerations such as these are by no means decisive, but it is interesting to note that our ordinary beliefs about ordinary material objects are very different: we are not naturally inclined to believe that questions about the existence and persistence of such things always have clear and unambiguous answers. If a house very gradually decomposes into a mound of rubble it seems unlikely that there is one particular point during the decomposition process at which the house ceases to exist. If we suppose that the house falls down small piece by small piece, with no sudden structural changes (such as sudden collapses of walls, roofs, or ceilings), then although there is always *something* there throughout the process, it is not always clear what *sort* of thing that object is. The same applies in reverse: suppose the house now in the process of decay was originally built piece by piece, brick by brick. A single brick or wall does not amount to a house, so at what point during the gradual construction process does a house come into being? There is certainly a house there at the end of the process, but again, it seems implausible that the house comes into being at any particular moment. There is a period during both processes—gradual construction and gradual decomposition—during which it seems there is no definite answer to the question of whether a house exists. This suggests that the synchronic identity of houses is not absolute. It also leads to a similar problem for diachronic identity. Suppose a house is damaged so severely that it seems impossible to say whether what remains is a house or a mound of rubble. A replica of the original house is then built on these remains, using a lot of new material. Does the original house survive? It is hard to say—all that is clear is that there is no clear and unproblematic answer to this question.

Various logical and semantic treatments of these problematic cases have been proposed. There is the option of accepting this sort of vagueness as ineliminable, and accepting that there are propositions with an indeterminate truth value, for example 'That thing there is a house'. There is the option of preserving bivalence by more less arbitrarily stipulating a precise point when an object ceases to exist. There is also the option of saying that there always *is* a precise point at which an object ceases to exist, we just can't discover where that point lies: vagueness in objects is only epistemic. I will not be attempting to establish which of these approaches is the most advantageous. The question I will be focusing on is whether subjects of experience are entities that can suffer the same kind of fate as entities such as houses, and be such that there are no unproblematic responses to questions concerning whether they have come into existence, remain in existence, or have ceased to exist. Are selves the sort of thing for which problems concerning seemingly vague or indeterminate existence *can* arise? If selves are entities whose existence is always and necessarily all-or-nothing, then such cases cannot arise. The Cartesian subject, a simple immaterial and continually conscious substance, is a familiar absolutist conception. But on the face of it at least, the C-theorist's view of the self is very different: the existence and persistence of a single subject requires a persisting potentiality for consciousness, not the continued existence of any kind of material (or immaterial) stuff or entity. If we take this view of the self, the question we need to address is whether or not the existence of C-systems is absolute.

There could easily be no one answer to this question. There may well be possible worlds where the existence of particular experiential powers is all-or-nothing, and likewise for C-related compounds of the same, and where as a consequence, the existence and persistence of subjects is invariably a perfectly determinate affair. Think of a world where exactly one hundred particles of a certain sort need to be bonded together into a specific kind of configuration before an experiential power—and hence a self or subject—of the simplest sort can exist. The instant the required hundred particles are suitably configured a simple subject comes into being; but if a single particle is removed from this minimal configuration, or the configuration changes in the slightest way, the capacity to produce the kind of experience required for a subject to exist is destroyed, and the simple subject is lost.

Perhaps worlds of this kind are possible. But there is no reason to think our world is anything like this. I have been working (for the most part) within a moderately naturalistic framework, and assuming that our own capacities for experience are grounded in the neurological structures of our brains. Our current state of ignorance concerning the relationship between matter and consciousness is such that even the most unadventurous assumptions we might make about this relationship are to some extent speculative. Nonetheless, one of the more plausible speculations we can make is that our capacity for consciousness is not grounded in configurations of a few primitive particles. A single neuron consists of billions of such particles, and it may be that tens, thousands, millions, or even billions of interconnected and biochemically supported neurons are required for even the simplest sensations. All we can be reasonably confident about is that something between one and several billion (appropriately interconnected) neurons are sufficient for consciousness. So let us assume this.[1] If the potentiality for experience (*our* experience anyway) requires this kind of highly complex molecular and biological structure, how likely is it that this potentiality is all-or-nothing? Whether or not our existence as subjects is absolute or not depends on how we answer this question. Although *any* answer we can come up with will involve some degree of speculation, we can at least clarify the issue.

I will start by looking at the relevant notion of potentiality at a general level, and try to distinguish some of the ways potentialities can be hampered, disabled, or degraded. We can then apply these distinctions to subjects, more specifically, human subjects and their brains—in ordinary and extraordinary circumstances.

10.2. SOME VARIETIES OF INCAPACITATION

Suppose an object x at time t possesses a potentiality P for producing effects of a certain type under certain circumstances. If we opt to individuate this capacity in a reasonably detailed way, then a characterization of P will take the form $P = [E, B, C]$, where E refers to the type of effect produced when the power

---

[1] Could *just one* neuron sustain consciousness? The idea might seem odd, but some are prepared to take it seriously: '. . . it is proposed that each neuron in the nervous system is independently conscious, with conscious content corresponding to the spatial pattern of a portion of that neuron's dendritic electrical activity. . . . The resulting scheme is one in which conscious behavior appears to be the product of a single macroscopic mind, but is actually the integrated output of a chorus of minds, each associated with a different neuron' Sevush (2004).

manifests, C the triggering conditions, and B denotes the part or property of x where the relevant causal powers reside—recalling our earlier terminology, B is the causal ground or *power-base* of P. As I noted in §4.5, there are different ways of conceiving of dispositional properties, for example some hold that dispositions arise by virtue of the interaction of non-dispositional properties with the laws of nature, others hold that some dispositional properties are primitive, others hold that all genuine properties possess both dispositional and non-dispositional aspects—a further option is to hold that no one such account applies to all dispositional properties. Given that we are primarily interested in materially grounded experiential powers in our world, and that we have no idea as to how our brains manage to produce experience, we are not yet in a position to know precisely how experiential powers should be conceived. Bearing this limitation in mind, let us press on.

To start with, let us say that P is an *active* potentiality of x at t if E would in fact be produced (by x) were C to obtain at that time, accompanied by the relevant background circumstances. When an object possesses an active potentiality it possesses a capacity in the most straightforward and unambiguous manner; the potentiality is primed and ready to unleash its effect as soon as the triggering circumstances arise. A bomb has an active capacity to produce an explosion if it will explode on being dropped. A battery-operated torch has an active capacity to produce light if it would do so when switched on. An entity x has an *inhibited* potentiality for producing an effect E if it possesses a power-base that is sufficient for the production of an E in the presence of C, but x also possesses features which would prevent the production of E were C to occur. In the absence of these internal inhibiting factors, the occurrence of the relevant triggering circumstances would result in the object's producing E. If something has an active potentiality, no such inhibiting agents are located within the thing itself. The inhibiting agents can work in at least two ways: (i) the triggering events are prevented from causing the capacity to be exercised; or (ii) the capacity is exercised, but something prevents the normal effect being produced. A piano's potentiality to produce musical notes would be inhibited in the first way if a damping material were fixed between the hammers and all its strings, so that striking the keys produced no sound; removing the damping device would rectify this, and change the inhibited potentiality into an active potentiality. A train's capacity for self-powered movement would be inhibited in the second way if by putting on all its brakes its engine can no longer move the train forward, even at full power.

An entity x has a *neutralized* potentiality if it possesses all the intrinsic causal factors for producing E in C, that is an appropriate power-base, but the prevailing background conditions are wrong, and as a consequence the presence of C will not cause x to produce E. Most objects possess their commonly recognized potentialities only relative to certain prevailing conditions: for example a match will only ignite when struck if it is in the presence of oxygen, a piano will produce piano-like sounds only if played in a medium with acoustic properties similar to those of air, a paperclip has the capacity to bend without snapping, provided it is not too cold. The relevant background conditions fall into two main categories: environmental and intrinsic. The atmospheric conditions needed for the match to strike or the piano to sound belong to the former; the temperature a paperclip must have to bend without snapping belongs to the latter—it is not the ambient temperature that matters, but the temperature of the metal itself. Since the 'appropriate' background conditions for a given capacity can be specified in different ways, the distinction between neutralizing factors and inhibiting factors is by no means always clear-cut, and certain cases of inhibition can also qualify as instances of neutralization. For example, the presence of damping material in a piano can be viewed as a case where sound-producing capacities are inhibited, but it could also be viewed as a matter of inappropriate background conditions, if one chooses to regard matters in this way.

A car with a damaged clutch may no longer have the capacity to propel itself along roads at high speeds, but it is a lot closer to having that capacity than a sack of potatoes. Many capacities are possessed by complex mechanisms of one kind or another (such as a car or a computer, or a brain), and depend on the proper functioning of many of the mechanism's parts. When the bearers of such capacities are damaged, it is intuitively plausible to say that the capacity can be lost or degraded to different degrees, depending on the degree of damage suffered: a car's capacity for self-powered motion is undermined by clutch-damage, but it is undermined to a greater extent in a car which has suffered clutch-damage *and* total engine failure. To accommodate this sort of case we can say that an entity x has a *defective* potentiality for producing E in C if it does not actually possess the causal capabilities (or power-base) required to produce E in C, but could acquire these if subjected to certain alterations of a fairly minor sort. For the reasons just outlined, powers can be defective to different degrees; when the damage to a car is very severe, so many new parts may be needed when it comes to be repaired that it may be unclear whether the original car has survived. The important point to note is whenever x possesses P, irrespective of whether P is active, inhibited, or neutralized, it possesses the appropriate power-base, but when an object possesses a defective potentiality P this power-base is lacking. If we take a strict view, a genuine or real potentiality cannot continue to exist as a defective potentiality; on becoming defective to the slightest degree the potentiality ceases to be.

Moving on, some potentialities are potentialities to *acquire potentialities*, usually with the proviso that certain background conditions obtain. A burglar alarm fitted to a house will be triggered (and hence make lots of noise) if windows or doors are opened, but only if the alarm is armed: an armed system has an active intruder detection capacity, a disarmed system does not. A disarmed system on a timer, a system which will arm itself at a certain time (as measured by its own internal clock) has the potential to acquire an intruder detection capacity: it has a *second-order potentiality*. Cases such as this could be interpreted in another way: we could say that the timed system *does* have a first-order intruder detection capacity, but an inhibited one. But there are other cases which are not open to this interpretation. A fertilized human egg does not have the capacity to think, but it has the capacity to gain this capacity if left to its own devices in the right sort of environment. These second-order potentialities are genuine rather than defective. The capacity a fertilized egg has to acquire the capacity for thought—by first developing into a more complex organism—exists in the form of an internal power-base which (under normal background conditions) does not need to be altered or augmented for it to develop in the required way. The newly fertilized egg's second-order capacity is not an inhibited capacity: its capacity for thought is not being blocked in some way, it has yet to develop. Of course, second-order potentialities *can* be inhibited, if there is an internal blocking factor which impedes development. They can also be neutralized, for example by freezing a fertilized egg. These second-order potentialities are merely at the first rung of a hierarchy: a third-order potentiality is the potentiality to acquire a second-order potentiality, a fourth-order potentiality is the potentiality to acquire a third-order potentiality, and so on.

Finally, we can distinguish *auto-activating* potentialities. These are first- rather than second-order capacities which do not require anything by way of a triggering event beyond the mere passage of time; on-going processes within the object will lead to the activation of the capacity in due course. Ordinary active potentialities will not activate unless the environment changes in the appropriate way. Fragility is a disposition which requires external activation (a sharp blow). But a radioactive substance will undergo decay of its own accord, and so its potential for decay is auto-activating.

10.3. BRAINS

How do these distinctions apply to a human brain's capacity to sustain or produce consciousness? I stress again that our ignorance means we must be cautious here, but we can make some reasonable surmises. To simplify matters let us say that a brain's *C-potential* (or its *C-capacity*) consists of all the different forms of experience it can generate; if a brain possesses a C-capacity it does so because it possesses or constitutes an appropriate power-base, or *C-base*.

The *active* C-potential of a typical (human) subject is responsible for that subject's entire phenomenal range, that is all the different forms and combinations of experiences they are capable of enjoying during their normal waking life, when none of their experiential powers are blocked or impeded in any way. If the triggering conditions for an active experiential power arise, the power manifests; an active power is not always being exercised, but it is ready to do so. Show a normally-functioning person a red object and they will experience red; make some noise and they will experience sound, tickle them and they will feel a tickling sensation—tell them the Earth is flat and they will think you are joking or deranged (probably). As I have already noted, some experiential powers belonging to the same subject are opposed, and so cannot be exercised at the same time, for example the capacity to have a visual field completely filled with blue, and one completely filled with red. But such powers are nonetheless active, since they would be activated by their normal triggering conditions, they simply cannot be active together.

There are various ways certain aspects of a brain's C-capacity might be *inhibited.* A blood clot or tumour might temporarily prevent one from enjoying a specific mode of sensory experience; remove the obstruction and normal service resumes. Drugs might produce the same sort of limited effect. More importantly, dreamless sleep could be seen as involving a temporary inhibition of a brain's C-capacity.[2] Tickle someone in a deep sleep and they do not feel anything; more generally, while we are soundly asleep our sensory systems do not respond in their usual way to their usual stimuli. But if the relevant systems are stimulated sufficiently strongly or persistently, we will generally wake up, and regain normal sensory awareness. An easy and straightforward explanation of these facts is available. Since the C-capacities of a sleeping subject can usually be quickly reactivated we have every reason to suppose that the brain's C-base remains perfectly intact during ordinary sleep. So perhaps what differentiates sleep from the ordinary waking state is that, during the former, the brain itself prevents our sensory capacities from being activated by their normal external triggers. If this is right, falling into dreamless sleep merely inhibits these capacities for a while, and since we generally wake up of our own accord, our C-capacities are auto-activating, at least in the case of ordinary sleep.

In fact, the difference between being awake and asleep is by no means so straightforward. There are empirical findings which suggest that although our sensory (or perceptual) systems *are* inhibited while we are asleep—both when we are dreaming and when we are not—there are also further factors at work. More specifically, while certain brain-systems must be active in order for the brain to be in a waking state, it is also the case that certain other brain-systems must *not* be active. One such system is the ventrolateral preoptic nucleus (VPN), which contains neurons that are active during sleep, and whose activity appears to be necessary for normal sleep: there is evidence that drugs which suppress the activity of this system promote wakefulness (Baars 2004). An example of the former type of system is the ascending reticular activating system: the cerebral cortex can only function in normal waking mode when it

---

[2] Assuming such a thing as dreamless sleep exists. While the assumption that dreaming is confined to REM sleep may be simplistic, it does not follow that dreaming occurs throughout all phases of non-REM sleep.

is receiving signals from the brain stem transmitted by this system; moreover, when this system is damaged coma results—and suppressing its activity by drugs produces unconsciousness. The reticular system is also thought to play a role in controlling the sleeping and waking cycle (and hence accounts in part for the fact that a sleeping person's C-potential is auto-activating—their brain 'turns itself on').[3] In the present context, the important point is that normal dreamless sleep seems to involve the brain's C-potential being both inhibited by internal factors, but also neutralized by various internal agencies, for example when the activity of the VPN makes the difference between a subject's being conscious or unconscious.

Although we would need a better understanding of the way in which neural systems actually produce experience to know precisely how to characterize an unconscious brain in terms of inhibiting and neutralizing factors, the key point for present purposes is that a brain can be *in perfect working order* at a given time, yet be incapable of exercising any of its experiential powers. This is by no means an uncommon predicament. Metal paperclips have the capacity to bend without snapping, but only if they are at the right temperature; a deeply-cooled paperclip is not in the right kind of condition to exercise its capacity for bending without snapping. In a somewhat similar fashion, a normal brain possesses a C-capacity, but for this capacity to be exercised the brain must be in a certain condition: there are certain systems inside the brain which must be active, systems which (presumably) could not generate consciousness all by themselves, and certain systems which must be dormant. A somewhat closer analogy might be a car with its engine ticking over; the car has the capacity to move under its own power, but for it to do so the clutch must be released, so as to allow the engine to move the wheels; a car's transmission system cannot move anywhere by itself, but a car cannot move unless it possesses such a system in working order, and appropriately engaged.

What of consciousness-eradicating general anaesthetics? Quite how these work is not yet fully understood, but they evidently alter the internal chemical environment in the brain in a way which renders an otherwise perfectly healthy brain incapable of producing experience: another instance of internal neutralization, but this time imposed from without. The notion of a neutralized potentiality is also needed to make sense of the condition of brains in rather less familiar conditions. Suppose advances are made in cryogenic techniques, and it becomes possible to super-freeze a brain, bringing an immediate halt to all neural activity, and then at a later time super-thaw it, without causing any tissue damage, or any impairment in experiential potential. It is very plausible to regard a super-frozen brain as still possessing the capacity for consciousness, but a neutralized capacity. The paperclip analogy seems the appropriate one here: a brain can only exercise

---

[3] The real picture is considerably more complex, and involves a greater number of inhibitory and excitatory mechanisms—for a taste of it see Pace-Schott and Hobson (2002).

its capacity for consciousness if it is at the right temperature, and it may be that the power-base associated with consciousness can remain intact at temperatures where it cannot produce consciousness.

10.4. CYCLICAL SUBJECTS

Suppose there were a species of subjects—that to which Maggot belongs, say—who sleep at regular intervals, just as we do, but for whom (ordinary) sleep is rather more profound. In this variant of the Maggot scenario, on falling asleep our simple subject does not merely lose consciousness, he loses the capacity for consciousness: his brain undergoes an internal modification which renders it incapable of producing consciousness for the next eight hours. Why? Because his brain's C-base undergoes quite widespread changes, and these alterations render all his experiential powers defective: their normal triggers produce no experiential response. After a period of eight hours, further changes occur in his brain, solely as a consequence of natural law, and his C-base is restored, along with a full complement of experiential powers. Maggot's experiential powers are thus *cyclical*: sometimes he has them, sometimes he does not. According to the C-theory, a subject only persists through periods of unconsciousness by possessing C-related experiential powers. This delivers the result that each time Maggot falls asleep he ceases to exist; the subject who awakes in his body eight hours later is a new, numerically distinct, subject. The trouble is that, intuitively, it seems wrong to say that *cyclical subjects*—as I will call them—cease to exist every time they fall asleep.

This problem has wider ramifications than might initially be obvious. Given our ignorance about the matter–consciousness relationship and the workings of our own brain, can we be sure that our own experiential powers remain intact during exceptionally profound brief periods of dreamless sleep? This is not very likely, granted—ordinary sleep does not seem to involve such profound neural changes—but it could easily be otherwise with some coma-like states. And we cannot rule out the possibility that there might be some subjects (e.g. Maggot, in the scenario just outlined) whose experiential powers are naturally cyclical. What can we say about such subjects?

There are several ways of approaching this issue. We could adopt a hard-line stance, bite the bullet, and hold that cyclical subjects would be consecutive or serial beings, and hence that a succession of numerically distinct subjects inhabit their bodies. Since I think this position is an implausible one, a solution which yields the result that cyclical subjects survive through their sleep cycles would be preferable. One way of arriving at such a solution would be to suspend the requirement that our account of subject-persistence be 'pure' or non-disjunctive. We could hold that in the case of cyclical subjects, when C-relatedness breaks down, sameness of body or brain takes over in securing subject-persistence. But I noted some reasons for rejecting a mixed solution of this kind in §4.1, and these reasons remain valid. It is implausible to suppose that a subject's continued existence is secured by entirely different factors at different times. Ideally, we want an account of our persistence that appeals to a single type of unifying relationship, one that binds all stages of a subject's life into a consubjective ensemble. One way to achieve this desideratum runs as follows.

Since a cyclical subject's defective powers are self-restoring, requiring no outside intervention (other than appropriate background conditions), we can regard their C-bases as possessing *second-order* experiential powers. They may lack experiential capacities in the ordinary sense of the term, but they have the capacity to acquire such capacities. Second-order capacities can be as real as first-order capacities, provided one condition is met: that the power-base of the second-order capacity is a system which does not need to be augmented or altered, relative to standard background conditions, in order for it to generate or acquire the relevant first-order capacity. Since cyclical subjects (of the kind we are currently concerned with) satisfy this condition, there is no obstacle to supposing that they possess second-order experiential powers during the periods when their first-order powers are defective. Hence the option exists for holding that a cyclical subject persists through periods of sleep by virtue of possessing experiential powers of a second-order type.

So far so good, but what we now need is a criterion of consubjectivity which applies to both first- and second-order experiential powers. We could say, simply, that first- and second-order powers are consubjective if and only if they have a common power-base. This would certainly do the job in the present case: when Maggot falls asleep the same physical systems which sustained his first-order powers sustain his second-order powers, as well as the first-order powers he has when he wakes up (or becomes able to). But while this might seem quite a natural solution—we are still defining subject-persistence in terms of experiential powers, of one sort or another—it is also true that we are now appealing to diachronic physical continuity in an essential way, something we have not hitherto been obliged to do.

There is an alternative route, one which allows us to continue to appeal to nothing more than experiential relationships in defining the conditions under which experiential powers are consubjective. We can achieve this by introducing a further species of potential co-consciousness. Two powers are *directly* potentially co-conscious, or DPC-related, if and only if they would produce co-conscious experience, if both were active. Let us now say that two powers are *potentially potentially co-conscious*, or PPC-related, if and only if one or both are second-order powers, and are such that if, contrary to actual fact, the second-order power (or powers) *were* first-order, they *would* be able to produce co-conscious experience, and so be DPC-related. This first step taken, we can now introduce the synchronic and diachronic forms of this relationship, *PPC$_S$-relatedness* and

PPC_D-*relatedness*. It is now a trivial task to incorporate these into an expanded definition of C-relatedness, one which embraces first- and second-order powers.[4]

If we want a way of linking first- and second-order powers without recourse to anything but actual and potential experiences and inter-experiential relations, the notion of PPC-relatedness does the trick, but not without a loss of simplicity. We are obliged to appeal to experiences a given power-base would be able to produce at a time t if it were physically different from how it actually is at t. Everything has a price; this loss of simplicity is the cost of purity.

Anyone disinclined to embrace second-order powers can adopt an alternative approach. While it is true that during their 'down-times' the power-bases of Maggot's C-system will not (and cannot) produce experience in response to their standard triggering circumstances, it is also true that, if left to their own devices, they will regain this capacity in a determinate period of time, thanks to their intrinsic constitution and the relevant natural laws. Such powers are, we might say, *nomologically self-restoring*. Needless to say, most defective powers do not fall into this category. (The computational capacities of my laptop changed from active to defective when it fell into a puddle; these capacities are most definitely not nomologically self-restoring, alas.) From a C-theoretical perspective it does not seem at all implausible to suppose that nomologically self-restoring powers can suffice to keep a subject in existence. Let us say that powers of this sort are *hibernating* during those periods when they are defective. We now need to specify the conditions under which hibernating powers are consubjective with (i) other hibernating powers, and (ii) normal non-hibernating powers. If we want to appeal as far as possible to experiential relationships, the obvious way to go is to rely on a version of the PPC-relationship that is defined in terms of hibernating rather than second-order powers. While this solution avoids recourse to second-order powers, it still has to appeal to counterfactual circumstances in which powers that are actually defective at a given time are not defective.[5]

10.5. CONGENIAL DECOMPOSITION

I want to turn now to the question of absoluteness. Save for the brief detour taking in cyclical subjects, we have been concerned thus far with normal, fully functional brains, systems which—intuitively at least—possess the capacity

[4] E.g. the account summarized at the start of §4.4 could be modified thus: the definition of S-relatedness in (1) is expanded to include PPC_S-related powers, and the definition of DPC_D-relatedness in (2) is expanded to include powers that are PPC_D-related.

[5] Although I cannot see anything illegitimate in so doing, it is also true that I criticized the Proximity variant of Foster's approach (in §5.4) for relying on other-worldly considerations of an analogous sort. The difference is that the appeal to counterfactuals currently under consideration only applies in the special case of cyclical subjects, whereas the Proximity approach uses it to deal with all lapses into unconsciousness.

required to sustain a subject in existence, but in situations in which this capacity is in some manner impaired or disabled without being eliminated. Cases such as profound dreamless sleep, anaesthesia-induced unconsciousness and cryogenic suspension fall into this category, as (arguably) do cyclical subjects. What can we say about the more difficult cases, those involving badly damaged or underdeveloped brains? The crucial distinction here is between brains which possess a genuine C-capacity and those which possess no more than a defective C-capacity. The issue we need to explore is whether a brain's C-base is something whose existence and persistence is all-or-nothing.

Although we know the neurophysiological structure the typical human brain possesses is sufficient for a C-capacity, and we also suspect that certain neural structures within the brain are necessary for consciousness, we are currently far from knowing all there is to know about the sort of neurological changes a human brain can undergo without entirely losing the capacity to produce experience of some kind. Nor do we know the minimum neurophysiological requirements for such a capacity; we do not know how simple a live and functioning neuronal structure can be and still be able to sustain experience of some kind. Nonetheless, the fact is that we are concerned with a capacity for a very distinctive sort of effect, conscious experience of some sort or other. Perhaps this fact is all that we need to determine whether the existence of a C-capacity is all-or-nothing. Unger's *spectrum of congenial decomposition* provides a useful way of approaching this question (1990: 60–6, 191–9).

Unger's spectrum consists of a sequence of cases. We begin with a normal human being, and by very gradually removing cells from this organism, one by one, and never replacing them, we end up with a single cell floating in a bath of nutrient fluids. It is useful to consider this case in first-personal terms: *you* are the person involved. At the start of the sequence, your C-capacity is wholly unimpaired, and indeed continues to be exercised for quite some time; but at the end of the sequence it seems certain that there is no such capacity, all that remains of your body is a single brain cell; if we take it that a single brain cell does not have the potentiality to produce consciousness, then at some point during the cell-removal process, or over some interval, this capacity ceased to be, and you with it.[6] This gradual decomposition is *congenial* because the cell-removal process is carried out in a manner designed expressly to keep you in existence for as long as possible. We begin by removing the cells that are least important to your survival, for example outer layers of skin cells. When removing a cell threatens to cause bleeding, appropriate steps are taken to minimize the risk to the remainder of the organism. If two cells are equally important, then one is arbitrarily chosen and removed before the other. As the decomposition proceeds upwards and inwards, and whole organs are first incapacitated and

---

[6] Anyone who thinks single neurons *can* sustain consciousness can suppose the spectrum terminates with some sub-cellular component, e.g. a single neuronal nucleus.

then removed, life-support machinery is brought into play to keep what remains as healthy as possible. Unger stipulates that: 'Matters are always made most congenial, or most conducive, for the candidate to be functioning optimally: They are most conducive, first, for the candidate entity to be alive and well, second, for that healthy living candidate to be thinking and experiencing and, third, for that living, thinking, experiencing candidate to be me' (1990: 62), What Unger refers to as the 'candidate' here is that part of what remains of your body after any given cell-removal that is the leading contender for being the causal ground for those mental processes and capacities that are necessary to your continued survival. So, as the rest of your body is gradually removed, especial care is taken to ensure that your brain receives the blood supply and nutrients it needs.

At quite an advanced stage along the spectrum all that remains of your body is your still-intact brain floating in a tank of nutrient fluids. When your sensory organs are removed, electrodes are fitted to the appropriate sites in the brain to keep you provided with sensory stimulation, the aim being to ensure your nervous system (or its remains) continues to possess and exercise its C-capacity for as long as possible. The sequence in which your brain-cells are removed is selected with the same goal in mind. At present we do not know what this sequence would be, but there must be such a sequence.[7] Given that conservative estimates put the number of neurons in the average brain at around a hundred billion, if the cell-removals take place at anything like normal surgical speed the entire process would take a considerable time. So, just as we grant our imaginary surgical team complete omniscience with respect to the neural structures that subserve consciousness, we grant them inhuman speed. Let us suppose the dismantling of your entire brain is accomplished in a mere eight hours. It may be that your diminishing brain cannot go eight hours without sleep, so at certain points, although you retain some experiential capacities, it may be that 'rest periods' are needed. If so, the cell-removal process is halted until your brain has recovered sufficiently to permit the reactivation of your C-capacities, at which point it proceeds as before.

At the far end of the spectrum only a single neuron remains, surrounded by all the life-support systems needed to keep it alive and healthy. Assuming that this neuron cannot generate experience of any kind, what can we say about the fate of your C-capacity? Remember that matters are so arranged during this spectrum of congenial decomposition that this capacity is exercised for as long as possible. Now, suppose we make the assumption that consciousness itself is absolute, that is, that a mode of being whose intrinsic nature is neither wholly experiential nor wholly non-experiential is an impossibility.[8] If consciousness is all-or-nothing, the

---

[7] If there are several equally good sequences, we choose one of the latter at random.

[8] At this point, the argument begins to diverge from anything Unger would endorse, since he rejects the idea that consciousness is absolute. His main argument for this rejection (1990: 203–6)

stream of consciousness produced by a brain undergoing congenial decomposition cannot fade away until there is no fact of the matter as to whether any experience is still being produced. Like a point of light receding into the distance, the stream can fade and diminish, but there comes a point when it vanishes altogether. It is certainly the case that as a brain becomes less complex as a result of progressive cell-loss it becomes unable to sustain the more complex forms of experience, such as conscious thoughts. But even simple forms of experience, such as sensations of pain or colour, have distinctive phenomenological characteristics; there is definitely something it is like to have experience of a visual kind, even if the phenomenal characteristics of the experience are not very clear or distinct (think of a blind person gradually regaining their sight, and the confusing nature of their very first visual experiences).

Bearing this in mind, let us return to the spectrum of decomposition and consider the final phases of your stream of consciousness. As the cell-removals continue, this stream becomes weaker and less varied, but it continues all the same. Then, all at once, with the removal of one particular cell, it comes to an end. Right up to this point there was experience, albeit of an impoverished kind, now there is none at all. Why think the removal of a single cell is the cause of the change at the experiential level? Because we are currently working on the assumption that experience causally supervenes upon the neurophysiological, so for any experiential change to take place, there must be a corresponding neurophysiological change. Prior to the removal of the critical cell, the remnants of your brain were active and sustaining a stream of consciousness; the bio-electrical supporting systems would have kept these remaining neural structures healthy and functioning in the same manner indefinitely. So the only significant change at the neurophysiological level which can explain the sudden cessation of consciousness is the loss of a further nerve cell; had this cell not been removed, your final stream of consciousness would have continued on. Furthermore, since matters are so arranged that your remaining C-capacity is being constantly exercised, your capacity for consciousness does not outlast your final stream of consciousness; this stream ends only when your capacity for experience is no more, and when this point is reached, you have ceased to be.

---

is far from conclusive. It rests on a spectrum of cases in which a brain is split into many parts, which continue to communicate with each other by radio transceivers; at the near end of the spectrum, when the brain is not separated into very many parts, the parts continue (jointly) to produce experience, but farther along the spectrum, when the brain is divided into many more parts, a 'grey area for consciousness' occurs. But if we envisage a world in which spatially separated brain-parts can generate consciousness at the near end of this spectrum, I don't see why they should not continue to do so farther along, or until they suddenly cease to do so when a certain distance threshold is reached. Also, at a more general level, and as I pointed out earlier (§8.3), Unger does not himself take the view that *we* would persist for as long as our capacity for consciousness persists: come the point when his psychological sophistication is no greater than that of a dog, Unger takes the view that he would no longer exist, in his stead is someone else, a sub-personal subject. I have given my reasons for rejecting this view.

Does this reasoning demonstrate that a brain's C-potential is absolute? At the very least it comes very close: it seems to show that whether a portion of living neural tissue possesses such a potential can depend upon the presence or absence of a single cell. What is striking is that the argument does not presuppose any detailed understanding of the neurophysiological underpinnings of consciousness (which is just as well since we lack such an understanding). But if the argument is successful, we can know that there can be a definite point at which a brain's capacity for consciousness disappears.

10.6. ASSESSMENTS

Does the line of reasoning sketched out above succeed in establishing that neural C-potential is all-or-nothing? It requires two substantial premises (i) that human experience is causally dependent upon the neurophysiological, and (ii) that experience is absolute. Neither of these assumptions is unreasonable. The causal dependence doctrine accords with the stance of moderate naturalism I am currently adopting. Our ignorance about the neurophysiological prerequisites for experience mean that we cannot say at what point along the spectrum someone's capacity for experience disappears, since we do not know how few (or which) brain cells a person needs to retain the capacity to have experiences. But the argument's conclusion is only that there has to be *some* particular cell whose removal would have a critical effect, in the envisaged circumstances. As for the idea that experience is absolute, I think this may well be the case: we are unable to conceive of a mode of being which is not clearly of an experiential kind, nor clearly of a non-experiential kind. We find the following idea readily intelligible: there are possible worlds in which only a single brief burst of experience occurs, and these worlds include something, for however brief a time, of a kind wholly unlike anything to be found in worlds in which no experience ever occurs. Although this form of absolutism is most at home in a dualistic setting, those who think consciousness is a physical phenomenon have the option of holding it to be a quite distinctive kind of physical phenomenon, one which is realized in complex neurophysiological states but not sticks and stones. Of course, someone hostile to the absoluteness (of experience) doctrine could argue that when we find out more about how matter gives rise to experience, everything will appear very different, and we will find there to be no sharp boundary separating material systems which are conscious and those which are not. But as things stand, this is speculation. The absoluteness of the experience doctrine may well be true, and I shall assume, tentatively, that it is.

But even with this assumption we should be wary of generalizing from a single imaginary case, especially one as contrived as the spectrum of congenial decomposition. First of all, the case involves certain questionable assumptions, and second, when we consider more realistic cases of death by brain degeneration (still from the perspective of moderate naturalism and the C-theory), some important differences emerge. The argument for the absoluteness of subjects based on Unger's spectrum is, for these reasons, problematic. By considering the following series of objections to the argument we can achieve a clearer perspective on the issue in question.

In the context of Unger's spectrum, there is no difficulty whatsoever in describing the conditions under which someone's C-capacity ceases to be. It is stipulated that this capacity is *being exercised* right up to the point when the cell-removal process finally gets the better of it, and so the capacity is no more when experience is no longer being produced. The sudden loss of any kind of consciousness—even though we might not be able to tell when it occurs looking on from the outside—at least allows us to state the conditions under which a C-capacity is no more. In real-life cases, however, we are rarely in a position to do this. Someone sliding into a deeper and deeper coma might have been unconscious for a considerable period before their C-capacity is finally obliterated by progressive neural degeneration.

While this is true, the fact that a capacity is not being exercised does not cast any shadow on the existence of the capacity itself, for it can be a perfectly determinate fact that should certain (perfectly standard) triggering circumstances arise, the capacity would be activated and a particular effect produced, even though none of this actually occurs and the capacity remains dormant. So the fact that a subject is unconscious when they die as a consequence of progressive neural deterioration does not, in itself, mean that there is not a sharply delineated point at which their brain loses the capacity to sustain consciousness. We may be unable to tell when this point is reached, but there might be such a point.

The very *congeniality* of Unger's spectrum distinguishes it from real-life cases of gradual brain-death. During the critical phase of this spectrum, we have a carefully selected portion of living neural tissue, call this N, hooked up to a mass of supporting equipment. Just before the final critical cell is removed, N is a power-base capable of producing experience of a primitive kind—in other words N is a neural structure capable of producing experience all on its own, when provided with appropriate stimulation. The supporting equipment not only keeps N alive and functioning, but provides the necessary stimulation to trigger its experiential potential. But in real-life cases, when a comatose brain is gradually deteriorating, even if a healthy N-type tissue mass could exist in such a brain, the remainder of the brain might be unable to provide it with the stimulation necessary to activate its C-potential. Does such a brain still possess a capacity for consciousness?

We might reasonably regard this as an instance in which it is indeterminate whether a brain possesses a C-potential. But this does not mean the existence of the C-potential is indeterminate; at most, what is indeterminate is whether the *brain* in question possesses this potential, and does so *as a whole*. The existence of the C-potential is secure in virtue of the existence of the healthy N-type tissues, which constitute only part of the remaining brain. These tissues constitute a genuine C-base because they are able to produce their normal range of experiences in response to their normal triggering conditions—or at least, their normal *local* or *proximate* triggering conditions. If N produces visual experience, then at the more extreme locations along the spectrum, these tissues will be being stimulated by electrodes—rather than signals passed along the optical nerve—but we can suppose (or stipulate) that the electrodes produce the same local changes in N as signals produced in the usual manner. Provided this condition is satisfied, we can say that a *part* of the comatose brain in question does possess a C-potential, but this potential is inhibited or neutralized by other parts of the same brain. But an inhibited or neutralized potentiality is still a potentiality.

But all this presupposes a sharp distinction between triggering processes and power-bases. Perhaps the brain does not work in this way. We have been assuming that N consists of neural tissues that produce experience when triggered by some process or event. For example, some individual neurons in N might require electrical or chemical stimulation, or perhaps the stimulation has to be applied to many neurons at the same time, or the concentration of certain chemicals throughout the entire tissue mass has to reach a certain level. But in actual fact the triggering process (whatever it is) may work by changing the intrinsic properties of N, thereby altering or augmenting its causal capacities. In which case, rather than saying N has the capacity to produce consciousness, it might be more appropriate to say that N has the capacity to play a role in a more inclusive consciousness-producing process.

The process which triggers N may well alter its intrinsic properties in some way, but this does not mean the distinction between triggering circumstances and power-base is no longer applicable. It is *usually* the case that the events which trigger the dispositional properties of complex material things affect their intrinsic features. When I flick a switch to turn on my radio the resulting changes are not confined to the spatial position of the switch: electrons flood through the whole system, creating a vast number of physical changes in various sub-systems. The same applies when I turn on my dishwasher or start my car. So the fact that N is changed by being triggered does not mean that N does not possess the capacity to produce experience: it can possess this capacity in just the same way as a radio can possess the capacity to produce sound, or a car-engine has the power to generate heat or motion. That said, it is certainly true that N can only produce experience if the right background conditions (temperature, pressure, etc.) obtain. But again, as we have already seen, this is how things are with most dispositions: my radio will not function in strong electro-magnetic fields, or in very high temperatures, or underwater. Quite generally dispositions exist as elements of a broader causal field.

There is a more straightforward objection to the argument for absoluteness. Even if we grant that removing a single cell at some point along Unger's spectrum could render a system such as N incapable of generating experience, this inability is relative to *normal* local triggering conditions. Consider the situation a few cell-removals along from the cut-off point. Although N is now incapable of producing experience in response to the range of (local) triggering events which would previously have sufficed, N is a lot closer to being able to produce experience in response to that range of triggers than a lump of iron or a hunk of cheese: N's C-potential is *defective*, in the sense introduced earlier, but only slightly so. Moreover, if we expand the original range of triggering conditions to include the immediate replacement of the crucial cells, N's C-potential would be immediately restored. Given all this, is it not more plausible to hold that N's C-potential gradually fades away as the cell-removals continue, rather than disappearing in an all-or-nothing fashion at one particular point?

The difficulty for the absolutist posed by this objection is quite general. Even if there is a sharp distinction between a brain (or any other complex physical system) which possesses a capacity for consciousness and one which does not, there are different ways of losing this capacity. Problematic borderline cases arise if the damage suffered *only just* obliterates the neural basis of consciousness—or what would ordinarily be regarded as such—and does so in such a manner that only relatively minor repairs to the brain are required to restore its C-potential. These minor changes could easily be viewed as reasonable extensions to the original (narrower) range of triggering circumstances for the relevant system. If it is nomologically impossible to perform such repairs there seems little doubt that the subject no longer exists. If, however, such repairs can be effected, and are in fact carried out, then the situation is quite different: it may well seem ridiculous to claim the subject died as a result of their injuries, and that the repairs made on the brain created a numerically different subject. Even if the repairs are not in fact carried out, or are beyond current (but perhaps not future) surgical techniques, provided the damage is slight and the damaged brain is preserved unchanged, can it be right to say the subject has clearly and definitively perished? Or suppose the damaged brain, if given enough time, has the ability to repair itself by regenerating the damaged cells?

The latter kind of case poses no problem. Damaged but self-restoring brains (or experience-producing systems) are simply another instance of the phenomenon of 'cyclical' subjects we encountered earlier, and the same diagnosis is applicable. Even though brains of such subjects no longer possess first-order experiential powers, they nonetheless possess second-order experiential powers, and these can be PPC-related to one another and first-order powers. The more difficult cases are those in which the brains in question will only regain first-order experiential powers with the aid of outside intervention, and so are lacking the second-order powers that can plausibly be regarded as being sufficient to keep a subject in existence. Cases of this kind pose a dilemma for the C-theory, but not an insuperable problem. There are two basic options: we can opt for tolerance, and allow a range of borderline cases, or we can opt for a strict response and say that as soon as a brain loses its C-potential, the subject it was sustaining no longer exists, and if the same brain later regains a C-potential, a new subject comes into being. There is something to be said in favour of each of these responses.

In favour of the tolerant response is the intuitive implausibility of regarding a seemingly insignificant amount of neural damage as fatal, especially if (i) the damage is not irreversible (at the moment there is not much we can do to repair neural damage, but this may not always be so), and (ii) the damage affects the brain's C-potential but leaves much of the subject's distinctive psychology (memories, personality traits, etc.) intact. Those inclined to adopt the tolerant approach can do so without abandoning the C-theory; all that is required is a minor modification. The C-theory states that a subject's persistence requires a continuous potentiality for co-conscious experience. If we want to say a subject can survive the envisaged neural damage we can correctly note that their brain retains a defective potentiality for experience for the period in question, and hold that a slightly defective potentiality for experience suffices to keep a subject in existence. And this is by no means absurd. After all, there is no denying that a slightly damaged brain is considerably closer to possessing a genuine C-potential than a healthy liver, since only very slight modifications to the brain would restore its full C-potential, whereas this is certainly not true of the liver.

But there is a downside. If we are prepared to accept that defective capacities for consciousness are sufficient to sustain a subject, we must also be prepared to accept a wide range of borderline cases, cases in which it is (seemingly) indeterminate whether or not a subject still exists or persists. For as I noted earlier, the notion of a defective potentiality is potentially very broad. There is certainly no sharp boundary at which a degenerating mass of brain tissues ceases to possess a defective C-potential; depending on the available medical skills and resources, it may be nomologically possible to reconstruct a brain possessing C-potential from the most unpromising materials. Degenerating brains are in one respect akin to houses falling into disrepair: there comes a point when it is not clear that the restored object is of the same kind as the initial object. They differ in that, at the moment at least, we can often restore even badly damaged houses to something closely approximating their original condition, but we cannot do so very much for brains. The tolerant approach has the perhaps surprising consequence that even if the existence of experiential capacities is an all-or-nothing affair, as the argument from congenial decomposition suggests it might be, the existence of the subjects that these capacities sustain is not.

As for the strict option, one thing in its favour is the possibility of avoiding difficult borderline cases. If the existence of our brains' C-potentials were in fact an all-or-nothing affair, then by defining our persistence conditions in terms of non-defective C-potentialities we could ensure that the boundaries of our lives are as clear and sharp as can be. Standing in the way of this appealing prospect is the intuitive implausibility of the idea that brief interruptions in genuine C-potentiality of the kind just discussed can be fatal, precisely the consideration that lends appeal to the tolerant approach. For reasons outlined in §1.1, it is unlikely that any account of self-identity could be fully compatible with all the intuitions imaginary cases are capable of arousing, and perhaps we are now confronting a case in point. But perhaps not. There are considerations which go at least some way towards explaining why we might find it difficult to reconcile ourselves to the idea that the loss of genuine C-potential puts an end to a subject's existence, even when in other respects their body and brain are in such good condition that if their C-potential *were* restored, the post-restoration subject would be psychologically very similar to (or continuous with) their pre-restoration predecessor. When these considerations are made explicit, the resistance to this idea significantly lessens, even if it does not altogether vanish.

Let us consider one such case, and call the pre- and post-restoration subjects X and Y. A useful first step is to consider more closely the relationships which continue to exist between X and Y in the absence of C-relatedness, namely psychological and bodily continuity. As we have seen, in the absence of consciousness or the capacity for it, neither of these continuities taken singly is sufficient to keep us in existence; they do not come remotely close. Why should the situation be any different when they are combined? Can adding zero to zero ever add up to anything more than zero? When X's C-potential disappears, X *qua* phenomenal subject ceases to exist, utterly and completely. And since Y is related to X by continuities that are insufficient to keep a subject in existence, Y cannot possibly be numerically the same subject as X.

Probing more deeply, we saw in §6.6 that although P-continuity is an important component of what matters in survival in the desirability sense of the term, by itself—in the absence of C-relatedness—it fails to conserve what matters in the prudential sense. Recall the case of informational teleportation, and the way in which the absolute rupture in C-relatedness prevents our self-interested concern extending to the P-related replica. Recall also the scenario in which C-relatedness and P-relatedness come apart, and the way in which our self-interested concern remains resolutely locked onto actual and potential phenomenal continuity. If our self-interested concern fails to pass through ruptures in C-relatedness in these sorts of case, why should it be any different in the present case? Where are the relevant differences? There are none.

There is yet a further consideration to bear in mind. Psychological continuity in the absence of C-relatedness is not sufficient to keep us in existence, but as we saw in §6.6 and §6.7, a case can be made for taking it to be a genuine mental relationship of a by no means insignificant sort. Since there is a real sense in which X's mind—or rather, one aspect of it—lives on in Y, it is scarcely surprising that we find it easy to believe that X survives the loss of his C-potential: a significant *mental aspect* of X does survive, even if X does not. Once this fact is fully and explicitly appreciated, it becomes easier still to accept that X and Y are distinct subjects of consciousness, despite our initial inclinations to suppose the contrary.

Pulling these various strands together, where do we stand? We are confronted with a choice: a strict version of the C-theory which equates subject-persistence with C-related experiential powers that are genuine capacities for consciousness, or a tolerant version that also embraces moderately defective experiential powers. I find myself equally well-disposed to both, others may be differently disposed. The strict version offers the advantage of at least the possibility of absoluteness for subjects such as ourselves, and this may well be a significant point in its favour.

But, as we have seen, whether subjects of our kind are beings whose existence is all or nothing depends on whether experience itself is absolute, and whether (non-defective) capacities for experience are absolute, and we are not yet in a position to be entirely confident about whether these conditions are satisfied.

We have been considering, from a moderately naturalistic standpoint, the ways subjects can cease to be, subjects whose mental lives depend on brains in the ways ours do. What can be said of the ways such subjects initially come to be? Is there a sharp boundary between being and non-being at the beginning of a subject's existence? So far as I can see, exactly the same considerations apply to both ends of a subject's career. A developing human embryo does not (I take it) develop the capacity for consciousness until its nervous system reaches a certain level of complexity. In its early days, an embryo is an entity which possesses only the capacity to acquire a capacity for consciousness. If experiential capacities are all-or-nothing, then there is a first moment at which a developing embryo acquires a genuine first-order C-potential; prior to this point the embryo possesses only a (slightly) defective C-potential: a small modification of its developing brain would cause it to possess a genuine C-potential. Those who incline to the zero-tolerance approach to borderline cases can say that subjects come into existence when they first develop active C-potentials; those who are more favourably inclined to borderline cases can hold that subjects gradually *fade into existence* as their C-potentials become increasingly close to active status.

But bearing in mind our earlier discussion of cyclical subjects, there is a further option which some may find attractive. Human organisms may not have *first-order* experiential capacities for the first few weeks or months of their existence, but they do possess *second-order* experiential capacities: they have the capability of developing first-order capacities if left to their own devices in normal background conditions. Second-order capacities cannot be related to first-order capacities by DPC-relatedness, but they can be so related by PPC-relatedness. Hence the option exists of holding that human subjects come into existence, as *potentially* potentially conscious beings, at the very moment of fertilization.

10.7. DEVIANCY

Take a heap of sand. Does it possess any experiential capacities? Of course not. But there is a way of re-arranging the heap's elementary particles so as to turn it into an organism indistinguishable from Maggot. Call the operations required to produce this transformation O. One of Maggot's visual capacities is for an *orange*-type experience, triggered, let us suppose, by circumstances of type C. We can now say that the heap of sand has a capacity for an *orange*-type experience, triggered by circumstances (O+C), where O turns the heap into something resembling Maggot, and C triggers the *orange*-type experience. The point generalizes. Take your capacity to visualize a Rembrandt self-portrait whenever you hear the word 'Rembrandt'. A pile of logs has just this capacity, but its triggering condition is rather more complex: it would first have to be turned into a being which resembled you. We can go further. A single hydrogen atom has the same experiential capacity: it is triggered by surrounding it with a human body of the relevant type, which is then exposed to the word 'Rembrandt'. The same holds for a region of empty space. It seems there are no limits whatsoever on the sorts of thing which possess experiential capacities, of any given kind.

If this reasoning were persuasive, then the distinction between genuine and defective experiential capacities would be undermined; worse, our grasp on what is involved in a thing's possessing a causal power would be undermined. How could it be otherwise if each and every object possesses each and every dispositional property? But of course the reasoning is not in the least persuasive: human brains have the capacity to generate experiences, hydrogen atoms do not; hydrogen bombs have the capacity to generate massive explosions, human brains do not, and nor do solitary hydrogen atoms, or points of empty space. Objects clearly *do* vary in their causal powers. So where does the reasoning go astray? What we need, it seems, is a way of distinguishing between deviant and non-deviant triggering events, for there is clearly something suspect about (so-called) triggering events which confer the power of conscious thought to lumps of rock, and devastating explosive powers to unoccupied spatial points.

One thing can be said straight away. In §4.5 we encountered a different kind of deviant triggering event, and I noted there that it is plausible to think that our ordinary thought and talk about dispositions is regulated by a (tacit) understanding of what standard (or non-deviant) triggering events are for a given kind of object. But it is one thing to say that we can recognize a non-standard trigger when one is presented to us, it is another to spell out precisely *why* a given case is deviant. Is it possible to say anything usefully informative about this? It is not too difficult to make some progress with the case of deviant triggers of the base-transforming kind. The trouble is, the most obvious and plausible way of explaining why such triggers are deviant might seem to threaten the autonomy of the C-theory.

Anyone trying to spell out precisely what is wrong with base-transforming triggers might reason as follows. Experiential powers are grounded in the laws of nature, they are *nomological potentialities*. Accordingly, we can straight away rule out of contention so-called triggering events which require a local suspension (or overruling) of the laws of nature. We need not regard a lump of cheese as possessing experiential powers on the grounds that a malicious minor deity could confer such powers on the lump by a wave of its magic wand if it so chose. We can confine our attention to combinations of power-bases and triggering events which produce their effects via the laws of nature. So far as these cases are concerned, a natural way of distinguishing between deviant and non-deviant triggering events is to hold that the former do not *augment* the properties of the object's power-base in ways that are causally relevant to its ability to produce the effect in question. Deviant triggering events, of the sort encountered above, do precisely this: they confer on objects power-bases which they previously lacked. An ordinary pile of logs has many dispositions, but the capacity to visualize a Rembrandt self-portrait is not amongst them; a triggering event which bestows this ability on the logs changes them massively (indeed, if we rule out miracles and magic, it would almost certainly eliminate them entirely). By contrast, when your capacity for this sort of experience is triggered by hearing the painter's name spoken aloud, the triggering event certainly causes changes to occur in your brain, but only of a minor kind—you certainly do not acquire experience-producing neural properties or structures that you previously lacked. Rather than unleashing *already extant* causal capacities, deviant triggering events *bring causal capacities into being and immediately activate them.*

This approach has some prima facie plausibility, but it will not do. As I noted in connection with Unger's spectrum of congenial composition, the events which trigger perfectly ordinary dispositions *usually* alter the causal properties of the object or system which possesses the disposition. When I switch on my radio and trigger its capacity to generate sound, I close a circuit within the radio, and allow current to flow along paths which were previously blocked. In so doing, I am altering or augmenting the causal powers of the radio in a way which is relevant to its ability to produce sound. Since similar considerations apply in a great many cases, the proposed criterion for deviancy clearly draws the line in the wrong place. However, a relatively minor alteration to the criterion improves matters considerably. What makes a triggering event deviant is not that it alters the target object, it is the *sort* of changes it produces. Generally speaking, dispositions are properties of objects of specific *kinds*, and specific kinds of objects have distinctive synchronic and diachronic identity conditions. The events which unleash an object's causal powers may induce changes in the object, but these changes must be among those permitted by the object's identity criteria, on pain of annihilating (and replacing) the object in question. Non-deviant triggers respect this constraint, deviant triggers (of the base-transforming kind) do not. Whenever I switch on my radio I change it in various ways, but these changes are among the kinds of change a *radio* can survive. It is otherwise with the changes that would need to be inflicted upon a lump of cheese in order to provide it with the sound-producing capabilities that my radio currently possesses: even if it were nomologically possible to transform the cheese in the required ways, the end result would not be a lump of cheese.

By way of an example that is more relevant to our main concern, we can consider one of Maggot's experiential capacities. Maggot possesses nine experiential powers grounded in three neural modules, his visual node V, his olfactory node O and his bodily-sensation node B, each of which possesses the power to produce three different kinds of sensory experience. Node V is a discrete physical structure. It is of course part of Maggot's body; it is embedded in his tissues and bodily fluids, and it is also connected to nodes O and B. But if V is removed from Maggot's body, and disconnected from B and O, it can still produce visual experiences, if appropriately stimulated (or so we can suppose). As a physical structure of a particular kind, V has its own synchronic and diachronic identity criteria, specifiable in bio-physical terms. As per usual, these criteria are such that V can survive some changes but not others: tickle V and its existence is not threatened, roast it with a blowtorch and it is gone in an instant. Some of the permissible changes V can undergo are produced by external agencies (e.g. the tickle), others are produced internally—as a living system, V is in constant turmoil.

The various changes V can survive correspond with the variety of different states V can be in, as specified by V's synchronic identity criteria. Among these permissible states are those V is in when it is producing experiences of types v_1, v_2, and v_3. Let us call these states S_1, S_2, and S_3 respectively. We can now define the various triggering conditions for the experiences V can produce in terms of these three states. C_1, the triggering conditions for v_1-type experiences, comprises the range of circumstances which cause V to enter S_1; C_2, the triggering conditions for v_2-type experiences, comprises the range of circumstances which cause V to enter S_2, and similarly for C_3, v_3, and S_3. These triggering conditions may be simple, but they need not be. There may be a number of different ways in which V can come to be in S_1. For example, certain types of signal passing into V through the optical nerve will cause V to enter S_1, provided at the time V is in one of a number of states $S_a \ldots S_i$. There may be another range of states, $S_j \ldots S_m$, which, should they occur, push V into S_1 in the absence of any optical stimuli—on these occasions Maggot hallucinates. There are other possibilities. For present purposes the key point is that the non-deviant triggering circumstances of v_1-type experience are all circumstances which cause a particular type of physical system to enter into one of its permissible states, a system which is *already in* one of the kinds of states permissible for it. The triggering circumstances do not *create* V-type systems, they do not change something which is not a V-type system into a V-type system, rather they act on a V-type system which already exists. Deviant triggering circumstances, of the kind which would convert a lump of rock into a V-type system *and then* produce experience, do not conform to this constraint.

The beginnings of a promising solution to the deviancy problem can now be discerned. Our ability to discriminate normal from abnormal triggering events is explained (in large part at least) by the fact that we work on the understanding that dispositions are possessed by objects of certain specific kinds—and these kinds are associated with specific existence and persistence conditions. If the causal powers we commonly recognize are constrained in this way, we avoid the absurd result that every physical thing, even regions of empty space, possess every possible experiential power. So far so good, but a different difficulty now looms. If we suppose this condition is built into our understanding of what counts as a non-deviant triggering event, then to what extent is the C-theory different from purely physical accounts of our persistence conditions? If (human) experiential powers are always possessed by physical systems of some specific *physical kind* or another, isn't the C-theory effectively equivalent to a version of the physical continuity theory?

Not at all, and for reasons which should by now be familiar. So far as the persistence conditions of subjects are concerned, it is quite conceivable that experiential capacities which reside in a succession of numerically distinct experience-producing physical systems, possibly of very different types, are C-related (diachronically) and so belong to the same subject. If I have been focusing latterly on subjects whose experiential capacities are grounded in a single biological organism it is because my main aim in this chapter has been to explore the implications of the C-theory for the issue of how sharp the temporal boundaries of subjects similar to ourselves can be. But the C-theory can of course apply to subjects whose experiential powers are entirely grounded in non-biological systems, and it can apply to subjects whose experiential powers are transferred from biological to non-biological systems: recall the consciousness-preserving NRT-procedures we looked at earlier. It should also be borne in mind that a single persisting experience-producing physical system may cease to sustain a subject (if it loses its experiential capacities) or sustain a succession of different subjects (if its experiential capacities are not diachronically C-related).

What of the synchronic level? The C-theory comes into play at a very general level: it tells us that for a subject S to exist at a given time t, S must possess one or more experiential powers at t. It has little more to say about subjects of the very simplest kind; if a subject possesses just one experiential power (for a primitive form of experience) at a given time t, the question 'What renders a subject's powers consubjective at t?' is inapplicable. But most subjects (it seems reasonable to assume) are more complex than this, and for such subjects the C-theory enters the picture once again: it provides us with an experiential criterion for determining which experiential powers belong to which subjects at any given time. To illustrate: we have assumed that Maggot's body contains three distinct power-modules, V, O, and B. What makes the experiential powers possessed by these modules consubjective? Not the fact that they are located within the same organism. Snip the connections and they remain within Maggot, but are no longer C-related, and hence no longer consubjective. But it is not the physical connections in themselves that render them consubjective: they could be indissolubly glued together, but unless they were C-related, they would not be consubjective. Indeed, there need not be *any* material connections at all between V, O, and B, they could conceivably be C-related at a distance. Individual power-modules may have physically specifiable identity criteria, but the conditions under which distinct co-existing power-modules are consubjective is specified in wholly experiential terms. The same point applies if we vary the scenario and suppose that Maggot's powers are all base-integrated. While there is no denying that some consubjective experiential powers are nomologically interdependent, as noted in §9.2, it is quite conceivable that nomologically interdependent powers could belong to different subjects; this sort of interdependence, in and of itself, does not make for C-relatedness and consubjectivity.

I will not go on, the main point should be clear enough. If experiential powers have bases or grounds which have physically specifiable identity conditions, then these physically specified identity conditions play a role in our account of subject-identity. But the role is a very limited one. Although our own experiential powers are grounded in certain types of physical system, being so grounded does not in itself render powers consubjective, and consubjective powers can (in principle) be grounded in different physical systems. In assigning powers to subjects, all the work is done by C-relatedness, which remains a purely experiential criterion for consubjectivity: simplifying only a little, so far as the C-theory is concerned, all that matters is whether experiential powers can contribute to unified states or streams of consciousness. Given the framework of moderate naturalism I have adopted it would be surprising if the existence and persistence of subjects were entirely independent of material considerations. We have seen that this is not the case. But we have also seen how limited a role these material considerations play.

10.8. TELEPORTATION REVISITED

The teleportation of macroscopic material objects is unlikely to be developed any time soon, and may indeed not be permitted by the laws in our universe—we do not yet understand these laws well enough to know for sure—but for my purposes this is largely irrelevant. Even if nomologically impossible, the procedure is a useful way of fleshing out the claim that it might be possible for psychological continuity to come apart from material and phenomenal continuities. To avoid needlessly complicating matters I have generally focused on a particular form of teleportation, one that is invariably a fatal procedure, at least if we take the C-theory as our guide to what is survivable and what is not. But for the benefit of those who take an interest in these speculative matters, it should be pointed out that the relationship between the C-theory and teleportation is rather more complicated than my earlier discussions may have suggested. Although some forms of teleportation are incompatible with one's survival, other forms are not. Since the issue hangs on the extent to which experiential powers are preserved (or put out of commission) by the particular process in question, this is the appropriate place to set the record straight.

The kind of teleportation discussed in §1.3 was of the purely informational variety. As will be recalled, a typical instance of this putative mode of transportation involves a person undergoing a destructive body-scan; the information gleaned from the scan is then stored in some passive medium—a large ledger, a computer's memory, a heap of plastic disks—and subsequently transmitted by radio waves to some distant location where it is used to construct an exact replica of the original person at the moment of their departure. Since, in our universe at least, objects such as ledgers and optical disks do not possess experiential capacities, this method of putative transportation would instantly annihilate the experiential powers of anyone making use of it. While it is hard to see how a process of this kind could be anything other than fatal from the point of view of the C-theory, there are conceivable forms of fast long-distance transportation that are far less hostile to phenomenal selves. Consider teleportation of the *material* kind, that is forms of teleportation which directly transfer a physical object to a distant location *without* first reducing the object to information, and without altering or diminishing the object's causal capabilities. If you had a teleportation machine of this kind and put your favourite painting in the transmission cubicle on Earth, you could be sure that the object which emerges from the reception cubicle on Mars is numerically the same object; not only qualitatively identical but composed of the same matter. If *you* were to step into the cubicle, your body would emerge on Mars a few minutes later, and you would do so too: if the causal capacities of your brain are unaffected by the transfer (let us suppose they are), its experiential capacities will be unaffected also—and if you choose to travel while awake, your stream of consciousness will exhibit just as much moment-to-moment phenomenal continuity as it ever does. Since variants of material teleportation that satisfy these constraints evidently preserve C-relatedness, from a C-theoretical perspective they are most definitely non-lethal.

As for whether material teleportation of this kind is a genuine nomological possibility in our universe, we do not yet know, but it might be. One promising option is the sci-fi staple of the wormhole: a short-cut through space–time that can, in principle, connect even the most far-flung regions of the universe. Travelling by wormhole can in principle be even faster than telegraphic teleportation, and since it does not involve any reconstruction or long-distance signalling—the interior of a wormhole is simply an ordinary expanse of space that is stretched in an unusual manner—it poses no threat whatsoever to the continued existence of one's experiential powers. Although the existence of wormholes appears to be permitted by the equations of general relativity, it is not yet known whether it will be a practical possibility to construct stable holes that are large enough for human-sized objects to travel through, but the possibility has not yet been definitively ruled out. Another possibility, perhaps rather more remote, is a variant of so-called 'quantum teleportation'. Under this procedure the quantum state of an object is embedded in an electromagnetic carrier wave after a destructive scan, and hence transmitted to some distant location where it is used to recreate an exact duplicate of the original object. On some views (cf. Greene 2004: ch. 15) there is no distinction between an object and its quantum state, so the re-created object *is* the original. But even if is the case, the prospects of successfully applying these methods to an object as complex as a human being are remote, to say the least.

One last point. Setting aside the as yet not fully understood subtleties of quantum entanglement and suchlike, the more familiar telegraphic informational teleportation may not be the dead-end it might seem. Variants in which the information gleaned from the destructive scan is stored for a time in some passive medium (such as a large ledger) may obviously and invariably be fatal. It is otherwise with *direct* variants, that is scenarios in which the scan data are transmitted directly to the reconstruction device, where they are immediately employed in the construction of a duplicate. Recall the cyclical subjects we encountered earlier in this chapter. I noted that it can seem implausible to suppose that a complete loss of experiential capacities is fatal if the loss is the by-product of a regular and reliable process which will restore the capacities if left to its own devices. In some such cases at least it is an option to hold that the system (or sequence of systems) that sustains the relevant process also sustains a single subject, by virtue of uninterrupted existence of second-order experiential capacities. Perhaps it is also an option to think of direct informational teleportation in a similar way: there is a controlled, reliable physical process, involving scanning machines, radio transmitters, and reconstruction devices which sustains a subject in being by sustaining second-order experiential capacities.

Standing in the way of this proposal is the time spent in transit. Travelling to Mars at the speed of light takes several minutes—can a sequence or pattern of radio waves really be said to possess even second-order experiential powers? Surely not; in which case, is it not clear that the subject has utterly ceased to be? Perhaps, but perhaps this does not matter: some might be prepared to admit the possibility of intermittent existence in such cases. For those who are not, there is another consideration to bear in mind. The special theory of relativity tells us that no time whatsoever passes for objects travelling at the speed of light. Photons do not age; from their point of view, they arrive as soon as they depart—and the same applies to the scan data transmitted during orthodox informational teleportation. Consequently, if you were to step into a teleportation cubicle on Earth and the destructive scanning process begins, there is a sense in which no time whatsoever would pass before the resulting information arrives at your intended destination and is processed by the reconstruction device. A lifeline of sorts for those unable or unwilling to pay the extra required for more traditional modes of transportation.

10.9. FROM EGOS TO C-SYSTEMS

The various issues I have been looking at over the past four chapters, although disparate, are all related by the theme of simplicity, in one way or another. Let us review the ground covered.

I began by considering two different ways in which subjects could be less complex than ourselves. One way is by possessing less complex minds, or what amounts to the same, less complex mental capacities. I suggested that there is no obvious obstacle to our accepting that some subjects—*simple* subjects—might have minds that are so rudimentary that they are capable of enjoying (or producing) only a few elementary forms of sensory experience. I then considered whether a subject need possess any mental capacities at all: could there be streams of consciousness that are not the product of nomological powers, and which are not associated with a dispositional psychology of any sort? It is difficult to know, but again it is hard to rule the possibility out altogether. I called subjects of this sort *minimal* because they possess so little by way of mentality. (Perhaps they do not possess *minds* in the usual sense of the term at all.) I called them *subjects* because I am assuming that we are essentially subjects, and because there is a plausible principle which entails that *we* could continue to exist in such a condition, as a stream of consciousness and nothing more. (The relevant principle is, of course, the S-thesis, the claim that co-streamal experiences are consubjective.) A thin, aetiolated existence of this sort would not be the one we would choose to have, if given the choice, but it seems to be a way we could continue to exist. Indeed, since a minimal subject's consciousness could resemble ours in all phenomenological respects, the idea that we could survive as a minimal subject is in many ways easier to accept than the idea (which I also defended) that we could survive as a simple subject.

It may well be that my defence of both these proposals—that we could survive as either a minimal or a simple subject—will fail to convince. This does not mean that the C-theory must be rejected, for the C-theory can be qualified in various ways. We might, for example, follow Unger (1990) in drawing a distinction between personal and sub-personal subjects, and take the view that we are essentially *personal* subjects, subjects with a certain degree or depth of psychological sophistication. We could take this option while still taking the C-theory as our guide to subject-persistence.

In this chapter I returned to a more mundane level, and examined the various ways in which experiential powers grounded in neural systems can be incapacitated. The main question here is whether the existence of our own experiential powers is absolute, or all-or-nothing. What we can say about this issue is limited by our understanding of the matter–consciousness relationship. Nonetheless, if we assume—as I do, tentatively—that the existence of experience is all-or-nothing, then a case can be made for regarding experiential powers as all-or-nothing also. Here too, however, there is a choice to be made, for there is also the option of taking a more lenient view, and allowing borderline cases. The significant point is that there *is* (or at least *might* be) a choice. It is often assumed—notably by Parfit—that the only way our existence could be an all-or-nothing affair is for our continued existence to depend on some 'further fact', over and above mental and physical continuities. But if I am right, this assumption is wrong. We need not suppose that our survival depends on such a further fact in order for our temporal boundaries to be sharp. There is at least the possibility that our existence is all-or-nothing, even though our existence just consists in facts about mental and/or physical continuities, or—adopting the perspective of the C-theory—in facts about the relationships between experiential powers.

Cartesian Egos have a two-fold simplicity: their existence is absolute, and since they are not composed of separable parts they are simple substances, in the metaphysical sense of the term. I argued in Chapter 9 that this second mode of simplicity is also available outwith a Cartesian framework. C-systems can also be regarded as being composed of inseparable parts, provided we recognize global phenomenal properties, and opt to individuate experiential capacities in a suitably discriminating way. Even if we choose a looser mode of individuation, it remains the case that our mental capacities are heavily interdependent, at both the functional and phenomenal levels. These interdependencies alone suffice to ensure that our minds are nothing like Hume's bundles. Unlike collections of twigs or heaps of pebbles, our minds are unified in deep and distinctive ways. We may not be Cartesian Egos, but in some significant respects we may not be so very different.

One final point. It is worth bearing in mind that moderate naturalism may not be true. Perhaps experience is wholly non-physical, perhaps experiential powers are only grounded in immaterial substances. Given the matter–consciousness mystery, this possibility cannot be entirely ruled out. How does the C-theory fit into the immaterialist's world-view? It is certainly compatible with standard substance dualism. Cartesian Egos have experiential capacities, and if we assume the consciousness of an Ego takes the form of a single unified stream of consciousness, we can safely conclude that the capacities of a single Ego will necessarily be C-related. Since this assumption is usually made, the C-theory could be viewed as an articulation of certain assumptions that most Cartesians make. But there are other possibilities, possibilities which cannot easily be ruled out given that we know nothing about the immaterial realm save that it is non-physical, and that mental states and capacities can be instantiated there. Perhaps there are immaterial worlds where immaterial substances as traditionally conceived do not exist; perhaps all that exist in these worlds are shifting formations of elementary immaterial ingredients, only some of which can sustain conscious mental life.[9] In this type of immaterial world, since typical subjects are composed of many parts, the question arises as to what distinctive characteristic these parts must possess in order to constitute a single subject. We now have a plausible answer: their experiential capacities must be C-related.

---

[9] See McGinn (1993) for a more detailed exploration of a similar speculation.

11
Objections and Replies

11.1. ONTOLOGICAL QUALMS

In its narrow guise the C-theory provides an account of our persistence conditions; in its broad guise it offers an account of what we are: I have suggested that we take ourselves to be C-systems. Although our own C-systems are embedded in a wider psychological system (they are parts of what I have been calling *extended* C-systems) and these wider systems are themselves embodied, by virtue of being F-related to a functioning human organism, neither our bodies nor our psychologies are essential to our continued existence. Leaving aside the (necessarily speculative) complications attendant upon the perhaps rather remote possibility of minimal subjects, C-systems are clusters of experiential capacities, distinguished by their ability to contribute to single streams of consciousness. While this view of ourselves carries with it a number of significant advantages (as I hope is by now clear), it is also unfamiliar, and in some ways quite strange—the idea that we are fundamentally nothing but clusters of causal potentials takes a good deal of getting used to.

Novelty aside, there will inevitably be those who are inclined to reject the C-theory, in both its narrow and broad forms, on grounds of principle. In this chapter I will try to do something to alleviate worries of this kind. Unfortunately, even if I could anticipate all the complaints that could be lodged against the sort of approach I have adopted, I would be unable to address them adequately here, so I will confine myself to considering a small selection of the more serious and obvious objections. One important point of contention is the strong realism with respect to experience that I have adopted, but as I noted at the outset, that conscious states are just as real and irreducible as physical states is something I am simply assuming for present purposes. Consequently, I will be concentrating on certain very general metaphysical worries, of the sort displayed in the following:

The C-theory is misguided, for it fails to conform to a fundamental aspect of our conception of what a self is. We manifestly do not take ourselves to be collections of states or events, we do not conceive of ourselves as happenings or processes or properties, we think of ourselves as being particular things, enduring objects—in traditional parlance, *substances*. By their very nature C-systems cannot possibly *be* substances, they can at most be properties *of* substances. Furthermore, since particular mental items—experiences and experiential capacities included—owe their individuality to the subjects that have them, attempting to explicate the identity conditions of mental subjects in terms of mental items is misconceived.

My imaginary critic is giving voice to several related objections. The first concerns the sort of thing a self is, if the C-theory is to be believed. Is a C-system the sort of thing we can plausibly take ourselves to be? Are C-systems sufficiently substantial to be selves? In the eyes of some, the answer will be 'no'. Michael Ayers, for instance, cites with approval Samuel Clarke, who found 'absurd and amazing' accounts which reduce 'a person to a "fleeting transferrible Mode or Power, like the Roundness or the Mode of Motion of Circles upon the Face of a running stream"' (1993: 281–2). There is a good deal that could be said on this topic—the topic of 'substance' continues to be as controversial as any in philosophy—but I will suggest that the self as construed by the C-theory is as substantial as it needs to be. The second line of attack aims to establish that accounts which reduce selves to systems of states or capacities are not merely odd, but are also metaphysically incoherent. Starting from the by no means wholly implausible premise that experiences and experiential powers are ontologically dependent entities—that they are modes or mode-like in nature—the argument leads to the conclusion that we cannot hope to construct an account of our identity conditions in terms of entities of this type. Since this is precisely what the C-theory does, this objection needs to be examined, and it will be. I will argue that there is indeed a sense in which experiential capacities are mode-like, but this does not preclude their being used in a constructive account of the self.

11.2. ISSUES OF SUBSTANCE

To the charge that Neo-Lockean accounts in general, and the C-theory in particular, cannot do justice to the substantial status of the self, there is a quick and easy response: 'Perhaps this is true, perhaps selves are nothing like ordinary substances, things such as cannon balls and horses, perhaps they are more like events or processes. So what? If selves are like this, then we are not the sorts of thing we are accustomed to thinking we are.' I have some sympathy with this reply. After all, one can take metaphysical considerations seriously without being metaphysically dogmatic, and resistant to novel ontological proposals. Faced with a conflict between some general ontological preconceptions (or prejudices), and a compelling account of my existence and persistence conditions, I would be inclined to allow the latter to override the former. But since others may be differently inclined, I would not expect this response to convince everyone.

There is a second quick and easy way of dealing with the insubstantiality objection. The C-theory provides us with a viable and well-defined sortal concept: that of a C-system. If to every distinct and well-defined sortal concept there corresponds an object of a distinct kind, then selves, as construed by the C-theory, count as genuine objects. What more could we want or need?

While this response goes some way towards meeting the insubstantiality charge, it does not go far enough. Earlier we encountered the concept of a *woofwagger*, that is a dog minus its tail on Mondays, Wednesdays, and Fridays, and a dog's tail minus the rest of the dog on Tuesdays, Thursdays, and Weekends. The simple sortal criterion of objecthood yields the result that woofwaggers are genuine objects, on a par with planets, people, and pigs. Many of us will feel uneasy with this, and for what might well seem perfectly good reasons. The idea that genuine objects can simply be defined into existence in this sort of way can seem suspect: it seems plausible to think that sortal concepts which pick out genuine substances reflect objective structures or patterns in nature, in a way that a concept such as *woofwagger* does not. (Perhaps woofwaggers are not odd enough for this point to be clear; they are odd things, but not as odd as *maggotholes*: each of which consists of all the maggots on a continent and the black hole nearest to the planet where the continent is to be found.) In a related vein, many of us find it plausible to think that genuine objects have a distinctive mode of unity, a unity that woofwaggers (and maggotholes) signally lack—think of the way the various parts of a living organism are related and work together. For these reasons, even if we recognize that maggotholes and woofwaggers are objects, they seem to be *arbitrary* in ways that more familiar objects are not. Adopting the simple sortal criterion means placing arbitrary objects on an ontological par with non-arbitrary objects. Isn't this reason enough to reject this criterion?

This case against the simple sortal criterion is by no means decisive, for the general distinction between arbitrary and non-arbitrary kinds of object may well turn out to be a hard one to defend. Is it not likely that beings very different from ourselves might have very different views as to what counts as 'real' or 'natural' when it comes to objecthood? Is the perspective of such beings any less valid than our own? Inspired by the desire for a truly objective criterion of objecthood, and seeing no other way to secure such a criterion, some philosophers recommend the adoption of the principle of 'unrestricted composition', according to which any occupied regions of spacetime, no matter how scattered in space or time, constitute an object (e.g. Sider 2001: 120). This view too has its appeal.

Happily, there is no need for us to enter this debate. Those who incline to the maximally liberal view will have no scruples about accepting the C-theory. If literally *anything*, no matter how bizarre, ethereal or scattered by the standards of common sense has the status of a genuine object, then C-systems will too. But equally, those of a more conservative disposition who incline to the view that there are at least some constraints on objecthood, and who as a consequence would wish to distinguish between sortal concepts which denote genuine objects and those which do not, also have reason to look favourably on the C-theory. For it is clear that the concept of a self, as defined by this theory, is quite unlike concepts such as *woofwagger* and *maggothole*. Objects such as these possess parts that are not unified in any obvious or significant way—true, even their widely separated parts are spatio-temporally related, but so too are the parts of *any* objects in any given universe. C-related experiential capacities are very different. The capacity to produce co-conscious experience is not only a genuine relation, it is obviously a *unifying* relation. And although the C-theory is concerned with experiential (and hence subjective) facts and relationships, it undeniably reflects an objective feature of reality in one significant respect: whether or not experiential powers exist, or can produce co-conscious experiences, is a fact about how the world is which is quite independent of our concepts and practices. Facts about the existence and persistence of subjects (as measured by the C-theory) are thus well-grounded in real features of the world, unlike the purely conventional boundaries between certain nations. Last but not least, the concept of C-relatedness is by no means an arbitrary creation. The concept was uncovered in the course of an inquiry into our own identity conditions; in conducting this inquiry, we were trying to isolate the strands of our life which are most essential to our own existence and persistence. What could be *less* arbitrary?

11.3. UNITY AND INDEPENDENCE

Selves construed as C-systems may have ontological credentials woofwaggers and maggotholes lack, but do they have the ontological credentials of planets and pigs? Our paradigmatic examples of genuine substances are, after all, entities such as these: persisting, unified, material things, of familiar kinds. There may be a sense in which C-systems are genuine objects, but are they the right *kind* of object? C-systems are composed of potentialities and nothing else; potentialities may be real, but since they are nothing more than *properties*, they are scarcely substantial, or so it could be argued.

The force of this objection can be diluted somewhat by reflecting on our actual condition. Even if we were to grant that C-systems are not substantial entities, human bodies and brains certainly are, and a typically embodied subject has both—even if subjects are not numerically identical with their bodies or brains. A subject who is F-related to a body is connected to their body in a far more intimate manner than mere physical contact or enclosure (and the latter, as we have seen, are not among the pre-requisites of effective embodiment). But while this is undeniably true, we are still left with the fact that *subjects themselves* consist of nothing more than collections of mental potentialities. Is this something we can live with? Can we really identify ourselves with entities that are as insubstantial as C-systems?

Those who find themselves disinclined to accept that they are C-systems need not reject the C-theory altogether. The preliminary form of the C-theory I outlined in §4.2 was formulated in terms of experience-producing *objects*, rather than experiential capacities. An object-based version of the C-theory can easily be obtained by substituting 'experience producing object' for 'experiential power' in the formulations of C-relatedness given in §4.4 and §8.5. Those who are reluctant to admit powers or capacities into their ontology may want to take this step. However, for reasons which will emerge, I do not think anyone else should feel obliged to follow suit.

The insubstantiality objection can be answered thus: 'You say you are an *object* not a cluster of properties, but *all* objects are nothing more than clusters of properties!' While this reply will only convince those who are already committed to bundle theories of objects, and the latter remains controversial, it also serves as a useful reminder that when it comes to the question of what counts as a 'genuine' object, very little is clear and uncontroversial. What does the charge of insubstantiality really amount to? It cannot plausibly be argued that real substances must be composed of *matter*. Cartesian Egos are not composed of matter, but few would deny that they are genuine substances—or would be if they existed—and the same could be said about God. Descending to a more mundane level, the single largest substance in our universe may well be spacetime itself—is spacetime a solid material thing? Clearly, if the insubstantiality charge is to pose a serious threat it must be construed in a more general way, along these lines: 'Selves or subjects are genuine substances. For an entity to be a substance, a real substance, it must satisfy certain conditions. Collections of powers or capacities manifestly fail to satisfy these conditions.' The difficulty here is in specifying the conditions for genuine substancehood. Debates about the concept of substance are as old as philosophy itself, and the debates continue; the concept is as contested as ever. To examine each and every influential conception of substance that philosophers have devised, and assess where the C-theory fits in, would be a tedious business, and would serve little point. Given the diversity of conceptions, we can confidently predict in advance that by some criteria, extended C-systems will successfully qualify as genuine substances, whereas by other criteria they will fail to do so. To expedite matters, and to illustrate the point, I will consider just only two conceptions of substance, two of the most influential and enduring.

According to Descartes: 'By *substance*, we can understand nothing other than a thing which exists in such a way as to depend on no other thing for its existence' (1984, 2: 210). Armstrong takes a similar view: 'I understand by a substance nothing more than a thing that is *logically capable of independent existence*' (1968: 7). And so have many others. For obvious reasons, we can call this the *independence criterion*, and objects which satisfy the criterion *i-substances*. There is no denying that this criterion reflects an ontologically significant distinction. Objects which do not depend for their existence on any other object undoubtedly deserve a special place in any respectable ontological scheme. That said, the independence criterion needs to be elaborated with some care if there are to be any i-substances at all. Those who believe the universe to be the product of divine creation have a problem here, although they can avail themselves of Descartes' response to the problem and distinguish between two classes of i-substance. On a more down-to-earth level, is a pig an i-substance? A pig has parts, and some of these parts—in particular, the elementary particles from which it is composed, assuming there are such—are themselves likely candidates for being i-substances. Yet clearly a pig could not exist unless its parts did too. The idea that a pig could exist without any other objects also looks implausible on the macroscopic scale: how long would a pig last in the harsh conditions of interstellar vacuum? Could *any* physical item, even an elementary particle, exist in the absence of spacetime?

I will not press these difficulties, for with suitably delicate manoeuvrings the independence criterion can be modified so as to accommodate them (Lowe 1994; Hoffman and Rosenkrantz 1997). The more relevant issue is whether subjects, in the guise of C-systems, can possibly be regarded as i-substances. It seems unlikely, at least for beings similar to ourselves. C-systems are composed of capacities, and generally speaking capacities are dispositional properties of objects, and I have been assuming that the same applies to our experiential powers. Given these assumptions, subjects such as ourselves will probably fail to satisfy the independence criterion, however it is elaborated. If selves consists of capacities, and these capacities are properties of certain physical objects, however these are construed, it makes no sense to suppose the capacities—and hence selves—could exist all by themselves. Of course the relevant assumptions may be mistaken. On one view, some dispositional properties are among the ontologically basic constituents of reality. If experiential powers fall, or could fall, into this category, then perhaps it is at least logically possible for there to be subjects who consist entirely of basic experiential capacities, capacities which are not possessed by or grounded in any material object, with the possible exception of space itself. While I believe it may well be possible to sketch coherent scenarios along these lines, certain rather extravagant metaphysical speculations are required, so I will not pursue the point here.[1]

If we concede the claim that subjects such as ourselves are not i-substances, we are not automatically obliged to deny that we are ourselves substances, for as I noted earlier, there may be other criteria for being a substance, criteria which C-systems satisfy. We do not have to look far to find a conception which fits the bill. Historically, the idea that substances are entities which are in some manner independent of other entities has co-existed with another idea, namely that substances are entities which have a genuine unity, a unity which

---

[1] Here is one way of putting some flesh on this speculation. Imagine a world containing only three persisting experiential powers, P, Q, and R, the activation of which produces experiences lasting one second of types X, Y, and Z respectively. The laws governing experience in this world ensure that (i) any two successive manifestations of these powers are co-conscious; (ii) that any occurrence of a Z-type experience is always followed by a manifestation of P, any occurrence of an X-type experience is always followed by a manifestation of Q, and any occurrence of a Y-type experience is always followed by a manifestation of R. It follows that the activation of any one of these powers sets in train a continuous stream of consciousness, consisting of the endless repetition of the same sequence of experiences. A little monotonous, but incoherent?

generally consists in a real and distinctive relationship between an object's parts or properties. Hume and Berkeley are perhaps the best-known advocates of a position of this general sort. (There are complications: Berkeley only adopted this view of material bodies, Hume extended it to minds as well, and was sometimes sceptical of substances in general). More recently philosophers such as Russell and Castañeda have advocated similar accounts, as have phenomenalists of one sort or another.[2] For the sake of terminological uniformity, I will call this the *unity criterion*, and entities which satisfy it *u-substances*. The idea that genuine objects, as opposed to their arbitrary or gerrymandered kin, are characterized by a distinctive mode of unity is, of course, one we have already encountered. If we find the idea that woofwaggers and maggotholes are genuine objects objectionable, even repellent, it is not just because these entities are unfamiliar, it is—in part at least—because their constituent parts lack the sort of unity that other things, *real* things, possess. If the independence criterion reflects a significant aspect of our understanding of concepts such as 'substance' or 'object', so too does the unity criterion, to no lesser extent.

The unity criterion, like the independence criterion, can be elaborated in different ways. Different sorts of object have different sorts of constituent parts, which may or may not themselves be substances, and these parts may be related by different unifying relations. These variations need not concern us here. Our only concern is whether C-systems satisfy the criterion, and of this there is no doubt. C-systems are composed of experiential capacities, and as I have taken pains to emphasize, these capacities are unified in real and distinctive ways. This point is by now so familiar that the briefest of recaps should suffice. The key relationship is co-consciousness, a primitive but real relationship between experiences. C-relatedness is defined in terms of this relationship, and as we have seen, experiential powers that are so related are interdependent in various ways. Experiential powers which can produce co-conscious experience are subject to C-holism: the experiential potential of any given power is affected by the powers to which it is DPC-related. Powers whose manifestations exhibit weak or strong impingement are interdependent in a more obvious way, likewise our powers for spatially and temporally structured experiences. Taken together, these different modes of unity and interdependence bestow a quasi-organic unity upon typical C-systems. If anything counts as a genuine u-substance, it is systems such as these, and so by this criterion at least, subjects are genuine substances.

I can see no further need to defend the C-theory against the charge that it commits us to conceiving of ourselves as non-entities. Entities such as pigs and planets may well satisfy both the unity criterion and the independence criterion, so they might reasonably be thought to be substantial in a way subjects (construed as extended C-systems) are not. But by virtue of satisfying the unity criterion in

---

[2] For a general survey, see Hoffman and Rosenkrantz (1997: 26–42).

so resounding a manner, subjects are undeniably entities, indeed substances, of an eminently respectable sort.

11.4. MENACING CIRCULARITIES

Does it even *make sense* to explicate the identity conditions of subjects of experience in terms of their mental states and capacities? Some philosophers insist that this whole approach is fundamentally misconceived. The line of argument I have in mind is familiar from chapter 3 of P. F. Strawson's *Individuals*, (1959) and has more recently been expressed in a forceful fashion by E. J. Lowe:

> What is wrong with the neo-Lockean theory is that, in purporting to supply an account of the individuation and identity of persons it presupposes, untenably, that an account of the identity conditions of psychological modes can be provided which need not rely on any reference to persons. But it emerges that the identity of any psychological mode turns on the identity of the person that possesses it . . . individual mental states are necessarily states *of persons*: they are necessarily 'owned'—necessarily have a *subject*. The necessity in question arises from the metaphysical-cum-logical truth that such individual mental states cannot even in principle be individuated and identified without reference to the subject of which they are states. (Lowe 1996: 25)

A central contention in Lowe's argument is that token mental items cannot be individuated without reference to their subjects. This claim is supported by two further contentions: first that all mental states necessarily have a subject to whom they belong, and second, that all mental states have the status of modes—they are ontologically on a par with scratches, surfaces, and dents. If the latter claim is right, then like all modes, mental items are essentially aspects or features of some substance, and in this case the relevant substances are none other than *persons*. From these points another follows: the attempt to account for the existence and persistence of persons in terms of relationships between their mental states cannot succeed, for 'the entities out of which [the neo-Lockean] attempts to construct the self—psychological states and processes—are themselves not individuable and identifiable independently of the selves that are their subjects, so that a fatal circularity dooms the project' (Lowe 1996: 8).[3] In evaluating Lowe's argument it will help if we clearly distinguish the four main claims:

A All mental items necessarily belong to some subject.
B All mental items have the ontological status of modes; they are features or aspects of subjects.

---

[3] Van Inwagen takes a similar line: 'We can't find out whether [a] situation contains a continuously existing thinker by first finding out whether it contains a "continuous consciousness" . . . I think of a sequence of thoughts as being thoughts of the same thinker just in virtue of their being modifications of one, continuing substance: the understander that stands under them' (1990: 206–7).

C Mental items cannot be identified or individuated independently of their subject.
D The attempt to explain or account for the individuation and identity of subjects in terms of relationships between mental items cannot succeed; any such account will turn out to be viciously circular.

So far as I can see, nothing of significance follows from (A) taken in isolation. Many neo-Lockeans would agree that all mental items belong to some subject, but they also believe that the existence and persistence of subjects can be explained in terms of relationships between mental items. Clearly, the more important claims are (B) and (C). If (B) were true, (C) would follow automatically, given the standard metaphysical construal of 'mode'. Could (C) be true without (B) also being true? Possibly, but it is not obvious how mental items could be wholly dependent for their individuation on their subjects unless they were modes of the latter. As for whether (C) entails (D), a plausible case can be made for thinking that it does—and it is certainly the case that the truth of (C) would pose serious problems for the C-theory. If all mental items owe their identity and individuality to the subjects to whom they belong, so too will experiences and experiential powers. In which case, the claim that experiential powers are consubjective only in virtue of the fact that they are C-related will be in jeopardy. If in order to exist at all experiential powers have to belong to subjects, then the ownership of powers is settled in advance, as it were, and so is logically prior to any other claims about the sorts of relationships which these items can enter into. It may well be that, due to the nature of subjects, consubjective powers can produce co-conscious experiences, but this is not what makes powers consubjective in the first place. Quite generally, if being consubjective is a logical pre-requisite of being C-related, we cannot hope to analyse consubjectivity in terms of C-relatedness in an informative or reductive fashion. Or so a critic might plausibly argue.

The key question, then, is whether (B) and (C) are true. I cannot see any good reason for supposing that they are, at least not in the way intended by Lowe.

When first introducing the notion of an experiential power, I suggested a number of factors could reasonably be taken to be relevant to their identity. In the first instance, two token powers are of the same type if they can produce experiences of the same phenomenal character; if we want a more stringent standard, we can say that to be of the same type powers must have the same triggering conditions. As for what makes token powers which are of the same type, and which exist at the same time, distinct from one another, I suggested that we could appeal to physical considerations, at least in worlds such as our own appears to be: if at a given time there are two powers, P_1 and P_2, which can produce the same sorts of experience, under the same triggering conditions, then the physical basis of P_1 will be numerically distinct from that of P_2. In human terms, P_1 will be grounded in either a different brain from P_2, or in a different part of the same brain. Given the various forms of power-holism we have recognized, this initial account is overly simple. To focus on just one case, in virtue of C-holism the precise experiential potential of a particular power depends on the other powers to which it is DPC-related. But the basic point remains: in individuating experiential powers in the envisaged way, we are making no appeal to subjects, we are mentioning only experiential manifestations and experiential relationships, physical bases and triggering conditions. And this puts us in a position to argue as follows. If experiential powers were merely modes of subjects, they would owe their individuality to subjects, and there would be no possibility of individuating powers independently of subjects; but since it is possible to individuate powers independently of subjects, powers cannot be modes of subjects. (B) is thus false, and the only obvious rationale for subscribing to (C) has been undermined.

This argument is simple but effective. It depends, however, on the legitimacy of individuating mental capacities—in this case experiential powers—by reference to their physical grounds or causes. Is this legitimate? Lowe argues not:

And why, it may be asked, should not the neo-Lockean simply say that mental states are states *of the body* . . . because by the neo-Lockean's own lights there can be no guarantee of a one-to-one correspondence between bodies (of whatever sort) and persons. Hence, in a case (however hypothetical) of co-embodiment by two distinct persons (as in the Jekyll and Hyde story), referring a mental state to a body will not determine to which person it belongs nor, hence, which token state it is. For persons cannot share token mental states, and so while it is left undetermined to which person a token state belongs, the identity of that token state must equally be left undetermined. (Lowe 1996: 31)

Reference to the Jekyll and Hyde story is perhaps misleading, since these two subjects (assuming they are such) could be regarded as inhabiting the same body successively rather than simultaneously. The real difficulty concerns simultaneous co-embodiment. Consider a case in which the same brain generates two distinct but qualitatively indistinguishable streams of consciousness, s_1 and s_2 at the same time. Assuming that this sort of case is logically possible, what is it that makes s_1 distinct from s_2? The appeal to differences in physical bases fails, since the capacities which generate s_1 and s_2 have exactly the same physical basis—to make life as difficult as possible we can stipulate that these capacities are not grounded in different parts of the brain in question. If as Lowe suggests, the neo-Lockean cannot rule out the logical possibility of this sort of co-embodiment, we need an alternative account of the individuality of mental states and capacities. It seems we have no option but to turn to subjects.

The neo-Lockean could argue that the kind of co-embodiment in question is a logical impossibility, and so the sort of case Lowe envisages simply could not arise. On some views of the experience–matter relationship this would indeed be the case—for example the Russellian form of the identity theory—but given the depths of our ignorance concerning the nature of this relationship, a defence along these lines would at present be inconclusive. A better response is to turn the tables. Let us suppose (as some do) that token experiences are immaterial particulars. Let us further suppose that it is at least logically possible for a single brain to generate two streams of (immaterial) consciousness, rather than just one. In such a situation, if we suppose that each of the two streams consists of distinct token experiences, and these token experiences are distinct in virtue of the fact that they belong to distinct subjects, in virtue of what are these *subjects* distinct? Since, by hypothesis, both subjects are enjoying exactly the same types of experience at the same time, it is difficult to see that anything *makes* these subjects distinct, so their distinctness is a basic fact which has no deeper explanation. I have no objection whatsoever to the idea that some entities are basic in this sort of way. If we individuate entities of type *a* by reference to their relationship to entities of type *b*, and we individuate entities of type *b* by reference to their relationship to entities of type *c*, we have to stop somewhere; there must be some entities which are not individuated by reference to anything else, otherwise we end up by going round in a circle (which may or may not be a problem) or with an endless regress. Perhaps spacetime falls into this distinctive category of entities that are basic from the point of view of individuation; perhaps some physical particulars do; perhaps subjects do. The problem for Lowe is this: if we allow subjects to be basic entities, from the point of view of individuation, why not token experiences or token experiential powers? What is to prevent our saying that in the relevant cases of co-embodiment, a single brain grounds two distinct but exactly similar C-systems, that is two distinct systems of C-related experiential powers of the same types?

The answer, I think, is that nothing does. But to accommodate the exotic possibility we are now envisaging, we do need to recognize a further way in which experiential powers can be individuated. Rather than holding that simultaneously existing powers for the same type of experience are numerically distinct by virtue of being grounded in distinct physical systems, we must hold that they can also be distinct by virtue of being able to produce numerically distinct token experiences. In response to the question 'Why think this brain sustains two C-systems rather than one?' we can simply say: 'because this brain can generate two distinct streams of consciousness', or 'because this brain possesses two distinct C-related collections of experiential powers'. If we are robust realists about consciousness, if we regard phenomenal items as being just as real as any physical item, this option seems quite intelligible. We might never be in a position, looking on from the outside as it were, to know that an otherwise typical brain is generating (or has the ability to generate) two indistinguishable streams of consciousness rather than one, but this inability does not matter: the logical possibility is there. So far as the issue of individuation is concerned, this option seems to make as much metaphysical sense as the alternative Lowe prefers, and is ontologically more economical, for we are not obliged to posit an additional entity over and above experiences and experiential powers.

Lowe anticipates a response along lines similar to this, due to Peacocke (1983), but argues that it is flawed. Could a single subject have two indistinguishable token experiences at the same time? Not if experiences are individuated in terms of subject, time, and character. Peacocke proposes an alternative way of looking at the situation: perhaps it is a necessary truth that a single subject cannot have two indiscernible experiences at the same time, but not because experiences are individuated in terms of subject, time, and character, but because subjects are individuated by reference to token experiences. In so-called 'split-brain' cases there is evidence to suggest that (different) parts of a single brain might be causally responsible for two similar states of consciousness, and Peacocke holds that 'if we do speak of two distinct minds or centres of consciousness in these circumstances, we do so because the token experiences are themselves distinct' (1983: 177). In response, Lowe insists that for this proposal to be viable we must be able to individuate token experiences independently of their subjects. With regard to this question, Peacocke proposes that token experiences might be individuated by reference to their phenomenal character, time of occurrence and their causes and effects. For Lowe this is problematic: 'such causal distinctions themselves cannot be made independently of any reference to subjects' (1996: 27). Irrespective of the sort of physical stimuli we might be dealing with, in order to be able to conclude that one (or two, or three) token experiences of a particular type ensued, we would *already* have to have reason to believe that the corresponding number of *subjects* were present to undergo these experiences: 'we cannot effectively motivate a claim that each stimulation results in a distinct token experience without relying on presumptions concerning the existence and identity of the prospective subject(s) of those experiences' (1996: 30).

But once again, and for reasons which should by now be quite familiar, this is unpersuasive. In arguing thus Lowe is relying on the very thesis that is currently in question, namely that token experiences depend for their individuality upon their subjects. As for the question of how token experiences are to be individuated if not by reference to their subjects, even if Peacocke's proposal is unsatisfactory, it does not matter. For as we have just seen, it is an option to take token experiences to be basic so far as their individuality is concerned.

One last consideration. Returning to the concurrent Jekyll and Hyde case, if we accept that it is logically possibile for a single brain to possess two distinct sets of consubjective experiential powers, there may be no answer to the question 'In virtue of what are there two C-systems grounded in this brain rather than one?' other than 'There are two C-systems because the brain can produce two indistinguishable streams of consciousness rather than one'. This position is open to an objection of this sort:

How can we be certain that *our own* brains are not like this? How can I be certain that as I think these thoughts, my brain is not generating another thought—or a thousand other thoughts—just like this one? Isn't the idea that there are a multitude of streams of consciousness being produced simultaneously with this stream of consciousness simply absurd?

I cannot see that it is. For if we adopt a sufficiently robust realism about states of consciousness—of the kind I am adopting here—the problem is surely epistemological rather than metaphysical. It is true that it is difficult, perhaps impossible in principle, for us to discover the truth or falsity of the experiential duplication hypothesis, but unless we subscribe to some form of verificationism, this does not in itself entail that the hypothesis is unintelligible or meaningless. The hypothesis that there exists a multitude of perfect duplicates of the entire *physical* universe is equally difficult to refute, but it is by no means obvious that this hypothesis is senseless. Even if inhabitants of each universe are unaware of the existence of the other universes (and we can stipulate that communication between distinct spatio-temporal systems is nomologically impossible), they are very much aware of their own existence, simply by virtue of being sentient, and surely this is enough to silence any doubts as to whether they exist at all. In an analogous way, the subjects of the duplicate streams of consciousness are aware of their own experiences (and hence existence). Of course, despite the intelligibility of the universal physical duplication thesis, nobody takes it seriously, and rightly so. The positing of unobservable entities is justified, but only if some explanatory purpose is served, but no such purpose is served by the positing of duplicate universes.[4] If we are entitled to ascribe a low probability to the physical duplication thesis on Ockhamist grounds of explanatory economy, why not the experiential duplication thesis also?

Moreover, if we do as Lowe suggests and take subjects to be our basic entities, we can pose an analogous question about the latter: How can we be certain that a thousand *subjects* are not associated with our own brains, thinking exactly the same sorts of thought, having just the same sorts of experience? As P. F. Strawson, admittedly in a somewhat different context, put it: 'when the man (a rational psychologist perhaps) speaks, we could suggest that there are, perhaps, a thousand souls simultaneously thinking the thoughts his words express, having qualitatively indistinguishable experiences such as he, the man, would currently claim. How could the man persuade us that there was only one such soul associated with his body? (How could the—or each—soul persuade itself of its uniqueness?)' (1966: 169). On either view, there is the bare logical possibility that there *are* a thousand subjects associated with each human body and brain; indeed, there

---

[4] Those who look favourably upon one or other forms of the Many Worlds interpretation of quantum mechanics *do* take seriously the hypothesis of multitudes of (near) duplicate physical universes, but in this case there are good (or at least respectable) scientific reasons for accepting the claim—see Deutsch (1997: ch. 2), and Barrett (2001). Similar remarks apply to multiple (sub-) universes postulated in 'inflationary' cosmological scenarios. The multiple-universe hypothesis I am considering currently is *mere* speculation: there is no empirical or explanatory reason for supposing it is true.

may be logically possible worlds where this is the case. But equally, on either view, there is no reason to believe that our world falls into this category.[5]

11.5. OWNERSHIP, ISOLATION AND HOLISM

So it seems that Lowe's circularity objection can be met. There is no need to appeal to substantival subjects in order to individuate mental capacities; alternatives are available which are both metaphysically intelligible and less profligate at the level of ontology. Before moving on, however, I want to probe a little deeper. Why can the doctrine that mental items in general (and experiences in particular) are dependent on their subjects seem plausible? Some of our earlier results are relevant here, and in more ways than one. There may indeed be a sense in which experiences and experiential powers are mode-like, but the sense in question is by no means inimical to the C-theory.

To start with, although the claim that experiences are dependent on their subjects can indeed seem compelling—I shall be examining why shortly—there are also considerations which suggest the opposite is true. Edges, dents, ripples, and holes are *obviously* dependent modes of objects in a way that experiences are not. It makes no sense to suppose that the entirety of a material object could be annihilated with the exception of its edges or corners, and the same applies to holes, dents, and ripples. If all the matter that constitutes your car were annihilated, so too would be the holes and dents in the bodywork; if all the water in the world's oceans were suddenly to disappear, so too would the ripples and waves on their surfaces. It is otherwise with respect to experiences: recall the world-gap case of §8.4, where *everything* is annihilated with the exception of our streams of consciousness, which continue on as if nothing unusual had happened. One reason for thinking that experiences are concrete particulars in their own right, rather than essentially dependent modes, is the ease with which it is possible to imagine a world containing experiences and nothing else whatsoever.

This sort of imaginary example is not conclusive, for it could be argued that in imagining such a scenario we are imagining a world which contains experiencing subjects (or portions of matter) as well as experiences, even if we fail to realize this. But there are further considerations which point in the same general direction. Recall some of the main positions on the matter–consciousness relationship. Traditional substance dualists do regard experiences as modes, but substance dualism is not the only available theory about the matter–experience relationship, and indeed, of the main options, it is the one I am least inclined

[5] And as I mentioned earlier, the (experiential) duplication hypothesis is probably only intelligible in the context of dualist conceptions of the matter–experience relationship. I don't think such conceptions can be ruled out, but equally, I don't think we can rule out the possibility that (our) experiences are brain states (or aspects of them).

to accept, at least in its classical Cartesian guise. Property dualism is the main immaterialist alternative to substance dualism, and property dualists explicitly reject the idea that experiences are modes: experiences are immaterial particulars that are generated by material processes, and may (perhaps) causally influence material processes. More significantly perhaps, if some form of materialism is true, experiences are themselves physical states, occurrences or processes. Some physical occurrences are naturally viewed as modes—ripples on a pond, or Clarke's Motions of Circles on a running Stream—but many are not. A bolt of lightning is a physical occurrence, but what physical thing is it a feature *of*? A star is an ongoing nuclear explosion, and so a physical process, but is it a mode or feature of anything? Events such as these can be regarded as particulars in their own right. They are, after all, things which have a full complement of features of their own—they are things which have shapes, boundaries, perforations and so forth. If we insist on saying that they are themselves features of anything, the only candidate is space itself, or the region of spacetime in which they happen. From this it follows that items of this kind owe their identity their spatio-temporal location, but this hardly sets them apart (or below) other kinds of physical thing, given the central role spatio-temporal location plays in the physical scheme of things. The materialist can now argue that since experiences are material states or processes, they should be regarded in just the same way, that is they have exactly the same ontological status as lightning bolts and stars, they are concrete material particulars, which are not modes or features of anything, with the possible exception of spacetime itself. And of course, as soon as we shift from a common sense conception of the physical to the sorts of conception to be found in contemporary physics, the situation changes once again, in a direction that is hostile to the notion that there is a meaningful distinction between physical *objects* and physical *processes*. From the perspective of quantum field theory, for example, seemingly object-like cannonballs and seemingly process-like waterfalls are essentially similar: both are composed of elementary particles of various types, and the latter consist of patterns of activity in the collection of underlying fields. Bearing in mind the unity criterion for objecthood, the fact that experiences are unified in a distinctive way might well lead one to the view espoused by G. Strawson: 'there are in fact no better candidates in the universe for the title "physical object" or "substance" than SESMETs [selves]. Certainly it seems that there is, in nature, as far as we know it, no higher grade of physical unity than the unity of the mental subject present and alive in what James calls the "indecomposable" unity of a conscious thought' (1999*a*: 128).

These considerations establish at least this much: the claim that experiences (and experiential powers) are parasitic entities, in the manner of edges, corners, or perforations, is far from being self-evidently true. Unless we espouse classical substance dualism (which Lowe for one is not inclined to do), why would anyone think that experiences are by their very nature modes of some substance? So far as I can see, the answer lies primarily in the idea formulated in (A) above: the metaphysical-cum-logical truth that token experiences are necessarily owned, they necessarily belong to some subject. In considering this ownership doctrine in Chapter 8 I made a number of relevant points, which are worth summarizing once again.

1 The idea of a free-floating pain does initially strike us as utterly absurd: surely a pain, in order to exist at all, has to be felt by someone or something. The Isolation Thesis—the claim that free-floating isolated experiences (or experiential powers) *can* exist—initially strikes most of us as absurd. But on reflection it soon seems less so. What would the conscious life of a very simple organism be like? Assuming there are forms of consciousness much simpler than our own, it is hard to rule out the possibility of very simple streams of consciousness; at any given moment, these very simple streams might have a phenomenal character akin to that of an isolated pain sensation, or an isolated bodily experience.

2 One reason the Isolation Thesis can seem implausible is that we find it impossible to imagine isolated experiences. But it is not surprising that we find this impossible. The inner component of the phenomenal background, a complex ensemble of experiences which together constitute what it usually feels like to be ourselves, is a constant presence in our consciousness. Whenever we imagine anything, the phenomenal background is there. This is why we literally cannot imagine an isolated sensation: any experience we imagine automatically occurs against the richer background of our consciousness. But this imaginative limitation does not entail that an isolated sensation is an impossibility in itself.

3 The Isolation Thesis would be absurd if the act–object or naïve perceptual (NP) model of consciousness were true. According to this doctrine, a pain sensation is a phenomenal content or object, and, to be experienced, such contents must fall under an act of awareness. Consequently, the idea that a pain could exist—as an experience—independently of the awareness of a subject, is an absurdity. But we have found no reason to think the act–object model is true. If the Simple Conception of experience is true, as I have argued, there is no need for a separate or additional awareness to turn a phenomenal content into an experience. Particular phenomenal contents are intrinsically experiential.

4 Would a stream of consciousness indistinguishable from our own, but not the product of a complex of experiential capacities, and not associated with a system of psychological capacities, belong to a subject? I can see no reason why we should say not. In taking a VR-4 trip, one's stream of consciousness is detached from both one's body and one's psychology, but is it not clear that *we would continue to exist and have experiences* during our VR-4 vacations? If so, then we must accept a special category of subjects, *minimal subjects*, which

consist of streams of consciousness and nothing more. Having taken this step, we see that there is a sense in which an isolated experience *would* belong to a subject, even though it is isolated. The subject in question is merely a minimal subject, but does this matter?

5 Perhaps isolated experiences and minimal subjects *are* impossible, either contingently or necessarily. It does not follow that experiences, or other mental items, are adjectival on subjects. There is a plausible alternative diagnosis: perhaps the impossibility of isolated mental items is a consequence of the essential systematicity or holism of the mental, perhaps mental items can only exist as integral parts of mental systems, systems which consists of various other mental items, each of which is also essentially systemic. I have argued at some length that there are interdependencies among a broad range of mental items, both phenomenal and psychological, occurrent and dispositional. Some of these interdependencies are essential, in that the items concerned simply could not exist in the absence of other mental items to which they are appropriately related; the relevant relations include both P-relations and C-relations.

This last point may be the most important. Recognizing that certain kinds of mental item can only exist when suitably related to others is tantamount to recognizing that the Isolation Thesis is false for a good many mental states and capacities of the sort with which we are most familiar: sizeable portions of our minds and our mental lives are composed of constituent parts which could not exist in isolation. However, once we realize that this is because the items in question can only exist when either C-related or P-related to other mental states or capacities, we no longer need to posit an additional entity, an underlying substantival subject, in order to accommodate this insight. Indeed, recognizing that a broad class of mental items are essentially system-bound gives us an explanation for why such items cannot exist in isolation, an explanation the substantivalist does not provide. If no positive account of the nature of the posited substantival subject is given, the claim that mental items cannot occur in isolation because they are modes of such substances looks to be nothing more than an attempt to provide a metaphysical gloss to an inadequately articulated intuition. But what can the substantivalist provide by way of a positive account of the kind of thing subjects are which is both informative and plausible? Surely the only such account would be of the form 'subjects are essentially substances which possess certain mental states and capacities', but since it is not at all clear how or in what manner this account differs from that provided by the C-theorist, we remain wholly in the dark as to quite what the substantivalist means by 'substance'. For do not forget that the C-theory provides a clear account of the kind of *entity* a self is: extended and effectively embodied C-systems, and C-systems are genuine substances in their own right, at least by the lights of the unity criterion.

At this point friends of substantival subjects might try a final manoeuvre, and argue thus:

Adopting the C-theory is tantamount to adopting the view that mental items are modes of substantival subjects, which is just the view we have been advocating. As you rightly point out, extended C-systems are substances, of a sort, and the components of a typical C-system cannot enjoy an independent existence, they are holistically interrelated and essentially systemic. We were right all along.

There is an element of truth here. Save for the case of the very simplest of subjects, C-systems are not composed of independent elements: the experiential powers responsible for most familiar forms of experience are systemic, and C-holism embraces all DPC-related powers. However, these dependencies are due solely to relationships which exist at the level of experiences and experiential powers. And as such they are entirely independent of *subjects* conceived as substances within which experiences and experiential powers inhere. Mental items can be mode-like without being modes of substantival subjects.

A few further words of caution are also due. In giving the various interdependencies which exist among mental states their full due, it would be a mistake to go too far, and regard experiential capacities as being precisely on a par, ontologically speaking, with archetypal modes such as ripples, perforations, and corners. First, it is quite possible that there are types of experiential capacities that are *not* essentially systemic (recall Maggot's mind, where only C-holism reigns). Second, modes such as dents and holes can only be individuated by reference to their substantival subjects, and as we have seen, experiential capacities are not like this. Third, it makes no sense to think that a particular dent, say, could be transferred from one thing (such as my car's door) to another (such as your car's door), but it does—or at least *may*—make sense to think that experiential capacities could be transferred from one C-system to another. If the parts of my brain responsible for my visual imagination were transplanted to your brain, which (we can suppose) previously lacked the relevant neural circuits, you would acquire some of my experiential capacities. The situation would be different if the holistic relations between experiential powers were of the token–token rather than the type–type variety. If this were the case, as I noted in §9.6, C-systems would lack logically detachable parts, and hence be simple substances, and so there *would* be a case for taking experiential powers to be something akin to modes in the traditional sense. But although we can choose to individuate in the token-specific way, doing so is not obligatory.

To sum up: is it the case that, as Lowe puts it, 'the entities out of which [the Neo-Lockean] attempts to construct the self. . . are themselves not individuable and identifiable independently of the selves that are their subjects, so that a fatal circularity dooms the project'? I have argued otherwise. Assuming both experiential realism and moderate naturalism, there is a strong case for supposing that otherwise indistinguishable experiences and experiential powers can be individuated in terms of their physical basis, or failing that, taken as basic. This point alone serves to put substantivalists such as Lowe on the defensive: if mental items such as these *can* be individuated in this fashion, without reference to any substantival subject, surely they cannot be modes of such substances? Latterly, I have been looking at the one consideration which might seem to provide a solid reason for accepting the mode-doctrine, the idea that experiential mental items cannot exist in total isolation. But on closer scrutiny, the assistance this brings to the substantivalist evaporates: to the extent that it is true that mental items cannot exist in isolation, this can be explained without adopting the view that the relevant class of items are modes of substantival subjects.

11.6. POWER WORLDS

I want to consider next an objection of a rather different kind. In §4.2 I outlined a number of related reasons why it is worth trying to develop an account of our identity conditions in terms of experiential capacities, rather than the things which possess these capacities:

- Although subjects of the potentially conscious (PCS) variety may well be able to differ in many ways, they have one feature in common: the capacity to have experiences. So if we want a maximally general account, framing it in terms of experiential capacities is the obvious way to go.

- Since an account along these lines abstracts from everything that is non-essential to our survival, if successful it would likely be more economical than the alternatives.

- Any given subject can survive any conceivable change save one, a change which eliminates its capacity for consciousness, so if the possession and retention of this capacity is necessary and sufficient for our existence and persistence respectively—and as we have seen there are good reasons for so thinking—then it seems self-evident that an account of our existence and persistence conditions should be in terms of this sort of capacity.

While these motivations for adopting a capacity-oriented approach carry a good deal of weight, some might be inclined to lodge an objection along these lines:

In effect, you are proposing to *dematerialize* the self without invoking immaterial substances, but it won't work. Since causal powers are always and necessarily properties of material objects, it is impossible to banish objects from an account of the self in the way you propose. So far as our material world is concerned at any rate, any self, at any time, will always and necessarily either be (or be composed of) one or more material objects. Consequently, framing an account in terms of casual powers, rather than the things which possess them, is a pointless and misleading endeavour.

So far as the proposed 'dematerialization' is concerned it is comparatively modest in intent. Given my agnosticism on the relationship between the physical and the phenomenal, I am neutral on the issue of whether or not experiential capacities are physical properties of a dispositional kind, on a par with mass or charge—but I am certainly not ruling this out. As for the issue of the precise relationship between powers and objects, if powers *were* necessarily features of material objects, it is by no means obvious that it would be illegitimate to identify ourselves with them: perhaps certain kinds of objects can consist of properties that belong to one or more other objects of other kinds.

However, so far as I can see, there is no good reason for supposing that experiential powers are in fact necessarily features of material things. Many philosophers who subscribe to the view that dispositional properties are generally grounded in non-dispositional bases do not rule out the possibility of there being *ungrounded* or *pure* dispositions. Indeed, there is a line of reasoning of a speculative—but by no means fanciful—kind which leads to the conclusion that all the *physical* properties that we ever might expect to be recognized by science are of this kind. Since this reasoning provides a further motivation for adopting the powers-version of the C-theory, it is worth exploring in a little detail.

Consider the scientific picture of the world, conveniently simplified. The physical world, according to our most basic science, is a world of particles, forces, and fields distributed though time and space. To keep things simple, let us suppose that scientists have discovered that there is just one kind of fundamental particle, an impenetrable atom of small but finite size, obeying certain (perfectly deterministic) laws of motion and particle–particle interaction. The physical world consists of nothing more than a collection of such particles spread through space and time, aggregated and interacting in various ways. Everything that is ever observed to happen in the physical world happens in accord with the known laws, and nothing happens which the known laws do not fully explain. Now, in this situation, and ignoring the question of how the physical world first came into being, scientists have what is sometimes called *a theory of everything*. There is nothing more for science to do; everything we might hope science could tell us about the world it has already told us. But despite this, it may seem that our knowledge of the physical world is incomplete. So far as the particles are concerned, our theory tells us that they are each impenetrable, occupying a certain volume of space and possessing various causal powers and sensitivities. Knowing everything about the causal powers of a particle tells us nothing of the intrinsic nature of that which *has* the powers, and neither does knowing that a particle is impenetrable to its kin. If we know two particles are impenetrable with respect to each other, we know that neither can occupy the space the other occupies, that each has the capacity to repel the other. But this tells us nothing about the intrinsic qualitative character of the material which pervades the interior of the particles. As for space, if we take space to be a physical entity of some sort, all we know is that it is the medium in which the particles exist and through which they move; our hypothetical completed science will tell us the geometrical structure of this medium, but nothing more; it will not tell us what the medium itself is like, in itself—and corresponding remarks apply to time.

One response to this situation is humility. We might hold that physical things do have an intrinsic nature, of some determinate kind, but accept that science can never tell us what it is.[6] But there is an alternative, and more economical position: we simply deny the existence of an unknowable intrinsic qualitative filling, we take the scientific description of the world to be complete. In so doing, we are subscribing to a view of the physical world as consisting of nothing but dispositional properties, bare dispositions that are not grounded in any categorical properties. On this view, the only features physical things possess are the causal and structural characteristics attributed to them by our physical theories. Physical objects are nothing more than variously shaped regions of space possessing various causal powers; an object's remaining unchanged at one place throughout a certain temporal interval would amount to a particular spatial region possessing a stable configuration of causal powers throughout the same interval, whereas an object in motion would involve a certain localized configuration of powers tracing out a continuous path through space. As for space itself, if our physical theory posits a substantival space (or spacetime), then it too can be construed in purely dispositional terms, as an extended field of potential, a potential for constraining and controlling the movements of the power-clusters that are constitutive of material objects. If space is relational, then the universe consists of nothing more than objects that are disposed to move in various ways with respect to one another—space itself has no independent reality.

A world of this sort, a world where all properties are purely dispositional—a *power world* as we might call it—is far from an idle fancy. The hypothetical physical theory outlined above is far simpler than the basic theories of current physics, which postulate a number of different elementary particles and fields, but it does not differ in the essentials: the properties our current theories assign to the objects and fields they recognize—properties such as mass, charge, spin, colour, and so forth—are purely dispositional in nature. So far as physics is concerned, an object qualifies as an electron (or a neutrino, or a down-quark) if it is of the right size, and *behaves* in the right sort of ways with respect to other objects and fields—there is no requirement or stipulation concerning intrinsic natures. Physical theories and physical concepts are thus purely *functional* in character: causal role is all that counts.

This fact has long been recognized: the atoms of Boscovitch's (1763) system were nothing but point-centres of causal influence, and the 'pure powers' metaphysic has had more recent adherents.[7] However, despite its appeal, there is

---

[6] The merits of this response are explored in Foster (1982, particularly chs 4 and 9), Langton (1998, 2004), Lewis (forthcoming).

[7] See, for example, Harré and Madden (1975); Shoemaker (1980), Hawthorne (2001).

a serious problem. With a little reflection, a world consisting of nothing but bare powers starts to look decidedly odd. The problem is not with the individuation of such powers. They could be individuated in terms of their relationships with one another, especially if there is a field of potential that can fulfil the role of a substantival space—this field could be taken as basic, and otherwise indistinguishable powers individuated by their locations within it.[8] Even in the absence of such a field, since the envisaged powers are all that exist in the worlds in question, they could reasonably be regarded as primitive so far as individuation goes. No, the difficulty is whether a world of this kind differs from nothing at all. Does anything ever really happen in such a world? On the face of it the answer is 'yes', since we can suppose that the powers can and do change their spatial locations and interact with one another in all manner of ways. But if nothing exists that is not a power, the envisaged changes can only bring about variations in one or more potentialities. It is not clear, to say the least, that a world in which the movement or activation of potentials can only ever bring about changes in other potentials is really intelligible. It is tempting to think that it is simply incoherent to suppose that there could be an *actual world* in which it is nomologically impossible for anything with a *non*-potential mode of being to exist.[9] There is a further and perhaps more obvious reason why the notion that we inhabit a pure powers world seems implausible: the world presented to us in our experience manifestly is not purely dispositional in nature. Since sounds, colours, textures—as they feature in our experience—possess distinctive intrinsic properties, we can be certain that our world contains something in addition to purely dispositional properties.

The latter fact suggests a way forward for an advocate of the pure powers thesis, a way of weakening the doctrine without abandoning it completely. A world which consists of nothing but dispositions for altering other dispositions may be impossible, but a world in which at least *some* dispositions can produce *something* with a qualitative or categorical nature may well not be. Accordingly, a world in which most (or all) physical things are purely dispositional, but where some physical things possess the potential to produce *experience* of some kind may well be logically possible, for experiences undeniably do possess an intrinsic qualitative character. Indeed, a world of this kind—a *P*-world* as we might call it—could easily have the appearance of a world very similar to ours, so far as its inhabitants are concerned. If phenomenal properties are non-physical, then

---

[8] Interestingly, Newton once contemplated allowing the spatial points themselves to be individuated by their relationships with each other: 'The parts of duration and space are only understood to be the same as they really are because of their mutual order and position; nor do they have any hint of individuality apart from that order and position which consequently cannot alter' (Hall and Hall 1962: 136). But as Nerlich (2005) observes, in Euclidean spaces all points are related to one another in precisely the same ways, and so no point is distinguished by its relations from any other.

[9] For variations on this objection see Blackburn (1990), Campbell (1976: 93–4), Foster (1982: 67–70), Heil (2003: 97–106), Robinson (1982: 115–21).

a P*-world may consist of nothing but bare powers; if phenomenal properties are themselves physical, then *most* of a P*-world could consist of nothing but bare powers—at least for worlds like own, where (it seems plausible to suppose) it is only when elementary physical items are configured in specific and highly complex ways that they start to be able to produce experiences.[10]

Returning to the topic in hand, the relevance of these very general metaphysical considerations is as follows. If P*-worlds are logically possible, and there is no obvious reason to think they are not, then there can be experiential powers that are ungrounded—or at least, that are not grounded in any object possessing a categorical nature. In which case, the claim that powers in general, and experiential powers in particular, necessarily possess non-dispositional grounds is false. And if we want a maximally general account of the identity conditions of subjects of experience, then we will need to formulate our account in terms of capacities, for in P*-worlds, with the exception of phenomenal states, everything that exists is purely dispositional in nature. Finally, since we cannot be sure that *our* world is not a P*-world, pursuing the capacity-oriented approach is simply prudent.

---

[10] Foster raises just this possibility: 'One possibility would be to try to specify the content of the powers in terms of the experiential responses of human subjects. Some powers (the first-level powers) would be specified as powers to affect human experience; others (the second-level powers), as powers to affect the spatiotemporal arrangement of the first-level powers; still others (the third-level powers) as powers to affect the spatiotemporal arrangement of second-level powers—and so on, as far as we need to go' (1982: 70). But he raises the possibility only to dismiss it. However, his grounds for so doing rest, so far as I can tell, on a conception of human subjects as non-physical substances, and his objections do not apply if we suppose the first-level powers produce experience *directly*. Further, even if we construe subjects in the way Foster does, the solution to the difficulty he raises—how can particular subjects related to particular parts of the physical world—can be solved by invoking the singular causal relations he himself defends elsewhere (1968, 1985: 254–63, 1991: 163–73).

12
The Topology of the Self

12.1. FISSION

Although we have by now covered a good deal of territory our various explorations have all revolved around a common point of origin. In effect, they have all been elaborations on a single plausible claim: that co-conscious experiences belong to the same self. This, of course, is the C-thesis, and the C-theory is already close by. If a self is an entity whose only essential attribute is the capacity to have experiences, it is but a short step to the conclusion that capacities for experience belong to the same self if they can produce co-conscious experiences. This conclusion is encapsulated in the Extended C-thesis, and the C-theory is no more than an elaboration of this. But while there is no denying that the C-theses have a good deal of intuitive plausibility we cannot conclude from this that they are invariably true; after all, the claim that the Earth is flat also has a good deal of intuitive plausibility. The most serious threat to the C-theses is posed by the possibility of fission.

Suppose a stream of consciousness could smoothly branch in the manner depicted in Figure 12.1. To make things as clear as possible, the stream in question is unrealistically simple: it consists of nothing more than a sequence of tones, and the contents of the post-fission branches are very similar. The tones are all of equal duration, and are half the length of their subject's specious present.

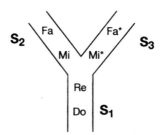

Figure 12.1 A branching stream of consciousness

We can further stipulate that this branching occurs without any rupture or diminution of phenomenal continuity, so that the final experience of the pre-fission branch, *Re*, is fully phenomenally continuous with both *Mi* and *Mi**, the initial (and numerically distinct) experiences of the post-fission branches. Since phenomenal continuity requires co-consciousness in its diachronic form *Re* will be co-conscious with both *Mi* and *Mi**. In itself this may not seem particularly problematic—we are after all dealing here with an unusual configuration of experiences. But matters soon start to look rather more problematic when we move from considering experiences to their owners.

Without prejudging their relationships to each other, let us call the subjects of the three branches S_1, S_2, and S_3, where S_1 is the owner of the pre-fission segment of the stream, S_2 and S_3 are the subjects of the left- and right-hand branches respectively. Since S_1's experience just prior to the branch-point is co-conscious with the initial experiences in S_2, the C-thesis entails that these experiences have the same subject, and hence that S_1 and S_2 are the same subject. Since S_1's experiences immediately preceding the branch-point are also co-conscious with the initial experiences in S_3, the C-thesis entails that these experiences also have a common subject, and hence that S_1 and S_3 are the same subject. If $S_1 = S_2$ and $S_1 = S_3$, then by virtue of the symmetry and transitivity of identity $S_2 = S_3$. Analogous considerations arise if we focus on experiential capacities rather than actual experiences. Suppose EC_1, EC_2, and EC_3 are the experiential capacities responsible for *Re, Mi*, and *Mi** respectively. If the Extended C-thesis is true, then since EC_1 and EC_2 can produce co-conscious experiences they are consubjective, and the same applies to EC_1 and EC_3. In which case, the symmetry and transitivity of identity entails that EC_2 and EC_3 have a common subject.

Is there anything standing in the way of our ascribing a branching structure of experiences and experiential powers to a single self? In some conceivable cases it can easily seem perverse to do anything other than precisely this. One such is a bifurcation which is both *very brief* and *highly asymmetrical*, in the manner shown in Figure 12.2. To make matters more concrete we can suppose that the depicted stream belongs to you. While changing a light bulb this morning you received a jolt of mains electricity, and this caused your stream of consciousness to briefly split in the manner indicated; the short-lived tributary lasted only a couple of seconds, and consisted entirely of tingling sensations in your right hand. Not surprisingly you noticed nothing untoward; the fact that these tingling sensations were not co-conscious with the main body of your experiences completely escaped your attention.

If a branching of this kind could occur, it seems quite natural to ascribe all the experiences to a single subject. There is a cost in so-doing: it is also plausible to think that at any given time a subject's consciousness is fully unified, that is to say that all the experiences which belong to the same subject at a given moment of time are mutually co-conscious—recall the $C^\#$-thesis of §8.6. If brief bifurcations in a single subject's consciousness could occur, then obviously there would be exceptions to the $C^\#$-thesis. Perhaps this is something we could

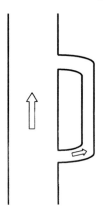

Figure 12.2 A radically asymmetrical bifurcation

learn to live with. Provided the bifurcation does not last long, there may even be *symmetrical* cases in which it can seem reasonable to suppose both streams have a common subject. In his well-known 'My Physics Exam' scenario Parfit imagines that he has the ability to divide his mind at will merely by raising his eyebrows; he is able to do this because he has been fitted with a device which blocks communication between his cerebral hemispheres. Faced with a tricky problem, Parfit decides to divide his mind for a period of ten minutes, so as to work on two different ways of tackling a question. During these ten minutes he has two streams of consciousness, each of which is served by a separate cognitive system. But since this division is only temporary, and only involves a single body, Parfit (quite plausibly) maintains that only a single person is involved, and hence concludes: 'We can come to believe that a person's mental history need not be like a canal, with only one channel, but could be like a river, occasionally having separate streams' (1984: 247).

Irrespective of whether Parfit's diagnosis of this case is correct, more radical divisions do not seem susceptible to the same treatment. In cases where the division is *complete* and *long-lasting* it can easily seem perverse in the extreme to hold that only a single subject is involved. This is especially clear in the context of the C-theory.

Modifying our original case, let us now suppose that each limb of the branching stream shown in Figure 12.1 has a character similar to that of a typical adult human (rather than a simple sequence of tones) and that the bifurcation is the product of a branching configuration of C-related experiential capacities. Such a configuration consists of a single earlier C-system (call it S_1) being C-related to two later and contemporaneous C-systems (S_2 and S_3). Putting flesh on the labels, we can suppose S_2 and S_3 entered the picture when the original subject's brain was divided into two halves, with each half being successfully transplanted into a new and independent body. Since according to the C-theory in its ontological guise C-systems are selves, we do not have the option of maintaining that the fission-products S_2 and S_3 are merely *parts* of a subject, or that they jointly constitute a *single subject with a divided consciousness*: if S_2 and S_3 are complete and distinct C-systems in their own right, each has precisely what is required to be a *self* in its own right. This quickly leads to a highly problematic result. For if S_1 and S_2 are C-related they are numerically identical, and the same applies to S_1 and S_3, and as we have already seen if $S_1 = S_2$ and $S_1 = S_3$ then $S_2 = S_3$. Although this is undeniably and unequivocally the result the C-theory delivers, how can it possibly be correct? How can *two* subjects be *one*?

If the identity of the post-fission subjects seems absurd from the perspective of the C-theory, it is scarcely less so from that of common sense. In the scenario we are now envisaging S_2 and S_3 have all the outward appearances of being two perfectly ordinary human beings, each getting on with their own lives in their own ways. S_2 is not directly aware of S_3's experiences, and vice-versa; at 3am after the transplant operation S_2 is safely tucked up in bed, while S_3 is dancing away in a nightclub; by noon the next day S_2 is out on an extended shopping trip while S_3 is catching up on lost sleep. It seems absurd to suppose S_2 and S_3 are one and the same self. How can a single self be both in motion and motionless, or conscious and unconscious, at the same time?

Hence the problem facing the C-theory. If C-systems can branch in the way envisaged, we are led to the seemingly paradoxical conclusion that distinct things are one and the same, that $1 + 1 = 1$ rather than 2. The only obvious way of circumventing this result is to hold that the original subject does *not* survive the division of its C-system. But this is highly problematic too. For we must now accept that there are circumstances in which subjects can be C-related without being numerically identical, and in which the C-theses are false. But how easy is it to believe that experiences can be co-conscious without being consubjective? Or that experiential capacities with the ability to produce co-conscious experiences could belong to distinct subjects?

There is a second difficulty, albeit of a less momentous kind. Parfit's verdict that only a single subject is involved in the 'My Physics Exam' scenario has some plausibility, but on the face of it this is a verdict the C-theory cannot deliver. According to the C-theory, facts about the existence and persistence of subjects are determined entirely by facts about actual and potential experiences, all other factors are irrelevant. When Parfit divides his brain his original C-system splits into two C-systems (or so it seems very plausible to suppose), and so far as the C-theory is concerned, this means two *subjects* come into existence—the fact that the post-fission C-systems are located in the same body is irrelevant, likewise the fact that the division is short-lived. Is the C-theorist committed to construing this sort of scenario in an intuitively implausible manner?

If so it would not necessarily be disastrous—most theories have *some* counter-intuitive consequences—but before arriving at any conclusions concerning this issue we need to decide on how best to construe fission itself, and this is what I will be concentrating on in what follows. Since I am particularly interested in what should be said about fission from the perspective of the C-theory, henceforth I shall confine my attention to fissions of the sort which are problematic from this perspective. Henceforth by 'fission' I mean a process in which a single C-system divides into two C-systems without any interruption in C-relatedness, that is in which a single earlier C-system is C-related to two (or more) C-systems at a later time t_2.

12.2. FISSION AS FATAL

Of course fission poses serious problems for other accounts of our persistence conditions, and the issue has been much debated in recent years. A good deal of this discussion has focused on Parfit's own treatment of the topic.[1] Parfit regards fission scenarios of the 'My Physics Exam' variety as a special case. In cases where the division is long-term (or permanent) and the fission-products go their separate ways, he argues that we have no option but to regard them as numerically distinct people—to do otherwise would put massive and unacceptable strain on our concept of personhood. The question then arises as to the fate of a person who undergoes such a fission. In Parfit's eyes, the most intelligible option is to hold that the pre-fission person ceases to exist at the point of division. If we were to say that the pre-fission person is identical with both post-fission people, then we would have to say that the latter were numerically identical with each other, which we have already ruled out. The only other obvious option is to hold that the pre-fission person is identical with just one of the post-fission people, but this is implausible too: fission (of the kind we are currently concerned with) involves a more-or-less *symmetrical* branching of the mental and/or physical continuities which determine facts about personal persistence. Hence the conclusion that fission is best construed as fatal. But Parfit also holds that it is hard to regard fission as we would ordinarily regard death. More specifically, it is hard to believe that *dividing* is anything like as bad as *dying*. The prospect of imminent non-existence is apt to provoke occasional feelings of dread even in those for whom life has lost its appeal, but the prospect of undergoing a fission which fully preserves mental and physical continuity is a far less momentous prospect. Given this, Parfit argues that fission teaches us a valuable lesson. If fission puts an end to our existence but is also nothing like as bad as dying, it seems we have no option but to conclude that what matters in life, in the moral and prudential senses, is not identity but the mental and physical continuities which normally

---

[1] See Parfit (1971, 1984: §89–90). On more than one occasion Parfit has remarked that it was Wiggins' ground-breaking discussion of personal fission which first drew him into philosophy (e.g. Parfit 1987: 19).

accompany identity. It is natural that we should assume personal identity is what matters because people's lives are, with few if any known exceptions, always linear. But reflecting on fission cases shows us that identity and what matters can come apart, and that identity in itself has little or no intrinsic value.

In more general terms, Parfit's argument is that we can come to accept the insignificance of our existence by appreciating that it consists in nothing more than the *linear* unfolding of the mental and physical continuities which constitute our lives, which although normally of this form, need not be so, as the possibilities of fission (and fusion) show. By understanding that self-identity corresponds to nothing more than a particular shape of life, our concern for our own persistence can, it is argued, properly transcend the boundaries of our own existence.

Modifying the C-theory so as to accommodate Parfit's conclusion could easily be done. It would suffice first to weaken the C-thesis, by holding that co-consciousness is sufficient for consubjectivity provided the stream of consciousness concerned is non-branching. We could then hold that although C-relatedness must take a linear form if it is to secure the persistence of a single self, and does not do so otherwise, it also carries much of what matters in life even in cases where a self divides. Of course, an account along these lines would not be entirely Parfittean—Parfit thinks it is P-relatedness that matters most—but as we saw in §6.6, this ceases to be plausible as soon as C- and P-relations are clearly distinguished.

However, whether it would be advisable to take these steps is altogether another matter. The point is simple but deep; but since by now it is also very familiar, I shall be brief.

Parfit's contention that fission is not as bad as an ordinary death is very plausible; likewise the claim that much of what matters in an ordinary life is preserved in fission. The trouble is, *so much* of what matters is preserved that it is difficult to believe that identity is not preserved as well. The force of this point is particularly strong when fission is considered from a phenomenal perspective. Consider a case in which the transition between pre- and post-fission streams of consciousness is subjectively imperceptible: the pre-fission stream flows on, phenomenal continuity entirely undisturbed, with a character that is in no way out of the ordinary. A division of this sort could easily be brought about using a variant of the VR-technology introduced earlier. If Parfit is right and fission is fatal, then when the division occurs the original subject ceases to exist and two new subjects come into being. But if this interpretation is correct, a subject can *cease to exist while their consciousness flows on*, without any interruption in phenomenal continuity. This is difficult to comprehend or accept. How could an experience which lies 'upstream' of my current experience belong to anyone other than me? Focusing on the point of division itself, how could a single unified conscious episode—such as the thinking of a single thought—belong to distinct subjects? More specifically, how can two experiences that are experienced together as co-conscious—such as *Re* and *Mi* in Figure 12.1—belong to distinct subjects? The claim that the experiences constituting the right and left halves of my visual field could belong to distinct subjects seems utterly absurd. Is the claim that the earlier and later phases of an experience of *Re-Mi* could belong to distinct subjects any less absurd? In both cases we are dealing with experiences that are experienced together, experiences that are parts of the same unified state of consciousness.

If it is difficult to take such alleged possibilities seriously—and it surely is—this is because it is difficult to see how an uninterrupted stream of consciousness, a stream whose successive phases are directly co-conscious, can be anything other than self-preserving. Or in fewer words: it is hard to believe that the C-thesis in its unqualified form could be false.[2]

12.3. CAN CONSCIOUSNESS DIVIDE?

We are confronted with an awkward dilemma. While it may be difficult to see how the products of fission can be numerically identical with each other, it is at least as difficult to accept that fission can be fatal. Since the dilemma is particularly acute when fission is viewed in phenomenal terms, some may be tempted by the thought that the phenomenal also holds the key to solving the problem. The evidence from commissurotomy operations suggests that it may well be possible to split an ordinary human brain into two independent working parts. Although the brain-splitting operations that have been carried out thus far usually only separate the cerebral hemispheres, it may one day prove possible to divide the lower brain too. As we have also seen, there is no reason to suppose that it is in principle impossible for the causal relations that are constitutive of psychological continuity to adopt a branching configuration: teleportation scenarios in which this occurs are easily conceivable. But is it equally clear that a *consciousness* could divide? It may be possible to divide a human brain into two parts each of which subsequently possesses the capacity for consciousness, but it does not follow from this that the original brain's capacity for consciousness remains intact throughout the operation, and unless C-relatedness is preserved throughout, the original subject will not survive. If it could be established that it

---

[2] Parfit certainly does not deny that fissions of this sort are possible: 'The division of one stream of consciousness might be claimed to be deeply impossible. But what has happened must be possible: and in the lives of several people this has happened' (1984: 278). Shoemaker, whose views on this topic are similar to Parfit's, is explicit on the matter: 'if fission were to occur in the middle of such a temporally extended awareness then the awareness itself would undergo fission and the later parts of it would not be copersonal either with each other or with the earlier part . . .' (Shoemaker 1984: 148). In other words, Descartes might, by undergoing fission, have ceased to exist at some point during the thinking of the thought *cogito ergo sum* leaving its completion to the new owners of his stream of consciousness.

is impossible for a stream of consciousness to smoothly divide, then we could be sure that C-relatedness could not bifurcate, and hence rule out the possibility of personal fission. Unfortunately, although it would make life a good deal simpler in more ways than one, I cannot see any reason for thinking that consciousness *is* indivisible.

If we had independent grounds for thinking that selves are necessarily indivisible then we could conclude, given certain other reasonable assumptions, that streams of consciousness and C-systems are indivisible. And there are of course many metaphysical systems—the various species of rationalism come most quickly to mind—which proclaim the simplicity and indivisibility of the self (or soul). However, within the confines of the experience-based approach I am exploring here, arguing from the nature of the self to the possible forms of consciousness is getting things back to front. I am taking the possible forms of consciousness as my principle guide to the nature (and possible forms of) the self. This said, if advocates of the simple unsplittable self had any compelling arguments for their position it would be a different matter, these arguments would have to be considered. But I am not aware of any such argument.[3]

Working within experience, as it were, what do we find? It is certainly difficult to imagine what it would be like for one's own consciousness to divide into two. There is no difficulty in imagining what each of the post-fission streams is like individually—they might each be quite unexceptional—but when we try to imagine what the actual moment of branching would be like we hit a wall. However, this is only to be expected. If a stream of consciousness were to divide without its experiential continuity being interrupted, the final pre-division experiences would be co-conscious with the initial post-division experiences in both newly created streams, but the latter experiences would not be co-conscious with one another. Yet any form of experience which can be faithfully envisaged in the imagination of an ordinary non-dividing human consciousness will be fully co-conscious, simply because all parts of an ordinary human consciousness are fully co-conscious, and since this includes the contents of the imagination, the distinctive experiential configuration of a dividing consciousness cannot be faithfully represented in our imaginations. In trying to imagine what such a fission would be like without fissioning ourselves, we *are* attempting the impossible. In the light of this, our inability to imagine what a branching in consciousness

---

[3] To take just one instance, in the Sixth Meditation we find Descartes arguing thus: 'the mind is utterly indivisible. For when I consider the mind, or myself in so far as I am merely a thinking thing, I am unable to distinguish any parts within myself; I understand myself to be something quite single and complete.' What sort of access does Descartes have to the self which allows him to state with confidence that it is without separable parts? Since Descartes regarded experiences as modifications of a substantival conscious substance, there is a sense in which we encounter the self in our experience. But since all we encounter are experiences, and these are evidently divisible into parts—just think of the right and left parts of your current visual field—it is far from clear how the character of our experience supports the indivisibility thesis.

would be like at the subjective level should not in itself lead us to suppose that it could not happen.

Is there any feature of consciousness itself that might preclude the possibility of fission? One view of the internal structure and composition of consciousness might seem to support the indivisibility doctrine: the awareness-content (or NP-model) we encountered in Chapter 2. Suppose it were the case that our experiences are unified by virtue of being presented to a single, point-like centre of pure awareness. If there are centres of pure awareness of this kind, they presumably lack constituent parts. If so, would it follow that they are indivisible? In one sense, yes. When compound objects such as amoeba divide they generally do so by splitting into two or more parts, each of which previously existed in the whole object. Clearly, an object lacking proper parts cannot divide in this sort of way, and the same might apply to loci of pure awareness. However, there are other ways in which one thing can become two. A geometrical straight line, as normally conceived, is composed of dimensionless points. Can such a line branch? Of course: all it takes is for two line-segments to emerge from a given point rather than one, as in the familiar Y-shape. Can we rule out the possibility that centres of pure awareness can behave in a similar manner? It is hard to see how.

However, since I can see no reason to believe that the NP-model of con-sciousness is true, such considerations are irrelevant. According to the Simple Conception outlined in §2.5 and assumed subsequently, a unified consciousness is a state of consciousness whose parts are connected by the co-consciousness relationship. It is difficult to see how this conception could provide us with a reason for supposing that consciousness is indivisible. What is there to *pre-vent* the co-consciousness relation holding between the component parts of a branching stream of consciousness? It is tempting to answer 'Nothing whatso-ever'—especially bearing in mind our earlier results concerning the diachronic unity of consciousness. Consider again the hypothetical branching depicted in Figure 12.1, where *Re*, the final pre-fission experience is co-conscious with the preceding tone *Do* and *Mi* and *Mi**, the initial experiences in each of the ensuing post-fission branches. This branching structure consists of three partially overlapping total experiences—*Do-Re, Re-Mi, Re-Mi**—with *Re* as a common part. Given the non-transitivity of the diachronic co-consciousness relationship it is difficult to see anything inherently problematic here: what we have is a collection of partially overlapping total experiences, and overlaps of this sort are a ubiquitous feature of non-branching streams. There is of course a difference. In a non-branching stream partially overlapping total experiences occur successively, whereas in the branching case, two such experiences occur simultaneously. That a branching stream of consciousness should contain different experiential relations than those characteristic of linear streams is only to be expected. The key point is that the internal inter-experiential relations are in both cases precisely the same: the relationships responsible for the experienced continuity of our streams of consciousness, namely partially overlapping total experiences and the consequent non-transitivity of co-consciousness, are also the relationships between experiences which would have to obtain if streamal branching were possible. Since we know these relationships can and do obtain, it seems that purely phenomenal considerations do not give us any reason for thinking that it is impossible for a stream of consciousness to divide.

The possibility or otherwise of a weakly unified consciousness is also relevant here. If a state of consciousness at a given time can vary in the degree to which it is unified—if *synchronic* co-consciousness can fail to be transitive—then it might be possible for a stream to branch in a gradual fashion. Such a stream would start off fully unified, and then becomes progressively less unified as time passes, until in the end there are two entirely separate streams. But if, on the other hand, synchronic co-consciousness is transitive, as I suggested in §8.6, then at any given time a stream is necessarily fully unified, and if streamal fission is possible at all, it must take place all at once rather than in a gradual fashion: a single stream of consciousness will *suddenly* become two entirely distinct streams. A fission of this kind is rather more dramatic than the gradual variety, but from a purely experiential point of view there is no reason to think it is impossible. The experiential structures involved are those we have just been considering.

12.4. OVERLAP TO THE RESCUE?

If we cannot rule out the possibility that a stream of consciousness might branch we must face up the dilemma posed by fission. Our earlier diagnosis left us in an uncomfortable position. It seemed that we either had to accept that fission is fatal and that the C-theses are false, which is hard to do, or we accept that the subjects which result from a fission—call them *fission-twins*—are numerically identical with one another, which is equally hard to do. There is, however, another option, a way of interpreting fission which does not require us to accept that fission-twins are numerically identical, but which also allows us to regard fission as identity-conserving. How is the trick worked? Surprisingly easily. Rather than supposing that fission involves a single person turning into two people, we hold that it consists in the separation and subsequent divergence of two already-extant but temporally *overlapping* people, both of whom persist through fission. Adherents of this approach hold that if (what seems to be) a person X divides into (what seem to be) two distinct persons, Y and Z, then although the latter are what they seem to be—genuinely distinct individuals—it is otherwise with X. Despite appearances, X is not one person but two temporally coinciding people, Y and Z, both of whom survive fission intact; what seems to be a single human body and mind is thus 'multiply occupied'.

In some ways this approach is attractive. Were it to prove viable, we would not be obliged to revise the C-theses, and we could reject Parfit's fission-based argument that identity and what matters can diverge. But of course, there is a downside: it is by no means obvious how what seems to be a single person could in fact be two. However, this matter is not as straightforward as it might initially appear. There are different conceptions of persisting things, and a state of affairs which seems absurd by the lights of one conception may be entirely unproblematic by the lights of another.

In its standard form—that expounded in Lewis (1976*b*)—the multiple occupancy doctrine is an offshoot of the perdurance conception of persistence. According to the view Lewis recommends, persons are not continuants in the orthodox sense, but rather maximal mereological sums of persons-at-times, or person-stages. A person-stage is simply the way a particular person is at a particular time, and for the perdurantist, persisting persons are composed of these parts in just the same way as a book is composed of a collection of pages, or a symphony is composed of a sequence of notes. This idea takes a little getting used to. We do not naturally think of person-stages as being *parts* of persons. The notion that when we see a friend across the street, examining the contents of a shop's window, we are not seeing the whole person but only a tiny part of them, strikes most of us as odd, at least on first encountering it. Most of us, if asked to come up with a list of our constituent parts, would mention things like arms, legs, or various internal organs, or cells, or atoms, or even sub-atomic particles or mental states of various kinds, but not items such as 'the way I was at noon yesterday'. This is because common sense recognizes *spatial* parts but not *temporal* parts. If the only parts that persisting things possess are necessarily of the spatial variety, then in encountering an object we cannot but encounter the whole thing each time we come across it, and what goes for encounters also goes for existence: if objects necessarily lack temporal parts, they must be completely present at all times at which they exist. In short, the endurance view of persistence would be correct and objects would be three-dimensional continuants that persist by being wholly present at a succession of times. But if, by contrast, objects did possess temporal as well as spatial parts, then persisting things clearly would not be fully present at any of the times at which they exist: if parts of them are located at earlier and later times, then at any one time they would be only partly present. Moreover, if objects do have parts existing at other times—if they are spread across time in much the same way as they are spread across space—then it seems obvious that the *whole* object consists of the complete collection of its spatial and temporal parts.

Returning to the case in hand, if we adopt the perdurantist view of persistence, and so hold that a person is identical with a sum of person-stages, then as Lewis points out, we can resolve the fission puzzle in a seemingly straightforward manner. Collections, or mereological sums, can partially overlap by sharing common parts, for example the sum of all animals on earth at the present time which have eyes and the sum of all animals which have tails overlap in this way. If persons are sums of this sort, perhaps they too can share parts. Siamese twins are a familiar example of distinct persons spatially overlapping, perhaps fission is a slightly less familiar case of distinct persons *temporally* overlapping, by sharing some (but not all) of their temporal parts, in the manner depicted in Figure 12.3, where A, B, etc. are person-stages.

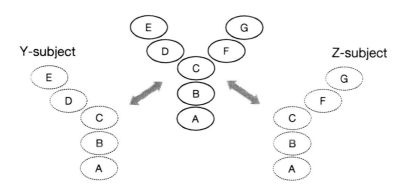

Figure 12.3 Fission construed as partial overlap

As can be seen, overlap by (temporal) part-sharing looks straightforward: one subject, Y, consists of the sum [A, B, C, D, E], while the second subject, Z, consists of the sum [A, B, C, F, G]. If we stipulate that each of these collections is C-related, then the stages in each collection will be consubjective. Hence to bring the C-theory into conformity with the standard form of perdurantism, it suffices to take ourselves (and others) to be identical with *maximal* aggregates of C-related person- or subject-stages. We want less-than-maximal sums to constitute parts of persisting subjects, rather than be subjects in their own right.

Lewis' resolution of the fission-puzzle has its advantages. It allows us to retain the idea that every uninterrupted stream of consciousness belongs to the same subject, and likewise for every C-related series of experiential powers. We are no longer being asked to accept that subjects can cease to exist without losing consciousness, or that experiences can be co-conscious without being consubjective. Moreover, from a general metaphysical perspective it provides us with a clear grasp on what fission involves. None of us has any difficulty in understanding what is involved when two paths cross: they share a common part or phase. Provided we accept that persisting subjects have temporal as well as spatial parts, we can construe fission in an analogous and equally unproblematic way. So should the C-theorists avail themselves of Lewis's proposal?

I think not. At the very least it is worth seeking an alternative. One reason for this is implicit in the preceding paragraph. Lewis offers a metaphysically perspicuous account of what fission involves *provided one accepts that persisting subjects have temporal as well as spatial parts*. While some are more than happy to accept this, many others are not—Wiggins, van Inwagen, Thomson, Geach, Mellor, Lowe, Johnston, amongst them. The debate between perdurance and endurance theorists shows no sign of abating, and it may well be that there will be no clear victor: we might well end up with two equally viable conceptual frameworks, two quite different ways of thinking about persistence, each with its own advantages and disadvantages. For this reason alone it would be a mistake to endorse an account of fission which is only viable within one of these frameworks. And as I stated at the outset, I am looking for an account of the self which is as neutral as possible with regard to broad metaphysical disputes such as this.[4]

There is an additional reason for dissatisfaction with Lewis' position. Although Lewis allows us to retain the doctrine that streams of consciousness are reliable guides to the persistence of subjects, this comes at a cost: consciousness is no longer a reliable guide to the *existence* of subjects. It is natural to think that a single stream of consciousness necessarily belongs to a single persisting subject, but if Lewis is right, this is not the case: there is no limit on the number of subjects to whom your current state of consciousness might belong—it could be one, but it could be two, or three, or even hundreds—it all depends on what happens (or does not happen) at other times. And this is not all. If we take consciousness as our primary guide to our persistence then Lewis' claim that the post-fission limbs of a branching stream of consciousness belong to numerically distinct subjects rings false. If I were in the position of seriously envisaging my current stream of consciousness branching, I would find it very hard to avoid concluding that *I myself* would continue to exist as the subject of *both* post-fission limbs. Since *my* current stream will flow into each of the post-fission limbs, how could it possibly be otherwise?

Although not an advocate of an experience-based approach to the self, Lewis is alert to difficulties of this kind. He suggests that prior to my fission if I think to myself 'If my consciousness flows on, *I* will survive' my use of 'I' lacks a determinate reference, since it could refer to either or both of the subjects who will subsequently separate. But while this would clearly be the case if 'I' am currently two distinct subjects, it is not easy to believe this is in fact the case. Lewis appreciates that he is requiring us to revise our ordinary criteria of synchronic identity, our ordinary ways of counting objects (and subjects). Returning to

---

[4] There is also a worry concerning the generality of the perdurance way of thinking. The four-dimensional view of continuants may be viable in a four-dimensional universe—a universe where all times and events are equally real—it is by no means evident, however, that it makes much, if any, sense in a *three*-dimensional universe, a universe where past and future events do not exist. (Here I use 'exist' to mean *exist simpliciter*, rather than *exist at such and such time*). I am not sure that we are yet in a position to be certain that our own universe is not of the latter kind, let alone other possible universes: presentism arguably remains a live option. See Dainton (2001, chs 6, 17, 18) for more on the case for (and against) presentism, and Merricks (1995, 1999) and Hestevold and Carter (2002) for more on presentism and endurantism. Robinson (1985) suggests a modified form of the overlap account is in fact available to endurantists; see Miller (2006) for criticism.

the case in which X divides into Y and Z, since it is not in doubt that X fulfils our ordinary criteria for being a single person—he has a single body, a single undivided brain, a single stream of consciousness—how can X possibly be anything other than a single person? Lewis concurs that there is a sense in which X is indeed a single person. He suggests that ordinarily, when counting persons, we do so using a weaker relation than identity, *identity-at-a-time*: two distinct continuants C_1 and C_2 are identical-at-time-t if and only if they both exist at t and their stages are identical (1983: 64). So in terms of this tensed identity relationship, Y and Z are one person prior to their fission, since they share their stages at all the relevant times, but two afterwards, since their stages are no longer identical. This may make sense in its own terms, but how plausible is it to suppose that we ordinarily count in terms of tensed identity rather than identity? Moreover, as Sider remarks: 'I doubt this procedure of associating numbers with objects is really *counting*. Part of the meaning of "counting" is that counting is by identity; "how many objects" means "how many numerically distinct objects". Counting must be by identity when we count objects not in time (numbers, for example), and surely we count persons in the same sense in which we count numbers' (2001: 189). Quite so.

Sider himself is no friend of the endurance theory, but he thinks the four-dimensionalist must do better than Lewis in accommodating the possibility of fission, so he offers an alternative (1996, 2001: 188–208). As we have seen, in its standard form the perdurance theory identifies continuants with the sum of their spatial and temporal parts—Sider dubs this *the worm view*. In its stead he proposes *the stage view*. According to the latter, continuants are identical with their momentary stages: strictly speaking, nothing—no *thing*, at least—lasts more than an instant. This might seem rather implausible, to say the least, but as Sider shows, it is by no means totally absurd. The stage theorist can, for example, accept that there are truths of the form 'I went to the cinema last week', even though none of us exist at more than one time. What makes this claim true, according to Sider, is the fact that someone other than me went to the cinema last week, a person related to me by a distinctive 'personal counterpart relation'—and the latter could easily be C-relatedness. For present purposes, the stage view is significant because it is immune to the counting problem that afflicts the worm theorist's treatment of fission. Prior to his division, X always consists of just one stage, and is therefore just one person. What makes it true to say that X will undergo fission is that he is related to two sets of simultaneously existing person-stages by the personal counterpart relation, rather than the usual linear succession. Unfortunately, this bonus comes at a significant cost. Whatever its other flaws, Lewis' worm theory could at least accommodate the intuition that we continue to exist for as long as our streams of consciousness flow on, or for as long as our C-systems persist. Since it turns us into momentary beings, Sider's stage theory does not. Parfit allows us to perish mid-stream, as it were, Sider does not allow us even to get that far. Hence so far as the experience-based approach is concerned, the stage view falls at the first hurdle.[5]

12.5. TIME TRAVEL AND DOUBLE EXISTENCE

Since construing fission in terms of temporary temporal overlap is by no means unproblematic, we need to look for an alternative. Ideally, as our consideration of Lewis' position has revealed, what the C-theorist needs is a construal that allows a single pre-fission subject to continue to exist as both post-fission subjects. In fact, this is not the absolute impossibility it might initially seem. In order to appreciate why this is so it will help if we return to basics. Why is it exactly that the notion that a pair of fission-twins might be one and the same strikes us as so bizarre? That *two* simultaneously existing entities of the same kind must be distinct—and so cannot be *one*—seems perfectly obvious. Suppose I pick up two billiard balls and hold one in each hand; what conceivable sense is there in the idea that they might be one and the same billiard ball? The same goes for ordinary human beings. The idea that two billiard players who are playing one another might be the same person may seem quite senseless. But let us run the risk of stating the obvious by probing a little more deeply.

As traditionally conceived, a continuant is an entity which can exist at different times with different properties. Continuants also have histories or careers which are continuous: they exist at an uninterrupted succession of moments. Or at least for the most part. There are certain complex artefacts, such as clocks, which can be disassembled into their component parts, and then reassembled from the same parts at a later date. Objects of this sort may be said to enjoy the possibility of intermittent existence. However, if the careers of continuants need not be continuous, it is natural to think that they must certainly be linear, or perhaps more accurately, *temporally linear*, since it is with time alone that we are concerned here. From a perdurantist perspective the career of a continuant consists of a succession of thing-stages, of a particular type, connected by the diachronic identity criterion appropriate to that type—which we can refer to as *R*. A temporally linear series of *R*-related thing-stages is one in which no stage is immediately succeeded, or preceded, by two (or more) stages which are *simultaneous* with one another. Switching from the language of perdurance back

---

[5] There is a quite different way of construing fission as separation, which merits a more detailed treatment than I can give it here. Mills (1993) argues that we will always be justified in viewing fission as involving the divergence of two *previously existing* streams of consciousness. While this would do the trick so far as the C-theory is concerned, I find Mills' argument for this claim unpersuasive. Summarizing rather harshly, Mills holds that we can legitimately dismiss the possibility of a single pre-fission stream on the grounds that if we accept it we would be depriving ourselves of knowledge we are confident we possess. But are we sure that fission always involves the separation of two streams rather than the branching of one? I cannot see that we are.

to that of endurance, a temporally linear continuant exists at a succession of times, and at each of these times it exists only once. Since it is difficult to envisage a single persisting thing having a career that is not temporally linear, it is natural to assume that persistence and temporal linearity go hand in hand. Once this assumption is made, it will also seem natural to suppose that two simultaneously existing continuants cannot be numerically identical—that a continuant cannot enjoy a *double existence* by existing twice-over at two different places at the same time. This relationship between singleness and time is particularly, perhaps uniquely, strong in the case of the self: the idea that *we* only exist once at a given time is an especially powerful one. 'Of all things existing now, there is only one *me*, and that is the thing thinking *this* thought *now!*'—there is no denying the appeal and plausibility of claims such as this.

However it would, I think, be a mistake simply to assume that the relationship between singleness and time enshrined in the temporal linearity principle is in fact a part of the unshakeable bedrock of our thought. Might there not be exceptions to the principle, even if only in exceptional circumstances? One such is a situation which is akin to the fission of a person—in that some have questioned its very possibility—but is nonetheless familiar from fiction and philosophy: time travel. If people could travel in time they could, by journeying back to the appropriate period, live once more through the very same hours or years in which they dwelled in their youth. If they wanted, such travellers could even arrange to meet their earlier selves. The fact that we can (at least initially) entertain such a possibility so easily suggests the concept of a continuant, more specifically, that aspect of this concept pertaining to its relationship to time, is more flexible than is commonly supposed: a time traveller meeting him- or herself is a case of the same embodied person simultaneously existing at different locations, or in other words, numerically the same continuant existing twice-over at the same time.

It might be argued that although we can indeed visually picture co-existing with our earlier (or later) selves in this fashion, no significant conclusion can be drawn from this case because time travel is in fact logically impossible. Against this, however, it can be pointed out that not only are the various arguments purporting to prove this impossibility of questionable cogency, but time travel seems to be a *physical* possibility in our universe. That one can, in a sense, travel into the future simply by moving very quickly with respect to someone else, is an accepted consequence of the Special Theory of Relativity. One could not meet one's future self like this, of course. However Gödel (1949) showed that the possibility of a thing travelling into its own past is contained in the equations of General Relativity. This is not the place to explore these issues, but we do not need to.[6] This is because the (good) arguments which purport to show time travel to be logically impossible are fairly abstruse, and the concept of a continuant is so basic, even if these arguments were sound they would not affect the limited claim

---

[6] For a survey of these matters see Dainton (2001: ch. 8).

I am making here, which is that we should at least hesitate before assuming that our general concept of a thing (or person, or self) is incompatible with double existence.

Fission, of course, is not time travel. But double existence is double existence. Why does the idea of persons leading a double existence strike us as so absurd in the context of fission but relatively banal in the context of time travel? The difference may be due partly to our familiarity with science fiction tales of time travel which result in double existence. But I suspect it may also be due to the fact that throughout the course of the relevant time travels we manage to keep a stronger grasp on the integrity of a single subject's persistence than we do when we think of fission cases. This is so because there is an important sense in which the temporal linearity of a time traveller's life is preserved. When we imagine a case of time travel, we tacitly assume the intrinsic structure of a traveller's life is no different from anyone else's: it consists of a succession of stages, each a little older than its predecessor. If a time traveller meets his or her earlier self, two stages of the same subject's life exist simultaneously, but they are (we automatically and rightly suppose) nonetheless separated by a linear succession of intervening stages, each a little older than its predecessor. Time travellers may jump back and forth through time, but they age one day at a time—just like the rest of us. Consequently, temporal linearity is preserved, since no stage of a time traveller's life is *immediately* succeeded, or preceded, by two simultaneously existing stages. Unlike a time traveller, a subject who undergoes fission seems to contravene the principle of temporal linearity, since the last pre-fission stage of their life is immediately followed by *two* simultaneous stages.

However, although a time traveller's life retains the property of temporal linearity in its own terms, it does not do so with respect to the rest of the world: a life which cuts back on itself, whose later phases occur before its earlier phases, is clearly not distributed through time in a linear fashion. One might take this as evidence that the picture of time travel we have been working with is paradoxical. But alternatively, one could argue that the paradox is only apparent, because it is obvious that implicit in the way we envisage time travel is a distinction between two kinds of temporal system: ordinary time, the time of the world as a whole, and a time determined by the life of a time traveller. Although the stages of the traveller's life do not occur in temporally linear succession in ordinary time, with respect to what it is natural to call the *time of his life*, they do. From the latter temporal perspective, each stage of his life is immediately preceded and immediately succeeded by just one stage, never two. In 'The Paradoxes of Time Travel' (1976*a*) we find David Lewis making just such a distinction—between what he calls 'external' and 'personal' times—as part of his defence of the possibility of travelling through time. External time is what a time traveller travels through, the time of his world; personal time is the time of his life, a temporal framework from within the perspective of which his life *continuously* unfolds, irrespective of any discontinuities in the path his life takes through external time. Accurate descriptions of events in terms of external time differ from accurate descriptions of the same events in terms of personal time, but they do so without contradiction, since such descriptions consist of true statements about different temporal relations.

The distinction between external and personal time renders intelligible double existence in the case of time travel, for if we allow that a time traveller's personal time is a legitimate temporal framework for the purpose of making sense of their life, then their double existence in external time is unproblematic. As we shall see, the same line of reasoning—to which I shall return in §12.7—can be extended to the double existence consequent upon personal fission, and renders it as unobjectionable as that brought about by time travel. But before venturing into these waters we need to take a closer look at the notion of personal time.

12.6. PERSONAL AND PHENOMENAL TIME

Lewis defines personal time in terms of an ordering relation among person-stages. Ordering the person-stages which comprise a time traveller's life in their personal time is a matter of ordering them as they occur successively in the traveller's life, as opposed to the order in which they occur in external time. Lewis suggests, convincingly, that this can be done in terms of the mental and physical continuities which characterize a life:

If you take the stages of a common person, they manifest certain regularities with respect to external time. Properties change continuously as you go along, for the most part, and in familiar ways. First come infantile stages. Last come senile ones. Memories accumulate. Food digests. Hair grows. Wristwatch hands move. If you take the stages of a time traveller instead, they do not manifest the common regularities with respect to external time. But there is one way to assign coordinates to the time traveller's stages, and one way only . . . so that the regularities that hold with respect to this assignment match those that commonly hold with respect to external time. With respect to the correct assignment properties change continuously as you go along, for the most part, and in familiar ways. First come infantile stages. Last come senile ones. Memories accumulate. Food digests. Hair grows. Wristwatch hands move. The assignment of coordinates that yields this match is the time traveller's personal time. (Lewis 1976a: 70)

It is important to note a point concerning the generality of the notion of personal time defined in this fashion. Those collections of person-stages which comprise the lives of individual people are determined by the diachronic identity criterion for persons, and since Lewis' method of assigning personal time coordinates is not restricted to any particular diachronic personal identity criterion, the concept of personal time is not hostage to any particular account of personal identity.[7]

---

[7] Lewis suggests that a set of person-stages are only to be assigned to the same person if they can all be ordered in a single personal time, and vice-versa (1976b: 74). Personal time and personal

If co-personal person-stages are tied together by psychological continuity, as Lewis himself believes, then ordering in personal times will be a function of patterns of belief formation, memory accumulation, causal connections between mental states, and so on. If co-personal stages are tied together by physical continuities, causal connections between physical states, biological process, and organic maturation will serve instead. But what if we are essentially subjects of experience, entities whose persistence conditions are as defined by the C-theory, rather than in terms of psychological or physical continuity, what sort of account of personal (or subjective) time can we give?

We cannot rely on factors such as organic maturation or memory accumulation, for although these will suffice in most cases, there are also conceivable circumstances in which a single subject persists through radical psychological and physical discontinuities. What we need is a principle for ordering the different phases of a subject's life which is applicable to subjects of differing forms and constitutions, irrespective of the (survivable) changes of a physical or psychological sort which the subject undergoes, or could undergo. It is clear what needs to be done: we must allocate mental items to personal times by the same principles as we allocate them to subjects. To start with, we can confine our attention to the experiential states and capacities which constitute C-systems, and seek to ground personal time systems in terms of relations between this sort of item. Since the relevant relations will be experiential, we can start by looking at the temporal relations between experiences.

Consider the plight of a solitary monad we can call *S*. To simplify matters as far as possible, let us stipulate that the possible world *S* inhabits contains nothing but a single linear stream of uninterrupted consciousness. This stream has a character and complexity similar to that of the average human being, there is only one significant difference: *S* never sleeps, or rather, never sleeps dreamlessly. Clearly *S* is a subject of an unusual, but not impossible, sort: in the terminology of Chapter 8 it is a minimal subject, a minimal subject who happens to be the sole occupant of its universe.[8] Now consider the temporal characteristics of this universe. Since *S*'s stream of consciousness is uninterrupted, it is safe to assume that all its experiences are temporally connected, that is they occur either earlier or later than, or simultaneously with, one another. Since the world we are considering contains nothing but *S*'s experiences, the only events which occur involve changes within and between *S*'s successive states of consciousness. A

identity will then go together, since irrespective of which diachronic identity criterion we favour, all and only those person-stages which belong to the same person will be ordered in the same personal time. This is reasonable on the assumption that it makes sense to ascribe a personal time to a person with a perfectly ordinary sort of life. So far as I can see, there is nothing wrong in so doing, there would just be little point in the exercise.

[8] Authentically *Leibnizian* monads have features that I am not assuming *S* possesses: for example changes in Leibniz's monads are driven by an 'internal principle', and they have 'perceptions' of which their owner is not consciously aware.

bare minimum of two time relations must be constructed from these materials, simultaneity and temporal succession (a metric might be desirable but is not strictly necessary). This is easily done.

We can begin with simultaneity. As a stream of consciousness unfolds, as it flows on from moment to moment, the various strands are bound together by synchronic co-consciousness. Synchronic co-consciousness is obviously a temporal relationship, and since experiences that are related in this way are *experienced* simultaneously, it is a temporal relationship of the phenomenal variety—a *phenomeno-temporal* relationship, as we might say. To know which of our experiences are related in this manner we need only introspect; there is no need to appeal to anything external to our own consciousness, there is no need to appeal to any objective or external temporal facts. So far as S is concerned, this is just as well, for there is nothing external to its consciousness at all. I have been talking about consciousness 'at a given moment', and while it is undeniably true that, as a subject's stream of consciousness flows on, its various strands are synchronically co-conscious from moment-to-moment, it is not only momentary (or minimally brief) experiences which can be related by phenomenal simultaneity, temporally extended experiences can be too. Two experiences of precisely the same duration which are synchronically co-conscious with one another from beginning to end can also be counted as occurring simultaneously, even though they both last for some time. If, as I have been tentatively assuming, synchronic co-consciousness is transitive, then at any given moment, every part of a stream is co-conscious with every other part. If synchronic co-consciousness is not transitive, it does not matter: if there are three experiences, and the first is synchronically co-conscious with the second, the second is synchronically co-conscious with the third, but the first and third are not co-conscious, the latter can still be counted as simultaneous in virtue of the fact that both are experienced as being simultaneous with the second.

Succession is similarly straightforward. Our solitary monad's stream of consciousness consists of a series of overlapping temporally extended total experiences, each of which has the duration of S's specious present. Any partially overlapping pair of specious presents will consist of at least three parts, p_1, p_2, and p_3, where p_1 is co-conscious with p_2, p_2 is co-conscious with p_3, but p_1 is not co-conscious with p_3. As we saw in §3.4, although the parts of a typical single specious present are all mutually co-conscious (some synchronically, some diachronically), they are also the realization of a temporal pattern, of an experienced temporal succession or flow. Irrespective of whether this pattern is simple or complex, since it has a direction it can be used to define temporal precedence. (Even the simplest sensations possess immanent temporal flow—think of the way a single tone, or a sensation of warmth, *continues on*.) Returning to our three stream-phases, if p_1 flows into p_2, and p_2 flows into p_3, then we can say that p_1 occurs before p_2, and p_2 occurs before p_3. Since 'occurs before' is transitive, it also follows that p_1 occurs before p_3, even though these experiences are not themselves co-conscious, and so are not linked by any direct phenomeno-temporal relations. If, on the other hand, p_2 flows into p_1, and p_1 flows into p_3, the temporal ordering is $p_2-p_1-p_3$, rather than $p_1-p_2-p_3$. Since the same reasoning applies to any series of overlapping total experiences, of any number or duration, we have a simple criterion for ordering the different phases of our monad's stream of consciousness, a criterion which is independent of physical and psychological continuities.

These ordering principles could be refined, but they will serve for present purposes, for they effectively locate each of S's states of consciousness in a single ordered time series. Let us call a time series that is generated by the relationships of experienced succession and simultaneity a *phenomenal time*. If this species of personal (or subjective) time is to apply to subjects such as ourselves, in a way which locates all our experiences in a single temporal framework—experiences that are co-streamal and those that are not—it needs to extend to experiential powers as well as experiences. The required extension is easily accomplished. Simultaneity for experiential powers consists in the experienced simultaneity of their manifestations. Two experiential powers are simultaneous in personal time if their (potential) manifestations are (or would be) experienced as occurring precisely together. One (phase of an) experiential power precedes (a phase of) another if the (potential) manifestations of the latter are (or would be) experienced as occurring after the manifestations of the former. Mental capacities which do not fall into the category of experiential powers are located in their possessor's personal time in virtue of their causal connections to their possessors experiential powers. A psychological capacity which can causally affect (in a suitably direct way) a subject's experiential core at a given moment in that subject's personal time exists at that moment in this personal time. Experiential powers can thus be located in a single dimension of personal time by virtue of the co-consciousness (synchronic and diachronic) of their actual or potential manifestations. And of course, according to the C-theory, it is precisely these relationships which render experiential powers consubjective. Just as experiential powers are aggregated into consubjective ensembles on the basis of their actual and potential manifestations, so too do they find their location in a personal time of the phenomenal variety. From now on, by 'personal time' I will generally mean *phenomenal time*.

Taking a further step towards the real world, what can we say about subjects and their bodies? A subject is *minimally* embodied (in the terminology of Chapter 7) in virtue of having a brain, or more generally, having mental capacities which are physically grounded. The physical ground of a subject's experiential powers have the same location in that subject's personal time as the experiences it produces, or could produce. A subject has a body in the more usual sense if they are *effectively* embodied, that is they have a body to which they are causally-functionally related in the appropriate manner. In virtue of these causal-functional relations, a subject's personal time can extend beyond the confines of their C-system: at a given location t in my personal time I am effectively embodied if my C-system is causally related to a body in the right sorts of way. Personal time, it should also be pointed out, need not be confined to a particular collection of subject-stages; events in the wider world, external to both the subject's mind and body, can be viewed as having a location within a personal time too. For example, any event simultaneous in external time with the stages of a time traveller's life can also be located in the latter's personal time. Indeed, as Lewis notes, personal time need not be confined to events simultaneous with stages of the traveller's life: if a time traveller were to die on his seventieth birthday while on a journey back to ancient Egypt, his funeral occurring three days after his death, we may 'add the two intervals and say that his funeral follows his birth by three score years and ten and three days of *extended personal time*' (Lewis 1976*a*: 70). A personal time may thus provide a quite general system for the ordering of events, and the same applies to phenomenal time.

12.7. NON-LINEARITY

We can now return to the question of fission. Although all the diachronic continuities ordinarily sufficient for the persistence of a single subject are fully preserved by a symmetrical fission, there seems to be an insuperable objection to supposing that these continuities can carry the subject in whom they originate with them: double existence consequent upon the breakdown of temporal linearity. However, if we view personal fission solely from the perspective of the type of personal time a dividing person would have, it soon becomes apparent that double existence is no more problematic than it would be in the case of backwards time travel.

Let us return to the predicament of our solitary monad, but now supposing that S has a branching stream of consciousness. Call the pre-fission branch of S's life A, and the two post-fission branches B and C. Let us temporarily ignore any apparent absurdity, and suppose that all three branches are in fact stretches of the life of one and the same subject. It follows that all three branches also belong to a common personal time, but a personal time of a distinctive sort: although all the stages in both B and C occur later than the stages in A, so far as personal time is concerned, there are no *direct* temporal relations whatsoever between the stages in B and C, by which I mean that no moment in B occurs before, simultaneously with, or after any moment in C, and vice-versa. For the stages in the B and C to be temporally related in one of these ways, they would have to be connected by the continuities which generate a phenomenal time-ordering, but they are not so connected: the relevant continuities run up through the pre-fission branch into the post-fission branches, they do not run *between* the post-fission branches. This is illustrated in Figure 12.4, where several brief temporal cross-sections of S's life are shown. Here relationships of synchronic co-consciousness (and hence phenomenal simultaneity) are depicted by double-headed dotted lines, and diachronic co-consciousness (and hence phenomenal succession) by single-headed solid lines.

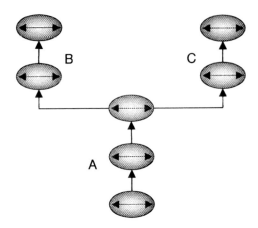

Figure 12.4 A branching in phenomenal time. Phases not linked by horizontal arrows are non-simultaneous

Branches *B* and *C* lie on the same page in this diagram but this spatial proximity has no temporal significance: there are no direct temporal relations between any phases of these branches. There are, of course, *indirect* temporal relations between the stages in *B* and *C*, since all stages in *B* occur later than the final stage of *A*, which in turn occurs earlier than all the stages in *C*. But this does not alter the fact that, so far as *S*'s personal time is concerned, none of the stages in *B* occurs earlier than, or later than, or simultaneously with, any of the stages in *C*, and vice-versa.

We have, then, a situation in which the experiences in the two post-fission limbs occur later than the pre-fission experiences, despite the fact that there are no direct temporal relations between the two post-fission limbs themselves. This state of affairs may seem very curious, perhaps even impossible: how can there be distinct moments in a *single* temporal system that are neither earlier nor later than one another? Given our experience of how our world is, this reaction is only natural. The incredulity can be tempered by reflecting on the differences between our world and that of *S*. The contents of our universe (or at least those parts of it to which we have access) are massively interconnected—by spatial paths, slow-moving objects, fast-moving particles, sound waves, electromagnetic radiation, and so forth—and things that are causally interconnected in this manner are inevitably temporally interrelated: objects and events that are not simultaneous occur earlier or later than one another. The world of our solitary monad is very different in this respect: there is an extreme paucity of connections between the contents of this world. This has the consequence that the disconnection of experiences produced by the splitting of the stream effectively splits time itself.

In fact, the temporal system *S*'s life creates or realizes is by no means unknown: a personal time of this form is an instance of the *branching time* familiar to temporal logicians, and widely employed in fields as diverse as quantum physics, computer science, and decision theory. There are different ways of characterizing branching time in formal terms, for our purposes an informal overview will suffice.[9] A time system can be thought of as a set of temporally connected moments. In a linear temporal system, such as we ordinarily assume our external time to be, every moment occurs either before or after every other moment. Such moments are said to be *strongly* connected. More precisely, a set of moments is strongly connected when each member of the set is linked to each of the others by one of the three direct temporal ordering relationships: occurring simultaneously with, occurring before, occurring after. Although we are accustomed to thinking of time as linear and strongly connected, there is no *a priori* reason to rule out the possibility of temporal systems whose moments are not all strongly connected. In a (forwards) branching time system, where the moments are distributed in a Y-shape rather than along a straight line, strong connectedness breaks down at the moment of bifurcation. All the moments in both post-bifurcation branches are strongly temporally connected to the moments prior to the division, since they all occur after that moment, and all the moments which preceded it. But they are not directly temporally connected to one another: the moments in either branch do not occur before, after, or simultaneously with any of the moments in the other branch. The moments in these post-bifurcation branches still count as belonging to the same temporal system in virtue of the moments in each branch being temporally connected (by the relation of 'occurring after') to all the moments *prior* to the moment of division. But given the lack of direct temporal connections between the branches themselves, the system as a whole is not strongly connected. The personal time of *S* described above consists of a non-linear temporal system of just this form, as would that of any subject who undergoes a symmetrical fission.

While the fact that *S*'s life realizes or creates a branching time is interesting in its own right, it has wider ramifications. So far as the interpretation of fission is concerned, it transforms the metaphysical landscape: the obstacles standing in the way of regarding the fission-products as numerically identical are no more. This is probably obvious in a purely intuitive way. The notion that the billiard ball you are holding in your right hand is numerically identical with the billiard ball you are holding in your left hand may well seem totally absurd. But vary the scenario: let us suppose that the entire physical universe has undergone a fission,

---

[9] For more detailed discussion of branching time see Prior (1967), Rescher and Urquhart (1971), and Belnap (1992).

of the kind familiar from the Many Worlds interpretation of quantum theory.[10] Let us further suppose that just prior to the bifurcation you were looking at a particular ball on the billiard table with a view to picking it up. In one of the resulting universe-branches you pick up the ball with your right hand, in the other you pick it up with your left hand. Does it still seem absurd to suppose that there is only a single ball involved? Indeed, does it seem remotely absurd to suppose that *you* exist in both branches, enjoying, after a fashion, a double existence? I suspect not.

But let us return to S and consider matters in a rather more sober way. The notion that a pair of fission-twins could be numerically identical is vulnerable to Leibniz's Law. An object can have different and incompatible properties at different times, but no object can have different and incompatible properties at the same time. If at noon one fission-twin feels sad and the other feels happy, it may well seem evident that we must be dealing here with two distinct subjects, not one. Thanks to the bifurcation of S's personal time, however, Leibniz' Law is no longer an obstacle to supposing that the subjects S divides into are one and the same. In one branch of his post-fission life S always feels sad, in the other branch he always feels happy, but it matters not: since these feelings occur in different limbs of his branching personal time they do not occur at the *same* time. In feeling the way he does, S is simply doing what any continuant does: having different properties at different times.

This is not all. Another obstacle to regarding fission as survivable is temporal linearity: it is difficult to see how a career that lacks this property belongs to a *single* persisting thing. A temporally linear series of thing-stages, it will be recalled, is one in which no stage is immediately succeeded or preceded by two (or more) stages that are simultaneous with each other. Or in the language of endurance, an object has a temporally linear career if it exists at a succession of times, and exists just once at each of these times. As is clear, the temporal linearity of S's life is fully preserved. Although the final pre-fission stage of S's life is followed by two post-fission stages, the latter do not exist simultaneously. Consequently, each stage of S's life is *followed in time* by just one stage. S exists at a succession of different times, and although S's life has an unusual shape, S exists just once at each of those times, and so is behaving in just the way a continuant should.

Since we have been looking for an identity-conserving interpretation of fission these results are of interest: it seems fair to say that when monadic fission is

---

[10] According to the most common version of the Many Worlds interpretation, each quantum interaction with different possible outcomes involves the entire universe branching (e.g. in one branch, Schrödinger's cat is seen to be alive, in the other it is seen to be dead). The history of the universe thus takes the form of an proliferating branching structure, with a branching time to match: each successive bifurcation creates limbs with no direct temporal connections between them, despite their possessing a common past. The related *Many Minds* interpretation restricts the bifurcations to the consciousness of the observing subjects—this also could be construed as bringing about branchings in personal time. See Barrett (2001) for more on these matters.

viewed as a branching in personal time it would be perverse *not* to regard the resulting pair of fission-twins as numerically identical. While this is undeniably a convenient result, it is important to note that viewing fission in this way is in no way arbitrary or unwarranted, for it could easily have been arrived at by a quite different route. Setting aside the problem of fission for a moment, suppose we have decided to develop a theory of personal time, using Lewis' account of the concept, or something similar to it. After employing the examples of time travel to provide the notion with an initial intuitive underpinning, we investigate other ways in which personal and external times could conceivably diverge. Philosophers hostile to the Kantian doctrine that we cannot conceive of a universe (construed as the totality of what exists) containing more than one time dimension have devised thought experiments in which a single individual is transported back and forth between universes that are not spatio-temporally connected to one another (e.g. Newton-Smith 1980: ch. 4). Evidently, the successive stages in the career of such a traveller will be ordered in ways which cannot be accommodated by any one external time system. Suppose such a traveller is just about to switch universe; the toothache he will feel tomorrow (in his personal time) will never occur in his current universe. Looking further afield, we might next wonder whether a personal time must share the same *topology* as external time. Might it not be possible for a set of co-personal person-stages to be so distributed through external time that they realize a non-linear personal time? How, for example, would a set of person-stages have to be organized if they were to realize a forwards-branching personal temporal system? The answer is not hard to find: all that is required is for the continuities which determine both personal time and continued personal existence to branch, such that no (direct) personal temporal relations exist between the post-bifurcation branches. Viewed from this perspective, and assuming the prior intelligibility of the notion of personal time, we would not think of such a life as being in any way paradoxical. More likely, any doubts we might have would concern the possibility of a life's *branching* in the radical way required. Fortunately, a good deal of work on precisely this topic has already been carried out: we need only turn to the literature on personal identity devoted to the problem of fission.

12.8. TIME AND TIMES

Earlier I suggested that when personal fission is viewed solely from the perspective of personal time, the double existence which ensues is no more problematic than it would be in the case of backwards time travel. It should now be clear why this is so. The lives of fission-twins do not run simultaneously (in personal time), indeed they are not directly temporally related (in personal time) at all; the predicament of a pair of fission-twins is precisely analogous in these respects to that of a time traveller who co-exists with a younger version of him- or herself.

In neither case is it absurd to suppose that a pair of fission-twins are identical both with one another, and with the person who divided into them. Or at least, there is no logical or metaphysical absurdity in this supposition. The very idea of two simultaneously existing people being one and the same may well strike one as absurd, but this absurdity is a consequence of the unfamiliarity of a novel possibility, rather than that which derives from the recognition of an impossibility posing as a possibility.

But we are not yet out of the woods. Personal fission may not be problematic viewed from the perspective of personal time, but from the perspective of external time nothing has changed: a pair of fission-twins exists simultaneously, and to suppose they are one and the same seems as problematic as ever. However, provided it is legitimate to regard the orderings of person-stages grounded in the unfolding of phenomenal continuities as genuinely temporal orderings, a question to which I shall return shortly, this conflict is innocuous.

In accepting that it is legitimate to talk in terms of certain people's possessing personal times we need not deny that these same people also exist in external time—which is just as well, assuming the people in question are not isolated monads. But in accepting the legitimacy of such talk we are recognizing that external time is not the only temporal framework within which the lives of such people may intelligibly be said to exist and unfold. Indeed, it is precisely because external time cannot accommodate the distinctively temporal relations we recognize as holding between the different stages of a single subject's life—a subject who has undergone fission, passage between temporally unconnected universes, or backwards time-travel, say—that we are led to think in terms of personal time at all. Consequently, for subjects such as these it is only to be expected that a career which makes sense (metaphysically speaking) in the context of one temporal system fails to do so in the other. A collection of co-personal person-stages which does not add up to a single coherent life when viewed from the perspective of one temporal framework may well do so when viewed from the perspective of a different temporal framework—and this is precisely the situation with which time travel, universe-switching, and fission confronts us. When a situation of this sort does arise, the fact that a subject's career looks impossible from one of the temporal frameworks it occupies is not in the least objectionable, it is only to be expected! There is a more general principle at work here which can usefully be made explicit:

The Temporal Parity Principle: if an object exists within more than one temporal framework, it is sufficient for its career to have an unproblematic form in *one* of these frameworks for the object to be deemed unproblematic from a metaphysical perspective.

This principle is tacitly at work in Lewis's treatment of time travel, and it seems eminently acceptable. The fact that personal fission appears problematic from the perspective of external time is not an insuperable barrier to everyone's recognizing that it is a perfectly legitimate form for a life to take, albeit in the context of an alternative (but well-founded) temporal framework, one grounded solely in the interrelations between the different parts of the dividing subject's life itself. Provided those whose lives conform to the structure of external time admit the well-foundedness of a dividing subject's personal time, there is no reason why they should not respect the perspective this time casts on such a subject's life.

One question remains: is it really legitimate to say that personal times are times? Granted, we can construct an ordering relation on the basis of the pattern of changes found in co-personal person-stages, but what reason is there to think such an ordering relation is temporal? There are, after all, plenty of ordering relations which are not temporal. David Lewis provides one answer to this question. He suggests that since time *per se* is external time, a personal time is not really time, but that this does not matter, for it can still resolve an apparent paradox of time travel. This is because personal time is 'functionally equivalent' to external (real) time, in that 'it plays the role in [the time traveller's] life that time plays in the life of the common person' (1976*a*: 70). I take Lewis' talk of 'functional equivalence' to amount to something like the following. Given that there may be sets of co-personal person-stages spread through external time in non-standard ways, personal time lends to those stages the same kind of coherence as that which exists between the stages of an ordinary life, a coherence which the intrinsic relationships between the stages demand we recognize. Personal time is the dimension which matters to a person with an extraordinary life in many of the ways that external time matters to a person with an ordinary life: it is the truer measure of the extent, order, and shape of their lives, in the sense that it is the dimension within which the successive stages of their lives are ordered as are the parts of ordinary lives through ordinary time. If personal times can fulfil many of the same conceptual functions with respect to unusual lives as external time fulfils with respect to ordinary lives, there seems to be no reason why they cannot be put to the same sort of metaphysical work, even if we prefer to reserve the word 'time' for external time.

This is fine as far as it goes, but we need to be clearer as to whether terms such as 'before', 'after', 'past', and 'future' and so forth, as they feature in a personal time, denote genuine temporal relations and properties, or merely functional analogues of these. There is a case for saying that to *be* functionally analogous they need to be temporal. If personal time is to have the same significance for a person with an non-standard life that external time has for a person with a standard life, then they must be able to think of events ordered by their personal time in properly temporal ways. If I were in the position of contemplating an imminent fission, in order for me to identify with my post-fission twins, I would have to be able to think of their experiences as lying in my *future*, as occurring *later* than my present experiences; thinking of their experiences as being located at a higher position in terms of a non-temporal ordering relation would not suffice. The same goes, *mutatis mutandis*, for the fission-twins produced by my division and their attitude to events in our pre-fission life. And from the external perspective, if you are to be able to make sense of my being identical with the fission-twins I divide into, then you must be able to think of my life in terms of a branching structure which is an alternative *temporal* system, for you must be able to make sense of the claim that my fission-twins do not live *simultaneous* lives.

However, the issue of whether personal times are truly *times* is far from being an entirely straightforward one, for there are very different views both as to the nature of external time and the factors which render person-stages consubjective and supply their personal-temporal ordering. On some views the order-generating relationships are of precisely the same kind. Suppose, for example, that the causal theory of time is true, and the temporal ordering of spacetime points is determined by the causal relations between them—if a point P_2 causally depends on a point P_1 then the latter is earlier than the former. If it were also the case that relationships of causal dependency generate the temporal ordering of person-stages in personal time, then it would be difficult to deny that personal temporal relations were properly temporal. At the other end of the spectrum, the same would apply in universes where certain forms of idealism is true, universes where everything is composed of experience; in universes such as these all temporal order is determined solely by phenomeno-temporal relations: by experienced succession and simultaneity.[11] We do not need to enter into details, for it is clear that in such worlds personal and external times would again be determined by precisely the same sorts of relationship. However, given the naturalistic framework I am working within, there is no reason to suppose that personal and external times will in fact be sustained by the same kinds of relationships. The nature and origin of time-order in our physical spacetime remains a matter of controversy: some appeal to causation, others to entropy, others to a primitive ordering relation among spacetime points, others deny that there is any objective difference between earlier and later.[12] We need not enter these disputes, for whatever the correct answer may be, it is unlikely to have much in common with the answer to the corresponding question concerning personal time. For as we have seen, if we adopt the C-theory, then the ordering relations in a personal time are purely phenomenal: experienced simultaneity and succession.[13] Does this divergence matter? I cannot see that it does. For is it not as clear as it could possibly be that the relevant phenomenal relations are genuinely *temporal* relations, irrespective of their relationship to the wider world? The temporal relations that fundamental physics supplies may be real enough, but they are not the only kind of temporal relations there are.

---

[11] See Foster (1982) for a variety of such schemes.

[12] Prominent advocates of these positions include Mellor (1998) and Tooley (1997), Atkins (1986), Maudlin (2002), Price (1996), respectively.

[13] What if the apparent difference between earlier and later in external spacetime is projected onto it by conscious beings, and lacks an objective basis? Although external and personal temporal orderings would now be connected, they would remain distinct: in such worlds personal times really are asymmetrically ordered—by experienced succession—events in external time are not.

Of course, personal and external times differ in other ways too. We ordinary people are fortunate in that the temporal system which lends most coherence to our lives is also the system which lends most coherence to the world as a whole. Those emerging from time travel, suspended animation or personal fission are less fortunate: the times of their lives and the time of their world no longer coincide. There are obvious disadvantages in this. A personal time is an ordering of events from the perspective of a single life, a life whose immanent temporal structure deviates from the norm. Since different (extended) personal times will order the same events in conflicting ways, the neutrality of external time with regard to specific personal histories would be reason to prefer it as a universal chronological standard. However, in the light of the points made above, there are strong grounds for supposing that it would be a mistake to allow the pragmatic superiority of external time when it comes to keeping track of the world as a whole to overshadow the merits of the case for treating personal times with the respect they deserve. Personal times are less than ideal as chronological standards for the world as a whole, and may have no place in fundamental physical theory, but they are grounded in experiential relationships which are themselves undeniably temporal, and which lend time much of the meaning it has for beings like ourselves.

12.9. ISSUES AND OBJECTIONS

The branching time interpretation supplies us with what the C-theory requires: a way of making metaphysical sense of the notion that post-fission subjects can be identical both with one another and the pre-fission subject who divided into them. Since this interpretation is neutral with respect to the issue of whether persisting things perdure or endure, proponents of both doctrines can subscribe to it. Perdurance theorists who take this step need not reject the standard Lewisian treatment of fission altogether. Instances of division to which the branching time interpretation is inapplicable can be interpreted in the standard manner, as involving two numerically distinct but partially overlapping four-dimensional objects. But for those cases where the branching time interpretation is applicable, perdurantists have the option of regarding the post-fission objects as numerically identical with both their predecessor and one another. And in the case of conscious subjects, this is a significant bonus—not least because it avoids the need to hold that what seems to be a single subject of consciousness is really two.

Its advantages may be significant, but there is no denying that the branching time interpretation takes some getting used to. Before proceeding further I will anticipate and respond to some objections.

A personal time can be extended beyond the events which make up a particular personal biography. If I had undergone fission, and now had a fission-twin, I would be able to locate events in my fission-twin's life, such as his suffering a sudden twinge of toothache, not only in external time, but also in my own extended personal time (i.e. my branch of 'our' mutual branching personal time). And of course, vice-versa: my twin would be able to date events in my life in terms of his personal time. Doesn't this conflict with the claim that, so far as personal time is concerned, there are no direct temporal relations between the lives of fission-twins?

Not in the least: the moment in my extended personal time at which my fission-twin's toothache occurs is a time which is (directly) temporally unrelated to, in particular non-simultaneous with, the moment in *his* personal time at which he suffers the same toothache (or more accurately, his *branch* of our common personal time system). We can both assign temporal coordinates to the same events, but so far as personal time is concerned, there are no direct temporal connections between the coordinate systems we use to assign times to events which occur after our division (we both assign the same times to events which occurred before our division).

But what of the attitudes fission-twins could be expected to have towards one another? If fission-twins are numerically identical, then surely each twin should feel as much concern for the other's present and future well-being as they do for their own. But this is implausible. Put yourself in the position of one of these twins. Would you dread your twin's visits to the dentist as much as your own? If you visited the dentist together, would you be as concerned with his pain as you would be with your own? Almost certainly not—no matter how firmly you believed you and your twin to be identical.

In fact, far from being incompatible with the identity of fission-twins, asymmetrical personal concern is entirely understandable on the assumption of branching personal time. For reasons which are not entirely clear, self-interest is temporally asymmetric. For example, present pain, and the prospect of future pain, worry us more than pain we have already experienced. This fact explains the pattern of personal concern it seems reasonable to ascribe to fission-twins. The experiences of a pair of fission-twins are only temporally related in external time. Because of their branching personal times, fission-twins have two presents and futures instead of the usual one. As a result, their personal concern will be doubly asymmetric: the usual temporal bias will be accompanied by a bias in favour of one of the two limbs of their branching life. For example, your fission-twin's visit to the dentist is a visit you make, but because it takes place in the other branch of your time, it is—in a sense—located neither in your present nor your future. Given the future-directed bias of self-interest, it is entirely natural for a pair of fission-twins who acknowledge their identity also to be relatively unconcerned with each other. Their attitude to each other's experience should be more like a non-branching person's attitude to their own *past* experience, that is to experiences belonging to the same system of (personal) time, but not lying in the present or future. And this, so far as I can see, is how it would be. Fission-twins who appreciated their identity would not be entirely unmoved by the lives they each lived. One might expect to feel proud or ashamed of one's fission-twin's deeds; but again, these are attitudes we non-branching people have towards our own past selves.

Fissions may be symmetrical from the point of view of satisfying diachronic identity criteria, but they may be radically asymmetrical in other ways. Suppose we accept the C-theory, and suppose you were to divide into a pair of fission-twins, who for convenience we can label BD_1 and BD_2. BD_1 has all your current mental traits and capacities, and gets to keep your current body. BD_2 has the intellect and experiential capacities of a typical mouse, is housed in a vat of nutrients, and supplied with the odd sensation. Do you still insist that you would be identical with both these entities? Presented with a forced choice scenario in advance, wouldn't you much prefer that BD_2 rather than BD_1 receive the pain on offer?

Of course I would. The fact that I will be numerically identical with both BD_1 and BD_2 does not mean I will have the same future-directed self-interested concern for each of my future selves. Why should I, given that they will be so different from one another? Since it seems reasonable to suppose that the capacity for suffering of a typical human being is greater than that of a typical mouse, I would naturally prefer that any pain be inflicted on BD_2. The fact that my self-concern (in both the prudential and desirability senses) would not be equally divided between my future selves is quite compatible with my believing myself to be identical, in the strictest and fullest sense, with each of them: any experiences BD_2 has will be experiences *I* have. A linear temporal analogy is relevant here also. I could be reduced to the condition of BD_2 without undergoing fission; although I believe I would be identical with the resulting subject (assuming C-relatedness is preserved). I would also go to great lengths to avoid such a state of affairs. If I knew there was nothing I could do to prevent this outcome—perhaps I will be diagnosed as afflicted with a new, incurable, and especially catastrophic wasting disease—I might well arrange for a speedy termination, and would certainly not place as great a value on the stretch of my life that I will spend in an attenuated condition as I would on the intervening period. Nonetheless, it would still be *me* who exists in this diminished condition.

Even if we accept the intelligibility of viewing fission as a branching in personal time, all sorts of obstacles of a mundane practical sort stand in the way of considering fission-twins as identical. A pair of fission-twins appear to all the world to be two different people, and indeed they are quite capable of leading completely independent lives. They are not at all like a single individual person. Although their common history and origin may lend support to the idea that they are identical, their manifest present separation supports the idea they are distinct; to such an extent that it is unlikely the claim that they are one and the same could long withstand the countervailing pressures of everyday life.

I do not claim that construing fission as a branching in personal time resolves all or even most of the psychological and practical problems to which a real-life personal fission would give rise. My concern has been primarily metaphysical:

accommodating the possibility of personal fission without having recourse to drastically revisionary schemes, and so rendering the fate of a dividing person intelligible in a way not otherwise possible. If one were to divide, one's relationships with one's friends, family, and property would be very inconveniently complicated; the very fact that one could have the sort of relationship with oneself that is normally only possible with others might well lead to novel psychological and legal complications. If I were to kill my fission-twin would it be murder or suicide? Or both? But then, there are many other *non-fatal* afflictions which have awkward practical consequences. In coming to terms with a pair of fission-twins the central and most pressing problem is deciding *who they are*. Are they identical with the person who divided into them, and so with one another, or are they not? Viewing fission in the way proposed allows us to give a definite answer to this most important of questions, the answer to which will largely determine how the fission-twins regard each other, and how they are regarded by others.

You favour the branching time interpretation over Lewis' partial overlap account because it doesn't presuppose the perdurance conception of persistence, and you want an identity-conserving interpretation that is equally available to endurantists. But there is at least one interpretation of fission which achieves the same ends but without the heavy metaphysical machinery. As is well-known, change poses something of a problem for endurantists: how can one and the same thing X be F and not-F? Doesn't this conflict with Leibniz' Law? Endurantists respond: 'Of course not. There's no contradiction because X possesses these incompatible properties *at different times*.' This tactic of circumventing Leibniz' Law problems by indexing property possession can be taken a step further. Why not also hold that property possession is indexed to both temporal *and spatial* locations. If we take this step then the fact that a pair of fission-twins Y and Z have different and incompatible properties at any given time t is no obstacle to also holding that they are numerically identical since they will each have a distinct spatial location at t.

That there is an alternative route to the same destination is a comforting thought, but there are at least three reasons for not dispensing with the services of the branching time approach. First, the proposed relativization of property possession to spatial locations is a modification of endurantism that not all endurantists will want to make.[14] Second, for the proposal to be viable for all subjects it must obviously be the case that all subjects *have* a spatial location. Anyone who is (like me) reluctant to rule out the logical possibility of immaterial subjects will in all likelihood also be reluctant to rule out the possibility that such subjects may inhabit entirely non-spatial universes (in the manner of our solitary monad

---

[14] In her otherwise plausible defence of the proposal Miller (2006) argues that the endurantists needs to admit relativization to spatial locations for another reason: in order to explain how a time traveller can be (say) standing and sitting at precisely the same time without contradiction. But Leibniz' Law difficulties of this ilk can also be avoided by recognizing the distinction between personal and external times.

S).[15] That it may be possibile for subjects lacking a spatial location to undergo fission poses no problem whatsoever for the branching time interpretation (as the case of *S* illustrates). Last but not least, as we have already seen, even if we set the case of fission aside, there are other conceivable situations—backward time travel, hopping between temporal dimensions—in which personal and external times come apart. Given this, and given the fact that fission creates a precisely analogous dislocation between these temporal frameworks, is it not entirely natural to construe fission as involving a branching in personal time? In so doing, aren't we merely being consistent?

If dividing subjects possess a branching personal time, and in virtue of this remains identical with the subjects they divide into, wouldn't the same apply to organisms such as amoeba which reproduce by fission? But then, accepting that human fission-twins would be identical seems to oblige us to view all those amoeba descended from the same parent as identical, as one and the same amoeba. Isn't this absurd?

If an amoeba were to travel back in time we would naturally distinguish between the relevant external times and a temporal ordering determined by the career of the amoeba. The same will apply quite generally: there is no need for the time-travelling object to be a living creature, it could be a table or a hunk of rock. A personal time can be viewed as a special case of *proper* time, as the physicists are apt to call it, and the latter is equally applicable to objects of all kinds. Since amoebic fissions yield two whole amoebae without rupturing the organic continuities which are sufficient to keep a living cell in existence, amoebic fissions pose precisely the same dilemma as the problematic kind of personal fissions. Given the analogies between the two cases, we have the option of applying the same medicine, and construing such fissions in terms of branching amoebic proper times, and more generally, accepting that the branching time analysis applies across the board, to all fission products, irrespective of their kind. While it may well seem odd that trillions of organisms scattered over the face of the globe are all numerically identical, we should remember that our ordinary ways of thinking are not always a reliable guide to metaphysical truth. We could further remind ourselves that we are under no obligation to revise our practices in the light of metaphysical discoveries if no useful purpose would be served by so doing: it would not greatly matter if we kept on counting amoeba and their kin in the usual way, even if the usual way does not conform to how things are.

While these considerations may suffice to meet the objection, there is an additional point worth noting. For the branching time interpretation to be viable in a given instance there must be compelling reasons for supposing that the fission in question results in a real disassociation of proper and external times, of a kind which results in parallel but non-simultaneous existence. In the case

---

[15] Cartesian soul-substances could be construed as having a location in physical space by virtue of their causal attachments to particular pineal glands.

of a time travelling amoeba—an amoeba which, say, is hurled a thousand years into the past, and then a million years into the future by a time machine—it is abundantly clear that successive phases of this organism's life (as measured by causal and biological continuities) are not successive in ordinary or external time, and consequently, this is a clear case in which proper and external times come apart. Since it does not involve any similarly dramatic dislocations, the fission case is more ambiguous in this regard: the successive stages of a dividing amoeba's career occur successively in external time, whereas in the time travel case they do not. Now, it is true that it is an option to regard the dividing amoeba's career as instantiating a branching proper time, and that by these lights there is a coming apart of proper and external times. But in the case of dividing subjects there is an additional factor: the presence of temporal relations of the *phenomenal* variety, the relations of experienced simultaneity and succession (either actual or merely potential). As we have already seen, these relationships are undeniably temporal in nature, and when a subject undergoes fission these relationship determine a branching temporal system. The presence of this additional and distinctively temporal dimension significantly strengthens the case for holding that there is real sense—a real *temporal* sense—in which the post-fission subjects do not exist simultaneously. Since this phenomeno-temporal dimension is (presumably) absent in the case of amoebic fission, the grounds for extending the branching time analysis to the latter are weaker, and the grounds for allowing our ordinary counting practices to override other considerations are all the stronger.

Accepting that a pair of fission twins are identical with both one another and the person who divided into them is one thing, but suppose each fission-twin subsequently undergoes division, and the process repeats down the generations, as it were. How plausible is it to suppose that thousands of people going about leading their separate lives, sometimes loving or killing one another, are all numerically identical?

Do numbers matter here? A sufficiently long-lived time traveller could arrange matters so that at a given time, a hundred or a thousand versions of himself co-existed. A particular personal time can loop back on itself (relative to external time) any number of times, and a particular personal time can undergo multiple and iterated branchings. The metaphysical situation remains the same. Surely the significant hurdle is overcoming the resistance to the idea that *two* seemingly distinct and perfectly ordinary people could be one and the same. If this is conceded, the objection has little force.

Numbers might matter for a different reason. Your interpretation of fission may be plausible for one-off occasional cases, but what if personal fissions were to become as commonplace as ordinary births? Wouldn't we quickly begin to regard fission-twins as distinct individuals? Suppose some unforeseeable catastrophe renders the entire human race sterile; although this change proves to be irreversible, a method of creating additional people by fission is developed, and to minimize difficulties, fission-twins are given psychologies quite different from that of the person who divides into them and from one another. C-relatedness is preserved through the fission process, but the resulting people regard themselves as distinct and unique individuals. In a situation like this, would it still be reasonable to regard fission-twins as numerically identical?

It is difficult to predict how, or even whether, a particular concept will evolve in response to radically changed circumstances. This said, I think it likely that there are circumstances in which we would find it useful to adopt a different conception of what we are, and so change our views as to the conditions under which subjects or persons persist. In the circumstances just outlined, it might well be natural and useful—although not inevitable—to adopt a revised version of the C-theory, and hold that a subject consists of a linear series of C-related mental capacities, and hence that personal identity is secured only by non-branching C-relatedness. In so doing, we would be allowing strong social and pragmatic pressures to override the thesis that co-conscious experiences (or C-related experiential powers) always, under all circumstances, belong to the same experiencing subject. But this concession does nothing to undermine the proposed diagnosis of the fission puzzle. My concern has been to suggest a way of making sense of fission which coheres with our *current* beliefs and values, and which does not require us to abandon or revise any of the most central and deeply held aspects of our understanding of the kind of thing we are, and the circumstances under which we will continue to exist. There is no guarantee that the relevant beliefs and values will not gradually evolve, perhaps in response to new practical possibilities, perhaps in response to more general ideological developments. In which case, neither the possibility nor the reality of fission will present the same puzzle as it does at present, and a quite different interpretation of what happens to a dividing self might well be appropriate. But we are not at present faced with a situation of this sort, and there is no point at all in revising our concepts and beliefs in response to hypothetical future circumstances which are at most logically possible, and may well be nomologically impossible, where these concepts and beliefs are both deeply held and perfectly adequate to our actual circumstances.

A further point. While it might well be a mistake to underestimate the mutability of human patterns of concern, and certainly a mistake to ignore the different ways of thinking and feeling which may, for whatever reason, appeal to subjects of a non-human sort, it would also be a mistake to underestimate the distinctive features of fission. Suppose there were a species of conscious beings who reproduced by way of division. Irrespective of what account of self-identity through time we adopt, the relationship between parents and offspring in this species is far more intimate than in our own case: a parent (for want of a better term) is related to both offspring in exactly the same intrinsic ways as would ordinarily secure their own continued existence. Unless the psychology and social norms of these beings are fundamentally different from our own, is it not likely that they will think of themselves as more closely related to their offspring than we do to ours? Reproducing by fission is *literally* a way of cheating death, standard biological reproduction is not. In a world similar to our world in many respects, but in which everyone is related to everyone else by virtue of prior fissions, it would be practical and natural to draw distinctions between individuals in much the way we do; but it would also be natural, and metaphysically justifiable, to regard these distinctions as being less deep than we do. In our world, consciousness is confined to closed discrete linear channels. In the envisaged world, consciousness flows along myriad intersecting branches of a single tree, a tree whose proliferating branches consist of C-related mental capacities. The difference between these two states of affairs is profound, and while we cannot predict with any confidence exactly how people whose lives are branches from a common stem would think of themselves, we can predict with some confidence that they would not think of themselves as separate from one another in the way we do.

12.10. FUSION

Now that we have an acceptable account of fission we are in a better position to tackle its temporal mirror image: fusion. Can the branching time interpretation be applied to cases in which two subjects become one? It can, but fusion also raises some additional complications, and I will be concentrating on these.

But first things first. Is fusion even possible? The considerations which suggest that it is possible in principle for a consciousness to divide do not seem to rule out the merging of streams of consciousness: precisely the same experiential structures are required, only in reverse. From a phenomenal perspective the possibility of a stream of consciousness possessing a branching structure, whether forwards (fission) or backwards (fusion), requires only that diachronic co-consciousness can fail to be transitive, as we know it can. In so far as we are concerned solely with the possible structures of consciousness, structures unconstrained either by contingent laws governing the possible patterning of experience and the relationship between consciousness and matter, fusion may well be just as possible as fission. If streams of consciousness can amalgamate, then so too can subjects, at least on the assumption that the possible forms of experience determine the possible configurations of C-related experiential powers, and not vice-versa. Of course at the human level, fusion is likely to prove even more difficult to achieve than fission. Whereas (human) fission could conceivably be produced by purely destructive means—severing the nerves connecting the hemispheres and relevant portions of the lower brain—fusion would require two already separated half-brains to be joined so as to produce a functioning whole, all without disrupting C-relatedness. Difficult in the extreme, but perhaps not beyond the bounds of nomological possibility. Even if it could be carried out, such a procedure would almost inevitably produce profound disruption at the psychological level, with the meshing of different and conflicting beliefs, memories, personality traits, and so forth—assuming that any psychological states survive the process, and the people involved are not mental duplicates. But from the perspective of the C-theory all that matters from the point of view of a subject's *survival* is that two C-systems could merge without loss or interruption of C-relatedness; the attendant psychological disruption is irrelevant. (Note also that severe mental illness may well produce a similar level of mental confusion within an ordinary human mind.) For present purposes, where our concern is with subjects in general rather than the human sort, it is sufficient that it cannot be ruled out that fusion is a possibility for *some* subjects of experience. The question now arises as to how we should interpret such cases.

The difficulty is analogous in many respects to that posed by fission. Our fusion-twins Y and Z each satisfy the synchronic conditions for being counted as distinct subjects in their own right, yet both are linked to a later subject X in a way which (by hypothesis) would ordinarily be sufficient for their identity with the latter: Y and Z are both C-related to X. Synchronic and diachronic identity criteria thus conflict, and what the latter would have us regard as a single subject, the former would have us regard as two. Various interpretations of fusion have been proposed. Parfit privileges synchronic considerations, and maintains that Y and Z should be regarded as distinct from both one another and the person they merge into, but since fusing would not be as bad as dying, we can again draw the lesson that the mental and physical continuities which matters in life can diverge from identity. Lewis takes a different line, and argues that the post-fusion person X is really two distinct but partially overlapping people of the four-dimensional variety, despite the fact that X has but a single body and a single stream of consciousness. But although fusion can be interpreted in these ways, it can also be interpreted in terms of the branching time proposal. Since the pre-fusion subjects are each C-related to their post-fusion successor, they can all be seen as occupying a common personal time, and moreover a personal time with a branching structure. This yields the result that Y and Z are one and the same person, living their lives in different branches of a common personal time, up until time t when they merge into X, with whom they are also identical.

The claim that fusion-twins are numerically identical doubtless seem even odder than the corresponding claim about fission-twins. Prior to their fusion these supposedly identical subjects differ in no way from the ordinary; their personal histories are no different from anyone else's. In the light of this, is it not absurd to suppose these subjects might, unbeknownst to themselves or anyone else, be one and the same? However, while it is certainly true that it would be impossible to tell by examining them at any time prior to their fusion that they were numerically identical, it is equally impossible to tell just by examining someone at a particular time whether they have undergone a *fission* at some point in their pasts. (This holds even if the person being examined only has half a brain: the other half may have been lost as a result of injury or disease). And as we have seen, this does not mean a subject at a time *t* cannot be identical with another seemingly distinct person who also exists at *t*. If an event in the past can make this difference, why not an event in the future?

Although appreciating this symmetry does something to reduce the qualms we might have about a symmetrical treatment of fission and fusion, some doubts may well remain. It is tempting to think that subjects who have not yet fused (but who soon will) are in some manner *less* connected to one another than subjects who share a common past by virtue of an earlier fission. I suspect there are two related considerations behind this intuition, one temporal and one modal. Since a future fusion has *not yet* taken place, how can it be right to say the personal time systems of the individuals concerned are connected to one another *now*? Suppose *Y* and *Z* do undergo fusion, and for this reason we claim them to have been identical with one another throughout their lives, specifically prior to their fusion. Although *Y* and *Z* have fused, it nonetheless seems possible that their fusion should never have taken place—*Y* could have died beforehand, for example. If this is possible, and it seems hard to deny as much, then the identity of *Y* with *Z* is a contingent state of affairs. But this conflicts with the disputable but widely held thesis that identities are necessary.

Neither of these difficulties is insuperable, but how we resolve them—and how we conceive of fusion—depends on how we think of time itself, more specifically, on what we make of the difference between past, present, and future. This is *the* great controversy concerning the nature of time, and needless to say there are very different positions that one can take on this issue. Rather than trying to establish the truth of any one of these positions, I will briefly consider the branching time interpretation of fusion from the vantage point of three of the main contenders: *eternalism*, the doctrine that all times and events are equally real, the *growing block view* associated with Broad (1923) and Tooley (1997), the doctrine that the universe is a four-dimensional block that increases in size with the passing of time, and finally (and very briefly) *presentism*, the doctrine that whereas the momentary present is real, the past and future are not.

Let us start with eternalism. If temporal location does not impinge on the reality of things and events, then there are (tenseless) facts concerning future individuals as well as facts concerning past individuals. Hence, from an ontological point of view, future and past are equivalent, both are perfectly real, both equally determinate. If this is not obvious to us (and it is not) it is because past events leave presently available traces of themselves in a way that future events do not—or so the eternalist will say. Given the ontic symmetry between past and future, if we suppose that *Y* and *Z* do undergo fusion at time *t*, that they do so—that they undergo fusion *at t*—is as much a fact prior to their fusion as it is after it. A branching in a personal time system which lies in the future is as real as a branching which lies in the past; in both cases every phase of a branching life is linked by C-relatedness. Accordingly, it is a fact that *Y* and *Z* share a common personal time prior to *t*, even if there is no evidence for this until shortly before *t*. And given this, it is also a fact that Y and Z are numerically identical with one another prior to *t*, leading different parts of the same life, concurrently in external time, but non-simultaneously in personal time. As for the supposed modal problem, it is not a problem at all. It would be a mistake to object that Y and Z cannot be identical because it is at least possible for their future fusion not to take place (even if in fact it does). If Y and Z are identical prior to their fusion, it is not possible that *they* should fail to undergo fusion. We can certainly envisage a possible world w that is indistinguishable from our world up until shortly before *t*, at which point the counterpart of Y (say) suddenly expires. But all this means is that Y-in-w is not identical with the actual Y, and likewise for Z-in-w and the actual Z. In all possible worlds where Y and Z exist after having been born as (seemingly) separate individuals, they undergo fusion at some point in their lives. The thesis that identities are necessary is perfectly compatible with holding fusion-twins to be identical prior to their fusion.

It seems that for eternalists fission and fusion are analogous in all metaphysically significant respects. The pre-fission phase of a forward-branching life is just as real *after* it has occurred as the post-fusion phase of a backward-branching life is *before* it has occurred: both are timelessly parts of the same universe. True, the doctrine that a single object can only have one origin is sometimes held to be a basic metaphysical principle. Since fusion-twins *do* have multiple origins, if we take them to be numerically identical, we must reject this doctrine—or at least, recognize that it only applies to objects whose careers are temporally linear. In any event, on reflection, is the idea that a single object can have two distinct beginnings any stranger than the idea that a single object can have two distinct ends, or a single person two distinct deaths? Subjects whose lives are non-linear will not conform to all the principles that hold true of subjects whose lives are linear, but since this is to be expected, why take it to be a problem? Eternalism has a number of counterintuitive consequences—most of us initially recoil from the thought that what will happen between now and the time of our deaths is as settled as what has happened between now and the time of our births. Since the eternalist view of non-linear lives makes additional demands, it is scarcely surprising that we find it even more difficult to digest. But this does not mean the view is false.

What of the growing block view? Fissions and fusions that lie in the past pose no new difficulties; since all parts of these branching lives are all equally real, just as they would be if eternalism were true. But it is otherwise with regard to presently existing subjects who have not yet undergone fusion but who may do so in the future. Suppose Y and Z are a pair of putative fusion-twins. Although at the moment they seem as distinct from one another as two individuals can possibly be, if we construe fusion in terms of a backwards branching personal time this is not necessarily the case. If tomorrow they undergo fusion they will then *become* one and the same, and hence from this time on their previous careers will be branches of a single subject's life, running parallel and simultaneously in external time, but non-simultaneously in personal time. If, on the other hand, Y and Z never undergo fusion, then they never become one, and so remain as distinct as they always appeared to be. We thus have a state of affairs that is peculiar, and perhaps perturbing: if Y and Z fuse they become identical, if they never fuse then they remain distinct, but for as long as their fusion remains a possibility then claims asserting their identity or non-identity appear to lack a determinate truth value. It is impossible to *say* for certain that they are identical or distinct because their status viz-à-vis one another is *not* (yet) settled! The identity of Y with Z is indeterminate not because they are vague objects with fuzzy synchronic boundaries, in the manner of a cloud, but because their diachronic boundaries are still in the process of forming. Of course, even if human fusion is nomologically possible—which it may well not be—we can say with some confidence that it is highly unlikely that any two humans will undergo it in the near future, and so, for better or for worse, it is highly likely that we are all distinct individuals. But while this may be reassuring, it is beside the point. Is the proposed way of thinking of fusion really intelligible?

Although the idea that our distinctness from one another might be less than fully determinate might seem bizarre, this indeterminacy is merely a special case of a more general phenomenon in growing block universes. Philosophers who accept the reality of the past while denying the reality of the future generally hold that statements about contingent future facts lack a determinate truth value; they hold, with good reason, that the principle of bivalence applies to statements about the past and present, but not to statements about the future. On this view it is only to be expected that statements about the past or present which depend for their truth or falsity on contingent future events will also be without a determinate truth value. If it is physically possible for a suitably modified human body to live on indefinitely (as some believe), then the proposition 'I am mortal' is currently neither true nor false, since there are no currently obtaining logically sufficient conditions for its truth or falsity. The statement 'Y is identical with X in virtue of a future fusion' belongs to the same category. As for the modal predicament, once identities and non-identities in growing block worlds become determinate they can be as necessary as can be. If Y and Z do fuse at some time t, then they are identical, and there is no possible world where Y exists but not Z and vice-versa. There are many worlds in which two individuals lead lives indistinguishable to those of Y and Z prior to their fusion and then go their separate ways, but none of these possible lives are possibilities for Y and Z.

If you are still finding it hard to accept that it makes sense to suppose that as basic a fact as your identity with another living person could depend on something that has not yet happened, a now-familiar analogy may help. As we saw earlier, most of us have little difficulty in accepting the idea that two contemporaneous people, who are seemingly as distinct from one another as they are distinct from anyone else, could nonetheless be numerically identical if one of them has travelled backwards in time. Imagine being confronted with your older time-travelled self. This person convinces you that he or she is indeed you. Given that you and the traveller are the same person, are you identical because of something which occurred in your past, or something that will occur in your future? The question is ambiguous. From the point of view of your older self, the answer lies in the past. But from the perspective of the younger you, the relevant facts lie in the future. You are identical with the older person standing next to you because of the path your life *will* take from this point on, not because of anything that has happened previously. You will continue to exist, until at some future time you step into a time machine, and travel back to meet your younger self. Your life is continuous with that of the time traveller, but the relevant stages of your life mostly lie in the future. Now consider your relationship with your fusion-twin. Again, we have two co-existing persons, who are identical because of the paths their lives will take in the future. Is the situation really so different?[16]

So much for the eternalist and the growing block conceptions of time, what of presentism? Interestingly, the most extreme form of presentism makes the problem go away. If the present is momentary, and we take the non-existence of the past and future to entail the absence of true propositions about past and future happenings, then it is difficult to see how fission and fusion are possible at all. All that ever exists—all that any present ever contains—is a certain number of presently existing momentary people. However, for obvious reasons this version of presentism lacks appeal, and most presentists hold that there can be truths about happenings at times other than the present, even though these times do not exist. Quite how this is possible is another matter, but for present purposes the details are irrelevant.[17] So far as the proposed treatment of fusion is concerned, those forms of presentism which accept truths about the past but not the future are in an analogous position to advocates of the growing block conception, whereas those who believe the future to be no less factual than the past are in a position analogous to the eternalist. So far as fission and fusion are concerned, plausible versions of presentism have nothing new to offer.[18]

[16] It is worth noting also that construing fission and fusion as involving a partial overlap of distinct perduring people, Lewis' preferred option, also leads to indeterminacies in a growing block universe. The problem is not with fusion—subjects who fuse begin as distinct and remain distinct—but with fission. For someone who *may* undergo fission it will be indeterminate beforehand whether they are one person or two (or more)!

[17] For discussion of some of the options see Bigelow (1996), Crisp (2003), Dainton (2001), Rea (2003), Sider (1999).

[18] This is as good a place as any to mention the following puzzle-case. Suppose you and I have both embarked on a VR-3 adventure, due to last several days. Unfortunately, thanks to an equipment malfunction, our C-systems collide in the following way. At the start of the adventure your C-system (and stream of consciousness) was transferred to one VR-machine, M1, and mine was transferred to a distinct machine, M2, but at precisely 3pm both our C-systems get transferred to a single VR-machine, M3. What happens to us? It depends on how the details are filled out. If M3 can generate two distinct streams of consciousness (composed of distinct token experiences) there is no difficulty whatsoever. This machine sustains two distinct C-systems, composed of distinct experiential powers; these powers may have overlapping material bases, and even precisely similar

12.11. THE MANY SHAPES OF LIFE

Interpreting fission and fusion in terms of branching personal times seems to be the only way in which the most pivotal elements of our conception of what our persistence involves and requires can be retained intact and together. Most significant here is the idea that there is a form of mental continuity which is sufficient to keep a subject in existence in *all* circumstances. As I suggested right at the start, if our thinking about selfhood and self-identity is regulated by any single unshakeable principle, it is that subjects cannot perish so long as their streams of consciousness continue on. If we also accept the possibility that streams of consciousness, and hence C-systems, can bifurcate and merge, then we are confronted with the problem of how strict numerical self-identity can be preserved under such conditions. This problem can be solved by accepting that the lives of those who divide or fuse are not metaphysically impossible or even especially puzzling, but simply the lives of those whose personal times are non-linear, in virtue of the different stages of their lives being distributed through (external) time in an unusual way. Of course, if personal fissions or fusions were to become commonplace there is no predicting the way concepts such as *self*, *subject*, or *person* might evolve. But this is a predicament we are not faced with. For as I have said before, my aim has been to show that the mere possibility of fission and fusion does not *now* oblige us to modify our actual conceptions of selfhood and self-identity.

The possibility that the life of a single subject can have a complex topology has intriguing ramifications. If iterated fissions and fusions are possible, the temporal architecture of a single subject may become indefinitely complex. Some comparatively simple possibilities are illustrated in Figure 12.5.

Those who believe in an afterlife which involves the merging of the consciousness of the individual into that of a wider super-personal self may find a use for the conclusion that fusion is identity-preserving. On a more mundane level, setting aside religious or supernatural considerations, there are implications for

---

triggering conditions, but they are distinct by virtue of being able to produce distinct streams of consciousness (see the tri-partite analysis of power-individuation). If M3 can produce just one stream of consciousness, and our C-systems smoothly merge, then it is equally clear what has happened: we have undergone fusion. By way of an extra twist, let's vary the scenario. We again suppose the machine can sustain only one C-system, call it S. If button X is pressed at 3pm then my C-system will merge with S and yours will come to an abrupt end (and so will you), whereas if button Y is pressed the reverse will happen. If neither button is pressed, both our C-systems are terminated. In the moments leading up to 3pm the ownership of S may seem disturbingly indeterminate: it could belong to me, or to you, it all depends on what happens at 3pm! Quite what we should make of this sort of situation depends on how we think of time. If the future is as real as the past, the ownership of S is settled prior to 3pm. If the future is ontologically open, then many future-oriented propositions lack a determinate truth value, and so the indeterminacy in the current case is not especially unusual.

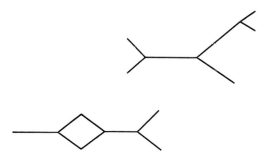

Figure 12.5 Non-linear lives can come in many forms

the boundaries of personal existence. For all its variety in other respects, the structure or form of an ordinary human life is terribly simple: a linear succession of experiences bounded by birth and death. It is easy to fall into the assumption that the life of an individual self is necessarily of this shape. We are accustomed to thinking of birth as the absolute entry into existence and of death as the absolute departure from it. These are prejudices which must be given up in the light of the possibility of non-linear lives. Fission brings with it the possibility of multiple deaths, fusion the possibility of multiple births; and putting these together we have the possibility that a single self could have a life with multiple branches, which have different beginnings and different endings.

Such a state of affairs is quite different from the kind usually envisaged by aficionados of metempsychosis. According to the latter hypothesis, the same self undergoes a succession of incarnations, entering a particular body at its birth only to transfer to another at its death; the self does not perish with each of its bodies, nor is it reborn with the birth of each new incarnation. The lives of the reincarnated thus have a standard linear topology, and if their existences are bounded at all they have a single beginning and a single end. In the light of these considerations, in cases of the sort shown in Figure 12.5 it might be thought appropriate to reserve the term 'death' for the termination of the last remaining branch of a subject's life—the 'partial death' which occurs latest in external time. Although this preserves some of the concept's accustomed force it still lacks some weight: death thus construed is still, in itself, no more than the termination of one limb of a subject's life, and as such it is an event which can occur more than once in the life of the same self.

Branching is not the only way in which a life can diverge from the linear norm. In a circular time, there is no first or last moment since every moment occurs both before and after every other. A subject with a circular personal time would have an unbounded existence; although it would be of finite duration, their life would be without a beginning or an end. Are lives such as this genuine possibilities? If time travel is logically possible, they may well be. Some of the most intriguing science fiction tales of time travel focus on precisely this possibility.

Last but not least, interpreting fission and fusion in terms of the realization of non-linear lives bears some similarity to Parfit's analysis. Parfit too recognizes that, in a sense, our lives do not necessarily have a linear structure. But although he holds that what matters in life can branch, he denies that the life of a single self can do the same. Since Parfit believes our mental lives can have non-linear trajectories but *we* cannot, he argues that it is a mistake to suppose death necessarily means the end of what we most value in continued existence. Although I have argued that both fission and fusion are identity-preserving, as we have seen latterly, this position is not incompatible with the view that death (in the form of the termination of one limb of a branching life) is not necessarily what it is usually thought to be. But also, unlike Parfit, I am not persuaded that what matters *can* be preserved in cases of non-linear lives if identity is not, since a significant proportion of our deepest personal concerns are so closely bound up with self-identity. Parfit is inclined to dismiss these concerns as irrational or merely sentimental, but it is not clear that he is right, all the more so since much of his case against the importance of identity rests on his claim that in fission and fusion identity and what matters come apart. Accepting the interpretation of these cases developed in the course of this chapter requires giving up some natural assumptions about the monolithic nature of time. But we have seen that there are independent grounds for questioning, and ultimately revising these assumptions. Changing our minds in the way I have suggested minimizes the re-conceptualization that accepting the possibilities of fission and fusion demands, and also ensures that our conceptual scheme remains centred over our most deeply rooted instincts concerning what matters in life. Can we reasonably ask for more?

13
Appendix: Reductionism

The term 'reductionism' has entered into recent discussions of person and their identity. Some theories are classed as reductionist, others as non-reductionist, where does the C-theory stand? Is it a reductionist theory? If so, is it reductionist to an extent that is objectionable or problematic?

In one respect the C-theory is not at all reductionist. It provides an account of the self in wholly mentalistic terms, and no attempt is made to reduce mental terms or concepts to non-mental terms or concepts, or to say that mental items are identical with, or constituted by, non-mental items. Taking experience seriously means taking experience to be an ineliminable component of reality. Moreover, if we take concepts such as 'person', 'self', 'subject', and 'experience' to belong to the same family, then the C-theorist's enterprise is a family business—all the concepts employed belong to the same circle. Yet, in other respects, the C-theory may seem very reductionist indeed: selves or subjects are equated with complexes of interrelated mental items. What could be more reductionist than this? To assess the extent to which the C-theory *is* reductionist, we need a clearer idea of what 'reductionism' amounts to. Parfit is largely responsible for introducing the notion into the field of personal identity, and has provided several characterizations of what a reductive account of persons would amount to or require—particularly in Part III of *Reasons and Persons*—but before commenting on these, I will make some general remarks.

Building on earlier results, in §8.2 I argued for a reductionist view of our *sense of self*. I suggested that the sense we typically have that particular experiences are things we are living through, or undergoing—the sense we have that there is more to us, as experiencing beings, than our current experiences—can be explained in terms of inter-experiential relationships, rather than a primitive quality of *mineness*. Although this is a perfectly legitimate use of the term, Parfit is generally concerned with ontology (what selves or persons *are*) rather than phenomenology (what it *feels like* to be a self), so I will be focusing here on reductionism about *things*.

Generally speaking the ontological reductionist typically aims to distinguish those kinds of entity which are ultimate or fundamental, and show that other kinds of entity only enjoy, by comparison, a derivative existence, or are somehow or other less than fundamental. Classical instances of ontological reductionism include claims that psychological states are dispositions to behave, physical objects are sets of sense data, numbers are sets of sets, persons are sets of experiences, and so on. Reductive identifications of this sort typically *identify* one sort of entity F with another sort G. Consider, for example, the phenomenalist claim that physical objects (F) are nothing but certain patterns of actual or possible sense data (G), and so physical objects are reducible to the relevant patterns of sense data. This can seem problematic if it is true that Fs *are* Gs, it may seem unclear whether this identification is in any way *reductive*. If Fs are Gs, then whenever an F occurs, so does a G, and vice-versa. If the existence of an F is necessary and sufficient for a G to exist, it seems odd to say that Fs have been reduced to Gs, for no ontological economy has been achieved—given the symmetry of the relationship, it is not clear why we should regard one of its terms as more or less fundamental than the other.

So far as I can see, and so far as concrete (as opposed to abstract) objects are concerned, there are two sorts of case in which we can find an ontologically significant asymmetry between Fs and Gs, the reduced and reducing entities; the first involves *conceptual* considerations, the second concerns *compositional* considerations.

A reduction by conceptual revision occurs when acknowledging the fact that Fs are nothing but Gs also means accepting that Fs are not the sort of things we previously thought. Suppose, for example, that we become convinced that ordinary material objects, such as tables, are nothing but collections of sense-data. This would not mean that tables do not exist, since they exist as much as they ever did, providing the relevant patterns of sense-data continue to occur. But in accepting this form of phenomenalism as true, those of us who were not phenomenalists beforehand would also be accepting that tables *as we previously conceived them* do not exist: we no longer take tables to be mind-independent material substances. Consequently, a reduction of Fs to Gs of this sort amounts to a form of revisionism: our understanding of what being an F involves, or might involve, is altered. This change in thinking counts as a form of reductionism because it brings about an ontological economy: a certain conception of what it is to be an F is no longer available to us. This does not necessarily amount to eliminativism, since so far as ordinary practice is concerned, the reduced or transformed concept can be as useful, even indispensable, as it ever was, and consequently used just as before. New converts to phenomenalism will not think about tables in all the ways they did before, but they will find no difficulty in applying the term in the customary way in their day to day lives.

The second, compositional, sort of reductionism derives from mereological considerations. Specifically, from its being true that F-type entities are wholly constituted from G-type entities, together with the fact that Gs are items which can exist independently of the complexes which are Fs. Setting aside phenomenalism, consider again the case of a table, and the matter from which it is composed. A table is wholly composed of atoms of various sorts, even if a particular table is not identical with any particular set of atoms in virtue of being able to gain and lose a few parts. But any atoms which do form part of a table do not have to: they can exist in no artefact at all, or in different combinations in a different kind of artefact. This amounts to a clear sense in which atoms are a *more basic* kind of physical entity than are tables. Consequently, there is a sense in which accepting that tables are always wholly composed of atoms permits an ontological economy, for it allows us to omit tables from our inventory of basic physical entities. What does 'basic' mean here? It does not correspond with epistemic priority, since we usually know a lot about tables before we discover anything about atoms. The use of the word would certainly be appropriate if we oriented our ontology by reference to scientific theory, in which tables do not figure at all. But there is a more general point too. Tables and their constituent atoms are related by an asymmetrical existential dependency: atoms can exist without being parts of tables, but tables cannot exist unless they have atoms as their parts (let us ignore the possibility of very exotic tables here). Some might baulk at calling this sort of re-conceptualization a mode of ontological 'reduction', and indeed there are occasions when this label might seem inappropriate. If one became convinced that tables were not physical objects but *Gods*, say, then it seems odd to say that tables have in any way been reduced. But since the task of formulating a notion of *ontological diminishment* promises to be a thankless one, I see no harm in the employing the term 'reduction', with the proviso that to reduce, in this sense, need not imply a diminishment or downgrading of the importance of the reduced items. Again, this form of reductionism does not inevitably lead to eliminativism. In many instances, the reduced concept is a useful one to have. Moreover, in some cases, there may be distinctive laws governing the reduced entities. For example, although organisms may be wholly constituted from atoms in the same way as tables, they may be subject to certain biological laws which cannot be reduced (in the way, perhaps, other laws can) to laws governing fundamental particles.

Both of these forms of reductionism can be applied to persons. Indeed, Hume (as commonly understood) combined the two. He argued that the more familiar conceptions of the self, as either a persisting material or immaterial substance, are false: there are no such entities, we are wholly composed of bundles of experiences. Since this is not how we normally think of ourselves, this is an instance of the first sort of reductionism. But also of the second, compositional kind: Hume argued that the particular experiences of which selves are wholly composed are akin to atoms, in that they can exist independently of any particular bundle to which they happen to belong.

As for the C-theory, it too is ontologically reductive, and perhaps doubly so. First of all, accepting the C-theory as an account of what we are surely involves a significant change in the way most of us are accustomed to thinking of ourselves. Rather than thinking of ourselves as human beings (a species of animal), we are required to think of ourselves as *subjects of experience*, or C-systems—as entities that persists so long as they retain a capacity for consciousness of any kind, irrespective of any other changes they might undergo. This conception of the self's nature bears at least some resemblance to one a good many people already hold, since many think they both possess and could survive as immaterial souls. Since adherents of this view also generally believe they could continue to enjoy a mental life of some kind as a soul, the latter notion has a certain kinship to the notion of a C-system. However, to the extent that a soul is taken to be a non-physical substance, accepting the C-theory still involves a significant conceptual revision. For according to the C-theory, a subject is not a persisting quantity of suitably organized non-physical substance, but rather a collection of experiential capacities—clearly an altogether different sort of thing.

This point ties in with the question of compositional reduction. Is the C-theory reductionist in this respect too? In one sense, yes. By taking a subject to consist of a C-related collection of experiential powers, typically included or embedded in a web of P-related psychological capacities, and effectively embodied by virtue of being F-related to a body, rather than being a body, we are committed to a view of selves as entities wholly constituted from component elements, lesser entities which only go to make up a single self in virtue of how they are interrelated. However, there is a significant divergence from Humean atomism. Most psychological capacities are essentially systemic, as are a good many experiential powers. Even if some types of experiential power can exist in very simple minds, or even in complete isolation—and this is debatable—no experiential power belonging to a complex C-system is a 'distinct existence': the experiential potential of every C-related power is affected by the remainder of the C-system, and so would be different if it existed in either a different sort of C-system, or all by itself. Extended C-systems are composite entities, but they are not, for the most part, composed of entities which could enjoy a wholly independent existence. This said, unless we individuate mental capacities in the strictest of ways, the same type of mental capacity can exist in different types of mind, and it may also be possible to transfer token mental capacities (or collections of them) from one mind to another.[1] So there is a sense in which mental capacities enjoy a degree of existential independence from the wholes of which they are parts, albeit a lesser degree of independence than physical atoms enjoy, and for this reason might be viewed as being 'more basic' types of entity than subjects themselves.

The doctrine that personal *persistence* can be non-trivially explicated can also be viewed as reductionist: those who subscribe to it reject the view that the identity through time of a person is a primitive sort of relation or fact, and hold instead that it consists in an earlier and a later person being related in various mental and/or physical ways. Since it concerns personal persistence, let us refer to this as 'persistence' or *p-reductionism*. This can be contrasted with ontological

---

[1] If we individuate experiential powers in terms of *token*-specific C-properties, then even God could not instantaneously replace my visual capacities with yours (by instantly switching around and reconnecting the relevant neural tissues). Type-holism does not have this consequence.

reductionism, the claim that persons *at* times are susceptible to an ontologically economizing reduction.

The p-reductionist is committed to at least this: that whenever a statement about diachronic self-identity is true, then so is a statement, or collection of statements, about other sorts of fact, and conversely, that whenever the statement, or collection of statements, of the latter sort are true, then some statement about self-identity is also true. But again, the holding of a symmetrical relationship between two classes of statements (or types of fact) does not seem enough here. For a reduction to take place there must be an asymmetry: the facts to be reduced, in this case those concerning the persistence of subjects through time, must obtain only *in virtue of* the reducing facts, which we are assuming here to be facts concerning the mental and/or physical relations between persons at particular times. Or in other words, if a statement about self-identity is true, it is true in virtue of other statements being true, statements asserting the holding of certain other relationships between selves. What is the content of the 'in virtue of' here? Admittedly, this can be a somewhat obscure notion, but in the present context, the claim will amount to something like this: statements about the persistence of subjects are not answerable to a distinctive *sui generis* category of facts ('bare identity facts'), but only to facts about certain mental or physical continuities—these are the only sort of facts that make statements about subject persistence true, they are the truth-makers of statements about subject persistence. The continuity facts may not be primitive either, but whatever further facts enter into their makeup, facts about subject persistence are not among them.

The C-theory is clearly p-reductive. Personal persistence is equated with subject persistence, and subject persistence is analysed in terms of C-relatedness. Consequently, at least in this framework, facts about our persistence are certainly not basic or unanalysable.

A p-reductionist, it should be noted, is not committed to the possibility of translating, without loss of meaning, statements about personal identity into statements which make no mention of persons or their identities, and the same goes for subjects and selves. In saying that personal persistence consists in the obtaining of certain facts concerning mental or physical continuities, the p-reductionist is not committed to saying that statements about personal identity *mean the same as* statements about these other continuities. To employ some further terminology, it is possible to hold personal identity to be weakly or *metaphysically* reducible, without also holding it to be strongly or *analytically* reducible. In the case of identity statements, the analytic variety of reductionism seems implausible. To say that an earlier and later person are identical is to say that the relation of numerical identity holds between them, and nothing more. Identity, as that relation which every individual bears to itself and no other thing, is as primitive a relation as any other, and it is difficult to envisage how a statement asserting that an individual designated X is identical with an individual designated Y could have just the same meaning as a statement asserting that some other relationship connects X and Y. All the p-reductionist need maintain is that the truth conditions for personal identity statements can be specified in terms of statements which make no mention of personal identity.

The same goes, *mutatis mutandis*, for the ontological reductionist and claims about personal existence. Consider again Hume's doubly reductive analysis. Such an analysans could not be substituted, without alteration of meaning, in very many statements featuring the analysandum, and the same applies to what the C-theory has to say about the kind of things we are. What the C-theorist claims our existence and persistence amounts to is certainly not what we ordinarily *mean* when we say 'X is a person' or 'X is the same self as Y' and suchlike.[2]

Four Parfittean Theses

In Part III of *Reasons and Persons* Parfit offers several different characterizations of what he takes reductionism about persons to amount to or require; in more recent writings (as yet unpublished) he clarifies the situation, and takes reductionism to amount to the following four claims:

R1: A person's existence just consists in the existence of a body, and the occurrence of various interrelated physical and mental states and events.

R2: Personal identity over time just consists in physical and/or psychological continuity.

R3: These continuities can be described in a way which does not presuppose personal identity.

R4: If we ask what unifies a person's consciousness, either at one time or over time, the answer cannot be that different experiences are all had by the same person. These unities must consist in the relation of these experiences to each other, and/or to this person's brain.

Terminological differences aside, there is nothing in R1 that the C-theorist would disagree with, and similarly for R2, provided we substitute 'mental' for 'psychological', so as to make room for the difference between the P-theory and the C-theory, a difference Parfit does not recognize. R1 amounts to what I have been calling ontological reductionism, and R2 amounts to p-reductionism. As for R4, the idea that the unity of consciousness consists of inter-experiential relationships is also something I would endorse, and I have tried to say something about the nature of the co-consciousness relationship. Although I reached the conclusion that nothing informative *can* be said about it (in phenomenal terms at least) this is progress of a sort.

While R4 clearly contributes to a reductionist account of personal persistence, its relevance to the ontological issue is less obvious. What has R4 to do with a

---

[2] For further varieties of reductionism see Garrett's (1998: 25 ff) useful discussion.

reductionist view of the sort of thing a self is? The answer is not hard to find. As Parfit sees it, the main way of being a *non*-reductionist is to believe that a subject of experiences is 'a *separately existing entity*, distinct from a brain and body, and a series of physical and mental events.' Anyone who took themselves to be a separately existing subject, in this sense, might also be tempted to explain the unity of consciousness in terms of ownership: experiences belong to the same person by virtue of being related, in the appropriate manner, to separately existing subjects of experience. If, on the other hand, we do not need to appeal to a separately existing 'owner' to explain the unity in consciousness, if inter-experiential relationships will do the job, there is one less reason for believing in separately existing subjects, and so one more reason for being a reductionist.

While this is reasonable enough, there are complications. Characterizing non-reductionism in terms of a belief in separately existing entities may seem puzzling, since Parfit also holds that reductionists who believe R1 and R2, who believe that the existence and persistence of persons just consists in various suitably interrelated mental and physical items, can also take a person to be an entity that is distinct from any particular series of these items: since our lives could have gone differently, we could each have had a different sequence of experiences, and so we cannot *be* any one such sequence. However, this is not necessarily problematic, for 'distinctness' does not entail 'separateness'. As Parfit observes, the reductionist can say that a person is constituted or composed of nothing but mental and physical states, even though they are not identical with any particular series or collection of such states. The non-reductionist who believes we are separately existing entities will, presumably, not want to say this, they will insist that subjects of experience are not constituted of mental states, they exist as separate substances in their own right. But again the situation is not quite so clear-cut. Parfit's main example of a putative 'separately existing entity' is the Cartesian Ego, which as traditionally conceived is *not* an entity that is wholly distinct or separate from its experiences: Ego and experience are related as substance and mode, experiences are *states of* subjects, rather than items that are separate or distinct from subjects. Note also, the fact that experiences are related by co-consciousness does not in itself undermine the Cartesian view: if Egos are essentially conscious substances, all their concurrent experiential states will be conscious with one another, as modes of a single conscious substance. As part of the case against the Cartesian view, we need to subject the thesis that experiences are mode-like to detailed scrutiny. This is something I have tried to do. I have argued that while there is some truth in the notion that experiences are not entirely independent particulars, this can be explained in terms of inter-experiential relationships and dependencies. There is thus no need to posit a substance to which experiences are related as modes.

There is a further issue concerning R4. In talking about the *unity* of con-sciousness, we might be talking about (i) the way simultaneous and successive experiences within a single stream of consciousness are related to one another;

or (ii) the relationship of consubjectivity, the fact that experiences can belong to the same subject. If we construe 'unity' in the latter way, then in rejecting the view that unity consists in consubjectivity we are merely rejecting the view that consubjectivity is a primitive fact—even the Cartesian has an account consubjectivity (in terms of consubstantiality). I assume Parfit means 'unity' in the first sense. The problem here is that in saying that 'These unities must consist in the relation of these experiences to each other, and/or to this person's brain' Parfit leaves open the possibility that consciousness has an act-awareness structure. On this view, it will be recalled, there is a special kind of experience, pure awareness, and this awareness is responsible for the unity we find in our experience. Anyone who believes in a separate awareness of this sort is but a short step from the separate entity view: the subject *is* the awareness, awareness and contents are distinct. So to defend the reductionist view that we are not separately existing entities, the act–object model of consciousness needs to be criticized and rejected. This too is something I have tried to do.

What of R3, the claim that the various continuities which the reductionist takes to constitute the existence and persistence of subjects 'can be described in a way which does not presuppose personal identity'? This seems true: in saying that experiential powers are consubjective if and only if they are C-related, and then spelling out C-relatedness in terms of the capacity to produce co-conscious experiences, we are describing the conditions under which these mental items belong to the same subject, both at and over time, without mentioning persons, selves, or subjects at all. Lowe says: 'To say that experiences are assignable to the same subject because they are "co-conscious" or "co-presented" not only gets the cart before the horse, but also reduces the self's unity of consciousness to an analytic triviality' (1996: 7). But surely, the claim that co-conscious experiences are consubjective would only be an analytic triviality if the C-thesis were an analytic truth. It is hard to see how it can be, since the *concept* 'co-conscious' is quite distinct from concepts such as 'consubjective' or 'belonging to the same self'. Some writers may take 'co-conscious' and 'consubjective' to be synonyms—they take 'co-conscious' to mean 'belong to the same subject or mind', but I do not. Nor do I take 'co-conscious' to mean 'belongs to a single consciousness, the consciousness of a single subject'. As I use the term, 'co-conscious' refers to an experiential relationship between experiences, not a relationship between experiences and subjects. Clearly then, to say that two experiences are co-conscious, and to say that two experiences belong to the same subject, is to say two quite different things.

If we say subjects have some property P, is this a belief we have about the sorts of things subjects in fact are, or is it because by 'subjects' we *mean* 'the sort of things which have P'? The general difficulty in drawing the line between concept and belief is particularly acute in the case of notions such as 'subject', 'self', and 'person'. Nonetheless, I think it would be plausible to say that there is a relationship of a broadly conceptual sort between the notions 'co-conscious' and 'consubjective', a relationship encapsulated in the C-thesis. This conceptual relationship, assuming it is such, stems from our understanding of what selves or subjects are, namely entities whose waking mental lives take the form of streams of consciousness. This is one *aspect* of what we take ourselves to be—one aspect of our ordinary understanding of 'person', 'self', and 'subject'. But concepts can be connected without being identical.

Parfit has put forward several further arguments in defence of the claim that the various mental continuities we might use to define the persistence conditions of person are conceptually distinct from concepts such as 'person', 'self', and 'subject'. One argument relies upon the claim that 'Though persons exist, we could give a *complete* description of reality *without* claiming that persons exist' (1984: 212). This is an intriguing claim, and I suspect that there might well be a sense in which it is true, but as Parfit himself notes, to be true of our world the supposedly 'complete' description has to ignore the contents of our thoughts—no one would deny that most of us *believe* that persons exist, and a complete description would mention these thoughts and beliefs. To avoid this problem, we can posit a race of people, such as the 'Humeans' I mentioned earlier, who do not think of their experiences in the ways we do: they recognize that experiences occur, and are interrelated, but do not ascribe them to *subjects*, they think of themselves as identical with sequences of mental and physical happenings. The trouble now is, although the Humeans might be able to provide a complete description of themselves in wholly impersonal terms—these are the only terms they would understand—do the Humeans mean by 'experience' what we mean by this word? I will not try to resolve these issues. Parfit's other arguments rely, in one way or another, upon cases of personal fission. He argues, for example, that in a case where a person divides into two, we have full preservation of mental continuity in the absence of personal identity. I have given my reasons for thinking that this interpretation of fission is not obligatory. But even if Parfit were right about fission, I am not sure that it would be right to conclude that there is no conceptual connection between the relevant concepts. For Parfit himself acknowledges that *non-branching* mental continuity, at least when accompanied by sameness of brain, is sufficient for sameness of person. Is this an empirical discovery?

Bibliography

Armstrong, D. (1968) *A Materialist Theory of the Mind*. London: Routledge & Kegan Paul.

——(1969) 'Dispositions are Causes', *Analysis* 30: 23–6.

——(1973) *Belief, Truth and Knowledge*. Cambridge: Cambridge University Press.

——(1997). 'What Is Consciousness?' In N. Block, O. Flanagan, and G. Guzeldere (eds), The *Nature of Consciousness: Philosophical Debates*. Bradford: MIT.

Armstrong, D. M., Martin, C. B., and Place, U. T. (1996) *Dispositions: A Debate*. London: Routledge.

Atkins, P. W. (1986) 'Time and Dispersal: The Second Law'. In R. Flood and M. Lockwood (eds), *The Nature of Time*, Oxford: Blackwell.

Ayers, M. (1991) *Locke—Epistemology and Ontology*, 2 vols., London: Routledge. Baars.

——(1993) *Locke: Epistemology and Ontology*. London: Routledge.

B. (2004) 'A Specific Drug for Consciousness?' *Science and Consciousness Review*, http://www.sci-con.org/articles/

Baker, L. R. (1999) 'Unity Without Identity: A New Look at Material Constitution'. In P. French and H. Wettstein (eds), *New Directions in Philosophy*, Midwest Studies in Philosophy 23, Malden MA: Blackwell.

——(2000) *Persons and Bodies*. Cambridge: Cambridge University Press.

——(2002) 'The Ontological Status of Persons', *Philosophy and Phenomenological Research* 65: 370–88.

Barresi, J. and Martin, R. (2003) *Personal Identity*. Oxford: Blackwell.

Barrett, J. (2001) *The Quantum Mechanics of Minds and Worlds*. Oxford: Oxford University Press.

Bayne, T. (2001) 'Co-consciousness: Review of Barry Dainton's *Stream of Consciousness*', *Journal of Consciousness Studies* 8: 79–92.

Bayne, T. and Chalmers, D. (2003) 'What is the Unity of Consciousness?' In A. Cleeremans (ed.), *The Unity of Consciousness: Binding, Integration, Dissociation*. Oxford: Oxford University Press. http://www.u.arizona.edu/~chalmers/papers/unity.html

Belnap, N. (1992) 'Branching space–time', *Synthese* 92: 385–434.

Berglund, S. (1995) *Human and Personal Identity*. Lund: Lund University Press.

Bermúdez, J. L. (1998) *The Paradox of Self-Consciousness*. Cambridge: MIT Press.

Bigelow, J. (1996) 'Presentism and Properties', *Philosophical Perspectives*, 10: 35–52.

Biocca, F. (1997) 'The Cyborg's Dilemma: Progressive Embodiment in Virtual Environments', *Journal of Computer-Mediated Communication* 3(2). Available online at: http://www.presence-research.org/

Bird, A. (1998) 'Dispositions and Antidotes', *The Philosophical Quarterly* 48.

——(2000) 'Further Antidotes: a Response to Gunderson', *The Philosophical Quarterly* 50: 199.

Blackburn, S. (1990) 'Filling in Space', *Analysis* 50: 62–5.

Blakemore, C. and Greenfield, S. (1987) *Mindwaves*. Oxford: Blackwell.

Block, N., Flanagan, O., and Guzeldere, G. (eds) (1997) The *Nature of Consciousness: Philosophical Debates*. Bradford: MIT.

Boscovitch, R. J. (1763/1966) *A Theory of Natural Philosophy*. Boston: MIT Press.

Brin, D. (2003) *Kiln People*. New York: Tor.

Broad, C. D. (1923) *Scientific Thought*. London: Kegan Paul, Trench and Trubner.

___ (1925) *The Mind and its Place in Nature*. London: Kegan Paul.

___ (1938) *An Examination of McTaggart's Philosophy*, 3 vols. Cambridge: Cambridge University Press.

Burke, M. (1994) 'Dion and Theon: An Essentialist Solution to an Ancient Puzzle', *The Journal of Philosophy*, 91(3): 129–39.

___ (1994) 'Preserving the Principle of One Object to a Place: A Novel Account of the Relations Among Objects, Sorts, Sortals and Persistence Conditions', *Philosophy and Phenomenological Research*, 54(3): 591–62.

___ (1996) 'Tibbles the Cat: A Modern *Sophisma*', *Philosophical Studies*, 84(1): 63–74.

___ (1997) 'Coinciding Objects: Reply to Lowe and Denkel', *Analysis*, 57(1): 11–18.

Campbell, K. (1976) *Metaphysics*. Encino: Dickinson.

Carruthers, P. (2000) *Phenomenal Consciousness: A Naturalistic Theory*. Cambridge: Cambridge University Press.

Chalmers, D. (1996) *The Conscious Mind*. Oxford: Oxford University Press.

___ (2004) 'Perception and the Fall from Eden'. http://consc.net/papers/eden.html

Crisp, T. M. (2003) 'Presentism'. In M. J. Loux and D. W. Zimmerman *The Oxford Handbook of Metaphysics*. Oxford: Oxford University Press.

Dainton, B. (1992) 'Time and Division', *Ratio* V, 2: 102–28.

___ (1996) 'Survival and Experience', *Proceedings of the Aristotelian Society* 96: 17–36.

___ (1998) 'Review of Eric Olson's *The Human Animal*', *Mind* 107: 679–82.

___ (2000) *Stream of Consciousness: Unity and Continuity in Conscious Experience*. London: Routledge.

___ (2001) *Time and Space*. Chesham: Acumen.

___ (2002) 'The Gaze of Consciousness', *Journal of Consciousness Studies*, 9(2): 31–48.

___ (2003a) 'Time in Experience: Reply to Gallagher', *Psyche* 9.

___ (2003b) 'Unity in the Void: Reply to Revonsuo', *Psyche* 9.

___ (2003c) 'Higher-order Consciousness and Phenomenal Space: Reply to Meehan', *Psyche* 9.

___ (2003d) 'Unity and Introspectibility: Reply to Gilmore', *Psyche* 9.

___ (2004) 'The Self and the Phenomenal', *Ratio* 17(4): 365–89.

___ (2005) (with Tim Bayne). 'Consciousness as a Guide to Personal Persistence', *Australasian Journal of Philosophy* 83(4): 549–71.

Damasio, A. (2000) *The Feeling of What Happens*. London: Vintage.

Dennett, D. (1982) 'Where Am I?' In D. Hofstadter and D. Dennett (eds.) *The Mind's I*. New York: Bantam Books.

Descartes, R. (1984) *The Philosophical Writings of Descartes*, 2 vols, trans. Cottingham, Stoothoff, and Murdoch. Cambridge: Cambridge University Press.

Deutsch, D. (1997) *The Fabric of Reality*. Harmondsworth: Penguin.

Devlin, C. (ed.) (1959) *Sermons and Devotional Writings of Gerard Manley Hopkins*. Oxford: Oxford University Press.

Dretske, F. (1995) *Naturalizing the Mind*. Cambridge, MA: MIT Press.

Drexler, E. K. (1990) *The Engines of Creation*. Oxford: Oxford University Press.

Egan, G. (1997) *Diaspora*. London: Orion/Millenium.

Ellis, B. and Lierse, C. (1994) 'Dispositional Essentialism', *Australasian Journal of Philosophy* 72.

Epstein, R. (2000) 'The neural-cognitive basis of the Jamesian stream of thought', *Consciousness and Cognition*, 9(4): 550–75.

Evans, C. O. (1970) *The Subject of Consciousness*. London: George Allen & Unwin. (Also available online: http://www.mentalstates.net/SOC.html)

Fine, K. (2003) 'The Non-Identity of a Material Thing and Its Matter', *Mind*, 112: 195–234.

Flanagan, O. (2000) *Dreaming Souls*. Oxford: Oxford University Press.

Forman, R. (ed.) (1990) *The Problem of Pure Consciousness*. New York: Oxford University Press.

Foster, J. (1968) 'Psycho-Physical Causal Pairings', *American Philosophical Quarterly*, V(1): 64–70.

——— (1979) 'In *self*-defence'. In G. F. Macdonald (ed.) *Perception and Identity*. London: Macmillan.

——— (1982) *The Case for Idealism*. London: Routlege & Kegan Paul.

——— (1985) *Ayer*. London: Routledge & Kegan Paul.

——— (1991) *The Immaterial Self*. London: Routledge.

——— (2000) *The Nature of Perception*. Oxford: Oxford University Press.

Frege, G. (1967) 'The Thought', In P. F. Strawson (ed.), *Philosophical Logic*, Oxford: Oxford University Press.

Gallagher, S. (1998) *The Inordinance of Time*. Evanston: Northwestern University Press.

——— (2003) 'Sync-Ing in the Stream of Consciousness: Time-Consciousness'. In C. D. Broad, E. Husserl, and B. Dainton. *Psyche*, 9(10), http://psyche.cs.monash.edu.au/v9/psyche-9-10-gallagher.html

Gallie, I. (1936–7) 'Mental Facts', *Proceedings of the Aristotelian Society*, XXXVII.

Gallois, A. (1998) *Occasions of Identity*, Oxford: Clarendon.

Garrett, B. J. (1998) *Personal Identity and Self-Consciousness*. London: Routledge.

Geach, P. T. (1962) *Reference and Generality*. Ithaca: Cornell University Press.

Gendler, T. S. (1998) 'Exceptional Persons: On the Limits of Imaginary Cases', *Journal of Consciousness Studies* 5: 592–610.

Gibbard, A. (1975) 'Contingent Identity', *Journal of Philosophical Logic*, 4: 187–221.

Gilmore, C. S. (2003) 'The Introspectibility Thesis', *Psyche* 9(5). http://psyche.cs.monash.edu.au/v9/psyche-9-05-gilmore.html

Gödel, K. (1949) 'A Remark about the Relationship between Relativity Theory and Idealistic Philosophy'. In Schilpp, P. A. (ed.), *Albert Einstein: Philosopher-Scientist*, La Salle: Open Court.

Greene, B. (2004) *The Fabric of the Cosmos*. London: Allen Lane.

Gunderson, L. B. (2000) 'Bird on Dispositions and Antidotes', *The Philosophical Quarterly* 50: 199.

Guttenplan, S. (1994) *A Companion to the Philosophy of Mind*. Blackwell: Oxford.

Hall, A. R. and Hall., M. B. (1962) *Unpublished Scientific Papers of Isaac Newton*. Cambridge: Cambridge University Press.

Hamilton, A. (1998) 'Mill, Phenomenalism and the Self'. In J. Skorupski (ed.), *The Cambridge Companion to Mill*, Cambridge: Cambridge University Press.

Harman, G. (1990) 'The intrinsic quality of experience', *Philosophical Perspectives* 4: 31–52.

Harré, R. and Madden, E. H. (1975) *Causal Powers: A Theory of Natural Necessity*. Oxford: Basil Blackwell.

Haslanger, Sally (2003) 'Persistence Through Time'. In M. J. Loux and D.W. Zimmerman *The Oxford Handbook of Metaphysics*. Oxford: Oxford University Press.

Hawthorne, J. P. (2001) 'Causal Structuralism', *Philosophical Perspectives* 15, 361–78.

Heil, J. (2003) *From an Ontological Point of View*. Oxford: Oxford University Press.

Hestevold, H. S. and Carter, W. R. (2002) 'On Presentism, Endurance and Change', *Canadian Journal of Philosophy* 32: 491–510.

Hoffman, J. and Rosenkrantz, G. S. (1997) *Substance*. London: Routledge.

Hofstadter, D. and Dennett, D. (eds) (1982) *The Mind's I*. New York: Bantam Books.

Holton, R. (1999) 'Dispositions All the Way Round', *Analysis* 59: 9–14.

Hopkins, G. M. (1959) *Sermons and Devotional Writings of Gerard Manley Hopkins*, ed. C. Devlin. Oxford: Clarendon Press.

Hume, D. (1739/1978) *A Treatise of Human Nature*, ed. Selby-Bigge. Oxford: Clarendon Press.

Hurley, S. (1998) *Consciousness in Action*. Cambridge, MA: Harvard University Press.

Husserl, E. (1991) *On the Phenomenology of the Consciousness of Internal Time* (1893–1917), ed. and trans. J. B. Brough. Dordrecht: Kluwer.

James, W. (1952 [1890]) *The Principles of Psychology*. Chicago: Encyclopaedia Britannica Inc. Available online: http://psychclassics.yorku.ca/James/Principles/

Johnston, M. (1987) 'Human Beings', *Journal of Philosophy* 84: 59–83.

——— (1989) 'Fission and the Facts', *Philosophical Perspectives* 3.

——— (1992*a*) 'Reasons and Reductionism', *The Philosophical Review* 101: 589–618.

——— (1992*b*) 'Constitution is not Identity', *Mind* 101: 89–105.

Jones, J. R. (1949) 'The Self in Sensory Cognition', *Mind* LVII.

Kirk, R. (1994) *Raw Feeling*. Oxford: Clarendon Press.

Kitaoka, A. (2006) 'Anomalous motion illusion and stereopsis', *Journal of Three Dimensional Images* 20: 9–14.

——— and Ashida, H. (2003) 'Phenomenal characteristics of the peripheral drift illusion', *VISION* 15: 261–2.

Kriegel, U. (2004) 'Consciousness and Self-Consciousness', *The Monist* 87: 185–209.

Langton, R. (1998) *Kantian Humility: Our Ignorance of Things in Themselves*. Oxford: Clarendon Press.

——— (2004) 'Elusive Knowledge of Things in Themselves', *Australasian Journal of Philosophy*, 82: 129–36.

Le Poidevin, R. (2000) 'The Experience and Perception of Time'. In Edward N. Zalta (ed.), *The Stanford Encyclopedia of Philosophy* (Fall 2000 Edition), URL = <http://plato.stanford.edu/archives/fall2000/entries/time-experience/>.

Lewis, D. (1971) 'Counterparts of Persons and their Bodies', *Journal of Philosophy*, 68.

——(1976*a*) 'The Paradoxes of Time Travel', *American Philosophical Quarterly* 13: 145–52.

——(1976*b*) 'Survival and Identity'. In A. Rorty (ed.), *The Identities of Persons*. Berkeley: University of California Press. Reprinted with postscript in Lewis (1983).

——(1983) *Philosophical Papers*, vol. 1. Oxford: Oxford University Press.

——(1986) *On the Plurality of Worlds*. Oxford: Blackwell.

——(1997) 'Finkish Dispositions', *The Philosophical Quarterly* 47(187).

——(forthcoming) 'Ramseyan Humility'. In Braddon-Mitchell and Nolan (eds) *The Canberra Plan*.

Locke, J. (1690/1975) *An Essay Concerning Human Understanding*, ed. P. Nidditch, Oxford: Oxford University Press.

Lockwood, M. (1989) *Mind, Brain and the Quantum*. Oxford: Oxford University Press.

——(1993) 'The Grain Problem'. In H. Robinson (ed.), *Objections to Physicalism*, Clarendon Press: Oxford.

——(1994) 'Issues of Unity and Objectivity'. In C. Peacocke (ed.), *Objectivity, Simulation and the Unity of Consciousness*. Proceedings of the British Academy 83.

——(2005) *The Labyrinth of Time*. Oxford: Oxford University Press.

Loux, M. J. and Zimmerman, D. W. (2003) *The Oxford Handbook of Metaphysics*. Oxford: Oxford University Press.

Lowe, E. J. (1994) 'Primitive Substances', *Philosophy and Phenomenological Research* 54.

——(1996) *Subjects of Experience*. Cambridge: Cambridge University Press.

——(2000) 'Review of A. Gallois' *Occasions of Identity*', *Mind* 109: 354–7.

——(2003) 'Substantial Change and Spatio-temporal Coincidence', *Ratio* XVI: 140–60.

Lycan, W. (1996) *Consciousness and Experience*. Boston: MIT Press.

——(1997) 'Consciousness as Internal Monitoring'. In N. Block, O. Flanagan, and G. Guzeldere (eds), *The Nature of Consciousness: Philosophical Debates*. Bradford: MIT.

Lyon, A. (1980) 'On Remaining the Same Person', *Philosophy* 55: 167–82.

Mangan, B. (2001) 'Sensation's Ghost: The Non-Sensory "Fringe" of Consciousness', *Psyche* 7(18).

Marks, C. (1980) *Commissurotomy, Consciousness and the Unity of Mind*. Cambridge, Mass: MIT Press/Bradford Books.

Martin, C. B. (1997) 'On the Need for Properties: The Road to Pythagoreanism and Back' *Synthese* 112.

Martin, R. and Barresi, J. (eds) (2003) *Personal Identity*. Oxford: Blackwell.

Maudlin, T. (2002) 'Remarks on the Passing of Time', *Proceedings of the Aristotelian Society*, 102(3): 237–52.

Maxwell, N. (1978) 'Mind–Brain Identity and Rigid Designation', *Minnesota Studies in the Philosophy of Science*, vol. IX. Minneapolis: University of Minnesota Press.

McGinn, C. (1989) 'Can We Solve the Mind–Body Problem?' *Mind* 98: 349–66.

——(1993) 'Consciousness and Cosmology: Hyperdualism Ventilated'. In M. Davies (ed.), *Essays on Consciousness*, Blackwell: Oxford.

Mellor, H. (1998) *Real Time II*. London: Routledge.

———(2000) 'The Semantics and Ontology of Dispositions', *Mind* 109: 757–80.

Merricks, T. (1995) 'On the Incompatibility of Enduring and Perduring Entities', *Mind* 104: 523–31.

———(1999) 'Persistence, Parts and Presentism', *Noûs* 33: 421–38.

Metzinger, T. (2003) *The Self-Model Theory of Subjectivity*. Cambridge: MIT Press.

Miller, I. (1984) Husserl, Perception, and Temporal Awareness. MA: MIT.

Miller, K. (2006) 'How to Wholly Exist in Two Places at the Same Time', *Canadian Journal of Philosophy* 36(3): 309–34.

Mills, E. (1993) 'Dividing Without Reducing: Bodily Fission and Personal Identity', *Mind* 102: 37–51.

Molnar, G. (2003) *Powers*. Oxford: Oxford University Press.

Mumford, S. (1998) *Dispositions*. Oxford: Oxford University Press.

Nathan, N. (1997) 'Self and Will', *International Journal of Philosophical Studies* 5(1): 81–94.

Nerlich, G. (2005) 'Can Parts of Space Move?: On Paragraph Six of Newton's Scholium', *Erkenntnis* 62(1): 119–35.

Newton-Smith, W. (1980) *The Structure of Time*. London: Routledge.

Noë, A. (2002) 'Is the Visual World a Grand Illusion?' *Journal of Consciousness Studies* 9(5–6): 1–12.

Noonan, H. (1989) *Personal Identity*. London: Routledge.

———(1991) 'Indeterminate Identity, Contingent Identity and Abelardian Predicates', *Philosophical Quarterly*, 41: 183–93.

———(1993) 'Constitution is Identity', *Mind* 102: 133–45.

Nozick, R. (1975) *Anarchy, State and Utopia*. Oxford: Blackwell.

———(1981) *Philosophical Explanations*. Oxford: Oxford University Press.

Oderberg, D. (1996) 'Coincidence under a Sortal', *Philosophical Review* 105: 147–71.

Olson, E. (1997) *The Human Animal*. Oxford: Oxford University Press.

———(2001) 'Review of Baker's *Persons and Bodies: A Constitution View*', *Mind* 110: 427–30.

———(2003) 'An Argument for Animalism'. In J. Barresi and R. Martin, *Personal Identity*. Oxford: Blackwell.

———(2007) 'What Are We?' *Journal of Consciousness Studies* 14(5–6): 37–55.

Pace-Schott, E. and Hobson, A. (2002) 'The Neurobiology of Sleep: Genetics, Sub-cellular Physiology and Subcortical Networks', *Nature Reviews Neuroscience* 3: 591–605.

Parfit, D. (1971) 'Personal Identity', *Philosophical Review* 80: 3–27.

———(1984) *Reasons and Persons*. Oxford: Clarendon Press.

———(1987) 'Divided Minds and the Nature of Persons' in C. Blakemore and S. Greenfield, *Mindwaves*. Oxford: Blackwell.

Peacocke, C. (1983) *Sense and Content: Experience, Thought and their Relations*. Oxford: Clarendon Press.

Perry, J. (1972) 'Can the Self Divide?' *Journal of Philosophy* 73: 463–88.

Persson, I. (1999) 'Our Identity and the Separability of Persons and Organisms', *Dialogue* 38: 519–33.

———(2004) 'Self-Doubt: Why we are not identical to things of any kind', *Ratio* XVII: 390–408.

Pockett, S. (2003) 'How long is "now"? Phenomenology and the Specious Present', *Phenomenology and the Cognitive Sciences* 2: 55–68.

Pöppel, E. (1985) *Mindworks: Time and Conscious Experience*. New York: Harcourt Brace Jovanovich.

Price, H. (1996) *Time's Arrow and Archimedes' Point*. Oxford: Oxford University Press.

Priest, S. (2000) *The Subject in Question: Sartre's Critique of Husserl in 'The Transcendence of the Ego'*. London: Routledge.

Prior, A. (1967) *Past, Present and Future*. Oxford: Oxford University Press.

Prior, E. M., Pargetter, R., and Jackson, F. (1982) 'Three Theses about Dispositions', *American Philosophical Quarterly* 19: 251–7.

Ramachandran, V. S. and Hubbard, E. M. (2001) 'Synaesthesia: A Window Into Perception, Thought and Language', *Journal of Consciousness Studies* 8: 3–34.

Rea, M. (1997) *Material Constitution: A Reader*. New York: Rowan and Littlefield.

_____ (2003) 'Four-Dimensionalism'. In M. J. Loux and D. W. Zimmerman, *The Oxford Handbook of Metaphysics*. Oxford: Oxford University Press.

Rescher, N. and Urquhart, A. (1971) *Temporal Logic*. New York: Springer-Verlag.

Robinson, D. (1985) 'Can Amoebae Divide without Multiplying?' *Australasian Journal of Philosophy* 63: 299–319.

Robinson, H. (1982) *Matter and Sense*. Cambridge: Cambridge University Press.

_____ (1994) *Perception*. London: Routledge.

Rorty, A. (1976) *The Identities of Persons*. Berkeley: University of California Press.

Rosenthal, D. M. (1986) 'Two concepts of consciousness' *Philosophical Studies* 49.

_____ (2003) 'Unity of Consciousness and the Self'. *Proceedings of the Aristotelian Society* June: 325–52.

Rovane, C. (1998) *The Bounds of Agency*. Princeton: Princeton University Press.

Ruhnau, E. (1995) 'Time gestalt and the observer'. In T. Metzinger (ed.), *Conscious Experience*. Paderborn: Schönigh Academic Imprint.

Russell, B. (1984) 'On the experience of time'. In *The Collected Papers of Bertrand Russell, Volume 7*. London: George Allen & Unwin.

_____ (1927/1992) *The Analysis of Matter*. London: Routledge.

Ryder, D. (2004) 'Critical Notice of Stephen Mumford's *Dispositions*'. http://homepage.mac.com/ancientportraits/drsite/paperlist.html

Ryle, G. (1949) *The Concept of Mind*. London: Hutchinson.

Schiff, N. D. and Plum, F. (2000) 'The role of arousal and "gating" systems in the neurology of impaired consciousness', *Journal of Clinical Neurophysiology* 17: 438–52.

Schwitzgebel, E. (2007) 'Do You Have Constant Tactile Experiences of Your Feet in Your Shoes? Or Is Experience Limited to What's in Attention?' *Journal of Consciousness Studies* 14(3): 5–35.

Searle, J. (1992) *The Rediscovery of the Mind*. Cambridge, MA: MIT Press.

Sevush, S. (2004) 'Single-Neuron Theory of Consciousness'. http://cogprints.org/3891/

Shoemaker, S. (1964) *Self-Knowledge and Self-Identity*. Ithaca: Cornell University Press.

_____ (1980) 'Causality and Properties'. In Peter van Inwagen (ed.), *Time and Cause*. Dordrecht: Reidel Publishing Co., 109–35.

_____ (1984) 'Personal Identity: A Materialist Account'. In S. Shoemaker and R. Swinburne (eds), *Personal Identity*. Oxford: Blackwell.

—— (1997) 'Self and Substance', *Philosophical Perspectives*, vol. 11: Mind, Causation, and World, 283–304.

—— (1999) 'Self, Body and Coincidence', *Proceedings of the Aristotelian Society*, suppl. 73: 287–306.

—— (2003*a*) 'Consciousness and Co-consciousness'. In A. Cleermans (ed.), *The Unity of Consciousness: Binding, Integration, and Dissociation*, Oxford: Oxford University Press.

—— (2003*b*) 'Realization, Micro-Realization, and Coincidence', *Philosophy and Phenomenological Research* LXVII: 1–23.

—— and Swinburne, R. (1984) *Personal Identity*. Oxford: Blackwell.

Sidelle, A. (2002) 'Some Episodes in the Sameness of Consciousness', *Philosophical Topics* 30(1): 269–93.

Sider, T. (1996) 'All the World's a Stage', *Australasian Journal of Philosophy* 74: 433–53.

—— (1999) 'Presentism and Ontological Commitment', *Journal of Philosophy* 96: 325–47.

—— (2001) *Four-Dimensionalism*. Oxford: Oxford University Press.

Snowdon, P. F. (1990) 'Persons, Animals and Ourselves'. In C. Gill (ed.), *The Person and the Human Mind*, Oxford: Clarendon Press, 83–107.

—— (1991) 'Personal Identity and Brain Transplants'. In D. Cockburn (ed.), *Human Beings*. Cambridge: Cambridge University Press, 109–26.

Sprigge, T. (1983) *The Vindication of Absolute Idealism*. Edinburgh: Edinburgh University Press.

—— (1988) 'Personal and Impersonal Identity', *Mind* 97(385): 29–49.

—— (1993) *American Truth and British Reality*. Illinois: Open Court.

Stace, W. T. (1960) *Mysticism and Philosophy*. London: Macmillan.

Strawson, G. (1994) *Mental Reality*. Cambridge, MA: MIT Press.

—— (1997) 'The Self', *Journal of Consciousness Studies* 4(5–6): 405–28. Reprinted in R. Martin and J. Barresi (2003) *Personal Identity*. Oxford: Blackwell.

—— (1999*a*) 'The Self and the SESMET' *Journal of Consciousness Studies* 6(4): 99–135.

—— (1999*b*) 'Self and Body', *Aristotelian Society Supplementary Volume*, 73(1)

—— *et al.* (2006) *Consciousness and its Place in Nature* ed. A. Freeman. Exeter: Imprint Academic.

Strawson, P. F. (1959) *Individuals*. London: Methuen.

—— (1966) *The Bounds of Sense*. London: Methuen.

Tooley, M. (1997) *Time, Tense and Causation*, Oxford: Oxford University Press.

Troy, C. (2005) 'What is a Disposition?' *Synthèse* 144: 321–41.

Tye, M. (1997) 'The Problem of Simple Minds: Is There Anything it is Like to Be a Honey Bee?' *Philosophical Studies* 88: 289–317.

—— (1995) *Ten Problems of Consciousness: A Representational Theory of the Phenomenal Mind*. Cambridge, MA, MIT/Bradford Book.

—— (2003) *Consciousness and Persons*. Cambridge, MA: MIT Press.

Unger, P. (1990) *Identity, Consciousness and Value*. Oxford: Oxford University Press.

—— (1999) 'The Mystery of the Physical and the Matter of Qualities: A Paper for Professor Shaffer', *Midwest Studies in Philosophy*, XXIII: 75–99.

Van Inwagen, P. (1990) *Material Beings*. Ithaca: Cornell University Press.

Ward, J. (1918) *Psychological Principles*. Cambridge: Cambridge University Press.

Whitehead, A. N. (1929) *Process and Reality*. Cambridge: Cambridge University Press.

Wiggins, D. (1968) 'On Being in the Same Place at the Same Time', *Philosophical Review* 77, 90–5.

_____ (1980) *Sameness and Substance*. Oxford: Blackwell.

_____ (2001) *Sameness and Substance Renewed*. Cambridge: Cambridge University Press

Wilkes, K. V. (1988) *Real People: Personal Identity without Thought Experiments*. Oxford: Clarendon Press.

Williams, B. (1970) 'The self and the future', *Philosophical Review* 79: 161–80

_____ (1973) *Problems of the Self*. Cambridge: Cambridge University Press.

Zahavi, D. (2005) *Subjectivity and Selfhood*. Cambridge, MA: MIT Press.

Zimmerman, D. (1999) 'Born Yesterday: Personal Autonomy for Agents without a Past', *Midwest Studies in Philosophy*, XXIII: 236–66.

Zimmerman, D. W. (2003) 'Material People'. In *The Oxford Handbook of Metaphysics*. Oxford: Oxford University Press.

Zuboff, A. (1977–8) 'Moment Universals and Personal Identity' *Proceedings of the Aristotelian Society*.

_____ (1982) 'The Story of a Brain'. In D. Hofstadter and D. Dennett (eds), *The Mind's I*. New York: Bantam Books.

_____ (1990) 'One Self: The Logic of Experience', *Inquiry* 33.

Index